On Foster ... Foster On

Dedicated to the memory of Sir Robert Sainsbury, 1906-2000

Introduction by Deyan Sudjic
Edited by David Jenkins

On Foster ... Foster On

Prestel Munich · London · New York

Die Deutsche Bibliothek –
CIP-Cataloguing-in-Publication-Data.
A catalogue record for this
publication is available from
Die Deutsche Bibliothek

Library of Congress
Cataloguing-in-Publication is available

Prestel Verlag
Mandlstrasse 26
80802 Munich
Germany
Tel +49 (089) 381709-0
Fax +49 (089) 381709-35
sales@prestel.de

175 Fifth Ave.
Suite 402
New York NY 10010
USA
Tel +1 (212) 995-2720
Fax +1 (212) 995-2733
sales@prestel-usa.com

4 Bloomsbury Place
London WC1A 2QA
United Kingdom
Tel +44 (020) 7323-5004
Fax +44 (020) 7636-8004
sales@prestel-uk.co.uk

Printed in Spain
ISBN 3-7913-2405-5
D. L. M-24966-2000

Contents

8   Exploring the City – Deyan Sudjic

24   On Foster

450   Foster On

786   Footnotes

790   Authors and Sources

800   Picture Credits

803   Index

'Given Foster's global reach few architects have had a more direct, personal experience of the impact of globalisation on the city, or have been better placed to see how ideas about urbanism and urban change have ricocheted around the world.'

Deyan Sudjic

The decisive shift in Norman Foster's work in the last decade has been a broad-ening of perspective. The studio has moved beyond a preoccupation with crafting the individual building and begun to operate at the scale of the city, as well as the spoon. In so doing it has of course drawn on concerns that were present in the practice's thinking even in the earliest days. Significantly, as Robert Stern, Foster's fellow Yale graduate, recalls elsewhere in these pages, one of Norman Foster's major works as a student during his time in America was the design of an entire city. And at the time, he was taught, among others, by Serge Chermayeff, just completing his influential book, *Community and Privacy*, a work that went to the heart of issues of contemporary urbanism.

Looking back at some of the writings about Foster's early work contained in this book, you find occasional suggestions that buildings such as the Sainsbury Centre, or IBM at Cosham were the product of an architect who was in some way deliberately avoiding any attempt to address the urban context. These critics seem rather wide of the mark. Even in his Team 4 days, Foster worked on schemes to create complete communities as much as on designs for individual houses. There was, as always with Foster, a search for the bigger picture. What has changed, however, is the architectural climate.

For a time the old idea that the architect could be involved in the physical shaping of urban context faded away in the face of a much more abstract view of what might constitute urban planning. Planning was seen more as a statistical and economic process than a physical and spatial one. That view has changed again in recent years. The idea that the city might be studied and interpreted, but not shaped, as if it were a meteorological phenomenon like rain, to be predicted but not induced, has been modified by the positive recent experiences of direct and rapid intervention in cities such as Barcelona and Bilbao. As a result, architects have once more been called upon to manipulate urban form in a whole range of cities determined to take command of their futures.

We have been reminded that architecture can have the power to symbolise a city or even a state. The reconstruction of the Reichstag offers a unique insight into the political nature of architecture and urbanism. This building now serves as the symbol of a reunited Germany and of a Berlin that has been transformed by the demolition of the Wall. Yet at earlier periods in its history, the building has been charged with equally significant and very different meanings. It was originally built as part of the Wilhelmine transformation of Prussian Berlin into an imperial capital for all Germany. It was the battleground of the German Left and Right in the 1920s, the subject of an arson attack in 1933 inaugurating the Hitler years, and was stormed by the Red Army in 1945. The marks of all these moments are still there, visible in the new Reichstag. Even the shape of the chamber is a political as well as a functional issue.

The one great unpredictable urban phenomenon of the 1980s was the astonishing growth of the cities of the Pacific Rim. In the course of a decade Bangkok, Kuala Lumpur, Guangzhou, Jakarta, Singapore, Shanghai and half a dozen other cities in the area were transformed. Foster has worked in almost all of them and it is an experience which more than anything has helped to shape his approach today. There are cities that turned from sleepy ex-colonial backwaters with cricket grounds and an atmosphere of tropical torpor, or down-at-heel ideological gulags, infested by bicycles and Mao suits with nothing on the shelves in the Friendship Stores, into the economic and urban powerhouses of the world.

It was a phenomenon that took the analysts of the urban world by surprise. They had been too busy worrying about the spectacle of the hollowing out of the cities of Europe into doughnuts dominated by tourism if they were lucky, and dereliction if they were not. A new crop of giant cities, some of which they could barely place on a map, was sprouting almost overnight.

The phenomenon of a city with a population larger than that of many European nations had once seemed to be the exclusive preserve of the basket-case economies, of malnourished peasants overwhelming cities incapable of supporting them, and of ecological and social collapse. The lurking paranoia of urban observers since William Morris and Ebenezer Howard is that behind the thin, fragile crust of urban order is another, nightmarish world, constantly threatening to engulf us. It is an image brought vividly to life by the raw, livid mouth of a Brazilian *favela*. To contemplate such a spectacle now is to stare into the same sort of abyss that so terrified the Victorians, and who developed their attachment to the rural ideal as an antidote.

Actually these new Asian cities were not nearly as alien as they initially seemed to European eyes. They were a distant reflection of the industrial cities of north-west Europe and the eastern seaboard of the United States in the nineteenth century. These had also been the cities that generated enormous sums of money very quickly, and they spent much of it on creating the attributes of city life that matched their high ambitions. Surveyors' grids were driven into empty landscapes to accommodate growth to come. The future was mortgaged to pay for sewers and power lines and bridges and transit systems. Universities, museums and hospitals were erected to convert these upstart newcomers into civilised world cities. Exactly the kind of projects, in fact, that Foster is building today in Singapore, Hong Kong, Japan and Malaysia.

Something irreversible and important has indeed happened to the history of the city in the last twenty years. Just look at the transformation of the Pearl River delta. Now a firestorm of development, spreading 100 kilometres up from Hong Kong across what was once the international frontier with China, through the Special Economic Zone of Shenzhen, up to Guangzhou, and back down along the other side of the delta through Zhuhai to Macao. This was farmland in the 1970s, a network of fruit orchards and fishing villages. The whole landscape has shifted.

For any architect, to take part in the creation of Hong Kong's new airport at Chek Lap Kok (1) – a process that involved building two major suspension bridges, 34 kilometres of motorway, a mass transit rail system, the removal of a mountain, and the creation of an artificial island, even the assembly of a fleet of ships to take the workforce to and from the site – and to see the enormous project completed in just four years, cannot but have served to affect their view of the world.

If there is one thing that has had more of an impact in shaping Foster's attitude to the city and to architecture, than the experience of working in this area, it is the relationship that he had as a young man with Buckminster Fuller. Even though Fuller was as much the product of the end of the nineteenth century as of the twentieth, and despite the temporary eclipse of his reputation as a visionary since his death, he has had a profound and continuing impact on Foster. The forms of the Autonomous House that Foster and Buckminster Fuller worked on together in the early 1980s prefigured such recent projects as the Swiss Re tower and the Greater London Authority building, whose forms are now achievable thanks to radical advances in computing power. In the same way, Fuller's dreams of large-scale city engineering have started to become a reality given the context of explosive urban growth in Asia. Fuller always had a sense of optimism, and of the possibilities of life; he did not allow himself to be burdened by its problems. It was a view that communicated itself directly to Foster. For Foster the city is about possibilities.

For all the dark side of urban life, the poverty that a city can conceal, the deprivation and squalor that persist, as well as the profligate way that it consumes precious resources and pollutes land, water and air, the city is still mankind's most remarkable, most significant creative invention. It is the focus of life and opportunities. It is the city that has become the primary economic engine, and not the national economy as a single entity. Cities attract the ambitious, the talented and the determined from all over the world to realise their potential. And cities do not remain static or fixed. They function in new and complex ways to reflect the changing nature of communications and technology.

Given Foster's global reach – with studios at different times in San Francisco, Hong Kong, Berlin, Tokyo, Singapore, Oslo and London – few architects have had a more direct, personal experience of the impact of globalisation on the city, or have been better placed to see how ideas about urbanism and urban change have ricocheted around the world. And the partnership's work has not been just a passive response to these issues, but has also been a positive intervention to achieve specific goals and targets.

Successful cities seem to belong to a self-selected group that set out to organise their futures. The old city boosters and their present-day equivalents, the big city mayors – a Giuliani from New York, a Maragall from Barcelona – or even more effectively the national leaders who have concentrated their attention on capital cities – Mitterrand in Paris, Mahattir in his new linear city outside Kuala Lumpur – seem to be an essential part of this equation. To succeed, these champions need a repertoire of tools and techniques.

It is significant that Foster has been sought out by a number of such mayors. There was Jean Bousquet in Nîmes, the very opposite of an Asian megalopolis, but still a city in need of the traditional skills of urban place-making that Foster brought with the *médiathèque* and the revitalised public spaces outside it. Foster's design for the metro in Bilbao was an early step on the path that the city took to redefining itself. In Barcelona, Foster's Collserola telecommunications tower was the most dramatic single image of the revitalised city.

Deyan Sudjic

Foster has found himself playing a significant part in cities that could be char-acterised as being at opposite poles. He and his colleagues have worked both in creating the infrastructure for the new Asian cities, and at the same time helping the older, post-industrial cities come to terms with their changing circumstances.

As an example of the latter, Manchester, the city in which Foster was born, had its own period of double-digit, Asian-style growth in the nineteenth century. It was the city that so alarmed Engels and Ruskin that the English-speaking world has suffered a permanent fear of unchecked city growth ever since. Foster was involved in plans for Manchester's bid to stage the millennial Olympic games in 2000. It was a project that had as much to do with the attempt to put Manchester into urban big leagues as it had with a love of sport. Foster provided a masterplan for the development associated with a proposed Olympic stadium.

And the practice's work in Duisburg, in the 'rust belt' of Germany, forms part of a scheme to allow a city that once depended on mining and heavy industry to reinvent itself in the image of the information economy.

For Foster, density is both a response to the imperative of responsible land and energy use, and to the creation of the appropriate qualities of urban life. Couple that with his inherent tendency to push the edges of any available envelope, and you end up with a project like the Tokyo Millennium Tower, originally designed for the Japanese construction giant, Obayashi, and later reiterated in several forms, first as the M Tower, then, on a much smaller scale, as the London Millennium Tower. Foster likes to compare two of the most densely inhabited spots on earth, Macao and Monaco, to point out that extreme density can be a way of life for some of the most affluent, and for some of the poorest, of the world's inhabitants. The Millennium Tower introduced the concept of 55,000 people living and working in a single building – almost twice as many as the population of Monaco.

The idea of the ultra-tall tower has haunted architects' imaginations over the years: Frank Lloyd Wright, for one, proposed the Mile-High Tower. And Foster's notion of an entire city in a single structure is, of course, not so far removed from Buckminster Fuller's projected dome to cover Midtown Manhattan; or, for that mat-ter, from the way that people actually live and work in Hong Kong. In Central and Kowloon every mall, office atrium and food court connects with the next to provide continuous air-conditioned space that avoids the outdoors altogether. Tip it up on

1>

its side, and you have something very like the Millennium Tower. With its lift shuttles in banks six high, like a vertical mass transit system, it certainly presents the possibility of pollution-free commuting. And it also reflects Foster's belief in the ability of high-density mixed-use structures that blur the boundaries between building types to make for a more vibrant city. Not just a residential building or an office building, but both. Add entertainment and a hotel and combine all four functions in a single building. And, of course, it presents the architect with the chance to address a far more interesting challenge than the single-use high-rise, which is quickly reduced to a problem of planning the lifts, the structure and the skin.

Just as globalisation is creating all the signs and symbols of a single metropolitan culture in which the same icons of corporate imagery appear everywhere, so we are discovering the necessity to find new ways of creating a sense of individual identity and difference. The more each city is shaped by the same forces, and the more they appear to become part of a single, global system, the more we look for ways of making a sense of distinctiveness and place. It is an issue that, with the global reach of architecture, is becoming increasingly pressing. What are the ways in which a high-rise tower can be tailored to the specifics of the Pearl River delta, or Korea, or Beirut? How should a civic building in Bahrain differ from one in Marseilles? Twenty years ago it would have been received wisdom that the cosmetic application of a vernacular style or motif would have been appropriate. That has never been Foster's approach – he has always looked for deeper predisposing characteristics: climate, *genius loci*, energy and the rest.

It is the difference between the generic building type, and the specific. The Hongkong and Shanghai Bank building in Hong Kong is a remarkable example of a building entirely specific to a place and to particular circumstances. It is a landmark building which serves to define context like no other. But it also results from the collaboration of a collection of global contractors – from Japan, the USA and the UK – and is the product of an architectural sensibility that relies on constant experimentation and exploration rather than on the pursuit of precedent. By reinventing the skyscraper, Foster made a building that seemed to define the city in which it stands.

It is the responsibility of every architect to design with, rather than against, the grain of energy considerations and sustainability. While the idea of using the

Deyan Sudjic

building fabric as a climate modifier is as old as architecture itself, the modern science of high-technology ways of dealing with the issue is still in its infancy. It is as yet a far from exact science; agreement has still to be reached on consistent ways of measuring energy performance in use, in construction, and over the long term. We are still in the early days of framing an adequate response.

The situation is analogous to the first days of flying, with many independent inventors experimenting with various approaches to getting the best out of heavier-than-air, powered flight. Was it the biplane or the triplane that offered the most productive direction? Would the engines face backwards or forwards? Each of these approaches ended up making aircraft that looked as if they belonged to entirely different species. In the same way there have been radically different approaches to sustainability in architecture. Do you design for long life, or low cost-in-use? Do you minimise the fuel costs of transporting materials to site? And there has been a tendency to assume that certain visual signals represent sustainability. So far these have tended to equate virtuous performance with so-called 'natural' materials and unambitious spatial qualities. But Foster does not see it this way. It is not what something looks as if it does, but how it performs, that matters. Don't forget that this is a man who was so struck by Fuller's question 'How much does your building weigh?' that he made a point of knowing down to the last kilogram.

The conventional wisdom is that a sustainable skyscraper is a contradiction in terms: skyscrapers are of themselves a type that can be equated with insensitive, exploitative, capitalist development; they are full of energy-consuming devices. But Foster has never had much time for this kind of hand-wringing hair-shirtism. Instead he adopts a cooler more calculating approach. The Commerzbank tower in Frankfurt, currently Europe's tallest high-rise, is not simply a building that is big for the sake of it. Naturally ventilated, thanks to the four-storey-high internal gardens which spiral up around the edge of the building, it is, in Foster's terms, all about sustainability.

The workplace is as much as anything the determining factor in shaping the geography of the city. The early industrial cities were all about concentration, the product of their dependence on the endurance of the pedestrian employing the only practical means of transport. That concentration is no longer necessary. And it is one of the major challenges traditional cities have to face.

The idea of the workplace as a democratic environment has been a key issue for Foster ever since Reliance Controls and the Fred Olsen Amenity Centre in the London Docks. It is a poignant witness to the pace of change that these revolutionary buildings have been demolished, superseded by shifts in the world of work.

In retrospect the Olsen project was the last gasp of the upstream dock industry in London. Built at a time when it was not yet obvious just what a dramatic change the containerisation of shipping would bring to London's thousands of acres of docks, Foster's project tried to create modern working conditions for an industry that was to turn out to be doomed.

The Amenity Centre was an attempt by a well-intentioned employer to address the positively medieval working practices of the dock industry, to abolish, as Foster himself once so eloquently put it, the 'distinctions between us and them, posh and scruffy'. And indeed it was a remarkable achievement. Britain suddenly seemed to escape from the black-and-white, cloth-cap and pin-stripe caricature of labour relations, to emerge blinking into a new world of vivid colour. Foster showed that it was possible to create a working environment for dockers that would be shown in the glossy magazines with its Eames chairs, carpets, restaurants shared between management and workers, venetian blinds, and even a view out over the river. Two radically different worlds, usually in collision, were for the first time brought together.

As it transpired, the Olsen company ended up following its rivals down river, leaving the building to be taken over by the London Docklands Development Corporation as its temporary headquarters. From here the LDDC was to address the regeneration of the whole area a decade before Canary Wharf was considered anything more than a place for tin sheds and back offices.

Interestingly, it is the Foster-designed Jubilee Line Underground station at Canary Wharf (2) that is making that development function adequately for the first time. And it has made possible the building of Foster's 40-storey Hongkong and Shanghai Banking Corporation global headquarters just a few hundred metres from the site of that original steel and glass box for Olsen.

Of course the nature of the workplace has shifted in the last 30 years. It is never just the form of the building itself that counts. It is the relationship of one worker to another; how the workforce get to work; the furniture that they use – an

Deyan Sudjic

issue that has increasingly been the focus of Foster's attention since the practice established a specific expertise in industrial design. But the ideas about a civilised workplace that shaped Olsen hold good for Commerzbank and Swiss Re, where it is still the idea of how the workplace 'feels' to the individual at the desk that drives the design.

We have been living on the investment that the nineteenth century made in infrastructure to make life in the metropolis possible. New growth, new technology, shifts in the landscape, and the urgent need to replace worn-out infrastructure, is leading to a new generation of large-scale projects to provide an essential new generation of infrastructure. It was Barcelona that demonstrated what an important symbolic as well as practical role this investment plays when it built the Collserola tower. And it was the investment in the Jubilee Line, the essential infrastructure project for Canary Wharf, which was vital to the development's success.

The city is shaped by a number of defining building types. The workplace is one; the public realm where individuals come together to feel that they are part of a larger whole is another. Such places can be defined in a wide variety of ways. The public realm is the traditional reflection of civilised urban values. The artefacts that the community chooses to put into the street and the quality of the materials underfoot reflect those values. This is something of which city builders have been well aware since the earliest days. And it is a memory that is reflected in Foster's work on the proposed partial pedestrianisation of Trafalgar Square as part of his 'World Squares for All' masterplan. But it is also defined through the invention of new kinds of social arena. And these are vital to providing a sense of identification with an individual city in the midst of an increasingly formless urban landscape.

The threat posed by a loss of this sense of communal urban identity is clear to see. Look at the way the privileged of Los Angeles seek to distance themselves from the city's ghettoes. Beverly Hills and West Hollywood have virtually escaped LA jurisdiction, as could be seen only too clearly when the rioters from Compton were left to burn their own neighbourhoods, but were repelled by force when they tried to enter Beverly Hills.

It can be dangerous continually to refer back to that traditional Greek type, the agora. Even if Hammersmith Broadway had been built as Foster planned, it would not have been a place where the citizens of west London gathered to discuss issues of state, or even to trade in the market place. It would just as likely have been somewhere that troublesome teenagers would have congregated at the burger bar in their back-to-front baseball caps and trousers three sizes too baggy. It's where commuters would have parked underground on their way to catch the Piccadilly Line into central London. And yet it would also have been an attempt at civilising a banal corner of London, a demonstration that it is possible to do things well. A demonstration that it is still possible to make a 'place'.

Such opportunities can come in unexpected corners of the city. The airport, for example, has come to play a role which goes far beyond its function as a place in which to board aircraft. It is a world of shopping and hotels, a place to eat and drink and meet people. Every year Gatwick, London's second airport, attracts 500,000 people (it could be more – it is difficult to count precisely) who are not there to catch a plane, to work or to greet or see people off. They come because it is a place to be. The airport is not tidily confined behind a perimeter fence. It spills over into the wider world as an essential part of the city. Moreover, it is a contemporary version of the city gate, a reflection of civic and national prestige.

The airport, alongside the museum and the shopping mall, has become one of the key public spaces that serve to define the contemporary city. A complex and multi-layered environment, the airport has developed a social hierarchy of public, private and semi-private spaces that are as intricate as any devised in the hidden courts of imperial Beijing's Forbidden City. There is the boundary set by customs and immigration officials, which delineates national from international territory; even though they may overlap spatially, both have their own circulation routes, their own restaurants and shops, their own identity. There is the frantic public world of the arrival and departure halls on the so-called 'land side' of this boundary, where people congregate. And behind the immigration security line, there is an even more tightly defended boundary, one that controls access to the aircraft itself, defending against terrorism and smuggling.

Airports are wealth generators. Every airline that flies into Hong Kong reinforces the city's pre-eminence as an airline hub, offering yet more destinations, and earning the city more money from landing fees. But Singapore, Kuala Lumpur and Bangkok are fighting to make themselves the primary hub for Asia. And the architecture of the airport is a vital competitive advantage in the struggle between them.

Deyan Sudjic

Foster's new terminal has given Hong Kong a second landmark of international significance. But it is not its sheer size that makes Chek Lap Kok so impressive. It is the sense of order and calm. Foster has eliminated as much of the visual noise as possible, restricting the range of finishes to a minimum. The structure is planned to make it as clear as possible in which direction passengers should be heading at every stage in their journey. And at the same time he has brought sunlight right into the heart of the building.

Chek Lap Kok is a powerful blend of the international culture of air travel, with the messy vitality of Hong Kong. Inside its vast spaces you find almost all the elements of a contemporary city: offices, a police station, a chapel, restaurants, shops. But the space is so big that, despite Foster's urge for order, the chaotic energy of the contemporary Chinese city outside the gates has managed to find its way into the very core of the airport without diluting the strength of the original concept. Alongside the boutiques of Cartier, Gucci and Harrods, there is the Fook Ming Tong tea house, and a restaurant that seeks to evoke a back-street *dim sum* cafe from 1930s Shanghai, complete with fibreglass-moon gate and ancient bicycles. There is a giant plastic giraffe poking its neck over the glass wall of the mezzanine in the departure hall, and the sports bar with its giant video screens, and a basketball court, jostling Foster's pristine flight monitors, around which in some places cans of cooking oil and empty vegetable boxes are stacked to shoulder height.

It represents nothing less than the creation of an entire city. And like every successful city it has the strength to outgrow the concept of its architect.

26   LL/LF/LE v Foster – Reyner Banham
34   Willis Faber & Dumas – Christopher Woodward
42   Grass Above, Glass Around – Reyner Banham
48   Speaking of the Sainsbury Centre – Doug Clelland,
      Ron Herron, Leon Krier, Theo Crosby, Robert Maxwell,
      Richard Rogers, Charles Jencks, John McKean
62   Energy: Issues and Attitudes – Loren Butt
68   Foster Associates – Reyner Banham
88   If You Ever Plan to Motor West – Martin Pawley
92   The Constructive Concept – Wilfried Wang
98   Gold Standard – John McKean
106   The Four Phases of Foster – Alastair Best
110   The Thing in the Forecourt – Reyner Banham
114   The Eagle has Landed – Jonathan Glancey
122   Royal Gold Medal Introduction – Robert Sainsbury
128   Royal Gold Medal Conclusion – Buckminster Fuller
132   A Building for the Pacific Century – Chris Abel
148   Foster Development – Alastair Best
154   Feng Shui: Applied Ecology Chinese Style – Hugh D R Baker
160   Hongkong and Shanghai Bank – Vittorio Magnagno Lampugnani
164   An Iron Will – Francois Chaslin
176   The English School – Martin Pawley
180   A Tree-House – Otl Aicher
184   The Years of Innovation – Martin Pawley
202   Architecture and Epistemology – Otl Aicher

220   From Hard to Soft Machines – Chris Abel

244   The Urban Dimension – Robert Maxwell

254   An Airport Where You Can Actually See the Planes – Jonathan Glancey

260   The Human Figure and the Molecule – Rowan Moore

266   Port Side – Martin Pawley

270   Team 4 – Richard Rogers

276   Century Symbol – Malcolm Quantrill

284   A Client's View – Kazuo Akao

288   The Tradition of Big Sheds – Martin Pawley

298   The Industrial Design of Buildings – Thomas Fisher

308   Silence and Memory – Luis Fernández-Galiano

314   Foster Mark Three – Deyan Sudjic

332   Reinventing the Skyscraper – Peter Buchanan

338   Hong Kong International Airport – Sebastiano Brandolini

344   The Impact of Yale – Robert A M Stern

362   Lifting the Spirit – Robert Hughes

368   Norman Foster, Urbanist – Rodolfo Machado

374   The River God – Jonathan Glancey

380   The Reichstag – Charles Jencks

384   On Norman Foster – Kenneth Frampton

404   When Democracy Builds – Peter Buchanan

420   The Architecture of Norman Foster – Joseph Giovannini

428   The Urban Room – Peter Buchanan

438   Norman Foster's Triumph – Kenneth Powell

'The staff tend to affect basic Brook-Street-temp gear – tan jeans, moustaches-of-the-month and accents that span the globe.'

Reyner Banham

Foster Associates have been getting their work on the fronts of architectural magazines again – not surprisingly. Glassy, simple, it's a colour photographer's dream. In real life, much of it is in places and circumstances where the general public won't get much chance to see it. So students of the contemporary scene should be pleased that Foster Associates now work in London's first storefront design studio, handily located in Fitzroy Street. Even so, it's easy to miss what's going on inside – the wall-to-wall, floor-to-ceiling glazing is flush, grey-tinted and highly reflective. With the sun at the wrong angle, the interior can only be seen if you get up on the rubber-paved podium and peer rudely through the glass at close range.

Inside you'll see a fully carpeted open-plan office à la mode, divided into workspaces by Herman Miller A0-2 'advertised in *Scientific American*' system furniture, in a colour gamut that tends to yellows and acky greens (1). A ditto-green wall down one side is punctuated by snub-cornered spaceship doors, giving access to kitchen, lavatories and the usual etceteras. On the other wall leans the boss's racing bike (yellow, naturally). The staff tend to affect basic Brook-Street-temp gear – tan jeans, moustaches-of-the-month and accents that span the globe.

It's a success scene; it's an architectural office doing its thing for fun and profit. The work style suits them, the product visibly suits the sort of client who wants to project a keen liberal image without ceasing to turn a fast buck.

Foster Associates' kind of architecture – lean, elegant, shiny, mechanistic – is the kind of thing that, for half a century, the Modern Movement believed itself to be about. Lightweight, standardised, advanced-technology stuff that the Masters of Modern Design kept trying to build all through the 1920s, '30s and '40s and finally got around to in the 1950s (except Le Corbusier, who'd given up trying). It seems that the professional establishment in architecture recognises that Foster Associates have achieved at least one of the ideals of the Movement, because one of their jobs – for IBM (of course) at Portsmouth – received the 1972 Royal Institute of British Architects' Architecture Award for the southern area of England, and duly appeared on the cover of the *RIBA Journal* last July. Its appearance in so prominent a place in that particular *RIBAJ* involved an irony so cutting as to be satirical and has had architects tittering everywhere.

To explain why requires a short excursion along the frontier between technology and envy. The converse of that RIBA award is architects wondering out loud how Foster 'gets away with it?' Nothing to do with financial skulduggery but about sheer nerve in making buildings. The walls of that IBM building consist of sheets of glass over twelve feet high, held in place by almost nothing; just aluminium glazing bars about an inch wide (4).

On 12 July the good old *Architects' Journal* published Working Detail No 408 (2, 3) (in a series that seems to have been running since Christopher Wren was a lad), which revealed that Foster had achieved this skinny detail at the top of the wall by securing the aluminium bar to a flat capping-strip of steel along the concealed edge of the roof behind. On 19 July a baffled reader writes to *AJ* expressing admiration for the way Foster Associates are developing 'invisible structures', but adding that: 'There seems to be a perfect vehicle for condensation … in the uninsulated mild steel roof capping. Perhaps Mr Foster would care to comment before we all start doing it.'

Certainly the absence of the usual clutter of gaskets, sealing strips, foamed polyurethane and general gunge at this point was impressive. Foster Associates clearly didn't see this as an inviolable trade secret. On 26 July Loren Butt, their mechanical engineer, wrote in a short, businesslike letter to the *AJ*, that the movement of conditioned air under this detail removed any risk of condensation, but that if they had applied anything to the underside of the steel, there might have been condensation between it and the metal, and 'the insulation has been specifically omitted in order to prevent a condensation problem occurring'.

One week later the full import of Butt's explanation dawned on Astragal, the *AJ*'s Pendennis: 'IBM's air-conditioning plant has to be on all the time at night and during the weekends to prevent condensation … heat has to be thrown at the glass wall – to be radiated outwards in vast quantities – to keep the building habitable. The process can only be extremely wasteful. Foster might now turn his back on lightweights and try to design heavy buildings which have many advantages – including an inbuilt resistance to condensation.' Anybody who has tried to cook in the kitchen of a Glasgow tenement with condensation streaming down its (heavy) stone-built walls, anyone who has battled with black mould growing in the standing water on the walls of a tower block built in the once-vaunted 'heavy prefabricated concrete panel' systems, is bound to wonder how Astragal can be so morally positive about so unreliable an 'inbuilt' quality – except that you can never be

Reyner Banham

morally positive in the real world without ignoring contingent factors. Who or what is Astragal that he can presume to ignore factors quite as consequential as these?

A crypto-LL/LF/LE is what he is! He, or one of his demi-independent writing limbs, must be an unavowed member of this new and officially sponsored amalgam of (mostly tame) young ecological radicals and good greying architectural liberals in waistcoats. The official backing comes from the RIBA (it's all a bit like the Festival of Light, somehow) and the unusually modish set of initials stand for Long Life/Loose Fit/Low Energy. This means that buildings ought to last rather longer than the current expectation of about 60 years; that they should not be too tightly tailored to their present functions, so that they can be adapted to other uses over time, not scrapped; and that they shouldn't consume heat, light and other kinds of energy at the wasteful rates now tolerated (not to say encouraged by present tax structures and the like).

All this high-sounding stuff was launched with due presidential pomp and circumstance in a lead editorial in the *RIBAJ*. That's right, irony-spotters, the self-same issue that belaurelled Foster's IBM building.

The PRIBA commended Long Life/Loose Fit/Low Energy to the membership as a 'study ... an attempt to work towards a set of professional ideas to meet the environmental crisis'. That may be how the President sees it. Some hairier adherents to the idea seem to see it as something of a crusade, not a study, and the initials as a kind of magic formula for 'solving' the environmental crisis.

Others, understandably, see it more cynically. Disgruntled RIBA members regard it as an attempt to distract attention from the internal political mess at the institute's headquarters. Trend-watchers saw it as a last desperate scramble onto Raine Dartmouth's environmental bandwagon before it rolled off to the Stockholm Conference with a nude at the prow and not a solitary architect on board.

All are agreed (me, too) that in plugging Long Life/Loose Fit/Low Energy as a quasi-political nostrum, the RIBA is attacking exactly the kind of architecture which it rewarded at IBM. That was specifically a temporary facility, tightly fitted round the client's functional needs, and consuming quite a lot of energy (chiefly because it is virtually impossible to run computers except in air-conditioned environments, and Foster Associates were capitalising on this fact to economise on structure). So the RIBA is speaking either with forked tongue or split personality.

Not that there's anything wrong with the RIBA doing some serious work on environmental problems. If the present alleged study has diverted talent into designing a Long Life-etc. campaign emblem (bearing an unintendedly ironic resemblance to the trademark of Kimberly-Clark paper, which has done so much to contribute to the world's waste-disposal crisis) it has also provided an establishment platform for serious eco-radicals like Andrew McKillop. But in going bull-headed for the slogan concept of LL/LF/LE, the RIBA must appear to be (as the President himself was admitting, almost as soon as that issue of *RIBAJ* came out) 'wanting to pre-empt the result of our study', and making serious research almost impossible. How could a well-intended operation (as I know it to be) have managed to get up the proverbial gum tree so fast?

2

One reason is the well-known polarisation effect, which eliminates third (fourth ... nth) alternatives in all quasi-political debate, and is very marked in architectural polemic. We go straight from high-rise to low-rise, from permissiveness to determinism, from scientism to intuitionism, Classical to Romantic, monumental to ephemeral; you have to be *for* or *against* Le Corbusier, New Towns, pneumatic structures; Utopia is always the opposite direction to the way we are headed. If people like Foster are building lightweight, short-life, energy-consuming, highly precise structures, and we are heading for an energy crisis, then the only salvation lies in the exact opposite of *everything* Foster Associates is doing.

I exaggerate, but not that much. There is another factor at work. In architecture, as in other arts of the possible, a problem is rarely perceived until the answer to it already exists. Architects, understandably, and for good reason as often as not, tend to work from example. When they see others doing it, they call it cribbing. When they do it themselves, it's called a fact-finding tour, or the 'study of typologies'. If the RIBA is plugging LL/LF/LE as the 'solution', the institute must have actual buildings in mind that exist.

They do. The original submission to Lady D made it easier to guess what they were, because it also mentioned heavy construction and less complicated exterior forms. And if ever there was a type of building that had tidy outlines, heavy construction, has lasted a long time, was designed to consume very little energy and is a loose fit on what goes on inside it now, it's the kind of building most of Britain's most influential architects were trained in – the Georgian terraced house! At

3

Liverpool, Cambridge, Edinburgh, Bristol (I can't remember the full list) and above all at the Architectural Association, generations of students have been conditioned by up to seven years of daily exposure to accept Georgian as a kind of universal environmental fail-safe. The Loose Fit myth in particular has been bred in the bone at the AA, which is located in Bedford Square, where other similar houses contain, without strain, functions as seemingly diverse as publishing, moral welfare and various other administrative all-sorts.

So radical eco-chic and greyheaded eco-told-you-so can unite on almost the only premises that all the generations of English architects hold in common. United, they have been saying some pretty alarming things already: one of the grey-heads, who is now delighted to find himself 'leading the profession from the rear', told this year's RIBA conference that for years 'we've been saying you could build buildings simpler, cheaper, better ... with fewer drains (spend the money on important things like decent brickwork)'. Did he really mean that architectural values are more important than health and life support? He's a nice guy, a humane guy. It just shows how silly the debate can get.

Each term of the LL/LF/LE slogan contains a potential silliness of this sort. If we are really going to be as short of land as is currently being doomsaid, then we shall need shorter-life buildings that can all be cleared away when they're not needed to free the land. Loose Fit may be fine for fundamentally similar functions like sitting at office desks in Bedford Square. But how many swimming pools, blast furnaces, cold stores, lifeboat houses and Anglican cathedrals are there in those admired purlieus? And how many cold stores, for instance, could be a loose enough fit to serve as Anglican cathedrals – though plenty of the latter might work wastefully as the former!

The biggest potential silliness concerns the relationship existing between Loose Fit and Low Energy. Holding forth about this kind of thing lately to a student at the AA, I was suddenly struck by the visible fact that adapting two Georgian front parlours into the lecture hall where we had found ourselves – a simple enough piece of loose fitting, you'd think – involved quite a startling amount of electric lights and similar gadgetry, whereupon a well-informed non-student voice from the floor volunteered the most up-to-date figures available: that the AA pays £900 per year rent and £2,000 per year for electricity. Even allowing that the AA currently pays a less than economic rent, the disparity should give the LL/LF/LE campaigners a pause.

Quite a long pause, we architecture-consumers must hope. Long enough for serious reflection, and genuine study. Such research may well show that the kind of adaptability sought in the Loose Fit concept can only be bought at an expenditure of energy that is too high to be acceptable when our energy sources are under strain; and that it would make better sense to design Tight Fit buildings that can take better advantage of the energy that's got to be used anyhow, Foster-style.

For the fact remains that there is no habitable building at all that doesn't use energy of some sort, and quite a lot of it. In Georgian terraced houses the energy source was called Serving Wench, and the fact that she doesn't appear on the architect's plan doesn't mean she wasn't there.

To go back to where we came in: you can only prevent humidity-saturated atmospheres from depositing moisture on walls by having warm enough walls, by throwing heat at them sometimes, in the manner that Astragal found so shocking. That is why you have put an infrared heater or a hot towel rail in your tiled bathroom, right? And if your bathroom has thick brick walls, they may dissipate less heat to the outside world than IBM's glass ones do. Except that you've also opened the window to let the bloody steam out, taking heat with it; and IBM has a closed and controlled air-conditioning system that knows, pretty accurately, where all its heat is going.

If the LL/LF/LE concept is ever properly studied, and the balance of trade-offs between its elements fully understood, it could be that someone is going to have to apologise to Norman Foster. They may have to, since he'll probably be PRIBA by then. If there's any RIBA left to be P of.

4

Reyner Banham

'Questions of scale are neatly avoided. What is the size of the building's subdivisions? Is it the interval of the scarcely visible floor-slabs, or the individually faceted and dynamic reflections of the sky, the buildings opposite or, occasionally, the building reflecting itself?'

Christopher Woodward

'The office building is a house, of work, of organisation, of clarity, of economy. Bright, wide workrooms, easy to oversee, undivided except as the organism of the undertaking is divided. The maximum effect with the minimum expenditure of means. The materials are concrete, iron, glass. Reinforced concrete buildings are by nature skeletal buildings. No noodles or armoured turrets. A construction of girders that carry the weight, and walls that carry no weight. That is to say, buildings consisting of skin and bones.'
Mies van der Rohe, *G*, 1923

'The surface of the Earth would change greatly if brick architecture were everywhere displaced by glass architecture. It would be as though the Earth clad itself in jewellery of brilliants and enamel. The splendour is absolutely unimaginable. And we should then have on the Earth more exquisite things than the gardens of the Arabian Nights. Then we should have a paradise on Earth and would not need to gaze longingly at the paradise in the sky.'
Paul Scheerbart, *Glasarchitektur*, 1914

Ipswich has accidentally become host to a building which materially realises these two early twentieth-century images (1, 2): ordered skin and bones and, almost, the Arabian Nights. After at least 1,200 years of fluctuating commercial activity it is now, with 120,000 people, the largest town in Suffolk, and was identified in the 1960s by two planning consultancies as an area suitable for expansion to meet the then Registrar-General's population model. Ipswich welcomed large firms decentralising from London, and a new but long-planned ring road skirting the dense medieval centre was built to serve these and the newish civic centre.

One of the world's largest firms of insurance brokers, Willis Faber & Dumas first considered moving out of the City some 25 years ago, and had already set up a satellite office in Southend. The imminent expiry of some of its London leases made the amalgamation of its scattered offices sensible, and these have now been condensed into a small City head office, and the much larger country head office – the present building which houses about 1,350 people on a one-hectare site.

Architects were appointed and a small client's committee was set up to plan the move, the management of a stock of temporary buildings in Ipswich and the new building. The ritual job evaluation exercise was carried out, the structure of departments and the relationships between departments were made explicit. This suggested that there was no particular relationship between departments, but that all should be near Accounts. Willis Faber's management was taken through careful discussions of the principles of office planning and the arrangement finally adopted grew out of these meetings. Special presentations, including drawings by an *Evening Standard* cartoonist, were made to explain the proposals to staff, stressing the high standard of working conditions to be expected.

After detailed exploration of several different ways of arranging the accommodation, office space and associated functions, with different storey heights, patterns of organisation, different ideas for the building's envelope, and the fixed constraints of the site, the present strategy emerged: a four-layer sandwich (3). Two floors of open office space are placed between two floors of particular, more differentiated functions: at roof level, a restaurant pavilion and garden; on the ground, entrances, swimming pool, computer and telephone exchange, and some plant. The site is marshy with a high water table and only one small basement connects the feet of two escape stairs.

This sandwich, theoretically indefinitely extendable because it is zoned horizontally, has been trimmed to the edges of the site, which the company had assembled to form nearly the whole of one block. One end of this, with its cottagey scale, is still clearly part of the medieval town, but the other, smoothly curved by the engineering works of the dual-carriageway ring-road, Franciscan Way, faces the stained, crumbling concrete of the largely unlet Greyfriars Centre. Approximately in the middle of the block stands the Unitarian Chapel.

The ruthless and apparently automatic way in which the shape of a plan has been determined more by the accidents of the site than by the building's internal organisation, has had a number of extraordinary effects. It has called for an architectural language which can do again what the corners of most Victorian blocks, especially pubs, did so well in towns not having the convenient assistance of an orthogonal street grid. The problems of form and meaning to which Townscape was addressing itself are neatly parried; the line of the street, its origin now as obscure as that of a country lane, can be reaffirmed, and the street itself transformed, but with materials and techniques only available within the last decade –

Christopher Woodward

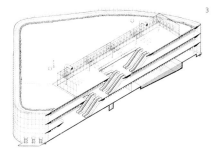

the technically brilliant skin of 4,000 square metres of 12mm, anti-sun, armour-plate glass in 930 panes, set out by computer but placed by suction pads (6).

Questions of scale are neatly avoided. What is the size of the building's subdivisions? Is it the interval of the scarcely visible floor-slabs, or the individually faceted and dynamic reflections of the sky, the buildings opposite or, sometimes, the building reflecting itself?

The entrance hall reveals what is not clear, at least during the day, to the passer-by who has not pressed his nose to the 12mm glass: the four floors behind the facade are connected to each other by six escalators (4) (on which the occupants are already learning to pose). This display is lit by large areas of rooflight set in the white-painted trussed roof of the restaurant four storeys above. On the long axis established by the escalators, placed behind them and behind a framed glass partition, lies the swimming pool, the level of its reflecting surface slightly above that of the surrounding floor; and beyond again stands the farther perimeter glass wall. Parallel with the axis, two long solid yellow tungsten-lit walls race across the green rubber floor.

This hall, again the result of an apparently simplistic planning decision, makes the organisation very easy to understand and to use, and carries two main redolences, neither necessarily intended by the designers. Firstly, there are reminders of the large rooflit and galleried hall, the floor of which served as arena for the exchange of wool, coal, shares or insurance risks, the galleries as divisible offices. The second, more likely, resonance is the Baroque celebration of vertical movement in a big space. Chicago's Rookery and Los Angeles' Bradbury Buildings (5) did this with delicate cast stairs and lift screens. Departmental stores still use escalators in this way, and the decorative style of the space, were it not for the quality of the daylight, suggests a very good California shopping centre.

What look at first sight like alarming geometrical risks have been taken in developing the plan shape from an irregular perimeter: the various sub-systems, whether derived or additive, appear to have been thrown together. At the entrance, one of the regularly spaced perimeter columns faces the user of one of the bank of revolving doors which are skewed to the main axis and not on it. On the office floors, the main 14-square-metre structural grid, while meshing with the openings for the escalators, casually peters out before it reaches the perimeter. At last a

5

fitting use has been found for those neat structural systems – coffered slabs, space frames – which always claim the benefit of allowing their columns to support them in non-regular places. The coffered slabs are now mostly covered up by the polished surface of the suspended ceiling, leaving the irregular grids poking through without the benefit of specific geometrical order.

But these risks, more apparent in the drawings than in life, always produce success: the systems are hardly ever allowed to touch, and never have planning or constructional modules seemed so unimportant. (There is one exception, on the ground and top floors, where heavy glazed black frames are brought out to meet the perimeter at right angles, trimming to the raking underside of the concrete slab edge. But here only the formal clarity falters; the technical requirements of the junction are answered with a large black rubber tube between frame and window.)

The two open office floors are models of quiet and pleasant efficiency. They seem to have fulfilled the promise of the planning of departments and sections using magnetic model furniture arrangements; and they allow the efficient passage of paper through the organisation, although this might later become less significant than the many telephone links, which are received in a new computer-aided silent exchange on the ground floor and which allow desktop print-outs on the office floors. To the main elements of escalator well and perimeter glass wall are added the yellow steel-partitioned cores, a serviced ceiling and floor. The ceiling, finished in reflective metal slats, handles generalised functions like lighting (fluorescent lamps in low-brightness fittings, producing a light that combines well with the daylight through the perimeter grey glass), air handling and sprinklers.

The suspended floor supplies electricity and telephone lines from an uninterrupted void below to people, furniture or machines placed anywhere on it. None of the modestly sized and delicate furniture is more than shoulder height, and its subdued colours against the yellow cores and green carpet reverse the more usual scheme of bright furniture scattered across a neutral background. 'Bright, wide workrooms' indeed. The calm simplicity resulting from an approach to the design of services that avoids some problems of more conventional arrangements and solves those remaining so elegantly, must derive directly from the engineers successfully embedded in the Foster practice. The attitude towards plant is instructive, for instead of being placed and identified in one monumental zone, it is scattered about in odd corners, sometimes 'centrally', sometimes next to what it is serving. A lot of plant is on the ground floor in rooms which differ little visibly (their firefighting arrangements are even more elaborate) from the offices and put on a modest display to the street.

The unwillingness of the designers formally to monumentalise any one of the main elements of the building – neither structure, services, nor the usual paraphernalia of modules – is offset by an obvious pleasure in showing how some things work: the exquisitely detailed white fibreglass trimmed escalators with their already cutaway diagram installed on their sides, the swimming pool plant, and the miniaturised cast-resin transformers of the two packaged electric sub-stations which take up only half the space of their older oil-filled counterparts.

The display of the building as an entity and such flagrant enjoyment of our present building techniques, may cause twinges of guilt in those affected by the too-quickly fashionable noises of reaction. We are now supposed to be hoarding energy, not appearing to delight in its consumption, however relatively mean this may be in an unconventionally thick, low building with unusually efficient lighting.

For only when the steel mills are cold, and managers ride to work on bicycles (with walnut handlebars if necessary) would these offices be unused.

The considered excellence of this building demonstrates conclusively that, in European Architectural Heritage Year, the heritage known in this country as Modern is not as dead as has been supposed, that some well-organised clients still recognise and want it, and that our maligned building industry can, when challenged, find the skills of management and craftsmanship that we too rarely demand in order to produce it.

Christopher Woodward

'Look upon its featureless facades, and you shall see every period of East Anglian urban architecture from Low Gothic to High Brutalist, and almost every catalogued historical detail from *abacus* to *zygus*.'

Reyner Banham

The Willis Faber & Dumas headquarters in Ipswich has taken just over two years to go from nine days' wonder to architectural respectability (RIBA Eastern Region award). But it remains almost as inscrutable as ever. It ought not to be. Most of us by now can 'read' a glass-walled office tower without difficulty. Many of us, indeed, are demonstratively bored by *having* to read them as often as we do. But then, what Foster Associates have designed in Ipswich is not a conventional rectangular tower, but a seemingly free-form four-storey plan, waving about as it pursues the outlines of its site, slickly clad in dark, unmodulated glass from eaves to pavement.

The decision to build in this way in the historical heart of downtown Ipswich can be defended – and has been – on purely functional and economic grounds, as architects are wont to do. But when you have said that, you have said nothing about why it is a controversial, important and (possibly) extremely good building to have on that particular site. All that part of the argument must turn about purely visual, formal and symbolic aspects of the design, because what Norman Foster has done is to mix, without apology, two completely different (some would insist, utterly opposed) sets of architectural approaches, expectations and customary usages.

In the traditions of the Modern Movement in Architecture, glass is of the party of order and hygiene. It stands for the replacement of the slums of the huddled poor by clean crystal towers. It stands for the illumination of dark places of vernacular superstition by the pure light of rationality. Worldwide, it has become the symbolic material of clarity, literal and phenomenal. As such it is, or was, universally delivered in crisp rectangular formats, pure and absolute, impervious to local accidents and customs. It was therefore appropriate to all the aspirations of the founders of the United Nations, who gave it canonical form in their headquarters tower in New York. Less felicitously it proved equally apt to the ambitions of great multinational corporations. Worse yet, to the avarice of downtown developers the world over.

In Ipswich, this last manifestation is represented, just across the street from Willis Faber & Dumas, by the Greyfriars Centre development. But the glass vision is there bowdlerised by the 1960s most favoured substitute for architectural thought, *béton brut* – off-the-form concrete, here so poorly detailed, so neglected and unloved, that it is already growing moss! The architecture of rationality runs down into the architecture of profit and loss; and being without profit, is accounted the deadest of losses.

Against this kind of design is normally set a different Modern tradition which has had many names at different times, but is most fully represented by the doctrine of 'Townscape' advanced by the *Architectural Review* in 1950 and elaborately developed over the years by the *Review's* two brilliant draughtsmen, Gordon Cullen and Kenneth Browne. It has had its triumphs – notably the Festival of Britain – and, in spite of attempts by writers in the *Review's* arch-rival *Architectural Design*, to prove the contrary, continues in the 'Contextualism' of sundry German, Dutch and Belgian gurus that *AD* is pushing at the present time. Essentially, it is an amalgam of picturesque contrast and surprise, with circumspect (and usually sentimental) respect for what the Italian phase of the movement would have called the *ambiente pre-esistente*, plus recycling, rehabilitation and so forth. Above all, not putting up standardised glass boxes all over the world.

That is the latter tradition that Foster's acquiescent pursuit of the boundaries of his given site appears to support. It's not what he usually does: his nearly complete Arts Hangar at the University of East Anglia pays no visible respect to anything at all in its surroundings. So he seems to have made even his faithful fan club uncomfortable, as well as making the opposition feel they are being got at. Yet he has, indeed, made his glazed perimeter follow the soggy curve of a post-war traffic improvement on one side, the irregular joggles of existing medieval streets on two others; and only on the fourth has he imposed a rationalised straight line on an irregular sequence of property boundaries – and that is the least seen of all the elevations.

But then to hang (literally) an uninterrupted and unaccented sinuous curtain of glass all round this 'historical' perimeter … for many good souls it's too much to take, even at the purely conceptual level. No, especially at the conceptual level, since, given the tendency of good-guy ideas to cluster, even when they have no logical connection, the Contextual, 'herbivore' approach has lately taken on board the moral load of energy conservation as well.

Now, 'everybody knows' that glass is an energy-wasteful material. Yet Foster Associates have the gall and (tough luck, herbivores) the figures to show that this is a reasonably energy-efficient structure – partly because its very deep-plan four-storey format gives a low ratio of glass to internal volume (and the glass is deeply bronzed as well) and partly because much of its roof is clad in one of the oldest and most reliable insulating materials known to vernacular wisdom – growing turf (1)!

Reyner Banham

But: turf on top of a high-technology building full of air conditioning, escalators, computers and stuff? Once again separate expectations, different architectural languages, have been shotgun-married without apology or regard for the niceties of academic discourse, where turf is perfectly acceptable as long as it is on small-windowed, irregular, technologically low-profile buildings. Academic polemicists might do well to remember that the man who reminded the present century of the roofing virtues of growing turf was none other than the true and only begetter of the universal, damn-local-traditions, glass-skinned, pure rectangular office block, Le Corbusier himself.

And so on. The pity of it is that much of this academic debate is about matters which are marginal and trivial to the important business of seeing the world better housed, better serviced, better symbolised – but which are matters suitable for academic debate. And Willis Faber & Dumas makes fools of them all. For what really hurts is that the building delivers precisely those anecdotal and serendipitous pleasures to the trained eye that the *Architectural Review* campaigned for 30 years ago and that the Contextualists have now rediscovered via linguistics and a kind of populist neo-Marxism … delivers all that by doing exactly the kind of architecture they would unobservantly claim couldn't do it.

As I recall, it is since Theo Crosby's rather Radical Chic 'Environment Game' show at the Hayward four years ago, that the cry has been for more craftsmanship, more detail, more decoration, more incident – all those qualities that the standard, off-the-peg, Minimalist glass wall could never give, and was therefore deemed uncultured and dehumanising. Foster's wavy wall, with its storey-high sheets of glass butted edge to edge without framing, is even more detail-free than glass walls usually are. Yet when you look at the building you see almost nothing but craftsmanship, detailing, incidents, decoration, historical values – all reflected from the buildings on the other side of the street.

Look upon its featureless facades, and you shall see every period of East Anglian urban architecture from Low Gothic to High Brutalist, and almost every catalogued historical detail from *abacus* to *zygus*. Spire and dome are there, chimney and gable, column and pilaster, arches round, ogival and pointed. Better still, by choosing your viewpoints with creative care, you can manoeuvre an artisan-Mannerist gable (reflected) on top of a modern matt-black metal ventilating grille

2

(real), and make them fit together exactly. Indeed, you need to keep your eyes peeled and your wits about you, because the facade can deliver sequences of this sort of effect quicker than you can keep up with at normal walking pace (2, 3).

The reason for this quick-change display of visual puns, oxymorons, metaphors and other tropes, is that the facades are curved but the glass is flat. So no two adjoining facets are in the same plane and thus reflect non-adjoining subject matter. Everything is reflected in tall vertical slices, with violent visual discontinuities between the content of one slice and the next. You may, for instance, on the in-curved side toward Friars Street, observe the same facing building reflected (in part) twice, several panes apart. The intervening facets are taken up with a quotation from a totally different building opposite, a short length of Willis Faber reflected at right angles to itself, and a tree apparently in a different part of Ipswich altogether.

These are exactly the kind of visual effects – surprise, truncation, concealment, confrontation – for which Townscape always campaigned. Looking back now on the discomfiture the *Architectural Review* clearly experienced when confronted with this building (that did so many things that the *AR* held dear by architectural means the magazine's editors affected to abominate) it would be difficult not to smile, but for the contemptible intellectual contortions the editors went through to find something definitively bad with which to damn it. After two pages of praising with faint damns, they finally produced their polemical master-stroke (sic) – the possibility of two such buildings: 'One Willis Faber & Dumas building may be a revelation, but two facing one another make a prison.'

Come off it! Two such facades facing one another would not (just) reflect a lack of craftsmanly detail on both sides of the street, but also – as in all facing-mirror situations – the viewer repeated to infinity in both directions. Not only does that flatter the viewer, but it is a form of ego massage which the editors of the *Architectural Review* enjoy all over their editorial offices every day of the working week, for their premises are notoriously the most bemirrored in the business. Perhaps they're just jealous. Perhaps it is not flattering to see a bankrupt ideological position reflected to infinity. Perhaps they should put turf on their heads and see if that looks any better.

Reyner Banham

'Foster is forcing us to eat soup with a fork, and with a very well-designed fork at that.'

Leon Krier

In August 1978, *AD* magazine (then a bastion of Post-Modernist thought) published a special issue on the newly completed Sainsbury Centre for Visual Arts (1).
It incorporated a critics' chorus of commentaries by several architects, a few
friends of Foster Associates, and some of the people connected with the building.
Their views covered the spectrum from laudatory to censorious. As *AD* concluded:
'The excitement and contention that has been the Sainsbury Centre for Visual Arts
suggests that it is indeed a polemical work of architecture.'

Doug Clelland

'Much Ado About Nothing or The Fetishist is Out': whether it is a 'shed' or an unintentional surrealism, a 'masterpiece' or an elitist 'sardine can', a 'foretaste of the
1980s' or 'a machine for displaying things in' with officially accepted 'snags', seem
trivial questions to me.[1]

    Whether or not Sir Robert Sainsbury's desire for 'informality' or his accolade
that the building is 'the gem of my collection' (would he dare say 'the most primitive rubbish of my collection'?) sets the tenor for appraisal; whether or not the
Hollywood pulp phrases of 'cathedral', 'enormous clarity and controlled reticence'
or 'classic simplicity' help us understand the building; whether or not the claim of
some pundits that even the declared aims of technical competence have failed is
more than sour grapes – all are debatable points.

    Perhaps in brief comments such as this, all one can offer are other clichés,
generalities and crumbs of wisdom, which neither add to the ego of the Foster factory nor deepen understanding of the building's place in contemporary life and its
architecture. However, my clichés, generalities and crumbs of wisdom are these:

1. The building, its location and its contents are all peripheral to the evolutionary
'theatre' of industrial society. Visual art centres (whatever the design) are containers of dead art; the building is on the edge of a campus, on the edge of a country
town on the edge of Britain; the collection does not rate placement in the first or
second divisions in terms of either size, range or excellence of type.

2. The building, not therefore being important, should be understood for what it is
– a *fetishist expressionism*. Like the sexual fetish of leather, this building celebrates

the cladding of the object – the aluminium trappings, clips, straps and other paraphernalia become the beloved. The fascination with the six-bolted interchangeable
aluminium, glass or louvred panel has kept Foster's team steadfastly (obediently?)
at work – will keep the visiting fetishist steadfastly (obediently?) at work –
expressing and revelling in the cool feel and sight of the aluminiumed ass. Yet what
a trivial and peripheral business is all that.

3. As *fetishist expressionism,* it can only be understood in its own marginal terms.
Just as with the life of leather, it is all-consuming for the few, uninteresting for the
many, and extremely boring for the discerning. To revisit this building or to use it
day by day is a bore.

4. The boredom inherent in the building is obviously not experienced or understood by the aluminium or glass fetishist, yet what I will call the one-dimensional
nature of the fetish is indeed a problem if we are to take this building seriously.
The structure and the texture of the thing is clear evidence of the UNIFICATION
and ultimate UNIFORMITY of technologically determined intentions in architecture. Since one has received such messages from the thing, nothing is left to
stimulate or to keep one inquisitive.[2]

5. That the patronage comes from supermarket supremos is clearly apparent from
the building. The graphic quality of the package is as good as a can of soup, and
the quality – at least cost philosophy – shines through in the price tag. Had the
building lots of car-parking around it, rather than East Anglian countryside, it might
actually be the archetypal Sainsbury's hypermarket – and this I am quite sure is
how most people will read it. When we cut all the crap, it is no more or no less
interesting than a can of Campbell's – no, Sainsbury's – soup. Pick up a
Giacometti, pass easily through the payout counter, and warm it up in the tranquillity of your home.

Well what is one actually saying? First, I do not find the building important,
relevant or interesting. Second, it is good to see a well-constructed object produced in Britain. Third, the building has all the short-impact graphic qualities of a

can of soup. Fourth, one must welcome pluralism in architecture,[3] and therefore inherently one must support particular interests be they vernacular or aluminium. Fifth, I find this particular set of interests of *fetishist expressionism* extremely boring and, if extended into town or campus planning, extremely dangerous, due to the extremely limited set of intentions lying behind the creation of the object.

To conclude with a banality (the editor will not allow an atrocity), this building and all its fellow travellers do not suggest an adequate architecture. Rather than a banner for the international scene, it is an interesting fetish from the *demi-monde*. I much prefer less illiterate architecture.

Ron Herron

I recently found myself buying an English architectural magazine other than *AD* for the first time in many years because it featured the Sainsbury Centre's 'shiny box'. This is an indictment not only of the magazines but also of the current boring state of architecture in England.

It is good to see an English architect muscle-flexing and producing work that is tough, obsessive and wilful, amongst so much work that is reasonable, sensitive and contextually proper.

The juxtaposition of the Sainsbury Centre and that icon of the 1950s, the University of East Anglia, with its stepped section, 45° geometry and flat-site, hill-town imagery, is to be enjoyed as much for their opposing ideologies as for their shared heroism.

One is immediately reminded of those earlier, 'shed' and 'kit-of-parts' images … the market hall at Clichy, the grandiloquent sheds of Konrad Wachsmann (not Mies), the potteries 'Thinkbelt' of Cedric Price, the Ford Tri-Motor, the People's Car of Hitler's Germany, and for me the Nissen hut in which I lived during my National Service in the RAF, in the service space between the two metal skins of which lived not service engineers but fieldmice.

This version of the much-loved 'well-serviced shed', although sophisticated, quite beautiful and a much-needed built model, suffers, as does its predecessors, from being over-concerned with dazzling us with its display of environmental hardware and technological symbols – the super-cool 'well-serviced shed' has still to be achieved, as has that other implied component, complete flexibility.

Leon Krier

'The fable of the fork and the soup': nobody could possibly have found a more remote spot to situate the only public building on campus. The idea must have been that the ever-empty bridges and decks separating the pedestrians from virtually non-existent traffic would perhaps become enlivened by strolling cultural tourists?

Having grown used to the industrial crudeness and brutality of Sir Denys' environment (it is difficult to imagine, but it was all designed from an office in dignified Queen Anne Street by architects who probably all live in Georgian or Victorian terraced houses) I was surprised by the elegance and dignity of Foster's Sainsbury shed. I was moved by its beauty in the same way I am moved by the beauty of an aeroplane, war engine or steel mill.

However, I know that these emotions have nothing to do with architecture, although Foster Associates have undoubtedly displayed art in the *wrapping* of their programme. One reason for my dissidence is that I think an 'industrial' shed or warehouse, however beautiful, is inappropriate to shelter artisanal art or cult objects, in the same way as it is inappropriate to frame a classical landscape painting with an extruded aluminium profile; everybody knows that.

Both these RIBA architects indulge in the same myth of serial production and standard details in a false myth of modernity.

We have to talk here about style because with Foster's and Lasdun's aesthetics we are not in the reality of necessity but of pure style or rather styling. Their methods of producing extremely small series have no more to do with industrial production in 1978 than would the construction of a Classical temple today.

Yet these two RIBA architects and their conscious or unconscious followers like to think that the aesthetic sense they display has something to do with our industrial civilisation, with this very moment in history, and probably with *Zeitgeist*.

I can affirm that their aesthetic sense is, at its best, nothing more than a *nostalgia* for outdated and objectively unnecessary industrial methods of production; and further, that the *Zeitgeist* reveals itself neither in the length of neoprene profiles, nor in the size of sheets of glass.

Both these RIBA architects sustain false myths, and, above all, they do it against any empirical necessity – and that is where the fraud, the false pretension, the mystification – their 'crime' – lies.

Another false *myth* is the appropriateness of large-span sheds for virtually any situation. Considering Foster's typological choice and its inner distribution, I felt that we are in the presence of an extremely stubborn man, who, given the opportunity, would force virtually everything, even his grandmother, into the same shed.

The size of the shed is not defined by its appropriateness for a certain social performance but purely by the size of the overall programme, the shed being apparently typologically 'neutral'. This is, of course, an imbecility and it forces Foster to locate working spaces in the middle of the landscape in eternal darkness.

Contrary to this, is it not true that industrial plants are always built to a constructional *type* that is most appropriate to the *type* of function or organisation they house? This is why an assembly line looks different from a design studio, or why a warehouse uses a different form of construction from that of a steel mill.

Foster's choice of constructional types is clearly *not* to do with any typological concern, but purely to do with style – it is to do with expressing and materialising a myth of industrial production. It is, therefore, to do with ideology. However he might want to escape the issue, his very 'neutrality, efficiency, and just doing the job-ness' are the materialisation of industrial ideology obsessed, it seems, with a little reflected *warehouse mentality*.

Foster is forcing us to eat soup with a fork, and with a very well-designed fork at that. If you are forced to eat soup with a fork you will most certainly damage your health, you might even forget about spoons.

Those who have not forgotten the taste of soup are now busy thinking about the nature and necessity of a spoon to eat the soup – if there is any left, that is.

Theo Crosby

In the early 1920s, when Wyndham Lewis asked architects 'where is your bullring for our healthy young bull', he wanted an architecture to complement the vigorous new painting. By the time the architects had got round to it, his bull had died. It is much the same with the Sainsbury Centre, for it reflects the aesthetic preoccupations of the 1950s, the reductionist impulse which had foundered by 1970.

It is a splendid building and, in its own terms, beautiful and successful. It is detailed with skill and resolution and it gives great pleasure.

But the bull is dead and we begin to look for something other.

First, a kind of ordered hierarchy which would make sense of the form – an entrance perhaps which is recognisable, part of a language.

Second, volumes which carry more than a single emotion – a meaning other than elementary function.

Third, reference to the place, to nature and to the past from which the future can be faced with secure continuity.

On all these counts it's a failure.

Robert Maxwell

The year of the Sainsbury Centre, as it happens, was the year I finally saw the Parthenon: both experiences were exhilarating.

The comparison is far-fetched, but not entirely pointless. One is a CELLA, the other a SHED – but both are strictly rational and fully frontal, with a portico at either end, one of which is clearly marked 'front' and the other 'back'.

Both are taut buildings; although with one it is purely visual refinement which animates the inert stone (as in the bowing up of the peristyle), while with the other, it is a technical refinement which stabilises the tense structure (as in the bowing up of the main trusses). The comparison can't admittedly go much further. To find something ancient to compare with the *space* in Sainsbury we have to advance to King's College Chapel, Cambridge, which is practically modern times.

Why such high-minded comparisons, which will probably be thought invidious by Modernist and traditionalist alike?

I'm sure Norman Foster had no images of ancient architecture in mind, and that he was bent on nothing but the severest practicality once the overall concept was fixed. But the conviction he has imposed on the concept has resulted in a fusing of form and content, so that the details are raised to the level of the ideology.

A living room for the arts may seem rather different from a house for the gods. Allow for two thousand years of history and science, and we can see that both buildings convey the central belief of their time: as the Greeks believed that the gods were fundamentally open to human ideas, we believe that the material universe is open to the human imprint, that it is *at our disposal.*

Corb's comparison of the Parthenon's Doric and the machine aesthetic is still to the point here. For Foster the machine aesthetic is, simply, the aesthetic of the

machine. The building is to be thought of as a machine – a bit of an airship, in this case. That a design aimed at creating a prototype should have archetypal aspects is not surprising. In Foster the Modern Movement lives – possibly to confound us all.

Richard Rogers

Let us not be mealy-mouthed. By dint of sweat, imagination and superb control Norman Foster, during the past five years, has produced two great buildings, which stand proudly and lonely amongst the mediocrity that surrounds us.

To stand outside the free-formed Willis Faber building and see the disciplined way it fills the site, the internal structure changing step as it nears the exterior, all wrapped in a no-hands, taut, tight, all-reflecting skin, or to stand inside and experience the heroic scale and simplicity of the Sainsbury Centre, fills me with wonder.

From the micro to the macro the Sainsbury Centre represents the rational marshalling of information and the orderly and elegant resolution of the problem of creating a modern temple for art, teaching, and the public. A true, uncompromising, machine expression of man against nature.

The glistening grey interior space is dynamic, Spartan and spare. Flexibility and enclosure are reconciled in the precise yet fluid machine environment. The lightweight, all-enclosing, zipped/unzipped skin wraps around Tony Hunt's brilliant semi-exposed skeletal structure, which contains the mechanical services. A shimmering changing light gives an ethereal steel substance to the interior, the open glazed ends framing the trees and lake beyond. For the first time, highly insulated prefabricated walls and the roof are the same, zipped together by continuous neoprene so that solid, translucent, and transparent panels may be interchanged in answer to the brief's changing needs both present and future.

The subtle layering of the exposed components in the interior and the drawing back of the glass skin at the ends to expose the structure gives those areas grain, scale and the easy legibility of an open-ended Meccano system. This goes beyond Willis Faber, where the monochromatic taut skin would have exploded if forced to incorporate other elements.

There are always concepts that we might question and challenge, but I prefer to recognise that this is a uniquely audacious and heroic statement carried out with perfect control. It offers food for thought and gives true delight.

Charles Jencks

Norman Foster's recently completed Sainsbury Centre in East Anglia is a typical Late-Modern building. Like Arata Isozaki's Gunma Museum, it is an uncompromising image of technology and repetition, and like Isozaki, Foster repeats an aluminium grid panel endlessly, as if it were the answer to everything – roof, wall and inside surface. This 'doing more' with 'less elements' is close to the Modernist incantation 'less is more', and like the former hocus-pocus it can sometimes work.

The excitement of the Sainsbury Centre is partly caused by such sorcery. The same 'superplastic aluminium' panel wraps around the (almost) flat roof, corner, and wall, thus giving a visual and semantic identity to elements which are conventionally distinguished by material and use. James Stirling plays the same trick in his Olivetti building and also places the gutter 'where it shouldn't be' (on the ground). In both cases the distortion of traditional syntax becomes a kind of magic, shrinking the building into a piece of domestic equipment: an Olivetti typewriter in the case of Stirling, and a computer cassette, or punch-card, in the case of Foster. But, and this makes the Sainsbury Centre Late rather than Post-Modern, the metaphor doesn't seem either intended or particularly apt for the function – in this case, viewing works of art. The criticisms of Sainsbury, and there have been some, often concern this metaphorical unsuitability. From the end elevation it looks like an 'aeroplane hangar' and even on the inside the grand space dwarfs the activities and the (relatively) minuscule works of art, as an aeroplane hangar would.

Like the Centre Pompidou in Paris (another Late-Modern 'museum' among other things), a single, linear spatial idea dominates all other concerns. But, and this is the point of Late-Modern sorcery, the vices of the work are, in a different light, the virtues. We overlook the homogeneity of the space *because of* its single-minded beauty. We suspend our disbelief, as we do before art, to judge it on its own terms; and these terms are, once again, extreme. The light quality of the ceiling is unlike anything we've ever seen before at this scale – shimmering, playful, iridescent, disturbing, like a thousand Bridget Riley optical vibrations laid end to end. It goes on buzzing and dancing overhead, with its 'motorised louvres', not for a hundred feet, but for over four hundred.

The conceptual logic is even more extreme. Basically the art gallery is *all* one building, a zone of services (WCs, stores, darkrooms etc.) wrapped *all* around

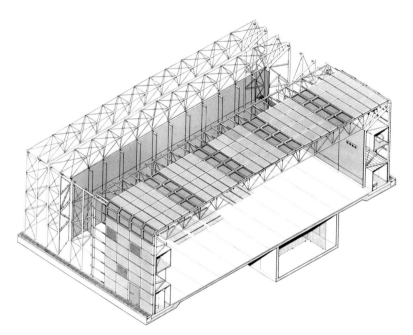

another building (the gallery and work areas). Like Cesar Pelli's work, the 'skin membrane' (2.4 metres wide) is *all* extrusion in one direction, so that the end elevation is *all* section (or a projection of it). Like Superstudio's Continuous Monument or Archigram's No-Stop City, the open space is isotropic – that is, *all* the same in every direction (except for differences in length). Like the 'well-serviced shed' idea of the 1960s, *all* the building fabric seems to come from functional requirements (structure and mechanical equipment). We might conclude that the Sainsbury Centre is an ultra-Modern building with no exceptions, ambiguities or second thoughts, which summarises *all* the extreme aspects of Late Modernism.

John McKean

We all know before arriving that it's a Contextualist's thumbed nose; that even if it looks like a shed it is amazingly, intricately inventive; that wall or roof panels can be changed from door to solid to window and back in the blink of an eye; that

vacuum-formed aluminium or mile-long neoprene strips are no mean feat; that, like all good Sainsburys, it's closed on Mondays.

But then it's dark. Bitter cold, driving sleet and snow as I walk the long narrow high bridge from the little town of Lasdun et al., towards the lighted hole, high in that huge grey shadow.

The glass airlock swings open.

Silver and grey, mist and sparkle into space. The soft warm purring mechanical inside, vast as the eye can see, which all our dreams know so well (the science-fiction hive; out of the tense, dark tunnel, suddenly into the glittering calm hum of the huge womb, onto a platform below which spreads out the secret space station, the underground city).

But here, somehow, it's theatrically friendly; an intimate hugeness; spacious to take the different pursuits, but − as among the 'living area' *Bürolandschaft* − small; and Superman's tiny crystalline lift; all at home within its shimmering louvred aluminium tent and black reflective gables.

I wonder what the Crystal Palace was like at night?

Critics' Chorus

'Energy is a servant not a master; it is there to be used, but used intelligently.'

The energy consumption of buildings is, and has always been, subject to the inter-action between physical, environmental, economic and social influences. The abnormally high oil price increases in 1973-74 changed nothing fundamentally but stimulated a new interest and attention to the subject. Some resulting influences have been good, some bad, some innocently misinformed. Energy has also become a platform for moralist and political comment, e.g., capitalism thrives whilst the planet's natural resources are squandered, polluting the environment into the bargain. Research has followed: low technology, e.g., windmills and solar panels, and high technology, e.g., fuel cells and thermoelectric semi-conductor materials. In the building industry new justifications for energy conservation tech-niques now abound; voices ignored in the wilderness for years are heeded for the first time. Governments identify energy as an issue that they must be seen to take seriously and inevitably demonstrate this by introducing more legislation.

Foster Associates' attitude to energy from the 1960s through the 'oil crisis' to the present time has remained consistent. Energy is a servant not a master; it is there to be used, but used intelligently. That obviously implies a concern for con-servation, but in the context of striving first for the highest possible standards of design and, in doing so, making buildings as effective as possible for the activities they house. The cost of energy used in most commercial and industrial buildings is a small part of the total cash flow they generate and as such should be kept in perspective. Energy conservation is just one of the main constraints of architec-tural design and can be acknowledged in positive ways; it should never be an excuse for poor design.

What are the factors influencing the energy consumption of a building? Basically they are its shape, the nature of its enclosing envelope, its internal light-ing and mechanical servicing systems, and the way these are run; very important too are its materials of construction, because the production and assembly of those materials also involves energy consumption. Reference to some aspects of the office building for Willis Faber & Dumas in Ipswich (1-3) will perhaps serve to illustrate some attitudes to the deployment of energy.

The building is essentially a deep-plan form, with artificial lighting and com-fort air conditioning used all year round; its main workforce of 1,300 people is housed on two floors, each of about 6,500 square metres gross area. Whilst a

shallow-plan form with natural lighting, radiator heating and ventilation by opening windows might be shown at a superficial level to use less energy, the loss of efficiency in terms of space utilisation, personal communications and environmental working conditions would make such a building relatively expensive to own in total.

The primary elements of the building envelope are glass on the vertical walls, and a landscaped roof. The function of the glass wall is twofold: to present a non-assertive appearance in its medieval market town surroundings, and to provide the best possible outward views for the occupants of the building, in order to enhance their working environment in an architectural sense. Some might see it as wasteful, but is it? First, its surface area is relatively small in relation to the all-important working floor area it encloses; second, it is a deeply tinted glass which absorbs daytime radiation and thereby reduces heat losses – even on quite dull days the effect is noticeable, and the savings show up on the main gas meter. Used in conjunction with a special internal louvre material, which controls glare without losing the identifiable details of the outward view, the glass reduces summer solar heat gains very much below that of ordinary clear glass and even below that of clear glass with view-obstructing venetian blinds.

The roof of the building, which is considerably larger in area than the vertical walls, has grass growing on it. The first aim of this was to give the users of the office space a positive amenity, which would be seen from the adjacent restaurant pavilion and would be there for them to enjoy during lunchtime relaxation. The roofs of so many office buildings are 'thrown away', i.e., covered with asphalt or allowed to become a repository for all manner of mechanical plant without much consideration for the visual consequences. But along with the amenity value comes an energy conservation advantage, and with that a solution to a particular construction problem: in order to grow grass on a roof it is necessary to build up a complex and deep layering of waterproofing membranes, insulation, drainage bed and, of course, fine soil. All this can't help but create an exceptionally good thermal insulation value, which in turn solves the structural engineer's usual problem of expansion and contraction in the building's main frame, because that finds itself virtually unaffected by outdoor temperatures under a thick insulating blanket.

The internal lighting of very deep-plan buildings poses special problems. The greatest of these is source glare, i.e., light directly striking the peripheral vision of

Loren Butt

the users' eyes. At Willis Faber this problem was solved by using light fittings deeply recessed into the suspended ceiling, with carefully shaped aluminium reflectors directing the light output downwards: as a result no direct light strikes the eyes (unless one looks significantly above a horizontal plane). The only real evidence that the lights are on is that there is very good light for working tasks and moving around the office space! Once again it works well first and foremost at design and environmental levels, but it also produces an energy-saving benefit: by controlling the light output so effectively the energy input to the lamps is much lower, about half in fact, than light fittings with diffusers at the ceiling plane.

The mechanical engineering systems for comfort air conditioning of the building embody a number of important decisions: some of these represent particular views which evolved over many years of experience. The building was designed before the oil crisis, but careful consideration was given to energy conservation through its mechanical systems. Many such systems exist and are popular in current new buildings: some of the systems have disadvantages, which should be (but often are not) weighed against their theoretical energy savings. The important disadvantages, apart from high capital costs and additional equipment space requirements, are increased complexity – therefore reduced reliability – and the need for numerous highly skilled operators if the full energy advantages are to be realised. As a result, the anticipated economies are sometimes not achieved.

The systems installed at Willis Faber took as their first requirements simplicity, reliability and low capital cost. Integrated as they are with the building fabric and structure, the mechanical and electrical systems have been found to give very good environmental standards at economical, but not the absolutely lowest possible, fuel consumption levels. In no small part this is due to the care taken by the building's small and efficient operational and management team, who are able to get good results because the systems are straightforward in their concepts.

More recently, the new Sainsbury Centre for Visual Arts at the University of East Anglia (4-7) probes some new approaches to low-energy design, using highly reflective and heavily insulated aluminium wall panels and attempting to exploit the natural buoyancy of warm air in high spaces to avoid mechanical cooling.

Much thought is given at present to the energy used in heating, lighting, ventilating and air conditioning buildings, and rightly so. But consideration ought

to extend to the energy used in extracting, processing, manufacturing, delivering and erecting the materials of which buildings are made. It is a difficult subject to pin down, but on approximations it is possible to arrive at energy inputs for construction which amount to five years' worth of 'running energy': given a service life of 20 to 30 years on much of the construction material, this 'capital energy' is clearly significant. Some materials are inherently energy intensive – look at brick or cement works, which belch waste heat (and other things) into the atmosphere.

Designing buildings in this energy-conscious time poses quite new problems, and these problems are not actually about how to achieve low-energy designs; much greater is the difficulty of making value judgements which will maintain a balanced view of energy in relation to all the other factors surrounding a building project, avoiding the comfortable refuge of reliable-looking technical calculations, or Building Regulations, or Codes of Practice, which sometimes deceive people into believing that building science is exact (it isn't!)

Because the realities are so complex, perhaps it is not surprising that new Building Regulations are being introduced that ludicrously oversimplify energy conservation by, for example, seeking to restrict the proportion of glass in a wall, irrespective of the relationship of wall area to floor area and irrespective of the passive solar heat gains which may offset or even exceed the heat losses of that glass. It makes life easy for many but enlightened designers are up in arms, of course, and no wonder. Computers are being wheeled forward to crunch numbers in quantity and demonstrate that the new regulations may make energy consumption greater in some cases. But even computers have to be programmed and at present they are usually fed data which is essentially based on steady-state heat flow conditions – the one thing which never actually happens in buildings! So one must be wary even of computer print-outs!

Recently, there have been nationwide government-sponsored campaigns encouraging ordinary folk to save energy: switch off lights, turn down the thermostat, insulate the hot water tank, use the car accelerator more gently. But very few people realise that in the United Kingdom about one-third of all primary energy used (coal, oil, gas and nuclear fuel) goes into electricity-generating power stations, which send out only one unit of useable energy for every four they consume. In other words, about one-quarter of the country's total energy consumption is

Loren Butt

thrown to the sky and winds in the giant cooling towers of our power stations. Of course, it's not intentional waste; technology hasn't yet got an answer to it. But people ought to know what's happening so they can make energy judgements in a properly informed manner.

As far as the future for energy is concerned, there is no real justification for the pessimism which seems to be so common today. Although it is entirely possible that fossil fuel reserves will eventually become exhausted, other sources of energy are available now. Even the technology for exploiting them exists already, albeit at high cost, but history clearly shows that even apart from new discovery, refinement steadily improves availability and lowers the real cost of everything technical. It seems bound to happen in the energy field, if or when the necessity arises. Indeed it is likely that as time passes, more and more energy will be needed. Why? Because energy is the catalyst of technological development and industrialisation, and that is really the only way in which living standards worldwide can improve – and in this context living standards means life expectancy, not television sets. The protagonists of a non-industrial society and autonomous rural living appear not to realise that it would simply be impossible for everybody to live that way: the UK can only support and feed 50 million people with a life expectancy of around 70 years each, by being an industrial nation.

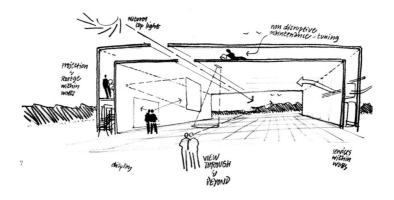

'… for everyday, ubiquitous, nine-to-five proof that Modern Architecture Lives – and thrives – the work of Foster Associates is at hand, at work and at our service.'

Reyner Banham

The collapse of the Modern Movement, when it finally happened, proved not to be as much fun as had been anticipated. The brave new Post-Modern world of stylistic pluralism, popular participation, architecture for its own sake, and all the rest of it, coincided with an economic recession that left the new *avant/arrière-garde* impotent to build. Even so, the most galling aspect of their unrealised millennium must be that 'that old Modern Architecture' survived as the dominant element in the new pluralism, is still producing the best buildings that are actually being built in Europe and North America, and is building them with its mythologies (social, economic, technological) still intact.

For proof, one has only to look at the work of Foster Associates. For overwhelmingly dramatic and rhetorical proof one might more conveniently turn to the work of Norman Foster's one-time partner, Richard Rogers, at the Centre Pompidou, still the only monumental building of consequence to go up in Europe in the 1970s. But for everyday, ubiquitous, nine-to-five proof that Modern Architecture Lives – and thrives – the work of Foster Associates is at hand, at work and at our service.

It is also controversial and contentious, chiefly because it suffers no false modesty and like all immodest building (that of James Stirling or Kisho Kurokawa, for instances) attracts far more hostile criticism than if it were modest and conventional construction with the same faults. For faults there are: none of us – not even Foster Associates – is perfect, and there never was a building that was exactly *au point* on the day it opened and there are few that are up to snuff a year later. But whereas leaks, drips, draughts and unwanted noises are understood to be 'in the nature of things' if 'the things' happen to be bricks, tiles and timber arranged in thick walls and pitched roofs, they are seen as 'the consequences of technological and architectural arrogance' if they are glass, metal and plastic, thin walls and flat roofs. In the former case faults are corrected as far as possible; in the latter case, also, they are corrected as far as possible – but in the meantime angry letters of denunciation appear in the press, and Astragal pontificates in the *Architects' Journal*.

These are not trivial matters nor storms in teacups; to build in unconventional materials and in forms not familiar to the untutored eye – to build Modern Architecture, that is – is still to practise 'the architecture of risk'. But whereas

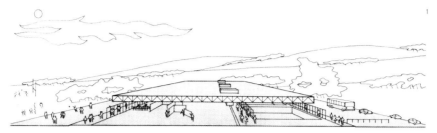

those who built Modern in the 1920s and '30s could do so in unsullied ignorance of what the consequences might be, and supported by a belief in the inevitability of progress (of whatever sort), we can no longer be so wilfully innocent. We *know* what are the consequences of abandoning the routines and traditions of four thousand years of architecture, and we know that progress is something that has to be *made*, is not inevitable, and goes only in whatever direction we will it, not automatically 'onward and upward'.

The risks in an 'architecture of risk', are therefore fundamentally different from what they were in Modern Architecture's Heroic Age – no longer Lucifer's attempt on the stars followed by a plunge to infernal depths, but the somewhat less-than-Miltonic risk of litigation, prosecution, persecution. It is no longer enough to promise performance and, on non-delivery thereof, plead that you are an artist and not a businessman; nowadays, he who promises performance must deliver – and that, of course, is what has prompted so many timid and incompetent souls to claim that measurable performance is not architecture's job.

Unfortunately it is. It becomes increasingly clear that the distinguishing feature of modern, corporate clients is not that they are faceless or bureaucratic but that they can count. They are numerate and measure architectural quality in figures. The architect who makes them promises must be able to deliver in measurable quantities, whether the units of measurement are BTUs saved by a factory for a manufacturer or votes delivered by a housing scheme to a tottering Labour majority.

Foster always thrives in these close-counting circumstances. He once said with real appreciation of a client: 'He's marvellous – every time he opens his mouth a quarter of a million comes off the budget.' And more recently he has had the temerity to answer Buckminster Fuller's non-rhetorical question, 'But what does your house weigh?' with a detailed weight breakdown of the Sainsbury Centre. It adds up to a remarkably modest total of 5,619 tons, or practically 70 cubic metres of building volume for every ton of structural weight – a figure that grows more impressive when it is realised that around four-fifths of that structural weight is the ground slab.

Four-fifths! It is the kind of figure that doesn't often become available, and it should give pause. Fetishistic concentration on only one kind of cost analysis and one kind of energy budgeting in building has effectively concealed the ridiculously

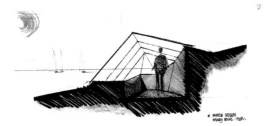

2

large part of the energy budget of any building that goes into rituals of extracting mud (aggregate, sand, cement, clay, rock etc.) from one part of the Earth's crust and dumping it on another. It is because this is so little known and so rarely discussed that many a proud claim for the energy-saving virtues of traditional heavyweight construction begins to crumble once the muck-shifting, rock-cracking and brick-baking have been added in.

Far from being energy-efficient, many so-called traditional methods of construction involve so vast an investment in mud-moving energy that it may not be amortised, so to speak, in the useful life of the building, and the total energy outlay may ultimately prove to be more than it would for a lightweight, 'high-energy' construction standing for the same length of time. Or may not be. We are still so unaccustomed to this kind of accountancy that we can rarely even guess the answer. This is not surprising: we have not usually needed to make such calculations until about a hundred years ago, and have only commanded the necessary environmental maths for the seventy-odd years since Willis Carrier wrote his first performance guarantee for air conditioning. In the same way, we have been able to get away with a view of architectural history which has automatically equated 'traditional' with 'massive' in construction and has dismissed lightweight construction as a modern aberration.

Yet history abounds – especially in the eastern and southern parts of England where Foster Associates have mostly worked to date – with examples of traditional lightweight construction: barns, sheds, clapboard houses. Indeed, what is salutary about so much country vernacular building is its ability to juggle together massive and lightweight construction as appropriate in the same farmyard, or even the same building, recognising that different functions require different shelter. But equally, in other parts of Britain, different functions are housed in identical shelter – be it light or heavy – where it is more appropriate economically to temper a less-than-perfect environment than it is to try to force a reasonably available building procedure to deliver performance it cannot.

The lesson of building history is not that one particular type of construction is superior or less wasteful or more natural than others, but that many modes of construction have long been understood to be subtly appropriate to different sorts and conditions of buildings and that you cannot tell which is the more appropriate

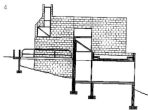

simply by looking – the proof is in the performance. This, alas, is beyond the mental capacity of too many of our architectural pundits and public mouthpieces who want immediate optical signals that a building is 'low technology' and therefore (as their limited understanding believes) not wasteful of energy and materials. Foster Associates have not offered these easy stylistic signals – indeed they have been at odds, at variance, with most of what has been happening in academic theory and editorial pontification of late.

Undisturbed by the Gadarene rush of theorists and moralists down from 'high' technology to 'low', Foster has gone the less facile route of 'appropriate technology' – a route easier to perceive now than it was ten years ago. Indeed, if he had said in 1968 that he was *not* pursuing high technology, he would have got a horse-laugh from most of his audience.

Yet the forgotten fact remains that his career in built work begins at the 'low' end of the scale. Although he first attracted attention with Reliance Controls and his Newport School Competition entry (1), derived from Ezra Ehrenkrantz's high-technology California-based SCSD system, the first built work to which his name attaches was a semi-subterranean coastal gazebo in Cornwall (2, 3), followed by a low-profile terraced housing project, a mostly subterranean house with canted glazed skylights protruding through greenery (4-6), and then a modest mews infill in Camden Town.

These projects have so much in common with the ecologically responsible and ideologically self-righteous 'solar' (etc.) architecture of a decade later that it is difficult at first to see them as in any way progenitors of, say, Foster's IBM buildings or of the Centre Pompidou. Yet the choice of the nomenclature 'Team 4' shows an awareness – of the name 'Atelier 5', matching the awareness of Atelier 5's masterwork at Siedlung-Halen – that grins through the apparent modesty of the architecture at Pill Creek.

Yet, almost immediately after these, came Reliance Controls – a building of stunning elegance and economy of means, one of those very rare European buildings that can be compared with the work of Craig Ellwood in California, and loses nothing in the comparison. It is not as skinny in its members as Ellwood's pencil-line-detailed XDS plant at El Segundo – yet like Ellwood, but unlike, say, Yorke, Rosenberg and Mardall in their work for Cummins Diesel or Wills Tobacco, Team

4 managed to eliminate the lurking monumentality of the Miesian tradition in metal framing. Whereas Mies (and Philip Johnson) still stood in the Neo-Classical tradition, Team 4 had escaped from it, not into the slightly vapid neutralism of Eero Saarinen's work for General Motors, but into something close to the tough self-sufficient indifference of the true 'architecture of the bottom line'.

But only '*something like*' – this is not indifferent but very consciously stylish, and this aware stylishness then remains a constant feature of the work of both of Team 4's successor offices, Foster Associates and Piano & Rogers. In both cases, but especially in Foster's, it is the stylishness that holds together a body of architecture whose devotion to 'appropriate technology' might have driven it apart into isolated works that were perhaps connected theoretically but not visually.

The point is worth pursuing further. Foster Associates' work is not stylistically unified; rather, a series of master-concepts – the glass box, the metal shed, the downtown polygon – have leap-frogged cyclically through their work, reappearing in modified form at each reincarnation. What continues consistently throughout is a fastidious, elegant but conspicuous minimalism in detailing, usually involving the edge-to-edge conditions of real or apparent lightweight materials.

Now, because lightweight materials are normally associated in the minds of architectural pundits (and bigots) with high-technology, high-energy structural systems, these buildings have given most observers the impression of a sustained devotion to high technology at whatever cost. Yet the actual energy range of Foster buildings is very wide, from the heavy servicing of the various IBM designs (where the demands of computers would require heavy energy consumption even in massive 'low-technology' enclosures with high heat capacity) to the relatively light servicing of the Sainsbury Centre for Visual Arts, or its cyclic predecessor, the Modern Art Glass plant (7).

Such devotion to the appropriate is – all too obviously – proper to responsible architecture and to the needs of clients, but it lacks that extremism that gives an architect a clearly definable position that can polarise opinion, for or against, in public debate or across the drawing boards in the studios of architecture schools. It has persistently driven critics, favourable as well as hostile, into imputing a devolution to high technology exclusively because that is what conventional opinion has always expected to find in architecture that uses glass and thin metal sections.

On Foster

7

Certainly, Foster Associates have not gone out of their way to evolve an architectural style or an iconography of details that says unequivocally: 'Look at me, I'm appropriate!' And they are probably right: the simple-mindedly Low-Tech have their windmills and *pisé* walls, the woolly-minded High-Tech have their highly coloured exposed duct-work; the 'appropriate tech' must have whatever is usefully at hand.

Where Foster's work so often startles is that this inevitable pragmatism, this lack of stylistic ideology, should be so recognisably stylish within a comparatively narrow range of stylistic possibilities. Narrow, that is, by comparison with Eero Saarinen who, once he had given up Mies-and-Water, thundered off with a totally different 'style for the job' with each successive commission. There is, as has been said, no single Foster style though the range of stylishness is close and connected. But none of the styles in the range specifically labels a particular type of quantity of servicing, and this makes life very difficult for the average hit-and-run journalist, or the lecturer playing solitaire with a hundred colour-slides in the AA Library. The rock-bottom, bottom-line fact about the work of Foster Associates is that you can't tell just by looking: you have to go inside.

Not that appearances are deceptive, but that our expectations of modern, unconventional buildings are unreliable, especially when the overall shape is not easy to read at a single glance, as at Ipswich. The wavy form of Willis Faber & Dumas (8), turning always (or nearly always) back on itself, away from the line of sight, contains more space than we can guess from without, but it is not immediately apparent on entry because the rising plane of the escalator through the generous central lightwell makes one look at, and think about, other matters. It is a building to be explored before it is understood, and for this reason its levels of technology, servicing and energy consumption are not to be read by snap judgement or any single viewpoint.

Its energy consumption is neither sensationally low, nor sensationally high – it is, in fact, rather lower than conventional professional wisdom has supposed, which must be a measurable comfort to the clients. The level of servicing is not sensational, nor the provision over-elaborate – just appropriate – and most of the environmental quality of the interior comes from the furnishings and fittings that define workspaces, control acoustics, frame views and have almost as much to do with the quality of the luminous environment as do the actual light fixtures.

8

In the end, one discovers that the highest technology in the whole complex is situated exactly where one received the first impression that this must be a high-technology building – in the outer skin. If anything about this building is *ahead* of the state-of-the-art it is the glass curtain wall around the perimeter. In it, the state-of-the-art finally catches up with an old Modern Movement dream, a dream as old as Mies van der Rohe's first skyscraper projects in Berlin – the dream of pure glass wall uninterrupted by gratuitous and light-wasting glazing bars. It is a dream that can only be approximated by the state-of-the-art, of course, because something has to support the glass and stop it falling out into the street.

At Ipswich that support has been refined away almost, but not quite, to nothing – a clamp bar to hang the glass from the top and a patch plate at each corner where four sheets meet. Otherwise there is nothing except a translucent line of sealant between each sheet and the next, optically lost in the inevitable refractions and reflections that occur at any cut edge in glass.

In this process of refinement we have, of course, lost an old friend, critical comforter and conventional indicator of the quality of a glass-wall architecture – the extruded alloy glazing bar. From Mies' Chicago work onwards, a quick run round the glazing bars would enable the viewer to sum up the quality of the whole – 'neat', 'pretentious', 'workman-like', 'scholarly', 'careless', or whatever. But at Ipswich you have to concentrate (as did the architects) on the glass itself and ask what it does and how well it does it – functionally, environmentally and visually – but not necessarily in that order, or in *any* order, since anything so simple must perform all of a piece.

By any standards, Willis Faber & Dumas would be a hard act to follow, and Foster Associates haven't even tried to follow, so far. The next downtown polygon, the Hammersmith Centre project (9), will be a very different kind of building, functionally, environmentally and visually. But even before Hammersmith was fairly under way, they had gone from a super-refined, single-element, single-material cladding to a more complex yet more simple wall and roof system – the Sainsbury Centre for the University of East Anglia. More complex in that three different types of panel for three different purposes are carried on subframes bolted to the main structure; more simple in that this is a vastly easier-to-comprehend, logical build-up of separable elements.

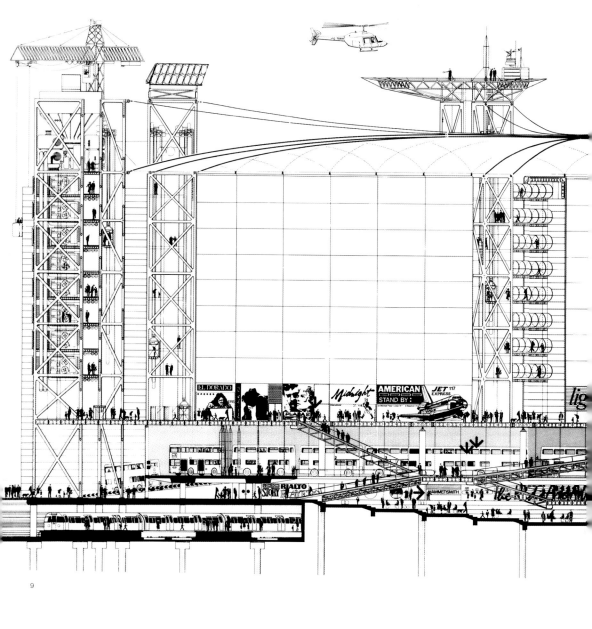

9

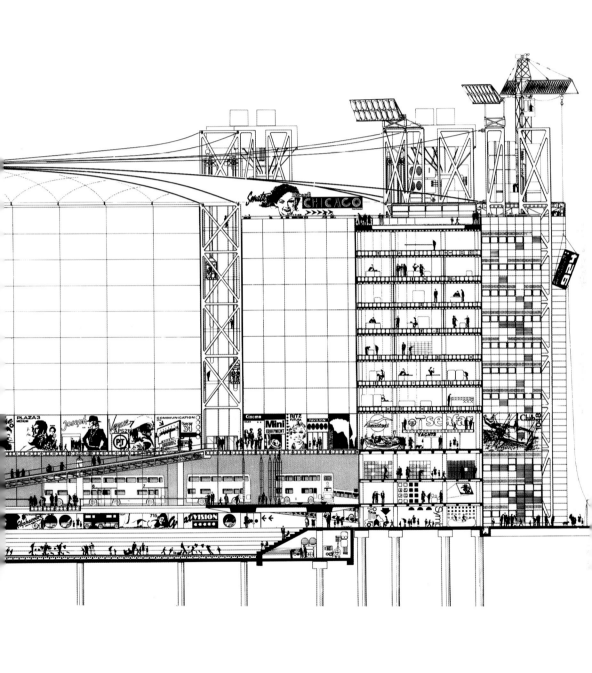

It is also simpler in that the Centre is not a complex form but the cyclical return of the supershed, long and regular in section, located not in a complex and heavily detailed downtown area but on a quasi-Palladian grassy knoll with a few rather distant sub-Capability Brown trees, in what remains of Earlham Park outside Norwich. If not a single glance, then certainly a short walk, will reveal the essence, if not the substance, of the building.

At Earlham Park, however, I must declare an interest. I went to Sunday School and early Communion across the main road at the Parish Church of St Mary's, Earlham; the park's grassy knolls were my nursery slopes for everything from sledging to sex; the only fish I ever caught were from the river that winds around the lower edge of the University site; and for a long time my main source of rubber for powering model aircraft came from cracking open golfballs that had come over into the park from the municipal course next door.

Any university building on that site starts with an advantage and a disadvantage as far as I am concerned. The advantage is that I know and understand the territory on which the building stands; the disadvantage is that the mere presence of the University of East Anglia offends me. Not − let me emphasise − because I am sentimental about the site, but because the location of the campus on the city's periphery instead of on a downtown site represents a failure of nerve that makes me ashamed of my native town.

So, given that the Sainsbury Centre was designed by an architect whom I respect, built by a construction company whose former head sat next to me at school, and located in a position I cannot approve, how does it rate?

Its relation to the earlier work, by Denys Lasdun and the local cathedral-menders, Fielding and Mawson, seems a bit offhand in spite of Foster's explanations. All the consultations with Lasdun and rationalisations about its relation to the various faculties seem as nothing compared to the topographical fact that it occupies the only decent parcel of land (views, trees, accessibility) remaining after Lasdun has finished − there really was nowhere else to put it without detriment either to the building itself or the campus as a whole.

Yet given its location as an end-stop to Lasdun's mighty pre-cast zig-zaggurat, it craftily underplays its role. In contrast to the implied permanence of Lasdun's concrete slabs and posts, the Centre's transparency and its visibly lightweight construction must inevitably be read as implying transience – even by so experienced a critic as Stephen Gardiner. Should the form-will of another generation demand the extension of Lasdun's project on its (by then) historical mould, then Foster's work, it is felt, could be disassembled to permit the extension, and itself erected elsewhere.

Or so says the common reading of architecture by architecture folks. Anyone who knows the East Anglian scene may read the matter differently. This is a landscape in which massive, Hun-proof, concrete blockhouses have been known to collapse in ruins during the lifetime of provisional hangars and sheds erected on a 'hostilities only' basis. There are farms that have been housed traditionally and for generations in 'temporary' lightweight barns, and in this admirable climate recycled London prefabs are still doing yeoman service to the local yeomanry almost a quarter of a century after their designed obsolescence dates.

The whole iconography of differences between permanence and obsolescence, as understood by the Modern Movement for most of the present century, becomes confused and irrelevant in East Anglia, where matchboard sidings on Victorian barns can look as immemorial as thatch on cottage roofs (which may be only ten years old). So, the fact that the three kinds of external panel on the Sainsbury Centre can be moved around at will and have no permanence of location does not ultimately call into question the permanence of the whole structure – any more than the ability to punch out the block wall between the frames of a standard 'Ministry' barn to make a new tractor access, in any way compromises the permanence or durability of the barn itself.

East Anglia, therefore, is not a bad viewpoint from which to scrutinise one of the most provocative aspects of Foster Associates' work: the air of impermanence. A pun is quite deliberately intended here; Foster *did* design an impermanent air structure (the Computer Technology temporary offices) at a time when other people were only talking about such matters. Its semi-transparency to light, including internal light, gave it a delicate air of transience, yet its form – like that of many other inflated structures – was not so different from that, say, of a long heap of clay piled at its natural angle of permanent repose. That particular form made functional and economic sense (something more bubble-like would have enclosed wasteful amounts of volume) but it still left a powerful sense of visual ambiguity, which is perhaps proper to an 'impermanent' structure – that is to say, any structure that can withstand ten winters or so, without containing all the redundancies which cause a traditional building to be strong enough to withstand a hundred in order to be sure of surviving one.

Inflatables anywhere constitute an extreme case of course – as do temporary buildings in East Anglia – but extreme cases can be indicative. Foster's sheds such as Sainsbury, Modern Art Glass and the Palmerston School (10) are middling rather than extreme cases, which is why they can be somewhat enigmatic, but the glass buildings do also constitute an extreme, and an indicative one. The problem here – and I suspect it had added animus and perplexity even to the environmentalist lobby's objections – lies in a seeming paradox between the known transience of the buildings and what appears to be implied by their highly reflective (and therefore visually impenetrable) rectangular format.

Now, pure, closed, impenetrable, rectangular blocks – by Le Corbusier at one extreme, and Minimalist sculptors like Donald Judd at the other – are supposed to bring us close to the 'permanent truths of geometry', form without compromise and therefore impervious to decay. As practical inhabitants of an ever-crumbling world, we know better, of course, but the Platonic tradition that invests so many fields of Western culture, and especially aesthetics, still conditions us to think that such pure forms are 'absolute' or 'natural beauty' according to Christopher Wren, or 'primary masses ... the most beautiful forms' according to Le Corbusier, and, in every case, lifted beyond the accidents of time and change.

So the economic logic which requires a building to be made thus because it is temporary collides with a cultural tradition which insists that buildings thus made must express permanence. Fortunately, a shift of viewpoint can come to our rescue: the light changes, reflection becomes transparency, we see, at Cosham for example, the apparently insubstantial and highly adaptable internal structure and furnishings, and we gain clues to its transient mutability. But they are recent, consciously learned clues; they don't have the ancestral power of the old Platonic prejudices. We have explanation but not satisfaction. The provocation remains.

It is, of course, only the inversion of a provocation that is as old as architecture itself. Eternity, permanence, is what architects have tried to build for millennia past, to guarantee a place in posterity for their lords and masters – and even in

Reyner Banham

10

their own lifetimes they have had to watch wind and weather dull the keen arrises, erode the proud outlines, and known that sooner or later the whole edifice would subside in its own dust. Still, knowing this, architects have learned to live with the recognition that 'a good design is forever' only in the mind, and a simple reversal of the polarities of permanent and transient helps us nowadays to deal with the provocations of transience in permanent formats, at least at the level of architectural surrealism.

At Ipswich, however, Fosters confront us with a more subtle and baffling contrast. The glass box of transience/permanence was understood – by Le Corbusier, explicitly – to be impervious not only to time and change, but also to *place*. The standard complaint about 'modern glass boxes that look the same all over the world' is a measure of the success of this proposition; modern architecture visits upon the site a concept that is indifferent to local history.

Willis Faber & Dumas is not. It sets its outline wavily to pursue the accidents of a site that is an accumulated record of civic process and private enterprise at a unique point on the Earth's crust over a finite timespan embracing the individual decision-making of former citizens whose very names are likely to be found in the city's muniments. By asking the already ambiguous glass box to come out of the architectural surrealism in which transience and permanence – the counted and the uncountable – were reconciled by an intellectual trick, and bending it to a format which is not symbolic of perenniality but is a continuation of local history by other means, Foster Associates have sprung the all-glass wall out of a kind of cultural preserve where its nakedness was masked by our Platonism, and made us look at it again as a visual fact.

At the same time, they have purified it, by removing all visible mullions and supports, even while they compromised it by bending it to the historical record. This in itself would have set the critics a tough task, but the matter is much compounded by the fact that the building reflects history not only topographically in its plan, but optically in its facades. When you look at Willis Faber you see the rest of downtown Ipswich, parcelled and splintered into tall vertical strips, edited and recombined, as it were, into architectonic relationships that don't exist in the real Ipswich, only in the reflection. This, whatever the architects may say, is a witty reconstruction of Ipswich as a kind of slide show or fold-out brochure of itself, and

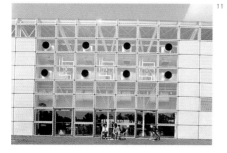

it is not likely to be entirely unwittingly witty because at least one of the design team, Birkin Haward, has close local connections.

The Sainsbury Centre (11-13) – to return to the original provocation of this disquisition on permanence and transience – is not involved with its surroundings. It may evoke echoes from all over East Anglia, everything from temporary barns to the old airship hangars at Pulham or Cardington, but it is crisply at variance with whatever traditions and visual habits have accumulated on the UEA campus. Landscape-wise its approach is diametrically opposed; Lasdun's buildings *are* the landscape, one whole side of the valley is now academic terraces in weather-stained concrete and weather-ravaged wooden window frames all looking half as old as time, suddenly.

The reason for the sudden ageing is, obviously, the contrast with the Sainsbury Centre, not only because Sainsbury is new, but because Lasdun's work by its very design is part of the landscape setting of Sainsbury, and is thus put at one with the 'timeless' elements of the site like the trees (some of which, however, and this being East Anglia I know, are younger than I am). In this landscape, the supershed sits as elegant and as Palladian as Le Corbusier's ideal Villa Savoye at Poissy, on a similar domed lawn shaven as close as Astro Turf. It is a defined form without ambiguities this time – its totally glazed ends enhance its definitiveness by revealing it as a straightforward half-tube of shelter, and the glazed entrance areas on its sides are seen as variations within a system (the pattern of the subframes comes through uninterrupted) rather than as breaches in the wall.

From within, the Palladianism takes a more dramatic turn. The glazed ends, with structure visible beyond the glass, embrace and frame a segment of the view, much as a Palladian portico would have done, and these two framed views (one down across the valley and the new lake, the other into a stand of trees that semi-conceal the underground service entrance) contain the kind of landscape elements, in the kind of painterly relationships that they might well have done in the eighteenth century. Whether this Palladianism is due to Fosters, or to the landscape consultant Lanning Roper, it is a slightly disorienting compliment to the county that contains parks like Houghton and Holkham and gave birth to Humphry Repton – disorienting because it seems so improbable in the context of such a sleek and undeniably modern shed. On the other hand, it is undeniably 'appropriate' in one

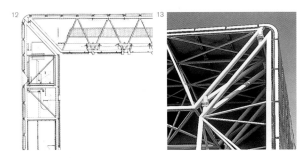

of the senses of that word that is not often employed around Foster Associates. But what about their usual sense of the word 'appropriate', what's the environment like when you go inside?

The issue is important because this is the building on which Foster Associates will be judged for a long time both by the general public, who will be more easily able to visit it than other Foster buildings, and by the body academic, who will have to work in it. From the latter there has been a certain amount of verbal flak ever since it opened. Much of this has been very like (some an exact repeat word-for-word) the verbal flak that has greeted every new university building in Britain since the war. Some of it has to be because it concerns the sort of mechanical faults that infect all new buildings, and some that are specific to highly glazed buildings: the faults will be cured, but neither forgiven nor forgotten – academics have elephants' memories.

More important are the pseudo-faults of human adjustment. The architects – any architect – may propose better ways of using buildings, or at least different ways, and invite the users to experiment. Being human, the users may decide not to bother, being academics they will be able to conjure up elaborate explanations for not bothering and putting all the blame on the architects. I happen to know some of the faculty and students who work in the Sainsbury, and continue to hope that they will judge more fairly and less lazily than their colleagues elsewhere.

Public opinion may leave them high and dry anyhow – there can be no avoiding the fact that the general consensus of opinion about the public gallery spaces, and about the building as a whole when viewed from the public spaces, is as favourable as it deserves to be. Like the almost-perfect glass wall at Ipswich, this interior is also the realisation of a Modern Movement dream – the dream of the infinitely flexible and perfectly conditioned art gallery.

That is a currently discounted dream. Galleries are now praised for their 'character', which all too often means lumpish masonry walls and randomly distributed shafts of eye-searing sunlight. One reason why this should be preferred to the possibility of bending the environment to one's will through high technology is that the technology has to be extremely high and expansive (as at Centre Pompidou) and may be allowed to stand uneconomically idle because the director is too timid or languid to make use of it (also, alas, as at the Centre Pompidou).

14

15

The Sainsbury Centre goes nowhere near these Pompidolian extremes – its servicing is less than absolute, its mechanical equipment is relatively modest, visible and easily understood, the overhead space is not be-jungled with dangling lamp-battens, and a great deal of its lighting is natural without being a nuisance. In other words, the technology is 'appropriate'. So conspicuously, yet unfussily, appropriate that Foster Associates have done another hard act to follow. If 'appropriate technology' is to be their slogan, then the Sainsbury will certainly be the example by which that slogan will be measured. They have set themselves the enviable task of, in future, creating buildings whose performance can satisfy numerate clients, and whose appearance can electrify the rest of us.

Waiting by the traffic lights at the Euston Road, I observed Norman Foster coming up alongside me in a Range Rover full of children and sporting equipment. He wound down the window and shouted, with ill-concealed glee, 'I've bought myself a glider!'

It was, in fact, a very high-performance Caproni two-seater sailplane (14-16). Everybody noticed that it was painted yellow, the colour of the Foster office in those days. One or two people remembered a previous architect sail-flyer in Britain, the late Kit Nicholson, and hoped Norman would not emulate him by crashing to his death in the World Championships. But Norman clearly loved the thing for its looks … and only later found in it the kind of symbolic meaning without which nothing is real in architectural discourse. 'It's incredibly high technology, you know, but it's more damn energy efficient than anything else around – and so-o-o beautiful!'

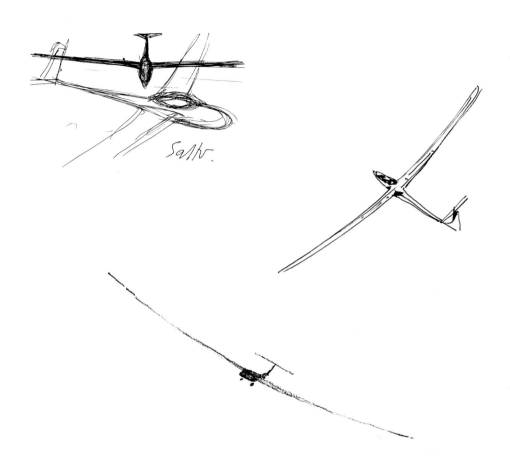

'Norman discusses the evolution of the structure with reference to his use of full-size mock-ups in the London office and workshop: the building site is not the place for a learning curve.'

Martin Pawley

Eight am, November 1982. Weather dark and drizzling. Temperature in the 50s. Visibility 500 metres or more. The tacho touches 5,000 in Norman Foster's white 911 Porsche turbo. Black whale tail, black leather upholstery, barely 2,000 miles on the clock, it flashes past the big rigs and the chaps in their Cortinas.

The undulations of the M4 unfold into a blur. Over the radio comes the news that a truck has jack-knifed after Exit 13. He reacts fast, corkscrews through a bunch of vehicles that look as though they are standing still, and zips down the Newbury off-ramp. Even through the lanes he still makes it to Swindon an hour before the hand-picked team of French journalists flown in by Renault to marvel at their £12 million Distribution Centre.

In the conference room of the rambling Bovis site hut chairs are being lined up, coffee and croissants displayed, and an easel is unfolded at the front. David Morley, project architect for the job although he only left the AA three years ago, arranges boards with images of earlier schemes so that Norman can talk the visitors through the project. The architect enters. He is wearing muddy boots – the Renault site borders a flood plain – and light brown cord trousers. A custom-knitted white sweater surmounts a pink shirt and largely concealed woollen tie. The two architects busy themselves arranging the exhibits. It is like the beginning of a thousand-bomber raid.

In come the French, led by the enigmatic Sebastian de la Selle – 'Coordinateur de l'Expression Visuelle' for Renault: the man responsible for matching the architectural quality of new Renault buildings with the imagined technological supremacy of Renault cars, and the patron of this present enterprise. Like many arbiters he is of unprepossessing appearance, green tie askew, baggy trousers, nondescript jacket. Not a bit like the elegant Geoffrey French of Renault UK, a Major Thompson look-alike who could sell Datsuns in Parliament Square with no trouble at all.

At length Sebastian calls the meeting to order and introduces Norman Foster, who steps to the easel. He announces that he does not wish to spend much time talking about the edifice that is just outside the door because it would be much more sensible to see it in the flesh. Nonetheless he does give a brief rundown, showing some of the earliest approaches to the scheme when it was raised, with car parking underneath. The planners were always obliging, he claims, allowing 67

per cent of the site to be used instead of the 50 per cent offered to Renault when they first considered moving from their unexpandable distribution centre in Reading.

The building itself, consisting of a cluster of 24 square modules, encloses 24,000 square metres but can be extended to 30,000. Norman discusses the evolution of the structure with reference to his use of full-size mock-ups in the London office and workshop: 'The building site is not the place for a learning curve.'

At the end of this introduction a Bovis operative enters with a bilingual invitation to don hard hats for the site visit proper and the delegation makes its way through mud and concrete to the vast double-height display area at the south end of the giant yellow and grey structure with its serried ranks of braced columns. The rain has stopped and brief flashes of sunlight illuminate the sharp sciagraphy of outrigged walkways and diagonal bracing rods.

The space under the floating, almost diaphanous, roof is enormous, with vast clear spans only just beginning to be filled with a tracery of triple-deck racking. The heavy concrete four-hour firewall separating the warehouse area from the showroom, mechanics' training bay and first-floor offices, makes a junction as final and clear as that between the train shed and the hotel at St Pancras. The mezzanine itself, formed in concrete for cost reasons connected with its own fire-rating, forms a third element, in this state of half completion difficult to assimilate properly.

What is clear about the building is its structure, enclosing space at half the cost of Foster's earlier IBM warehouse and using about half as much steel per square metre. Despite the logic of its 'endless umbrella' form, it is difficult to describe simply. The roof-decking itself is apparently so light that its rockwool insulation was necessary for loading purposes. And even a rank amateur can see that all the tension members dipping through the cranked steel beams in a catenary curve must puncture the PVC roof surface every time, like the 16-metre columns themselves. There is time to marvel at these roof-penetrating junctions – over three hundred of them – and find out that they are simply made by wrapping the tube itself in PVC fabric and passing a circular patch down the length of it to bond the whole assembly to the PVC roof membrane.

In the case of the junction between the profiled wall-sheeting and the near-beamless edges of the roof, another kind of technology transfer is employed. The large relative movement of the floating structure with its light roof-decking and

Martin Pawley

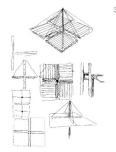

light panel walls is such that no rigid junction could do the job. Several complex moving joints were designed but the final solution involved the use of a thick neo-prene fabric, similar to that used for the skirts of hovercraft. Compression-bolted to roof and wall-edge profiles, this large flexible connection is held firm by rows of stainless-steel coil springs, pulling down like the cover-tie on a trailer.

The glazing itself, each large 10mm sheet drilled and fixed to steel subframes with four bolts tightened on rubber washers, is installed to such tolerances that only silicon mastic joins the separate panes on the outer face. Although daring, this is less remarkable than the planned use of the same silicon to hold the glazing in position by tension in the Hongkong and Shanghai Bank.

After perhaps 40 minutes wandering through the cavernous spaces of the Distribution Centre the party returns to the site hut and embarks in a fleet of vehicles for lunch. Sebastian de la Selle, who has already contrasted the new Centre with what he says in French is called 'a shoebox in a beetroot field', waving his arm airily in the direction of the Anchor Butter warehouse a mile or so away, pauses before Norman's Porsche. He confers with a colleague in French and, when Norman appears, wonders aloud whether he has ever tried a Renault Alpine. Norman says no. 'Pity', says Sebastian before stepping into a Renault 18, the car company's bid for a place in the fleet market that is the *raison d'être* of the whole French invasion of Swindon.

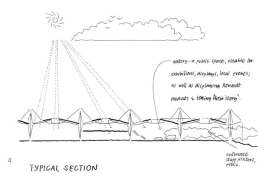

gallery - a public space, useable for exhibitions, displays, local events; as well as displaying Renault products & telling their story'.

entrance
staff, visitors,
public.

4   TYPICAL SECTION

'The "constructive idea" has its followers, but it is too early to decide whether the Renault Centre's structural virtuosity will assume the same architectural significance as Beauvais Cathedral.'

Wilfried Wang

There could have been no greater contrast between two architectural schools of thought than that evident in the current three exhibitions on display at the Institut Francais d'Architecture.

Located in an eighteenth-century *Hôtel Particulier*, a typical Parisian town house organised around a courtyard, the exhibition rooms for the work of Jean Prouvé, Norman Foster and Adolf Loos have been accommodated in the remodelled left half of the Institute's building.

The strength of the opposition between Prouvé and Foster on the one hand, and Loos on the other, lies in their attitude towards the expression of the architectural whole. Loos saw architecture as 'built thought', where the concept of constructional honesty was to be subservient to the concept of cultural ethics.

Loos advanced the idea of 'visual correction', which the ancient Greeks had perfected with the Parthenon, to one of 'conceptual correction'. Hence the principal facade of the Michaeler House (1) consists of two separate entities, the domestic and the commercial parts. They seem structurally independent, as the lines of the supports do not match up.

Contrary to this position, then, both Prouvé and Foster have continued a tradition in which the architectural object clearly expresses its constructional origin. Each junction of different elements or materials explains its constructive *raison d'être*.

Jean Prouvé, who is 82 this year and who has been accorded the three largest exhibition rooms at the IFA, has worked since 1930 towards the industrialisation of construction. The ideological reason behind this sustained interest lies in his belief in modern constructional economy. This preoccupation grew out of a recognition of the housing crisis during the inter-war years.

Since then, his involvement with metal prefabrication saw the realisation of the Maison du Peuple at Clichy (2), designed in collaboration with Beaudouin and Lods in 1983. Its primary qualities, a wholly integrated programme, a mobile, lightweight, constructional system with relocatable floors, anticipated similar concerns in Piano and Rogers' Centre Pompidou.

The accompanying book to the exhibition, *Jean Prouvé, l'idée constructive,* is overly pessimistic in its suggestion that Prouvé is a master without a school. The unquestioned ascendancy of industrialised production from the turn of the century reached a peak in architectural circles in the 1960s to mid-70s.

Casabella, for instance, used to include an issue on prefabrication every year. In the United States and Europe the curtain wall has become the symbol of the operability of the urban desert, of corporate blandness, rather than the firm image for which the companies had laid on the architects.

It is in this cultural climate that the concurrent remarks by Dominique Clayssen, author of the aforementioned book, and Annelle Lavalou, co-organiser of the exhibition, have to be seen. Despite a vast series of buildings with which Prouvé has been involved, such as the conference centre at La Défense, the UNESCO office in Paris and the Free University in Berlin, a feeling of bitterness, of lost opportunities, of an architecture that awaits its future, remains.

Prouvé's international recognition, which came in recent years in the form of the Auguste Perret Prize by the UIA in 1963, the Erasmus Prize of 1981 and the Grand Prix for architecture given by the City of Paris in 1982, was underlined by the personal letters written to him on the occasion of this exhibition.

James Stirling, Oscar Niemeyer, Michel Ecochard, Berthold Lubetkin, Paul Virilio, Alison and Peter Smithson and Norman Foster paid their respects to Prouvé's innovative and visionary abilities. The Smithsons see his work as the direct continuation of an artistic engineering spirit which had Eiffel and Citroën as its precursors.

Norman Foster – whose Renault Centre at Swindon (3-5) is exhibited in what is rather euphemistically called the 'galerie d'actualité', a single room connecting the Prouvé and Loos exhibitions – clearly holds Prouvé in high regard. Foster's own handwritten letter confirms this by its extensive quotes from the French master on the subject of the need to fuse material and technology with human needs.

Lubetkin, in his more emphatic manner, implores the reader to see that 'the future of mankind should be governed by reason and not by his machines. We have atomic bombs – should we be forced to use them?'

Lubetkin's and Prouvé's ideological positions are probably shared with reticence by their English counterparts. The parallels that do exist between Foster and Prouvé remain at the process-oriented, rapid construction, and lightweight prefabrication level. That their aesthetic attitudes mirror each other is of a certain interest.

In Prouvé's Grenoble exhibition centre a vast square of 36 metres is supported at each corner by four cylindrical sections, which are welded to the I-beam crossmember of the upper structure and which come together in an inverted pyramidal

Wilfried Wang

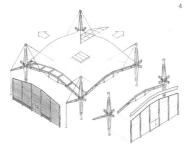

3

footing. A set of four of these bundled columns gives a table-like rigidity, which relies entirely on the bending stiff connections achieved through the splayed junctions.

Foster's Renault Centre has similar properties. Four sets of columns create a rigid 24-square-metre frame; the main mast is surrounded by eight sets of splayed tension rods which are connected to the cross and diagonal beams, thereby ensuring downward and upward bending stiffness.

While the Grenoble building relies on internal corner-plates to resist diagonal deformation, the Renault Centre exhibits a more expressive solution by the diagonal beams. These structural principles, which are not unlike that of an umbrella, have something of the thinness of Gothic columns and arches. Indeed, Prouvé's smaller schemes for houses and schools recall the resoluteness of the Gothic builders: to achieve structural integrity with an efficient use of materials, while bearing witness to an extreme elegance.

The lightweight gestural roofs of Prouvé's schools, the slight curvature of the bent metal cantilever, could be seen as a contemporary solution to the edifices of the medieval *architecte bâtisseurs*.

The Renault Centre is a step away from the trabeated yet portal-frame-like Sainsbury Centre. With its ambiguous directionality, the Renault Centre is evidently more adept at growth and contraction. The planning problems remain: although showrooms and offices can be contained relatively easily, there is no specificity about the external appearance. The arts centre at Norwich had a front, back and sides; the Swindon building seems to have sides only.

It is of course highly speculative to suggest parallels between the German post-war period where the impulse of Peter Behrens' Doricist AEG Turbine Factory in Berlin gave way to the Gothicising 'democratic cathedrals of labour' by the *Gläserne Kette*, and here, where the seeds of the Sainsbury Centre have flowered into the Renault Centre to become work environments. But when other architects such as Rogers at Fleetguard, or Piano in Italy, tackle similar steel structures, emulation by younger architects is not far away.

The 'constructive idea' has its followers, but it is too early to decide whether the Renault Centre's structural virtuosity will assume the same architectural significance as Beauvais Cathedral, or whether we shall see a prolonged constructional competition for this ultimate corporate symbol.

'Clients are brave to take on Foster, for he may reorganise their idea of their own organisation through meticulous and inventive searching for a brief.'

John McKean

The Foster style cannot be ignored. It is immediately apparent at the practice's new office, the ground floor of an old central London block. Between structural masonry, glass; no name or other distinguishing symbol visible to the street; only one bay, its glass, set back, is not blanked by perforated full-height metal louvres. On approach, the glazing vanishes automatically, inviting one to step up onto the deck, inside the cavernous white and grey space (3-7).

Islands of grouped white plan chests are plinths to models; deeper inside, at vast drawing boards and under red anglepoises, sit the designers. The firm, grey suspended floor hides servicing, allowing uninterrupted tall space. In the bays, marked by a rhythm of old columns and deep cornices, are slightly dropped acoustic ceilings. Background noise is low; telephones and typewriters do not distract. Large, low, white tables are rock solid on their Foster-designed minimal structures. Plain walls contrast with three large, glossy photographs: a sailplane, a view out through the Eiffel Tower, and a microchip blown up and multiplied to look like ordered city squares – three city icons for Foster.

The nearest model shows all Portland Place, with the BBC and the Langham Hotel in the middle. It is the project of the moment. Norman Foster, recovering from an intensive weekend with 40 people from BBC Radio, bounds calmly across: 'This incredible weekend, like running two marathons. Thursday was a sample day in the life of BBC Radio, ten hours non-stop; and then the weekend, Friday night to Sunday night, more or less all day and night, talking.'

Having recently won the commission, after six months' vetting in competition with, initially, nine others, he is full of ideas but not drawings. But even though he will give no details of the BBC building (1,2), discussion about it raises the questions that are consistently prompted by Foster's buildings. These include: what is the practice's role as designers in the definition and identification of the project; what is their view of the relationship between technology and art, and whether architecture can result from single-minded pursuit of the goal of technical efficiency; and what is the rationale for their neglect of the experiences to which architecture must give form, such as movement through a series of articulated spaces and, particularly, the first gesture of the threshold?

How does Foster see his role as the BBC's architect? 'One of the difficulties today is that traditionally architects are trained to think that somebody's going to tell them what to provide, and that is their starting point. The idea that their skill could be helpful at an earlier stage, for example through *specific exercises* to demonstrate the potential of ideas, without starting the design of a *specific building*, is largely discounted because it isn't seen to be part of the creative process. Yet in many ways it is intensely creative.'

1

With so many new buildings, Foster suggests, the best that one can normally hope for is 'an early conversion', but here, with an attitude they have developed since the Fred Olsen project in the late 1960s where traditional management/worker divisions were cut across, the practice has been involved before any brief has been formulated. 'For me, Olsen was the first time I really got personally involved in being able to see the relationship of that kind of creative discussion to be as significant a part of the design process as putting pencil to paper,' says Foster. 'This BBC weekend has been valuable beyond all expectation, because of the relaxed openness. In the knowledge that no lines have been drawn, the group talk in ruthless down-to-earth aspects and at the same time fly kites, float really quite way-out possibilities. Most importantly, we find out what might be the tender spots, contentious issues, early in the game.'

When asked about the rumour that he had developed a lift that will go down, along under the street and up again, Foster laughs at the success of the myth: 'Certainly we have, just as a matter of interest, gone through the patent process on this. There are a number of things where we go through the patent process, but it's very peripheral. Generally when we do develop something, like the Ipswich glass wall, we have warranties, which transfer design rights to industry, making a conscious trade-off and not tying us into a technical franchise and marketing situation. We have now developed a device, yes, which will move people vertically and horizontally without transferring from one vehicle to another. How far it is, in the end, applicable to this project, I don't know.'

Norman Foster is, as Peter Cook might say, particularly good at making functional noises. And this raises the second question: are his buildings mechanisms or architecture? 'But technology is simply the making of things,' he claims, 'and the making of things can't by its own nature be ugly or there would be no possibility for beauty in the arts, which also include the making of things. Actually, a root word of technology, *techne*, originally meant *art*. The ancient Greeks never separated art from manufacture in their minds and so never developed separate words for them. The way to solve the conflict between human values and technological needs is not to run away from technology. That's impossible.'

So is the technological sophisticate also, then, a noble savage, unencumbered by such problems as ambiguity, irony or just the contradictions of our self-conscious times? Is he free to focus all energy on solving 'functionalist' problems of how, without wondering why or what, letting dazzling perfection of means blind the question of ends?

The 'how' is something Norman Foster delights in stretching to the limit (even, at times, seeming to topple over that limit into science fiction). It could become an obsessive pursuit; yet the certainty and calm in the total comprehension of one's tools and their confident use is most appealing (and of course link Foster to Jean Prouvé, Walter Segal, Buckminster Fuller and other eccentrics).

Prouvé is an obvious master. The quotation about art and technology is taken, unchanged, from the notes Foster supplied for the current Prouvé exhibition in Paris. Foster took it, unchanged, from Robert Pirsig's *Zen and the Art of Motorcycle Maintenance,* 'as he says it so much better than I could have'. Yet is there not a sentimental trap in believing, as Pirsig might suggest, that to make *anything* well is a substitute for making the *right* thing? An internal ambiguity about ends is central to the art of our era. This is clear as Foster, starting from Pirsig, continues the argument: 'It is not plastic as a material that would upset somebody, but rather the connotations that plastic has taken on, by inference, of inferior design. If you ever get the chance to look at a racing sailplane in glass fibre and carbon fibre, you'll see what I mean. It's unbelievable. Beautiful. That's why I took to gliding in the first place: the actual tactile quality of the machine, even if it never flew, frozen in space.'

And so to the third question: are there not universal human experiences to which architecture must give form, one of which, the threshold, is so memorably stated in Aldo van Eyck's definition of any building as that building entered? The works of Foster Associates have tended simply to avoid these issues of place and human experience. At times it seems they have gone out of the way to find sites with the least possible contextual reference, being at home in the industrial estates of Thamesmead, Tibshelf and Greenford.

The Eiffel Tower is Foster's icon for 'economy, elegance and an unerring eye for proportion'; to him 'it does more with less'. His anecdote that the vertical column of air over its base to the top weighs more than the steel of the tower itself is startling indeed; a comment worthy of his other friend and mentor, Bucky Fuller. But it does more of *what* with less? It is a context-less (and architecturally useless) object, an icon for architects as misleading as the glider/sculpture and the microchip pattern-making.

Lloyd Kahn, author of the *Domebooks* and converted to 'more with less' by Bucky Fuller in the 1960s, more recently thought again: 'Don't worry about how much your building weighs. It doesn't have to fly.' Perhaps it is revealing that Foster stresses looking at his buildings from a distance, and how well they appear on film because it appeals to escapist fantasy. Both the TV films that have been made of his work concentrate on the air, on magical views from the air, and on that magical, immaterial material, glass: buildings are tiny, shiny jewels, not to be scuffed or bruised in everyday life. Such films, though they show interiors, avoid the threshold entirely, whether at Olsen, Willis Faber or the Sainsbury Centre – avoid the harder architectural task of the moment of entry. At these buildings, entrances are insignificant holes in tight, hermetic skins. Breathtaking internal spaces are usually countered by the antisocial hard shell. Sometimes reflective, where the citizen feels scrutinised by the hidden gaze behind the Mafioso shades, they are always, as also at the sadly aborted Hammersmith roundabout project, a clear barrier.

Foster talks of BBC Radio becoming more approachable, of enlarged public accessibility and of participation: but how can these be achieved with the vocabulary he has developed? 'A recurring theme in my conversations over the weekend was echoing the dissatisfactions of buildings that are hard-edged,' Foster begins, before moving on to praise for buildings like 'the Galleria in Milan, the Corn Exchange in Manchester, even, in a most gentle sense, the peristyle and steps of All Souls' opposite ... Yes I accept your point about entrance. It *was* almost as if one needed Braille to find a way into Willis Faber (pause). It was built a long time ago, we had other priorities; and we are changing.'

Norman Foster now talks of 'a village', of the qualities of tiny holes and routes through dense urban places. A pedestrian street through the ground floor of the new BBC buildings is floated: 'I don't really feel we have as dogmatic or fixed a

John McKean

vocabulary as you might see from the outside.' But doesn't his own new office remain the conditioned reflex? Foster laughs and changes tack: 'The Hongkong Bank is designed to invite people in, to break down the scale of the larger entity, and to develop a progression from the outside through a sequence of spaces.'

There is an immediate contrast with the classic skyscraper: 'Take the Seagram. Now that's got to be the most beautiful skyscraper ever. But deposit yourself by magic inside it; once you've gone through that "one-shot" reception entrance, which is stunning, you could be *anywhere*! Hongkong explores the idea of involvement and the identity of individuals and groups within it. You come into the plaza – it's quite large, with sunlight scooped in and reflected from below from the very Victorian pavement of cast glass – moving into the entrance lobby and travelling by high-speed one-stop lift to the main reception space (of which there are a number up the building), opening onto a double-height landscaped area; and then up or down by escalator, through smaller scaled atria.'

Foster is clearly fascinated now by the vertical 'villages' in the Hongkong Bank, by the possibilities of newly sensitive public/private boundaries at BBC Radio. All this might just lead his architecture in new ways – or do we just hear his language bending in the prevailing wind? Certainly he exudes conviction, confidence and credibility.

Foster claims he is 'relaxed and not blowing big trumpets', but there is nifty footwork involved in coordinating *The Gold Medal*, a TV programme (in a series which Foster describes as 'on moguls of industry – I'm the odd one out') and two current exhibitions abroad – the Renault building alongside Prouvé and Loos in Paris, and the Hongkong Bank alongside SOM and Johnson at the Museum of Modern Art, New York.

Hardly a low profile, I suggested, but he refutes this: 'We say yes to some invitations, and resist the pressure of others.' Norman Foster was described in a recent TV profile as an 'architectural megastar'. Despite being a word coined by Dame Edna Everage, it seems to have been used without irony. Foster still argues, stirringly, that 'architecture should be about issues of today, not nostalgic retreat or nervous breakdown'. But more and more his observations of the issues of today are becoming social, based on human activities, and evidenced in the modification of BBC offices by making hatches, removing doors, building 'homes' or private empires, in the meanings and values of this cluttering, and in encounters – as on the escalators at Willis Faber: 'I found that people talk to each other across escalators, or wave, or crack a joke. People never do that in lifts.'

Clients are brave to take on Foster, for he may reorganise their idea of their own organisation through meticulous and inventive searching for a brief. (It also means they are not surprised by the end product.) Brave, also, to accept his architecture, for his process ensures that the buildings will never appear expected, however quickly they become accepted after the first shock. And it is brave, too, to give him the Royal Gold Medal now, when he deserves it. For, unlike most other recipients, he may deserve it again, a quarter of a century later. And we might then be surprised to see that he received it at an early stage in an extraordinary career.

3

John McKean

4

5

6

7

'Somewhere at the heart of it all, then as now spectacularly difficult to pin down, lurked the contradictory figure of Foster himself: edgy, gum-chewing; exuding chutzpah.'

Alastair Best

If genius could be described as the infinite capacity for being dissatisfied, then Norman Foster, this year's RIBA Gold Medallist, is unquestionably a genius. He is also a congenital optimist; a refreshing quality he shares with his mentor, Buckminster Fuller. But to the outsider perhaps Foster's most remarkable trait is an uncanny ability to diagnose the nature and working processes of big institutions. It is this that has made him such a successful corporate architect. For it was undoubtedly his instinctive grasp of the nature of the BBC anthropology ('a collection of warring tribes') as much as any demonstrable design skills (although these are highly developed too) which carried the day in the limited competition for the design of the new headquarters in Portland Place.

Foster's career to date resembles a military operation, conducted in four phases. Phase one (Commando period) saw the formation of Team 4 (1) with Richard Rogers, Wendy Foster and Georgie Wolton and the commission to design an electronics plant for Reliance Controls in Swindon. Credits for this mould-breaking light-industrial shed have always been shared jointly between Foster and Rogers. Yet with its lean lines, rigorously stripped bare of inessentials, Reliance has always seemed more the work of Foster the Classicist than Rogers the Romantic. Indeed, it may be seen as the precursor of a number of the industrial buildings that followed when, after the disbandment of Team 4, the Foster office established itself in Covent Garden (4) and began attracting an enviable list of industrial clients – Fred Olsen, IBM and Iann Barron (then of Computer Technology) among them.

I remember the office of this second (Beach-head) phase quite well. Its atmosphere was curiously hard to describe. The general impression was of galvanic creative forces barely under control. Somewhere at the heart of it all, then as now spectacularly difficult to pin down, lurked the contradictory figure of Foster himself: edgy, gum-chewing, exuding chutzpah. In some ways this was the most exhilarating Foster phase. It was characterised by a fevered, *Boy's Own Paper*-ish admiration for technology in all its forms and an endearing reverence for transatlantic business practices, imbibed during Foster's graduate spell at Yale.

The third (Frontal Assault) phase saw Foster Associates installed in a Herman Miller Action Office in Fitzroy Street – a sleek paradigm of the type of corporate client they were out to attract (2). It was London's first architectural shop

window (neon sign and all) yet, as an interior, Fitzroy Street was singularly lacking in charm. With its acidulous lime-green paintwork and jet-black services core, reached by submarine doors rimmed, inevitably, in neoprene, it resembled the offices of an advertising agency or even an airline, rather than an architectural practice. Yet this was the setting for the great period of consolidation (most of the 1970s) during which Foster designed what is commonly reckoned to be his best building so far: the Willis Faber & Dumas offices in Ipswich.

The move into the present building in Great Portland Street (3, 5) marks the final (Big Punch) phase in Foster's career. The offices themselves, large and airy and white, sealed off from the street by 'Sainsbury' louvres, offer a much more relaxed and congenial working environment than their predecessors. Yet they are also less personal, an inevitable result of Foster's rise into the big international league. Commissions such as the Hongkong and Shanghai Bank – widely tipped as the world's most expensive building – are highly labour-intensive, and one notes the inevitable drawing-board fodder hived off in the basement. Yet, if some of the informality and fizz of earlier days has evaporated, the buildings themselves are growing in complexity, size and assurance. Norman still looks unstoppable.

Alastair Best

2

4

5

3

'... Foster's emphasis on structural rationalism puts him in the
oldest tradition architecture
knows, and right in its forefront,
since old Vitruvius ... always
put Firmness or Solidity ahead
of Utility or Beauty.'

Reyner Banham

The outstanding thing of the past summer, by my reckoning, has been the thing standing out in the forecourt of the Royal Academy – a sample, as it were, of the structure and glazing of the Hongkong and Shanghai Banking Corporation's new headquarters building in Hong Kong, designed by Foster Associates. The why and wherefore of its standing there is that it is an exhibit in the RA's annual summer show but too big to go inside the building – but see below for a possible alternative reason so shocking as to be interesting.

It is, in any case, occupying some of the most desirable parking space in the West End, but what makes its presence provocative is less that architecture should be deemed more important than parking, than that it should be publicly displayed at all. To admit any work whatsoever of Norman Foster's to these sacred precincts will be seen as a deliberate flouting of the Academy's most cherished traditions – at least by the lunatic core of the New Architectural Tories, whose main mouthpiece these days seems to be the 'Nooks and Corners' column in *Private Eye*.

For some months past, Foster – even more than Richard (Pompidou) Rogers – has been the prime object of their paranoia, and not just because he is so successful and has such very rich clients. His so-called High-Tech architecture is hated in itself, partly because it allegedly doesn't work, but more especially because (*Private Eye*, 1 July) it avoids 'the development of tradition' as well as a whole litany of other things.

Now one could reasonably argue that Foster's emphasis on structural rationalism puts him in the oldest tradition architecture knows, and right in its forefront since old Vitruvius (a Roman building contractor much cited by New Tories like Roger Scruton) always put Firmness or Solidity ahead of Utility or Beauty. Finding reasonable ways to make buildings stand is what architectural tradition has always been about. But that's not what the New Tories are on about: for them *tradition* means the comfort of never being exposed to anything they haven't seen before.

In this sense, the offence given by Foster's thing in the forecourt is deeper and weirder, because they have half seen it before. So let us be clear what it is they are seeing. The finished building, right on Statue Square on the Hong Kong waterfront, will consist externally of large areas of glazing, forty-something storeys high, with all the structural elements and most of the mechanicals on the outside of the glass. But what you will notice will be the quadruple 'masts' that hold the whole thing up.

According to the hand-out from the Foster office, the thing at the Academy shows 'a full-size section – a typical storey-height – of the aluminium cladding which encloses each mast, the glazed external curtain-wall system with integrated sun-louvres, and the raised aluminium flooring'. What you see, therefore, are four stout grey columns with equally stout grey connecting pieces, some flooring, and two double-storey glazing units rising tall and slender above the columns.

The flooring is a bit numb to look at, the glazing system much more interesting because you can see the literal nuts and bolts of its construction. But what are chiefly notable are the columns, not because you can see their nuts and bolts (you can't) but because for anyone who remembers what the history of architecture looks like, they are provocatively reminiscent of something old, fusty and important.

It took me a moment or two to work out what it was, but when I did, I was hugely amused. Whether the Academy, or Foster, deliberately meant it, the whole thing notably recalls one of the most traditional (in the New Tory sense) of all forms of architectural education, the exemplary sample from a historical masterpiece. Since such samples would necessarily be rather large – a bay from a Gothic chapel, the frontal from a Renaissance palace or, famously, a set of columns and a length of entablature from a Greek or Roman temple – they wouldn't go inside the building and had to stand – you guessed? – in the school forecourt.

The classic examples were at that most 'traditional' and influential of all such institutions, the Ecole des Beaux Arts in Paris, but poorman's versions were at most of the imitating schools; and the lineage extends forward in the direction of modernity and Foster by way of the utopian project for a *Cité Industrielle* done in the early 1900s by that dissident student of the Ecole, Tony Garnier. It was modern in that the drawings show the courtyard covered by a glass-and-steel roof, but resolutely traditional in that the columns, three in number, were clearly offered as objects of emulation, something for the student body to copy, study, ponder in their quest for firmness, utility and beauty.

Could it be that the Royal Academy, which has been a school of architecture in its time as well as an annual jumble sale of art-products … could it be that the Academy, traditionally Tory to the core, is offering these four columns as an example for the young to copy, study and ponder? Well, they must have put them there on purpose … Moreover, the layout of the courtyard ensures that the statue of Sir

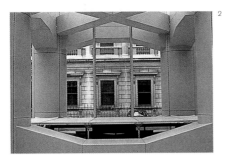

Joshua Reynolds, the Academy's founder and a great believer in the exemplary method, cannot but appear to be pointing at it with his outstretched brush hand, as if calling it to our attention.

Oh, sure, it may be entirely unintentional. Except that Sir Hugh Casson, the Academy's President – an architect and a Modernist of sorts, and a frequent target of the Tories' scorn of late – has been known to identify himself with Sir Joshua on at least one previous occasion. Not long after acceding to the position, he sent a missive to various friends, which showed a drawing of the Academy with himself replacing the Founder on the sculpture's plinth, and crying 'Help!' Sir Hugh is not everybody's favourite architect (not mine for starters) but I know that he was sincere in his desire to 'do something about the old Royal Acad' and is too smart and erudite (I think) to have missed this one.

It could indeed (and tough luck, 'Piloti' of *Private Eye*) be a sly endorsement by Sir Hugh of the toughest and most aggressive style of Modernism available at the moment, and an assertion that the truest tradition of architecture is constructive, not decorative (a proposition that his words bear out more often than his works). If that is true, then the cherished illusions of the self-styled traditionalist wing of architectural opinion have been neatly turned back-to-front and against them. They are mocked in their erudition, and that always hurts (said he with feeling!)

Of course, rule-book Marxist explication would put all this on one side and say that it is simply the head of a typical bourgeois institution acknowledging the power of his true masters, the great international banks. And if you were the head of a typical focus of bourgeois ideology as permanently strapped for cash as the RA, would you not be tempted to make the odd conciliatory gesture towards Big Money?

But if you were offering an academic exemplar for study, copy and contemplation, you might go further and fare worse. In the whole world, the Rogers and Foster offices know more about the making of hardcore, High-Tech architecture than anybody else does. If that kind of architecture is your bag, these nuts and bolts, claddings and exposed metal sections are just the kind of thing to stand in your forecourt.

'Foster has charmed, if not tamed, advanced building technology. He is like Gresley, Lyons, Mitchell and Chapman – very stylish.'

Jonathan Glancey

'Note that the most highly industrialised objects – on wheels, in flight or fixed on the ground – are most subject to renewal and constantly improved in quality, even in terms of price. Building is the only industry that does not advance.'
Jean Prouvé, *The Organisation of Building Construction*, 1971

Norman Foster commissioned John Batchelor to draw the pull-out detail sheet you will find in this issue of the *AR* (2). John Batchelor? The name might not seem familiar at first in architectural circles but a vast number of British architects born from the mid-1930s onwards will recognise his talent. John Batchelor used to produce those superb cutaway drawings of rockets, ships, planes, cars, trains and cranes for *Eagle* (1), probably the finest boys' comic ever published and an inspiration to a generation of British architects and engineers. *Eagle* was thoroughly optimistic about the benefits and possibilities of modern technology and complemented a bedroom cluttered with Meccano sets, dismantled Raleigh racers, Dinky cars and Ian Allan's *ABC of British Railway Locomotives*.

The first generation to grow up with John Batchelor and *Eagle* came to maturity in the late 1950s and early 1960s. Their by now deep-rooted love of machinery burst out in the white-hot technological revolution of the Wilson era (1964-70) in *Archigram* and plug-in cities, in a respect for the writings of Buckminster Fuller and the buildings of Jean Prouvé. The men who had inspired the comic's vision were now in touch with a new generation inspired in turn by the pages of the comic. Norman Foster is of that new second generation.

But, though fascinated by technology, what characterised this generation of British architects was its connection with the British tradition of designing elegantly, of visual integration, of the sensual machine. The French have produced some of the most unmatchable and efficient machinery this century, but no matter how efficiently the machines perform they often look ugly – a mass of complex plumbing, true 'Bowelism'. Look at the original corrugated steel Citroën 2CV (3) or Chapelon's magnificent compound locomotives for the French railways ... or Jean Prouvé's buildings.

By contrast the British have aimed for smooth surfaces, concealed or neatly tucked-away plumbing, ducting and wiring. They seek the curve, the rounded edge, flush panelling. Look at Gresley's Pacific locomotives for the LNER (5), William Lyons' E-type Jaguar (4), and Mitchell's unparalleled Supermarine Spitfire. The sleek and the

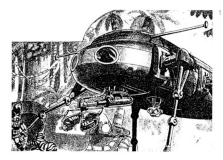

smooth, the thoroughbred, the well-mannered machine, mechanical successor to the racehorse. Now consider the Sainsbury Centre, probably Norman Foster's best-known building. The form is sleek and smooth, the guts of the building, although beautifully detailed, largely hidden away from sight: note the complete resolution of the flowing surface, the sense of visual inclusion, of togetherness, propriety, good manners. Set as elegantly into the East Anglian landscape as an English Palladian house in its park it is yet a part of the world evoked by *Eagle*, of Meccano and Colin Chapman's Lotus cars.

Several of Foster's buildings closely resemble those by Prouvé (the Communist Party Headquarters of 1970 could be the starting point for Ipswich; the exhibition hall at Grenoble, 1967, for Sainsbury; and the National Ministry of Education project, 1970, for Hong Kong). But whereas Prouvé is blunt and prosaic as a blacksmith in his craft, Foster is loquacious and poetic. Foster has charmed, if not tamed, advanced building technology. He is like Gresley, Lyons, Mitchell and Chapman – very stylish. Yet it is just this 'stylish' label that Foster would like to avoid. Being labelled 'stylish' suggests a lack of seriousness, conveys a sense of being more concerned with show than go. He shouldn't worry. It is just this sense of style that ranks him with the best British engineers.

Of course there is a lot more to him than that, but here is the essential difference between young (Foster) and old (Prouvé) masters of what neither would want to call High-Tech. Norman Foster always wanted to be an architect but had no concept of how one *became* an architect. And although he admired, from Art 'O Level' days, the buildings of Le Corbusier and Frank Lloyd Wright, on the one hand, and Palladio and Hawksmoor on the other, he could see no obvious connection between contemporary and historical architecture. Nor was there an obvious connection between his passion for machinery – model aircraft, trains, Meccano sets, bicycles – and architecture. Buckminster Fuller and Jean Prouvé were not names on the lips of British schoolboys. The connections had yet to be made and Foster's introduction to the world of architecture after a spell pen-pushing in Manchester Town Hall's Accountant's Office (Waterhouse's spatially satisfying Neo-Gothic building was the compensation at this point in an uncertain early career) and after National Service in the RAF (specialising in electronics) was to design a traditional brick house while working on the cost side for a local practice.

Jonathan Glancey

3

But once into the university system he left traditional brick houses far behind. Yet as a student Foster earned money producing architect's impressions for building-site hoardings and, influenced by the contemporary *AR* (the days of Eric de Maré, Gordon Cullen, Ian Nairn …), won an RIBA measured drawing medal for a highly detailed representation of a post-mill.

If Sainsbury can be interpreted as a contemporary Grecian temple then Foster's education at Manchester University should be remembered. Like many of the less 'progressive' schools at the time students were still required to draw the Orders and holidays meant sketching Tuscan villas as well as the sneak trips to the Scandinavia of Jacobsen, Utzon and Erskine. Around this time when Foster had begun to integrate his own intentions, the connections between Siena and Cape Canaveral, the architectural engineering of Buckminster Fuller and the automotive engineering of Colin Chapman fused. The *Eagle* had landed.

Discussing his office's most recently completed and most articulated project, the Renault Centre (9), Foster says: 'There is no need to expose everything or conceal everything. One has to integrate. Renault is surprisingly Classical in what it suppresses' – rather like Bulleid's 'air-smoothed' Pacific for the Southern Railway, 1940, or the Comet jet airliner of 1949, or NASA's spaceshuttle (7) – all reference points.

In discussing Foster's projects there is a temptation, to which most critics have succumbed, to look at individual buildings (or even details) as if they were isolated objects. We look at a photograph of a Foster building, out of context, in the same way as we look at a photograph of a car or plane or spaceship. We rarely see him in context – here is a street, the third building along is by Norman Foster … but a visit to Foster's spare white office hardly leads us out of temptation. Large photographs of disassociated *objects* line the walls – NASA lunar module (10), Saturn-Apollo gantry (original painting by John Batchelor – Foster collects them) – whilst between the space-programme-style desks sits a model of a Buckminster Fuller geodesic dome.

It *is* hard to see Foster as a Contextualist despite the nature of the geometrical relationship between Sainsbury and Lasdun's Inca pyramids at the University of East Anglia, in spite of Willis Faber and its urban setting. Because of their striking, unfamiliar shapes and because of the sleek, glossy materials they are constructed from, Sainsbury and Willis Faber stand out like a man without a hat at Goodwood. Sainsbury is a Classical temple whilst Willis Faber seems like some Spielbergian

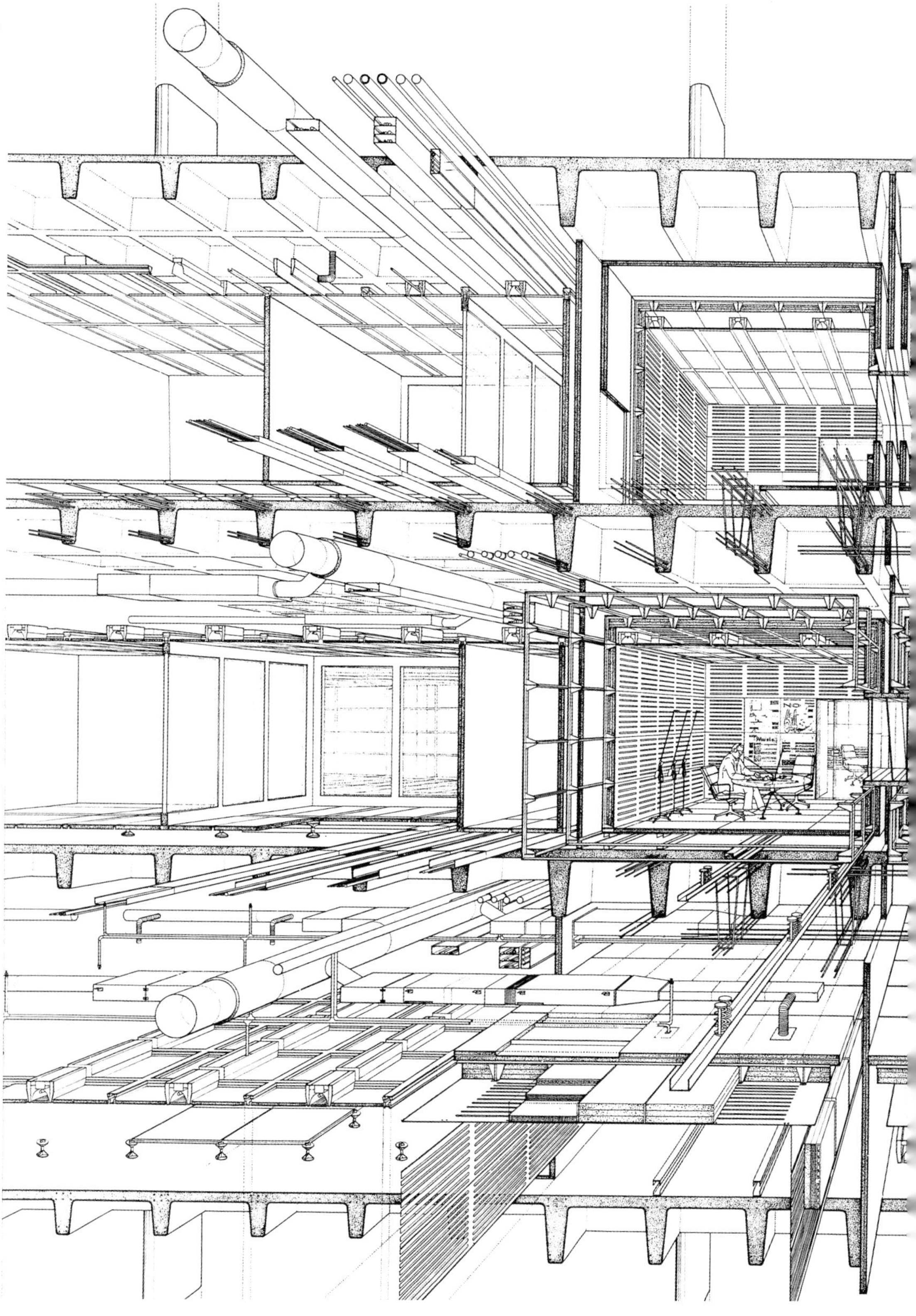

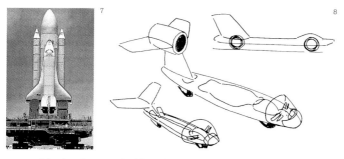

spaceship that has settled into the weave of the town, opaque and visually silent by day, transparent and winking with ethereal light after sunset.

And the Hongkong and Shanghai Bank has never, of course, needed to be a contextual building. The island thrives on cheek-by-jowl contrasts, its aggressive commercial character reflected in the nature of ever taller and glossier buildings. Foster's wins hands down on style even before one begins to think about the subtlety of the Prouvé-inspired interior planning.

The abandoned Hammersmith project too, although ostensibly concerned with the quality of urban life in a messy part of road-raped London, is essentially a glorious contemporary castle. It offers to protect those who use it, cocooned inside a hermetic world. It makes few concessions, and perhaps it doesn't need to, to the surrounding urban chaos. Yet Foster is a long-standing fan of Gordon Cullen and Townscape. He wants to be seen as a Contextualist. If so his real opportunity has just come with the BBC commission in London's Portland Place (6). And it comes as no surprise that Foster should have chosen Cullen to make sight-line drawings of the scheme. The BBC, because of its location on the site of the Langham Hotel, must be a contextual building. So will it be clad in stone or some new blend of stucco? No and again no.

Foster is certain that the architect should employ contemporary materials and avoid those where either development has come to an *impasse* or where the necessary craft is missing (he would build in brick if the body of skill were there to make daring brick structures). Anyway, he argues, Portland Place has seen successive waves of building materials without (until the intrusion of the Langham Hotel) upsetting the nature of the street. Where Robert Adam used bare brick trimmed with stone and John Nash used brick sheathed in stucco, and at Broadcasting House Val Myer used a Portland-stone-clad steel frame – at the new BBC building Foster will use the latest materials whilst respecting and hopefully adding to the character and quality of this broad and subtly curved avenue.

Certainly Foster should be happy working in this urban context, for today's streetscape has as much to do with the *objects* that inhabit or pass through or above it – cars, buses, taxis, delivery vans, telephone boxes, parking meters, airliners and helicopters – as with the objects that *define* the street, i.e., the buildings themselves.

The BBC is not only important because it will show us something of Foster as urbanist but also because it links Foster's talent to a public corporation. His interest

9

in planes (8), cars, trains suggests that here is an ideal designer of railway stations, airports (will Stansted ever emerge?) and motorways. Rich corporations can pay for the stylish delights of Ipswich, Norwich and Hong Kong. Public bodies might not only have more difficulty in finding the necessary cash but also rarely nowadays have the vision to employ imaginative architects. Charles Holden had the eagle-minded and generous Frank Pick as a patron when he built that classic series of Underground stations on the Piccadilly Line extensions (1930-33).

Nikolaus Pevsner has compared Frank Pick with Lorenzo the Magnificent and the Medicis. Norman Foster won't find such a patron in the public domain as easily as he has in the wealthy private sector. Yet money is not, or should not be, a constraint. Foster says that if all he could afford, or all that society allowed him, was breeze-blocks then he would attempt to build imaginatively in these normally bleak building blocks. Like Jean Prouvé he finds it hard to forgive the architect who expresses reservations about his own completed buildings: 'I would have liked to, *but* ...'

At 47 Norman Foster has a long way to go as an architect. It's unlikely that he will relax, although he could afford to do so. He certainly has no intention of going into bulk architecture, of administering a large office churning out Sainsbury and Renault replicants. Each project will remain an experiment. Yet maybe just as he reconciled the independent machine with the rooted building Foster might now make links between his earlier concrete and ivy-strewn buildings and the glistening steel structures of today. Architects like Prouvé and Foster have advanced the state of the building art but nature should not be forgotten in all this passion for machinery and new materials. The path from Renault could lead to a post-industrial Arcadia or to a self-referential Utopia. Apolitical, pragmatic and Classicist as he is, Norman Foster is probably striking out for the former, but the second-rate puff of 'High-Tech' that skids along in the *Eagle's* slipstream is sadly dragging us along to the latter.

'... I wasn't wildly taken with a lady who looked around the Centre, turned to me and said: it's so beautiful – if only you didn't have these works of art in it.'

Robert Sainsbury

A short while ago my wife and I were talking to a senior member of the architectural profession about Norman Foster and his Centre for Visual Arts at the University of East Anglia at Norwich – Norman's first major non-industrial, non-commercial building. Suddenly our friend exclaimed in obvious amazement: 'My God, you mean to say you're still on speaking terms with your architect!' Well I wouldn't be standing here if we were not indeed good friends with Norman.

As our experience of that building has grown, so, if possible, has our admiration for Norman. Our gratitude to Foster Associates remains undiminished. An examination of the varying relationships between professional people and their clients would certainly be very revealing. However, I am only concerned today with the rapport between Norman and ourselves resulting, I like to think, in a truly productive relationship, the sort of relationship in which I believe Norman is at his greatest, one which we found unbelievably stimulating. I hope therefore, that you will excuse me talking about the Sainsbury Centre but really I am not qualified to speak on this particular occasion about anything else.

When Norman accepted the commission, the precise site hadn't even been chosen. There was no written brief – in fact there never was one. Norman's task was to give substance to a somewhat ill-defined concept. We wanted him, in providing a home for our collection, to give members of the University and visitors the opportunity to look at works of art in the natural context of their daily work and life and, above all, to enjoy our collection as we have done. Sensual enjoyment is no bar to the pursuit of knowledge or intellectual understanding.

All this called for a place in which people could relax, look at works of art in a leisurely manner if they so wished, work, read a novel or just dream away. Such a place would surely appeal equally to outside scholars and lay members of the public as to men and women in the University. That was Norman's brief, if you can call it that, and it was to be developed and elaborated in the course of many, many hours of discussion and travel during the planning stage.

Norman himself has stated that the building attempts a sensitive but positive response to the collection. Undoubtedly the building provides to a marked degree the sought-after environment. It equally satisfies the particular gallery needs of a somewhat eclectic collection containing a great deal of sculpture. It is, in our opinion, the measure of Norman's imagination and flexibility, quite apart from his innate

brilliance as an architect. I would add that as we find the building completely satisfying visually, we did not contradict the person who suggested that Norman's
building was the greatest work of art in our collection, although I wasn't wildly
taken with a lady who looked around the Centre, turned to me and said, 'It's so
beautiful – if only you didn't have these works of art in it'.

It was, I think, that great American architectural writer, Ada Louise Huxtable,
who said that architects are passionate people. That may or may not be true, but
what is certainly true is that Norman's building has aroused extraordinary passions
amongst architects, architectural writers and art historians. There has been, on the
one hand, intense admiration. On the other, apart from genuine disapproval, there
has been a great deal of ill-informed, even hostile, criticism and of course many
attempts by writers just to appear clever. My personal prize goes to the description of the building as 'fetishist expressionism'.

It is to me extraordinary that so many commentators, when assessing the
building, have ignored the present-day needs of an art gallery. As the selected site
had no defined area, the size and configuration of the building were determined by

1

Robert Sainsbury

the initial planning. Now there are numerous advantages in the flexibility provided by having column-free gallery spaces: 18,000 square feet on the ground floor and 5,000 square feet on the mezzanine. In the first place, an unencumbered space vastly increases the display potentialities. The importance of this is usually underestimated. I believe that the usefulness of museums should be determined not just by the number of people who visit them but also by the extent and quality of their experience, and that, in my opinion, is largely conditioned by the way objects are shown. The more I realise the generally deplorable standard of museum display and lighting in this country, the more I am thankful for what Norman has made possible at the University of East Anglia.

There is an idea around that small objects cannot be satisfactorily displayed at the right height for the average adult in free-standing places of the appropriate size. The same argument can be applied to paintings and drawings, all of which are displayed at UEA on screens related to the human scale. The screens can also be used to break up the space and as backgrounds to the free-standing cases.

Naturally an integral part of the display is the lighting, and possibly Norman's supreme achievement at the Centre is the quality of overall light and the lighting of the individual works of art. This is achieved by a combination of natural lighting, controlled by photoelectric cells, and manually controlled artificial lighting at ceiling level directed at the works of art. There is therefore no lighting in the cases and there is no heat generated in the tops of the cases. And when the spotlighting is turned off, special security lighting is turned on. All lighting locations are accessible from walkways running across the building within the roof trusses, so no machinery has to be brought in at floor level to change bulbs or adjust fixtures.

One cannot of course consider the lighting of a gallery without at the same time considering the allied and controversial problem of conservation. Whilst appreciating what we owe to our conservators, I do not consider it necessary always to pander to their frequently changing requirements, or to endorse the practical absurdity of having a drawing, which can be properly viewed and studied while on display, kept in a suitably constructed vault and brought out only occasionally for the benefit of scholars. The answer at UEA, apart from the strategic placing of certain works, lies in the perfectly reasonable rotation of the permanent collection. Incidentally, I believe the latest formula used by the experts is to relate length of display to intensity of light. With special exhibitions there is a means of taking protective measures for groups of sensitive works.

Apart from display, there are other major advantages of open gallery spaces. Sophisticated detection equipment does not necessarily minimise invigilation costs – something to which I think some architects might have paid more attention. At UEA the entire display and reception areas can be invigilated by three guards – one at the top of the spiral staircase leading down from the upper entrance, one on the mezzanine, and a third watching the monitor. There are naturally no circulation problems – in fact the Centre allows complete freedom of movement, even for the disabled, in accordance with the basic concept, and plenty of space in which to sit and relax.

It will be understood that the University was specially concerned with minimising running costs. The building is a practical realisation of Norman's concept that high technology can equate with low energy consumption. As he has explained, through the design of the spaces and the nature of the enclosing wall, combined with the engineering of air movements he has attempted, I consider successfully, to provide an alternative to air conditioning with its high running costs.

Ladies and gentlemen, I have said enough of the building, and I will simply add a postscript. A well-known American architect recently asked me for the 'bucket' rating of the Centre. One bucket, two buckets, three buckets? I was pleased to be able to say that the Centre does not need buckets.

Buckets or no buckets, I still believe strongly that an ongoing relationship, as at UEA, between architect and client is of paramount importance. This creates a better chance of ensuring maintenance of standards and long-term satisfaction with the building for both parties. I am proud that my family's name is associated with Norman Foster's building, and very proud to support him here today.

2

Robert Sainsbury

'Society is highly specialised: specialists don't ever see what is going on in the next laboratory, so there is very little integration of the information accruing to the doing of more with less.'

Buckminster Fuller

I was born in 1895 and I have lived through very great changes in the potential and accomplishments of humanity. I would like to put our experiences here into perspective so you can understand what is going on in relation to where humanity may be going.

When I was born, reality was everything you could see, smell, touch and hear. The year I was born the X-ray came in. You couldn't see it. The year I was born, the wireless came in. You couldn't see it. When I was three, the electron was discovered. When I was entering Harvard in 1913 my physics book had yellow pages pasted at the back called 'Electricity'. We were entering an era of invisibility. Development is being conducted in the realms of reality not directly contactable by human senses.

I would like to point out the relation of this to structures and buildings. We have in the universe a tendency to expand and contract and in this expanding and contracting the expansion that we call radiation brings about pressure, compression, and the gravity copes with the other tendency and pulls the thing together. Gravity is tension, radiation is compression, and all buildings, structures, all interaction, every realisation physically is in play with that push and pull. We entered the Stone Age absolutely ignorant. We put a stone on top of a stone. It would sit there. We would make a pile of stones and try to put a stone on the side and it wouldn't stay there – it fell. It needed tension to hold it there. Throughout the early years of masonry and architecture we had a compression-resisting capability of 50,000 pounds per square inch in masonry, but it only had 50 pounds tensile strength. The best we could do for tension was wood and the average available strength and quantity was 10,000 pounds per square inch tensile strength against 50,000 compression. So we had *five times* capability compressively as we had tension. Everything we call architecture came out of that kind of condition.

In 1851, we took out production steel for the first time. Production steel came to 50,000 tension. Tension changed its parity with compression for the first time in history. A few years later, in 1883, Roebling built the Brooklyn Bridge, got the steel up to 70,000 with higher carbon. During the Second World War chrome nickel steel provided 350,000 tension capability. Seven times that of mild steel – the same weight of material – the same bulk. Most recently we have got up to 600,000 per square inch tensile strength in carbon fibres. One-quarter the weight of steel. So we have 48 times the strength in the same bulk and weight of steel. And that's why MacCready was able to have his pedal-powered plane flown across the Channel. No radio, television nor newspaper mentioned anything to do with increase of tensile capability, because it is invisible.

Society is highly specialised: specialists don't ever see what is going on in the next laboratory, so there is very little integration of the information accruing to the doing of more with less.

After Trafalgar in 1805 the East India Company College was set up here and all the data of exploring round the world for two hundred years was put in this college. Thomas Malthus (the first human in history to have the total vital statistics around a closed systems sphere) was made Professor of Political Economics. He came to the conclusion that humanity was reproducing itself at a geometrical rate and increasing its life support at an arithmetical rate.

Quite clearly, the vast majority of humanity was doomed to go through life in great want and pain. Ninety-eight per cent of humanity was illiterate at the time. Sixty years later we have Darwin going around the planet developing his theory of evolution – survival of the fittest. By this time information was gathering quite rapidly. Contemporary with him was Karl Marx. Then, it was thought there were two classes of human beings – different blood stocks. If you were of royal stock, you always married into that blood stock, but the worker was something completely different. As far as the socialist was concerned, the workers were the fittest to survive, because they knew how to handle tools and nurture seeds; the capitalists were parasites. The capitalists said: 'We go along with Darwin and Malthus too. We are on the top of the heap because we're the fittest. The workers are dull – no imagination, no daring, no venture. We're just full of it – life needs us very badly.' All political economics are based on 'it has to be you or me'. What was not foreseen at that time was the telegraph – 1810, just after Malthus said what he said, we began to do a lot more with less, invisibly.

I kept track of all those technologies when I was in the Navy in the First World War. I got myself into the technology of more environment-controlling with less.

When we developed the first geodesic dome, the two largest domes in the world were St Peter's in Rome and the Pantheon. St Peter's is around 30,000 tons – about the weight of the *Queen Elizabeth 2*. When I developed the first

geodesic dome of 150 feet it came out 30 tons – one-thousandth of the weight of St Peter's. I have been trying very hard to get the world of architecture, the accrediting boards of the societies, to require that all drawings of any buildings made by any draughtsman or any architectural students should always have the weights of the materials.

In 1970 we crossed a threshold where it could be demonstrated that if we took all the metals being put into armaments and put them into 'livingry', within ten years we could have all humanity living at a higher standard than anyone had ever known on a completely sustainable basis while phasing out all further use of fossil fuels and atomic energy. In 1970 it became evident in engineering that if we kept track of the whole thing on a planetary basis, for the first time in history it did not have to be you or me, it became adequate for both. War became obsolete but you couldn't get the word around because everyone was so specialised. I want to be sure that you really know we do have the option to make it, instead of blowing ourselves to pieces in half an hour.

The invention of humans in the universe gave them access to the great design laws of the universe; we have the choice of destroying ourselves or taking care of everybody and living in the universe in an entirely new kind of way.

Architects have a very extraordinary responsibility – they really do have a responsibility for putting things together. Darling people, I want you to realise that in the era of specialisation the architect is really the only person we have whose business is with *everything*, but we have not been able to exercise very much because big money has been running. I have been round the world now 50 times and I have seen in the last eighteen years all these buildings coming up. Bangkok was a lovely little city and they filled up the canals and now there's all these great skyscrapers; and why are they there? They're there because that is the way you make most money with your land – nothing to do with what's good for humanity.

'The only proper word to describe the sort of care and finesse involved in the making of purpose-made "High-Tech" architecture such as this is craftsmanship.'

Chris Abel

Money is, and always has been, the beginning and end of everything in Hong Kong. Originally founded – with the help of a little gunboat diplomacy – to force-feed China with British India's lucrative opium, the 145-year-old colony has grown to be one of the largest financial and trading centres in the world.

Conspicuous wealth abounds in the city, amongst both Chinese and Caucasian elites. But the obsession with making money is by no means confined to the super-rich, who live on the upper slopes of Victoria Peak overlooking the harbour. Nor even to the merely well-off who live, inevitably, further down the Peak, at Mid-Levels. It seems to affect Hong Kongers of every race and station, fuelling a frenzy of economic activity, both large and small scale, which gives the place its reputation as a money machine. Over the years, these energetic entrepreneurs have been reinforced by a constant stream of immigrants, mostly refugees from across the border, just bursting to join the great game, make this money machine work for them, too, and – who knows – maybe one day join those who have already made it to the Peak.

Anything goes in the streets of *laissez-faire* Hong Kong, and the irrepressible vitality of Hong Kongers is released here in a Jane Jacobs-style fantasy of compressed human activity and colour. Forests of gaudy signs, emblazoned with Chinese characters or familiar Japanese and Western brand names, reach almost into the middle of the street, as if to tell you what Hong Kong is all about, and why most of the people crammed into those awful apartment blocks towering above choose what they have over the alternatives they or their grandparents escaped.

Not surprisingly, Hong Kongers will say that it is the banks that *really* govern this Asian Eldorado. The colonial apparatus merely facilitates the rest, and provides an occasional ceremonial flourish. It is therefore entirely fitting that Hong Kong's first architectural monument of global significance should be a bank building. It is also fitting that the bank in question should be the Hongkong and Shanghai Banking Corporation (also known as the Hongkong Bank). Not only does the Bank enjoy a premier position in the local economy – it is one of the two note issuing banks – but it also enjoys a special place in local folklore. Almost as old as the colony itself, it is identified with Hong Kong's success story. So long, it is said, as the twin bronze lions (3), Stitt and Stephen, guard the entrance to the Bank, so will Hong Kong prosper.

More than that, the Bank has a record as an innovator in its choice of architecture, notably for its last headquarters, built in 1935 on the same site beneath the Peak as the new building. Already confident then of the Bank's future, the general manager, Vandaleur Grayburn, instructed his chosen architect, G L 'Tug' Wilson, senior partner in the Hong Kong firm of Palmer and Turner, to 'build the best bank in the world'. The completed building (1, 2) aroused as much excitement and controversy in its time as the new headquarters has. Its main tower, 220 feet high, made it the tallest building between Cairo and San Francisco. It was done out in Art Deco, and it had a vaulted ceiling decorated with a splendid mosaic. But it was the technological innovations that made the building truly unique in the region. High-tensile steel, not previously used outside North America, was used in the stone-clad frame. It had high-speed lifts and air conditioning, both rare in Asia at the time, and it had provision on the roof for a landing pad for autogiros. The impressive-looking building still appears on old Hong Kong banknotes, a potent symbol of the powers-that-be in Hong Kong.

Then came the turn of Foster Associates to answer the very same magisterial decree. The Bank was also more specific about its latest needs. True to its innovative style, it has achieved its present position in the banking world's top twenty largely by being able to respond quickly to changes in banking methods and technology. Functional and technological flexibility were therefore essential: enough to keep the Bank on top for another 50 years.

The programme could have been made in heaven for Foster. Even so, elegant 'serviced sheds' of the kind his practice is renowned for, do not necessarily provide much of a precedent for the special problems of building flexibility into a high-rise structure. Compelled to rethink common assumptions and solutions, Foster found the usual 'kebab of shallow floors' skewered on to a central core to be wanting from every viewpoint: socially, functionally and visually – all in all 'joyless'.

The result is a building quite unlike any normal suspended floor structure – which usually also features an obtrusive central core as the main support, floors all hung straight down from the top – let alone any bog-standard office tower. Notwithstanding the much publicised use of bridge building techniques, it looks like, and in principle behaves much like, a series of stacked portal frames. Moreover, it bears a marked visual resemblance to the stacked timber structures with over-

hangs that are typical of Chinese and Japanese Buddhist temples, forms referred to by Foster as source images. The decreasing intervals between the double-floor-height suspension trusses also have an intended foreshortening effect, reinforcing the likeness to the Oriental model, as well as making the building appear to be taller than it actually is.

In addition to their function as horizontal structural zones for trusses and braces, the double-floor-height spaces serve to integrate a whole host of unique features. By breaking up the building into distinct spatial units, Foster sought not only to avoid the monotony of looking up at nothing but identical storeys, but also – more importantly – to introduce a sense of identity to the main operational functions of the Bank. The vertical breakdown into blocks of floors, or 'villages', as Foster likes to call them, lends a spatial focus to the principal organisational divisions within the headquarters: local main branch operations down near street level; electronic data processing further up; then international operations and senior executive offices, and finally special services and chairman's apartment on the uppermost floors. A smaller, streamlined block of VIP dining rooms with a helicopter pad on the roof tops the building out (12).

In between these units, the upper three double-floor-height zones accommodate the larger communal facilities, such as staff dining and conference rooms. Setbacks at each of these levels have the effect of emphasising the breakdown on the outside of the building, as well as serving as refuge terraces in the event of fire (a mandatory requirement for all high-rise buildings in Hong Kong). It was also intended that the terraces be landscaped to create a series of 'hanging gardens' for recreation, but the idea was unfortunately dropped by the Bank.

However, it is the ingenious vertical circulation pattern which gives the organisational structure of the building its most original twist. Foster had experimented in the three-storey Willis Faber & Dumas building with replacing lifts by escalators as the principal means of getting up and down an office building. The success of that experiment encouraged Foster to use a combination of lifts and escalators for the Hongkong Bank. For most of the building's height, the high-speed lifts stop only at the double-floor-height spaces which, along with everything else, provide reception and interchange points. Intermediate floors, starting above the banking hall atrium, are served by escalators. So you choose which floor you want to go to, take a lift

which whisks you up at twenty feet per second to the nearest reception point, and then travel the rest of the way in more leisurely fashion, up or down – whichever the case may be – by escalator. No more waiting, no more cramped lifts, or at least, fewer of them, and at spatial and capital costs comparable with the number of extra lifts that would otherwise have been needed to service a building which houses 3,500 employees.

The pleasure ride on this seemingly endless cascade of moving stairways throws open floor upon floor of vast areas of virtually unimpeded space (the large-span structure yields a remarkable 75 per cent useable floor space, as against the usual 60-65 per cent for office towers). Cellular offices are generally kept to the minimum possible, and those that have been included are grouped 'inboard' around the escalators, well back from the exterior curtain walls, so as not to hog the spectacular views towards the harbour on one side and the Peak on the other.

The extreme transparency of the whole arrangement is in part a reflection of the Bank's expressed desire that everybody working in the building should be visibly accountable to everybody else. Some managers were apparently not too happy at first about the lack of privacy, nor about losing such prized managerial privileges as offices against a window wall. Presumably other office workers, who gained the views they might not have otherwise had, are happier with the arrangement, though they, too, have to cope with the overexposure. Foster's own penchant for see-through structures and wide open spaces is also familiar enough. But the detailing of the computer-type raised floor, as well as that of the partitioning system, points to other influences of a regional origin.

The removable floor-panels, made of a lightweight aluminium honeycomb sandwich similar to the floor panels used in Boeing aircraft, have a grey metal trim around the carpet finish, so that the floor grid is clearly visible from end to end of the building. It looks like, and dictates, the internal planning in much the same way as the Japanese tatami mat. The partitions, which, logically, are hung down from the floor above, are 100 per cent demountable and confirm the source of inspiration: they were in fact designed by a Japanese member of Foster's Hong Kong-based design team. Not only do the proportions of the glazed panels mimic Japanese form, but in the executive offices on the top floors, where senior staff are allowed a measure of privacy, the translucent panels are made of 'shoji glass'. Composed of two panes of laminated glass with a thin white layer of fibreglass pressed between, it passes well enough for the real thing.

It is no coincidence that, along with his visits to Hong Kong during the design of the project, Foster made two trips to Japan (4), which apparently left a deep impression. Not altogether surprisingly, the spare but elegant traditional domestic architecture of Japan struck a special chord of empathy. A comparison with the earlier pilgrimage by Frank Lloyd Wright is irresistible. It is not so much, therefore, that Foster has come away from Japan with a whole new outlook. But something like a recognition, a certain crystallisation of ideas already nurtured, has taken place.

Nothing superfluous intrudes on these austere, flexible open spaces, in which, Japanese fashion, anything can happen, but only if it is *allowed* to happen. Even the subdued colour scheme suggests the influence of *shibui*, the word for 'sober and refined' Japanese taste. Foster's renowned care and control over every aspect and tiny detail of his buildings is much in evidence in these interiors, as elsewhere, put to service in the projection of a twenty-first-century corporate image of High-Tech banking efficiency: a smooth-running money machine like the city itself, only more elegant. No place for clutter here.

The computer-type floor itself was designed in anticipation of the paperless office, and allows for unforeseeable changes in desktop data retrieval systems. It also provides for an unusual system of air conditioning, in which fresh air is blown *up* from small vents in the floor panels. The height to which the air is blown is sufficient to refresh the volume in which people circulate and work, and no more. This highly efficient system is fine-tuned to keep down energy consumption by a computerised building management system (the computers are located on level 27, from where – note the phrase – 'the building is driven'), which also keeps similar tabs on other services, as well as maintenance jobs to be done, qualifying the building as one of the new 'smart' generation.

All cabling and ductwork is tucked away beneath the raised floor. The only services to get any direct exposure, *à la* Willis Faber & Dumas, are the escalators and lift shafts, which are clad in tinted glass to reveal supporting frames and moving parts. Even the prefabricated service modules on the outside have their separate character fudged somewhat. Each stack of structurally and functionally independent modules is clad in a continuous sheath of aluminium panels (of the same type

5

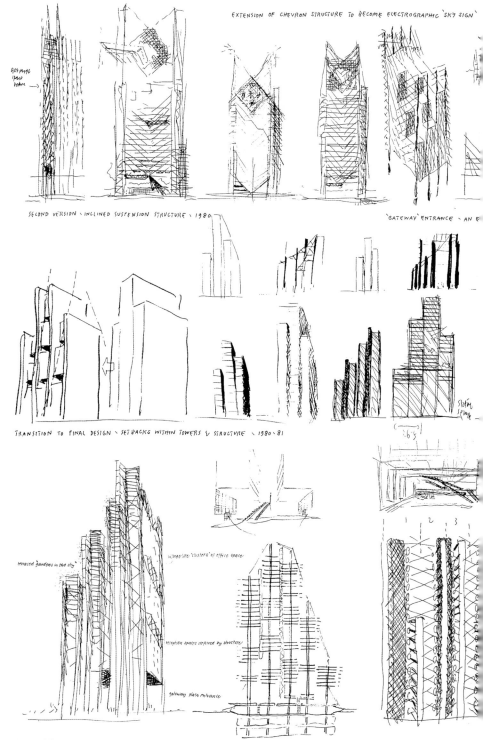

EXTENSION OF CHEVRON STRUCTURE TO BECOME ELECTROGRAPHIC 'SKY SIGN'

SECOND VERSION · INCLINED SUSPENSION STRUCTURE · 1980

'GATEWAY' ENTRANCE · AN E

TRANSITION TO FINAL DESIGN · SETBACKS WITHIN TOWERS & STRUCTURE · 1980·81

terraced gardens in the sky

triangular 'clusters' of office space

reception spaces defined by structure

gateway plaza entrance

RECURRING THEMES · RICH MIX OF SPACES & ACTIVITIES WITHIN A GRID OF STRUCTURE & TOWERS FOR VERTICAL MOVEMENT & SERVICES

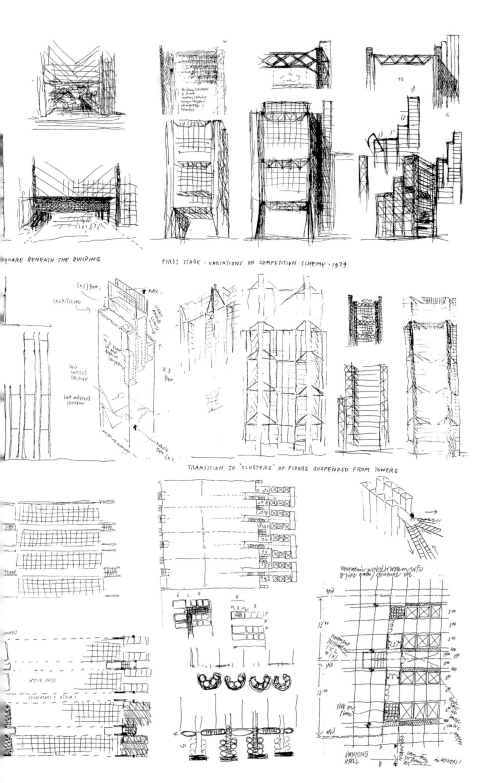

SQUARE BENEATH THE BUILDING

FIRST STAGE · VARIATIONS ON COMPETITION SCHEME · 1979

TRANSITION TO 'CLUSTERS' OF FLOORS SUSPENDED FROM TOWERS

as the floor panels), so that the stacks read together as homogeneous vertical shafts, not unlike the medieval-looking service towers of Louis Kahn's laboratory building in Philadelphia, rather than the 'plug-in' sort which they really are.

All this visual restraint begins to weaken, though, the further we go up, where the setbacks necessitated by shadow regulations begin to cut into the building. On a typical office floor in the lower sections, filling the full three bays, the open construction of the gigantic steel masts has a muted impact on the acres of open space. But from where the progressive setbacks start to reduce both the number and the length of the floor bays, the structure makes increasingly dramatic spatial and visual intrusions into the interior. With each structural member beefed up to as much as twice its size with corrosion and fire protection, aluminium cladding and tolerances in between, these already massive columns and cross-pieces begin to take on very aggressive manners. Coming across one of the masts in the more confined spaces of the upper floors is like finding an oil rig where you expect to find a Japanese tea house.

6

Towards the top of the building, where the floor bays draw further back to reveal the full assemblage of masts, trusses, and now 'flying' cross-braces, the structure takes over completely in an unabashed display of naked brute strength. The impression that the building is incomplete at these levels is reinforced by the sight of sturdy maintenance cranes perched atop some of the masts, looking much like the construction cranes which had been placed in similar positions in the process of bootstrapping the structure up into place.

Up here it is all pure megastructure stuff, overwhelming in its delight in what advanced engineering can do for architecture, and taking it for granted that the visual excitement is more than enough compensation for the loss of human scale. But in the same way that the bared structure of the Eiffel Tower (another favourite source image of Foster's) relates to the scale of Paris and not to the people in the restaurant enjoying the view, so does this Godzilla-strength structure relate, if not to the inhabitants of the building itself at these heights, then to the population of Hong Kong looking *down* on the roof space of the Bank from the skyscraper apartments of the Peak rising up behind.

The latent conflict of scale also surfaces in the multi-purpose, double-floor-height spaces. While it may have seemed like a good idea to take advantage of

these generous spaces for larger communal functions, the amenities are dwarfed by the muscular trusses and cross-braces, which inhabit the same volume. No matter what, it is impossible to shake off the feeling that one has stumbled into some outsize converted attic, where people and furniture have to make the best of what room they can find between the rafters.

But if things go somewhat awry in these areas, they are set to rights in the building's centrepiece, the banking hall and atrium. The Bank wanted a symbolic focus to replace the much-loved vaulted banking hall of the previous headquarters. Foster obliged. The entry alone is as calculated a piece of architectural hype as there has ever been. By reducing the building's 'footprint', the 100-foot span structure made it possible to create an open public plaza underneath, connecting the busy Queen's Road and Des Voeux Road thoroughfares at the front and back, and pulling pedestrians into the very bowels of the building. In the middle of this sweeping space two escalators span the height from plaza floor to banking hall – the odd angle was determined by the Bank's feng shui man as the most propitious for the Bank's future – to scoop up customers and deposit them back down again (6, 7). They pierce a glazed, lightweight catenary structure, appropriately nicknamed the 'underbelly', which seals off the central bay beneath the atrium, whilst affording passers-by on the plaza a clear view 170 feet up through the middle of the building.

If you do not know what is in store, the glance upward from the plaza can knock you back. Given the power of the present set-up, it is hard to imagine what the reaction would have been if Foster had been permitted to carry out his intention of putting a glazed floor into the plaza, so that atrium, plaza, and the lower banking floor at basement level could be experienced as one continuous vertical space. The sensation of walking across such a space, especially at night, with the plaza floor illuminated from below, regrettably has to go down as one of the great might-have-beens of architecture.

Never mind. The design as built has thrills enough. Joining the slow and lengthy procession leading upwards and seeing the reflections in the glass panels of the 'underbelly', the sensation is not unlike surfacing from a swim in the depths of some huge pool. Looking down on the same procession from inside the banking hall, seeing passengers popping up one by one through the glistening transparent membrane, miraculously dry from their ascent, you get an analogous impression.

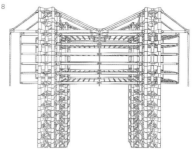

8

9

But you look *down* when you have first recovered from looking up. The immense void of the atrium affords the extraordinary dimension of complete north and south facing cross-sections through ten storeys. Standing at a point midway up the atrium, one looks from corner to corner through a whole stack of transparent floors, with apparently precious little to hold them up apart from some slender 'sky-hooks' hanging down in the middle. This 'look-no-hands' effect is only slightly mitigated by the sight of the mammoth masts and cross-bracing at each end of the atrium, and the trusses overhead. The uninstructed brain is not sufficiently accustomed to the logic of suspended floor structures to do away with a felt need for visible – meaning solid – load-bearing support, spaced at decent, reassuring intervals through the floorspaces. And whilst the logic of the structure may be spelt out with painstaking care on the outside of the building (8, 9), where the eye and brain can more easily grasp the thing in its totality, reason and imagination both falter inside at the sight of a building that not only has no middle – atria are common enough in themselves – but also seems to be almost completely devoid of any kind of intermediary support.

There is a lot more that is Gothic than Classical in all this structural and spatial magic, contrary statements about Foster's work notwithstanding. If the 'medieval' service towers, 'flying braces' and 'incomplete' appearance of the building had not already prompted the idea, then the soaring proportions of the atrium (read nave) and the great translucent eastern window, easily justify the building's popular description as a 'cathedral of commerce'.

Perhaps too easily. For the familiar Western concept, apt as it is, diverts attention away from those other, regional attributes already spoken of. It is something of a paradox that an advanced technology building such as this, put together out of parts manufactured in so many remote locations, mostly in the industrialised nations of the West, should have any regional character at all. But that quality of structural and spatial transparency which Foster has long sought, and which is the keynote of the whole building, has, as Foster has now discovered at first hand, many more Oriental than Occidental precedents. And if the balance between brute structure and fragile interior is upset on the highest floors, then it is in the central space of the atrium that Godzilla and Madame Butterfly come closest together in an unexpected but convincing harmony of opposites. Perhaps the sight of so many open

Chris Abel

floors floating effortlessly one above the other creates a sufficient spectacle to counterbalance the display of raw strength put out by the support structure. Or maybe the brain does dimly sense, if only at an unconscious level, something of the causal connection between all that overbearing strength on the one hand, and all that lightweight transparency on the other, the cunning result of a diversion of forces away from the expected places to be concentrated elsewhere, in fewer but greater amounts.

And to cap it all, there is the 'sunscoop' (10, 11). More Heath Robinson than Buck Rogers, this incredible device consists of two banks of mirrors, each the full length of the atrium, one positioned in the double-height space which forms the roof of the atrium, the other stuck out on huge brackets on the south face of the building. The exterior, computer-controlled mirror is moveable, rotating on its axis to track the changing angle of the sun, so that it directs the sun's rays into the building to strike the interior mirror at a constant point, fortunately at a sufficient height so as not to blind the employees working at the same level. The beams of sunlight thence bounce down through the atrium, washing the interior from west to east with an intense pool of sunlight that cuts straight through the glazed 'underbelly' to illuminate the plaza underneath. Pedestrians move about on the plaza far down below, with their shadows cast by bright sunlight that just ought not to be there. It is an awesome experience.

But if the sunscoop is the most spectacular demonstration of Foster's ability to push building technology to its limits, the entire construction speaks of a level of technique and precision engineering that cannot help but change customary perceptions of relations between technological means and ends, perceptions still shaped by decades of orthodox Modernist ideology. It is the story of the making of this building which, in the final analysis, tells us the most of what it portends for architecture in the late twentieth century, and even beyond.

But here we encounter something of a dilemma, requiring a small digression, because the use of advanced technology in building is supposed, by definition, to preclude the very kinds of human skills involved in the making of an artefact that make this unique building comprehensible for what it is. For according to the way we were once taught, and not so long ago, the use of advanced technology in building implies *standardisation*, of the components, and of course, of the looks of

a building. And so, by and large, it has come to be. Foster's own earlier 'off-the-peg' concoctions helped to keep the faith alive. But now here we have Foster and his team producing an advanced technology building in which there is hardly a single component that has not been *tailor-made* for the job, and with *machine-made* precision. There is repetition, yes. But when you go to a manufacturer and tell him to make something for your building that he has never made before for any other building, and will probably never make quite the same way again, then you are *not* talking about standardisation.

The only proper word to describe the sort of care and finesse involved in the making of purpose-made 'High-Tech' architecture such as this is craftsmanship. And if we have to bend our categories to accommodate the notion that technology of this standard not only does not exclude, but actually *necessitates* craftsmanship of the highest order, then so much the better, because otherwise we shall not be able to make room for one or two related notions of no small consequence. For was it not also once fervently preached that a rebirth of architecture in the twentieth century could only come about through an alliance of craftsmanship with industrial technology? Only it was also then assumed that the inevitable, and desirable, consequence was mass production of the end product, which made the whole idea meaningless. But here we have an advanced technology building, a sophisticated machine, purpose-made by craftsmen using other machines in a manner not significantly different, in terms of the quality of human control over product, from the way we are accustomed to seeing tools used in more traditional forms of building.

So what is there now then, to hold up this long delayed rebirth? For that is what this building confronts us with: the conclusion that the standardised Modern architecture we have come to know, but not love, was after all a historian's decoy; that the *real* thing, having undergone the necessary mutations for survival, is only now beginning to emerge; that, in sum, what is authentically 'modern' in twentieth-century architecture has to do neither with fluctuating aesthetic preferences nor dubious social engineering, but with certain innovations in mechanised *technique*, the full development of which is at last becoming clear, and turning out to be very different from the popular characterisation.

The problem, it will doubtless be argued, is that this is a very special and very expensive building – though contrary to rumours, it was built according to target (when inflation is accounted for) and ahead of a tight schedule – and that the sorts of technology and skills involved are unlikely to be repeated too often.

Enter the robots. The US firm of Cupples, who had previously clad most of the world's tallest buildings, had to undertake a major retooling in order to meet Foster's stringent requirements for this job. Amongst their new acquisitions were a number of computer-controlled machines, including robot welders, to cut, fabricate and assemble the complex aluminium cladding, made up of thousands of pieces, mostly of different shapes and sizes.

It was suggested many years ago that the flexible, computerised techniques of production being introduced into other industries might be used to create a new kind of building industry, free from the tyrannies of standardisation. Picture programmable, adaptable machines turning out small batches of high-technology components, tailor-made for specific buildings in specific places, and for specific clients, at economic rates previously thought feasible only with mass-production methods. Now here they are, 'smart' tools helping to make 'smart' buildings; the advance guard of a new generation of machines that are going to transform the way buildings are conceived and built in the next century. So it is not too bold to suggest that the supreme level of megascale craft involved in the making of Foster's 'one-off' building might herald something of a much wider range of possibilities. And if it is true that the death of Modern architecture may have been greatly exaggerated, then it is also doubtful that the customised, machine-made products we shall in future call 'modern' will look much like the standardised, defunct model.

The phrase 'made in Hong Kong' has not always implied the very best that money can buy. But buildings of this quality do not just happen anywhere, at any time. They happen because a rare combination of circumstances leads them to happen. That does not just mean that an innovative, perfectionist architect was lucky enough to have an innovative, perfectionist client who wanted the best and had enough ready cash to be able to afford it. Nor was the Hongkong Bank merely maintaining a well-established tradition and standard when it demanded once again to have 'the best bank in the world'. With '1997' closing in, and the Sleeping Dragon next door waking up at last to claim its rightful place in the world and with it the territory of Hong Kong, the whole project is a calculated gesture of self-confidence designed to steady the nerves of Hong Kongers for the changes ahead.

146

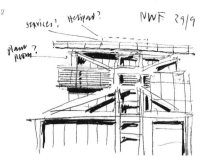

Such gestures do not come cheap. But there are still other considerations which put this extraordinary venture in proper perspective. Hong Kong is no longer just the Crown Colony of Hong Kong. It is one of the 'four tigers', or 'mini-Japans', which, along with Taiwan, South Korea, and Singapore, comprise the front line of the burgeoning Pacific Rim economies. Many analysts go so far as to claim that the global centre of economic energy has already shifted away from the West, and that it is the nations of the Pacific region, centred on, and pulled along by the Japanese economic locomotive, and also now by the newly liberated Chinese economy, which will dominate in the next century. It is towards this larger, Pacific stage, that Foster's subtle regionalism is appropriately directed. And if this building points the way towards one kind of rebirth, then that architectural event pales in comparison with the other awakening it also symbolises.

Soon enough, I M Pei will complete his building nearby for the new Hong Kong branch of the (mainland) Bank of China. At 935 feet, the Dragon's tower will loom high over the Hongkong and Shanghai Bank headquarters. But Stitt and Stephen are back in position, and looking across at the Bank from Statue Square it is easy to share the confidence of the Hong Kong businessman who, when asked what he thought about '1997', said that: 'For a while we were afraid that China was going to take over Hong Kong, but from the way things are now going over there, it looks as though Hong Kong will be taking over China.' The showdown approaches, but, standing firm, legs spread wide apart, High-Tech guns blazing, the building demonstrates Hong Kong's machismo for all the world to see. Hong Kongers have got their money's worth, just as they like to.

Chris Abel

'Foster is not, of course, a believer in architectural determinism; but he has always maintained that a better working environment can improve morale and labour relations and he has used these arguments with brilliant success.'

Alastair Best

It is tempting, to anyone trying to make critical sense of Foster's career, to regard the Hongkong Bank as the great central masterpiece, the culmination of over twenty years' astonishingly fertile practice and the almost inevitable outcome of a series of ambitions which have never faltered. And in many ways it is. The Bank develops and enormously enriches ideas foreshadowed at Willis Faber (the moving staircase combined with atrium) and at Sainsbury (extensive prototyping of prefabricated components). But one of its most significant features is new in Foster's repertoire: the spatial variety made possible by opening up the building at street level and suspending the office floors in stacks from bridge-like trusses. Willis Faber and Sainsbury, by contrast, are sealed containers: the most seductive examples available of architecture as industrial design. Also new in Foster's work is the emphasis on *movement*. After the somewhat constrained circulation of Sainsbury, the Bank provides an exhilarating journey from public, to semi-public to semi-private and finally to private space.

Norman Foster and Richard Rogers are the only architects of international status who are now practising with their Modern Movement ideals more or less intact. Both cling tenaciously to an architecture which is anti-suburban in form, committed to social integration, and wholly, even ostentatiously, dedicated to technology at its leading edge. These are values worth fighting for, but they are out of fashion. Those who have abandoned the struggle – through fecklessness or expediency, or both – must now watch from the ten guinea seats while Foster and Rogers carry on the heroic struggle alone. Heroism is unfashionable too; yet we admire courage and virtuosity, and although we may reassure ourselves from time to time with the cosy reflection that all this Late-Modern stuff is drenched in self-parody, we cannot escape experiencing the frisson of excitement, the sense of danger, which all Foster's work conveys. A E Housman once famously assessed poetry by its effect on the hairs at the back of his neck: if they bristled involuntarily, then it was the genuine article. Judged by this criterion, Foster is a very great architect indeed.

It is perhaps inevitable that one should bracket Rogers and Foster together – although I happen to believe Foster to be Rogers' superior as an architect – for despite the strong dissimilarities in their work, their careers have followed similar paths and their personal and professional lives were once closely intertwined.

They came to architecture, however, by very different routes. Rogers, as Bryan Appleyard's newly published biography (Faber & Faber) vividly demonstrates, was a late developer, somewhat *dépaysé* after what sounds like an idyllic and cultured Italian childhood, a school drop-out, and, to begin with at least, a rather indifferent performer at the AA School of Architecture.

Foster was not so much a late developer as a late starter. He began life in the Accountant's Department at Manchester City Hall and only switched to architecture after National Service in the RAF. Both experiences were crucial. Of Waterhouse's magnificent Manchester City Hall interior, what struck Foster most of all were the details: the handrails and the light-fittings, even the glass-sided water cisterns in the lavatories. But apart from this very significant revelation – for what impresses again and again in Foster's work is precisely the beautifully judged sense of detail – very few of Foster's admitted 'influences' could be described as buildings by well-known architects. What fascinates Foster is the language of assembly: the grading of components, the pared-down junction, the smooth immaculate fit. His office walls are adorned with blown-up details of key images of heliostats and Airstream caravans, for he belongs to the last generation of students to be weaned on the seductive imagery of *Vers une Architecture*. It is hardly surprising that a book which twins the Parthenon with the cockpit of a Caproni sailplane on a double-page spread should have left an indelible mark.

National Service in the RAF as an electronics engineer was the second formative experience of Foster's professional life. It instilled a love of flying and aircraft and the desire – seen by some as quixotic – to reproduce the svelte and energy-efficient forms of the flying machine in his own architecture. Nor did the built forms on the airfield escape attention. Foster recalls how he worked in a turf-covered hangar (1) ('high on camouflage, very low on natural light'), and it is not entirely fanciful to look forward from this to the turf-covered roof garden at Willis Faber (3) or the sleek, ground-hugging form of the Frankfurt Athletics Stadium (4), or even (a personal favourite of mine) the Computer Technology air tent (2).

In the same way, the problem of introducing natural light into a deep plan has been a recurring preoccupation. It was completely ignored at IBM Cosham, the interest of which extends little further than the glass skin; partially solved at Willis Faber by punching a central lightwell into the heart of the plan; and brilliantly

2

3

4

handled at Sainsbury with its filigree of trusses, grilles and catwalks. The Hongkong Bank's 'sunscoops', which direct light beams into the atrium, provide another solution; their precursors are the tracking mirror systems, designed to harness the low winter sun, which Foster mounted on top of the unbuilt 'office in a forest' for Fred Olsen at Vestby on Oslo Fjord.

The third and much the most important influence on Foster was the time spent in America on a Henry Fellowship at Yale. Here he met Richard Rogers and became acquainted with Californian architecture – notably the work of Craig Ellwood and Charles Eames, and Ezra Ehrenkrantz's SCSD schools system. At Yale he sharpened up his drawing technique under Paul Rudolph (the exploded section and heavily shaded elevations with which all Foster buildings from Reliance Controls on are presented owe something to Rudolph) and came under the spell of Serge Chermayeff, whose theories of community and privacy are resurfacing with interesting results in the Bank. 'I have always believed,' he told the RIBA during his Gold Medal address in 1983, 'that architecture is about people – at one extreme is the private inner sanctum that it can create, at the other extreme are the outside public spaces ... In between the public and private domains the edges can be consciously or unconsciously blurred, to create or modify communities by sustaining, erecting or breaking down social barriers.'

Those who argue that 'people' are precisely what Foster's architecture is not about would claim that this is the empty rhetoric of a man who seems to shun personal relationships and whose buildings, for all their technical brilliance, are cold and inhuman. I think they are wrong and I feel that Foster's motives are entirely genuine. They are rooted in standard Modern Movement ideology and in his observed experience of American corporate culture. Foster's early work is characterised by a perfectly orthodox social commitment which saw architecture as the instrument for improving the lot of the working man – by, for instance, sweeping away false barriers between management and shop floor.

One detail from this early phase sticks in my mind. Foster Associates, retained to convert a small canning factory for Iann Barron's rapidly expanding Computer Technology, installed a fitted carpet on the factory floor. This had a dramatic effect on the working habits of the staff (6), who began to work with almost obsessive neatness, and it also demonstrated that in the new clean industries the

old divisions between white-collar and blue-collar workers need no longer apply. Nothing at all remarkable now, but in 1968, on a scruffy trading estate in Hemel Hempstead, it was a mild sensation.

Foster is not, of course, a believer in architectural determinism; but he has always maintained that a better working environment can improve morale and labour relations and he has used these arguments with brilliant success. At Willis Faber, for example, he was able to convince the client that an Olympic-size swimming pool should be the centrepiece of the main entrance, on the grounds that recreation should form an integral part of the working environment. In the same way Sainsbury is an essay in the art of persuading wary dons of the inherent dangers of a Two Cultures mentality. All this 'strategic questioning' is the architect's stock-in-trade but Foster has developed it into an art form in its own right. It has enabled him dramatically to alter or extend his brief, or, as at the BBC, to let the brief slip through his fingers. An architect less concerned with 'challenging preconceptions' (a favourite Foster phrase) would, perhaps, have achieved *something* at Portland Place. Instead, the constraints of the site and the shambolic and impenetrable corporate culture of Broadcasting House have deprived central London of one of its few chances of acquiring a serious Modern building.

The proposed Radio Centre at Portland Place and the proposed *médiathèque* at Nîmes, captioned in Foster's own unmistakable hand, which appeared on the May 1985 cover of the *Architectural Review,* told all: 'No diagonals in structure – must *not* look industrial' (5). This is not so much a loss of nerve, as a sense of realism. Or has Foster, while attempting to resist it with every weapon at his disposal, begun to see the virtues of Contextualism in certain circumstances? I think it very improbable that Foster is distancing himself from past concerns – drawings of Stansted's terminal and of the Athletics Stadium suggest not – but he could claim that his work shows an increasing preoccupation with light, space and movement. And he would be right.

'The worker in the Bank, where the office space has been passed as "harmonious" by the feng shui geomancer, feels better integrated with the company and its fortunes.'

Hugh D R Baker

Feng Shui: Applied Ecology Chinese Style
– Hugh D R Baker, 1986

The special issue of the Japanese magazine *Process Architecture* on the 'Foster Tower', contains the following statement: 'Foster's design for the Hongkong Bank building was influenced by a variety of sources outside the traditional building industry, from the Concorde design team to a feng shui expert.' One wonders how many readers would have understood the reference to feng shui. What is it, and why should it influence an advanced design and engineering project?

Feng shui is a Chinese term, which translates literally as 'Wind and Water'. Nature is at the heart of feng shui, as the name implies, and its philosophical origins can be traced back to early Chinese ideas of the unity of man and nature. In the West there was the pathetic fallacy, where nature was invested with human emotions and was thought capable of reflecting man's mood. In China there was feng shui where man did not influence but, rather, was influenced by nature. Feng shui has been defined by J J M de Groot as '… a quasi-scientific system, supposed to teach men where and how to build graves, temples and dwellings, in order that the dead, the gods and the living may be located therein exclusively, or as far as possible under the auspicious influences of Nature'. It is not difficult to detect a note of scepticism in de Groot's writing, but other non-Chinese observers have been far more scathing. E J Eitel, writing in 1873, calls feng shui 'a farrago of nonsense and childish absurdities'.

Most Westerners, however sceptical, would probably agree that surroundings can have an influence on quality of life – a house at an airy location in a beautiful setting may be expected to have a happier resident than would a smoke-begrimed house next to a city cesspit. But feng shui goes much further. It says that a properly located house will not only make the residents happier, but that they will also live longer, be healthier, have more sons, and get richer. It claims that the correct siting of a temple, a village, a government building, or an office can similarly affect those who worship, live or work there. And because feng shui is part of the Chinese religious system, which includes ancestor worship, there is great emphasis on the correct siting of graves, so that ancestors and descendants alike can benefit from nature's good influence. No doubt it is this extension from the idyllic to the supernatural that makes Eitel describe feng shui as 'the foolish daughter of a wise mother'.

In theory all feng shui sites face south and the direction in which a site faces is always thought of as south whatever the true direction may be. The back of the site, the north, is usually protected by a hill or grove of trees or even a high wall, all to keep the baleful north winds from sweeping over the site and dissipating the beneficial airs. The south is often called the Vermilion Bird, the north is the Black Tortoise, the west the White Tiger, and the east the Azure Dragon. A good site will take account of the position and comparative strengths of the physical landscape in each of these four directions. It is very necessary, for instance, to balance the White Tiger with a stronger Azure Dragon. This is because tigers are dangerous animals which are harmful unless under the control of dragons, the only beasts which can control them and turn their strength to good account. So if to the west there is a high hill, then it is necessary for there to be another hill at least as powerful looking to the east.

1

Straight lines in the form of rivers or roads are much feared in feng shui because they are thought to be like arrows threatening the site, or else like drains running off all the beneficial influences. Perhaps even worse are those features of the landscape that cannot easily be seen by the untrained eye – they may all, unsuspected, be causing problems. Altogether feng shui is an extremely complicated business – much too complicated for the layman to comprehend and manipulate; and so there exists the need for the specialist to interpret, advise and locate. The specialist is called a feng shui gentleman or, more correctly, a geomancer.

The geomancer needs little equipment other than a special compass set in the middle of a large number of concentric circles. Segments of the circles are marked off and identified by symbols, and he can interpret the significance of a site's alignment by reference to these. A client might ask him to locate a new house in such a way that there will be sons born to the occupants, or perhaps so that academic success will come to those who live there. By choosing to face the house in a certain direction the geomancer will hope to maximise the required benefits.

Feng shui is made more complicated by the fact that good sites are not easily found, and that when found they do not necessarily confer all-round benefits. A site might be good for creating wealth but poor at producing sons, or good for examination success but short on longevity. Moreover, the size of some sites is quite limited. Some excellent grave locations may only be able to take one or two sets of bones. Some building sites may only accommodate a small house, or perhaps a limited number of storeys. Even when a good site has been found, the slightest error in alignment can negate its beneficial effects – or even produce harmful ones – or one of the surrounding features may change, thus destroying the good effects associated with it.

Hugh D R Baker

Feng shui, then, is a belief that the environment can be tapped for the benefit of those who live, work or are buried in it. Because it is not easy to understand, it is necessary to have (paid) specialist help. Because the system is complex and fragile, it is easy to mismanage and constantly goes wrong. Because it affects everyone, it can be used not only to create good effects, but also to explain 'bad luck' or failure. Is your business going downhill? Blame it on grandfather's grave. Is your wife producing daughters not sons? It must be because the house has been built slightly out of line.

In one case in Hong Kong, a family was very distressed that a grave it had had expensively sited by a geomancer had failed to produce good effects. 'Oh,' said cynical friends, 'you know geomancers: they only promise good effects after 70 or 80 years, by which time they have spent their fee and died!' A second opinion was sought. The second geomancer pronounced the site excellent, but said that the grave had been built six inches too low down the hillside, thus missing the vital spot where the benefits were located. In another case, two clans point proudly to the deserted ancestral hall of a third clan which has died out in the village: 'We did it by paying a geomancer to misalign a brick in the wall, and so we got rid of them!'

So feng shui can become a weapon in the hands of the aggressive or the ambitious. If your neighbour annoys you, you can go secretly to his ancestors' graves and by cutting down a tree, or perhaps by diverting a stream, ruin his luck. If you want your business to succeed, ask a geomancer to site your office in such a way that it will give you an edge over your rivals. If you are jealous of your elder brother, get the geomancer to site your father's grave so that it benefits the number two son rather than number one, then you as second son will do better than he.

Feng shui is not a moral system: it will work as well for the wicked as for the innocent. It could be called a philosophy of greed, for it plays a zero-sum game with the good in the landscape. That means that no one can escape its influences, for there are bound to be evil people looking to monopolise good influences at the expense of others. And so there has to be defensive feng shui as well as offensive. Much activity is directed at making sure that other people are not scoring at your expense, and at warding off possible malign influences from inadvertent or unavoidable poor siting.

Many Chinese believe that the feng shui of Government House is what makes Hong Kong prosperous. Over a century ago Eitel reported: '"Why", they say, "there is Government House, occupying the very best spot on the northern side of the island,

Koo Pak Ling
古柏靈

screened at the back by high trees and gently shelving terraces, skirted right and left by roads with graceful curves, the whole situation combining all that feng shui would prescribe. How is it possible that foreigners pretend to know nothing of feng shui?"'

Governors of the territory do not comment, but their civil servants and their policies have been recognising the existence and power of feng shui for many years. When a new road is built in the rural areas, it is quite common for the government to pay large sums of money to local villagers as compensation for damage to feng shui. And when new government offices are built, it is not unknown for geomancers to be called in to help in planning the layout.

And so with the Hongkong Bank. A feng shui expert, Koo Pak Ling (1-3), was retained to advise on the plans long before they were implemented, and his specialist view was consulted at various stages of the project. He is not a designer or an architect: it was not his function to make the building 'look Chinese'. He was there to ensure that feng shui principles were not violated and that the siting, the construction, and the fitting-out were as closely in harmony with the surroundings as possible. Norman Foster was so impressed by the importance placed on Koo Pak Ling's advice that he discussed the project with him during the design team's first visit to Hong Kong. Koo sketched his impression of the most favourable direction from which to enter the building (4) – not directly from the front but angled to one side – advice that was followed through to the final design.

It was not his advice that caused the demise of the Chevron scheme (5, 6), as the directors were sufficiently concerned by the symbolism of the downward-pointing 'arrows' to raise their own objections, but he was on hand to oversee the positioning of the main escalators during their erection. Later, it was he who determined the position of the furniture in senior executive offices, and had potted trees and foliage strategically placed to hide areas of the interior that he found dangerous in feng shui terms. It was he who supervised the moving of the famous bronze lions from their place outside the main door of the old building to two carefully chosen temporary positions, and finally back to their posts in front of the completed tower. There they protect the fortunes of the Bank and, it is claimed, Hong Kong, while bringing luck to any passer-by who touches them.

The site itself was not, of course, of his choosing, but it has proved itself (to the believer's eye at least) by the success of the Bank over so many years of operation

Hugh D R Baker

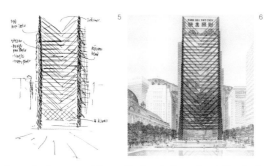

from that same address. It stands in a direct line between Government House and the harbour, so it has a very powerful protective Black Tortoise composed of the Peak and the Governor. In front of it are the waters of the harbour, and water which cannot be seen to flow away is indicative of wealth in feng shui terms. Across the water are the Nine Dragon Hills of Kowloon, permanent markers of good fortune and a stately presence. To the east and to the west, White Tiger and Azure Dragon ridges sweep down to the harbour, cradling the Bank's site. No road points arrow-like at the building, for in front of it is Statue Square, and the main pedestrian way to the Bank runs alongside the Square and only then disgorges people at an angle towards the carefully aligned escalators.

All that sounds nonsensical to scientific ears, but there is an uncanny echo of much of it in that special issue of *Process Architecture* on the Bank project: 'The strong influence of the surrounding topography in sheltering the site is apparent, particularly for winds from the south coming over the Peak. This is, of course, a direct reflection of the original reason for the founding of Hong Kong, whose sheltered harbour …' The geomancer and the research team of the Boundary Layer Wind Tunnel Laboratory of the University of Western Ontario seem to speak the same language, though perhaps one is a poet and the other has only plain speech.

Western interior designers go to great lengths to furnish space in ways that help relaxation or concentration, and they choose colours to harmonise with function. Chinese geomancers position desks, re-site doors and change colour schemes to harmonise with an overall view of man's place in his surroundings. The aim of both is similar: to tune the relationship between life and environment. The worker in the Bank, where the office space has been passed as 'harmonious' by the feng shui geomancer, feels better integrated with the company and its fortunes. Feng shui may go beyond what Western rationalism can accept, but it is more than 'a farrago of nonsense'.

'Foster's ambition goes beyond the evocation of yet another grand metaphor of the technology of steel, be it an Eiffel Tower or a Cape Canaveral launch-pad: it deals with the possibilities of architectural metamorphosis offered by technological invention.'

Vittorio Magnagno Lampugnani

Hongkong and Shanghai Bank
– Vittorio Magnagno Lampugnani, 1986

After working together on Team 4, Norman Foster and Richard Rogers went their separate ways, each carving out a distinct architectural path. While both remained faithful to the concept of an architecture tied closely to advanced technology, these two English architects moved in opposite directions: where Rogers explored the aesthetic potential of supporting structures displayed on the outside of buildings, Foster, instead, designed buildings that were less exaggeratedly High-Tech, though equally radical in their way, clad with a refined 'skin' of steel or glass. The emblematic building of the former is the Centre d'Art et de Culture Georges Pompidou in Paris (1972-77, with Renzo Piano); that of the latter is the Sainsbury Centre for Visual Arts in Norwich, England, of 1974-78.

But with the skyscraper for the Hongkong and Shanghai Banking Corporation in Hong Kong, Foster, surprisingly, took a considerable part of the supporting structure onto the outside. The consequences of this for the finished building are both positive and negative: positive because the huge steel beams articulate the functioning of the tower and turn it into an engineering icon; negative, because the steel beams, plated with fireproof and anti-corrosive aluminium, lose much of their elegant immediacy as a result of this complex and weighty 'padding'. Foster is very much aware of both the advantages and disadvantages and it is not by chance that in his early designs for the project he considered using a stainless steel structure treated with fireproof paint, with a sophisticated water-cooling system as an added protected against fire.

The plating of the supporting structure affects the building functionally, conceptually and aesthetically, but does not compromise its *raison d'être*. Foster's ambition goes beyond the evocation of yet another grand metaphor of the technology of steel, be it an Eiffel Tower or a Cape Canaveral launch-pad: it deals with the possibilities of architectural metamorphosis offered by technological invention.

The Hongkong and Shanghai Bank is nothing less than a new type of skyscraper. Conventional skyscrapers – from the pioneer experiments of the Chicago School during the last decades of the nineteenth century to the more recent structural *tours de force* of large American practices such as Skidmore, Owings and Merrill – follow the same basic pattern: an internal core of services (lifts, stairs and service plant) which also serves a structural purpose, with floors stacked one on top of the other around it.

Foster breaks with this tradition. His tower comprises eight giant interconnected masts which leave the heart of the building free. Fixed to these, at varying intervals, are five gigantic Vierendeel beams, which vertically structure the interior. From these, 47 floors, divided into groups, are suspended by steel cables. The result is in many respects revolutionary: a large central atrium, ten storeys high, which spatially reflects the tower concept; a surprising sense of unity between the groups of floors, visually connected by their shared view over the atrium and functionally connected by escalators; and an extreme transparency which makes the building particularly luminous, resembling the fascinating visions of crystalline towers elaborated during the 1920s by Ludwig Mies van der Rohe.

But is it really high technology that has effected this evolution in the form of the skyscraper? The doubt is legitimate: the Monadnock Building, 1884-91, by Daniel Burnham and John Wellborn Root – one of the star turns of Chicago's heyday – is entirely constructed of conventional brick; and the structural technology of the Hongkong and Shanghai Bank building is not a recent development. It is true that only now has an architect applied that technology to invent a new type of building, but even here the role of that technology is equivocal. If, on the one hand, it is the necessary premise of the new building, then on the other, it threatens to overwhelm with its exhibitionism, baring its structural all, sometimes in places where discreet dissimulation would be more appropriate, and obscuring the clarity of the overall design with a surfeit of clever devices.

For the generation of Antonio Sant'Elia, enthusiasm for technical expertise was an understandable historical condition; for that of Archigram, a forgivable attitude of ironic refinement; for Foster's generation it risks becoming a limiting and dangerous ideology. Only if technology is met with a refusal to be enchanted, and is redirected to serve the purpose of architecture – to create rational spaces for humanity – will it regain its positive role in the history of building.

'Foster's buildings are technical contraptions; they come from another planet; they are uncon-cerned, tolerant, amnesiac Martians who land on Earth with remarkable ease.'

François Chaslin

Otherworldly – that is what is most striking about the architect Norman Foster. For although the precision-assembled materials and technologies of his architecture embrace a certain kind of reality, Foster seems always to be aspiring to an elsewhere, another world. Another world, partly that of a long-gone age – the world of industrial pioneers, the mystical and fascinating world of Jules Verne – but on another level, a world too of contemporary futurism, space conquest, science fiction and cartoon strips; a world of suprahuman places whose controlled environment is inhabited by soulless beings moving in the eternal microclimate of a capsule, unworried by petty concerns or conflicts, their trouble-free existence bathed with a light and an atmosphere which have no substance.

These two dream worlds, two Utopias conceived a century apart, combine two visions of technology: that of the nineteenth century – the archaic modernity of the age of steam, the Crystal Palace of the 1851 Great Exhibition (1), the Eiffel Tower with its fusion of riveted beams, the Galleria Vittorio Emanuele II in Milan, the lifts and metal staircases of the Bradbury building in Los Angeles; and the otherworldliness, too, of contemporary contraptions – big bridges, articulated cranes like gigantic animal structures, astounding pipelines, the vast crop sprayers of the American plains (3), telescopic pylons, forests of support cables; and then too, toys like Dinky cars, electric trains, model aeroplanes – those things which bring out child-like faculties. Norman Foster is such a dreamer: 'American Airstream motorised caravans lost in the Colorado desert, the Apollo landing craft or a space buggy on the surface of the moon, are for me evocative of autonomy and freedom,' he confesses.

Is he not himself Superman, flying solo in his gliders and helicopters, above this confused world – free, airborne and able to reach Asia or the Americas in no time at all whenever he feels like it? Is he not the model for the man of the future, cut off from everyday human burdens, pursuing Icarus' dream of impossible weightlessness? He regrets that the foundations of the Sainsbury Centre are four times as heavy as the building itself. Weight has nothing to do with him; his buildings are slimmed down to the limit and only the Earth itself stops them from taking off.

Foster's single-minded individualism is exceptional – modern architects long-since reverted to the notion of the team project: they like to ally themselves into rival tribal groups. But Foster adamantly refuses to be lumped in with the 'High-Tech' style developed in recent years in England. He recognises no professional peers; rather he prefers to disassociate himself from the rest. Neither does he recognise any influences on his work other than that of Jean Prouvé and Buckminster Fuller. He seeks his models elsewhere, as a voluntary exile, in the engineering architecture of the past century or in a completely different technical universe – that of offshore rigs, Cape Canaveral launching towers (2) and the operation theatres of advanced medicine.

And, indeed, his work is vigorously questioned by a British architectural establishment, which pretends not to understand why we find his work so interesting. In this era of value crises, economic collapse, rapid erosion of the old city fabric – and of the economic and social fabric too – to them the growth of High-Tech seems to signal a cynical victory over accepted liberalism. No doubt they see it as an attack on tradition, proper priorities and everyday problems; a taste for superficial Modernism, a self-promoting and world-deceiving vision accompanied by the indecent euphoria surrounding a few spectacular *tours de force* which seem designed to hide the irredeemable decline of British society.

And it is true that, while a whole system of production was in the process of collapse, a new type of building emerged, as though the High-Tech style and certain types of more or less international precision industries were inextricably linked. The clarity, elegance and precision of these new buildings is in notable contrast to the ruined industrial landscape of some parts of Europe. High-Tech is the style, the trademark, of the most active factories, the symbol of industrial success – and that irritates some people.

The phenomenon is worldwide. Schlumberger built with Renzo Piano at Montrouge and with Michael Hopkins at Cambridge; Foster worked for IBM at Cosham and Greenford; Nicholas Grimshaw designed for them at Winchester, while Piano designed the firm's travelling exhibition. Richard Rogers' ultra-sophisticated buildings proclaim the contemporaneity of several companies: as at Quimper for Fleetguard, where he has designed the European bridgehead and distribution centre of a powerful multinational company of American origin (it was built at the same time as the Renault Centre at Swindon); or the microchip factory for Inmos at Newport (contemporary with Grimshaw's work for DEC); or PA Technology, the international centre for technology and science at Princeton. Rogers' new headquarters for Lloyd's, in the heart of the City of London, bears witness to the blatant appearance of High-Tech in that commercial and financial holy of holies.

Francois Chaslin

Certainly, High-Tech is the style of the industrial shop window. It is equally the style of some museums: latterly Beaubourg; soon the Menil collection at Houston; previously the Sainsbury Centre for Visual Arts, in East Anglia; now for the future Contemporary Arts Centre at Nîmes. In Paris, the future pyramid at the Louvre and the great glazed bays for the Villette Museum of Science and Industry have been assigned to the British designers Peter Rice, Ian Ritchie and Martin Francis. High-Tech is the style of prestige. And it was not born in Great Britain by chance; for it began long before the present crisis.

Doubtless it has its roots in certain aspects inherent to British culture, notably in the major role played in it by the machine, the poetic universe of technology, and industrial archeology, and that long-standing element in art criticism dating back to the eighteenth century, to Edmund Burke and Sir Uvedale Price and to the Industrial Revolution which plays on two types of beauty: the picturesque and the sublime. High-Tech is sublime. It also owes something to the never-extinguished memory of the astounding architecture achieved by the Coalbrookdale foundry and at Birmingham – that forebear of modern building fabrication, the successful prototype of a jointed, demountable construction composed of interchangeable elements. Above all, it owes a debt to Archigram and, in general terms, to the atmosphere created in the late 1960s by the magazine *Architectural Design* – the 'instant cities in progress' and 'plug-in cities'; that frenzy of mobility, experimentation and utopianism, which combined cranes and helicopters, mobile homes and dirigible balloons, Japanese metabolists, Kurokawa's Nagakin Tower, motorised caravans, Frei Otto's tented structures and inflatables, megastructures, capsules, Buckminster Fuller's geodesic domes – lines of enquiry we thought had sunk without trace with Californian hippies but which, as Europe turned its attention to Italy, to urban concerns, typological morphology, history and historicism, were being tenaciously re-honed in readiness for this spectacular resurrection of modern thinking.

If Prouvé is the most obvious influence on Norman Foster, they could hardly be more different as people. Prouvé was a blacksmith all his life, the solitary manual worker, the 'little manipulator of sheet metal', the modest but gifted industrial innovator. Foster breathes cleaner air; he is more conceptual and less in contact with materials. Utterly imbued with the notion of interchangeable technologies, he claims to find more pleasure and relevance in visiting aeronautical shows than building exhibitions. With a sort of power-drunkenness, Foster seeks the most advanced and efficient techniques on the international market – at 'top level'.

For his remarkable Hongkong and Shanghai Bank (which he proudly describes as 'the most expensive building in the world') he worked with British Army bridge construction experts and with the designers of Concorde. The concrete was French, as were the security doors; the steel was British; the lifts and curtain walls American; and the weather sealants were part Japanese, part French. Typhoon resistance was tested in Ontario; the lighting was tested in Innsbruck. The ready-equipped sanitary modules were imported from Japan, while the foundations were hand dug and the scaffolding that overran the tall metal structure was traditional, in bamboo (9).

With Foster, there is an obvious desire to be different, not be considered as merely one of a group representing a hypermodern alternative to Post-Modernism. Behind his cool remoteness, doubtless he is conscious that he is not one of them, that he has cut his ties with the antiquated world of his fellow architects, that he no longer uses the same tools nor shares the same concepts, that he does not think or work as they do, nor does he design in their way.

His own preliminary design takes the form of models, sometimes dozens of them for a single project; full-size mock-ups and prototypes of technical details, of structural nodes or constructional methods. He likes to sketch the whole – firm, assured sketches where the massing is decisively organised; schematic drawings showing clearly worked-out options, with brief explanatory handwritten annotations and a few arrows – to show openings providing light, air and views; the circulation systems; and to pick out major compositional elements.

They are drawings that seem to remove all areas of mystery. They are analytical and educational; their purpose is clearly to reinforce each stage of Foster's unique working process. And they are used to maintain a dialogue with his clients, too, for he really does seem to keep his projects in a fairly fluid state for a long time. The computers he recently acquired in such abundance should further increase his ability to produce numerous fully worked-out images representing provisional solutions, which remain open to discussion and can be altered radically should the need arise.

In many ways, Foster's approach is like that of an industrial designer: there is the same absolute perfection of high-performance floors, the same constant oscillation between form and use, the same desire to fuse both into a homogeneous whole.

Francois Chaslin

And, indeed, the critical terms used of his work raise the question that has lingered since the origins of modern architecture without ever being satisfactorily answered: why is the design of a building so different from the design of a technical entity, a machine, a refrigerator or, come to that, a piece of furniture or a car?

It was at the very beginning of the 1920s that Le Corbusier wrote: 'It is not seemly that a gentleman of good standing should sleep on a Breton bed in his Parisian mansion; it is not seemly that a gentleman who owns a saloon car should sleep in a Breton bed,'[1] and showed, in the pages of *Vers une Architecture*, under the heading 'Eyes which do not see', the Voisin Sports Torpedo of 1921, ocean liners, Farman 'Goliath' biplanes and the cockpit of the extraordinary Caproni triple hydroplane (4) 'showing how plastic organisms are created in response to a well-stated problem'.[2]

Industrial design has reached the level of high art with Foster. His buildings are, in fact, machines – finely honed, robust mechanisms which give the impression of being ceaselessly cared for by a team of technicians who maintain performance by oiling and adjusting the cogs. Even those who are disparaging about them recognise the supreme elegance of Foster's buildings which, incidentally, British critics enjoy comparing with the improvised, crude and ill-connected aesthetic of French design, whether the work of Jean Prouvé with its touchingly handcrafted quality (a view which fails to take into account Prouvé's flawless glazed facade for the Communist Party Headquarters in Paris which is just as sleek, pure and smooth as the Willis Faber building it influenced) or the design of our cars (which may be justified in the case of the extraordinary but appealing 'ugliness' of the Citroën 2CV, but certainly has no bearing on the DS, produced by the same manufacturer).

But the fact remains – Foster's concern for style is unique. The calm emanated by each of his details is impressive, each effect being flawlessly restrained, each technical miracle smoothed out, delicately powdered and rubbed down until all the difficulties have been overcome. Foster's architecture seems effortless for it is free of extraneous expression and constructional eccentricity, unlike some other High-Tech buildings. It is not an architecture that seeks to draw attention to itself by unexpected lyricism or obtrusiveness, rather, it basks in a completely controlled serenity. Generally speaking, it is neither structurally exhibitionist nor does it bristle with complex mechanisms or projections. From this point of view, it is astonishing to compare

5

6

photographs of the Hongkong and Shanghai Bank as it was during construction – extraordinarily lively and dynamic with the tremendous clash of metal structures, with crane-booms apparently locked in swordplay on top of the skyscraper as it was raised upwards – and the building as now finished, pacified and calmed, where each element is integrated with rigorous discipline.

'Nothing should be exposed, nothing hidden, but everything integrated,' Foster said of his Renault Centre at Swindon (5), which nonetheless is the most romantic of his buildings. Foster's confidence in modelling and construction can be seen growing from one project to the next, from the mid-1960s onwards. He began with a stripped-down form of industrial warehouse: off-the-peg, standard-section beams and lattice girders with fairly straightforward fixings; square and 'I'-section RSJs; diagonal cross-bracing; lightweight panels and envelopes. Next, welded portal frames – still a relatively simple form of Meccano. And then, for the Fred Olsen passenger terminal, a frugal box, clad with corrugated sheet metal. Even then, comparison of the accumulated sectional perspectives prepared for project after project seems to show parallels emerging, which trace a course, the stages of development defining an evolution of growing sophistication and increasing strength. The spindly, harsh forms acquire substance and, at the end of the buildings, the glazed flank wall, sliced as if dissected to reveal the anatomy, is each time more subtle. Simultaneously there emerges a more perfect control of the curtain wall – the joints, well-defined openings, sleek glazing and the abstract play of reflections. Then, at the Sainsbury Centre in East Anglia, comes a masterful breakthrough, the three-dimensional structure is exploited to the full to infuse a new breath of life.

At the Renault Centre, the supports for the flexible, wide-span portal-roof structure project above the roof, masts and cables being freely displayed against the sky, creating a new sensation of suspended animation, unearthly quiet, frozen flight and supreme stability. Discreet and refined, certainly – but one senses a desire to break out from the smooth surfaces, the uniform completeness of the contours; a wish for the building to be more pointed.

Without going to the 'Gothic' extremes of some other High-Tech architects – the projections, the mass of cables and beams, the taut surfaces and strong articulations – Foster the 'Classicist' likes angular images more than he did. He has allowed the skeleton to emerge from behind the flesh, the frame from behind the

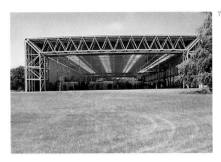

7

suppleness. At the Renault Centre, the exposed innards, the structural expression, is reminiscent of the constructional forms – the *pattes de poulet* and the *pattes de cerf* metal joints – illustrated in Viollet-le-Duc's instruction manuals (6). It is a laying bare of the building's anatomy, a dissection of its structural properties, an architectural stripping down of a kind unexpected from this supreme exponent of the smooth-skin aesthetic.

The same expressionist bias exists in the furniture Foster has designed. The slender joints, splayed supports, clearly visible bolts, tie-rods and handles, the resemblance to a water-boatman or a giant mosquito, give an almost parodic dimension. More fluid than Hopkins, less angular than Piano, more homogeneous than Rogers' Lloyd's building, the finishes in Foster's buildings generally exploit the full potential of pressed sheet steel or cast metal. They give the impression that Foster likes Jaguars and Porsches, aeroplanes, high-speed trains, big trucks, high-quality bodywork and spacecraft. Everywhere, design sensuality pervades. Foster acknowledges that he is indebted to his admiration for John Batchelor, whose drawings of racing cars, jet fighters and flying saucers were published in the boy's paper *Eagle* during the 1950s.

Foster's buildings are technical contraptions; they come from another planet; they are unconcerned, tolerant, amnesiac Martians who land on Earth with remarkable ease. One only has to see the serenity with which the most urban to date of Foster's buildings, the Ipswich office for Willis Faber & Dumas, has taken its place on a humdrum site, the series of concavities and convexities coolly reflecting the surrounding townscape, integrating, defining and domesticating the chaotic environment; or with what aristocratic disdain the Sainsbury Centre (7) sits on English parkland, like an ultra-light temple or some weird aircraft (a helicopter perhaps).

Foster has always sought the fluid and avoided shock or conflict, introducing freedom of movement to encourage circulation and communication that will be as clear and legible as his sketches. Above all, he likes all forms of efficiency, speed of travel, ease of interchange, which for him obviously represent an important element in happiness. The escalator, at Willis Faber, and above all, at Hong Kong, holds an essential place in the architectural composition. It is Foster's mechanised equivalent for the grand staircase. It is the efficient, unobtrusive movement and silent gliding that pleases him, the *nihil obstat*.

'Social contact in natural, open space also suggests freedom of movement,' he says; hence he builds into his plans equality for the individual at work. There are no doors in the Willis Faber building, no individual offices for the directors, no apparent hierarchy, but an opening up – a policy of 'democratic' transparency in professional and social relations.

In his own office in Great Portland Street, London, the same neutral, undifferentiated and theoretically open atmosphere reigns. In principle, Foster's workspace is identical to those of his colleagues – except that it is bigger, emptier and more impressive. But nobody walks across it: it is a no-go area, isolated by a kind of taboo. Everybody can see him, but, more importantly, he can see them. This panoptical system creates a strange sensation of collective control, of a calm that weighs too heavily and of repressed individualism. There are no cubbyholes or private corners; Norman Foster's architecture does not seek to provide separate or secluded places. It does not lend itself to the protection of the personality, to providing the means of sheltering or hiding, but creates an unrelieved environment where public and private space are combined in a 'relaxed' coexistence, smooth interchanges softened by use. All is visible and clear, restrained by an impeccable integrity. Everything is in order, in its proper place. Visual contact is constant. In this world without physical barriers, with its clarity of spaces and behaviour, orientation is instant. Everything is assumed to be faster and easier. Even leisure is integrated and takes its place in the rationalised working day. The canteen, swimming pool, gymnasium and, especially, the lawn on the roof are major elements in the architectural and social organisation of the Willis Faber offices, which are themselves (visually) open to the surrounding neighbourhood. A utopian, if somewhat totalitarian, desire to set an example to the passing public holds sway.

As for the 'green' on the roof, so far from the ground and in the middle of town, is it not yet another demonstration of Foster's desire to extract himself from reality? At one point he envisaged it as a glazed dome, a capsule with controlled, constant conditions – an echo of the science fiction that still inspires him. Always hanging over him is an obsession to control energy, the quality of the air and the atmosphere. He has dreamed of the capsule ever since the Air-Supported Office for Computer Technology, erected in Hertfordshire in 1970, to be followed by preliminary studies with Buckminster Fuller (the Climatroffice of 1971) and a later project – the

Francois Chaslin

autonomous house with controlled microclimate – right up to the glazed gardens on top of the Hongkong tower. Yet, sometimes, the little sun he likes to add to his sketches sends a few shivers up the spine; even the plants themselves are treated without the least hint of pastoral or rural spirit. They too are regulators, technical tools to guarantee the optimum levels of comfort from a hygrothermic and psychological point of view. And that is the very nub of the matter – the fundamental ambiguity of Foster's work.

Even though he makes a point of stressing the humanitarianism which lies behind his every principle, and claims to be preoccupied with subjective realities (no sooner said than he renders them objective), with the quality of life, his architecture remains cold, sometimes almost clinical in its perfection. It is not clear where to draw the line between the natural and the artificial. Has not his concern with lighting incessantly nullified light? Has he not subjugated that too – controlled it, filtered it, softened it, reflected it and redirected it, taken it in hand? And, like the lighting, which is never direct, air too must be conditioned and humidified until the silence of the environment is broken everywhere by the clicking of ventilator outlets for the air-conditioning system. Energy is conserved in the same way as human effort is saved – we are all mechanisms, which must not be allowed to go to waste.

Hence perhaps the filtered, pleated, regularised aesthetic so characteristic of Foster – the corrugations of cladding panels or roofs, the louvres of screens or blinds that come between the viewer and the landscape, perforated aluminium, sunbreaks, the leaves of suspended ceilings, semi-transparencies, screens, translucencies. Things must be softened, given texture, substance added to metallic structures.

The highly ordered abstract beauty of Foster's buildings again brings us back to the cold notions of the sublime. It has a grandeur and a rare capacity to fill us with wonder; it is great and noble; it is a magnificent achievement of the imagination. But, from time to time, it radiates a fascinating sense of impersonality, not to say inhumanity. The architect himself is not unaware of this glacial tone, this abstract quality – otherwise he would not employ photographers who accentuate the effect – as in a photograph of the Fred Olsen building roof (8), where a desert of corrugated metal sheeting stretches to the horizon; to the left, in the middle distance, two men are seated on a chimney stack, apparently waiting for Godot, while, miles behind them in the background, smoke rises from a factory chimney. It is a real nowhere place.

And in how many other images are to be seen thin human forms, silhouetted against sheets of glass, solitary, faced with their own reflection in the relentlessly closed facade? The great paradox in Foster's work is this mixture of humanity and inhumanity. His architecture absorbs and overcomes all contradictions and puts them into play. Confrontations are toned down and all functional, technical and psycho-social problems supposedly resolved at a stroke. Human intelligence remains supreme, the human brain triumphs once and for all.

And in that, too, it is a utopian architecture. As arbitrator between contradictions, it is not an architecture that shows the least inclination to parade itself through excess, nor to express superabundant vitality like some other High-Tech architectures. When it is lyrical at all, its lyricism is tempered; its complexity is monitored, restrained, played down. Everything about it is methodical and prescribed, reasoned and Classical. The asymmetry of the Hongkong and Shanghai Bank tower is tightly controlled, rigorously constrained and the *tour de force* resides precisely in the immutable propriety, the perfect decorum of this puritanical, worthy and arrogant achievement which is so sure of its strength.

It is a self-controlled architecture, full of tact and some arrogance. Calm, courteous and, above all, efficient, never showing his feelings and always suppressing his impulses, Foster the man is something between a gentleman and an anonymous agent for social organisation. Self-control is an aid to social control. All spontaneity is subjugated in the name of this activity; each gesture is measured, disciplined and cultivated. A utilitarian moral perfectionism reigns, a somewhat metallic coldness of the spirit that methodically and objectively rationalises each and every action. All the rest is literature ... it is a Modernist vision of the 'systematic and rational shaping of the moral world in its entirety', as prescribed by Max Weber in his book *The Protestant Ethic and the Spirit of Capitalism*. It would seem to mean changing the individual to achieve a more general benefit – hence the iron will.

Francois Chaslin

'With Norman Foster, clients, historians and critics alike are dealing with a sharper, more elusive intelligence. Like his consciousness and his public persona, Foster's buildings are less accessible and more seamless in their declension from concept to detail.'

Martin Pawley

Thirty years ago there was no British architect of world importance. Sir Edwin Lutyens was dead, Sir Howard Robertson was a disappointment, Sir Albert Richardson had become a joke. True, there were planners like Max Lock and Lord Holford whose influence in the developing world persists to this day, and there were practitioners like Basil Spence, whose name was (unjustly) a household word for scandalous Modernism. There were even *avant-garde* figures, like the Smithsons, with an intellectual reputation overseas. But there were no native stars to compare with such living modern pioneers as Wright, Le Corbusier, Gropius or Mies; or even their younger successors Saarinen, Niemeyer, Rudolph and Johnson.

In part, of course, there were good economic reasons for this paucity of genius. Britain was a small country again after two hundred years of empire. Divesting itself of colonial possessions, ground down by war and reconstruction, it was given over to the levelling work of the New Jerusalem and its own brand of social architecture. Not without interest of course. But lacking the arresting quality of the inverted pyramid museum, the sweeping concrete airport bird or the mile-high tower with its nuclear-powered elevators.

Thirty years later the same country has a gross national product smaller than that of what was formerly the Russian-occupied zone of Germany. It has a trade deficit on everything except oil, and the legacy of its social architecture, like the legacy of its welfare state, is a spiral of debt, maintenance and class conflict. In foreign eyes the country is a paradigm for post-imperial decline. But industrially doomed, culturally dependent, technically backwards as it is, Britain does at least have one thing going for it: three world-class architects – James Stirling, Richard Rogers and Norman Foster.

In the 30 years since 1956, modern architecture has moved from centre stage to shredder, while history has emerged from the shredder to take centre stage in a massive scissor movement that destroyed the careers of devoted Modernists and resurrected those of diehard Classicists.

Among the very few whose prospects escaped were the three men whose work is now celebrated by the Royal Academy (1-3). Like the national economic death slide that each succeeded in countering, the historical backlash has left them unscathed, even Stirling, who was the most modern and is now the least. Because of this it can be said that their careers have no historical inevitability. Stirling,

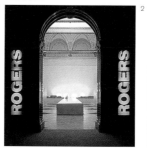

Rogers and Foster are originals. Two provincial, one foreign, all unknighted, all beneficiaries of an early exposure to America, all born outside ruling-class life.

Notwithstanding the enormous popularity of old buildings in the land, in the end even the most thoughtless and reactionary planning officers, patrons and clients are compelled to contemplate the shock of the new in relation to great commissions. And when they do, they think about James Stirling, Richard Rogers and Norman Foster first. All three have international reputations, proofed against the sneers of English philistines by past commissions in dollars, deutschmarks and francs, and protected against the mockery of critics by medals of solid gold.

It is because of his internationally tempered reputation that James Stirling was awarded the rump of the Old Mansion House Square commission by Peter Palumbo; it is because of the French presidential seal upon the Centre Pompidou that the world's most famous two-centuries-old insurance brokers came to commission the spectacular £160 million Lloyd's building from Richard Rogers; it is because of the response of foreigners to the electrifying Dolby hush of the Sainsbury Centre for Visual Arts that the old colonial Hongkong and Shanghai Bank (4, 5) came to commission from Norman Foster the magnificent £600 million grey-framed tower that presides over the only classical harbour frontage in Hong Kong.

Stirling is variously viewed by his peers as a turncoat Modernist and unprincipled panderer to decadence, or as a brilliant creator of styles – always one step ahead of his imitators. Enigmatically, he included in *James Stirling: Buildings and Projects* (Architectural Press, 1984) a photograph of Le Corbusier autographed 'To Jim 29.8.65'*. This relic of an old relationship serves to remind us that his is a political, as well as an aesthetic, reputation. His switch from Modern to Post-Modern is an exact parallel to the move from Liberal to Conservative that made the career of Winston Churchill, or the move from Labour leader to coalitionist that ruined the career of Ramsay Macdonald. To disinter Stirling's creative stature from this controversy is possible but fruitless. It requires the admission of criteria that cannot be usefully applied to the work of either Rogers or Foster.

Where Stirling now lays claim to the vocabulary of architectural history as a kind of exterior decoration for his wilfully geometric works, Rogers and Foster cleave to the notion of themselves as technological designers deploying the entire resources of science and engineering to 'get the functions through'. An aesthetic

appraisal of Stirling's Clore Gallery at the Tate, or his much-acclaimed Stuttgart Staatsgalerie, cannot be duplicated at Lloyd's, or at Willis Faber & Dumas, or even at the abortive BBC project, which represented Foster's closest brush yet with townscape and the burden of architectural history. Rogers, it is true, speaks of Borromini, Brunelleschi and Sir John Soane, as well as Buckminster Fuller, claiming that their synthesised influence is constantly with him in his High-Tech ventures. But this smacks of the politics of architecture rather than the psychoanalysis of design.

Of the three, Foster shows the greatest evidence of that liberation from current intellectual categories that is the hallmark of the independent mind. Stirling's work is immediately accessible to clients and critics on the international academic circuit of architectural culture. Rogers has his own easy-going reputation, wedded to a free-thinking technological bohemianism, which makes friends everywhere.

With Norman Foster, clients, historians and critics alike are dealing with a sharper, more elusive intelligence. Like his consciousness and his public persona, Foster's buildings are less accessible and more seamless in their declension from concept to detail. In each there is immense complexity and the total clarity of an idea carried through without compromise.

But while today we honour three great British architects, a glimpse into the future might reveal that in the year 2086 there will be only one whose work will be universally thought to have displayed the timeless combination of innovation and completeness that we concede to have been achieved by Sir Joseph Paxton.

* Editor's note: This was a typically robust Stirling joke: Le Corbusier drowned two days earlier, off Cap Martin, on 27 August 1965.

'A building without a tree
is like a lost child.'

Olf Aichter

The most architectonic works of nature are trees: their structure – how they hold out their leaves towards the sun – is still unsurpassed by technology. No technical form has arms that, in relation to the material outlay, stretch as far as those of beech trees, like those of Savernake Forest in Wiltshire, say – large, spreading monoliths with the disposition of autonomous individuals. No work of technology can compare with them: stretching upward from one point and supported on a single column, the trunk, they develop a volume large enough to achieve the maximum surface area required for the assimilating function of the leaves.

Norman Foster lives on the edge of a park in Wiltshire; his boys played there before they left home and went to university.

A building without a tree is like a lost child. Building and tree complement each other, whether the ornamental tree on the boulevards of Paris or the protective tree that watches over a farm. The solitary building without a tree is exposed, defenceless against the weather. Tree and building complement each other without surrendering themselves or their sovereignty. But they have common laws. Both have an evolved, constructive character. They contain and envelop the light that is appropriate to man, the light that falls through trees, not the relentless flood of light in a desert. If the imagined world of the architect has no trees, it is impoverished, empty.

Perhaps this has to do with the fact that man, seen in the light of historical development, comes from the trees. From our understanding of ontogenesis, we know that every individual works through the developmental history of his species in shortened form. For a time the human embryo even begins to grow gills. Life originally came from the water.

But perhaps we live through the stages of our developmental history not only in terms of nature, but also in terms of culture.

All children build huts, houses, camps; and they all dream of a house in the trees, of a house in the uncovered heights, beneath which lies the world. Here one can be entirely sovereign, independent, unburdened, removed from the bustle. One can be oneself.

Another device of this kind is a wall: the wall around a monastery, around a yard, around a house. It protects and also delineates, creating its own territory. But the house in the trees needs no wall. The whole world is there at one's feet. One

lives with the birds, with the sun, with the clouds, with the wind, and with the land beneath. One just needs a rope-ladder that can be drawn up.

The tree-house is more than a child's dream. The architect may have designed it for his children; but it can also be a space for a way of life, for man as he would most deeply like to be. We do not dream only of a freedom in which everyone has equal rights, we dream also of a freedom that consists in living just for oneself – without claim, without obstacles, without pressures. A house in the trees would suffice for that.

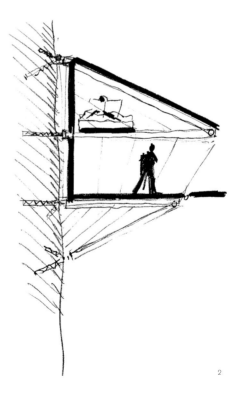

'By learning more about his client's needs than the client himself knows, Foster ... has frequently been able to move from a situation of inferiority to one of superiority – and redraft the user's definition of what he needs from his building.'

A building, a plan or a project by Norman Foster is always interesting – all the more interesting for being at once as useful as a pair of jeans or a bicycle, and as beautiful as a violin or a racing yacht. A shop for Joseph Ettedgui; a plan for the harbour at Saint Helier in Jersey or the island of Gomera in the Canaries (1); an office building for a multinational corporation or a sports hall for a German city; a project for a flying club or a private house – the scale is unimportant, for every one displays the same qualities of lucidity, conviction, completeness and, ultimately, perfection. Each comes from the application of an intelligence and creative ability that is unique. If it is a building it will not be built to a style – Modern, Post-Modern, Revivalist or Futuristic. Instead it will be a complete answer to a series of problems that locks into its site with the same conviction that it locks into its economic purpose and the lives of those who will use it.

At the beginning of the 1970s, Norman Foster was a promising young architect with a small office in the West End of London and a short string of unusual commissions behind him. The buildings he had designed included an 800-square-metre inflatable office for a computer company, which was erected in 55 minutes. It depreciated in one year at a cost of £10 per square metre including furniture. Another project was the 15,000-square-metre air-conditioned headquarters for IBM, a structure that (to its corporate surprise) the company discovered would cost less than the equivalent accommodation in temporary wooden huts. Another client had, no doubt to its equal corporate amazement, been convinced by the architect that better space planning would obviate the need for a new building at all. That was the Foster of 1971, an architect known, where he was known at all, for his unorthodox approach and his capacity to produce remarkably advanced buildings at a remarkably low cost.

It is one measure of the following twelve years of achievement that on the evening of Tuesday, 21 June 1983, when he rose to accept the award of the Royal Gold Medal for Architecture from the hands of the President of the Royal Institute of British Architects, his reputation was no longer that of a promising designer, but of a world-famous architect. He was in 1983 already a man in the throes of one of the most prestigious commissions of modern times: the 47-storey, £600 million, 100,000-square-metre new headquarters for the Hongkong and Shanghai Banking Corporation – a structure that, when it was completed, was destined to

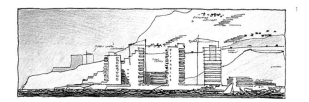

be recognised not only as a work of sublime architectural genius but also as the most expensive building in the world.

Though few could have foreseen it in 1967, the break-up of Foster's Team 4 partnership with Richard Rogers, shortly after the completion of the award-winning Reliance Controls building in Swindon, marked the debut of a powerful and wayward force in world architecture. Foster's period of apprenticeship, remembered as a time of 'guinea-pig clients who were really relatives', had ended long before. Now four years of close association with another gifted architect were over too, and he had crossed an important threshold.

Largely unknown outside the profession, Foster was destined within a decade to triumphantly execute commissions of such seminal importance that they elevated him above the battleground of modern versus traditional values that raged throughout the rest of the profession, giving him the almost magical immunity from stylistic controversy that he retains to this day. In the short space of time covered by the design and completion of three major British buildings – the offices for insurance brokers Willis Faber & Dumas in Ipswich, the Sainsbury Centre for Visual Arts at the University of East Anglia, and the Renault Distribution Centre in Swindon – Foster was to pass through a period of unprecedented creativity, the results of which were not so much national as international in their impact. Taken together, the built and unbuilt projects of this period revealed a rare capacity for innovation coupled with an intuitive grasp of the synoptic needs of broad outline and structural detail. At a more fundamental, but frequently overlooked, level they gave evidence of an organisational and logistical capability that few British architects have ever been called upon to deploy.

As his practice steadily grew, Foster moved his office twice: from Covent Garden to Fitzroy Street, and from Fitzroy Street to Great Portland Street. Varied industrial, commercial and planning projects for such clients as the Department of Education and Science, London Transport Executive, the Fred Olsen shipping line (2), IBM and Computer Technology tested his abilities and prepared the ground for buildings that were to follow. As he himself is the first to agree, each of these projects contributed to its successor in the most direct and fundamental way.

Without the 1967 Newport School study, with its deep plan and steel-lattice roof service distribution system, there would have been no 1968-70 Operations

Martin Pawley

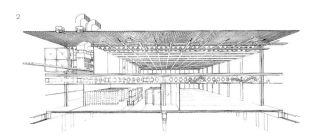

2

and Amenity Centre in London's Docklands for Fred Olsen and, in due course, no headquarters for the London Docklands Development Corporation, the then unborn organisation that was destined to take over the building in 1981. Without the neoprene and aluminium floor-to-ceiling glazing at Fred Olsen, there would have been no air-conditioned space-frame over a glass box at IBM Cosham. Without IBM Cosham, no suspended glass facade at Willis Faber & Dumas. Without the huge floor plates and escalator circulation at Willis Faber & Dumas, no confident mastery of vertical movement and no Hongkong Bank in its present form. A similar progression can be shown to run from one of the alternative roof structures considered for Willis Faber & Dumas, through the massive 1977-79 Hammersmith redevelopment project for London Transport, to the 1981-86 Frankfurt Athletics Stadium – and even to the 1987 King's Cross transport interchange scheme. Yet another line can be shown to connect the structural concept of the 1974 78 Sainsbury Centre for Visual Arts with the unbuilt 1978-79 project for the architect's own house. A fourth can be discerned in the progression from the 'umbrella' structural system of the 1980-82 Renault Distribution Centre to the omnidirectional, space-enclosing structure for the London's third airport at Stansted in Essex.

The immense variety in the nature and scale of Foster's work during these years is not, however, its most remarkable feature. Of far greater historical significance is its supremely innovative nature. None of the buildings completed in this period is conventional or traditional, and the departure from standard practice begins early, with the writing of the brief, and ends late, with the pattern of project management during construction itself. In a way that was perhaps foreshadowed by a sequence of drawings produced in 1970 to show how the structural system evolved for Reliance Controls developed first into the monocoque structure of a proposed passenger terminal at Millwall Docks, and then into the evanescent nylon-reinforced PVC envelope of the Computer Technology Air-Supported Office, each project represented a step towards a new approach to architectural design and practice.

Today this approach can be seen to have drawn closer and closer to the omnivorous methodology of industrial product development, and farther away from the traditional architect's manipulation of visual images. In this sense Foster's

buildings and projects of the decade to 1983 are not only numerous, diverse and complex, but conceptually uncharted as well. Though to a lesser extent than the global component sourcing brought to such a triumphant pitch of organisational perfection in the specification of the Hongkong Bank (4), Willis Faber & Dumas and the Sainsbury Centre and Renault Centre (3) were all buildings whose key architectural elements were developed with the indispensable aid of the research and development engineers of major international component manufacturers. As such, they had to be conceived in an entirely novel way. The structural and cladding elements that gave each of these buildings a unique identity were not taken from standard ranges or chosen from catalogues, but envisioned in the architect's office and developed by the manufacturer according to the architect's specification.

Foster not only designed and built landmark buildings in the years before 1983; he designed and built them in a way that had never been successfully achieved before – even by the pioneers of prefabrication who, 50 years earlier, had called for the creation of a whole new building components industry. Although confined to individual buildings, Foster's architecture succeeded precisely where theirs had failed. Instead of demanding the replacement of an old industry, he achieved the same goal by stretching its capacity and forcing the pace of development amongst the established manufacturers of steel, glass, plastics and alloys.

In comparison with the design leadership that was necessary to produce the suspended Pilkington glazing system at Willis Faber & Dumas, the superplastic aluminium cladding at the Sainsbury Centre or the vast, undulating, seamless PVC welded roof at Renault, Foster's capacity to master the administrative complexities generated by major commissions, rapid growth, repeated office relocation and fluctuating workload during the years to 1983 falls into its correct perspective. For his real achievement was the sustained innovation that was the end-product of this management triumph. It is a measure of his diverse abilities that he was able, during this short period, to deploy not only the traditional architectural skills of clear thinking, programming and delegation, but also serendipitously to attract and maintain the allegiance of a growing number of gifted staff, manage the massive expansion of his office, and lose neither his overall direction nor control of the fine-tuning of projects that were so complex and diverse that they would have driven lesser men into a hopeless morass of indecision and compromise.

Martin Pawley

4

So universally accepted now is Foster's reputation for combined attention to strategic thrust and crucial detail, that it is not widely appreciated that the skills that enabled him to gain it were self-taught, and learned in a remarkably short space of time. It is a testimony to the rapidity of Foster's own learning curve that many people still do not know that, prior to the Hongkong Bank, the practice had never built a building more than three storeys high.

It is perhaps inevitable that the magnificent achievement of the Hongkong Bank should become the lens through which the entire Foster *oeuvre* to that point has come to be viewed. This is understandable, but it presents a problem to the historian, for it becomes as difficult to concentrate on the work of the architect before that epic voyage of discovery as it is to study the career of Winston Churchill before the Second World War, or to consider the work of Ferdinand Porsche before the design of the Volkswagen. In all such cases, the only way to approach the earlier period without hindsight is to seek out threads of meaning that are not only perceptible before the great event, but still exist after it. In the case of Churchill one such thread is to be found in his historical writing. With the immortal engineer it might be considered to be his transcending interest in power transmission. With Foster the key is, perhaps surprisingly, the indissoluble link between the redefinition of the brief and the achievement of a new architecture.

The Austrian psychologist Alfred Adler (1870-1937) is best known for the importance in the structure of human personality that he ascribed to the will to dominate. In this connection Adler invented the term 'lifestyle' – since debased and misused until it has come to mean little more than a collection of consumer choices. What Adler meant by it originally was the unique process by which every individual in a competitive situation endeavours to move from a subservient to a commanding role. In Adler's original formulation, an individual's lifestyle was the behavioural technique he or she evolved in early childhood for dealing with feelings of inferiority. Properly understood this lifestyle can not only be recognised in individual responses to personal experience, but can also be seen as an integral part of the creative personality.

Architects, designers, artists and creative individuals of all kinds continually confront challenges in their professional lives, all of which can be analysed in Adlerian terms. Successful creative individuals surmount or rationalise these challenges; if they did not they could not survive in an environment dogged by frustration and disappointment. When a designer surmounts a challenge to the authority of his or her conception of a project, he or she does it – according to Adler's analysis – by converting the threat of inferiority, or defeat, into superiority, or victory. In this sense, lifestyle becomes more than a part of their personality, it becomes a professional tool that makes them successful where others fail, and drives them on when others fall back. In the Adlerian sense there is a way in which Foster's characteristic initial approach to any architectural commission – which takes the form of an energetic research phase designed to enable him, if necessary, to seize the initiative from his client by challenging the precepts of the brief – can be seen as a classic manifestation of the successful professional lifestyle. By learning more about his client's needs than the client himself knows, Foster the architect has frequently been able to 'move from a situation of inferiority to one of superiority' – and redraft the user's definition of what he needs from his building.

There is evidence of the remarkable success of this technique from Foster's very earliest commissions to his most recent. It is a thread that runs right through his work in the decade leading up to 1983 and beyond. In psychological terms, an important part of Foster's astonishing success as an 'advanced technology' architect, in an era that professes to distrust advanced technology, is to be found in the very early moves prompted by his lifestyle. Of course, this technique alone can never guarantee success, but lifestyle coupled with a carefully developed reinforcing expertise is a powerful combination. As a firm today, Foster Associates deploys powerful design skills and more research and development expertise than ten conventional firms of architects. But Foster's ultimate skill is his first line of attack – the practice knows how to seize the initiative by questioning and rewriting the brief by analysis – and this is a skill that has grown from the personality of Norman Foster himself. As an architect he has never hesitated to question any prospective client's conception of the kind of building, plan or organisation that he needs, even when such questioning might appear to endanger his own position at the very beginning of delicate negotiations. It is a bold course, and it is not always successful, but time after time it has laid the foundations of great architecture.

Foster has always been dedicated to the business of solving organisational, environmental and people problems rather than inventing architectural imagery. As

Martin Pawley

Foster himself put it in 1970: 'Clients tend to put problems to us in building terms but, with analysis, the solutions to those problems often emerge as not architectural at all. In this sense we are a new kind of architectural office, a bridge between the potential of new ideas and their realisation in practical terms. Each project, for us, is a kind of challenge to do more with less.'

In one case – that is dramatic in its illustration of the difference between this approach and the understandable desire of most young and ambitious architects for work at any price – a client approached Foster for a new building but was convinced by dispassionate analysis that the real answer lay in a more efficient pattern of space utilisation within his existing buildings. Berco Corporation actually bought space planning, not architecture, from Foster. Instead of a building, the company was rewarded with a pioneering example of a technique that was soon to become a recognised discipline in itself.

Needless to say, doing more with less did not always mean convincing a potential client that a new building was not needed. On a subsequent occasion it meant pioneering something that ten years later was to become famous in city office development as the American technique of 'fast-track construction' – the deliberate overlapping of briefing, design and construction stages and the elimination of a single main contractor through the exercise of expert project management and the use of multiple prime contracts with different suppliers.

Where Berco had retired satisfied without a new building, Foster's next client found himself enthusiastically commissioning a 10,000-square-metre head office building when his initial approach had been about the organisation of some temporary hutted accommodation. This client was IBM, the UK subsidiary of the American computer giant, which in 1970 submitted part of its decentralisation plan from central London to Foster for analysis. After considering the economics of moving the corporation's head office to temporary buildings on a pilot site for five years, Foster concluded that rapid construction of a single-storey, air-conditioned glass box with a vast 10,000-square-metre floor area would actually be cheaper – as well as reducing the site coverage to create more car-parking. As a computer company, IBM was in the business of logic and it knew how to be convinced.

The decision that no new building was necessary for Berco, and the decision that a new building would be better than a temporary collection of huts for IBM,

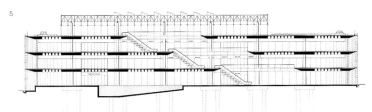

5

are examples of Foster's Adlerian lifestyle in professional action. At Willis Faber & Dumas, 1971-75, it expressed itself again, but this time in the leap of imagination that led from the conventional notion of a multi-storey office building on an irregular site, to a three-storey, deep-plan structure with 100 per cent site coverage. Once again an essentially conservative corporate client – one of the longest-established insurance brokers in the world – allowed itself to be convinced by logic. 'Willis Faber & Dumas never in their wildest dreams expected the sort of building they ended up with,' recalls Foster. 'What we achieved was an architectural coup. We captured the spirit of the company.'

Foster's design sketches for Willis Faber & Dumas perfectly reflect the process of questioning and probing for the initiative that enabled such a coup to take place. They start with an awkwardly-angled geometrical building that leaves slivers of its amoebic medieval site on all sides; from there they develop into various ziggurat forms which are dismissed as structurally unsatisfactory; and finally they venture into a fully glazed envelope with an inverted ziggurat within. 'Great possibilities! But we lack time and technical expertise,' noted Foster at the time – and indeed this idea was not to be developed until later, for the Hammersmith redevelopment project and, more recently, at King's Cross.

The final solution to the problem at Willis Faber & Dumas (5, 6) only emerged after all these possibilities had been pursued to the limit. Eventually the sketches begin to define with increasing confidence the wide structural grid, stepped escalator circulation, faceted, transomless, mullionless glass walls, and the helipad-equipped roof garden of the final version. Today Foster's sole regret is that the proposed *porte-cochère* entrance to the reception was not retained.

At the Sainsbury Centre for Visual Arts, 1974-78, the Foster process of analytical redefinition was more complicated. The Sainsbury collection and the accommodation for the Arts Department of the University of East Anglia were not only originally conceived as occupying separate buildings, but the architectural commission itself was at first to have been shared between Foster and the Dutch-Indonesian architect Kho Lang Ie. The tragic death of Kho Lang Ie early on in the project inevitably led to a reassessment of the whole commission and it was only then, after considerable discussion between Norman Foster, Sir Robert and Lady Sainsbury and the University authorities, that the single-building solution emerged.

When it did the project was one of breathtaking simplicity. The Sainsbury Centre (7, 8) is a 120-metre long inverted 'U' with two 7.5-metre legs joined by a 35-metre roof. The structural 'U' shape is built up from welded-steel tubes so as to create a 'thick wall' effect. Within the 2.4-metre zone between the inner and outer skins are located lobbies, lavatories, stores, darkrooms and plant. Far from being two buildings, the Sainsbury Centre brings the collection and the department together in a single, astounding interior space with its own advanced artificial and daylight control system. The 'thick wall' concept creates a simplicity and purity of outline, inside and out, that is as different from the 'bolt-on' appearance of his former partner's Centre Pompidou, in Paris, as it is possible to imagine. At the Sainsbury Centre everything that is not space is hidden within structure, and where there is no structure – as at each end of the great inverted 'U' – there is glass. As Foster's former associate Richard Horden has said, the building is 'about light and space never achieved before'.

In one way the building for Renault at Swindon, 1980-82, is unique in that there was no apparent redefinition of the brief in the early stages. Sebastian de la Selle, Renault's 'Coordinateur d'Expression Visuelle' at the time, commissioned Foster after visiting Willis Faber & Dumas and the Sainsbury Centre and, apart from the exigent functional requirements of the building, the French car company had no preconceptions about the design. Foster was asked to provide a vast 30,000-square-metre enclosure for parts storage, training, showroom and office purposes, with the prospect of a later enlargement to 40,000-square metres. With the brief established, the expression of lifestyle here took the form of an abandonment of the previous Foster trademark of enveloping form, and the adoption instead of a structure-driven umbrella roofing system. This consists of a forest of 59 steel masts supporting projecting beams with over 300 steel tension rods. At Renault the conventional wisdom that roof penetrations should be avoided is stood on its head: there are no less than 456 separate penetrations of the huge, continuous, solvent-welded PVC roof membrane in the form of structural members, rooflights and smoke vents. The result is a radical silhouette in which structure, for the first time in Foster's work, completely dominates the building's appearance.

We should also note two further examples of analytical brief redefinition in Foster's career. The first, and perhaps most dramatic, occurred at the competition

8>

stage of the commission for a new headquarters for the Hongkong and Shanghai Banking Corporation, which started out with two options already prepared by the client. It was only at the end of a research phase, equalled by none of the other invited entrants, that Foster was able to win the commission by proposing a third solution that transcended both original strategies. More recently, the King's Cross redevelopment project – which began with Foster being asked by London Regeneration Consortium to contribute a single building to a masterplan prepared by another firm of architects – quickly evolved into a commission to prepare an alternative masterplan. This masterplan featured the creation of a large park and a complex transport interchange (9), clear-spanned by an advanced-technology envelope, neither of which had existed in the earlier version.

These examples of the application of Foster's design lifestyle to the practice of architecture clearly show the pattern and force of a technique that can be detected throughout his career. In each case the same analytical skills are deployed from the very first moment of client approach, and it is in the exercise of them that the seeds are planted for his unique buildings. As the artist Ben Johnson – who has executed remarkable paintings of many of Foster's buildings, including several bold interiors of Willis Faber – once said: 'I know it is the "concept" of that building that created the masterpiece, because I watched what happened to the people who came from the old office in Southend and went to work there. It transformed them; it turned them into better, healthier and happier human beings.'

While it is partly due to their unique process of inception that Willis Faber & Dumas, the Sainsbury Centre for Visual Arts and the Renault Distribution Centre attract the admiring and the curious from all over the world, there is another powerful reason for the unique status they hold in the architectural firmament. Not only are they buildings that emerged from a new process of design, but they are also the sole masterpieces of a discredited era. In conception they are all buildings of the 1970s (although Renault came at the very end of the decade) and the 1970s were the years of the death of Modern architecture: a time that by common agreement produced few architectural landmarks.

The decade of the 1970s was a period of ideological bankruptcy in politics, economics and architecture. It marked the end of many of the unquestioned certainties of the post-war years; the end of unquestioned deficit spending by the governments of the Western nations; the end of unquestioned public-sector investment in housing and social welfare building; the end of unquestioned cheap energy and guiltless environmental damage; and the end of an unquestioned public consensus in favour of Modern architecture. If a single date must be assigned to the commencement of this era of disillusionment, it is not the parochial but much-quoted 15 July 1972 when the low-cost public housing project of Pruitt Igoe was filmed being dynamited to the ground in St Louis, but 6 October 1973 when engineers of the Egyptian Army bridged the Suez Canal under fire and began the Yom Kippur War.

From that war flowed the Arab oil embargo, and from the oil embargo the massive inflationary shock to the economies of the West that resulted from an overnight 500 per cent increase in the price of Middle Eastern oil. Adjustment to this shock, and the state of economic and political uncertainty that accompanied it, was the story of the rest of the decade. It was a time of fear, a time of disaster, and a time of opportunity. From the wreckage of the old socialised states of Europe emerged new political and economic attitudes, and nowhere more drastically than in Britain. From the 1973 oil embargo onwards, successive governments struggled to maintain the status quo and failed. Modern architecture, its limitless state funding removed, drifted from the penumbra of mild disappointment into a black pit of public loathing. Slashed budgets and abandoned plans downgraded the built environment and as the environment deteriorated so the architects who had built it were blamed for its failure. It was not a good time to be a Modern architect.

But notwithstanding the well-documented manifestations of this era of uncertainty – the property boom, the energy crisis, the three-day week and the winter of discontent – Foster's architecture not only survived but prospered. It prospered because by its very nature it contrived to connect itself to the public consciousness, not with the past – the post-war architecture of social welfare that had failed – but with the future. The future of an advanced-technology, 'more-for-less', design science that would manifest itself in a new kind of architecture. In addition to their technological ingenuity, their speed of erection and their economy, their appearance as something utterly different to the heavy *béton brut* of the final years of public-sector Modern architecture, Foster's buildings of the 1970s possessed another quality that was unique: they radiated competence, control, performance

and beauty in an environment of fear, incompetence, failure and ugliness. The magnetism of those buildings, perhaps their true significance, derives from this.

Willis Faber, the Sainsbury Centre and Renault were each in their way buildings of crisis. They were designed and constructed at a time of inflation, strikes and recession, but there was nothing about them that spoke of failure or even half-failure. They were something in the field of architecture that had not been seen for 50 years: they were triumphs of anticipatory design that radiated new possibilities. Like the early villas of Le Corbusier, the prefabricated housing of Ernst May, and the whole creative ethos of the Bauhaus, they were socially and environmentally predictive. Foster's buildings showed how people might live and work in another way in the future – once the bad times were over. Just as the early skyscraper projects of Mies van der Rohe radiated an order and optimism belied by the inflationary chaos of Weimar Germany, so Willis Faber & Dumas, the Sainsbury Centre and the Renault building promised a better ordering of the elements of life and a new harmony after the passing of the 'winter of discontent'.

Unlike many of the buildings of the 1970s – London's Alexandra Road housing scheme (10) is a classic example – Foster's buildings were not rearguard actions fought by the old Modernism. Instead they were the pioneering structures of another, newer rationality. Light, where Alexandra Road was heavy; private, where Alexandra Road was public; fast, where Alexandra Road was slow; innovative, where Alexandra Road harked back to a concrete technology that was new in the 1920s; each of Foster's buildings in its way was a promise for the future.

Fifteen years before 'Big Bang', Willis Faber & Dumas had open-planned, 4,000-square-metre office floors, complete with under-floor servicing, still – at the time of writing – larger than any dealing room in the City of London. Designed before the Yom Kippur War, it anticipated the energy crisis in an uncanny way with its heavily insulated grass roof; deep plan, giving minimal surface area for internal volume; and power by natural gas. Although it was under construction during the February 1974 crisis of the three-day week when the normal 40-hour working week was cut to 24 hours, it was completed ahead of schedule by a characteristically masterful reprogramming of construction to anticipate material shortages.

Like the 1971 IBM building, which absorbed an 800 per cent increase in computing power over fifteen years without structural alteration, or the Hongkong

Architecture and philosophy have few points of contact, so it is assumed. But that is only how it seems. In metaphysics, at the beginning, there is a creator who made the world in the same way as an architect, a master builder. The world did not become, it was created.

We do not know what God is; but we know what an architect is and so he has been elevated to the ranks of the divine. Since then we have interpreted the world as planned and ordered. We can no longer imagine an unplanned world, even though it now seems most likely that it was. The image of the creator who makes a plan and realises his work according to it – the image of the architect – is so dominating that it not only disguises God but also, in our culture, guides our understanding of the world as being a planned one.

Everything the world is has come into being according to a grand scheme of things; it was created according to a plan which is present in our thinking as an inscribed structure that can no longer be erased.

An opposing proposition could run: the world is that which has come into being, and that which might occur, according to the rules of probability and chance. It is a game and its rules are the rules of play. On this understanding, the world would not be determined by eternal laws, but by continual variation, continual discovery and continual design. Certainly not without rules of play but, just as certainly, without metaphysical direction.

But what would be the point of a philosophy that was not dedicated to timeless laws? For the Greeks, for Plato and Aristotle, and still for Whitehead and Russell, the subject of philosophy was the general law of regularity; this was even so for the early Wittgenstein.

There would never have been a Greek philosophy, an Occidental form of thought, and never a European Enlightenment had there not been this image of the architect, who created the world along ordered lines that we now recognise as laws. Philosophy, as the highest knowledge, only manifests itself if it is possible to explore and reveal such laws; and, in particular, metaphysics is only possible if the order underlying these laws can be established. But is this image of the architect correct? Do architects really work like this? Do they design in this way?

We wish to know what the world is, how it evolved and how it will develop, what our place in it is, and what determines and should determine our lives. Thus we pursue metaphysics, wishing to look behind things, beyond what is given. Moreover, our critical understanding and our analytical reason have posed the question: 'What can we really know and hope?' The question of the meaning of the world is not so much a problem of the world, as our own problem, a problem of knowledge.

Epistemology today has taken over from metaphysics. Anyone who wants to find out the meaning of the world must first find out how we obtain what we know.

One of the first to reverse the problem of philosophy was William of Ockham (1285-1348) who addressed himself to the question of whether general concepts have reality, or whether they are products of thought. What is humanity? Is it a superior principle, which makes possible the individual person, or was the person there first? Is the sum of people then formed what we call humanity, in which case is 'humanity' just a word?

The ancient image of the world collapsed when this kind of question was asked. The concept of the 'modern' emerges; the *via moderna* displaces the *via antiqua*.

The ancient world treated knowledge as an objective problem, as a problem of how one ordered the things of the world. In Ockham, knowledge results from sensory appreciation by which true knowledge is incorporated into the subject. Ockham felt himself forced into the position of Adam: he gave things their names. In antiquity, knowledge was seen as a constituent part of reality, a conceptual appreciation of the world. For Ockham, knowledge was a creative act of word and concept formation. A concept like 'humanity' is not the name of something existing in its own right, but only an invention of people. Only after people existed could there be concepts that attempted to define the individual.

But for Plato, just as for Aristotle, man was the result of a general idea of 'man'. The idea of man existed before the person and was paramount to the individual, who was merely its embodiment. It was the architect of the world who created the human being; the individual was merely a pictorial representation of this. The Old Testament, which is contemporaneous with the Hellenic age, is based on these same ideas.

Plato assumed the existence of an independent realm of ideas, in which the true, the good and the beautiful were at home. According to his understanding, this kingdom of ideas lay beyond the observed world, which was only a diluted realisation, or materialisation, of this spiritual cosmos of fundamental ideas. Pure ideas were, however, inadequately reproduced in this materialisation. Matter, the corporeal, allowed pure ideas to appear only in unsatisfactory form; everything corporeal is incomplete, just because it is corporeal.

According to Plato, knowledge of something comes about through our remembering the idea that lies at its creation. We have access to the eternal values and truths through our soul, which derives from beyond the beginning of time. Three factors may have led Plato to this concept of knowledge.

First, in the tradition of Pythagoras, Plato was concerned with mathematics; above all with the ideal basic forms, which are still called the 'Platonic bodies' after him and which are still the basic elements of architectonic construction. It is evident that in the world as it exists, there is no ideal sphere, no ideal cube, no ideal pyramid: bodies can only exist in perfect form in the purity of concept.

Second, man perceives himself as a divided being. His psyche and his spirit are quite often in conflict with his body. He lives between inertia and an erupting will; he lives between drive and control; and his corporeality often stands in the way of his pure aims and intentions.

Third, Plato was offended by the political development of his city state, Athens. It was too emancipated and liberal for him, principally because of the influence of the Sophists and their critical, analytical thinking. A conflict of generations became evident, into which Socrates was also drawn by the accusation that he was corrupting young people.

Plato's criticism comes down to this: we must do as the ancients did. The corruption of the world derives from the betrayal of eternal ideas, eternal values and eternal laws. The ancients conquered the land, founded the new city states, drew up constitutions, and their laws provided for the domination of the unfree and the slaves and for the best regulation of the business of the city. They set up institutions of science, and provided for the pursuit of truth, of the beautiful and the good.

We are familiar with these arguments; the implication is that Plato was an arch-conservative and approved of an authoritarian rather than a democratic way of life. In his political writings he called for a council of the wise as the highest political arbiter. The democratisation and opening-up of society down to the slaves went too far for him. Only the educated appeared to him to have access to the realm of justice and truth, which lay in a spatial and temporal world beyond. Similarly, the aesthetic roots of elegant proportion and Classical form lay in a superior realm and were as binding as the laws of mathematics.

Aristotle was a pupil at the academy founded by Plato. A generation younger; he wanted to see political conditions not circumscribed by eternal laws, but determined rather by the principle of the common good. By this he meant that which is due here and now in the interests of everyone. He pursued truth not in a distant realm of ideal being, in some storehouse of eternal values; he looked for it in the world, in the things themselves. He also, however, stuck to the idea of plan. The plan was something definitively valid, a ready-made a priori principle. Things separate out into their plan and their realisation. It is as with a sculptor: he has an idea, an imagined form, and must hew it out of the stone as well as he can. According to Aristotle, things can be divided into form and matter. Form and matter were the basic concepts of his philosophy – form described the spiritual principle, and matter the bodily principle.

Man is both form and matter; his consciousness is the forming principle. As such, it can also take the forms of other things into itself, stripped of their matter. By abstracting from experience and perception, one comes to know and see the inbuilt plan of things.

It is no longer the realm of ideas which makes knowledge possible, but the experience of the world as it is; and the formal principle, which constitutes things, does not lie in the beyond, but in things themselves as their forming principle. Aristotle also assumed that matter discloses the spiritual principle only incompletely; for him matter is needed merely for the individuation of a general idea. The individual person, even Socrates, even Aristotle himself, is thus only the accidental individuation of the idea of the person. Humanity, the idea of the human, comes before the individual.

Even the early Christians, into the Middle Ages, inclined towards this Classical philosophy. But according to the Christian view it is the individual, and no longer humanity, who stands before God. From Jewish history and the Jewish religion there develops the idea of the uniqueness of each human being, in character, disposition and behaviour. And God is no architect, who has drawn up a world plan according to which everything comes into being and develops; God is a god of history, who leads his people home from banishment, who quarrels with them, punishes and yet loves them. God is a god who speaks to everyone, disputes with them, even when someone – like Job – despairs in him. In the Jewish consciousness, the world exists in time, it has history, it develops. Much of this informs the convictions of the Christians. Christianity, however, did not break the cultural framework and the cultural fetters of antiquity for some time. The first church fathers carried on with Neo-Platonism, and Thomas Aquinas, in his *Summae*, still used the categories of Aristotle.

However, the question of how a plan arises was not one that the ancients asked. How indeed does a plan arise?

The ancients regarded a plan as given; as a principle outside time; as a preordained structure according to which everything and its development is determined; and as the generality that determines the specific.

We now know from biology that there is no plan for the development of a species, be it man or a bird. The blackbird was not always as it is today and will one day no longer be as now. Perhaps two species will develop out of it. It is the adaptations of individual blackbirds that determine their behaviour and their bodily form, modifying them in often tiny steps. Through cross-breeding within a species, subjective experiences and alterations enter into the total population and determine its development. Perhaps one day we will need two words for 'blackbird', because the species has divided into types with two patterns of behaviour which can be readily distinguished by their appearance. The species, the generality, thus stands below the individual. It is the individual that determines the species, not the other way round.

The general, in terms of the communal, certainly exists; as the denotation of a group. But the general as the pre-planned, as the already given, as the determining guideline, exists neither in nature nor in the history of humanity.

That does not mean, however, that there is in the world only the single, only individuals. Individuals gather in organisational forms, whether families, work units, or states. Marriage is thus no less real than the individuals who form it. It is not merely a name or a concept. But it is only real in so far as it is realised by individuals. Marriage as an eternal institution, as a superior authority, does not exist (in the sense of Plato's values), however often the opposite is claimed today.

The plan of the world is merely the adaptation of individuals to the world, whether singly or in groups. This plan can never be established in advance, even when in retrospect it proves to be meaningful. Every individual carries in his cells the development code in which the experiences of adaptation accumulated by the entire species are stored. This code is handed on in reproduction. It guarantees the pattern of behaviour of the species as thus far developed. But it says nothing about how the individual will behave in specific situations; the individual will indeed behave within the frame set by the pattern, but yet so freely that new patterns of behaviour can enter into the genetic code, no matter how these new patterns are generated and triggered.

There is a plan for creatures, for men and blackbirds. That is their behavioural code, their inherited knowledge, their genetic code. But this plan says nothing about how they will actually behave in their lives, and also nothing as to whether this plan undergoes modification through the behaviour of the individual in the course of its existence.

Thus it is the behaviour itself, the adaptation to the environment and to other individuals, it is the ability to respond to the given surroundings, it is the search for a proper balance with the given conditions and the attempt to optimise such relationships, which determines the plan, and not only the plan of the species but also the plan of the world.

More recently, modern science suggested that there were constant laws of nature. There was still reason to assume a world plan and thus also an architect of cosmic laws. However, with the acceptance of a more mechanistic world – as a kind of mechanical system or machine – in place of the architect there began to appear the engineer.

Since the Earth began, the sun has risen every day. Will it rise tomorrow? Is that a necessary law? No. Of course it will rise tomorrow, but one can think of the possibility that it will never do so again. We now even have sufficient technical imagination to conceive of an end to the Earth. But the probability that the sun will never rise again is so small as to be nil. And yet the extraordinary could happen. When a raindrop falls on the ridge of a roof, what is the probability of its running down to the left or to the right? It is half and half. The regularity of the process is such that there is no regularity. Every prediction is false or accidentally correct.

Otl Aicher

Modern research into states of chaos, which is predominantly concerned with liquid or gaseous currents (and what does not flow?) sees the world in alternatives. Yes and no, like this or like that: that is the law of the world.

How then does a plan arise? How does an architect's knowledge come about?

Norman Foster's practice is unusual in its results. It is certainly unusual as far as the work itself is concerned: its quality, its appearance, its constructive genius. But first of all it is unusual for the fact that the practice has no style. Every piece of work turns out so differently that one does not know what to expect next.

No less unusual is the fact that the practice possesses what may be the most highly developed design method. (Perhaps this is the reason for the originality of every design.)

Whether one takes the designs for Renault or the Sainsbury Centre, or even the Hongkong Bank, one finds alternative designs for every job. At least two designs are confronted with each other. For the Sainsbury Centre there is one concept with a solid portal structure and another with lattice supports; for Renault there is an umbrella concept, with a support in the centre of the roof area, against a tent solution with four supports at the corners. The Hongkong Bank had to be the best answer to a false premise: the client wanted to have the new building grow so that the old one could remain standing until the new was finished. Thus one arrives at a building which is a bridge, growing in segments from the rear to the front. There are numerous variants, which describe opposing positions, not just stages of development. This means that Norman Foster always allows for twice the development outlay, compared with other practices, because there are always at least two design approaches. The drop of water can run to the right or to the left.

Le Corbusier could not have permitted himself such opportunities because the artist-architect has only one throw, even at the development stage. Mies van der Rohe did not need them because he had an established style.

With Foster, the alternative designs are not merely stages: they are fully worked out as designs. This way of working requires alternatives to be so perfected that their final results can be compared. That need not mean that the designs also run parallel in time – they can just as well be developed one after the other – but their comparability must be ensured through complete execution.

210

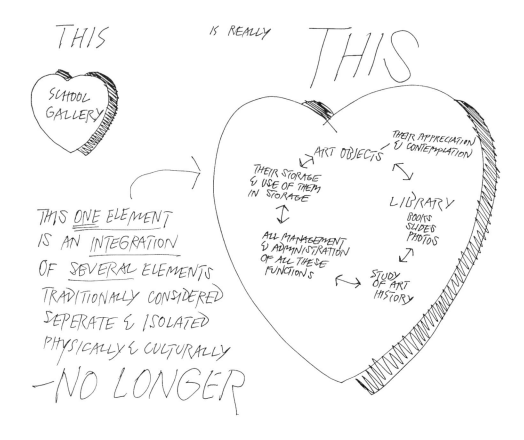

THIS

IS REALLY

THIS

SCHOOL GALLERY

THIS ONE ELEMENT
IS AN INTEGRATION
OF SEVERAL ELEMENTS
TRADITIONALLY CONSIDERED
SEPERATE & ISOLATED
PHYSICALLY & CULTURALLY
—NO LONGER

ART OBJECTS

THEIR APPRECIATION
& CONTEMPLATION

THEIR STORAGE
& USE OF THEM
IN STORAGE

LIBRARY
BOOKS
SLIDES
PHOTOS

ALL MANAGEMENT
& ADMINISTRATION
OF ALL THESE
FUNCTIONS

STUDY
OF ART
HISTORY

Comparability is undertaken through the representation of the design in perspective drawings of the closest approximation to reality, in technical drawings – particularly for details – and in models of the highest quality. Reality is exalted.

In every attempt at a solution, the representation of an idea is not enough; rather it is a matter of positive proof. The construction must be developed, the organisation rehearsed, the building technology defined. Only with the highest possible development of the scheme can a qualified yes or no be issued.

At the start of a design there is the brief, followed by an analytical consideration of the field of action. One investigates the local conditions and also other examples, insofar as such are built. The first data for conceptual ideas grow from this analysis. They are captured in many drawings.

The real concept appears in the form of sketches. Often the final version is clearly anticipated in little sketches, at least as far as the appearance and cultural climate of the building is concerned.

Norman Foster is a great draughtsman, but in a way that differs from what one expects from an architect. He has a clear inner image but a line that only hints generously. The language of his drawings is that of Giacometti. He seeks an inner reality and captures it in indications. He is already going through his buildings or around them, testing the character and atmosphere that they produce.

Other drawings capture technical or constructional ideas. For Norman Foster, the building is always the built, the constructed building: it gains its character from constructional characteristics. What is sought is not merely a building by its organisation and appearance alone, but also a new and appropriate construction.

A concept, however, is a long way from being a design. There now begins a phase of discourse. The building is discussed and brought into rational distinctiveness. Seeing becomes making. The drawings assume the size of drawing boards. Ideas now become testable. But alternatives still develop continually, captured as the inevitable outcome of discussion.

Then the rigour of the factual appears. Only what works counts here. This rigour is not hostile; it is not the obstinacy of the material world. On the contrary, the factual inspires, it is the source of new possibilities, technical possibilities. In wrestling with what works and what does not, with what can be made and what cannot – even when it has never been made before – there arises this special form of architecture which knows no style, either constructionally or aesthetically. At this point too the alternatives emerge. The counter-design joins the design.

There develops an architecture of which it may be said that the spirit resides in the material. It is the struggle with construction and technique that produces the essential object; not as a necessary struggle, but as one that is sought after. Similarly, in this architecture the organisational form of a building is not something that has to adapt to the architectonic form: in a castle one can accommodate an office or a hotel as well as a monarch. The organisational form is the result of discussions, which can involve reference systems as well as discoveries; the investigation of new joints for example.

Good cooks can never be convinced that there is anything more important than the ingredients themselves, the material that constitutes a particular cuisine. Forget the recipe and sense how to release the nature, the content, the character, the charm of what one has bought fresh at the market. This is what good chefs manage to blend into what they cook.

It is of the greatest importance to make this point, if one wants to describe how knowledge comes about. If they have any respect for the job, an architect or a cook cannot allow themselves, like Plato or Aristotle, to regard the ingredients as something secondary or even inferior. They do not need to be materialists, even if convinced that spirit resides in matter and that it is the spirit that sets matter free.

The spirit that sets matter free, however, has to be extracted from it. The most demanding part of the design process lies there: in explorations, experiments and studies; in countless series of tests and fresh starts with models and prototypes; with the help of one's own efforts and in consultation with others – all to achieve the essence of an optimal solution.

The architect is no more intelligent than his material, but the material says nothing to an architect who is not intelligent. He stays unenlightened. But what is an intelligent architect? One who asks the right questions. Not one who knows better.

Is the process of acquiring knowledge in design therefore a passive one? Does the designer only take part in what is already given? Not at all. Design is a creative process. In a certain sense, the material is passive. It exists only in certain ordered forms and these must be found. Design is the production of technical and constructional forms, and the transformation of a programme into an organisation.

Otl Aicher

2

Material in architecture never occurs in its raw state. Steel, for example, is always formed for a special purpose, either as sheet or rod, profiled or corrugated, appearing in the building as support, truss, tension or compression beam, as link, joint, screw, rivet or slat. And concrete exists as wall, slab, support or pillar, as joist or as column head, and is always differently reinforced according to function. Material is never the passive matter of Aristotle who presides only over art, not industry, and who, as with the activity of the sculptor with stone, describes a neutral situation. His interest in the organisational forms of matter was limited. He considered plants and animals to be made from the same material. And in art, even now, the material is treated as tending to insignificance.

Design is an intellectual ordering, a clarifying of connections, a defining of dependencies and a creating of weights. It requires of the designer a special mental capacity to see and to establish analogies, connections and fields of reference.

The architect is no scientist. He does not think in the categories of logic; he draws no conclusions, even when he judges. He assesses situations, relations, fields of reference. He practises not algebra but geometry. His thought is not linear, from conclusion to conclusion, but develops rather in nets, structures and connected systems. The values by which he judges are those of the optimal form of life, the organisational form which sets a building free.

When a design in this sense has been completed, it is not yet at an end. The regard for actual circumstances, the respect for the real, is so great that only the one-to-one model, the full-size mock-up, can grant the security of a definitive judgement. If the mock-up is good, the design is approved.

But the challenge of matter is still not over; the dialogue between the possible and the definite is not yet concluded. When the stage of construction is reached, one again starts with a model or prototype, at least for those parts, described by the concepts of design and discovery, which are newly conceived and found. Once more the dialogue between conceptual and technical possibilities gets under way, and the test-for-real tells whether one has succeeded in gaining a new approach out of the domain of what is technically feasible. The mock-up is tried and tested and exposed to every eventuality. A prototype comes into being.

It is clear that an architectural practice like that of Norman Foster works with methods that are also applied in the development of industrial products. In industry, the following stages are distinguished: brief and programme; concept; design; model testing and modification; technical drawing; and development of proto-types. Only then can production begin; and while in production the outlay on time, material, work, and costs is continually minimised. With increasing complexity in a job, there exists the tendency to extend these basic stages and to increase the outlay on development. Nowadays, development encompasses broad areas of research and it integrates interdisciplinary concerns. The design of a car, a calcu-lator, a robot, and even a good saucepan, is a widely based collective effort.

Modern technology has also given an important boost to the dematerialisation of matter. The fact that matter only appears in organisational forms has already been pointed out. It follows from this that matter, where it is not just 'there' but is harnessed to processes, must be subject to control.

An aeroplane does not fly if it is not controllable, and a calculator does not calculate if it is not operated on the basis of a given programme. In a helicopter, there are over 30 elementary forms of movement, governed by hand and foot, which, by means of the most complex technicalities, operate the steering mecha-nism. Matter also has a fourth dimension; it has a form of behaviour. Very important philosophical concepts, such as those of software and hardware, stem from this, even though they are concepts of a pragmatic philosophy. Software is a pro-gramme for the organisational form of the machine's matter, which in turn is itself organised matter. Does Plato catch up with us in the end? Is there a spiritual el-ement, an idea, which technology just activates?

Wrong. The control programme for a machine's field of action is part of the machine itself, emerging from it as specific possibility. What is new in our consciousness is, perhaps, that programme and control have a presence in reality. We understand material increasingly as activated and organised matter and, as such, it becomes a machine of one kind or another. And machines are determined by a programme and are in need of control.

There is no realm of architectonic ideas in the architecture discussed here, and no code of aesthetics. It stands quite in contrast to current architectural theory.

This theory would have eternal architectural ideas, such as the column, the portal, the hall, the roof, the arcade, the gallery. The task would then consist of giv-ing these eternal ideas a contemporary form according to the measures of

Classical proportion. Architecture becomes a dialogue transcending time, with one and the same problem, manifesting itself in the quotation of previous solutions.

Philosophically speaking, one is back again with Plato, as is discernible also in the renewed currency of the Greek column and the Classical triangular, the segmental and, above all, the broken pediment. Once again, the material is secondary to the spirit. Whether concrete, steel or stone, it is used as though it is some sort of dough, ready to be manipulated into any form.

We are back with the old function of the Classical, to secure domination by evoking eternal and spiritual values. However, each personal and individual life is a progress from experience to experience, from bitter insights to happy memories, from narrow horizons to wide ones, from the landscapes of childhood to those of real life, from satisfaction to doubt, to disgust and then back to joy. Life is design and fate combined; one is thrown in and yet has it in one's own hand.

Life is not Classical. The Classical is a feature of rule, whose legitimisation it serves, as the guardian of the eternally true, good and beautiful. Classicism is the aesthetic expression of the conservative: the consolidation of what always was and, thus, the consolidation of power. Power is that which would like to stay as it was. Nothing on Earth wants to stay as it was as much as power. And it persists with all available means. It sets itself against the course of the world, against the strength of life. Thus the attempt to perpetuate a philosophy of the established, the Classical.

But there is more to say about present-day architectural theory. The talk is of Hegel; one strolls along the paths of the dialectic, as the epistemological form of absolute reason.

It is quite right to understand the modern as the antithesis of historicism. While the modern is certainly a dialogue with the newly emerged mechanised world, its original motivation was liberation from the aesthetic ballast of ornament and historical elements.

To build with historical dress was once the highest form of cultural consciousness, even though it was also an alibi for economic decline. The antithesis to this was pure building. The new spirit of the age, Hegel's *Weltgeist*, of knowledge of the world, demands a synthesis of the two. Pink and turquoise steel girders spring from brown stone cladding, Bauhaus geometry unfolds under the ledges of the new Neo-Classicism.

Otl Aicher

Doubts must be raised over whether the dialectic can be validated as the key to understanding the world, and as a programme for the future, when what is produced most obviously is kitsch. Though its philosophical method may appear to be sound, at least as a principle sanctioned by Hegel and his followers, what sort of spirit of the age is this, that produces a stew of inconsistency and renunciation of thought?

Hegel's ideal state seems already to be inconsistent with the epistemological principle of the dialectic. What was first the principle of morality, whereby people were expected to conduct themselves, became the principle of power and of conquest – conquest of neighbours and conquest of the whole defenceless world.

This ideal state then became the principle of economic rationality and of the planned welfare economy. Now it has degenerated into an overblown bureaucracy of tax-gathering and security control. Today the state is an institution which endlessly levies taxes to maintain and secure its own existence, two-thirds of which is superfluous. Has not the spirit of the age similarly degenerated from the great *Weltgeist*, along with its spiritual principles of progress and liberation?

What shall we think of Hegel's eternal laws, when Plato's eternal ideas have already left us in the lurch? What sort of system is it, what sort of epistemological principle, that reduces the dynamic of world events and cultural progress to a logic which produces mere nonsense: Neo-Classicism *à la* Bauhaus. At least those architects are more consistent who, for the sake of conserving what exists, regard Albert Speer as the most significant architect of this century. Speer adhered to the eternal architectonic ideas. True, a portal was twenty times higher than a normal portal; the window was so huge that it could only be opened mechanically; the foot of a pilaster – just the foot – exceeded five times the height of a person, and one storey came to the height of four or six ordinary storeys. The dome of St Peter's was to fit a hundred times into his dome, while next to his triumphal arch the Trajan Arch was just a garden door.

It may be that one can still relate this to Plato. Plato did not discuss size. Nevertheless, it remains sheer inhumanity.

How do insights occur in architecture, how does knowledge come about? Architects are not philosophers. Architecture and philosophy hardly touch each other. Architecture has a depth to which philosophy has rarely descended.

That could change. If philosophy wishes to concern itself further with the question of how knowledge comes about, it must address itself to the making of things and the way knowledge can arise from the manufacturing process.

This path has been blocked or made difficult because philosophy appears to profit from the condemnation of matter, of the bodily and of embodiment.

The antipathy to the body, or spiritual arrogance of Western philosophy has led finally to the material, in the form of organised technology, overcoming us like a foreign power. We were not prepared for this; we failed to recognise this power, and have neither coped with it intellectually nor been in any position to control it. The disaster of the present world is complete.

Philosophy would benefit from analysing and learning to comprehend processes of knowledge at the point where knowledge takes place. There are architectural offices that are like epistemological workshops. Here intellectual discussions crackle, problems arise without announcement, must be tied up and resolved, tamed by rational demystification. Things are discovered and rejected, formulated and forgotten, systems of order are sketched and relations determined. Whole search-Commando units seek an opening and a way out, and a single idea brings light. Thesis is pitted against thesis. The search is not for the eternal truth, not for the eternally beautiful. It is about what is right.

And its authority is continually questioned by tests, experiments on models, trial arrangements and dummies. One pursues lines of thought as much as columns of figures and rows of data; one changes view from inner imagination to calculation, and what the one divides up, the other must coordinate. It is an adventure where ideas and requirements reside in one concept and condense into one design, one form. Views alternate with darkness; there is a struggle and a sigh of relief, pressure and freedom, and nothing is more blissful than to have brought a problem to its solution. Applause would only disturb.

In essence, knowledge is work: work in the form of making and in the form of producing models that can be compared. Knowledge is the naming of differences. The one that is more correct is shown in the alternative. The architect works thus. Nature works thus.

By what method is the world likely to have been planned? There has been only one philosopher who was an architect at the same time: Ludwig Wittgenstein.

Otl Aicher

After he had written the celebrated *Tractatus Logico-Philosophicus,* he built a house for his sister in Vienna. This altered his philosophy and he developed a second. He had discovered the knowledge that comes from making. In the place of knowledge, eternal knowledge, there came what is right, the rules of the game which result from use.

Ludwig Wittgenstein, perhaps the most important philosopher of this century, developed two philosophies. The first did not satisfy him. He had built a house.

On Foster

'For all Foster's achievements in improving the quality of the workplace … breaking down the professional and class barriers between the architect's studio and the factory shop floor to bring architecture into the new Machine Age may turn out to be his most significant social accomplishment.'

Chris Abel

The First Machine Age meant many things to architects. From nineteenth-century writer Horatio Greenough on, it meant drawing lessons from ocean-going liners and other mechanical and engineering achievements of the time, to point out how inefficient and otherwise outdated contemporary architecture was.[1] To Futurists like Antonio Sant'Elia, it implied that buildings and even whole cities should be designed to emphasise mechanical speed, both in streamlined architecture and exaggerated, criss-crossing movement systems. To Constructivists and others, it included more pragmatic considerations, such as making the most of new light-weight materials and construction techniques. To Bruno Taut and the members of the Glass Chain, it was synonymous with a transparent 'glass architecture', thinly framed in rolled steel and suffused with natural light. But above everything else it meant struggling – first like the Deutsche Werkbund and, later, like the teachers at the Bauhaus – to reconcile the art and craft of architecture with the new machinery of industrial production.[2]

The transition to the new Machine Age was marked by equally spectacular advances in technology, dramatised in the 1960s by Russian Sputniks circling the Earth and the answering American Apollo Space Programme that put man on the moon. As with the earlier change of gear, the social effects were profound. From providing mechanised benefits for the elite, modern industry graduated to providing similar benefits for the masses. Automobiles, domestic appliances and communications are now available to most of the population of the industrialised world, and television, according to Reyner Banham, is the 'symbolic machine of the Second Machine Age', joining the older technology of mass production with the new technology of mass communication.[3]

For better or worse, television has made its predicted impact, and created the 'global village'. But the true symbolic machine of the Second Machine Age, better known as the Computer Age, turned out to be not the one-way unresponsive TV, but the two-way computer, especially the 'user-friendly' personal computer. And it is around the versatile microprocessor – rather than the inflexible mass-production line – that the emergent architecture of the Computer Age centres.

It is against the background of this transition, and its meaning for architecture, that Norman Foster's achievements must be measured. The contrast with the failures of earlier generations of architects to fulfil the promises of the First

Machine Age makes those achievements all the more remarkable. For the fact is that the Foster team's mastery of the techniques and tools of machine production is a rare exception to the general professional record. As forecast, factories now turn out practically all parts of buildings by industrialised methods. But they do so without any significant participation by architects, whose role in building production is reduced to the job of assembly, selecting from catalogues components that have been designed and made by other people. To all intents and purposes, the profession remains just where it was when the first Modernists issued their rallying calls – detached from, and ignorant of, the means of production.

Something went badly wrong. But what? The commonly accepted version of Modern Movement history has it that the deciding battle for industrialised building was enjoined in the 1920s and '30s, and won in the '40s and '50s, with the general acceptance of Modern architecture. But not only was a vital part of that battle – gaining design expertise with the new tools of machine production – never even won, it was hardly ever properly begun.

The main obstruction was invariably ideological in kind. Joseph Paxton's prefabricated iron structure for the Crystal Palace (1) created an enduring model for an architecture of the First Machine Age, built with the most advanced industrialised materials and techniques of the day.[4] But Paxton's use of a limited variety of structural and cladding elements based on a single glazing module grew amongst his later admirers from a practical concept of modular construction, appropriate to a single large-scale industrialised building project, to an idealised concept of a universal architecture of standard forms.

The obsession with standardisation for ideological rather than industrial reasons runs like a common thread through much of the history of the industrialised building movement, shaping the main course of events and often negating positive economic and social benefits that might otherwise have occurred. The general drift was already apparent in the nationalist Deutsche Werkbund's efforts to reconcile design with industry on the basis of a purely qualitative interpretation of standards, meant to confirm Germany's place in the modern world.[5] It reappeared to inspire Le Corbusier to compare the Parthenon with automobiles and aeroplanes as examples of the same evolutionary 'product of selection applied to a standard'[6] and to shape all his early architecture. Le Corbusier's prefabricated dwellings at Pessac had little to do with either industrial or social realities,[7] but his Modulor geometric system of proportion had a profound influence on later efforts at modular coordination; a largely pointless exercise since it too demonstrated 'little authentic contact with (production) engineering'.[8]

The same pattern of thinking seriously undermined Walter Gropius' well-meaning efforts at the Bauhaus to bring designers to work together with industry; the Bauhaus workshops remained essentially craft-based and few prototypes coming out of them ever went into industrial production.[9] And it doomed to consumer rejection countless later schemes, including the most promising, such as Gropius' later collaboration in the United States with Konrad Wachsmann on the standardised 'Packaged House' project.[10]

For all their protestations of a new partnership with industry, most of the early Modernists only toyed with the idea. What was at stake was a general consensus on the 'new style' rather than any genuine understanding of industrial production methods.[11] Even the 'machine aesthetic' was misunderstood and made to conform to preferred Platonic images.[12] In the end, they nearly all stuck to the same Olympian role of architect-as-artist that was most revered by the profession before the advent of Modernism. Only Mies van der Rohe, having spent much of his youth in his father's stonemason's yard, seemed able to form an effective working relationship with industry.[13] Ditching most of the dogma that accompanied Modern architecture even before he moved across the Atlantic, Mies freely translated his early experiments with 'glass architecture' into an industrialised language for corporate America, an aspect which has often distracted European critics from the quality of his building technique.

It is no coincidence that industrial design emerged as a separate profession in the 1930s independently of any formal schools of art or architecture; and not even in Europe, where industrialisation was conceived, but in the US where fledgling designers had fewer academic or professional preconceptions to wrestle with. Significantly, the first designers willing to court industry also came from various commercial backgrounds, such as advertising, commercial art and even stage design, and had no misgivings about working in a competitive or industrial environment. The most successful of them, such as Walter Dorwin Teague, Raymond Loewy and Henry Dreyfuss, also quickly grasped the importance of mechanical

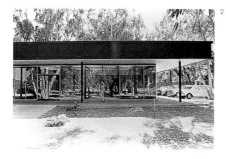

efficiency as a factor of good design. Working hand-in-hand with production engineers, they designed or redesigned everything from cameras and refrigerators to telephones, which both looked and worked better than existing models.[14]

The notable exception to the familiar post-war catalogue of failures in this area was also American. Impressed by his studies of the British approach, at least with the theory if not the practice, Ezra Ehrenkrantz spelt out much the same ideological message in *The Modular Number Pattern*: standardisation, with a limited number of sizes carefully selected for their combinatorial value, and modular coordination, providing a numerical measure for determining those standard sizes.[15]

Ehrenkrantz nevertheless brought an American brand of realism to producing his factory-made Southern Californian Schools Development, or SCSD building system (2), even if it was to mark yet another professional retreat. Like the pragmatic American pioneers of industrial design, Ehrenkrantz understood the value of high performance in functional, structural and mechanical efficiency – factors that were eventually to account for most of the success of the SCSD project. But recognising that the weaknesses of the European building systems he had studied were largely due to their architectural designers' lack of industrial expertise, he handed over final responsibility for product design to the manufacturers themselves. The four major component sub-systems for the SCSD project were, accordingly, all designed by the manufacturers' own designers. Architects were confined to writing performance specifications for each component and, as usual, were assigned the task of assembling the results.[16] In effect, the Ehrenkrantz formula completed the process of professional emasculation begun with the onset of the First Machine Age, and only further distanced architects from any direct contact with the means of production.

Foster's entry into the field coincided with the same turbulent period of the 1960s in which Ehrenkrantz produced his SCSD system. Much of Foster's early work was subsequently influenced by the SCSD model. As well as offering economic advantages and ease of prefabrication, the highly flexible structural and planning concept suited his functional and social aims of providing for changes of use and improving the workplace, a strategy effected by pooling resources and encouraging conventionally separate classes of workers to share the same spaces and amenities.[17]

The unitary building form with its regular open structure and roof-and-services 'sandwich' first appears in the Newport School competition of 1967, but was soon adapted as a general-purpose building type in the proposals for the Olsen Amenity Centre at Millwall Docks in London, which brought dockyard workers and management together for the first time within the same building. Both projects were crucial in gaining the experience needed for the IBM Pilot Head Office at Cosham, which was built as temporary accommodation – and for the same cost as the equivalent 'off-the-shelf' structures – but which pleased IBM sufficiently to make it a permanent regional headquarters.

IBM Cosham (4) was followed by the Factory Systems studies of 1969-72 (3), and the building of IBM Technical Park at Greenford, 1975-80, which included mezzanine floors, as opposed to the usual single-storey configuration. These are only the most obvious members of the same building type. If consistent elements such as the full-height glass walls are ignored, and attention concentrated on the deep-plan configuration, the post-and-beam structure and the roof-and-services 'sandwich', then it is possible to also include the Computer Technology Centre in Hertfordshire and the scheme for the VW-Audi headquarters at Milton Keynes, all from the same period.

But if his early architecture is influenced by the SCSD building type, Foster never accepted the implied defeatism in Ehrenkrantz's approach to product design, which left architects bereft of any direct design role. The Foster team's highly professional skills as both industrial designers and architects separates their factory-made architecture from that of the industrialised building movement as a whole.

The same professionalism, involving increasingly close working relations with industry, had led Foster and his team to overturn popular myths about the way buildings are made in factories. For all his refinement of similar building types and respect for qualitative standards, Foster never fell into the same trap as other designers in confusing such standards with those having to do with processes of industrial production. As Foster explains, when an architect orders a component from a catalogue, such as a window, he usually imagines that the component is lying around the factory somewhere all made up and ready to go. Not so. Most products ordered from a catalogue are not standard items at all, but are made to order. What the factory actually has at hand is a range of industrialised materials

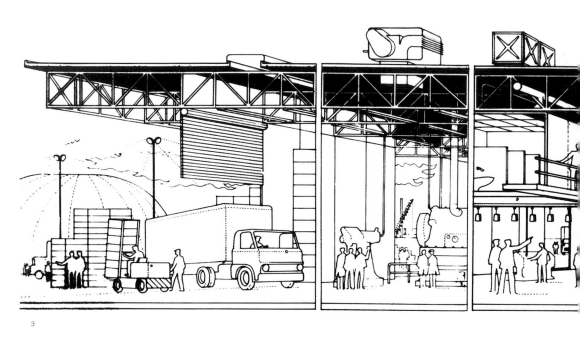

3

and products in sheets or lengths, which are cut up and assembled as required. Some factories might keep a limited stock of the most popular size ranges of assembled components, but even then the selection is dictated by customer preference. It has nothing at all to do with economic or technological constraints of industrialised production, as modular mythology would lead architects to believe.[18]

While flexibility of planning grids may require the use of fixed forms and size ranges within each building, manufacturers are not so constrained in the manufacture of their products, and cannot be if they wish to reach the largest and most varied market. If a designer cares to take the trouble, therefore, as Foster proved, it is possible in many cases to persuade a manufacturer, at little or no extra cost to the client, to modify his product to suit a particular project or situation.

For this reason, comparisons between Foster's work and the use of 'off-the-shelf' components by other designers, exemplified in the house in Pacific Palisades by Charles Eames (5), can be misleading, and do little justice to Foster's greater involvement with industry.[19] Such practice, however, is rare, and Foster learned early in his career that to get the most out of industry it was necessary, as he puts it, to 'cheat the system and penetrate an organisation in order to get through to the shop floor'. He recalls his experience with the Olsen Amenity Centre project, when, having learned that no British manufacturer could supply a suitable glazed-wall system in the eleven-month design-and-build period of the contract, he flew over to Pittsburgh in the US to discuss the project with the PPC Company, whose glazing system seemed to fit the bill. Met at the airport by a company representative, Foster was told that he would be taken directly to meet the vice-president at the head office. Foster respectfully replied that he would prefer to talk to the people involved in drawing up and detailing the components he wanted to use. Told that such operations were not carried out in Pittsburgh, but in Dayton, Ohio, Foster was on the next available plane. In Dayton he worked round the clock with the company's designers, and after a week returned to his own offices in London with the drawings he required. The elegant glass skins of the Olsen Centre and IBM Cosham buildings were produced in just this fashion as an adaptation of an existing curtain-wall system, modified to work as a ground-supported, free-standing element with minimal interruptions to the smooth, reflective qualities of the glass.

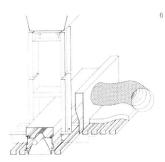

From persuading manufacturers to adapt their products to suit his particular requirements, Foster and his team soon became immersed in the full process of product design, development and manufacture. In practice, up until the collaboration with Tecno on furniture production, the Foster team had mostly been restricted to designing custom-made components for each building project as it came up, though they were frequently designed with some kind of wider application in mind. This restriction could be viewed as a blessing in disguise, for it forged Foster's expertise in developing high-performance components for economical small-batch production, a major factor in preparing his team for the technological innovations to come.

The key to Foster's approach to component design, just as it is with space planning and with the design of the overall enclosure, is integrated design aimed at maximising performance.[20] This approach, which Foster calls 'design development', is strongly influenced by Buckminster Fuller's philosophy of 'doing more with less', whether that be materials, weight or energy.[21] It is symbolised by the images of ultra-lightweight aircraft, with which Foster frequently concludes presentations of his work, as well as by his own personal passion for flying gliders. It is also cogently summarised in the terse statement made by Jean Prouvé – another keen glider pilot and source of inspiration – in criticism of architects' obsessions with modular coordination: 'Machines are seldom built with parts selected from various sources; they are aggregatedly designed.'[22]

What Prouvé expressed and what Foster discovered for himself is a basic principle of manufacture: if a product is to be designed for maximum efficiency, then its constituent parts must be integrated in the manner that most closely approximates to the desired performance specification for the whole. In sum, the approach substitutes high performance for high-volume production as the main criterion for good industrial design.

One way to achieve high performance is to get a single component to do what was previously done by many different ones. Among the first purpose-made component systems designed by the Foster team was the aluminium suspended ceiling for the Willis Faber & Dumas building (6). Though it has received less attention than the more striking glass wall, in some ways it demonstrates the Foster approach to industrial design even better. The parabolic reflectors in the ceiling, for

example, do with a single, integrated component what is usually done with several separate systems, providing support for the ceiling, plus light, plus air distribution, plus sprinklers, together with power distribution for the floor above. The ceiling itself is made up of simple, but non-standard, aluminium channels spanning between the reflectors and, though it was the first of its kind to replace the conventional suspended panel system, development and production costs were kept within conventional cost limits by virtue of the scale of the contract.

As for the glass wall, the near-seamless curtain still defines the state-of-the-art in 'glass architecture' (7). Mies would without doubt have applauded that gossamer skin, with its Minimalist aesthetic, craftsman-like detailing and reflected images of the old market town of Ipswich. But so also would have Camillo Sitte, whose 'artistic principles' of urban design[23] inspire much of Foster's sympathetic approach to dealing with problems of urban context.[24] The decision, for example, to make the perimeter of the building follow the existing street pattern led directly to the curved lines of the wall. To achieve this, the Foster team virtually created a new kind of glazing system. The patch plates and other components were already available, but they had never been used in this way before, to hang a glass curtain from the top of a multi-storey building or to follow a curved perimeter. Much ingenuity and adjustment to parts was needed to take up differential movements between the glass skin and the reinforced-concrete structure. All of which involved pushing materials and technology – not to mention the manufacturers – to the limit of their abilities.

For all its technological sophistication, much of Foster's work, as he readily points out himself, involves using conventional building materials in a new way – as with the glass wall at Willis Faber & Dumas. In the same fashion, he argues for factory-made buildings on the straightforward grounds that it is easier to ensure quality control and raise performance standards in a factory than on a building site. His work in the developing world is also marked by a notably conservative technological attitude. In their Regional Planning Study for the island of Gomera, in the Canaries (8, 9), the Foster team recommended labour-intensive industries, mud-brick housing and energy from windmills, while the structure for the Televisa Headquarters in Mexico City is no more advanced than reinforced concrete, albeit used in an exceptionally graceful manner.

Chris Abel

Where appropriate, however, Foster frequently steps outside the architect's normal compass of interests to borrow ideas, materials and techniques from other, technologically more advanced, sources such as the aircraft and automobile industries. The emphasis here is on the word 'appropriate'. Foster sees nothing extraordinary in pushing at the boundaries of building technology, if that is what is needed to get the best job done. Architects have always done that, he insists, and rejects the 'High-Tech' label, which has been foisted on his work. On a visit to Florence he wondered, for example, if Brunelleschi's contemporaries called him a 'High-Tech' architect for advancing building technology in the construction of his dome for Florence Cathedral (10).

Technology transfers from advanced industrial sectors, though already evident in early projects such as the Air-Supported Office for Computer Technology, 1969-70, nevertheless play an increasing part in Foster's work from the Sainsbury Centre onwards. As with the interchangeable cladding panels for the Sainsbury Centre, the choice of materials and techniques is usually made in order to achieve maximum performance whilst keeping tooling costs to a minimum. This is an essential consideration given the limited production runs for which Foster typically designs. The research and development costs incurred are generally borne by manufacturers eager to extend their product range and technical experience.

The use of superplastic aluminium for the Sainsbury Centre's cladding panels was one of the first uses of the material in the construction industry and it was chosen for its special properties. Developed for the aircraft industry, the light-weight composite material becomes highly malleable when heated, and can be stretch-formed into rigid shapes using compressed air presses and low-cost tools. The panels may look as though they were stamped out on expensive presses and mass-production lines in accordance with Modernist folklore (the raised surface of the original design is suggestive of the panels on the same Citroën vehicles that inspired Le Corbusier's naming of his 'Maison Citrohan' project) but they were not.

The neoprene jointing system running between the panels is equally ingenious and an archetypal product of Foster's integrated design approach, providing in a single component a weatherproof connection between adjacent panels, a continuous gutter system for roof and walls, and an expansion joint (11, 12). As with all Foster's component designs, the design development process involved

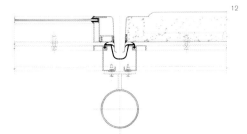

making and testing full-size prototypes. In one such test, a group of panels was bolted together on their aluminium subframe and subjected to a simulated 120-mile-per-hour rainstorm: the panels and jointing system held up splendidly, not leaking a drop, but the test rig was blown over.

The single-span, hangar-like structure of the Sainsbury Centre was the first of a series of advanced structural types connecting Foster with those designers who believe, with Viollet-le-Duc, that 'architecture can only equip itself with new forms if it seeks them in the rigorous application of new structure'.[25] Large-span enclosures of advanced engineering sheltering structurally independent mini-buildings first appear in Foster's work in the Buckminster Fuller-inspired Climatroffice project, then at the Sainsbury Centre, followed by the unbuilt scheme for the International Energy Expo at Knoxville, of 1978 (also done with Fuller), and most recently in the new terminal for Stansted Airport.

Each of these structures took Foster and his team into new areas of precision engineering. For example, in order to allow the cladding panels for the Sainsbury Centre to be interchanged at any point on the exterior, the aluminium subframes had to be fixed to within tolerances of plus or minus 3mm over the full length and breadth of the 133 x 35-metre structure. Precision of this order is a form of technology transfer in itself and is found more often in mechanical engineering than structural engineering.

The prismatic steel structure for the Sainsbury Centre was mostly concealed on the outside by cladding panels and on the inside by automated, light-sensitive, perforated louvres, and was only bared at each end to form impressive 'porticoes'. The reticence did not last. In his more daring experiments, which placed increasing emphasis on the structure's expressive qualities as well as on ever higher performance, Foster and his engineers combined new and old structural forms to create hybrid forms which sometimes defy conventional description.

For example, in the Renault Centre (14) of 1980-82, steel trusses are part-cantilevered, part suspended from slim 'mast' supports and steel cables, but also link together in two directions to act as interlocking, rigid portal frames. The design and manufacture of the structural components entailed a similar hybrid approach, involving both First Machine Age and Computer Age technologies. The behaviour of the structure is so complex that it could not have been designed without the

13

help of computer analysis and simulation, while the spheroidal graphite cast-iron fixings on the structural masts, which anchor the cable stays, were made using sand moulds familiar since the Industrial Revolution. Each structural component was carefully designed with the engineers at Ove Arup & Partners to communicate the task it was made for, as well as to perform in the required manner. The contrast with the smooth, unbroken skin of the Sainsbury Centre could not be greater and the Renault Centre marks the beginning of a new phase of structural expressionism in Foster's work, which can be thought of as almost Gothic or Oriental in quality.

If the Renault Centre is Foster's first unequivocal work of structural expressionism, it also marks a high point in the technological shift, begun at Willis Faber & Dumas and continued at the Sainsbury Centre, from ready-made to custom-made factory components. Almost all the major component systems at Renault were designed and manufactured for the job in hand. As with other projects, materials and techniques were also freely borrowed from outside the building industry: the flexible joint between walls and roof, necessitated by differential movements in the lively structure, is made from the same fabric used for the skirts of hovercraft; while the foam-filled, steel cladding panels, with their unusually fine profile, were made with existing tools used in the manufacture of wall panels for caravans. Despite being custom-made, the use of a small variety of repetitive units and low-cost tools helped to keep total building costs down to the same as those for a standard industrial 'shed'.

All of Foster's previous achievements in factory-made building craft, advanced engineering and structural expressionism were eclipsed, however, by the Hongkong Bank. Foster's earlier tower projects for the Whitney Museum (13) and the Humana Corporation in the US, show simple, monolithic shapes with integrated skins and strutures. The tower for the Whitney Museum, especially, looks something like a vertical Sainsbury Centre, with similar cladding and rounded edges reinforcing the unitary appearance of finite form. The structural concept for the Bank, however, is closer in spirit to the indeterminate 'megastructure' projects of Japanese Metabolists and especially to the projects of Kiyonori Kikutake.[26] Foster even outdoes the Metabolists in flexible structures since, as actually built, their spaces are usually fixed for all time in concrete. The suspended floors of the Bank are also fixed, but the staggered gaps left in one side of the structure to meet daylight regulations can, if circumstances should ever permit, actually be filled in to produce another 30 per cent of useable space. The sturdy maintenance cranes atop each of the steel 'masts' add to the appearance of a structure still in the process of erection.

The urgency of the building programme as well as the restricted site and lack of suitable local industrial capacity necessitated a maximum level of prefabrication, involving manufacturers as far apart as Japan, Europe and the United States in the most complex exercise ever undertaken in factory-made building for a single structure. The fabrication of the unique suspension structure alone set new standards of building craft on a hitherto unheard-of scale. The enormous stresses placed on the steel 'masts' for the eight structural towers, for example, required technologies and welding techniques more in common with the offshore oil production industry – with which the Foster team had previous experience working on projects for prefabricated accommodation units – than with building construction. In appearance, they actually resemble the legs of a North Sea production platform.

Similarly, the concentration of forces in the giant trusses required very exact heavy engineering of a kind not normally associated with building construction at all, but with suspension bridges and with civil engineering projects with large moving parts, such as the Thames Barrier. The spherical bearings used to connect the truss members, for instance, have to cope with extremely high loads – 2,000 tons at level 13 – pulling different ways on a very small area of steel. The tolerances involved in manufacturing the bearings and the solid steel pins that they hold – 0.033mm between bearings and tongue plates, and 0.25mm between pin and bearings – brought forth the sort of perfectionist attitudes and skills from Dorman Long, the British steel fabricators, that one thought belonged to another age. By all accounts, there was a remarkably high degree of personal commitment by the key men on the job. Interestingly, the father of one of the men who directed this job had been responsible for the steelwork of the Bank's 1935 headquarters, also fabricated by Dorman Long.

What was true of the structure was also true of the building's other innovations. Almost all the component systems set new standards of performance and industrialised technique, even where existing products were used. The exposure of the support frames of the Otis escalators and lifts, for example, necessitated

their complete redesign, an approach carried meticulously through to the lift controls, where even the circuit boards are exposed.

Most of the major sub-systems also involved technology transfers of one kind or another, with research and development costs being shared between the manufacturers and the Bank. The removable panels for the computer-type raised floor system (15), for example – developed, like the escalators, from similar ideas used at Willis Faber & Dumas – are made from a lightweight but rigid aluminium honeycomb sandwich material used in the floor panels of Boeing aircraft. With their prominent edge trim, they strongly resemble the traditional Japanese tatami mat and dictate the planning grid in much the same manner. Added together with such other Oriental qualities as the delicate transparency of the skin, contrasted against the bold structure, they produce an impression of a design inspired as much by Eastern as by Western sources.[27]

The Foster team's earlier projects for the offshore oil industry also came in useful in the design of the factory-made service modules. The modules contain the air-handling plant and lavatories for each floor, and are built like shipping containers as rigid boxes, ready to be transported and hoisted into place either side of the main structure – the same aluminium honeycomb material used for the floor panels is also used to clad the service modules. The arrangement not only freed up the internal spaces in the manner of Louis Kahn's articulation of 'served' from 'servant' spaces,[28] but also enabled the 'plug-in' modules to be installed ready for use while the main structure was still going up. The contract was won by a Japanese consortium – not surprising since Japanese industry is the most advanced in the world in the field of prefabricated services. What impressed Foster most was the Japanese attitude towards quality control: shoes were left outside the prototype, engineers entering only in stockinged feet: literally, a 'gloves and socks' operation.

Design of the environmental services also took the Foster team into the new but fast-growing field of 'smart buildings', a technology with far-reaching consequences for the future of responsive forms of architecture.[29] In *Soft Architecture Machines*,[30] Nicholas Negroponte extrapolates from experiments in artificial intelligence to forecast 'intelligent' environments able to comprehend and respond to users' needs on a fully interactive basis. Foster's architecture is firmly set in a similar direction and has been so for many years.

Chris Abel

16

Previous experiments with responsive environmental control systems include the 'tuneable light box' for the Sainsbury Centre. In his 1973 project for an office building at Vestby in Norway, Foster also proposed both a light-sensitive skin and an external tracking-mirror system designed to bring as much of the low winter sun into the building as possible. This 'sunscoop' idea reappears at the Bank in built form (16), directing sunlight into the atrium at the heart of the building. The Bank also incorporates an 'intelligent' environment in the form of a computerised building management system – overseeing everything to do with environmental control from the floor-based air-distribution network to maintenance schedules – that is not only capable of monitoring the performance of the various systems it controls, but also of improving their efficiency.

However, the most important innovations were to come from the design and manufacture of the building's cladding systems. To understand their full significance for the future of industrialised building is to engage in a kind of 'gestalt switch' involving some of the most fundamental assumptions concerning the nature of craft versus machine production.

While generally drawing admiration for Foster's infinite care and attention to detail, the growing proportion of custom-made parts which go to make up Foster's buildings, even before the building of the Bank, has generated considerable confusion amongst architects who still associate industrialised building exclusively with mass production. The confusion is understandable, but it is erroneous.

In the earlier work described above, Foster showed that by careful planning and design it is possible to adapt existing industrialised products, even produce new ones, without getting involved with the expensive, fixed-purpose production lines and special tooling required for mass production, such as in the automobile industry – long the favourite model among industrialised building enthusiasts. The penalty is the reduction in variety, which production runs for single building projects generally necessitate, resulting in a building with a highly uniform character. In effect, while Foster's design approach contradicts the still widespread assumption that industrialisation of building necessitates standardisation among different building projects, it still implies standardisation within any single building project itself.

However, innovations in automated production machinery in the consumer industries mean that – planning grids and other constraints notwithstanding –

architects may soon no longer need to accept even this limitation. Though special purpose mass-production lines still play an important part, their role in the manufacture of consumer goods, including automobiles, has been increasingly displaced over the last quarter of a century by more flexible production machinery, much of it now computer-controlled (19). All of which means that industry is better able to keep up with ever-growing consumer demand for more variety and choice of product.[31]

The revolutionary consequences of this trend towards increasing variety and smaller batch production in industry were spelt out by Stafford Beer in his seminal paper on the 'cybernetic factory' of the future, written in 1962.[32] Based on cybernetic theory and advanced computer science and technology, Beer visualised a sensitive industrial 'organism' capable of responding to the fast-changing needs of a true market-orientated economy, turning out customised products as easily as standard ones on variable, computerised production machinery. By the mid-1960s there were already around 50 versatile industrial robots in use in the West. And at least one adventurous concern, by the name of Molins Machine Company, which has a highly variable product, was turning Beer's Computer Age vision of flexible production lines into reality.[33] Twenty years later the number of 'high-level' robots in use around the world had grown to nearly 23,000,[34] of which – as might unfortunately be expected from past performance – few belonged to the construction industry.[35]

Foster's architecture demonstrates his unique grasp of these fundamental changes in industrialised technology. By refusing to accept conventional building practices, and increasing the level of his demands for high-performance, custom-made products, Foster and his team have led the way in encouraging a notoriously conservative building industry to catch up with other industries in confronting the new technological era, and meeting individual consumer needs and values. Paradoxically, what may have appeared to some architects like craft technique imitating machine production is turning out to be more like machine production imitating craft technique.

If Joseph Paxton's standardised iron structure for the Crystal Palace with its minimal variety of cladding parts still epitomises the concept of factory-made building in the First Machine Age, then the first major building of the Computer

Age is the Hongkong Bank, with its thousands of different cladding parts made with the help of robots and other 'smart' tools of production.

The exposed treatment of the suspension structure furthers the trend towards a richer structural expressionism in Foster's architecture, and the cladding was carefully designed so as not to interfere with that quality. The mast, trusses, suspension rods and cross-bracing all required layers of corrosion protection and fireproofing, which in turn needed some kind of maintenance-free cover. In order that the structure beneath all this should be still expressed as directly as possible, it was necessary for the finished aluminium cladding to follow the complex geometry of the structural members as closely as possible. Changes in the diameter of the columns, corresponding to vertically decreasing structural loads, greatly multiplied the variations, necessitating the design and production of thousands of separate pieces of cladding, with almost as many variations in shape and size (17).

Problems such as these called for a major retooling by Cupples Products, the American firm selected for the job, including the purchase by them of state-of-the-art computer-controlled production machinery. A computerised sheet-metal fabricator was used to cut the intricate and varied patterns for the customised panels (18), while the complex shapes were formed under microprocessor control on flexible hydraulic presses. Two Unimate industrial robots were also purchased and programmed to perform the high-quality, full-penetration welds required on the two-storey aluminium truss mullions supporting the curtain walling, which, like the main structure, have to withstand typhoon wind-loading conditions.

It is at this point that popular beliefs concerning the nature and cost of automated production lines break down. The high cost of conventional, fixed-purpose automated machinery of the sort still used to make engine blocks, for example, can only be justified by producing tens or even hundreds of thousands of identical components. The computerised machinery Cupples acquired also involved a sizeable capital investment but, because of its inherent flexibility, it has almost unlimited capacity for use on other jobs requiring similar manufacturing operations. Initial investment costs do not therefore have to be recouped by producing the maximum possible number of the same component, but can be amortised over a very wide range of different products.

Tecno's production line in Milan for the Nomos furniture range (20) confirms the direction in which the furniture industry as well as the building industry is now headed. Tecno's reputation and experience as a furniture maker is of the highest rank. The Tecno mode of operation, combining the use of modern materials with craft techniques and the most sophisticated computerised production machinery – as well as its highly flexible method of subcontracting work out to a network of specialised firms as necessary – was ideally suited to Foster's need for an innovative manufacturer.

Based on his earlier experiments with furniture design, first for his own offices and then for the Renault Centre, the Nomos range was Foster's first product design aimed specifically at the open market, and it encapsulates much of his design approach (21). Foster himself describes furniture design as 'architecture in miniature', and the similarity between the furniture and the architecture, especially in the case of the Renault Centre, begs comparison with the furniture of other distinguished architect-designers working with industrialised materials.[36] The clear articulation of the different parts of each piece of furniture, and a delight in solving the way they come together, is typical of the furniture by Charles Eames, for example, and he shares the same professional attitude as Foster towards working with industry.[37] The name 'Nomos' also says much about his approach. Taken from the Greek word for law, it also means rhythm, or the beat and measure in music. It is difficult to think of a more appropriate name for the work of an architect who lays so much emphasis on structure and process in the making of things.

Early versions of the adjustable steel and aluminium worktop – the centrepiece of the range – were handcrafted, involving 66 different welds. The Nomos version retains the same essential design, with its main support beam or 'spine', onto which legs and everything else are fixed, but it is made differently. Instead of welding parts together, Tecno devised a unique pressurised plug-in jointing system for the beam and a computerised production line on which to manufacture it. Consisting of four computer-controlled machines, arranged in a circle, each machine performs a different operation on a steel tube, which is fed in at the beginning of the line. The first machine cuts the tube to the required length; the second drills the fixing holes into the beam; the third expands each fixing hole so that it forms a raised edge ready to receive and cover its steel plug; and the fourth forces a plug into each hole at very high pressure. The plug itself has fixing holes into which other components of the table are screwed, so that the number of welds needed to put the table together is reduced to six. Each operation can be reprogrammed to provide as many variations as are needed, enabling Foster and Tecno to offer a considerable number of options within the basic range, making it one of the most versatile furniture systems on the market.

Like the machinery Cupples bought to produce the parts for the Hongkong Bank, the production line at Tecno was purchased initially for the Nomos range. But the machines can be used separately or together just as easily – and are already being so used – to make other products. The same is true of the other robotised and computerised machinery to be found elsewhere on the Tecno shop floor.

Commenting on the contemporary industrial organisation of the 1960s, typified by the fixed-purpose mass-production line, Beer wrote that the only way such corporations could survive was by paying advertisers enormous sums 'to make less mutable an environment to which the [industrial] organism cannot adapt. If the dinosaur can no longer live in the world, the world must be turned into a dinosaur sanctuary.'[38] But as the computerised production lines at Cupples and Tecno demonstrate, that need no longer be the case. Beer's cybernetic factory has come to stay.[39]

In *The Illusion of Technique*,[40] William Barrett defines a machine as 'an embodied decision procedure. By going through a finite and unvarying number of steps it arrives invariably, so long as it is not defective, at a definite result.' Barrett warns of the danger of applying the same kind of restricted operational logic to complex human issues, and points to the totalitarian society described in B F Skinner's novel *Walden Two*[41] as an ominous example of deterministic ways of thinking.

Similar warnings have been regularly sounded by architectural writers, from William Morris' nostalgic rejection of industrialised society as a whole,[42] down to David Watkin's critique of historical determinism in architecture.[43]

History justifies the warnings, but they are founded on a definition of 'machine' which has hardly changed since those two arch 'metaphysicians of mechanism', René Descartes and Isaac Newton, used the machine model to try to explain the workings of the universe.[44] That definition is now outdated, and if mechanical metaphors have shaped much of human thought in the past it is also

becoming increasingly clear that the word 'machine' in the Computer Age no longer means what it used to. It is therefore reasonable to expect corresponding adjustments in language and thought, no less in architecture than in other spheres of human endeavour.

Understandably, William Morris and his followers in the Arts and Crafts Movement saw nothing in industrialisation but 'hard' machines, rigid mass-production lines, human alienation and a block to artistic expression. What they could not see was that industrialisation would not always have to mean such things. Neither is it necessary to subscribe to any mystical *Zeitgeist* in order to recognise the impact of technological change on society, or to want to get the most out of the available materials and tools of modern industry, as Foster does. Failure to do so would mean a tragic loss of opportunity to take advantage of the new technology to create a more responsive architecture.

Unlike the machine models of the First Machine Age – but like the computers that are increasingly used in their design, manufacture and day-to-day operation – Foster's architectural 'machines' are designed for interactive use. They might also be called 'soft machines', not just for their adaptability or 'smart' environmental control systems but because they exhibit a responsive character in the way they are made. Anything but the stamped-out replicas of early Modernist ambition, they look like the finely crafted, custom-made machines they are. As such they resolve some long-standing architectural conflicts of aims.

The Bauhaus failed to deliver the 'new kind of collaborator for industry and the crafts' promised by Gropius,[45] because neither he nor any of his colleagues could bridge the gulf between the creative and craftsman-like attitudes and skills taught in the Bauhaus workshops, and the technological and commercial realities of industrial production. Foster's work demonstrates that the gap between the art and craft of architecture and the machinery of industry can be bridged after all, but

Chris Abel

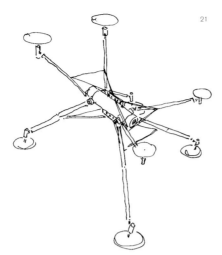

only by dispensing with orthodox Modernist dogma on standardisation. And that goes for even conventional production machinery.

With the general introduction into the building industry of Beer's cybernetic factory, the gap promises to be reduced still further, to the point where it may become meaningless.[46] As Foster puts it: 'The concept of a new era of craftsman-ship – "handmade by robots" – opens up an exciting prospect in which technology can design out standardisation and produce richly customised one-offs.'[47]

There was always more than a touch of hypocrisy in the way the early Modernists approached the industries they held up as the future providers of homes for the common man. It was alright to symbolise the machine in stucco, but actually getting down to the factory to work with the people who really knew what machines were all about was another matter. For all Foster's achievements in improving the quality of the workplace in his buildings, breaking down the profes-sional and class barriers between the architect's studio and the factory shop floor to bring architecture into the new Machine Age may turn out to be his most sig-nificant social accomplishment.

'Le Corbusier and Louis Kahn are important influences in Foster's development, and if he is not original in terms of the theory by which he operates, he is certainly unique in the degree to which he subjects the ideal object to circumstantial stress and distortion.'

Robert Maxwell

In the realist tradition of writing, 'a novel will be deemed successful if the reader is persuaded that the picture is not the writer's composition but life itself, making its appearance on its own authority'[1] In exactly this sense Norman Foster's version of functionalism is realist in intention, aiming to present a view of design in which the solution has emerged from the raw material of circumstance. To this end he labours indefatigably to sift the raw material of circumstance in search of certain advantages by which space and structure may be defined in relation to stated needs and goals. The needs and goals stated are generally those of the client; those of the architect are subsumed and have to be inferred from the work as a whole.

The extreme formal precision of Foster's output makes it clear that this emphasis on the programme is counterbalanced by some principles of design that derive more from the ideal than the circumstantial. The decisions about exactly which circumstances will contribute to the final solution remain hidden within the operational mysteries of the office. At the same time, there is no reason to doubt the architect's good faith, nor his dedication to the hard work of programme analysis, nor his sensitivity to social aspects of architecture. If this sensitivity has a spatial dimension, that after all is the architect's expertise, his professional contribution.

For example, in his design for a Special Care Unit in Hackney, 1970-72, for children with cerebral palsy, his analysis of needs focused on the incontinence of the children, for which the remoteness of standard toilets was little help. He then produced an unusual layout where the core of toilets, divided only by low screens, is more readily accessible, and allows for both supervision and privacy.

Along with improved functional efficiency comes a benefit in terms of a sense of spatial continuity and communal lightness. The 'solution' is not typologically unique, but partakes of a general approach to the fitting-out of activities derived from Miesian and Corbusian concepts of the free plan. It is analogous to the use of shoulder-height dividers to define architects' workstations in the 'office landscape', providing a carefully measured mixture of individual privacy and competitive continuity.

One can speak, then, of a constant search for a formal order that is presumed to be initially hidden within the raw material of the programme. One must also be allowed to speak of a search, within recognisable formal solutions, for certain variations and transformations that will sharpen these forms with new programmatic life. This dialectical relationship is not essentially different from that identified by Le

Corbusier in his famous essay 'In Defence of Architecture'. Nor is it very different from the dialectic expounded by Louis Kahn as the conflict between the will-to-form of an object and its embodiment through a process of design that adapts to circumstance.

Le Corbusier and Louis Kahn are important influences in Foster's development, and if he is not original in terms of the theory by which he operates, he is certainly unique in the degree to which he subjects the ideal object to circumstantial stress and distortion. Yet this never reduces the object to a mere accessory to the programme; as the product of a well-defined process, it always radiates an intensity and a self-awareness that speaks of aesthetic closure and stylistic measure. It is necessary therefore to go a little further in attempting to define the ideal qualities that he pursues through his designs.

Within the tradition of Modernism in which Foster has placed himself, there is clearly to be found the retention of a certain machine aesthetic. This is no longer the somewhat abstracted aesthetic of the heroic Modern period but more a latter-day imitation of machines, an imagery of some literalness which can also be, on occasion, quite surreal. In his most extravagant building to date, the Hongkong and Shanghai Bank, there are intimations of the bridge, the engineer's shed, the space rocket. In probably his least extravagant building, the Air-Supported Office, 1969-70, there are intimations of the airship. Foster has repeatedly stressed the need to seek technological means outside of the standard building tradition, with its reliance on wet trades and weight, and this search has led in the direction of lightweight materials and flight technology.

If the oil rig is the paradigm of the braced platform, the helicopter is the paradigm of power in reserve. But perhaps most attractive is the glider, the paradigm of minimal power, of beauty produced by circumstance (wind currents, clouds). This image is potent in Foster, insofar as it suggests an energy efficiency derived entirely from shape and structure. It is significant that Foster's longest-standing partner, Loren Butt, is an engineer specialising in energy. The ideal of energy utilisation is the principle of elegance, as it is the ideal of mathematical proof, and it is *elegance* of the object that Foster pursues in the aesthetic dimension. For this reason the play of circumstance is an essential part of Foster's method, and Banham is correct in stressing in his work the ideal of 'appropriate technology' rather than any doctrinaire addiction to the attractions of 'High-Tech'.[2] No Foster building can be adequately explained without regard to the circumstantial, whether this be located in the programme as such, or in the detail accounting whereby the programme is represented in form.

We come now to the question of the urban context. Clearly the physical context of a Foster building is part of its circumstantial genesis, and also dialectically of its circumstantial aura, and the definition of appropriate technology cannot proceed without taking into account the whole idea of appropriateness to the site. As a maker of elegant objects, which draw at least part of their unexpectedness from some internal principle of organisation, Foster has a peculiar responsibility in dealing with the external pressures present in the urban context, the more so as these are as much social as physical, and he has always presented himself as sensitive to social factors.

This is almost a novel question, since the greater part of Foster's work to date has been on isolated or 'greenfield' sites. But with his office building for Willis Faber & Dumas, 1971-75, we come squarely up against the urban context.

The *Architectural Review*, in publishing a review of this building,[3] was concerned that it introduced a negative factor into the townscape, since its entirely glazed walls offer no incident of scale or character, but blankly reflect the surrounding buildings in a fractured, surrealist manner. What would happen, the *Review* asked, if the adjoining buildings in turn were replaced by similar reflecting glass objects? It is true that Willis Faber & Dumas is disconcerting in that its appearance fluctuates between two contradictory extremes: when the internal lighting is stronger than the outside light level, it displays its structure as a three-storey building; at other times the glass wall becomes a reflecting barrier, as impregnable as granite.

However, before dismissing it as entirely negative to the townscape, it is worth asking what it does, if anything, in recognition of its urban setting. The positive aspects may be summarised as follows: the building reinforces the given street pattern; in avoiding the conventional organisation into 'podium' and 'tower', it conforms to the planners' preference for a three-storey envelope (a partial fourth storey is virtually invisible from the street); and the face towards the old Unitarian Church, and its garden setting, is classically orthogonal in disposition, creating a pleasant civic square on the side facing the medieval town. Since on the opposite side, the medieval street pattern no longer holds, and a loose suburban pattern takes over, the offence offered by the glass fortress is hardly egregious. Nevertheless, it is startling to come upon, and it embodies, in a novel form, the conflict between the internal world of the

client and user, and the external world of citizen and shared convention. Foster is in the habit of seeking advantage for his client, and he enjoys rejecting conventional wisdom, so we shall expect to find other instances of this conflict.

The BBC Radio Centre project, 1982-85, is such an instance. The glazed mall which bisects it diagonally is positioned to provide a pedestrian link between the north-east corner of Cavendish Square and the bend in Regent Street at Langham Place, doubly articulated at this point by the curved front of the old BBC building and the circular portico of John Nash's church (1, 2). The internal system of office layout is made orthogonal to this mall, with the advantage that this produces considerable variation of depth within the envelope, giving cross-axes of different lengths. At the perimeter, just as at Willis Faber & Dumas, a secondary columnar system parallel to the street elevations sews the edge to the street pattern. The use of a diagonal geometry is only apparent at the points where the transverse axes meet the periphery with fire stair exits. The internal layout has thus been conceived in order to make sense of the pedestrian flow through the building, and to orient the building as a whole towards the civic register of Cavendish Square, All Souls' Church, and the 'parent' building.

It is characteristic of Foster that the civic dimension should be recognised in terms of pedestrian flow, a factor both social and operational but also physical and measurable. What is absent is the use of figuration by means of traditional architectural motifs that gesture towards the civic context as a historical continuum. There is no trace here of the Post-Modernism of facades, and this is clearly a point of honour with the architect, an expression of his ideological commitment to functionalism. This is not to say that we are dealing here with an architecture of degree zero, that the objects produced are devoid of ideological stance and are in some sense objective correlates of the programme. As we have seen, the programme is as much penetrated by a selective sensibility as are the formal means adopted. The approach encompasses both an apparently objective web of circumstance, and a circumstantial aura that expresses contingency as an absolute value. For this reason, the resulting architecture is not manifestly 'civic', even in the reduced sense allowed by Giorgio Grassi, but remains in some way hostile to the historical context and reformative towards it.

The conflict between internal programme and civic context is perhaps at its most poignant in the case of the *médiathèque* at Nîmes (3, 4). The programme has all the potential provocation of a populist demonstration, a provincial Centre Pompidou, but

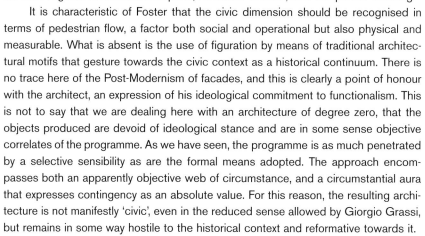

Robert Maxwell

THERE IS NO
'LANGHAM
PLAZE' - NASH
HAD A GARDEN
HERE -

COMPARE
THE
AGRESSION
OF THIS
CORNER
WITH
THE
'INVITATION'
OF
ALL SOULS !

NOTE HOW THE LEVEL
CHANGE LIFTS YOU
ABOVE THE TRAFFIC
- VISUALLY BUT ALSO
SMELLS - A BETTER
PROSPECT THAN
PAVEMENT LEVEL.

NOTE HOW THE
PERISTYLE IS
INVITING - A PUBLIC
SPACE - A SYMPATHETIC
GESTURE - PEOPLE SIT
ON THE STEPS EVEN
IN THE COLDEST
WEATHER !

NF

it is pointed irrevocably towards the flank of the Maison Carrée, the most perfect relic of antiquity in France. All of Foster's studies for this commission reflect a certain agony in dealing with the tension between these polar references. It is not surprising that one senses here the shadow of Louis Kahn, who in his own work made a change of commitment between the claims of the future and those of the past.

In Foster, the issue of spatial direction, of longitudinal frontality, is tied up with the concept of the industrial shed. The shed is one of the recognisable types in his repertoire, since it embodies the principle of serial construction with regular structural elements, as first demonstrated in the Crystal Palace. The shed in its pure linearity is the prototype for the Modern Art Glass building, 1972-73, and the Sainsbury Centre, 1974-78, and it reappears in other projects, most surprisingly perhaps, in the high-rise format of the Hongkong and Shanghai Bank, 1979-86. While the form is generated from the need to reconcile serial structure with the rational disposition of the service elements, it does have the inevitable consequence of producing directed space, and this quality of space appears to be actively sought and enjoyed for its own sake.

At the Sainsbury Centre, the ends of this spatial flow are marked by external recesses, which have the feeling of being porticoes, even in the absence of formal entrances. One can make a direct comparison between the 'portico' at the outer end of the Sainsbury Centre and the evident portico at the outer end of the Palazzo dei Congressi at EUR. Both have similar spatial properties, and both recognise the technological counter-motive in their lattice-work, in the main structure in the former, in the window mullions in the latter. There is a further irony in this comparison because Libera was forced to insert an order of giant Tuscan columns in his portico (in the corresponding one at the other end of the building), whereas at Nîmes, Foster was narrowly able to avoid incorporating an array of Classical columns surviving from the old Municipal Theatre.

In any event, the overhang of the roof at the outer end facing the Maison Carrée has all the qualities of a civic portico, if not a Classical one. Moreover, as we can see from the four intermediate steps by which the design evolved, the architect was not only concerned with his civic duty towards the monument, but with the need to recognise also the bias of the civic space as determined by the frontality of the Maison Carrée. This is reflected variously in the use of splayed sides, and in the off-centre placement of the glazed atrium which extends back through the space. A further

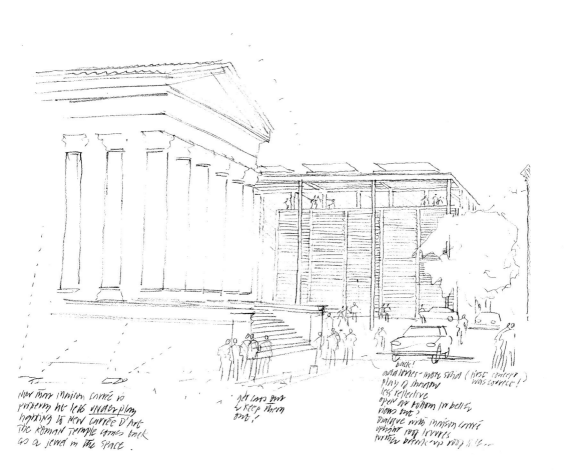

Now from Maison Carré to perform the less vivid plan heading to New Carrée D'Art The Roman Temple comes back as a jewel in the space.

get cars out & keep them out!

back!
add lines - more solid (first concept was correct!)
play of shadow
less reflective
open air bottom in belly, views out,
balance with Maison Carré
upright roof louvres
twisted break-up roof etc...

5

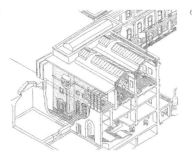
6

reflection of the civic role of the building is evident in the adoption of a monumental form in the serial staircase, which joins the main public floors and confirms the directionality of the space. This is far removed from the mechanical aspect of the external escalator at Centre Pompidou. The *médiathèque* thus reveals in Foster a sensibility towards civic convention, even if his method constrains his response.

Urban design is not a major factor in the case of the additions to Burlington House for the Royal Academy (5, 6), since the effect on external space is minimal, although the changes will allow the public to use a new entrance courtyard and appreciate an unfamiliar aspect of the building. What strikes one about these proposals is the efficiency and discretion with which the new elements have been incorporated, while allowing the existing features, such as the main monumental staircase, to be better enjoyed.

With the small Thames-side development at Chelsea Reach (9), there is a delicate balance struck between the symmetry of the three elements of the plan and the asymmetrical dominance of the higher volume alongside the river. This plan enables us to see the essential rationalism within Foster's sometimes sensational images.

In the case of the building for the Royal Thames Yacht Club, in Knightsbridge, the rationality is compromised by the sensational accent placed on the two elevators, brought forward and exposed outside the main entrance, although approached in use from within – a play reminiscent of the escalators at Pompidou, similarly displayed on the outside, but approached from within. In such cases one senses the architect's need to balance discretion with physical vigour, like reasserting youth against age. But one may certainly question whether the exhibition of moving parts is not already falling into the category of cliché. In this case it appears to diminish unfairly the status of the small Neo-Classical building standing on the left of the entrance.

The scheme for Paternoster Square (7, 8, 10) has something in common with the BBC Radio Centre, in the way that office space is broken down and differentiated by the use of toplit access elements. Since the site is irregular anyway, there were no inhibitions against allowing these channels to run north-south, in varying lengths, reinforcing a directionality towards the public space around St Paul's Cathedral, and incidentally towards the River Thames, Europe and the sun. The south face of the new complex would clearly be a place of public amenity, with a certain democratic aspect as each section of offices reaches its place on the barrier facing the Cathedral. The

Robert Maxwell

9

building height is moderated, as with Willis Faber & Dumas, and the result is more like a kind of kasbah than the mishmash of standard office buildings that is due to be replaced on this site.

Yet one may be forgiven for questioning the adequacy of such an organisationally systematic complex as a setting for the City of London's greatest monument. St Paul's itself is, in Foster's terms, a dishonest building, since its entire upper storey has no other function than to screen the essentially Gothic organisation of the nave and aisles. The honesty in which the Modern architect takes such pride, his constant efforts to be transparent towards the programme, seem in this context to be trivial and somewhat puerile. The selection of what is to be given significance remains hidden and doubtful. The approach allows an organisational order, certainly, but is organisation a sufficient principle of art, as Hannes Meyer proposed? It is interesting that among Foster's analytical sketches there is one that shows some diversity of character among the pieces, suggesting that the layout is a masterplan or structure plan, capable of providing 'a basis for individual identities and separate design responsibilities'.

In that admission there is a whole world of adjustment still to be made. It expresses a dissatisfaction with the implied uniformity of corporate offices, but it also limits the scope of individual identity to what is consonant with the dominance of an organisational system. It is the pressures of the functional tradition, with its emphasis on transparency towards the programme, which limits the accommodation with the flow of history and civic convention. Yet, such is the eagerness with which others have all too readily embraced appearance, dissimulation and accommodation that our impatience with Norman Foster is mixed with gratitude.

10

'Could airport design recapture the romance of *Casablanca*? Foster, a keen flyer, believed it could.'

Jonathan Glancey

The new terminal at Stansted Airport opens for business next Tuesday. From then on 8 million passengers a year will pass through, rushing to catch cheap flights to the sun or nervously tiptoeing into the long and intimidating 'green channel' customs hall, the longest yet built. As they do so, how many will ponder the design of what must be the most logical and best-looking airport terminal yet built in Britain?

You cannot blame people if they are dismissive of airport design. Few post-war airport buildings this side of the Atlantic have been works of architecture. At best, they have been highly serviced sheds that have grown in piecemeal fashion in response to the inexorable increase of air traffic.

As a result, air terminals are among the most confusing of public buildings. Stansted, however, is one of the simplest and least demanding. Its inner workings are all but invisible to passengers. While not self-effacing, the new terminal has been designed to be as easy to use as possible, the antithesis of the typical labyrinthine modern airport that demands stamina, patience and cat-like cunning from passengers if they mean to board a plane.

In recent examples, such as Gatwick North, the logic of the building guides you into garish shopping malls with their gewgaws and burgers. Having escaped from the shops, you struggle under the glare of fluorescent lights shining with all the energy Sizewell B can muster, under low, suspended ceilings, across acres of jazzily dancing patterned carpets, accompanied by a horde of baffling signs. Finally, without having glimpsed so much as a tailplane, nose cone or undercarriage, you are herded into the workaday, open-plan, office-style interior of an anonymous airliner.

When Norman Foster was asked to design the new terminal at Stansted, 30 miles north-east of London, he started from first principles. Could a modern airport building achieve the compelling simplicity of a tent, a weighing scale and a short walk across tarmac to a piston-engine biplane? Could airport design recapture the romance of *Casablanca*? Foster, a keen flyer, believed it could.

Stansted stands in a bleak, windswept and gently rolling stretch of Essex countryside. Foster's building is about twice the size of Lord's Cricket Ground, yet slips quietly into its setting. On a cloudy or misty day the silver and grey, steel and glass building is almost invisible. But it is not hard to find. Network SouthEast trains from London's Liverpool Street hum into its vast undercroft (1). Ramps, lifts and escalators take passengers up one floor to the check-in desks. Taxis and cars,

meanwhile, drop passengers off at check-in level. Cars and coaches park down-hill and out of sight, surrounded by newly planted poplars, silver willows, silver birches and clipped hornbeam hedges.

Close up, the exterior of the building is imposing: the best-looking tin shed you have ever seen. The interior is like the underside of some giant metallic sun-shade or umbrella. From almost any point inside the building you can see all four walls and all four corners of the roof. You are unlikely to get lost.

If you walk in a straight line from the entrance, you will come to the check-in desks, security, passport control, departure lounge and transit to the satellite to which your plane is attached. At no point are you misdirected from your waiting plane. So much so that you can see the tailplanes of the aircraft as soon as you enter the terminal. And, because of this, signs are few and far between.

'The best sign system', says Foster, 'is no sign system. The ideal is an envi-ronment where people can actually see what they need without the need for signs.' Arriving passengers will find this true. The path from satellite and transit through passport control, baggage reclaim and the Gulag-style, 236-foot customs hall to trains, coaches, cars and taxis is obvious and direct. The only large signs are blue plastic pictograms designed to draw your attention to the lavatories. Gone are the usual police-black-on-yellow signs, invisible to anyone without twenty-twenty vision.

Whether arriving or departing, passengers move through the building under the airiest roof this side of London Zoo's Snowdon Aviary. This giant umbrella, 50 feet high, is supported by 36 tree-like columns (2) spaced at 120-foot intervals. Each houses all the heating, lighting and air conditioning the building needs, as well as information for passengers (including large analogue clocks: Foster is rightly suspicious of digital clocks that convey no sense of passing time).

For the first time in a modern airport building the roof is clutter-free: no sus-pended ceiling, fluorescent lights or mysterious, dust-gathering ducts, tubes and pipes. Nothing distracts from the purity of the roof's design and from its principal job of holding the Essex weather at bay. In fact, the roof does more than keep the rain out. It also lets in light from four triangular windows set into the top of each of the 121 lightweight domes. This obviates the need for artificial lighting during the day: sunlight alone brightens the vast under-roof space, while at night the under-side of the roof glows from lamps shining, glare-free, from the building's columns.

Jonathan Glancey

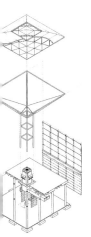

The only unpleasant light is that which shines from the inevitable airport shops (3). Stansted might be the model of a logical airport building, but it cannot escape our insatiable lust for trinkets. After heated debate, architects and client agreed on a compromise. The shops have been housed in custom-made cabins plugged into the floor and shrouded neatly by walls and roofs designed by Foster Associates. By placing the shopping 'street' across the main avenues of arriving and departing passengers, it is just possible to ignore them altogether and travel light. However, despite the best efforts of Norman Foster, Spencer de Grey, his project architect, and Winston Shu, architect in charge of the terminal's interior, the shops are as daft and as patronising as ever. Here is a 'Casey Jones' burger joint. Casey was the American locomotive engineer who took the throttle of the Cannonball Express; yet, here he is popping up to sell burgers in an English airport. They might at least have changed his name to Biggles.

The shops reach their climax in a court in the centre of the terminal, with more themed and graphically packaged eateries. These are only partially redeemed by Brian Clarke's impressive stained-glass murals and illuminated stained-glass tower.

If, during a prolonged delay, you start wondering where all the heavy-duty equipment is (none is on show) you might be interested to know that it lurks below in a vast undercroft that shelters the British Rail station as well as the baggage-handling system. By hiding away the mechanical organs of the building, the architects have assured us that when the building is in everyday use, its great public floor will be largely free of maintenance staff poking their heads into the recesses of suspended ceilings while mysterious fluids drip onto the fitted carpet.

Although they diminish the integrity of the building, shops and fitted carpets (do you expect carpets at Paddington Station?) cannot in the end detract from Stansted's functional elegance. It is the first of a new generation of high-quality, energy-efficient British public buildings (and the first public building designed by Foster Associates).

When you dive through the clouds in your charter jet and spot this silver machine, you will have no doubt that air travel has, for the first time in years, been rewarded with its own special breed of architecture. At the very least, Norman Foster's Stansted will take the strain out of the irksome trek through the ramshackle shopping malls that currently pose as airport buildings.

4>

'If St Paul's has the theatricality of a Rubens, then Foster's work has the dispassion of a Dutch landscape.'

Rowan Moore

Christopher Wren, as is well known, is buried beneath the dome of St Paul's. When the time comes (one hopes, a distant one) to inter Norman Foster, Stansted Airport, his greatest monument in this country, will offer no such obvious place of rest. This is not only because the crypt of Stansted is a flurry of trains, cars, coaches and air conditioning, but also because it reflects the contrast between processional cathedral and the dispersive, centreless airport.

Sir Christopher and Sir Norman are each the most esteemed architects of their generation. Are their most imposing buildings informed by the same eternal verities, or at least by some common Englishness? The bracing and perhaps illuminating truth is that the two buildings could hardly be more different.

Some differences are obvious. One building is secular, and the other religious; one is made of steel and the other of stone; one grows out of a densely inhabited city, and the other occupies a slight rise in a flat and largely empty landscape. Other differences grow from these simple facts. At St Paul's, structure, light, materials and detail are orchestrated into the hierarchical progression from portico to dome and from street to sky. The cross-section reveals a continuous tapering and thinning of the massive masonry as it rises from the ground, and the detail progresses from the naturalistic carving and almost domestic window surrounds at street level to the idealised forms of the skyline. Wren was happy to resort to illusion to sustain the representational order of his cathedral: to give his dome due prominence over London he gave it an exterior much higher than its interior, and he erected dummy walls to conceal the structure supporting the nave. These deceptions have been offending purists ever since.

At an airport, where the ritual of religious service gives way to the Brownian motion of travellers, such hierarchies would be senseless. Airports are not finite, privileged spaces, but immense junction boxes, places where the tissues of transport momentarily intersect. It is impossible to say where the building ends, and at what point it has merged with flight.

Foster does not attempt to structure all this flux into any rhetorical or illusionistic order. Indeed, his statements on Stansted dwell on the need to minimise physical and visual interference, so as to allow for change and to merge with the overwhelmingly horizontal landscape in which it stands. 'The form and external appearance of the terminal are designed to have an unassertive and low profile,' say

Foster Associates: one imagines that this was not Wren's intention in designing St Paul's. Stansted builds up to no climax, and the plan of the building is the same regular grid of column and dome at the periphery as at the centre. Where the dome of St Paul's is the Cathedral's culmination, the 121 shallow domes of Stansted Airport give equal status to the entire enclosure.

This does not mean that the Airport is merely neutral. Rather it achieves coherence through the consistency and clarity of its structural logic. It is a conceptual as much as a perceptual order, achieved by simplification, and by allowing the innate qualities of the building's elements to speak for themselves. The light at Stansted, by day and night, is well considered, but it aims at no effect, and the lightweight steel superstructure and the concrete base are simply juxtaposed, with no attempt to manipulate the progression from one to the other. If St Paul's has the theatricality of a Rubens, then Foster's work has the dispassion of a Dutch landscape.

Such consistency is easier to achieve in a field in Essex than in the centre of an ancient city, on a site loaded with associations, and when designing a building burdened with the political and religious aspirations of a nation. Wren's Great Model design is certainly less compromised than the finished building, and was preferred (it seems) by both Wren himself and by successive generations of architectural historians. Like Wren's post-fire street plan for London, it is one of the great might-have-beens of British architecture but, like the London plan, it had to give way to more mundane considerations. While the street plan conflicted with patterns of private land ownership, the over-centralised Great Model took too little account of the liturgical patterns of Anglican worship.

St Paul's was also a product of a lengthy gestation and birth. It is ten years since Foster was first consulted on Stansted and four since construction began, but Wren's involvement with St Paul's began before the Great Fire of London and continued virtually until his death, over 50 years later. The design of the dome and west tower were not finalised until construction of the nave was well advanced, and some details, such as the bathetic balustrade along the skyline and Thornhill's illusionistic painting inside the dome, were made against the architect's wishes by a younger generation of know-alls. Such continuous change would be impossible in a machine-made structure like Stansted, where the building is conceived in advance of construction.

Rowan Moore

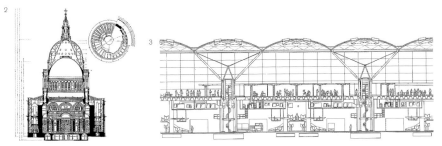

These factors combine to militate against conceptual purity in the Cathedral and against complexity in the Airport. As a result the Airport (perhaps paradoxically) attains an architectural ideal more readily than the Cathedral, but this is as much a reflection of the two architects' personalities as of their circumstances. Although both are structurally inventive, Wren's ambitions were more complex, and he was always prepared to sacrifice consistency in order to remain within the restraints of the Orders, or to satisfy the demands of his historical imagery. Were it possible, it would be hard to imagine a fruitful dialogue between Foster and Wren, since Wren would be likely to dwell on the subjects of his writing, which include Noah's Ark and Solomon's Temple, while Sir Norman might discuss optimum passenger convenience and internal flexibility.

Foster, like Wren before him, pursues a non-architectural interest with enthusiasm. Foster likes to fly helicopters and light aeroplanes, which is presumably why Stansted is among the most convincing of his creations. In this comparison you might expect the pilot to be the pragmatist and the astronomer the speculator, except that modern aviation is rather more abstract and harder to visualise than seventeenth-century science. In volume 3 of the official record of Foster's work, he illustrates his love of flying with the navigational diagrams he uses on a particular flight to Germany. These images have a gnomic beauty, but they are baffling to the layman. Wren's speculations, by contrast, such as his design for a weather clock, have a toy-like immediacy, and are as symmetrical and Classical as his buildings. Like his architecture, his science expresses itself readily in visual imagery, whereas Foster's buildings have some of the inscrutability of his flight-path diagrams.

Of course, both architects can be said to belong to the same Western tradition. Both are in some sense Classical. The hypostyle hall, of which Stansted is a modern incarnation, has a venerable tradition, and Foster refers to his columns as 'trees', a metaphor that goes back to ancient Egypt. Wren's Classicism is less generalised, and refers to models in antiquity and the Renaissance, in particular St Peter's and Bramante's Tempietto. Both architects modify these traditions in a characteristically English way, tempering the idealism of foreign influences with an enabling pragmatism.

The main difference is that in Foster's case these influences are Buckminster Fuller and Mies van der Rohe, not Bramante and Vitruvius. The light, symmetrical

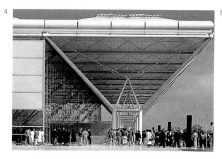

pavilion on a solid base recalls Mies' National Gallery of Berlin, and the idea of a single roof enclosing many functions goes back to Fuller's much-drawn but little-built geodesic domes.

Stansted Airport and St Paul's are brought together by the secular quality of modern cathedrals, and by the aura of worship that surrounds technology. Now that churches are used more by tourists than by worshippers they feel very like airports, while the extreme regularity and perfection of a structure like Stansted gives it the air of a temple.

But these are only very general similarities, and the fascination of the two buildings lies more in their differences, which are characteristic of the time as well as the individuals who produced them. The cathedral was, curiously, an even rarer commission in seventeenth-century England than in twentieth-century England, with only St Paul's to set against Coventry and the two at Liverpool: but the airport may fairly be called an archetypal building of the present. This has not stopped most airports being little more than very large and very complicated bus shelters, but Stansted is part of a growing number of projects that celebrate this central part of modern life. The airiness of the interior evokes the ideal, if not the actual experience of flying. Its structure, like that of aeroplanes, is of a minimal lightness.

Each building is not only of its time, but unimaginable in any other. It would be no more possible to build St Paul's now than it would have been to build Stansted after the Restoration. We lack the masons, the carvers and the metalworkers, and any building so dominating and so unfamiliar would be howled down by planners and conservationists. Where Wren assumed that the best stage for an architect was the centre of a great city, our most confident productions, like Stansted, are reserved for anonymous tracts of landscape.

One the product of a centralised, the other of a decentred world, St Paul's and Stansted are both compelling and moving buildings. This is not because they both rework the same ancient formula, but because they respond, with intelligence, passion and genuine originality, to the unrepeatable and unprecedented conditions of their respective periods. The hierarchy and symmetry of St Paul's recall the human figure, while Stansted has the more abstract structural logic of a crystal or a molecule, and, like these natural phenomena, the works of Foster and of Wren intrigue because they are so unalike.

Rowan Moore

6

7

'Asked years later why he had chosen the then unknown Foster Associates for the Millwall project, Fred Olsen gave a reply that Norman Foste still quotes with pride: they asked the right questions.'

Martin Pawley

They swore it would never work. But it did. Conclusive proof that the most intractable managerial problems can have architectural solutions, the Fred Olsen complex changed the way a company operated.

Even the fastest building methods are slow compared to the unpredictable movements of the economy, and commissioning a new building can be full of pitfalls. The benefits of successful collaboration between architecture and business, however, can be considerable. A classic but little-known example is Foster Associates' work for the Fred Olsen shipping line at Millwall Dock between 1968 and 1970. Now long-since demolished, following the closure of the London Docks and removal of Olsen's operations to Tilbury, the two buildings that resulted went on to enjoy a second life as the first headquarters of the London Docklands Development Corporation.

When approached by Olsen, Foster Associates was one-half of a dissolved partnership operating from a Hampstead flat. Both Norman and Wendy had worked with Richard Rogers on the design of a new factory in Swindon called Reliance Controls. This building had excited considerable interest, partly because its design was elegantly and uncompromisingly modern, but also because it had been com- pleted in less than a year, was designed to expand to four times its size without any disruption to production, and, most important of all, embodied a number of revolu- tionary management ideas. In effect, Reliance Controls was one single 3,200- square-metre space with a single entrance for both management and workers, a shared canteen, and open-plan offices separated from the central production space only by glazed partitions.

Labour relations at that time in the Port of London were notorious. On his first visit to Millwall Dock, Norman Foster found the accommodation for dockworkers to be primitive and barbaric. There were racially segregated lavatories, no permanent canteen facilities and only huts for shelter. Foster Associates asked for time to study the entire Olsen operation in Millwall and, after a swift but penetrating analysis, pro- posed an architectural solution to the labour relations issue and other problems.

Foster's design solution enabled the company to segregate passenger and cargo operations and centralise its administration and labour force in a new, strategi- cally located amenity building erected to unprecedented standards of comfort. Headed by Fred Olsen himself, the Norwegian management reacted favourably to the plans; Olsen's London people initially opposed them. As Foster recalled years

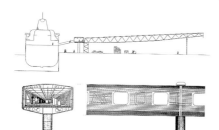

later: 'In the end we were allowed to proceed with the project very much against their will. How could we possibly have dockers in the same building as management? They were dirty, they swore. The secretaries would walk out. It was unthinkable.'

Unthinkable or not, Foster Associates completed the design and construction of the new facilities in little over a year. One element was a simple raised corrugated steel tubular structure called the Passenger Terminal. This passed over the quayside to enable passengers to enter and leave the Olsen ships from deck level with their baggage travelling by conveyor beside them, clearing the quayside itself for cargo operations (1). Though barely a building at all in the conventional sense, this adroit structure simultaneously revolutionised one part of dock operations and facilitated the construction of a two-storey amenity centre, a 2,500-square-metre, glass-clad, air-conditioned building demonstrating an elegance and refinement unprecedented in dock areas. Located on the quayside between two vast transit sheds in what had been a 27-metre-wide firebreak, it provided large clear-spanning areas on two floors behind front and back mirror-glass facades using an advanced American neoprene glazing system (3).

Internally the building provided new facilities at quay level – principally lockers, lavatories, washing and storage areas for up to 240 dockers, as well as a full-scale restaurant and relaxation area (2). The first floor consisted of one 47 x 27-metre deep-plan open office space for the 60-strong managerial and administrative staff. Both ground and first-floor accommodation were superbly detailed with all services concealed in the roof zone and complementary carpet, ceiling and furniture colouring to provide a purposeful but civilised and calming environment.

The success of the Millwall project was extraordinary. It was right on cost and right on schedule. The operation of Olsen ships was simplified and speeded up; the company's labour relations set new standards for the industry. Olsen decided to commission more work from Foster Associates, but changes in the shipping industry prevented the completion of all but a Regent Street travel centre.

Asked years later why he had chosen the then unknown Foster Associates for the Millwall project, Fred Olsen gave a reply that Norman Foster still quotes with pride: 'They asked the right questions.'

Martin Pawley

'I remember … a client asking me what I thought his damp-proof membrane was made of and finding it was the *Daily Ma*, painted black; unplanned-for springs of water bursting into beautifully conceived living rooms; and our precious unopened drawings being used by contractors to wrap their fish and chips.'

Richard Rogers

Norman and I met in 1961 at a reception for students from Britain who had been awarded scholarships to American universities: he had a Fulbright, the best. We were going to Yale to study with Paul Rudolph, although we both wondered whether we should have not applied to Penn University where Louis Kahn taught.

There were some thirteen Masters students working on the top floor in Louis Kahn's beautiful Yale Art Museum. Rudolph expected full commitment, 24 hours a day, with surprise tutorials at 2am. Those who collapsed at their drawing boards didn't make it. Fortunately, there was a couch on which we took turns to sleep. The four English students didn't take kindly to being 'taught'; being somewhat older we questioned, talked, objected and tried to avoid drawing. One day a plaque appeared over the English group's work tables – 'start drawing' – which we answered with 'start thinking'. We certainly learned to work extremely hard and to use our eyes, not an English tradition.

Philip Johnson and Jim Stirling were among our critics. The historian Vincent Scully was at his peak; his lectures were great theatre and attended by hundreds of students from all the faculties. He stressed the difference between Europe and the States, opening our eyes to America, to Richardson, Sullivan, Kahn and especially Frank Lloyd Wright. Norman, Su Rogers (who was taking a Masters in City Planning), Carl Abbott, a classmate, and I set out in Carl's VW Beetle to see every Wright building in Illinois and Wisconsin. They made a deep impression on all of us.

For the second semester Serge Chermayeff was the visiting professor. He was as academic and European as Rudolph was visual and American. Instead of designing beautiful buildings, we researched the concept of the city in terms of the hierarchy between the private and the public realm. We believed everything he said. His concise intellectual framework is still with us.

The two star pupils were Eldred Evans, urbane and mysterious, with cool, beautifully controlled, unfinished, geometric drawings, and Norman, who had left school at sixteen, gone into the Air Force and worked his way through Manchester University and eventually to a Henry Fellowship to Yale. A brilliant, versatile and concise thinker, Norman immediately became a great friend. We discussed and argued about everything. Our backgrounds were very different. His was industrial Manchester while mine was Italian; he was as brilliant a draughtsman as I was a poor one. Norman, a natural leader, would have succeeded in any profession.

These were wonderful heady days. I especially remember Norman's stunning office design, a series of strongly articulated towers marching round the corner, where office space was supported by a structural service core with great splayed feet; and a design for the Yale science campus which, to the horror of Paul Rudolph, we did together. These two projects, partially based on Kahn's concept of served and servant spaces, inspired much of my later work, as well as some of Norman's such as the Hongkong Bank – a truly seminal building.

Before leaving Yale, Norman, Su and I designed a small Wright-influenced house for old friends of mine, Michael and Pat Branch, in Kent. Never built, it was conceived in Naum Gabo's house, where Su and I lived to the music of Ella Fitzgerald and Elvis Presley. This was the beginning of our partnership. America enthralled us with its scale, energy, optimism and openness. We travelled by thumb, by car and by Greyhound bus, voraciously absorbing the culture, both of the massive open spaces and of the tall, taut, energetic cities. Norman, Su and I ended up working in San Francisco: Norman for Anshen & Allen and others on a new campus for UC Santa Cruz, Su for the US government and I for SOM. Su and I returned to Britain, drawn by the opportunity to build a house for Su's parents in Cornwall and by the prospect of the Branch house. A few months later Norman joined us and the two Cheesman sisters to form Team 4.

I had met the sisters Georgie and Wendy Cheesman at art school in Epsom in 1953. Wendy was still at the local convent. I have never met anyone who could laugh as Wendy did, or who was so gentle. The sisters were brilliantly inquisitive, fiercely intellectual and bohemian, battling to break away from a very dominant, successful and conservative Lloyd's broker father who had no time for the arts. Georgie, Wendy and I became inseparable and decided to try to become architects: ten years later we set up office together. Norman had never met them before returning to England and was more than a little surprised at their eccentricity.

Wendy rented an Edwardian two-roomed flat in Belsize Park. She slept and lived in one room and the other was our office (1). From the beginning we went from crisis to crisis. Within a few months, the only registered architect, Georgie, had resigned. She could see there was little room for a wonderfully strong and intelligent loner. This left Norman, Wendy, Su and me and a letterhead that read 'Team 4 Architects'. There followed a series of hilarious episodes with the four of

Richard Rogers

us trying to persuade some friendly architect to lend us their name, at the same time staving off the Architects' Registration Council and the Royal Institute of British Architects, and trying to get through our professional practice examinations.

None of us appreciated the difficulties of running a practice without experience. I remember episodes such as crying under a tree on Hampstead Heath and thinking, 'I will never be an architect'; a client asking me what I thought his damp-proof membrane was made of and finding it was the *Daily Mail* painted black; unplanned-for springs of water bursting into beautifully conceived living rooms; and our precious unopened drawings being used by contractors to wrap their fish and chips.

We searched for a magician, an experienced assistant who knew the answer to everything from plumbing to construction and law, but to no avail. During those early years some brilliant young assistants joined us, among them Frank Peacock, who was a traditional carpenter and a beautiful draughtsman before becoming an architect. He was also a wonderful craftsman, whose building knowledge helped us through those terrible early days. John Young, who was in love with technology, design and construction, and Laurie Abbott too, joined us as third-year students. Laurie used to file down even the finest nibs to get a more incisive line. An enthusiastic racing car designer and driver, he brought a fresh approach to architecture and technology. On the backs of these three our practice was built.

We worked fifteen hours a day, seven days a week. No one invited us to dinner as we would invariably fall asleep during the first course. It took the team three years to build the Brumwells' Creek Vean house, the first house to win an RIBA Award. This slowness of production, when related to the national housing shortage, stimulated us to reconsider our architectural direction.

Looking back, the 50 or so different designs we prepared for the house under the kind eye of the Brumwells, gave us the opportunity to work through a wide range of approaches and ideas. The Jaffé house in Radlett sowed the seeds of future, more geometrically ordered projects. In between, we designed what in conceptual terms was probably the most important project of our Team 4 period, a large planning scheme on some 300 acres at Coulsdon, Surrey, for Wates Homes, including detail drawings for one section of about 120 houses. The scheme incorporated many of Chermayeff's theories on privacy and community and the definition and separation of public and private realms.

While on the West Coast, both Norman and I had been excited by the Californian Case Study Houses of Eames, Soriano, Ellwood and Neutra, and a little later with the School Construction Systems Development programme of Ezra Ehrenkrantz. The use of standard lightweight industrial components and flexible plans in these projects led to an approach which broke away from the Classicism of Mies van der Rohe, and the organic naturalism of Frank Lloyd Wright, both then major influences. In 1965, Jim Stirling recommended us to Peter Parker to build a 30,000-square-foot factory in Swindon in ten months for Reliance Controls at a cost of £4 per square foot. Reliance Controls gave us the opportunity to change the direction of our work.

By now Wendy and Norman were married. Their once clearly defined edges had become blurred. Wendy, the wonderful, sensitive bohemian, and Norman, the natural leader, had become an interdependent team. Their first two children, Ti and Cal, and ours, Ben and Zad, were playing around the office. There was practically no work. Norman and I worked on every project as a team, each idea was forged out of heated discussions and tested out on rolls of yellow tracing paper.

After some five years of an intensive and stimulating relationship, where everything under the sun was argued about, Norman, Wendy, Su and I were beginning to grow apart. The divorce was difficult, jealousy tore us apart and it was not until Renzo Piano and I were building the Centre Pompidou five years later that the four of us became friends again.

Norman was as enthusiastic about Centre Pompidou as I was about his Willis Faber & Dumas and Sainsbury Centre buildings. His support gave me great strength and once more our meetings and discussions took on an excitement lost for a decade. Wendy, Norman, Ruth and I even talked seriously of linking up again when Centre Pompidou was finished.

Though the partnership never materialised, Norman, Wendy, Ruth and I became very close. We both adopted boys, Jay and Bo from Arizona. Ruthie's restaurant became a base for planning the future and employed our elder sons. Tragically Wendy died in 1989.

Richard Rogers

'Here in the Century Tower, the feeling is that of being in the very pounding heart of Tokyo, at the very centre of the modern world.'

Malcolm Quantrill

Theory for Norman Foster cannot be divorced from the nature of materials, the problems of component production, and the art of construction and assembly. Consequently, the design process in the Foster office requires a concentration and continuity of effort that 'brings to the final product the quality of the original thought'. This constitutes the heart of Foster Associates' reputation: that over the years confidence has grown in their architecture precisely because of the persistent emergence of strong ideas that are brought to perfection in the design process. The clarity of these ideas and their resolution has developed a consistent language in many ways limited in its expression but with the poetic economy of the *haiku*.

All this surely helps explain how an extremely fastidious Japanese client came to commission the Century Tower for his Obunsha Publishing Group from Foster Associates. Certainly, the project has roots and origins in the Hongkong Bank. The Japanese developer, Kazuo Akao, who has been the patron of such artists as Richard Long and Carl André, got to know and admire the Hongkong and Shanghai Bank. He paid many visits to Hong Kong, staying in the adjacent Mandarin Hotel, in order to study the building in detail and become thoroughly familiar with its unique architecture. Akao then invited Foster to Tokyo in November 1986 and commissioned Foster Associates to provide an innovative solution for Tokyo of comparable boldness. But Century Tower is not a small-scale version of the Hongkong Bank. It is quite another building, for a very different context: it has its own logic and must be judged on its own terms.

In the Hongkong and Shanghai Bank Norman Foster reinvented the skyscraper, returning to the original Chicago invention, followed in turn by Mies van der Rohe, of giving prominence to the expression of the primary structure. The irregular massing of the Hongkong Bank responds to the constraints of zoning codes. Similarly, the variation in height of the two towers of the Century building in Tokyo's central Bunkyo-ku district is a response to building regulations. The two-tower solution originated from constraints that allow 21 storeys at the front (south) of the site, but only ten at the rear (north), an enclosed lightwell linking the two parts up to the tenth floor. While the revision of zoning regulations during the design process eventually maintained the south tower at 21 storeys, the north tower was allowed to rise to nineteen. The upper two floors of the south tower are occupied by Akao's own offices and private penthouse residence.

The outer form of Century Tower is deceptively simple, contained from north to south within the four eccentrically braced frames (EBF) (3) that define the two towers and the continuous narrow atrium between, providing column-free office space (5) and giving the basic seismic shock resistance. Main structural floors, known as stability floors, are double height, with mezzanines suspended between them on north-south hangers for all but one such floor (level seventeen north tower, level nineteen south tower) in both towers above entry level. The towers are slung, like a series of stacked bridges, over a three-level basement. This basement has parking at the lowest level, with a museum for Akao's collection of Oriental antiquities at level B2. Public access to the museum is from the entry level, in the central area between the towers and under the atrium to the office floors.

To the east and west the towers are enclosed by movement-resistant frames (MRF) that define the boundary between master (lettable) space, and the slave (service) elements. At levels eleven and nineteen the towers are linked structurally across the ends of the atrium on the movement resistant frame. Along the western edge these conventional beam and column frames give access to the main bank of twelve passenger lifts, all of which go to floor nine. From nine to level nineteen, six faster lifts give access to the upper floors. These lifts on the western side are arranged behind an effectively continuous transparent glass wall, and they provide excellent views across Tokyo on the ascent. On the eastern edge, the towers project beyond the atrium and the MRF to house the escape stairs, lavatories, service lifts and other services, providing the only two opaque surfaces on the building's exterior. The lavatories are all unisex cubicles, with occupancy signals in the access areas similar to those found on aircraft.

The atrium (4, 6), or what Norman Foster calls 'the slot', between the towers, which is essential for bouncing light through the building on both axes, is the most daring and innovative part of Century Tower in the context of Japanese office design. Prior to this design it had not been permitted in Japan to combine an open central shaft or atrium with adjacent open-access floor space. Previously, all Japanese atrium buildings were required to have enclosed floors at all levels, with the additional provision of fire shutters. Foster Associates' ingenious solution to this problem has two components. The first is the provision of smoke-activated shutters, which descend from both the main and mezzanine floors 1,500mm towards the continuous glass balustrades at the floor edges. This accelerates the flow of air from the atrium into the smoke-affected floor. Fans located in the outer corners of the building then draw the air across the floor diagonally, sucking the smoke out of the building away from the atrium to avoid the migration of smoke into the central slot. The effect of the smoke baffles, descending from the upward-splayed soffit of the mezzanine ceilings, is reminiscent of the brake-flaps on aeroplane wings. By avoiding opaque barriers on either side of the atrium the building remains transparent on both axes, so that the unique pattern of Tokyo's jumble and confusion is visible from almost every point of the interior.

The south tower of the building fronts onto a busy thoroughfare at the canal's edge adjacent to a major railway line, with the entire EBF forming the south facade. This frame is the most forceful expression of the interlocked systems of logic that make up Century Tower. It is most clearly viewed from across the Kandagawa Canal just before taking the Ochanomizu Bridge. Close up, the legs of the EBF form a portico, or gateway to the main entrance, which is set back at a slight angle from the pavement line. The entrance lobby is already revealed through the plate-glass screen that stretches beneath the EBF between the service bays to west and east. A single, four-blade revolving door brings us into the lobby. Once inside, the choice is between the bank of lifts to the left (serving up to the ninth or changeover level) and the reception desk to the right.

Straight ahead are twin water tables, recalling the ritual of purification, which frame the staircase down to the museum. These water tables, made from polished black Zimbabwe granite, were designed by Richard Chaix to overflow at their edges and feed the waterwalls that descend into what Norman Foster has dubbed 'the cave'. Beyond these waterwalls a public tea house stretches towards the rear wall, looking onto the catenary roof above the restaurant and an exclusive health club located in the basement on the northern boundary of the site. The diagonal legs of the EBF structure are the only interruptions to the clear flow of the lobby from south to north. Beneath the dimmer-controlled illuminated soffit, the feeling of transparency and abundant natural light is immediately evident. The essential tranquillity of the lobby is reinforced by the gentle sound of water flowing down the waterwalls and the soft grey surface of the flame-finished black Zimbabwe granite floor.

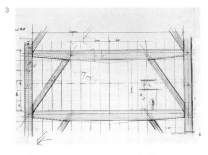

Approaching the site along the canal from the south, we see both the eccentrically braced frame and the higher thrust of the service banks to both towers. This composition reveals the basic components of the building form. The EBF displays the cross-site structure, while the service bays mask the posts and beams that make up the MRF. Within this simple relationship of structural frames, the one transparent and the other opaque, a complex interplay of technology and industrial design is worked out in the floors, ceilings and other interstices of the building. From the distance, the super-scale and brilliantly reflective frames of the EBF facade contrast with the rugged slatting of the service banks and the skyward thrust of the red and white communications mast. Century Tower offers a ritual refinement of structure in the EBF frames, but the muscularity of the supporting service bookends is undisguised. Indeed, from the exterior it seems to combine a High-Tech rationale with the aesthetics of Expressionism. The mark of a Foster building is often made by this combination of refinement of detail with an almost raw freshness of the whole event, like silk and sharkskin.

The pattern of the building's structure-form logic is directly expressed by colour coding of the finishes. All the main structure, both externally and internally, both the EBF and the MRF, is covered in warm grey panels. For the externally exposed structure these are the 25mm aluminium sandwich panels made by Cupples of St Louis and previously used for the Hongkong Bank. Steel linings are substituted, for economy, on the inside linking beams for the EBF. All the secondary structural elements are indicated in light grey. The services are coded in silver throughout, consistent with the reflector strips for ceiling lights. And finally, all infill panels are white.

The quality of finish throughout is consistent with the highest standards of industrial design. This is the result of the closest collaboration between the architects, contractors and specialist manufacturers. For example, the substitution of steel cladding panels inside the building for the Cupples' honeycomb aluminium was possible because the Japanese producer managed to eliminate the welding spot effect normally present in flat steel sheet, and also avoided surface distortion. Similarly, the mullions for the double-storey windows to the south and north sides of the building (behind the EBF) were developed as a single 450mm-deep section necessary for wind bracing. Santoprene gaskets, rather than neoprene, are used

both between cladding of main structural elements and between different elements as boundaries of building trades. The santoprene gasket allows for a neater connection since it can be directly heat-welded in place.

In contrast to this elemental separation, the whole success of the horizontal services, both in the raised floors and the suspended ceilings (i.e. above and below the structure) depended not only upon the rationalisation of subcontractors' work but also on the integration of lighting, heating and air-conditioning installations, and power and data facilities. The result is the clean lines of the ceiling patterns, with lighting, sprinklers, heating, air conditioning and other necessary outlets all incorporated into the silver service strips between the white ceiling panels. This ceiling system allows for complete flexibility in the employment of standard, off-the-shelf partition systems for the cellularisation of any floor space, with fixing sockets located midway between the service strips. Similarly, special distribution boxes were developed for the raised floors to accommodate power and data outlets, and these are now in standard production for general distribution. This level of collaboration in industrial design and production is essential in Foster Associates' quest for the integration of design, materials, manufacture, assembly and quality of finish.

Unlike the Hongkong Bank, Century Tower is not a corporate headquarters but a private, speculative office venture, with special functions for the client and owner at the upper and lower extremities of the building. Already established as a prestige space in Tokyo (it was only opened at the end of May 1991) both the design department of the building's main contractor, Obayashi, and Japan Air Lines have leased space in Century Tower. But what is it like as a working environment? If appearances are to be believed, the bright and airy continuity of the interior provides a new model for the speculative office.

Although there is the potential for cellularisation of the individual floors, the concept is rather one of universality of space and view. Privacy is not so much a visual concept in the new corporate office, which is more concerned with the work being done rather than spatial status. Here in the Century Tower, the feeling is that of being in the very pounding heart of Tokyo, at the very centre of the modern world. This impression is not possible in a conventionally planned office tower. In Century Tower the workers are suspended in the city. The Tower is literally the

5

city at work within itself. In the tradition of Frank Lloyd Wright's Larkin and Johnson Wax buildings, the status of the workplace has been elevated. But, importantly, Wright's temple of work as represented by the Larkin building is replaced here by a series of bridges that afford changing landscapes of light and view and being. Although the Century Tower is certainly an efficient machine for working in, it is more. The differences are immediately evident in the entrance lobby and confirmed by moving about the building. While the EBF establishes a formal, ritual character to the building's exterior, and this sense of ritual is reinforced by the water tables in the lobby, the very essence of the building in use centres on informality, flexibility and comfort.

The distinctive form of the EBF frames, reminiscent of temple gates with their diagonal thrust across the facade, combines with the stepped service shafts to create a vigorous new landmark on the Tokyo skyline. Within the building the essential tension of the EBF structure dissolves, partly in the pattern of main and mezzanine floors, but mostly through the continuity of light and space that permeates the whole interior. If Century Tower is outwardly a symbol of the new Tokyo, inwardly it represents the triumph of design and technology in orchestrating an ideal working environment.

6

'On his visits to Japan, Norman Foster has shown a great deal of interest in traditional Japanese architecture. Indeed, his own work might have been inspired by the aristocratic spirit of the Heian, or Kamakura, or Muromachi periods of architecture: unconsciously, they seem to blend with his own aesthetic of effortless transparency.'

Kazuo Akao

I first came across Foster's work in the spring of 1982. The Japanese newspaper *Nikkei News* issued a special edition about Hong Kong which included a full-page advertisement for the Hongkong and Shanghai Banking Corporation showing a photograph of its proposed new headquarters building. The image was very powerful and, for some time afterwards, I found myself thinking about the building. The name of the architect was not mentioned, but I was able to find that out for myself.

Norman Foster's work was not widely published in Japan at that time, and I had to consult the foreign architectural magazines to learn more about his projects. The more I found out, the more absorbed I became. Finally, in April 1986, I made my first 'pilgrimage' to the newly completed headquarters in Hong Kong. Unfortunately, it was just before the official opening ceremony – which took place in June – so I could only see part of the building and I had to make a second visit. It took three visits before I saw the whole building and felt I really understood it – five visits, in fact, if I include the times I dropped by on my way to other places.

I was struck by the sheer power of concentration that had obviously gone into the building's detailing, and by the strength of its structural expression. The latter created an impressive 'character' that was clearly visible outside the building, and even more so within. The more I learned, the more strongly I felt that here was a building of supreme quality, executed with absolute confidence and without compromise. I was deeply moved by the spatial experience that had been created: I had never encountered anything like it before.

The more I understood Foster's work, the more critical I became of modern buildings in Japan. In my opinion, architecture is the property of the whole nation; it should belong to everyone. Borrowing Norman Foster's own expression, architecture should represent the 'quality of an idea' most appropriate to a particular time and place. In the early 1980s it was rare to come across architecture of such conviction in Japan.

For me, this 'quality of an idea' is the essence of Foster's work. Immaculate craftsmanship is found in every part of his detailing; the most appropriate technology is employed during construction; there is constant research into a wide range of technical innovations, some well beyond the sphere of the building industry. All play a significant part. Innovative ideas about structural design and, of course, the creation of large flexible spaces – given life by natural light – are also

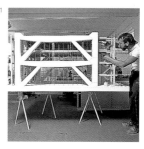

central to Foster's work. All are brought together to establish an architecture of quality. Technology is not seen as an end in itself, and to flaunt it would be inappropriate. For Foster, technology is the means by which quality can be achieved: whether a quality of materials, of fabrication or of assembly. I believe this is a common philosophy, which permeates all his work.

'Lightness and transparency' are other essential ingredients of Foster's architecture — and is another reason why I am so deeply committed. But this is not a simple transparency: it is invested with a nobility of character. On his visits to Japan, Norman Foster has shown a great deal of interest in traditional Japanese architecture. Indeed, his own work might have been inspired by the aristocratic spirit of the Heian, or Kamakura, or Muromachi periods of architecture: unconsciously, they seem to blend with his own aesthetic of effortless transparency. It is this spirit of the old Japanese culture — so apparent in Foster's architecture — that is missing from much contemporary architecture in Japan.

My commitment to Foster's architecture grew during my visits to the Hongkong and Shanghai Bank and I decided to invite him to Tokyo to discuss a new project. Our site at Ochanomizu, where Century Tower now stands, was badly in need of total redevelopment.

We met for the first time in November 1986. It was a fruitful meeting and, during the site visit and briefing, we discovered we had many things in common. I remember Norman Foster commenting that he thought it an 'interesting' site. A month later, in New York, the provisional contract was signed, and in February 1987 I made my first trip to London.

At our first meeting in Tokyo, Foster's design team had been provided with many documents relating to planning and building regulations in Tokyo. These are complex issues, so I was hardly expecting what I found at Foster Associates' office: in just a few months, they had produced study models (1, 2) exploring the designated floor area ratio, site coverage and setback requirements, as well as numerous concept sketches and drawings. Considering the tremendous disadvantage of being foreign to Japanese culture and regulations, their achievement in such a short period seemed remarkable. And it was not only their speed that impressed me; their persistence in searching for the best solution was also apparent. The twin-tower concept was outlined in the earliest sketches, but already it had been examined, re-

Kazuo Akao

examined and compared exhaustively with many alternatives.

This constant search for improvement continued as the project evolved. Foster Associates were keen on design development, a system that guarantees quality through the progressive use of small-scale models, full-size mock-ups and production prototypes. I attended some of the review sessions myself, including those for the lifts, and witnessed how the designers identified problems and areas of concern so that they could make improvements at every stage.

Century Tower is primarily a tenanted office building, but it also includes a museum, a restaurant and a 'tea house' which are all open to the public. These are intended to make the building more accessible, and also to enhance the quality of the office environment.

It was my intention that Century Tower should symbolise the corporate philosophy of the Obunsha Group by its quality. I believe we have achieved our aim. Apparently, the design quality of the Hongkong Bank is guaranteed for 50 years: I hope that Century Tower will promote the benefits of architectural quality in Japan for even longer.

'The 50,000-square-metre Stansted Airport terminal, 30 miles north of the centre of London and 14 miles from the M25 orbital motorway, is a Big Shed. In fact it is one of the largest and most beautiful Big Sheds that has ever been built.'

Although it was ten years in the making, Foster Associates' new £200 million Stansted Airport terminal building and its satellites sprang suddenly into the public consciousness. This was because throughout the 1980s, while it made its way through outline and detailed design, official and unofficial approvals, and finally construction and fitting-out, the architectural issue that obsessed England was not the potential of advanced technology construction, but the challenge posed by the architecture of the past.

It was the issue of the relationship of modern architecture to historical architecture that gave force to the interventions of Prince Charles, interventions that set the agenda for the media reporting of architecture during the decade. During this time the whole concept of architecture as an independent creative discipline fell into disfavour. Such was the power of the historical conservation lobby that nearly 500,000 old buildings were granted immunity from alteration or demolition. The emphasis on historical architecture in an urban context was reinforced by the most popular new building of the 1980s – a London office complex disguised as a row of large Georgian houses designed by the Classical Revival architect Quinlan Terry – and by the unsuccessful outcome of the greatest architectural adventure of the decade, a bid to erect a posthumous Mies van der Rohe building in central London.

In England there has always been a tendency to emphasise historical urban issues because the intelligentsia lives and works in historical towns and cities, often in the oldest and most picturesque quarters. Furthermore, today's architectural critics and commentators tend to be unfamiliar with the issues of economic policy and construction management that underlie most commercial construction. A surprising number cannot drive and thus never travel the motorways. Most have never visited a factory or a distribution centre, never travelled to an offshore oil platform, never seen a container port or cargo ship. Their ignorance of all these matters contributes powerfully to their vision of the world. It explains why they concentrated on historical towns and cities while the economic infrastructure of the nation was being assembled elsewhere.

During the 1980s, a new architecture was being built in non-historical England. While forests were being cut down to provide paper to debate the merits of the various proposals for an extension to the National Gallery in London's Trafalgar Square – in the end no more than a small building on a site that had been a car-park for 40 years – all over the country millions of square metres of business park and distribution centre floor space was being constructed at breakneck speed.

Outside the towns and cities, at a thousand motorway access points, whole new commercial complexes were springing up with no reference to the supremacy of history at all (1). This new 'abstract urbanism' was ignored by architectural critics; yet in economic terms it outweighed in importance all the 'Fine Art' architecture of the preceding quarter century. Today, after a decade of frenzied construction, these offices, manufacturing and distribution parks boast over 300 million square metres of new serviced floorspace. They are the new operational centres of the British economy. Their architecture is the architecture of 'Big Sheds'.

Big Shed architecture is not small, vertical and ornate like the historical architecture upon which most English cities concentrate. It is vast, horizontal and plain, as befits the unobstructed road sites upon which it is built. In such areas, steel-framed, flat-roofed, laser-levelled floor-plates of 25,000 square metres are not unusual, and 50,000 square metres is not unknown.

In some parts of the country these great boxes of Big Sheds line the horizon like stationary sleeping cars. Cheap offices or expensive distribution centres, they are inscrutable from the outside but conceal secret inner worlds. Some contain extraordinarily expensive mechanical handling equipment. Often they are air conditioned or refrigerated; their operations are controlled by computer from hundreds of miles away. These enigmatic Big Sheds are not national but international in their design. They are the unacknowledged International Style architecture of the world consumer economy.

They are also the first steps towards the realisation of the supra-architectural megastructures dreamed of by Richard Buckminster Fuller in the 1950s. They are the buildings of the 'flatscape with containers' that Reyner Banham first wrote of in 1966, the 'non-plan' cities of the future that Cedric Price visualised in 1969. The 50,000-square-metre Stansted Airport terminal by Foster Associates, 30 miles north of central London and 14 miles from the M25 orbital motorway, is a Big Shed. In fact it is one of the largest and most beautiful Big Sheds that has ever been built.

Although possessed of a world reputation for fine art architecture of the highest aesthetic importance, Norman Foster has also had a long association with Big Sheds. In some ways he can claim to have invented the genre. Beginning in 1966

3

with the electronics factory at Reliance Controls, designed in association with Richard Rogers, he went on to design a succession of commercial and industrial buildings and projects in the years that followed. As early as 1972 he was working on a major expansion of the conventional limits of the Big Shed. Working for an international leisure consultancy, Foster Associates designed two large motorway-access single-storey structures intended to enclose shopping malls and leisure parks. Each one was to have provided 40,000 square metres of serviced floorspace beneath a space-frame roof – by comparison with the modest 3,200 square metres enclosed at Reliance Controls.

In 1974 another client commissioned what might have become the largest Big Shed in Britain if it had been built, a mammoth 160,000-square-metre distribution centre for German cars at Milton Keynes (3).

In these unbuilt projects, as well as more modest completed industrial units like the 2,000-square-metre SAPA extrusion factory at Tibshelf, and the much smaller 850-square-metre showroom and warehouse for Modern Art Glass at Thamesmead (2), the origins of the vast terminal building at Stansted can be seen. Like Stansted, all these projects were large, horizontal 'umbrella' enclosures that hugged the landscape and were plugged into an existing transport infrastructure. The proposed German Car Centre at Milton Keynes in particular, with its almost military landscaping of long earth berms, massive 24-metre structural bays, 800-metre frontage and full-length open bay along one side used as a giant *porte-cochère*, prefigures many aspects of the 50,000-square-metre Stansted terminal.

All the Foster Associates' Big Shed buildings of the 1970s were prophetic in their emphasis upon ground-hugging horizontality and existing transport infrastructure. Seen in retrospect, their work of nearly twenty years confirms that the idea of huge, flat rectangles of serviced floorspace, cruising half-buried through the landscape like submarines running on the surface, yet connected by the umbilical cords of access to road and rail networks, must have taken root in Norman Foster's mind at the end of the 1960s and worked through one commission after another to achieve its most developed realisation.

Nor did this idea affect only commercial projects. The Sainsbury Centre for Visual Arts of 1974-78 is an art gallery, but it is also a Big Shed, a five-times-larger version of the Modern Art Glass factory of five years before, connected by the same

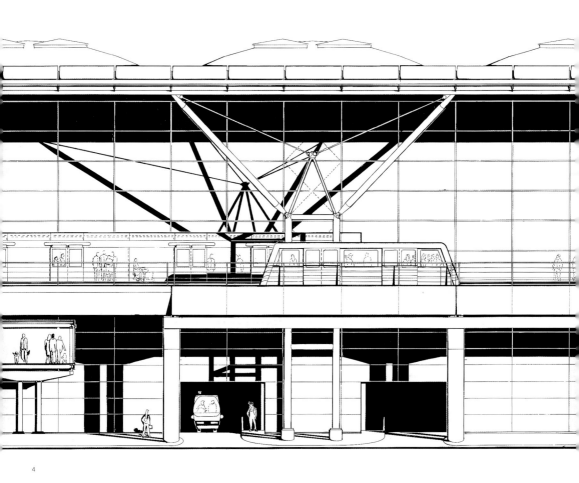

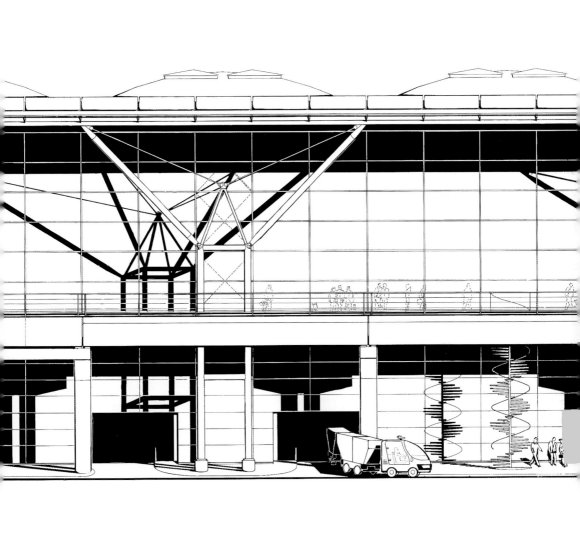

5

ribbon or road to the rest of the country. In this sense it is linked to the 24,000-square-metre Renault Distribution Centre of 1980-82. There Norman Foster raised the size of the floor-plate by six times again and even returned to the giant mode of the German Car Centre with the same 24-metre bay width, but the same matrix of existing transport infrastructure remains.

In 1981, when the Renault building was still in the process of design, the outline commission for the Stansted Airport terminal arrived. Despite having only one runway, Stansted Airport is destined to become the third great London airport, after Heathrow and Gatwick. Today it accommodates up to 8 million passenger movements a year: fully expanded with four satellites it will be able to handle 22 million. True to Big Shed genealogy, the accommodation of these passenger movements revolves around transport infrastructure.

At Stansted (4-6) the heart of the operation is a covered intersection of three transport systems. The most important of these is the existing 227,000-square-metre former United States Air Force runway, one of the longest in England, built in the mid-1950s to receive military transport aircraft en route for Germany and underused ever since. The others are the M11 motorway, giving access to the M25 and the entire national motorway system, and the new twin-track rail spur off the main London to Cambridge route that permits express shuttle trains to run direct from beneath the Stansted terminal to Liverpool Street Station in the heart of London in 40 minutes.

Foster Associates' task at Stansted was to enclose the passenger and baggage facilities and movement systems that would make this tri-modal transport interchange operate smoothly and, as far as possible, on one level. This resulted in the conception of a single large 'umbrella' roof covering an immense public concourse with submerged servicing and a new railway station. There were, from the beginning, three overriding architectural requirements: minimal structure, maximum use of daylight, and maximum concealment of services.

Foster Associates started with the 'umbrella' roof that would enclose all functions. They took an abandoned, centrally supported roof module system, originally sketched out for the Renault building, and began to develop it further. Using tension members within splayed struts, and setting a square shell of roof deck between each central support, they were able to push the column spacings out to

Martin Pawley

36 metres. Suspended glass cladding for the walls and more roof daylighting than had ever been incorporated into any previous Big Shed building – with a promised saving of 500,000 kilowatts of lighting electricity a year as a benefit – enabled this 'umbrella' to become almost the sole visible part of the building.

The roof in particular possesses an extraordinary visual lightness. Before the cladding was installed it resembled an enormous formation parachute landing at the point of touchdown. Today it still floats 15 metres above the grey granite-paved concourse, barely apparent to the airport users below. There is no lighting, heating or service function of any description attached to the underside of this cluster of metal shells, not even a sprinkler system. Nor above it. Where the Renault roof membrane (7) was penetrated by 90 steel columns and 360 tension rods, Stansted's roof membrane is continuous, with no penetrations, no expansion joints, not a single rainwater pipe. It is the most breathtaking roof since the Middle Ages.

At concourse level, all that is visible of the mechanism that sustains this epic roof are the rows of squat quadruple tubular column structures containing the square risers for a dense mass of servicing technology. Above are the splayed struts of the parasol roof: below is what is in effect a 9-metre raised floor. This is the deep 'undercroft' that contains the railway station, the mechanical handling equipment, heating and cooling machinery, servicing and communications technology, all hidden underground in the same way that a ship's engine room is hidden below the waterline. Right down at the bottom of this 'engine room' are the shallow pad foundations for the roof.

Using the topography of the site, the architect was able to plant a forest of 36 quadruple tubular steel trees at centres of 36 metres. The trunks of these trees rise to a height of 12 metres but at 9 metres they are connected by the *in situ* coffered concrete slab of the concourse. At 12 metres the branches of the trees spread out to support the roof shells 24 metres above the undercroft floor.

Like all truly large horizontal buildings, Stansted terminal is difficult to view adequately except from the air. The topography of the site makes it difficult to see from a distance on the ground, and its ingenious changes of level – ground level becomes basement, first floor becomes ground – mean that it is only from the large car-park to the south, or from the access roundabout, that the way in which it plunges into the landscape like a huge ship into a giant wave can be understood.

Martin Pawley

Once inside, the terminal itself is spectacular in a surprisingly understated way that is better experienced than described. Apart from a modest use of stained glass in the region given over to a complex of concession cabins on the concourse, it is the austere and unnerving quality of space and light that strikes a visitor, rather than any design feature, rather like the experience of the Sainsbury Centre but on a vaster scale. The grandeur of the grey Sicilian granite floor in what is, after all, a public service building is not obvious but subliminal. The structural steelwork is simply painted. Only the fire-hose reels in the 'trees' glisten in stainless steel, echoing the shape of the analogue clocks above them.

At the time of writing, only one arrival and departure satellite is in use (the second is still under construction and a further two can be added) and this is reached by a rail shuttle transit system. The satellites, each one nearly one-third as long as the terminal, have braved an inadequacy of resources that stems from their relatively late inclusion in the design. Ingenuity and discipline alone, coupled with vast areas of glazing and a cheap form of metal cladding on plywood, are not really adequate to overcome the narrowness and Spartan perspective offered by their almost penal interiors.

In the earliest design configuration, the aircraft at Stansted were to have docked on the north-west side of the terminal and the passengers were to have walked straight through it to their surface transport in the simple manner of air travel in the 1930s. This was Sir Norman Foster's ideal. In the end, operating requirements, security and cost made this idea unrealisable. Thus what has survived is horizontal, but not without considerable changes in level. The huge, squat Big Shed of the terminal itself is landscaped with a muscular grandeur appropriate to the openness of the site and to the vastness of the great runway and its associated transport infrastructure. It is an envelope as economical as that of the Hongkong and Shanghai Bank was expensive; a structure as light as that of the Sainsbury Centre was heavy – and an authentic milestone on Foster Associates' road to the eclipse of history and tradition in architecture.

'Unlike most current modes of architectural production, Foster's method emphasises interdisciplinary teamwork rather than personal expression, user needs rather than formal conventions, clarity rather than complexity, functionality rather than imagery, invention rather than consumption.'

Thomas Fisher

As you approach the terminal at London's Stansted Airport (1) the building seems buoyant, almost effervescent, with its undulating roof of domes seeming to float above improbably thin steel struts. The same rarefied quality appears in the vast open space inside, where elements that clutter most airports – signage, TV monitors, display boards, lighting fixtures, safety equipment – have been gathered into 24 elegant black boxes integrated into the building's columns. Stansted terminal is a modern *tour de force*, reasserting the value of the free-plan and flexible space.

But it is something else, something even more important than a well-designed airport. In an era when so many buildings come wrapped in styles unrelated to their use or structure, Stansted – and indeed most of Norman Foster's work – shows the power of a design process that refuses to separate aesthetics from function or technology. This refusal is not just some tenacious strain of Modernism. It goes to the heart of what ails this profession, because the more we separate aesthetics from programme or 'technics', the more we play into the hands of those who would like to portray all architects as building decorators or arrogant 'artistes'. Whether or not you like the look of Foster's buildings, none of us can afford to dismiss the thinking behind them.

Some critics might argue that Norman Foster, too, is something of an artiste, an international design star whose 250-person staff turns out High-Tech buildings from its high-ceilinged workroom overlooking the Thames in London. And some architects might have a hard time relating to Foster because of the scale of his commissions and budgets; his firm's bank building in Hong Kong, for example, constructed for about $800 per square foot, is still one of the most expensive structures of its kind in the world.

But such scepticism, while understandable, misses the underlying relevance of Foster's architecture. The value of what he does has little to do with the size of his commissions (which actually varies considerably) or with the stylistic similarities among his buildings, and everything to do with his method of working, which involves trying to solve the greatest number of problems with a minimum of means.

This approach might best be described as industrial design applied at an architectural or urban scale. Unlike most current modes of architectural production, Foster's method emphasises interdisciplinary teamwork rather than personal expression, user needs rather than formal conventions, clarity rather than complexity,

functionality rather than imagery, invention rather than consumption. As the Spanish critic Josep Maria Gil Guitart recently described it: 'Foster and his team do not wish to complicate life. The departure point for their work is always conceptual simplicity with a view not to excluding variables, but to eliminating the superfluous.' Recalling Buckminster Fuller's admonition, Foster describes this as 'doing more with less'.

It is true that the differences in scale between industrial design and architecture limit the relevance of the one to the other. We rarely get a chance, for example, to build prototypes of buildings and test them the way a company can a car or a computer. But the fact that industrial design has never split aesthetics from function and technology makes it a process from which we might learn how to repair that split in our own discipline.

There are some incentives to do so. While the architectural profession has been struggling in recent years, industrial design has undergone a renaissance, at least in terms of interest and investment by the business community. And it isn't hard to see why. The industrial designer's ability to derive form from technology and to justify beauty in terms of function plays well in a culture that, rightly or wrongly, views aesthetics as a matter of personal preference and utility as the primary way to measure design's value. What Foster has done is show how those values can work in our favour.

One of the aspects of our field most at odds with industrial design is that of personal expression. While there will always be limited demand for designers known for their signature style, most architects face a situation which is inimical to personal expression, having to share leadership of the building team with construction managers, project managers, and the like. This rather more humble position is better suited, I think, to the more egalitarian notion of teamwork common among industrial designers.

Foster's office demonstrates the difference. As Foster describes it, their process 'is the opposite of much that has been academically taught. The architect is not handing down from above, passing the parcel to the specialist who waits in line to be told what to do. Each individual has the potential for creative input.' From the conversations I've had with some of Foster's long-time consultants, this process is well liked. It also seems to be a way to generate new design ideas. In

Thomas Fisher

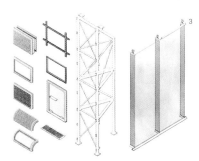

a well-functioning team, says Foster, 'it is the personal chemistry and mutual respect that enable anyone on the team to challenge anything and everything'.

Indeed, Foster is somewhat unusual among design stars for his admiration of anonymous industrial designers. As Foster puts it, they are 'often hidden in bureaucratic and business organisations, or sometimes in independent consultancies. Their main role, in essence, is problem solving. It is this fundamental aspect of their work that is so often overlooked.' Such praise of the anonymous designer is part of a larger belief that design must reconnect to ordinary people and the commercial world if it is to have any effect. 'There is a tendency among designers', adds Foster, 'to overindulge in the more superficial aspects of their trade to the exclusion of the fundamental problems. The ensuing dialogue, with its overtones of "good taste" and mystique, is largely irrelevant to a world going about its business.'

It is not just the nature of teamwork, but the nature of the team members that distinguishes this process. Most architects are accustomed to depending on clients for information and on local consultants for the expertise necessary to design a building. But industrial design, perhaps because of the mobility and utility of its products, has a somewhat different emphasis. More attention is given to actual user needs, as opposed to what the client says those needs are, and a greater willingness exists to tap expertise from around the world.

For Foster, the search for global expertise is due, in part, to the location of the firm. 'We're on a small island with an eroded industrial base', says David Nelson, a partner in the firm, 'so we have to go farther afield for consultants and manufacturing expertise.' And the intensive research phase that Foster's staff engages in at the beginning of most projects is a search for expertise of a different kind: 'We talk a lot to the users of a building', adds Nelson, 'because it gives us ideas about how to do things. They are experts in what they do, so it's important to go beyond the figurehead client.'

This intensive user input often leads Foster's office to question things in the building programme. Most of us acquire the rather bad habit in architecture school of not questioning (for fear of reprisal?) the programme requirements given by our studio design professors. When that carries over into practice, however, it puts the architect in the position of passive acceptance of what clients ask for, even if that is not in a client's best interest or what the building users actually want or need.

'We listen carefully to clients,' says Nelson, 'trying to really understand what they are saying and playing it back to them with the hope of making the brief better.' The critic Martin Pawley has described this process as a 'will to dominate' on Foster's part: 'By learning more about his client's needs than the client himself knows,' writes Pawley, 'Norman Foster the architect has frequently been able to "move from a situation of inferiority to one of superiority" – and redraft the user's definition of what he needs from his building.' But Nelson says that makes it sound more arrogant than it really is. 'We offer suggestions of how to improve a project, but we certainly accept it when a client isn't convinced.'

The counter-argument to this questioning of need is that it can anger or alienate a client. But, if the questioning is aimed at reducing the cost or improving the efficiency of a project, it can please the client immensely.

Foster and his staff also frequently question the way building products are manufactured and how they perform. Here too many architects have become rather passive, assembling buildings with products identified and largely accepted as shown in the manufacturers' catalogues. The origin of this practice lies not in architecture school, I think, but in our consumer-oriented culture, which encourages us all in the mistaken belief that the superficial variations among the thousands of products available to us can compensate for the lack of real differences among them. The result of this consumer attitude is not just diminished performance in buildings, but a diminishing of the architect's influence.

Foster argues that by pushing manufacturers to do better and by becoming 'integrated into the "how and why" of the making of the building, the architect comes closer to the heart of the project'. It certainly increases control over both the function and the aesthetics of what goes into a building. Says Nelson: 'When manufacturers say things have to be certain ways, it's amazing what the question "Why?" produces. You end up with a dialogue with them and with improvements that neither of you would have come up with in isolation.'

Nelson admits that this pursuit of innovation has risks: 'You have to be cautious; no client wants to be a guinea pig, so if something is new, you have to ask yourself why you are doing it in the first place. Also you have to have a back-up.' When Foster developed with H H Robertson the raised floor for the Hongkong Bank (4), with its honeycomb-core aluminium panel technology borrowed from the

Thomas Fisher

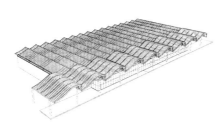
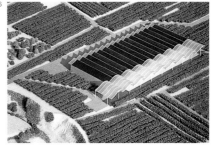

aerospace industry, 'we had a fallback', says Nelson, 'of a standard computer floor that would not have performed as well, but that would have sufficed'.

What about the criticism that most projects and most clients cannot absorb the cost of such product innovation, even if architects were inclined to pursue it? Nelson acknowledges that architects' fees in the UK tend to be higher, on a percentage basis, than they are in North America. However, if the product innovations result in lower construction or operation costs – as is almost always the case with improvements that Foster's office pursues – then clients must decide whether or not to spend money up front in order to save it later.

Although Foster's challenges to clients' briefs or manufacturers' products often end up saving money or improving performance, the firm's work is still widely seen as being expensive. This is due, in part, to the media. His large, high-budget projects get most of the press, but he still does the kind of project his firm first gained prominence for: low-cost industrial and warehouse structures. His office recently designed an 80,732-square-foot office, warehouse, and showroom for the furniture company Tecno (5, 6), which came in at under $100 per square foot.

It is a different kind of economy, however, that makes the firm's work so impressive. In architecture, we tend to think of economising by lowering the quality of finishes or reducing the size of a building. Foster, however, views economy more the way an industrial designer does: using the most minimal means available to solve the greatest number of problems. 'The designer's task', says Foster, 'could be summed up as analysing set problems in the widest sense and organising the best available resources to achieve the highest-performance solution in the most economical manner.'

This economy of means can lead to low first costs. But in Foster's work it results more often in buildings with long-term flexibility and performance. The Stansted terminal had a budget that was not extravagant, but took into account long-term costs: as servicing and processing requirements at airports change, the mechanical plenum underneath the building and the concourse's demountable partition system will certainly make the structure adaptable at less expense.

Stansted also shows that economy of means does not necessitate expressing all of the technology in a building. While some of Foster's early work, up through, say, the Hongkong Bank, expressed structural and mechanical elements on the outside of the building, the recent projects have become less assertively technological. I think some of this comes from a shift in the firm's work towards a more environmental position, where, because of passive solar and ventilation strategies, the buildings have become more analogous to tools like umbrellas or lenses than to machines.

Still, the machine seems to remain a sticking point in the minds of many architects when it comes to discussing Foster's work. One reason for that, I think, is the belief that industrial design processes automatically lead to standardised products. A building can never be as standardised as, say, a motorcycle or an aeroplane. But, this association of machine production and standardisation is fast becoming obsolete as computer-controlled equipment allows machine-made components and systems to be customised to a degree never before possible.

Indeed, critic Chris Abel has argued that the 'cybernetic factory' envisioned by Stafford Beer in 1962 is now here. 'Beer', writes Abel, 'visualised a sensitive industrial "organism" capable of responding to the fast-changing needs of a true market-orientated economy, turning out customised products … on variable, computerised production machinery … Foster's architecture', continues Abel, 'demonstrates his unique grasp of these fundamental changes in industrialised technology. By refusing to accept conventional building practices, and by progressively increasing the level of his demands for high-performance, custom-made products, Foster and his team have led the way in encouraging a notoriously conservative building industry to catch up'.

Behind Foster's employment of industrial design methods is, as David Nelson puts it, an 'Englishness'. In the country where the Industrial Revolution first flourished, Foster's office seems less afraid of embracing advanced technology than architects have been in North America. Indeed, Foster, as the Gold Medallist at this year's AIA Convention, expressed some envy of the mighty industrial base at our disposal and asked why architects here do not take more advantage of it.

Another 'English' aspect of Foster's work is its craft orientation. He seems to share the goal of the nineteenth-century Arts and Crafts movement in England of reconnecting design and fabrication. But unlike the reactionary anti-machine character of that earlier effort, Foster's method gets at the problem in a different way, by making machine production more craft-like.

Thomas Fisher

Finally, the analytical and empirical nature of Foster's thinking also has a peculiarly 'English' character. It is a mode of thought that values clarity, prizes precision, and respects facts – a welcome alternative to some of the fuzzy, jargon-laden thinking in our field. There are, of course, limits to what empirical analysis can achieve, as Foster himself now seems to recognise. The rational systems approach that characterised his early work, like the Sainsbury Centre for Visual Arts (2, 3), is now weighted more heavily by cultural, contextual, and climatic considerations, as in the Reichstag project (7, 8).

Every designer's method is, to some extent, personal and unpredictable. And every discipline, even if two are as close as architecture and industrial design, has unique qualities that are not easily transferred. Still, there are aspects of Foster's industrial-design approach that have wide relevance to our field as an explicit model or at least as a gauge against which contrary methods can be more accurately measured. Either way, if we can reconnect the aesthetic, programmatic, and tectonic aspects of architecture, we will all be better off.

7

8>

'Norman Foster is not an everyday author; but the fascination of his reductive forms comes from the dissolution of his authorship into an architectural degree zero that becomes a hopeful Esperanto.'

Luis Fernández-Galiano

We do not know Norman Foster well. His public image is that of a champion of British High-Technology and the head of a huge firm with offices in different time zones of the planet; his best-known work, the Hongkong and Shanghai Bank, sharpens this futuristic and muscular profile of his with its colossal frame and galactic atrium; and both his training in the engineering tradition and his penchant for aeronautics help to mint a robust, metallic and demiurgic personage. Yet his career as a whole depicts something closer to a meticulous and laconic architect whose efficient elegance is the apparel of an intelligent pragmatism, and whose silent clarity expresses a cold optimism, at once timid and haughty. His latest museum projects, all embedded in historical contexts, clearly illustrate this quiet and luminous quality of his architecture, which exalts the pre-existing with the quiet virtuosity of the new.

In all five cases – the Carré d'Art *médiathèque* in Nîmes, the Joslyn Art Museum in Omaha, the Royal Academy in London, and the projects for the British Museum and the Prado – Foster has had to face up to buildings held by their respective communities to possess architectural merit, historical meaning and emotional value. In each case he has responded by physically and symbolically subduing his intervention in a serenely natural manner that seeks to prolong the useful life of the historical complex by regenerating its internal organs and improving the urban quality of its immediate surroundings. Over and above the diversity of material, climatic and cultural contexts, which has occasioned a visible diversity of strategies, the five projects share a refined and silent subordination of the new to the old. The luminous fissure of the Sackler Galleries at the Royal Academy (4), the stony pink box of the Joslyn Art Museum (5-7), the glazed courtyard of the British Museum (3), and the light, sculptural podium of the Prado project (8), all defer to the hierarchy of memory, and even the Nîmes *médiathèque* buries more than half its volume underground so as not to compete with the delicate scale of the Maison Carrée.

The *médiathèque* (1,2) may at the outset seem unique among the five, since it presents itself as an autonomous, prismatic and free-standing building. But it clearly falls in line with the series when we consider the architect's very pertinent approach, whereby the site of the project is not just the excavated lot but the entire area of the square, including the Roman temple. In deference to the latter,

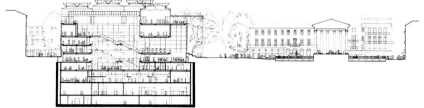

several floors are submerged, brightened up by a large atrium whose latticework filters the intense Mediterranean light; in homage to it, the facade is bedecked with a svelte and airy metal portico; and as a gesture of urban respect the entries are arranged along the diagonal line that links the Arènes amphitheatre with La Fontaine gardens. The building is organised by a sober and refined grid of cylindrical concrete pillars placed at 6-metre intervals, which evoke Classical pilasters in their union with the enclosing walls. With the interior bathed in a striped opalescent light, the prism acts as the busy backstage of the brightly illuminated square, where, on the carpet of stone, the temple is the soloist.

In Omaha also, Foster bows to the order of the place. Here the Classicism is Art Deco, with a charm of its own, and the architect again avoids the spectacular in what happens to be his first American building. Avoiding the fuss of a first, the extension of the Joslyn Museum is contained within a neutral, almost trivial box, lined with the same pink marble that was used in the original building – even extracted from the same Georgia quarry. The anonymous and analogical modesty of the approach does not prevent him from exploring the use and regulation of Nebraska's intense light through the ingenious section of the skylights in the exhibition galleries; or from restructuring the immediate surroundings by emphasising the main entry with a landscaped amphitheatre, and setting apart the vehicular access and the parking lots; or from stressing the importance of the pre-existing building by segregating the extension with a light glazed element, which brings natural light into the atrium and visually articulates the various volumes – the latter a solution that is also used in the Madrid and the two London projects.

The slot of light separating the two historical buildings that make up the Royal Academy is the most characteristic feature of the project, for which Foster has filled the void with vertical circulation elements to provide access to new toplit exhibition galleries. Clearing and illuminating the area, like an archeologist he discovers the seventeenth-century facades hidden behind the walls of the nineteenth-century extension, and reveals them by building the stairs, the elevator and even the floorings from glass, so that all transit needs are met by transparent or translucent elements that open up a new perception of the pre-existing buildings.

Similarly, though on a much larger scale, the project for the British Museum calls for the demolition of the book storage areas which cluttered the space

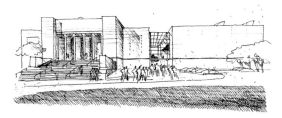

between the perimeter of Sir Robert Smirke's original inner courtyard and the large cylindrical volume of the Reading Room, built in the centre of the courtyard in 1857. The resulting space, flooded with light from a huge glazed roof, reveals the original courtyard's hidden facades, a brilliant excision that improves the building's circulation and integration with the surrounding urban fabric while recovering the dignity of its historical parts.

Similar is the strategy for the Prado, which starts with the sensible premise of building only within the limits of its site, maintaining the Church of the Jerónimos and the Museum of the Army as they are, and doing away with underground passages. The buildings are instead connected to each another by a landscaped walk. The extension *per se* is a podium stretching Villanueva's building to the rear and on the Goya side, toplit through skylights and a glazed gap respectfully left between the new structure and the old. The new construction – containing foyers and public services, a gallery for temporary exhibitions, a hall for various functions, offices, ateliers and a garage – is never higher than the pavements of the adjacent streets, so that these are extended into the staggered terraces of an open-air sculpture plaza. To the north of the museum, a new public square reconstructs the original topography of the zone while allowing direct access through the higher Goya entrance, although both the lower door of this facade and that of the Murillo facade are maintained in the new circulation system.

As with Foster's other museum projects, the reorganisation and functional fitting-out of the historical building combines with an extreme deference to the artistic and sentimental values of the past; with an intelligent and subtle use of natural light in the underground areas of the new construction; and with an ambitious yet cautious refurbishing of the immediate urban context, which is placed at the service of user need and memory, and wherein the new construction plays a role that is as efficient as it is silent. In the Prado, this silence allows some whispers – the raised square that appears at the northern end of the main facade or the terraces of the rear facade, articulated by stairs and skylights – urban whispers that hardly reveal the massive alteration of the architectural organism, rejuvenated by a careful scalpel that prolongs the museum's continuing existence amongst us.

Beyond technical refinement or functional clarity, what is astounding about Foster's work is his radical stripping of architectural language, which achieves the

7

Miesian 'almost nothing' through an empirical exploration devoid of rationalist Platonism. The clear geometry and efficient shapes of his buildings, eschewing both dogmatic idealism and romantic machinism, quietly express their structures while incorporating the flexibility to accommodate varying future uses. Such universal, elemental and complete openness was at the heart of the modern revolution and its generous and stubborn pursuit of objectivity. But also residing in this supreme surrender to external reason – whether of place, technique or use – is the poetic tremor that accompanies the deliberate abandonment of subjective vanity. Norman Foster is not an everyday author; the fascination of his reductive form comes from the dissolution of his authorship into an architectural degree zero that becomes a hopeful Esperanto.

8

'Foster's studio had seen so many bright young architects pass through it that he had if not exactly a school … at least a "tail" of architects, responsible for much of the wave of building in London during the 1980s, who were putting his methods to good use.'

Deyan Sudjic

There are many Norman Fosters. Perhaps the earliest to have made a mark on the world of architecture is the young student, who can be seen shyly peering out of the black-and-white snapshots taken of him in the company of the almost equally youthful Richard Rogers when they were both postgraduates at Yale (1). They huddle together in their overcoats against the winter chill of New Haven. They catch the train to Manhattan for bruisingly dry Martinis at the Four Seasons with James Stirling. They worked with Serge Chermayeff to explore the nature of the modern city. They collaborated on designing megastructures.

This was Foster as the personification of the ambitious Brit abroad, the bright young working-class Englishman from Manchester, for whom the spur of America and its uncomplicated social structure was an escape from the claustrophobia of post-war Britain. This was the brilliant student who reinvented himself in America, for whom design was an escape hatch from the bleaker aspects of British life.

Simply to have travelled to America at this period was enough to be different from his peers who had stayed at home. It was to have experienced at first hand what the builders of the California Case Study houses were up to, to have used commercially available colour film, to have seen Airstream trailers close up (2), to know about Charles Eames and Buckminster Fuller. It was enough to set yourself apart from the everyday reality of Britain, where such things were known only at third hand from blurry illustrations in magazines, and seemed like no more than colourful fairy tales from across an Atlantic that still took three days to cross.

In America, it was taken for granted that architecture was about optimism and a sense of possibilities in a way that Britain, which had only just escaped from shortages and rationing, found impossible to comprehend. And Foster, apparently effortlessly, adopted those easy, optimistic assumptions. But as things were to turn out much later on, Foster's discovery of Fuller was not just to be confined to an enthusiasm for the imagery of the geodesic dome. It was also about discovering a sweeping sense of scale, of not being afraid of making large plans. It helped prepare him to make the ambitious kind of statements that characterise his work, in a way that seemed uncomfortably out of place in the Britain of his student years.

Then there was the Norman Foster who emerged after the dissolution of Team 4 – the practice that he and Rogers established when they returned home – still a young man, but by now in a hurry to reinvent the architectural profession.

This was a moment when architects were divided between the large commercial firms who got most of the work but none of the critical attention, the submerged nine-tenths of the profession as it were, and the charmed circle of small practices who built the art galleries and universities that accounted for a tiny fraction of Britain's buildings, but for almost all of what was conventionally understood as its contemporary architecture.

Foster, with his crew cut and polo neck, hardly fitted the conventional image of either architectural camp. The big firms offered nothing but business-like pragmatism, the small ones carried on as if they were country doctors or family solicitors. Or prima donnas. Exposure to America, and his own natural predispositions, left Foster with an abiding impatience with each of these models. The turbocharged, even ruthless quality of Foster's own work was instantly apparent.

He presented himself as a problem solver, he was refreshingly free of sentimentality, and was as likely to ask a potential client 'Is your new building really necessary?' as to offer heroic form-giving exercises involving tracing paper and soft pencil sketches. His favourite word at the time was 'systems'. He delighted in appropriating technology from industries more advanced than construction for use on the building site, or better yet, for prefabrication off-site.

Even at this early stage, there was always an ambition to Foster's practice that seemed larger in scale than the material he was working with. Each project was always beautifully rendered – Helmut Jacoby was an early discovery (3) – and when it was completed, it was equally beautifully photographed. There was a sense of keeping an eye on the future and the place of the practice within it.

And yet, if Foster was enthusiastic to embrace the language of business-like technology, the reality was that he began his practice at a moment when there was a still unbridgeable gulf between those architects who treated the profession as a business, and those who were concerned with architecture for its own sake.

It wasn't just the architects on opposite sides of this great divide who saw themselves as belonging to different worlds – it was their clients too. The kinds of people who commissioned office blocks and corporate headquarters in the 1960s tended to regard architecture that could be considered as art with an innate sense of scepticism. In their eyes this was a form of self-indulgence. To be seen to care about architectural quality at this period, was to be accused of spending too much

tax-payer or shareholder money. Bland or banal building might actually be more expensive than a building of genuine architectural quality, but the very fact that it camouflaged its cost behind a slovenly exterior disarmed all criticism. Ugly buildings had – perversely – become synonymous with value for money.

Foster tackled this muddle-headed thinking head on. He talked about his work in terms of efficiency and value for money. He made his office, first in Fitzroy Street, then in Great Portland Street and finally in Battersea, look like a machine humming with efficiency. He had IBM as a major client. He looked for new methods of construction. He explored new development and contractual techniques with the intention of building well, but quickly.

Yet Foster was still essentially part of the architectural community. And there was still something of the poetic analogy in his work: it was often the dream of mechanisation rather than its substance that counted in the way he presented his work. Despite the visual clues given by his office, he was anything but a businessman-architect. To hire him was considered to represent an adventure by most of his clients. He was anything but a conventional choice of architect. And he was anything but a conventional designer.

This was the Foster of the Willis Faber & Dumas building (4) and the Foster of the Sainsbury Centre. The image that the office projected of itself was smooth, efficient, and technocratic. But it still used Rotring pens and tracing paper as its principal design tools rather than computers. The staff numbers were still small, and the ethos of the practice was not so different from that of a score of similar bright young offices. Being small was still seen as a virtue, even if it might have been a virtue conjured up out of necessity.

But despite the air of quiet pragmatism, the office's output was anything but pragmatic. Each building that came out of the office was an event; each seemed to be the product of entirely fresh thinking – a leap in a new direction, rather than a refinement of what had gone before. You could not say that this was an office that designed glass buildings, nor that it specialised only in steel. It was ready to experiment with anything, though there was not, it is true, much in the way of brick.

It was a period when the practice was finding a voice. Certainly there was a clear attitude and vocabulary emerging. The early projects reflected Foster's discovery of Buckminster Fuller, in that there was a predisposition in favour of the lightweight, and making the most of the minimum of materials. But it still allowed for buildings of such individual genius and unpredictable inventiveness as the Willis Faber & Dumas headquarters – with its black glass, grand piano super-structure, with its resonances of Mies van der Rohe's free-form glass towers from Berlin – as well as the pristine Classical elegance of the Sainsbury Centre.

The pattern began to change with the building of the new headquarters for the Hongkong and Shanghai Banking Corporation – another completely original solution, a reinvention of a familiar building type. Until they won the commission in an invited competition, Foster Associates had essentially followed the traditional pattern of the small creative British architectural office. Like many others it was based on the dedication of a band of slightly unworldly enthusiasts, living for archi-tecture with no strategic sense of the wider world. It was important to share certain values and assumptions if you were to continue to belong to this world. To deviate from them was to risk ostracism, to be ejected from the club.

To be part of the architectural culture of the early 1970s, it was a given that the office would be managed by architects. And for such architects, running the practice, hiring, management, job-getting, financial planning and all the rest of it, were almost always treated as side issues. The only really important thing was to design buildings, and to maintain a structure that put the creative architect at the top of the tree, responsible for all decisions. This was still a time when the archi-tectural profession continued to be tightly regulated: limited company structures were banned; unlimited liability partnerships were still a professional requirement. Fee-cutting, advertising and building industry directorships were all taboo.

In this view of the architectural world, professional management was regarded as, at best, a distraction. A prerequisite to this approach was that the office stayed small. An office that followed this path could never rise much beyond about 30 people. But even after the Hongkong Bank came into the office, Foster deliber-ately maintained a practice with just such an ethos. For even though the Bank commission was one of the largest of its kind, it was mainly coordinated from Hong Kong, where a substantial team was established to build the project, employing upwards of a hundred people.

Consciously or unconsciously, it was an arrangement that worked in such a way that the expansion needed to cope with a job of its complexity and scale never

Deyan Sudjic

5

touched the London office, which continued to maintain the character of a small and intimate organisation. The infrastructure and the scale of operation needed to make the Hongkong Bank a reality were kept at arm's length.

Thus it was that Norman Foster remained the quintessential English architect, even when he was first beginning to make a mark outside the narrow world of architecture. It was a caution that perhaps provided the reassuring sense of security that comes from familiarity. He might have had a few unfamiliar characteristics, such as piloting his own aeroplane, but he still spoke the language of the architectural world, even as the Royal Academy's 'New British Architecture' exhibition of 1986, bringing together Norman Foster, Richard Rogers and James Stirling, turned him into a national figure. So much so that his reputation had reached the point where Foster had joined the roster of celebrities promoting Rolex wristwatches, and he was part of *Vanity Fair's* recreation of the famous Beaux Arts Ball, which New York's most celebrated architects from the 1930s had attended dressed as their own buildings (5).

It was the Mark Three Foster that really broke the mould: the post-Hong Kong Foster. The scale and complexity, the ambition and sheer dynamism of the Hongkong Bank moved Foster out of the purely British context, propelling him onto the world stage. And having crossed that threshold, he became an architect who was able to transcend the division within the profession between the critically acclaimed and the materially successful.

By the middle of the 1990s Foster was unique among British architects of the post-war generation in that he had become a dominant force both in the quality and the quantity of his work. This had not been seen in Britain since the days of Lutyens, who dominated the profession in a way that Foster has come to echo. And like Lutyens, Foster is now in demand to design both giant corporate buildings and individual houses.

But the transition was not immediately apparent. The shift in perceptions of Foster was almost covert at first. It seemed for a while – to the world outside the office at least – as if things had gone quiet for Foster Associates, as the practice was then called. For various reasons – the accidents of cancelled commissions and shifts in programmes, as well as the sheer length of time taken to complete large-scale projects – there was a gap between the opening of the Hongkong

6>

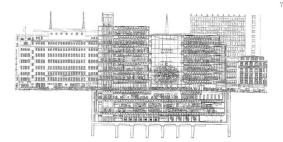

Bank and the completion of the next major Foster design. A gap that stretched almost to the end of the 1980s, and was wide enough for it to seem as if the adventure into building on the scale of the Hongkong Bank was a one-off, rather than a settled new direction for the practice.

The exhibition at the Royal Academy (6) was certainly a watershed for Foster – but it was not quite the immediate new beginning for his career that might have been expected, even though it attracted so much attention. The stunning photographic images of the Bank and the huge models of it that dominated the Academy exhibition brought home to a British audience just how remarkable a project the Bank was. It went a long way to overcome the tendency of the insular architectural community in Britain to discount the significance of buildings that were not within easy reach of central London. And it did much to change the sense that the architectural community in Britain lived in an embattled enclave.

For years there had been a feeling that architecture was cut off from the other visual arts as well as from a wider public. The success of the Royal Academy show demonstrated that architecture could take its place alongside art in the Academy's galleries. And that it could attract a large audience as well. But the other scheme that Foster exhibited at the Royal Academy – the new headquarters building for BBC Radio in London (7), which was envisaged for the site of the former Langham Hotel, and which should have seen the triumphant unveiling of his most significant project in Britain and the natural next step in his career, consolidating the achievement of the Hongkong Bank – turned out to be a memorial for a dead design.

This was the most complex, and potentially the richest and most rewarding urban problem that Foster had yet addressed. But the building was cancelled while the exhibition was still being planned. Instead of building itself a contemporary civic monument, updating the inheritance of the Reith years, the Corporation opted for a banal metal box in suburban White City. It was a decision that said a lot about the state of contemporary British culture.

The walls of the Royal Academy were crammed with countless study models that showed every twist and turn in the project's troubled history, betraying Foster's fondness for the model as a design tool, and also his way of exploring every potential option to the full before finally committing himself to one approach rather than to another.

Deyan Sudjic

But it is hard not to interpret the display not so much as an exposition of a design process in minute detail, but as a memorial for a great deal of futile effort. And as such, it sharply brought home the precarious nature of architectural practice. Critical success, and the successful completion of one giant project, is no guarantee that there will be a steady flow of similar work to follow. And in the end, the critical reputations of architects of Foster's kind are based not so much on ideas as on completed buildings.

Nor are these fluctuations simple abstractions. They are fluctuations that can have painful consequences for individual careers and livelihoods. The period after the completion of the Bank certainly faced the firm's directors with some difficult decisions about the number of employees that their shifting workload could support. Teams and expertise that had been built up over several years had sometimes to be dispersed. The concomitant to this was that the Foster office by the 1980s had become one of the most important training grounds for young creative architects drawn in from around the world by the opportunity to work on what were widely seen as some of the most exciting projects available anywhere.

Until the BBC project, the majority of commissions that came Foster's way were of a nature that required pristine 'object' buildings on out-of-the-way sites. The BBC, by contrast, would have been the centrepiece of one of London's great urban set pieces, the culmination of the eighteenth-century expansion of the capital north, towards Regent's Park. Thanks to its site it could not fail to engage in an intimate dialogue with Nash's bravura church of All Souls', with its conical spire, just across the street.

The office had worked long and hard on the project, wrestling with the complexities of modern broadcasting technologies, and with the symbolic qualities of housing a national institution such as the BBC in a building that would be appropriately dignified, and yet democratically transparent. It had to deal with a site that required a building which simultaneously closed a vista, turned a corner and formed part of an urban block.

These were issues to which Foster, when he had previously had to address them, albeit on a much less demanding scale, had responded with ingenious sleights of hand. His formal buildings had denied the very existence of formality and symmetry. Think, for example, about the way in which the Sainsbury Centre's

8

umbilical glass bridge, uniting it with Denys Lasdun's concrete university mega-structure, had finessed the issue of a formal connection by approaching it at an oblique angle, rather than head-on.

His contextual buildings had actually denied context. Think of the way that the Willis Faber building addressed its context by not addressing it at all, but by ingeniously adopting that black glass skin which insinuates itself into the lanes and pantiles of Ipswich with a plan that has no sharp edges, and a facade which literally reflects the city around it rather than trying to look like it. Foster makes connections by stripping back the detail: two walls will meet at an oblique angle and appear not to touch at all. Ceilings do not touch walls, they stop short of them. Walls do not touch the ground, rather they are insulated from it.

But with the BBC, there could be no hiding behind this kind of sophistry. The Langham Place scheme was the first project for which Foster had to play the game of architecture according to rules that were not of his own making. Until then, he had always been able to sidestep them, to pull a rabbit out of a hat, to find a new way of doing things. And the BBC was all the more impressive a design for the fact that it didn't try to beg any questions, but addressed the high game of architecture.

But it was not built, despite all the energy that had gone into it. The thinking that went into the BBC project helped to inform Foster's unsuccessful submission for the Paternoster Square competition to replan the setting of St Paul's, demolishing the crude structures of the 1950s to renew both architecture and planning concepts. Projects like this marked the rediscovery of masterplanning in the city context, an activity that had all but vanished after the 1970s, as planning became dominated by mathematical rather than physical models.

The BBC and Paternoster Square marked a rediscovery of modern physical planning, not just by Foster, but by the architectural profession at large. But, in the event, neither was built. Nor was the spectacular plan for Televisa (8), the Mexican broadcasting company, which came into the Foster office at almost the same moment that the BBC project was cancelled. Televisa was characterised by a soaring roof that embraced the clarity of Stansted Airport, and prefigured the economy of means of the roof for the new Hong Kong airport at Chek Lap Kok.

There were a number of other schemes that came to nothing in this period. The projected athletics stadium in Frankfurt, for example, and the masterplan for

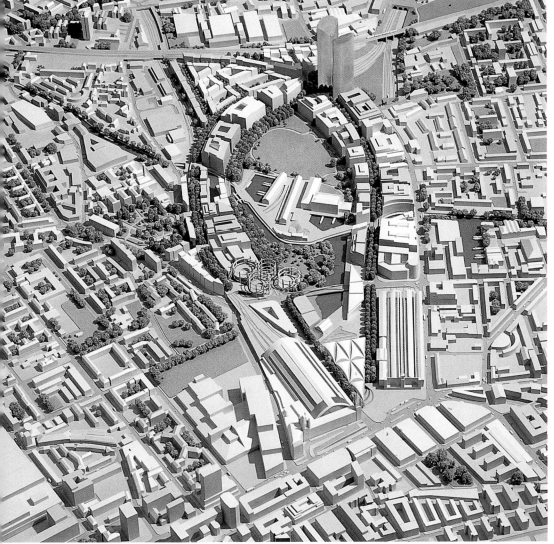

the redevelopment of a massive 52-hectare site around the King's Cross railway terminal in London (9), which gave Foster the chance to work on the scale of a city and to draw in teams of other architects on a collaborative effort. And the other projects that the office was working on, in particular the scheme for London's third airport at Stansted, but also the Carré d'Art in Nîmes and the American Air Museum at Duxford, moved so slowly that there was nothing to be seen of them until well into the 1990s.

Meanwhile, London in the second half of the 1980s was going through one of the most feverish building booms that it had ever seen. Great tracts of the city were reconfigured as Fleet Street was turned over from being the traditional preserve of the newspaper industry to an enclave dominated by the American banks. The docks were resurrected from derelict wasteland into a facsimile of the World Financial Center in Manhattan. In the process, architects grew prosperous and confident, and the profession shed the last traumatic memories of the collective nervous breakdown it had suffered in the 1970s when it had had to face society's disenchantment with the failed Utopia that it had offered in the 1960s.

Architecture in the 1980s became part of the fashionable agenda again. It rediscovered the glamour that it once had. This was the design decade; the Alessi kettle, the Eames chair – and Foster's Nomos table for that matter – became its essential props. The smart advertising agencies used them to establish their credentials as being in touch with the mood of the moment.

The decade saw the beginning of the revitalisation of the purist-influenced approach to architecture that is often called Modernism, in opposition to the decorative playfulness of Post-Modernism. And cool Modernism became the definitive image for a wave of smart galleries and boutiques. This phenomenon, with which Foster is often associated, is presented as a stylistic revival, a resurrection of the aesthetic of Modernism, and recycled, shorn of the original social content.

Certainly there are some examples of this. Richard Meier, for one, has played a limited set of variations on themes originally created by Le Corbusier. But this is not an interpretation that applies to Foster. His work is not so much a resurrection of the original Modern Movement pioneers, despite the resonances of Mies van der Rohe in the Willis Faber building in Ipswich or of the Le Corbusier of the Algiers period in the massing of the Hongkong Bank, but is part of a continuing

tradition of lightweight, unrhetorical architecture that owes as much to the California of the post-war boom as to the radical Europe of the 1920s.

It is often claimed that the Modernists, for all their dreams of a machine age, in fact knew precious little about how machines actually worked. That they made buildings which looked as if they had sprung from a production line, but which were actually made laboriously by hand. It is not a charge that is entirely justifiable: Jean Prouvé, Buckminster Fuller and Charles Eames knew what went on in factories and on production lines, and Foster learned to understand the potential, as well as the limitations, of technology. His work is clearly influenced by the refined beauty of the components employed by the aerospace industry, but it is not simply a superstitious reproduction of its imagery. It takes those techniques and materials as its starting point, and applies some of the same concerns to architecture.

Foster is first and foremost an instinctive architect, rather than an intellectual: his architecture is informed by an optimistic embrace of the potential of technology, a spatial vision, but most of all by an aesthetic sense. In contrast to Richard Rogers, whose work is an elaboration and a celebration of structure and connection, Foster's is about refinement, the omission of the inessential, smooth skins and sparing palettes.

By the 1980s his work was already emerging from its original identification with High-Tech, a phenomenon given an important boost by the designs for the Royal Academy and for the Carré d'Art in Nîmes. In both cases history and context took a leading role. Foster's studio had seen so many bright young architects pass through it that he had if not exactly a school or a group of followers, at least a 'tail' of architects, responsible for much of the wave of building in London during the 1980s, who were putting his methods to good use.

But Foster found himself almost marginalised in all this activity. While Terry Farrell changed the face of central London, completing giant new structures at Alban Gate, Charing Cross and Vauxhall, and Richard Rogers beat him in the competition to design the new Lloyd's building which became the most conspicuous architectural embodiment of the period, Foster was working – in the UK – on little more than a small speculative office development at Stockley Park, a relatively modest redevelopment of the *Sunday Times* building on Gray's Inn Road for ITN, and the mixed-use building in Battersea to which he eventually moved his own studio.

Foster did, in fact, work on a design for a high-rise office tower at Canary Wharf, the archetypal 1980s building site, but it was just before the site's owners were forced into bankruptcy as the 1980s boom turned to the bust of the early 1990s. It would be almost a decade before Foster would realise a high-rise tower at Canary Wharf, this time for HSBC – his old Hong Kong client. He did work on a couple of high fashion projects in the champagne-swilling 1980s – Katharine Hamnett's Knightsbridge store, a scheme for Esprit's headquarters in San Francisco and a shop for them in Sloane Street – but both of them ran out of steam.

And yet, despite all these apparent setbacks, the Foster operation in London was expanding rapidly. When the team that built the Hongkong Bank came back to London, the office grew quickly. The new terminal for Stansted Airport eventually got the go-ahead; Century Tower (10), an office tower in Tokyo, was built at breakneck speed; and the Carré d'Art in Nîmes eventually received the funds it needed to be built. At the same time, the practice was doing all that it could to adjust itself to the increasingly global world of architecture.

The Hong Kong office closed in 1986, shortly after the completion of the Bank, but Foster quickly went back to Asia to pursue further projects in Japan. Mainland Europe was also an important place to be for Foster: first in France, then Spain and Germany. This was an acknowledgement of the realities of a global culture. American architects built Canary Wharf, just as British architects such as Foster now work throughout the world.

Foster's student days in America had opened his eyes to the world beyond Britain's sometimes narrow and insular view of the world. The experience of building the Hongkong Bank brought home the global nature of the building industry, to say nothing of the dynamic nature of the tiger economies of the Pacific Rim. It played an important part in shifting Foster's focus. And it did something to the nature of his approach to design. Foster was transformed from a purely English architect into a designer with a global perspective. He became more than the product of English High-Tech, with its schoolboyish enthusiasms.

While the boom of the 1980s marked the high tide of Post-Modernism, distinguished by heavy-handed playfulness and colour, Foster maintained a coherent belief in the architectural vocabulary which marked his mature approach. It was distinguished by a cool austerity that seemed to reflect the values particularly of

European clients at the time, who felt uncomfortable with the element of fancy dress that Post-Modernism seemed to represent. And as the attractions of Post-Modernism faded, Foster's restraint became, if not a uniform for confident corporations, then certainly an architectural benchmark.

It was a two-way process. Foster's exposure throughout Europe and Asia and his confidence with large visions allowed him to adopt the aspirations of the cultures in which he worked. It is interesting to see how often Foster was able to build close personal relationships with his clients. It is no accident that he designed not only the Carré d'Art for the city of Nîmes but also a new house for the city's mayor. Just as he built not only Century Tower in Tokyo, but also a house for its owner.

It would not be an exaggeration to say that the rapid growth which characterised the nature of the Foster office in the 1990s, when it completely destroyed that old distinction between business architects and art architects to become one of the world's largest practices, was based on achieving an understanding of the nature of construction in the 1990s. The firm was big but, more to the point, it had found a way in which to impose some sense of order on the chaotic wave of building that was transforming the Pacific Rim.

That way included not just an aesthetic discipline which gave Foster's work a distinctive signature and, even more importantly, a coherence from one project to the next, but also an organisational structure which made the whole undertaking possible. The firm expanded in its ambitions, and in its size. It turned itself from a studio into an office and then into a series of offices around the world. It went from an intimate group of architects, to a highly organised structure, in which every creative architectural employee seemed to adopt, both literally and metaphorically, the handwriting of its founder.

These are all difficult achievements to pull off, and are just as much accomplishments as is the ability to design great works of architecture in isolation. And, in this sense, it is perhaps one of the greatest achievements of Foster's career that he was able to create an organisation that could be relied on by the most demanding of worldwide clients to produce architecture on demand of such distinction.

And yet it would have been hard to predict all this in the building that Foster completed in London after the Bank which attracted the most attention. This was the creation of the new Sackler Galleries at the Royal Academy: a project that is

13

all but invisible on the exterior and which exists only in the interstices of the complex web of historical layers of the old Academy building (11, 12).

In comparison with the Hongkong Bank or the terminal at Stansted Airport, it was a tiny project, and yet it allowed the practice to reflect deeply on its attitudes towards architecture; about the issues of spatial hierarchy and context; about the relationship of one historical period to another; and about the creation of spaces that can sympathetically accommodate great works of art – a reflection which could be seen as introducing a new richness to Foster's work, and to his ambitions.

The project came at the time when the office was also thinking about the issue of context in Nîmes, where it was not only working on the Carré d'Art – a building which had as its immediate neighbour the Maison Carrée, the ancient Roman temple at the heart of the city – but was also looking at ways in which architecture could make sense of the shape of the city as a whole. Foster produced a strategy for linking the heart of the city with the airport on its periphery, for making sense of its existing public spaces, and for giving a presence and a dignity to the major boulevards.

As at the Royal Academy, Foster was interested in the creative tension that comes from juxtaposing new with old. But unlike what might have been expected from a younger Foster, the Royal Academy work takes care to respect the grain of the building as he found it. It is not confrontation for confrontation's sake. Foster searched for a way of unlocking extra space within a complex building. And he used the architectural detail of Modernism not to show off in an egotistical way, but to create a coherent and refined space. The Royal Academy was the first in a continuing line of projects in which Foster found sympathetic ways of confronting history. It was followed in due course by the new German Parliament in the Reichstag (14) and then by the Great Court at the British Museum (13), both of which are large-scale, contemporary interventions in the context of historical – even iconic – national buildings.

But Foster wasn't only designing at the scale of the city and the individual building. This was also the time when he was working for the Italian furniture company, Tecno, at the scale of the desk, the drawer, and the workstation. This was a range of furniture that had its origins in prototypes developed for the office's own use. The experience of working with Tecno brought direct experience of working at the scale of industrial design, an activity that is inevitably rather different from that of architecture. It was a chance to build up expertise in this area that the practice has gone on developing.

In the language of the pioneers of the Modern Movement, here was an architecture that truly went from the scale of the spoon to that of the entire city. And an architecture which had the coherence and internal logic to move effortlessly from one to the other.

14

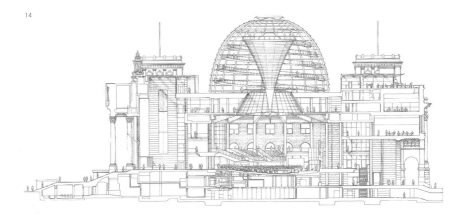

'The Commerzbank tower turns the conventional skyscraper inside out, opening it up to natural light, fresh air and abundant vegetation, which pervade the whole building, penetrating right into its empty core.'

Peter Buchanan

Foster and Partners' Commerzbank in Frankfurt, like the Renzo Piano Building Workshop's Debis building in Berlin (1), is a corporate headquarters in Germany – a country that takes social and environmental matters seriously. So both complexes include a glass-roofed space used by both public and corporation, and the towers of both have a secondary outer glass skin that achieves energy efficiency by allowing even the highest offices to be naturally ventilated for most of the year. Debis is one of a group of buildings by Piano, in an area masterplanned by him, that together are creating their own context as a new urban quarter; the Commerzbank fits into existing urban fabric. Yet it is Commerzbank that is the more generic solution. Although both buildings have lessons to teach about achieving energy efficiency while maintaining a sense of contact with the outdoors, the Commerzbank offers a prototype for the future by showing how a tall building can also be a vibrant social mechanism.

At 258 metres tall, and 298 metres to the top of its mast, the Commerzbank Headquarters is Europe's tallest building (4). But other than in size, it does not seem from a distance much different from other towers clustered in Frankfurt's financial centre. This impression is misleading, for the building's height is one of its less significant aspects. What Foster and Partners have achieved is nothing less than the reinvention of the skyscraper. Certainly there is precedent for the design in unbuilt projects by Jean Prouvé and Amancio Williams, in SOM's triangular tower in Saudi Arabia and Ken Yeang's 'bio-climatic' towers in Malaysia. But the Commerzbank synthesises the inspiration of all such precedent along with very current concerns and state-of-the-art engineering. The result is innovative not just technically (in its structural and servicing solutions) but also socially, as well as in its 'green' strategies to conserve fossil-fuel energy and fresh water while bringing the pleasures of natural light and fresh air, and the close proximity of plants, to everybody inside. Moreover, around its base, lower parts of the same new complex retain the street alignment, scale and mixed uses of the surrounding nineteenth-century buildings (2).

The conventional skyscraper wraps its offices around a central core to achieve maximum efficiency in the proportion of the plan that is lettable and the minimal length of external wall to enclose it. If the tower rises as a sheer Miesian rectangle, then it does so set back across a lifeless plaza, destroying the contiguity of

street facade and urban fabric. If it rises and steps back from the street line or is very tall, then its lower floors tend to be so deep in plan that most of their occupants might as well be underground. Throughout such buildings, where each floor is dismally similar to the others, there is a total dependency on energy-consuming and spirit-sapping artificial light and air conditioning. These buildings are efficient only in relation to initial capital costs and net-to-gross floor area ratios. But in terms of the far higher energy costs over the life of the building, and even more so in terms of the health and happiness of the workers inside (whose salaries will typically account for very many times the capital costs), such buildings are extremely inefficient.

The Commerzbank tower turns the conventional skyscraper inside out, opening it up to natural light, fresh air and abundant vegetation, which pervade the whole building, penetrating right into its empty core. The usual central core of structure, circulation and services has been removed, leaving a void filled with light and fresh air, and replaced with three compact cores at the corners of an equilateral triangle. Between these cores span pairs of huge Vierendeel trusses, each eight floors deep, the outer one of which bulges in a curve outwards (the stability ensured by the wide-legged stance of the cores is therefore further enhanced by the tower's structural performance as a tube – a solution devised by structural engineer Chris Wise of Ove Arup & Partners). These Vierendeel trusses support the secondary beams of the column-free offices, which all have windows facing outwards or inwards. On each level only two sides are filled with offices. The third side is left open as one of the four-storey-high 'sky gardens' (6) that step up from one side to the next in a helix that rises through the building. It is through these sky gardens that the central void and the inner offices that overlook it get most of their natural light and all of their fresh air.

These sky gardens provide an interesting outlook for the inward-facing offices (which the Bank's employees now consider to be more desirable than the outward-looking ones), most of which overlook two gardens, one as a foreground to the sky above, the other to the city below. The landscaping of the gardens (as well as the colour-coding of the cores) aids orientation: those facing west have North American trees such as maples and cedars, the east-facing have Asian bamboos and Oriental pines, and those facing south have ancient olive trees and

Peter Buchanan

[...]
Un joc de miralls
permet de veure l'altre banda
del poema.
[...]

Ein Spiel von Spiegeln
erlaubt, die andere Seite
des Gedichts zu sehen,

Mediterranean herbs. People in the sky gardens further animate the view, for these spaces are social foci, with coffee bars and seating tucked amongst the plants. They are thus intrinsic to Foster's vision of the tower as a 'community of villages', with each garden as a village square-cum-green for the 240 employees who directly overlook it.

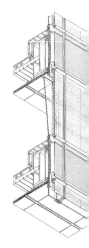

Significantly too, these gardens are part of a hierarchy of social foci. Ranging upwards from the shared offices, these include also the widened circulation areas of the 'combi-office' layouts, which accommodate 30 people on each floor between pairs of cores, and the glass-roofed 'plaza' adjacent to the bottom of the tower (3). The latter houses a restaurant that is open to the general public who reach it by climbing very broad steps from Grosse Gallusstrasse to the north and curving past the spectacular but too-stark reception area in the base of the tower, or more directly by stairs from the Kaiserplatz to the south. The plaza is thus on a pedestrian thoroughfare and acts not just as a social focus for all Commerzbank employees – the 1,200 in the old tower retained on the same block as well as the 2,300 in the new tower – but also as a social link between Bank and city. After lunching here, employees in the tower report that they enjoy taking coffee in a different sky garden to those they used on the previous few days.

Gusting winds and rain usually make it impossible to use opening windows and natural ventilation on tall buildings. This problem has been resolved here by having a secondary external glass skin with horizontal vents below and above the base and head of the motorised, bottom-hung inward-tilting windows (5). These windows are controlled by those working next to them, although they are automatically sealed shut by the computer-controlled building management system (BMS) if temperature, weather or pollution conditions become extreme. The 'breathing wall', in combination with chilled ceilings and the admission of heat-purging cool night air in summer and convection heaters under the window sills, allows the building (in Frankfurt's relatively temperate climate) to be naturally ventilated for more than 60 per cent of the year. Motorised venetian blinds in the 165mm cavity between external rain screen and inner wall are also under the control of the BMS. When the sun strikes these faces they are automatically lowered, their blades being angled to exclude sun in summer and to reflect sun deep into the offices in winter.

Peter Buchanan

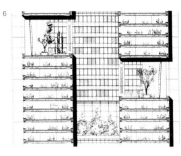

The inward-looking offices need no protective rain screen, so their windows open directly off the central void. This gets fresh air from the pivoting windows at the head of the glazed screens that enclose the sky gardens and slope so as to reflect high, hot sun downwards. In mid-winter, when these are closed, the plants help re-oxygenate and humidify the air, which is warmed by the low sun that penetrates the glazing. Because the height of the central void would have resulted in strong updrafts caused by 'stack effect' convection, it has been closed between reception lobby floor and roof into twelve-storey segments by three intermediary glazed diaphragms.

If one could ignore the drama of its vistas and vertiginous spaces, the Commerzbank is not, as an object, one of Foster and Partners' more exciting and elegant designs. Partly this is due to the inevitable blandness of the fully-glazed external skin (adapted and specially coated to minimise radar reflections), as well as some awkwardness in parts of the public level, and partly due to a relatively constrained budget. But the building deserves to be one of the architect's most influential. Foster has often talked about the importance of social and environmental issues, yet has seldom delivered these as convincingly as here.

But even skyscrapers such as this have negative consequences: they overshadow their neighbours and accelerate winds, so destabilising the local microclimate, as well as overloading the local transport infrastructure. So medium-rise buildings with internal atria or courts, along the lines of Arup Associates' buildings at London's Broadgate, represent a better model for the city of the future – which would once again have a continuous physical and social fabric, and an outdoor public realm suited to the Mediterranean-inspired al fresco lifestyle that is spreading to wherever and whenever climate permits. But if skyscrapers continue to be built, then Commerzbank provides the model that deserves to be emulated – if only architects would accept a good idea when they see it and not feel compelled to seek originality in the spurious formalisms of which Commerzbank is almost entirely devoid. This last point might suggest that the blandness and inelegancies of form and detail that distress some of Foster's fans, are partly what makes this building seem so convincing and authentic, and so available as a prototype.

'The illusion is that the light does not radiate from a given point, but resides in space while occupying it, much as the sound of an orchestra occupies an auditorium while bouncing off different surfaces.'

Sebastiano Brandolini

The numbers alone, in this new Hong Kong Airport, are mind-boggling and it would take a new metric system to understand them. We are assured that like the Great Wall of China, the Airport is recognisable from space – and we can only believe it. Various sources speak of 370,000 cubic metres of concrete for the passenger terminal, 67,000 tons of steel reinforcement, 8 kilometres of expansion joints, an overall surface area as large as Soho in London, and a luggage hall more spacious than a football stadium. We are assailed by a mixture of dizzy figures and triumph, just at a time one hears so much about the risk of collapsing Far Eastern economies. Moreover, the awe-inspiring Chek Lap Kok Airport, with its grandiose connecting infrastructure, is the project which more than any other has described the continuity between Hong Kong's past and future; from British Crown Colony to ward of capitalist China.

A super-monument to man's progress? An intelligent machine governing nature? The model for an ideal city dedicated to transport? The answers and the criticisms may be varied, but no major airport – European or American – can call itself so modern. By comparison, the others are all jumbles of bits and pieces, where systems have devoured architecture; they are eternal demolition sites and stop-gap projects.

Those who until 6 July had been accustomed to land at the old Kai Tak Airport were privileged to feel that they were already in the heart of Hong Kong before actually getting there. Those were the days when washing-lines flapped close to the wingtips of jets, and the characteristically tropical sour smell of rot wafted into the terminal. Kai Tak Airport was in the city; and the difference between inside and outside was almost nil; it was like arriving by train, with passengers plunged straight into the hyperdensity and round-the-clock congestion of Hong Kong. At Chek Lap Kok, Norman Foster's pencil and the Mott Consortium's organisation have imposed a decidedly different atmosphere. It is sunny, unlimited, clean, unobstructed and calm, and the ceilings are high. The Airport is a monument to contemporary China and Hong Kong presented to half the globe's population, which lives within only a five-hour radius by plane.

The new runways, terminals and buildings annexed to Chek Lap Kok (which means 'goldfish') rest on what was previously a mountainous island. This was flattened for the purpose, squared and linked by a rail and road suspension bridge

(the longest in Asia) to Central, the main underground station in the city's business centre. This new place is linked to the sea rather than to the topography of its surrounding land. The shape of the island and the arrangement of the buildings on it – the project's townplanning – were already defined by the masterplan design. This, with a peremptory logic, laid down the delicate meeting-points between management aspects and architecture, without which the role of the various players cannot be outlined and the unity indispensable to decision-making would be lacking.

Henceforth, 'completion times were the essence of the project'. They were not just deadlines, they governed the actual idea of the architecture. It is amazing how cleverly Foster manages in the forms of his architecture to represent the links (in his view indissoluble) between time, production systems and functional schedules – without, however, letting himself be swayed by construction systems or practical engineering. Those who compare Foster to an engineer fail to grasp the superior quality that he adds to plain technology.

Foster knows how to represent the organisational machine at the close of the twentieth century, just as Paxton did with the Crystal Palace. As we walk the thousand metres and more that divide the entrance wall from the embarkation gates, we notice the absence of all intermediate scales of architecture, creating direct switches from the scale of the infinitely large to that of the infinitely small. Foster and the Mott Consortium have reduced to a minimum the compositional elements of the Airport, which was not designed in the traditional sense, but organised and programmed. Compared to Stansted, as well as Chek Lap Kok's larger scale, it is easy to notice that here all the elements of design have been abandoned in favour of the overall perfection of the outer shell. The risk was that of producing a general sense of anonymity. The intelligent totems supporting the umbrella roof at Stansted have given way to round pillars that seem to vanish into an inner volume so vast that the eye is lost in it.

As at Stansted, here too the roof catalyses our curiosity, especially if we are in the departure hall or in the long embarkation fingers. The roof (2), comprising a series of barrel arches leading towards the gates, is conceived as a perspective that channels us in the right direction. Towards their sides the arches get lower, though without being flattened. The top of each section incorporates a skylight composed of triangles, which continue the pattern set by the structural ribs of the crossed arches below, screening the light and reflecting onto the intrados of the roof. The geometry must have been complicated to design, but it is easy to perceive and conjures up the magical feeling of being inside a vast lighting fixture.

The illusion is that the light does not radiate from a given point, but resides in space while occupying it, much as the sound of an orchestra occupies an auditorium while bouncing off different surfaces. The shape of the roof screen causes a special gravitational sensation to reverberate in the air, almost as if we were in a pressurised interior capable of inflating its surroundings. In a place acting so directly on our senses, it is difficult to grasp distances. Foster solves the problem of the project's immensity by means of illusion, by the articulation of light and perfectly matching material, reflections, minute details, proportions and rhythms, in a smoothly calibrated and impeccable scene in which we ourselves become actors and must prove ourselves worthy. This is his image of an ideal and perfect world. For Foster, computers and technology are parts of this imaginary world. And one of its great merits is that it never slips into authoritarianism. We ordinary mortals may perhaps not deserve it, but it does allow us to dream.

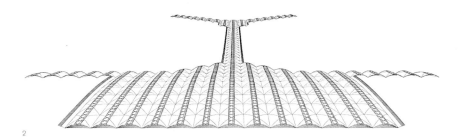

2

3>

'One day Foster and his compatriots found posted above their desks a sign that read: start drawing. The English response was to post another sign that read: start thinking.'

Robert A M Stern

'Yale opened my eyes and my mind. In the process I discovered myself. Anything positive that I have achieved as an architect is linked in some way to my Yale experience.'
Norman Foster, 1994[1]

Norman Foster is without question one of the most accomplished and influential architects of our time. What interests me in particular about Foster's career is the continuing exchange of English, European, and American techniques and ideas. The Anglo-American part of this exchange has its practical, experience-based beginnings in 1961 at Yale University, where both Foster and I were architecture students. Our time at Yale School of Art and Architecture had a profound and differing effect on each of us, leading me to question the then 'constituent facts' of Modernism and modernity, and Foster to open up his work to the various 'constituent facts' of the American experience, including its vast landscape and its unabashed commercialism.[2]

In 1951, ten years before going to Yale, Norman Foster, aged sixteen, had already begun to develop a healthy interest in architecture, in part stimulated by trips to the local public library in Levenshulme, the Manchester suburb where he grew up. It was there, as he recalled recently, that he '… discovered the different worlds of Frank Lloyd Wright and Le Corbusier. Imagine the contrast of a house on the prairie with a villa on a Paris boulevard. Yet I remember being equally fascinated by both at the time.'[3]

At just the moment that Foster was educating himself in the history of architecture, however, he was called up for two years' mandatory National Service, which he elected to serve in the Royal Air Force. Following his return to civilian life and his subsequent graduation from Manchester University School of Architecture, Foster arrived in New Haven in the autumn of 1961 aided by a Henry Fellowship which each year enables selected British students to study either at Yale or Harvard universities while their opposite numbers study at Oxford or Cambridge. Foster was a Guest Fellow in Jonathan Edwards College, one of Yale's residential colleges modelled on those found in Oxbridge. Interestingly, Foster had been offered a Fulbright Travel Scholarship but declined the award because it would have inhibited his freedom to work in the United States.

Foster's decision to go to Yale was not easily arrived at, nor did the value of the place immediately manifest itself to him. For a time he wondered if he might not have done better to have gone to the University of Pennsylvania and studied under Louis Kahn. Soon enough, however, Foster found Yale to be a liberating place, alive to the possibilities of architecture as an art and to the cross-currents of prevailing styles, ideologies, and passions.

A small school, at the time – really a department in the School of Art and Architecture – Yale was dominated by two great teachers: the architect Paul Rudolph (1) and the architectural historian Vincent Scully. There were, of course, other permanent faculty members but the great strength of the school lay in the interplay between Scully and Rudolph and, in turn, in their interplay with a host of visiting critics, including American architects such as Philip Johnson, Henry Cobb, Craig Ellwood and Ulrich Franzen, to name a few. They were joined by Europeans such as Frei Otto, Henning Larsen and Shadrach Woods and especially the British architects James Stirling and Colin St John Wilson.

In Foster's year at Yale, the Masters class benefited not only from his presence but from that of two other brilliant English students: Eldred Evans and Richard Rogers. The confluence at Yale of the three – who had not known each other in England – proved to be remarkably important for the future of architecture, as was their interaction with American students in the class, such as Carl Abbott, as well as others in the four-year-long baccalaureate programme, including Charles Gwathmey, Jonathan Barnett, M J Long, David Sellers, Peter Gluck and David Childs.

Paul Rudolph's Yale was a phenomenon, a surprise newcomer on an American architectural scene dominated by Harvard since the late 1930s when Walter Gropius took over as chairman of its architecture programme. When Rudolph became head of Yale's programme in 1958, the school was in a state of disarray, despite a burst of energy in the early 1950s when George Howe, assisted by Louis Kahn and Philip Johnson, had revived it. Following Howe's retirement, in 1954, the school became rank with contentiousness under his short-term successor, Paul Schweikher; but Rudolph's regime changed all that. By the time Foster arrived, Yale occupied a position of international prominence in architectural education. Arguably it was the most talked about architecture programme in the world.

Robert A M Stern

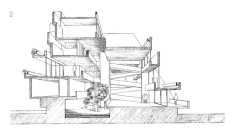

2

Rudolph's appointment had required a great leap of faith. He was no 'educator' in the generally accepted sense of the term, but he was a brilliantly talented architect, whose reputation rested on the bedrock of a dazzling series of small houses, mostly in Sarasota, Florida. In the late 1950s Rudolph's practice was blossoming. His first major work, the Jewett Arts Center at Wellesley College, was nearing completion and was already regarded as a serious challenge to the uniformity and placelessness of the American version of the International Style, which Gropius and Breuer had advocated at Harvard in the 1940s.

Rudolph was not only not an educator, he was not very well educated himself. He was in no way like his courtly and well-connected predecessor, George Howe, who had come from wealth, attended Groton and Harvard with Franklin Roosevelt, and spent four years in Paris at the Ecole des Beaux Arts. Rudolph, a Methodist minister's son raised in a variety of Southern towns, lacked cultivation and was brusque in a way many found refreshing – and many did not. He had studied at Alabama Polytechnical Institute (now Auburn University) and although he had gone on to complete two years in the Masters class at Harvard, at the time of his appointment to Yale his professional academic experience was confined to a succession of posts as visiting critic at a dozen or more provincial universities. Rudolph, 40 years old when he took over Yale, was not that much older than some of his students whose education had been interrupted by the Korean War.

Rudolph lacked a theory of education, and he did not seem particularly interested in developing one. But he was intensely interested in the 'learning process'. He viewed the art of building in strictly heroic terms and passionately believed in the capacity of the architectural idea – and the architect – to prevail over day-to-day circumstances. For him theory was synonymous with the big idea that carries the day: 'Theory', he said, 'must again overtake action … Architectural education's first concern is to perpetuate a climate where the student is acutely and perceptively aware of the creative process. He must understand that after all the building committees, the conflicting interests, the budget considerations and the limitations of his fellow man have been taken into consideration, that his responsibility has just begun. He must understand that in the exhilarating, awesome moment when he takes pencil in hand, and holds it poised above a white sheet of paper, that he has suspended there all that will ever be. The creative act is all that matters.'[4]

On Foster

3

The zenith of Rudolph's effectiveness as a teacher can be said to be the years 1960-63, when his career as a practising architect was in full flood and he worked intensely on the design of the watershed building that would become the new home of Yale's School of Art and Architecture.

Vincent Scully was the other important guiding force at Yale at the time. Scully played a key role not only as a brilliant Professor of Art History, but as an active participant in the crits and juries in the design studio. Cut from the same cloth as Malraux or Camus, Scully was an engaged intellectual. Typical of his often controversial stands on contemporary architecture was his endorsement of the, then vigorously debated, late work of Le Corbusier. Scully, a local boy from New Haven, was a graduate of Yale College and its graduate school. He had seen active service in the Second World War and had been teaching at Yale since the late 1940s.

By the 1960s, Scully's lectures were the stuff of legend; indeed, he was among the first of the academic media stars, working with film-makers and frequently quoted in the press. David McCullough, in a profile of 1959, in *Architectural Forum*, dubbed Scully an 'Architectural Spellbinder'.[5] Scully's theatrical lectures electrified his audiences, challenging architects and would-be architects while fostering a profound interest in the built world among Yale's other undergraduates who would carry this new-found awareness to their work in different fields.

Scully taught a generation to view buildings as the embodiment of ideas and ideals. He also taught them how to see, bringing inert matter to life as – with a scholar's knowledge and an actor's passion – he brought out the empathetic relationship between mankind and masterworks of the built environment, be they Greek temples sited in the landscape or the taut abstractions of post-war industrialization.

To a remarkable extent, Scully's perceptions helped to shape those of his most talented students – including Foster – and his powerful convictions became central to his students' own concerns about architecture. At the deepest level, Scully's influence was based on his feeling for the interrelation of man, building and place. And his reach extended far beyond the lectern; he published prolifically in the early 1960s, completing monographs on Frank Lloyd Wright and Louis Kahn, as well as *Modern Architecture: The Architecture of Democracy* and *The Earth, the Temple, and the Gods: Greek Sacred Architecture,* both published in 1962.

Robert A M Stern

In specific historical terms, Scully stressed the great differences between European and American architecture, elevating the latter from its then lowly status as a mere footnote to the former. He dramatically and memorably presented the work of Henry Hobson Richardson, Louis Sullivan and particularly that of Frank Lloyd Wright, as part of a continuum across national borders yet uniquely expressive of American issues of landscape and culture. In 1999, when accepting one of the architectural profession's highest honours, the Pritzker Prize, Foster pinpointed a key aspect of his teacher's impact, asserting that 'the insights of Vincent Scully ... opened my eyes to the interaction between the old world and the new'.[6]

Louis Kahn was another highly consequential force at Yale when Foster arrived, although he was no longer teaching there. Kahn and Rudolph did not get on and the University of Pennsylvania, Kahn's alma mater, offered a more convenient, and to his mind congenial, setting. Kahn nonetheless seemed ubiquitous. Scully had got to know Kahn during the architect's Yale years in the 1940s and '50s and Scully's lectures often promoted and interpreted new projects by Kahn long before they were published in the journals. As a result, Kahn's work was vigorously debated in the Yale studios.

Kahn also came to New Haven for juries and public lectures, a typical one of which was published in 1965 in volume 9/10 of *Perspecta*, the student-run Yale journal which had begun publishing in 1952.[7] Perhaps Kahn's biggest impact on Yale architecture students in the early 1960s was through his Yale University Art Gallery, completed in 1953, an epochal building which married the influences of Mies van der Rohe, Le Corbusier and Richard Buckminster Fuller. The building exerted a powerful, positive influence on virtually all those students who spent seemingly endless days and nights in its extensively glazed, concrete-trussed, fourth-floor drafting room.

During the early 1960s the presence of brilliant visiting English architects immeasurably enriched the New Haven scene and brought to it a much-needed cosmopolitan approach that Rudolph's inherent provincialism lacked. The English offered an alternative way of looking at things. Their admiration of the uninhibited formal exuberance of American architecture, especially roadside and other commercial vernacular work, came as a surprise to the locals who were still embarrassed by the absence of high cultural aspirations in so much native building.

Moreover, the English not only seemed to admire some of the everyday build-ings that embarrassed the Americans, they also found most American high art efforts pretentious. According to M J Long – a Canadian educated at an American college and a student at Yale between 1960 and 1964 – the English afforded a nexus of countervailing criticism against '… the forced and rather blowsy monu-mentality prevalent at the school'. In the mid-1970s, Long recalled the English influence at Yale:

'The English used "humble" materials (brick rather than concrete) and displayed a natural reticence which sometimes emerged as anti-monumentality. They talked about Aalto as much as about Corb. They showed that it was not necessary to resort to anaemic form as an antidote to overblown form – their buildings at best had a kind of animal toughness and boniness. It was a set of images which we could use and it took hold, just before Moore and Venturi pointed to the possibil-ities in traditional American wood buildings and gave to others of us a similarly useable alternative set of images … They were also interested in issues of plan-ning and saw them in design terms … And they were never anti-intellectual; on the contrary, they were highly articulate and historically conscious.' [8]

Among the visiting British critics at Yale, James Stirling exerted the most pro-found and lasting influence.[9] In a break with the historical 'know-nothingism' of the 1940s and '50s, Stirling made it respectable for Yale students to consider the past. In this he was complemented by Philip Johnson who in 1959 began a lec-ture at Yale by writing on the chalkboard: 'You cannot not know history.'
To students who were still in the thrall of anti-traditionalist Modernism, Stirling offered a strong dose of its opposite – a Modernism that drew from both the Modernist and the pre-Modernist past. Like Paul Rudolph, Stirling tended to see history as a justification for romantic formalism, but Stirling's grasp of the past was deeper and broader. Stirling was keenly aware of – and troubled by – the limited definition of modern architecture that had come to be accepted. In his essay, 'The Functional Tradition and Expression', published in 1960 in volume 6 of *Perspecta*, Stirling not only made a plea for an expanded vocabulary of form but also exposed his own work to direct comparison with the best of the past.

Robert A M Stern

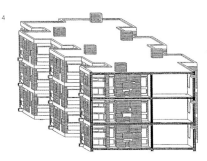

He showed Blenheim Palace alongside unidentified medieval fortifications and walled cities as well as passed-over nineteenth-century English brick vernacular architecture and the late work of Le Corbusier, which he suggested did not subscribe to the extreme reductionism of the Cubist work of the 1920s, or similarly Minimalist work by Gropius and Mies van der Rohe. This was remarkable and largely new to American architects, and perhaps also to Foster who first got to know Stirling at Yale.

Though in one sense Stirling's argument suggested that enriched form should arise from a more careful and imaginative representation of a building's functional programme, on the other hand, he chose to illustrate his text with images from the past coupled with those of his own recent work. To be 'modern' was no longer enough. Stirling presented Trinity College in contrast to his and his partner James Gowan's Churchill College scheme of 1958, as well as a traditional English farmhouse paired with his own Woolton house of 1954, and nineteenth-century English commercial and industrial buildings seen in counterpoint with his and Gowan's Ham Common flats of 1955-58 (4).

As a result of their publication in *Perspecta*, Stirling and Gowan's housing projects at Ham Common, and Stirling and Alan Cordingley's work for Sheffield University became stylistic touchstones for Yale students, and for Rudolph as well. At a time when heroic, self-invented and self-inventing architecture was very much the model, Stirling's bold move to show how his and Gowan's work derived from the forms of high and low buildings from the past was almost unique.

Three other Britons, Colin St John Wilson and Alison and Peter Smithson, significantly contributed to Yale's intellectual climate, although they preceded Foster by a year and had no direct contact with him at Yale. Nonetheless, their impact on the school was still apparent in 1961-62. Colin St John Wilson – 'Sandy' to students and faculty alike – offered a yet more complicated reading of the recent past than did Stirling. Wilson loved things American in a way the British often then did: he loved jazz, especially Miles Davis, when most young Americans were not that interested in it, preferring folk music or rock and roll. Yet despite his love of jazz – and English Pop Art – he was appalled by pop culture as it really was in America, sharing with many American intellectuals a dislike of commercial design that Peter Blake would elaborate upon in his book, *God's Own Junkyard*, of 1964.

5>

Alison and Peter Smithson were better known for their writings and exhibitions than for their buildings, although Scully admired extravagantly their school at Hunstanton and showed it in his classes. Of the Smithsons' ideas, that of 'ordinariness' proved the most compelling. The idea rooted itself more deeply and lastingly into the Yale psyche than any other, resonating for years to come, perhaps as an antidote to Rudolph's heroic bluster.

Another British influence on the early 1960s Yale scene – disproportionately strong perhaps given the brevity of the contact – was that of Peter Reyner Banham, an engineer turned architectural critic and historian, who was at Yale in 1960-61 and returned in the spring of 1962 to visit the recently completed Morse and Stiles Colleges, a posthumous work of Eero Saarinen. Perhaps the most emblematic American architect of his generation, Saarinen was a graduate of the Yale architecture school and a close advisor to Whitney Griswold, the Yale president whose passionate support of modern architecture fuelled the university's extensive post-war building programme.

Saarinen's proto-Post-Modernist Morse and Stiles residential colleges 'disgusted' Banham 'at sight' and still appalled him four weeks later when he slammed them in a review in the *New Statesman*, stating that there were 'no extenuating circumstances' to justify the design for which 'the client gave the architect plenty of rope'. Although Banham disliked Saarinen's special kind of concrete, he really saved his venom for what he lambasted as 'Gordon Craig-type scenic effects' which he felt were achieved at the price of the 'medieval standards' of the accommodation.[10] Banham had already denounced Saarinen, architect of the US Embassy in Grosvenor Square, London, as one of America's 'most trivial performers'.[11]

For many in New Haven, Banham's hatchet-job on the Yale residential colleges went too far in a too public way. Not content to take a swipe at the recently deceased Saarinen's design, he also went after the architect's wife, the art critic Aline B Louchheim, dismissing her as the 'formidable Saarinen widow', and then lamented that the dormitories employed 'that creeping malady that causes an increasing number of returning Europeans to say "Yale is a very sick place", the malady of gratuitous affluences irresponsibly exploited … '[12]

Such was the backdrop of stimulating, if sometimes overheated, design and intellectual debate that greeted Foster in 1961. In Manchester, lacking a grant and

forced to fund his own way through his studies, he had been compelled to live at home and to work at an array of part-time jobs, from manning the night-shift in a bakery to being a bouncer in a rough cinema. New Haven, in contrast, offered the luxury of time to study and think and debate.

While the students in the architecture department were intensely focused on their work as designers – the drafting room was open to students 24 hours a day – the programme of studies also encouraged students to pursue interests in architectural history and planning and, in fact, whatever else attracted them from among the university's broad course offerings. Moreover, in a time when there was still comparatively little cross-fertilisation among cultures, Foster and the other Britons then studying in the architecture department – together with Rogers' wife Su, who was studying for a Masters degree in City Planning – found themselves challenged, even confounded, by the American way of doing things.

This situation was exacerbated by the fact that the English visitors were a little older than most of their American counterparts. They considered themselves to be not quite students – or at least in a different league from their Yankee student cousins. The English would-be architects did not want to be instructed *per se*, preferring to discuss, debate and deliberate at length; they put off committing their ideas to paper for as long as possible.

One day Foster and his compatriots found posted above their desks a sign that read 'Start drawing'. The English response was to post another sign that read 'Start thinking'. While these strikingly different approaches produced a certain degree of tension, their juxtaposition ultimately proved fertile ground for Foster's imagination. Foster has said of his time at Yale: 'Looking back with the perspective of nearly 40 years, I can see that our practice has been inspired by those polarities of analysis and action.'[13]

Though the American and English students differed in many ways, Foster got on quite well with his American classmates. In particular, he formed a close friendship with Carl Abbott (6), who was from the west coast of Florida. Abbott would return to Florida after his time at Yale – and a stint in London where he worked with Foster and Rogers during their Team 4 partnership – to establish his own practice in Sarasota which to this day extends the spirit of Rudolph's early architectural achievements in that city.

While at Yale Foster also began a lifelong friendship with Richard Rogers. How amazing that friendship was between two gifted students who would later practise together. How ironic, as well, that the two architects who, working separately, would subsequently dominate British architecture for decades, first met as they prepared to leave their home country – at a reception for English students who had been offered Fulbright Travel Scholarships.

Both Foster and Rogers were bowled over by Yale – each in his own way. Rudolph's driven and hard-driving working and teaching styles were a complete surprise. He constantly pressured students to work fast and around the clock and would stage surprise late-night crits. Foster found his pressure-cooker methods exhilarating. A superb draughtsman and model-maker, Foster was used to racing the clock; having worked his way through school in Manchester he understood that time was precious.

Foster recalls: 'Rudolph had created a studio atmosphere of fevered activity, highly competitive and fuelled by a succession of visiting luminaries. Crits were open and accessible – often combative. It was a "can-do" approach in which concepts could be shredded one day and reborn overnight. The only criterion was the quality of the work presented – the architecture of the drawings and models. There was no room for excuses, no substitutes of rhetoric.'[14]

At Yale Foster learned to look hard at what was around him and what was on the drawing board before him. As Rogers, who later described his time in New Haven as 'wonderful heady days', would note, the Britons at Yale learned 'to use our eyes, not an English tradition'.[15] In the studio the importance of 'using one's eyes' was stressed most of all by Rudolph who was brilliantly and instinctively visual. In the lecture hall, this same approach was emphasised by Scully. So compelling did Foster find Scully's presentation and interpretation of Wright's uniquely American architecture that on one short, between-terms break, he, together with Carl Abbott and Richard and Su Rogers, squeezed into Abbott's Volkswagen Beetle and visited nearly every Wright building in the Midwest.

Foster's first studio project at Yale not surprisingly reflected Rudolph's influence. Rudolph had assigned the design of a public high school (2), a relatively workaday building type, which – three years earlier – he had raised to the level of architectural art in Sarasota, Florida, by imaginatively translating Le Corbusier's

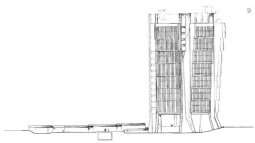

9

High Court Building at Chandigarh through the medium of American technology and the realities of American programmes and budgets. At the final project crit, Rudolph praised Foster for 'thinking like an architect', even if the trees in his Rudolph-inspired renderings 'looked like cauliflowers'.[16]

Foster considers his project for an office building (7-9) to be the best of his Yale work. The design problem Rudolph assigned was once again a reconsideration of one of his actual commissions – in this case his massive concrete, Blue Cross-Blue Shield building, completed in Boston in 1960. Foster's project consisted of a cluster of towers which marched round the corner, 'where office space was supported by a structural service core with great splayed feet',[17] as Rogers later put it. The project incorporated a structurally expressive building profile, exposed service elements, and a strong programmatic mix that represented a distinct break with the Rudolph model and strongly suggested spatial and structural lessons learned from Louis Kahn.

Foster's design also stood in sharp contrast to the prevailing open-field neutrality pioneered by Mies van der Rohe. In Foster's design the areas of office space were broken up into column-free sections spanning concrete towers that housed vertical services, surely an anticipation of his Hongkong and Shanghai Banking Corporation Headquarters building in Hong Kong, an architectural and engineering *tour de force* completed in 1986.

While at Yale, Foster and Rogers collaborated on a studio design problem, the Pierson Sage Science Laboratories (10) in the Hillhouse section of the University's campus – a complex actually entrusted to Philip Johnson, whose resulting Kline Science Center deferred to the site's older medieval-inspired buildings by Delano & Aldrich and others, while incorporating the misconceived, Modernist, Gibbs Physics Laboratory designed by Howe's short-term successor as architecture department head, Paul Schweikher.

In this project, Rudolph challenged the students to consider not only programmatic requirements but also what he believed to be the deplorable state of contemporary architecture as a whole. His brief stated: 'This is an urban problem. It is also the problem of the architect, as planners and developers have failed to rebuild our cities. They are obsessed with numbers (people, money, acreage, units, cars, roads, etc.) and forget life itself and the spirit of man.'[18]

358

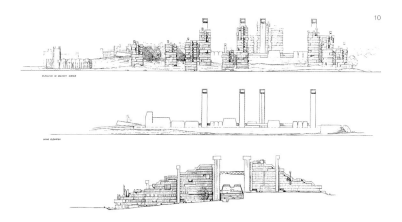

10

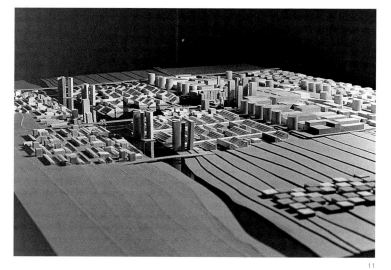

11

Robert A M Stern

According to Rogers, he and Foster worked on the project together, 'to the horror of Paul Rudolph'.[19] Nonetheless, their scheme was a marvel, introducing to the local scene, and perhaps to American practice as a whole, a megastructural approach that was a radical departure from the typical, isolated, building-by-building campus model. Foster and Rogers proposed a central spine of car-parking, from which lecture halls and other facilities projected at right angles forming wings that stepped downhill to confront existing buildings at an appropriate scale.

Though the scheme's megastructural scale and diagrammatic approach were distinctly English, or at least not American, there were aspects to the proposals that were quite familiar – especially the Kahn-inspired service towers. Philip Johnson, one of the guest jurors at the final review, adopted a typically robust approach to architectural criticism. He took a strong dislike to the buildings placed on top of the spine. After staring at the balsa wood model of the project, he proceeded to crush these blocks in his fist, saying, 'have to do something about these'.[20] Whatever the project's weaknesses, however, Foster and Rogers' explosion of scale and their ability to command the entirety of the large and complex site were nothing short of astonishing.

Foster's last Yale project was for a new city (11). The project was realised in collaboration with four other students but verbally presented for jury review by Foster, who had been elected by his co-designers to act as spokesman. It was clear even then that besides talent and drive Foster possessed an attribute deemed by many to be quintessentially that of American business practice: the ability not only to work in a team but also to become its leader. The design of the new city incorporated aspects of Foster's earlier office tower project, constituting a form of self-quotation that had characterised the urban proposals of Le Corbusier and Frank Lloyd Wright.

Foster's scheme was developed under the guidance of the European-born Serge Chermayeff, who Rudolph had brought to Yale from Harvard in a deliberate, if possibly misguided, attempt to lodge an anti-heroic, anti-aesthetic point of view in the curriculum. Whatever the complex intentions behind Chermayeff's appointment as Professor of Architecture, his influence, particularly on Foster, was lasting and profound. Chermayeff added a distinctively European seasoning to the already rich Anglo-American soup.

360

Foster has argued that, 'My timing at Yale in 1961 was more fortunate than I could ever have foreseen because it marked the change of leadership to Serge Chermayeff. He was as European as Rudolph was American. It was not just in dress or manner, but deeply rooted differences in philosophy. For Chermayeff debate and theory took precedence over imagery – questioning was to the fore, analysis dominated action.'

Ironically, the European influence at Yale emanated not only from the Russian-born Chermayeff but also from the quintessentially American Rudolph; as Foster has noted: 'In some ways I went to Yale to discover a European heritage because America had embraced émigrés such as Gropius, who taught Rudolph at Harvard and who was, I quote, "his point of reference".'[21]

Foster's project for a new city, executed while he was studying with Chermayeff, was decidedly European, with rationally sited *Siedlung*-like rows of houses punctuated by towers. In a way, the project directly illustrated the theoretical studies which would lead to Chermayeff's book, *Community and Privacy* (13), co-written with Christopher Alexander and published in 1963.

After completing his studies at Yale in 1962, Foster was invited by Chermayeff to stay in New Haven and join him as a research fellow. Tempted as he was, Foster chose instead to work as a city planner in Massachusetts before moving on to San Francisco to work with John Carl Warnecke and Anshen & Allen who were engaged in planning a new University of California campus at Santa Cruz. Rogers was also working in California at the time and the two young architects were excited by Ezra Ehrenkrantz's School Construction Systems Development programme.

Through journals and Scully's lectures they had already been introduced to the California Case Study houses designed by Raphael Soriano, Pierre Koenig, Craig Ellwood, Richard Neutra, and Charles and Ray Eames, which they admired. Of these, the house that the Eames built for themselves in 1949 in Pacific Palisades (12), with its creative assemblage of off-the-shelf industrial components, exerted a lasting influence on Foster's work. So too did the compelling imagery of Koenig's hillside Case Study House #22 with its impossibly slender cantilevers. Foster was also captivated by the forms of American technology: highways, Airstream trailers, and the rockets and launching pad structures of Cape Canaveral.

Robert A M Stern

However, it was not just specific American buildings, nor even American approaches to architecture, construction and large-scale planning, that captured the young Britons' imaginations as they criss-crossed the country together. It was the entire sweep of the continental landscape and the national character that fired them up. As Rogers has said: 'America enthralled us [with] its scale, energy, optimism and openness. We travelled by thumb, by car and by Greyhound bus, voraciously absorbing the culture, both of the massive open spaces and the tall, taut, energetic cities.'[22]

For Foster, Yale was in some ways emblematic of America: 'The emphasis on tangible results in the studio summed up an American world in which everything was possible if you were willing to try hard enough. For me that was a breath of fresh air ... America gave me a sense of confidence, freedom and self-discovery.'[23]

In 1963, Foster returned to England where he joined Richard Rogers to found the trendsetting firm Team 4. The remaining two of the 'four' were the architect sisters, Wendy and Georgie Cheesman, although the latter was a member in name only; as the only qualified architect of the group, it was she who initially allowed Team 4 to meet the legal requirements of architectural practice. Soon enough, however, Foster would be on his own. After only four years together, in 1967, Team 4 split up. Foster and Wendy (by then his wife) established themselves as Foster Associates and pursued an independent architectural direction quite different from Rogers', although the three of them remained close.

Foster's is an architecture which, in its functional rigour, compositional clarity, and high finish, as well as its concern with means of production and far-reaching issues of urban planning and the social context of buildings, continues to reflect his experience at Yale and in America. It inspires architects everywhere to realise the expressive possibilities of advanced technology and the sheer optimism of the act and art of building. Most of all, in the generosity of his open-mindedness, Foster has demonstrated, as too few architects do, that 'architects learn from architects, past and present'.[24]

'The ideal of humane efficiency, understood as social respon-sibility, undergirds all Foster's work. No living architect has thought more closely about the ecological effects of his buildings

Robert Hughes

The annual Pritzker Prize – $100,000 plus a gold medal – is by far the most prestigious award in architecture today. It is like the Nobel Prize for literature or for the promotion of peace, though not as hotly debated, there being no architectural equivalent to Dario Fo – still less to Rigoberta Menchu. It is given not for promise but to uphold the ideal of excellence. Twenty men (but no women) have received it since Philip Johnson got the first one in 1979; they range from Mexico's Luis Barragán to Italy's Renzo Piano, from Britain's James Stirling to America's Frank Gehry. This year's laureate is another Brit: Norman Foster, 63. 'Every award is special,' says Foster, 'but there's only one Pritzker. It's a recognition of the importance of architecture itself.'

Foster, like his former partner Richard Rogers (who has a peerage, but no Pritzker as yet), is a pivotal figure in British architecture. But his buildings have risen all over the world, from Germany to China, and at present his practice employs some five hundred people. His influence on the profession is enormous. His 1986 tower for the Hongkong and Shanghai Bank in Hong Kong, for instance, reversed the general dogma that a high-rise office block had to have a solid central core: it is not a 'block' but a frame, a vertical web whose generous, open, ground level has become a Sunday gathering spot for Hong Kong's Filipina maids. It has probably done more to change the way people think about what Foster calls 'the culture of office buildings' and the relation of the corporate to the public domain in a city's matrix than any other twentieth-century structure.

'Sire, do not talk to me of small projects,' said the great Cham of Baroque architecture, Gianlorenzo Bernini, to Louis XIV after the Sun King lured him to Paris. Foster is too much of a democrat to echo that sentiment, but it's a fact that his imagination runs naturally on the epic scale and that, more surprisingly, large size doesn't diminish the humanistic and spiritual qualities of his buildings.

The most heartening and invigorating thing about Foster's design sense is its clarity, the insistence that the poetics of a building must grow out of its legible and fully expressed structure. Foster has never been even faintly tempted by the clutter of second-hand allusion and quotation that infested so much Post-Modernist building in America and elsewhere – the kind of stuck-on, boutique historicism represented by Philip Johnson's 1984 Chippendale-top skyscraper for AT&T in New York City, or Robert Stern's recyclings of the Shingle Style. It may be that

PoMo quotation, of which a gutful has been served up over the past 25 years, served a useful purpose in reminding architecture's public that, yes, there was indeed a vast repertory of form and ornament on which early, messianic Modernism had turned its back. But it was mostly skin deep, and it kept turning into a kind of false nostalgia – a parallel to the rash of 'heritage' fetishism in the 1980s.

An accumulation of signs can carry architecture only so far, because architecture in its root and essence is very much more than sign language. Yesterday's ironies wrap today's garbage. Architecture has to go deeper, find real human needs and deal with those. Foster likes to list them in simple terms: the structure that holds a building up; the services that enable it to work; 'the ecology of the building – whether it is naturally ventilated, whether you can open the windows, the quality of light'; the mass or lightness of its materials; its relationship to the site, the street and the landscape view; the symbolism of the form. All these, he argues, must be accounted for 'whether you are creating a landmark or deferring to a historical setting'.

Foster can handle both with equal aplomb. In 1993 he completed a cultural centre for the French city of Nîmes (1). It is right next to the city's most famous Roman monument, the so-called Maison Carrée – a Corinthian temple dedicated to Augustus' sons in the year AD4. It was Thomas Jefferson's favourite Classical building – in fact, Jefferson based his whole conception of Neo-Classical architecture on it – and one obviously had to approach such a historical object with caution. Would the solution be a pastiche historical arts centre? Foster was sure not. 'I went there incognito before the competition was announced,' he recalls. 'I walked the site for hours. The challenge was to do a contemporary building that could face the Roman temple directly but not be intimidated by it.' The result, a crystalline rectangular structure with sunscreens, does exactly that. Its transparent grid defers to the pillar-and-architrave opacity of the ancient stone building without mimicking it.

The same kind of thinking occurs in Foster's project for the British Museum. When its library moved to massive new premises 1.5 kilometres away, it left behind one of the great English spaces: the 1857 Round Reading Room designed by Sydney Smirke, with its shallow dome, surrounded by an 8,100-square-metre internal court. To demolish this masterpiece would have been unthinkable. It had

3

to be preserved, and Foster's scheme for so doing entailed sweeping away the clutter of now obsolete book-stack buildings from around it and covering the court with a light glass-and-steel roof, creating Europe's largest enclosed space, which will function as the access core of the museum.

Foster's genius – the word is hardly too strong – is most apparent in his structural thought. He has often been called a High-Tech architect, but actually, despite the complexity of some of his designs, the buildings don't brandish their technological language as gee-whiz metaphor; they use it as an essential tool of spatial effects and structural needs, always seeking the most elegant and succinct solution. 'The idea of High-Tech is a bit misleading,' Foster says. 'Since Stonehenge, architects have always been at the cutting edge of technology. And you can't separate technology from the humanistic and spiritual content of a building.'

Ever since his student days at Manchester University in the 1950s (a working-class boy, he paid his way through school with a variety of jobs, including a stint as a bouncer in a rough cinema), Foster loved utilitarian buildings: barns, factories, windmills. He did measured drawings of them when other students were drawing buildings they had never seen: Greek temples, Palladian villas. Foster would learn from those too, but his immersion in a common language and use translates into a feeling of rightness, which works as completely in small structures as in large. A fine example of the former is the entrances to the subway system he designed for Bilbao in northern Spain: hoods of glass (3), like segments of a nautilus shell, ribbed with stainless steel, which curve downward and carry the eye to the spaces underneath – by far the most elegant subway entrances since Hector Guimard's Art Nouveau designs for the Paris Métro a century ago (2).

He learned from other structures too. As a kid he built model aircraft, and as an adult he flies real ones, both fixed-wing and helicopters. He did his National Service in the Royal Air Force and regards the time he spent working in a hangar as a big influence on his later designs. Way back in the genetic code of his buildings is a feeling for hangar-like lightness, strength and frugality of consumption that came out brilliantly in such projects as his 1981-91 design for the airport at Stansted in England. Earlier airports had large concentrations of ductwork above their ceilings for air conditioning, lighting and electrical services; Foster rethought this completely and realised huge savings in structural mass and energy

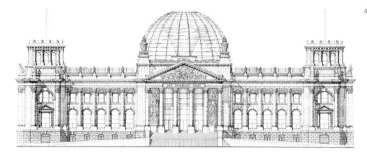

4

consumption could be made by shifting the utilities underground, leaving a floating roof and walls that could open to natural daylight. This changed architects'
thinking about airport design worldwide, and every major airport built since –
Hamburg, Stuttgart, Kuala Lumpur – has followed Foster's design insight.

He would reapply the lesson himself eleven years later in his $20 billion
design for the world's largest airport, Chek Lap Kok, in Hong Kong – the last
megastructure spawned by the floundering 'tiger economies' of Asia. Foster envisaged it as a 'horizontal cathedral', with its airy, Y-shaped passenger terminal under
the great wing of its roof. It had teething troubles at first – there were cargo and
passenger delays when it opened last July – but now, according to Wan Wai Lun,
corporate affairs officer of the Hong Kong Airport Authority, 'it's incredibly efficient
and caters to the passengers' needs'.

The ideal of humane efficiency, understood as social responsibility, undergirds all Foster's work. No living architect has thought more closely about the
ecological effects of his buildings. In his brilliant 1991-97 design for Frankfurt's
Commerzbank, the tallest office building in Europe (5), he brought off the seemingly impossible feat of building a supertower that could use natural ventilation (as
against fuel-gobbling air conditioning) during 60 per cent of the year. 'Anything
that reduces energy consumption and cuts down on greenhouse gases is good
news,' he says. In his redesign of the Reichstag (4), the seat of German government in Berlin, Foster has carried this out to an extraordinary degree. He noted
that the old Reichstag, heated and cooled by fossil fuels, produced 6,400 metric
tons of carbon dioxide a year. Foster came up with a system of 'driving the building' with renewable vegetable oils such as rapeseed for fuel. Its carbon dioxide
emissions have dropped 94 per cent, to 400 metric tons per year. The waste heat
is converted into cooling capacity, and the small heat surplus is dumped into
aquifers 300 metres below ground level, where it is stored and recovered in winter.

You can, of course, do a building that's eco-responsible but aesthetically
worthless. The crux of Foster's achievement is to have designed megastructures
that are at the forefront of eco-design as well as beautiful in their own right. He is
a fine detailer – everything from the junctures of a beam to the cladding to the
door handles comes out of the same relentless aesthetic concentration. But on
the wider scale, Foster is also one of the great living manipulators of light and

Robert Hughes

transparency. No other government building in the world, for instance, can boast anything as outright exhilarating as the great inverted cone sheathed in 360 mirrors that floods the Reichstag with daylight.

Light is part of the very subject matter of Foster's buildings, along with steel, glass and stone. When Foster speaks of 'the spiritual dimension' of architecture, and its power to 'lift the spirit', he's talking about the action of light in space. Anyone who supposes that technology, or the exacting use of modern materials, implies a break with the past should look at Foster's work – and learn.

5

'Historical modernity has produced such a large quantity
of bad urbanism ... that it takes
effort to see that the continuatio
of modernity in which Norman
Foster is engaged can in fact
produce appropriate urbanities.'

Rodolfo Machado

After the year-long process that led to the selection of the work of Norman Foster as this year's winner of the Veronica Rudge Green Prize in Urban Design, my colleagues – George Baird and Christine Boyer – and I were almost surprised, chuckling at the unexpectedness of our own choice. It was unexpected, first, because of the award's global egalitarian agenda: wouldn't it be nice, we had asked ourselves, to be 'correct' and sprinkle the world evenly with this award in urban design? So, after casting our nets far afield for projects in India, for instance, or Brazil, or Australia, it was unexpected, but perhaps predictable, to find a winner so well placed at the centre of European architecture, and, in many ways, so close to us.

What was most unexpected though, was to give Norman Foster a prize in urban design, because the culture of architecture has kept him ensconced in the niche of 'master architect', the thoughtful detailer of contemporary buildings embodying the essence of what is usually referred to as English High-Tech. What we have found is the urbanist in Norman Foster, and that is quite something because, to my knowledge, nobody has yet properly recognised this important aspect of his work.

We set out to find excellence – and we have found it in his work; we set out to find lessons, relevance, social significance, and confirmation of the healing capacity of good, built urban design – and we have found it in the work of Norman Foster and his many collaborators at Foster and Partners.

Given Norman Foster's centrality in architecture, one should ask: why have the critics and the academics been silent about his urbanism? This is strange, considering that in the last 30 years, almost every important critic – from Banham to Frampton, to mention just the English – has written about this abundant body of work. Thus we should speculate.

Is it, perhaps, because of the 'punch', the forcefulness of Foster's architecture? It is, it seems to me, as if the sheer brilliance of the technical resolution has had the power to erase other relevant issues in the work of Norman Foster; it is as if the transparency of the ever-present glass surfaces has rendered the urban issues invisible; it is as if the seemingly immaterial glass floor of the Bank in Hong Kong, suspended like a cloud over a spectacular public place, has rendered the very strong public floor underneath irrelevant. Or more recently, in the case of Frankfurt's Commerzbank, it is as if the glass-enclosed gardens were not, essentially, urban places – veritable meeting grounds. Granted, these projects are not examples of the traditional way to do urbanism.

Traditionally, urbanism has to do with sites larger than a block, containing an impressive amount of infrastructure and at least a few buildings. For me (and for most of my colleagues in the Urban Design Program, I dare say) urbanism is not simply a question of size but of quality; urbanism, as a practice, produces urbanity and, in that sense, Foster and Partners' skyscrapers in Frankfurt and Hong Kong are urbanism.

Therefore, I would like to suggest that urban design is not defined by an object, but rather by a process, by a way of thinking, by a particular body of knowledge that is brought to bear on the object – any object and at any scale.

Another intriguing reason why Foster's urbanistic performance has remained unacknowledged, I speculate, is its modernity (this may sound paradoxical and sad). Historical modernity has produced such a large quantity of bad urbanism (culturally irresponsible, alienating urbanism – we all know the rightful criticism it has received since the late 1950s) that it takes effort to see that the continuation of modernity in which Norman Foster is engaged can in fact produce appropriate urbanities.

If I may digress, I would like to add that this could, in fact, be a great lesson for the American New Urbanists, if they could simply shed their historicist stylistic preferences and consider the language of modernity as another useful strategy. In America today, in people's minds, the conservative iconography of the New Urbanism stands for 'good urbanism', and all that looks modern becomes 'bad urbanism'; this is a terrible perception and a sad state for the practice. The work we honour here helps to prove how wrong that assumption is.

Thus, in awarding the Veronica Rudge Green Prize in Urban Design to Norman Foster, we are, in a way, interpreting his work, claiming it as urbanism, and recasting a practice. We are comfortable and delighted with all of these operations, because we believe that the vision of urbanity that they promote will further the cause of urban design, and that is what we, at Harvard, are about.

At another level, it is also fascinating, instructive, and reassuring to look today at the work of Norman Foster, because his designs for the public realm have had the power to redefine the cities of Bilbao and Nîmes. This, of course, is due equally to his talents and to the talents of the city administrators who have retained the services of Foster and Partners. One cannot but wonder at the intelligence of those officials who commissioned an architect to design a metro system, and at the savvy of those who commissioned a modern architect to design a square around a

Rodolfo Machado

4

Roman temple! How wonderfully daring, how 'unsafe', how distant from the prevailing logic, which blindly states that only those who have done something once can do it again. I must confess that I look at those events with lust and envy and cannot but reflect, by contrast, upon the situation of urban design in North America: who are our clients here and how do they proceed?

Enough digression: back to the work in question and the fascination it provokes. The fascination comes from the beauty of the urban places, from the totalising, relentless, perfectionist detailing of the construction, from the sense of pleasure – visual, tactile and also intellectual – these places induce.

In Bilbao (5) we see a manifestation of the toughest kind of regional infrastructure – a metro system – rendered with the humanistic qualities that characterise a well-inhabited domestic realm, but without any of the faux cosiness, the studied disorder, or the condescending 'warmth' one usually finds in those public places whose designers set out to produce a 'humane' environment.

It is equally fascinating to find, in Nîmes (1-4), face to face (or, more precisely, 'face to cheek') with the Maison Carrée, a cool, highly appropriate, and minimal version of Classicism, a most responsible modernity indeed, one not afraid to unsettle the dominant critical ideologies of the times by revealing its Classical underpinnings.

These public works are instructive in an exemplary way: they demonstrate that transportation infrastructure can be conceived as public architecture (and that great benefits can be obtained from such an agenda); that to make iconic public architecture today as was done in the past is OK, and moreover, that the city's self-conscious image-making yields good marketing, as demonstrated by the much-loved 'Fosteritos' representing the new Bilbao; that to build public places around a monument of Classical antiquity need not be an act of mindless mimicry; that a respectable contextualism need not be about style; and that legibility, ergonomic correctness, atemporality in language and permanence in building are obviously significant qualities for an urban product to possess.

The lessons coming from these two enlightened European cities – Nîmes and Bilbao – are reassuring and optimistic, in times when little about urban design lets us feel so. These works demonstrate that what we teach and preach can be possible, that the desirable can be made real, and that the power of the urbanist's imagination can better civic life.

Rodolfo Machado

'Foster has been chosen to represent a new epoch in London's history: his design suggests openness, democracy and energy.'

Jonathan Glancey

The Fosterification of London continues apace. It has become almost commonplace to say that no architect has so dominated the capital since Sir Christopher Wren with St Paul's, or Colonel Richard Seifert with Centre Point. This raises one obvious question: why? And beyond that, what does it mean? In a country that has famously been associated with conservatism and conservation, what does it say about us that we now seem to be favouring the glassy, airy charms of Foster over the brawny, bulky, tweedy architecture of English compromise?

Norman Foster (now Lord Foster of Thames Bank) has never been a political figure in the manner of his friend, rival and former partner Richard Rogers (Lord Rogers of Riverside). Yet he has been able to realise his vision on a scale that falls to very few in his profession. Foster has usurped the territory of the big commercial players, those firms of architects who since the mid-1950s have modelled them-selves on American firms such as SOM (Skidmore, Owings and Merrill) who made architecture into a slick and highly profitable business. SOM took architects away from pipes and bow ties and into the world of natty suits, fast-track construction, accountants, lawyers and public relations.

It was SOM, and the firms that aped it across the world, that have been respon-sible in great measure for the way, better or worse, our city centres have looked over the past 40 years. At best they have produced office towers of great sophistication, the equivalent of Abstract Expressionist canvases. On a normal day (don't even think about a bad one) they have invaded our cities with slick, gimcrack office blocks that have been designed first and foremost as machines for making money in and with the good grace and manners of the Krays and the Richardsons.

This left the 'art' architects out in the cold, or when there was money available in the public sector (something you will have to explain to your children one day when they ask: 'What was the public sector?') designing agreeable buildings such as uni-versities, hospitals and local authority housing (another one to explain to the children).

What Foster has done, and where a part of his considerable genius lies, is to reconcile the roles of the commercial and the 'art' architect. His buildings flatter the sensibilities of both business leaders and the sort of people for whom a day spent in a museum is worth more than all the sums added up in all the computer ledgers in the City of London. But Foster knows well that in 1999 those museums are very likely to be funded to a large extent by the business corporations he flatters with his

fluent, sassy buildings. In other words, Foster has found an architectural path that brings together the needs of both art and commerce. His 500-strong international practice, Foster and Partners, has the technical ability, the financial skills and the sense of timing which are inherent in top American firms, and the artistry and imagination of the most innovative architects and engineers of the past half century. It is a remarkable and rare achievement and needs to be pointed out if we are to understand why Foster has such a command of our urban landscape at the end of the twentieth century.

It is also important to recognise his appeal to the Blair government, which, although it has a very long way to go in helping to steer the architectural and building world along a path that will encourage the best of design in our cities, wants to present the kind of dynamic, modern world view that Foster has done since he began work more than 35 years ago. Foster's is the architecture of New Britain as New Labour dreams of it, although it is important to stress that the government has picked up on Foster's vision rather than the other way round.

And yet this star man has come down to Earth very successfully. If you seek his monuments, take a trip along the Thames from Battersea to Canary Wharf: you'll find them, and these are only the buildings nearing completion and not the ones that already exist. Starting at Foster's office overlooking the Albert Bridge at Battersea (2), we have some time to relax before chugging through the old City centre. As the boat passes the South Bank, you'll pass (though not see: it's a mile or so away) the great green dome of the British Museum on your left-hand side. The Great Court that Foster is shaping there will be a major new public meeting place, a kind of glazed forum as well as the hub of the museum itself. It's a huge project and opens one of the better acts of the Lottery Follies being played out by architects on behalf of the strange and secretive Millennium Commission next year.

Coming up dead ahead between Blackfriars and Southwark bridges is the Millennium Bridge (3, 4), a graceful arc across the river that will take pedestrians from the City of London to Southwark and, specifically, from St Paul's Cathedral to the Tate Gallery of Modern Art (converted from the former Bankside Power Station by the Swiss architects Herzog & de Meuron). It has been designed in collaboration with Sir Anthony Caro, the sculptor, and Chris Wise, an engineer with Ove Arup & Partners. It opens with the Tate in May. On our right, shortly after the bridge, is the

Jonathan Glancey

3

site of the long-awaited headquarters of the new Greater London Authority (GLA) (1), the glass eye from which the first elected mayor of London will survey the capital and decide what to do about the traffic and a public realm that has all but fallen apart in an age of deregulation and privatisation. Foster has been chosen to represent a new epoch in London's history: his design suggests openness, democracy and energy. We just have to hope that the GLA will live up to these ideals.

Past Tower Bridge we reach Thatcher Towers, aka Canary Wharf, the extraordinary concatenation of sub-Chicago architecture. Here Foster is adding not just a new seventeen-storey headquarters for Citibank, and a 200-metre-high glass tower for the Hongkong and Shanghai Banking Corporation (whose headquarters in Hong Kong he designed to universal acclaim between 1979 and 1986) but the means to reach them: Canary Wharf Underground station, one of the cathedral-like public buildings realised by the Jubilee Line's project manager, the architect Roland Paoletti.

Stop here and contemplate: we may never see public architecture of this ambition and calibre in private, pirate New Britain again. It is fascinating to see Foster at Canary Wharf creating space for public service that is in every way the equal and possibly the superior of that he is shaping for the business community. One more bend in the Thames and we come to land beside the Dome on the apex of the North Greenwich peninsula. The vast wave-like transport interchange building that will serve the dome by way of Underground, bus and taxi is yet another Foster project.

And no, I haven't forgotten – on our way back to civilisation down river, as we watch a wonderful panorama of the City of London hove into view – the vertiginous steel-and-glass spiral Foster is designing for the Swiss Reinsurance Company that will rise above the old Baltic Exchange site. This has been called a gherkin, but owes nothing to the pickled state of much of the homespun architecture that the City, among other commissioning bodies, is struggling to come to terms with. It is, rather, a way of looking at the city office tower that is as fresh as SOM's designs were in New York and Chicago 40 or more years ago. Foster may indeed be over-producing, yet until fellow architects find alternative or parallel ways to express art in commerce, and commerce in the art spirit of our age, his sheer professionalism will keep them wandering, jealously, in the wings.

'Architect and government accept that the building must symbolise events even when tragic, making this one of the few significant public monuments of our time.'

Charles Jencks

Ever since the Reichstag was burnt in 1933, it has been associated with Hitler's rise to power and the question of whether Germany can nurture a viable democracy. As a late nineteenth-century Classical pile, the architecture symbolised the heavy, Prussian imposition of power. Few of the *Deutschen Volke*, whose name is grandly inscribed on its pediment, loved it. So its renovation as the seat of government for the united Germany has been surrounded by controversy, and only by a small majority was the decision made to move the Bundestag from Bonn to Berlin.

After 1945, German architects dissociated themselves from the tainted Classicism of Albert Speer, and this led to two main styles: the Expressionist work of architects such as Hans Scharoun, and the lightweight Modernism epitomised by the all-glass architecture of the previous Bundestag. Furthermore, since the utopian writing of Paul Scheerbart in 1914, avant-garde Germans have associated glass architecture with openness. According to his humorous panegyrics, the glass building of the future will change every aspect of life – expose all deceit, make cheating husbands faithful, show what's going on behind closed doors and, inevitably, be good for government, since politicians in smoke-filled rooms will have to conspire in full public view. Glass transparency leads to political transparency.

Given this background, it is not surprising that the new, renovated Reichstag, by Norman Foster, is something of a magnificent fishbowl, and a light, elegant contrast to its heavy container. In several ways it is a convincing expression of the new German democracy. The citizens are encouraged by the see-through planes to climb all over and through the building (1,2) to discover what their representatives are up to. At night the parabolic dome lights up like an Expressionist beacon of hope, the radiant crown of crystal that so many 1920s architects put at the centre of their utopian schemes. By day one sees tiny figures walking up and down the helical ramps and traversing the four corners and terraces of the old building. Curiosity and beauty, two powerful architectural motives, are thus used to get the public involved with their city and government: fantastic views over the previously divided metropolis are given spectacular framing by the architecture.

More than this, it makes a positive drama of traversing recent German history. Scorch marks from the 1930s fire remain, shrapnel wounds from 1945 are preserved, graffiti by the Russian occupiers are accentuated. History is thus confronted and turned into a form of realist ornament, rather than being whitewashed

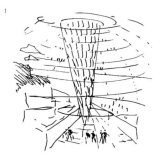

over, as it has been in Russia and Japan. Signs vary from Russian slogans and swearwords to 'Mockba', Moscow, the equivalent of 'Kilroy was here'. Architect and government accept that the building must symbolise events even when tragic, making this one of the few significant public monuments of our time. Foster even tried to redesign the fat German eagle, symbol of imperial history, and put it on a diet, but his efforts were frustrated by traditionalists and the previous designer's family. Undeterred, and discovering that his see-through building would result in the eagle being seen from behind – backwards – he overlaid the fat one with an elegant offspring and thus managed to symbolise at a stroke the dialectic between new and old. Time is once again brought into architectural expression.

Aspects of the new Reichstag do, however, raise some questions of design and symbolism. Foster's neutral, horizontal grammar of glass windows conflicts with the vertical forms of the old Reichstag and also his own diagonal ramps. Conceptually, the glass wall is a stretched skin that has no visible supports, but actually these supports are neither strong enough to contrast with what exists, nor set at an angle to counter the incline of the spirals. Furthermore, the central fountain of mirrors is reminiscent of an Art Deco lighting fixture, or even the sacred altar of a new sect: that is, it's more a religious icon of unity than a political sign of pluralism. It also shoots down into the general assembly like an incoming missile.

But these are minor flaws in a structure that is basically right, and exhilarating. It celebrates the city, democracy and even the ecological potential of new technology. Not only is the building energy efficient, but Foster has also designed a heating and cooling system that runs on vegetable oil. Such technology is dramatised as an essential part of the architectural experience, so when you climb up the thin hovering ramps and seem to fly over the city, you pass within touching distance of an extraordinary invention, a gigantic blind that rotates with the sun and cuts down glare and heat. This ascent then culminates in a giant, open-air oculus, like the Pantheon in Rome, a round disc that transforms the sky visually into a dome. Thus the whole building can be experienced as climb through German history to present politics and then to the cosmos, an appropriate and moving narrative.

Charles Jencks

'Perhaps in the last analysis
Foster's work may not be neatly
subsumed under the Corbusian
term "engineer's aesthetic" since
in many instances the aesthetic
and the engineered form cannot
be prised apart.'

Kenneth Frampton

'Foster always thrives on these close-counting circumstances. He once said with real appreciation of a client: "He's marvellous – every time he opens his mouth a quarter of a million comes off the budget." And more recently he has had the temerity to answer Buckminster Fuller's non-rhetorical question, "But what does your house weigh?" with a detailed weight breakdown of the Sainsbury Centre. It adds up to the remarkably modest total of 5,619 tons, or practically 70 cubic metres of building volume for every ton of structural weight – a figure that grows more impressive when it is realised that around four-fifths of the structural weight is the ground slab.'
Reyner Banham, Introduction to *Foster Associates*, RIBA Catalogue, 1979

American Affinities

Within this laconic observation, written in that punchy style for which Banham was justly famous, lies a particular ideological affinity that requires to be elucidated if we are to appreciate the origin of Foster's work and the nature of the stance that he has adopted towards the opportunities and complexities of the late twentieth century. As the quote implies, Fuller may also have been seen as a kind of catalyst linking Banham to Foster and vice versa. This tends to be confirmed by the concluding chapter of Banham's *Theory and Design in the First Machine Age* of 1960 where Fuller is advanced as the only scientific architect of the twentieth century. A decade later the work of Fuller will not only serve as a role model for Foster, but the man himself will become a direct mentor, collaborator, and friend. Throughout the 1970s this peripatetic eminence will be whisked off on the occasion of his London stopovers to visit the latest of Foster's achievements. Foster testified to this 'dymaxion' affinity when he remarked in 1986 that, 'The association with Buckminster Fuller as friend, ally, and collaborator lasted from the late 1960s until Fuller's death in 1983. The practice joined forces with Fuller on a number of projects.'

In 1971, Foster collaborated with Fuller on the design for a multi-purpose underground theatre, to be built beneath the quadrangle of St Peter's College, Oxford, and in the same year they jointly explored the idea of the Climatroffice (1), based in part on one of Fuller's earliest geodesic works, the St Louis Climatron of 1960, and in part on his magnificent geodesic sphere erected as the US Pavilion at the Montreal Expo of 1967 (2). The Climatroffice, accommodating a maximum

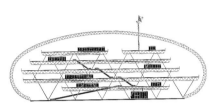

amount of office space within a minimal envelope (and hence *dymaxion*) was under discussion while the Willis Faber & Dumas project was on the drawing board. Its application on the Ipswich site would have produced an envelope of striking sculptural character. There followed a collaboration between Fuller, Foster and Shoji Sadao, Fuller's associate in New York, with the common aim of designing a pavilion for the International Energy Expo in Knoxville, USA.

Shortly before his death, Fuller was again engaged with Foster Associates on the design of an Autonomous House (3) in which the inner and outer domes of the house would have been able to rotate independently of one another. Half glazed and half solid, the glazed half would have been able to follow the sun during the day, while warm or cold air circulating in the space between the skins would have maintained an appropriate temperature. As in the Climatroffice, the cooling properties of certain plants were also to have been involved in helping to maintain a homeostatic microclimate.

An adherence to Fuller's dymaxion principle, or 'maximum advantage gain for minimum energy input', was to characterise Foster's work from the outset, although his first efforts in this direction were hardly of the High-Tech, lightweight structural range that one normally associates with Fuller. On the contrary, the initial Team 4 partnership, formed by two British members of a postgraduate Masters class at Yale University, with two architect sisters, Georgie Wolton and Wendy Cheesman, first took a decidedly low-tech approach to the issues of building economy and energy conservation. This much is evident from their early joint work in Cornwall – the Creek Vean house of 1964-66, designed for a steeply sloping river-front site in the Fal Estuary, together with some stepped terrace housing projected for a nearby site of similar nature.

Like their unrealised low-rise housing project for Coulsdon, Surrey (5) and their Franklin mews house, all these early works attempted to satisfy certain ecological and topographical criteria. These may be summed up as firstly, minimising the disruptive impact of the work on the site and secondly, maximising the work's capacity for conserving energy. A typical work of this earth-bound, mixed-media period was the so-called Skybreak House built in Radlett, Hertfordshire, between 1964 and 1966. This was a load-bearing, brick, cross-wall house which could hardly be further removed from Fuller's geodesic preconceptions. That this was a

matter of conscious policy at the time is born out by Foster's retrospective description of the work:

'This house was designed to reconcile the owner's needs for family living and occasional large-scale entertaining. It stands in the midst of suburban housing on a steep slope facing the Green Belt to the north. A series of platforms follow the slope: a single-storey brick cross-wall with piers divides the house spatially into a series of toplit zones and serves to carry the lightweight roof deck ... The concept reconciles fine views to the north with sun penetration into the heart of the house and was a forerunner of later projects which combined deep plans, toplight and flexibility on a larger scale ... The detailed design of the house, like others of this period, combined traditional materials with factory-made components ... '[1]

Given the markedly technological character of their subsequent careers as two separate offices, it is somewhat surprising that the early work of Team 4 should have been so ecologically disposed.

During this period Team 4's work became less involved in integration with a specific site, and more object-oriented. This is especially true of Reliance Controls (6), realised in Swindon in 1966. This drive towards the dematerialised production object came into its own in Foster Associates' Fred Olsen Amenity Centre, built in the London Docks from 1968 to 1970 – an object which declared its self-effacing autonomy by asserting itself as little more than a mirror image of its environment (cf. Ben Johnson's super-realist painting 'Dock Reflections' of 1970) (4).

In terms of American themes one must acknowledge the latent presence of the American architect Louis Kahn in much of Foster's work, above all Kahn's methodological distinction between *servant* and *served* space. This first announces itself in the Sainsbury Centre for Visual Arts, 1974-78, where the main volume is the *served* space and the interstitial volume between the skin and inner louvred membrane, occupied by the steel structure and the mechanical services, is the *servant* space. In fact, one of the most ingenious aspects of the building is the way in which the louvred ceiling and side walls of the hangar allow visual penetration into the interstitial space; while the gallery volume is precisely defined one may still perceive both the welded, tubular steel trusswork and the service ducts.

6

A similar distinction between *servant* and *served* also informs the *parti* for the canonical high-rise structures of the Foster office: the Hongkong and Shanghai Bank, Hong Kong, 1979-86 (7), and the Century Tower, Tokyo, 1987-91 (8). While the structure is separately articulated, partially as an exoskeleton in the first instance and as portal frames in the second, the service cores in both cases – that is to say escape stairs, elevator banks, lavatories and duct shafts – are pushed to the ends of the open office floors as the *served* volume, the vertical cores, themselves play the role of the *servant*.

Well-serviced Anonymity

A shift towards what Cedric Price has characterised as 'well-serviced anonymity' will eventually distinguish the work of the Foster office from that of Richard Rogers. Thus, where the Reliance Controls factory was to indulge – like Eero Saarinen's plant for Cummins Diesel at Darlington of 1965 – in a post-Miesian emphasis of the constructional process, exposing the steelwork together with its cross-bracing and corrugated cladding, the more discreet articulation of the kit-of-parts in the Fred Olsen Centre had little impact on the external expression of the building, except to stress the thin gasketed joints of the envelope that created an all-but-seamless mirror effect.

This penchant for Minimalism merits further examination. No two buildings could be more different in this regard than Foster's Sainsbury Centre for Visual Arts, Norwich, 1974-78 (10), and the Centre Pompidou, Paris completed a year earlier to the designs of Richard Rogers and Renzo Piano. Where the former comprises a hermetic hangar that all-too-rationally envelops everything including its structural frame, the latter exposes not only its principal structure but also its primary circulation and duct systems, engendering a manifold of piped services as a kind of figurative play against the curtain wall of the building (cf. the picturesque, High-Tech approach taken towards services in Richard Rogers' Lloyd's Headquarters, London, realised in 1986). Aside from the questionable role played by exposed ductwork in the presentation of a public building, the two structures may also be compared in terms of their relative maintenance. While both buildings have not been that easy to maintain over the years (they have both been re-clad at different times), the exposed services of the Centre Pompidou have surely been a

greater liability, not to mention the glazed tubes of the pedestrian escalator and *passerelle* that were difficult to keep clean from the very beginning.

Foster's predilection for precisely articulated dry construction, along with 'well-serviced anonymity', led throughout the 1970s to a series of systematically designed, lightweight industrial sheds. The day-to-day production of medium-sized, partially prefabricated, lightweight structures enabled the Foster office to evolve a relatively open building repertoire and a syntax that was both economic and elegant. Unlike other High-Tech approaches, Foster was able to escape an a priori fixation on a particular technology. Thus, these well-serviced sheds varied considerably in their form from the impermanent, tunnel-like inflated PVC structure, designed in 1969 – and erected in a matter of hours – for Computer Technology, to the neoprene gasketed glass box (equally impermanent in theory) built as a 'fast-track' building for IBM at Cosham, in 1971. A similar range is evident as one passes from the stressed-skin, corrugated-metal Passenger Terminal built for Fred Olsen in Millwall Docks, in 1970, to the steel portal structure realised for Modern Art Glass, at Thamesmead, in 1973.

IBM Cosham was a seminal building for Foster Associates in that it united for the first time the perfect Minimalism of a gasketed glass curtain wall with the universal servicing matrix concept borrowed from Ezra Ehrenkrantz's prefabricated SCSD California schools system. Here Foster was able to combine a universally flexible service grid in the depth of the roof trusses with a flexible, anonymous glass perimeter. In his retrospective appraisal of the building Foster emphasised the mutual flexibility of both the plan and perimeter: 'Major internal changes over the past ten years have been helped by the ability to pop in external doors in lieu of the gasketed panels which otherwise complete the external cladding vocabulary.'

That the environmental serviceability of this lightweight physical fabric should depend, in the last analysis, on the continual maintenance of the air conditioning has been confirmed by Loren Butt, who was responsible for its mechanical engineering. With the continual maintenance of a warm internal climate the usual deleterious 'cold bridge' effects such as condensation simply do not arise. Clearly, such conditions can only be maintained by permanently heating a fully glazed building, although such a provision was essential in any case given the optimum internal temperature that had to be maintained for the computers within.

Bürolandschaft to Carré d'Art

The German concept of *Bürolandschaft*, or 'office-landscape', is equally applicable to the *parti* of two major Foster works realised in the second half of the 1970s – the Willis Faber & Dumas insurance company headquarters (13) completed in Ipswich in 1975, and the Sainsbury Centre for Visual Arts built on the park-like campus of the University of Norwich from 1974 to 1978 – and it remains a strategy in much of Foster's current work.

The application of the concept to the organisation of modern office space was pioneered in the United States, most notably in Frank Lloyd Wright's Larkin Building of 1902-06. Other syndromes accompany this open office form as it slowly becomes the ideal *modus operandi* of modern tertiary industry. Thus as information handling succeeded manufacturing as the main form of productive employment in the second half of the twentieth century, there was a certain penetration of the ways of the factory into those of the office – the counting-house transforms itself into the workshop rather than the other way round.

At the same time, however, the received mode for marketing consumer goods shifts from the street workshop, which since the Middle Ages had combined both production and selling on one site, first to the specialised shop and then to the arcade as an assembly of such shops and finally, around 1876, to the multi-storied space of the department store (cf. Gustave Eiffel's Bon Marché department store built in that year). A comparable evolution towards unencumbered, open, toplit and sidelit space may be found in the evolution of the greenhouse and its progressive application to the accommodation of large universal exhibitions, from Paxton's Crystal Palace of 1851 to Contamin and Dutert's Palais des Machines of 1889 (9). A similar trend is visible in the evolution of the nineteenth-century railway shed, culminating in W H Barlow's St Pancras Station, London, of 1867, with its 275-foot clear-span ferro-vitreous roof.

Whether acknowledged or not, certain aspects of this mixed heritage seem to be embodied in the genesis of both Willis Faber & Dumas and the Sainsbury Centre. With regard to the latter we are led to ask whether this mixture of *Bürolandschaft* with the large single-span shed is really an appropriate space for an art gallery. For while the curator of the collection is surely free to arrange and rearrange art works on mobile screens as he or she sees fit, a doubt lingers

Kenneth Frampton

2

nonetheless as to whether a hangar is truly conducive to the contemplation of art. This potential mismatch becomes even more problematic when one recognises the fact that there is no acoustically isolated volume within which to give lectures. Whatever else it might have been – museum, conservatory, art school, senior common room, or lecture hall – it is also, above all else, an undecorated shed. It is this, perhaps more than anything else, that points to the emerging strength of the practice – its determination to continue with the Modern project as the invention or adaptation of received prototypes to suit new typical conditions or programmes in the late modern world.

In the Willis Faber & Dumas building, by contrast, the *Bürolandschaft* model was relevant from the outset, while at the same time the undecorated shed was deftly integrated into the surrounding urban fabric. Indeed, paradoxical as it may seem, Foster was able to arrive at a compromise between the building as a free-standing technical object and the building as a contextual response: here an irregular plan extends the continuity of the fabric in terms of both topography and time. As Banham, once again, has written with provocative insight:

'[Willis Faber] sets its outline wavily to pursue the accidents of a site that is an accumulated record of civic process and private enterprise at a unique point on the Earth's crust over a finite timespan embracing the individual decision-making of the former citizens whose very names are likely to be found in the city's muniments. By asking the already ambiguous glass box to come out of the architectural surrealism in which transience and permanence – the counted and the uncountable – were reconciled by an intellectual trick, and bending it to a format which is not symbolic of perenniality but is a continuation of local history by other means, Foster Associates have sprung the all-glass wall out of a kind of cultural preserve where its nakedness was masked by our Platonism, and made us look at it again as a visual fact.'[2]

The Platonism alluded to in this passage is of course none other than the monumentality of Mies van der Rohe's late Neo-Classical manner (12), adopted after 1945 as the received American corporate style. However, one can hardly overlook the earlier precedent established by Mies' glass skyscraper proposals of

the 1920s (14) wherein he imagined an undulating sculptural high-rise clad entirely in frameless glass. With this astonishing proposal Mies not only anticipated the faceted cladding of Willis Faber & Dumas but also the essential precepts of its aesthetic character. Thus, as he wrote in 1921 of his Friedrichstrasse proposal: 'I have discovered by working with actual glass models that the important thing is the play of reflections and not the effect of light and shadow as in ordinary buildings.'

That Willis Faber is a full-size realisation of this Miesian intention is borne out by the undulating distorted streetscape reflected in the surface of the structure. This reflected context disappears totally at night, along with the glass wall when the building is lit from within.

While the realisation of this concept would have been unfeasible before the advent of silicon sealants, credit has to be accorded to Martin Francis and the Foster Associates' team that developed and detailed the necklace-like curtain wall. The flat, plate-glass 'beads' that make up this 'necklace' are in fact held together at every corner by patch plates, sealed with silicon, and hung like transparent chain mail from the concrete cornice at the top of the building. The architect's description of the progressive evolution of this wall is a casebook example of the Foster method at its best:

'An awareness that glass is at its strongest in tension prompted the concept of a glazed curtain suspended from the top edge of the building. Unfortunately we were unable to convince anyone outside the office it was technically feasible. For this reason all the interior perspectives of that period show a steel mullion system designed for the project and testbedded on a smaller installation in Thamesmead. Eventually, however, enough calculations and technical details emerged to convince specialist suppliers and subcontractors that the idea was not only viable but also looked very attractive in cost terms (hardly surprising since it reduced the major elements down to just glass and glue).'[3]

But Willis Faber was not just a *tour de force* of innovative technique or a judicious upgrading of the office landscape approach of the 1960s. On the contrary, it was the invention of a unique, hybrid type. Part department store and part flattened office space, the building was devised to accommodate a totally new

modus operandi; that is to say it facilitated an innovative approach towards the organisation of office work and towards the welfare of the firm's employees.

The building comprises two deep office floors sandwiched between two predominantly social floors, the first of which is situated around the entry concourse on the ground floor. It consists of a swimming pool and a coffee bar, together with plant rooms, computer space and loading docks. The second provision is located on the roof and comprises a glazed restaurant surrounded by a lawn that extends out to the parapet. As in the department store type, all the floors are served by up and down escalators running through a large atrium, enabling light to descend freely from the roof to the ground.

A perennial theme borrowed from the teamwork ethos of the office is also evident here: namely the elimination of closed offices for executives. This gesture points towards a democratisation of the workplace, as does the maintenance of a single high standard of finish, equipment and glare-free lighting throughout. At the same time, however, it also facilitates a certain increase in the level of mutual surveillance and control. Thus, as in Frank Lloyd Wright's Larkin Building, by which it was surely influenced, a kind of panoptic transparency prevails.

As with Herman Hertzberger's Centraal Beheer offices (11), Willis Faber & Dumas moved out of London in order to benefit from lower land values and reduced staff costs in the provinces. With its palm-filled, toplit winter garden, Willis Faber met the criteria of Herman Kahn's future workplace inasmuch as it placed a greater emphasis on social interaction and recreation than hierarchic control. This strategy was adopted, as Foster is at pains to stress, not for philanthropic reasons but because it guaranteed a socially productive instrument of higher overall efficiency, whilst exploiting the last available square foot of the site. With its mixed lineage, running from Wright's Larkin Building to Mies' glass skyscrapers, Willis Faber & Dumas proffers itself as a decentralised productive unit, precisely scaled to the emerging era of global communication.

The Carré d'Art in Nîmes, France (15), completed in 1993, comprises an art museum, a *médiathèque* and library, and had to respond to the powerful presence of the Roman temple known as the Maison Carrée. This canonical cultural institution succeeded in resolving the anomalies inherent in the *Bürolandschaft* space of the Sainsbury Centre. Here, in a louvred glass pavilion that is even more

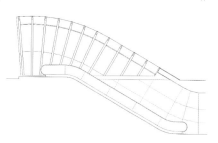

dematerialised than the Sainsbury Centre's hangar volume, the various spaces demanded by the different users are precisely distinguished from one another, while still being encapsulated within a single glazed prism, itself sustained by a systematic column grid.

This is still perhaps the most *contextual* work of Foster's career, not only because of the way its mass is handled in relation to the Roman temple, but also because of its carefully calibrated response to the site and the Mediterranean way of life. This is succinctly stated in Foster's summary of the project:

'The design has been influenced by the vernacular architecture of the region, with its cool courtyards, steps and terraces, and the Roman grid pattern of the city centre. The Carré d'Art attempts to combine these themes in a modern way. Half of its nine-storey structure is buried below ground in order to respect surrounding building heights. At its heart, a five-storey internal courtyard exploits the lightness and transparency of modern materials, especially clear, translucent and opaque glass.'[4]

It is significant that the Carré d'Art, together with the Metro in Bilbao (16, 17), should have prompted Foster's receipt of the much-coveted Veronica Rudge Green Prize in Urban Design, in 1999, given under the auspices of the GSD, Harvard University. Rodolfo Machado's appraisal of the award reveals the values that influenced the jury's decision:

'In Bilbao we see a manifestation of the toughest kind of regional infrastructure – a metro system – rendered with the humanistic qualities that characterise a well-inhabited domestic realm, but without any of the faux cosiness, the studied disorder, or the condescending "warmth" one usually finds in those public places whose designers set out to produce a "humane" environment ... These public works are instructive in an exemplary way: they demonstrate that transportation infrastructure can be conceived as public architecture (and that great benefits can be obtained from such an agenda); that to make iconic public architecture today as was done in the past is OK, and moreover, that the city's self-conscious image-making yields good marketing, as demonstrated by the much-loved "Fosteritos"

representing the new Bilbao; that to build public places around a monument of Classical antiquity need not be an act of mindless mimicry; that a respectable con-textualism need not be about style; and that legibility, ergonomic correctness, atemporality in language and permanence in building are obviously significant qualities for an urban product to possess.'[5]

'The Tall Office Building Artistically Considered'

At the other end of the global spectrum in terms of investment and technological rhetoric, the Hongkong and Shanghai Bank (18-20), realised on the Hong Kong waterfront, is evidently an instrument of much greater potency. It is one of the most significant and distinguished high-rise office structures built since the golden age of the American skyscraper in the 1920s and '30s, notwithstanding the preva-lence of the Miesian high-rise paradigm in the 1950s which, in terms of tectonic integrity and urban responsiveness, culminated in Mies' Seagram Building, realised in the very heart of New York in 1958. Twenty years separates the closed competition for the Hongkong and Shanghai Bank of 1979 from the realisation of Seagram. It may be noted that these were the years in which American military and economic pre-eminence began to wane; the years, in fact, in which the Far East began to emerge – as Herman Kahn had prophesied it would – as the economic giant of the future. With this new global formation one witnesses not only the tri-umph of multinational capitalism but also, from the mid-1970s on, the techno-economic restructuring of Europe in which high technology began to play a more salient role. The inauguration of the Anglo-French Concorde service in 1979 is symptomatic in this regard.

With the realisation of the 180-metre high Hongkong and Shanghai Bank, Foster entered a new scale of global and technological achievement. An account of its evolution and production reminds one of nothing so much as the conceptual prowess and organisational method that went into the erection of the Eiffel Tower. One hardly knows which to admire more – the final tectonic result or the techni-cal know-how. It is surely this last which is in a class of its own. For while we have become accustomed in assembly-line production to the transhipment of certain components and materials across great distances, to have prefabricated and shipped large-scale building elements, constructed to fine levels of tolerance (as

little as 3mm in some instances) and to have fitted them into their appointed positions without difficulty, is an achievement of a totally different magnitude.

Symptomatic of this was the forging and transhipment of the entire tubular steel superstructure by British Steel, which, at 34,000 tons, was the largest single constructional order for the British steel industry since Sydney Harbour Bridge. The aluminium cladding, prefabricated in the United States, was of a comparable order of magnitude and precision. No less remarkable, although closer to the site geographically speaking, were the Japanese metal-clad service modules, each fully equipped down to the smallest piece of sanitary hardware. They are particularly impressive when one recalls that, on delivery, these elements were hoisted into position by cranes mounted on the top of the ever-growing superstructure. These metal boxes needed only to be plugged into the rising power lines and plumbing ducts to become immediately serviceable.

The 47-storey Hongkong Bank is made up of three visually distinct bays, each with a different ultimate height. Since the entire structure is suspended, these bays jointly bridge over an unobstructed plaza at ground level. This covered public space serves as a direct extension of the adjacent Statue Square. It is typical of the servo-mechanistic approach taken towards the entire building, that the open flanks of this portico are provided with retractable screens that will automatically close in the event of a typhoon. They are of the same gossamer, High-Tech order as the glass floor to the central atrium, which hovers over the open portico like the underbelly of a glazed dirigible. This catenary membrane is pierced by two equally transparent escalators which, aside from providing continuous access to the main banking hall above, are also auspiciously aligned according to the augural precepts of feng shui geomancy. The geometry of these escalators introduces an organic inflection into the work; one that is comparable to the asymmetrically stepped, setback skyline of the building in cross-section, crowned by mantis-like mobile cleaning cranes.

Perhaps the most impressive part of the Bank is the ten-storey high atrium, which rises up above the public concourse. As an ultimate *machine à travailler*, this building is equipped with a number of ingenious mechanical devices, including a large, adjustable, mirrored 'sunscoop', mounted outside the structure, which is designed to reflect sunlight down into the atrium. The atomistic composition of

Kenneth Frampton

these giant mirrors returns us to Foster's habit of looking outside the building industry for his more technologically advanced components. Thus, the 480 annealed mirrors that make up the external reflector of the sunscoop are of the type more commonly employed in solar power stations. In this instance, the sunscoop is powered by a computer-controlled motor, which allows it to continuously track the path of the sun.

Despite its high cost, the primary advantage of the suspension structure was that it avoided the necessity for a central structural core. This enabled Foster to make a more efficient use of the available floorspace, yielding a far higher net-to-gross ratio than is commonly attained in high-rise office accommodation.

Faced in shades of automotive silver-grey, this High-Tech structure can be seen as one of the prime multinational corporate symbols of the 1980s. Identifiable with finance itself, it stands forth in the Hong Kong conglomeration as an ultimate sign of power and prestige. It is ironic that it should be the ultimate Constructivist manifestation of the century, particularly since this vision has been realised without the revolutionary Socialist connotations that Constructivism once implied.

Despite its brilliance, the Hongkong and Shanghai Bank also displays some of the limitations of the Foster approach: first, perhaps a certain disingenuity with regard to the topographic complexities of the site, and second, a reluctance to deal with aspects of a complex building programme that are non-instrumental. However, the Hongkong Bank ultimately achieves a successful contextual inflection, in part through the public space afforded by the 12-metre-high concourse beneath the building, which sensitively integrates the vast volume of the structure into the adjacent street fabric, and in part through the staggered formation of the building mass, which enables the complex to be read as a continuation of the atomised, high-rise fabric of downtown Hong Kong. This is a perceptual effect comparable to the subtle concatenation of the Rockefeller Center in New York, in which a single development is broken down into a series of parallel slabs of varying height, the lowest of them subtly layered into the block fabric. The Bank's dull silvery grey metal facade only enhances its contextual potential since it looms out of the 'mist' of Hong Kong as the most discreet and elegant skyscraper the world has ever seen.

22

From Roofwork to Earthwork

The Renault Centre, Swindon (21), completed in 1982, is a *tour de force* in structural expression. Along with the Hongkong and Shanghai Bank, it represents a decisive break with the received Foster paradigm, since here the structure is rhetorically expressed as a modulating exoskeleton running throughout the length and breadth of the building. This is a radical departure from the principle of enclosing a structure within an all-enveloping membrane. Conceived as a kind of flexible 'tensegrity' network, the Renault Centre consciously departs from the bulky, unarticulated, windowless mass-form that has become the norm in out-of-town warehousing. Instead, a structural counterpoint of post-tensioned steel pylons, taut guying cables and perforated steel arches animates the flat Wiltshire landscape, appearing on the horizon like the dematerialised 'domes' of some Oriental pavilion.

The roof, consisting of a two-way symmetrical grid of steel decking, is ingeniously supported in its interstitial valleys by cylindrical masts, cable-stayed from their apexes above the roof, which support the underlying steel structure. Like Max Bill, in his Swiss Landesausstellung Pavilion of 1963, Foster is deeply indebted in this work to the model of the Crystal Palace of 1851, and even perhaps to Bill himself. Like these lightweight, prefabricated precedents, the Renault Centre's hollow cylindrical columns also double as rainwater downpipes.

As in Paxton's Crystal Palace (22), symbiotic techniques drawn from other fields are integrated into the construction. Thus, where the Crystal Palace was a synthesis of greenhouse technology and the mid-century infrastructural know-how of railway engineering (Paxton's engineers, Fox and Henderson, specialised in railway construction), Foster's Renault Centre employs a nut-jacking system originally developed for stressing nuts in marine boilers, together with a flexible fascia made from a neoprene-coated nylon fabric developed for the skirts of hovercraft. Of a similar order is its pioneering use of spheroidal graphite cast-iron bearings (strong as steel and half the price) and a new form of bolt-suspended, flatbed armour-plated glass.

The Renault Centre fulfils Foster's intention of providing flexible, multi-use, well-lit space. It is as suitable for the storage of automobiles and their components as for the purposes of public reception, product display and the training of personnel. It not only serves its purposes adequately but also presents an effective

23

technological image for a leading automobile company. An essential part of its poetry derives from the fact that its lightweight perforated steel frames and similarly perforated aluminium mullions, respectively finished in 'Renault yellow' and bare metal, represent only too well the lightweight French engineering tradition of which Renault was an important pioneer, not to mention the reference to the master *constructeur* Jean Prouvé, whose spirit seems to inform the structure.

At a modular level the Renault Centre served as a prototype for the terminal building at Stansted (23), the third London airport, which Foster completed in 1991. Here the exoskeleton roof of Renault is transformed into a domed roof made up of 18-square-metre modules, reiterated 121 times to cover a square plan area with 198-metre sides. The shallow 'domes' that form the roof rise to 3 metres at their crowns and are carried on tree-like steel columns placed at 36-metre intervals throughout the terminal. These 'trees' support welded tubular steel 'branches', which splay upwards at 45° from a 4-metre-high datum above concourse level.

The terminal building comprises a single volume poised on top of an undercroft housing mechanical services, baggage facilities and main-line rail connections. The glass-sided terminal is divided by low partitions into departure and arrival concourses running side by side within a single shed. On the model of the nineteenth-century railway terminus, every effort has been made to allow passengers the maximum freedom of movement, and to afford visual access to the means of transport – in this case, a clear view of the aircraft. While there is ample provision for the extension of the terminal laterally, the two fronts to roadway and runway are conceived as fixed planes, thus allowing for expansion while retaining both the basic image and the approach to the terminal as stable conditions.

The Ecology of the Commerzbank

As we have seen from the painstaking evolution of the final form of the exoskeleton in the case of the Hongkong and Shanghai Bank, Foster patently recognised that a key to mastering the challenge posed by great height was to break down the scale of the vertical form through some kind of horizontal modulation. Thus the office would return to Louis Sullivan's problem of *The Tall Office Building Artistically Considered* of 1896. However, instead of opting for the suppression of the floors through stressing the mullions, in order to emphasise the unity of the

24

shaft – the quintessential solution to the skyscraper from Louis Sullivan's Guaranty Building, 1896, to Mies van der Rohe's Seagram Building – Foster deployed a megastructural exoskeleton as a way of modulating the high-rise form.

With the 53-storey Commerzbank, completed in 1997, Foster would address the issue of height by partially suppressing the structure and by inserting suspended gardens (24), which form large spatial 'slots' in stepped formation around a triangular central atrium running the full height of the building. For the rest, as the office description informs us: 'Lifts, staircases and services are placed in the three corners, in groups, to reinforce the village-like clusters of offices and gardens. Pairs of vertical masts, enclosing the corner cores, support eight-storey Vierendeel beams, which in turn support clear-span office floors.'

Here the high-rise – the tallest in Europe – comes to be modulated through the pursuit of an ecological form, in which the atrium functions as a natural ventilation shaft. By virtue of the four-storey-high 'sky-gardens' that spiral around the building, each desk is afforded a lateral view over a suspended green space. With the additional device of double-layered solar walls built into the perimeter of the building, each office is provided with the possibility of natural ventilation, since the tower supports its own microclimate inside and out.

Engineer's Aesthetic and Architecture

This dyad so categorically posited as a symbiotic opposition in the first chapter of Le Corbusier's *Towards a New Architecture*, of 1923, has in many ways been integrated as a dialectic into a great deal of Foster's practice. This is particularly true of those works where the structure assumes a decisive instrumental character, as in the Barcelona Telecommunications Tower – the so-called Torre de Collserola – completed on a mountainside overlooking the city in 1992 (25), or the Bilbao Metro System, the first 61 kilometres of which were opened to the public in 1995. In both instances these were precisely engineered solutions that incorporated certain values, that is to say they were motivated by visual concerns that could not be reduced to superficial aesthetic effects.

In the first instance it was a question of allowing the profile of the mountain to remain as unencumbered as possible by elevating the various transmitters and microwave dishes halfway up a 288-metre cylindrical, tapering tower, 4.5 metres

in diameter at the base, with a suspended platform stabilised by Kevlar cables. This is a Constructivist solution with a capital C and a paradigm that has many antecedents, not least of which is surely the long-forgotten Skylon erected for the Festival of Britain of 1951 to the designs of Hidalgo Moya and Felix Samuely.

The second instance, Bilbao Metro, offers the Basque public one of the most subtly lit, dematerialised subway systems devised anywhere in the last 30 years, providing a quiet, well-organised environment in which to wait for equally efficient trains. With its suspended circulation decks and panelled walls it is a question not only of what it amounts to in phenomenological terms but also of the way in which it has come to be built. It is this last that assures the liberative aesthetic effect; and this judgement also surely applies to the 'slinky', totally glazed subway entrances, which rise to the surface in a way that is both self-effacing and assertive.

Something must also be said at this juncture about the way in which Foster has always worked in close association with the very best structural and mechanical engineers, from the inception of the practice. It is this that places him, along with a number of other so-called 'High-Tech' practices such as those of Renzo Piano and Richard Rogers, in a class of architects that have consistently enlisted the services of consulting firms of the calibre of Ove Arup & Partners, Buro Happold and RFR – and through these agencies worked with such distinguished engineers as Ted Happold, John Thorton, Chris Wise and the late Peter Rice.

Today Foster and Partners is by any world standard a global practice, and has been so for some time. However, what distinguishes the Foster office from other corporate enterprises of a similar genre (from HOK, for instance, which is still the largest worldwide) is the conscious cultivation of flair, intelligence, teamwork and precision within the firm, as it has evolved under Norman Foster's leadership, passing from one generation to the next. So, far from being just another corporate practice, Foster and Partners is a culture of architecture in the deepest sense of the term, much like Skidmore, Owings and Merrill and Mies Van der Rohe were in the early years of the Pax Americana after the Second World War. Nothing could be further from the contemporary American corporate tradition, where there is no culture of architecture strictly speaking, where expediency rules, and where engineers are largely kept at arm's length by the architect and vice versa.

Reinterpreting Typeforms

In some 30 years of continuous practice, after projecting and realising over two hundred designs of widely varying scale and scope, it seems clear that on balance Foster has been at his best where he has been able to encapsulate the problem as a generic type, that is to say a work which, while it is relevant to a specific brief and site, also has general ramifications that go beyond the particular solution. This, in my view, is the way in which the office keeps its faith with the 'unfinished Modern project' which was the fundamental agenda of the Modern Movement in the inter-war years. Thus a Foster design, at its best, is not only a response to a particular site and brief but also a self-conscious interpretation of the programme to such a degree as to reinterpret a received typeform to meet the needs of an emerging era. Hence the inestimable contribution that Foster has made to the design of post-Miesian office space or, as we have seen, the equally pertinent formulations brought to bear on the problem of the high-rise.

'There is no point in inventing anything unless it is an improvement,' to quote Adolf Loos' provocative slogan. And while many architects would like to justify their work in terms of this principle, there are very few who are truly able to do so. The Foster office at its best has been able to adhere rigorously to the ethical implications of this aphorism. There are two things that surely follow from this. The first is that not all of the practice's works are able to attain this 'generic' level; and the second is that the typeform, once it has been formulated, will be reiterated to some extent in other works by the practice, which is, after all, what a typeform is for.

With regard to this last we may surely cite the Century Tower in Tokyo of 1987-91, as a reworking at a smaller scale of ideas initially broached in the Hongkong and Shanghai Bank. This is evinced not only in the use of Kahnian servant shafts, plugged onto one side of the complex, but also in the layering of the twin office slabs and the deployment of portal spans on each floor in such a way as to modulate the height. Here we may also remark on the relation between the generic and the specific; for where the tower form is somewhat typical, the glazed catenary roof over the swimming pool and fitness centre is quite specific, not only to the client but also to the social and aesthetic mores of Japan.

By the same token, one may see the ITN Headquarters in London (26) of 1988-90, as a sober reworking of the atrium of the Hongkong and Shanghai Bank

Kenneth Frampton

27

together with cylindrical concrete columns such as Foster was to use in the Carré d'Art in Nîmes. Similarly, it is possible to argue that the National Botanic Gardens for Wales, projected in 1995, are a partial reworking of the Climatroffice; just as the Exhibition and Conference Centre (27), completed on a disused harbourside in Glasgow in 1997, is a partial reinterpretation of the typeform of Utzon's Sydney Opera House of 1957-73, or perhaps, in part, of Fumihiko Maki's Fujisawa Gymnasium in Tokyo, of 1984-86.

A received typeform has perhaps never been more directly addressed by Foster than in his designs for the Sackler Galleries of the Royal Academy of Arts in London, completed in 1991. In this instance it was a matter of replacing the nineteenth-century Diploma Galleries on the top of the Academy and devising a much more efficient mode of accessing them. This involved inserting a new glass stair and elevator shaft into an existing space between the seventeenth-century Burlington House and the Victorian gallery extension beyond. Foster was able to reinstate the galleries as a kind of *répétition differente*, respecting the deportment of the traditional gallery space but detailing it in such a way as to reveal its struc-tural dependence on a new steel armature.

Perhaps in the last analysis Foster's work may not be neatly subsumed under the Corbusian term 'engineer's aesthetic' since in many instances the aesthetic and the engineered form cannot be prised apart. And by a similar token we may also surely say that the 'architecture' of the firm is not so much architecture in the old classic, artistic and humanist sense, as it is *Baukunst* – 'building art' – in what we may reasonably identify as the reborn medieval sense, where invention, tradi-tion, sensibility, know-how and craft are unified in one moment, and where the authorship is no longer a single individual but a supremely intelligent team, rising and falling across time and space according to a singular aim.

'The view up through the dome to the people on the ramps is reminiscent of frescoed ceilings such as those of Veronese, with skies full of leaning and flying people. And the trick of reflecting down so much light would have been the envy of architects such as Neumann and Bernini.'

Peter Buchanan

The seat of a national government is one of the most symbolic of buildings, if for no other reason than that it inevitably comes to represent its country. It is also a repository of the nation's traditions and ideals, the place where its destiny is determined. Such a symbolically loaded building might, therefore, seem unlikely to be commissioned from a foreign architect. This might be expected to be particularly true of a country such as Germany where the sense of nationhood has historically been rooted so much in 'blood and soil', whereas in countries such as Britain, the US or France it has rested much more in democratic institutions. Yet it is precisely this elevated status of the democratic institution, the Bundestag, and its democratic processes that the transformed Reichstag now so aptly houses and symbolises, by introducing a dialectical play between old and new, solid and transparent, vertical and horizontal, and by evoking the very German ideal of the *Stadtkrone*.

Yet there are many twentieth-century precedents of national parliament buildings designed by foreign architects, although they are mostly for ex-colonies, built by architects from the colonising country. The three most famous were all designed for outposts of the former British Empire, but by non-British architects. The Punjabi and Bangladeshi governments turned respectively to the Swiss-French Le Corbusier, and the Estonian-American Louis Kahn, for assembly buildings in Chandigarh (1) and Dacca (2). Two of the most revered modern architects, Le Corbusier and Kahn were to help advance these countries into the modern age. Yet ironically, both designed buildings that even at the time seemed more archaic than modern, and to many today seem excessively primitive. They are, however, also highly charged and timeless masterworks, not least because they deliberately evoke local tradition.

Both Le Corbusier and Kahn drew on historical themes from East and West to symbolise the dignity, solemnity and seriousness of government. At Chandigarh the plan evokes the Classical elements of K F Schinkel's Altes Museum while the portico is capped by an Indian parasol roof which, seen end on, suggests the horns of the local cattle Le Corbusier liked to sketch. Dacca's plan recalls compositional themes found in Mughal and Roman architecture. Both buildings play circular forms against rectilinear: each of their assembly chambers is circular in plan (that at Dacca is chamfered into a polygon), organised around a vertical axis that rises to a distinctive lantern filtering natural light down into the hall.

The invitation to those entering to lift the eyes, and the emphasis on the vertical axis, inspire awe and spiritual aspiration, raising these halls into hallowed precincts where debate should be measured and inspired. The lantern, in each case, also announces externally the presence of a chamber that is otherwise buried among surrounding spaces. At Dacca the circular hall rises above the surrounding spaces. At Chandigarh, this theme is extended; besides the dominant form of the projecting assembly chamber, there is a smaller pyramidal roof above the council chamber.

The third former British colony in this selection, Australia, chose through competition the Italian-American architect and acolyte of Kahn, Romaldo Giurgola, to build its new Parliament House in Canberra. His design fuses architecture and topography, burying the building beneath the existing Capital Hill. This richly allusive building evokes key elements of Western architectural history, from Queen Hatshepsut's Temple onwards, as well as depicting Australian and Aboriginal motifs. The public can walk up the hill to a four-legged flagpole which marks both the summit and the Members' hall between the House of Representatives and the Senate chamber below. As now at the Reichstag building, people can ascend above the politicians visible in the hall beneath them. They can also circulate around the complex at first-floor level and look down on the politicians from galleries around the central Members' hall and the two chambers. Like the chambers at Chandigarh and Dacca, these are capped by, and toplit through, conspicuous and distinctive lanterns that are substitutes for a form which has generally been taboo for modern architects: the dome.

Throughout the twentieth century, architects sought less symbolically fraught alternatives. Consider how Erik Gunnar Asplund's Stockholm Library focuses on a drum with a white interior which is an apt metaphor for Scandinavia's pale and misty skies; or the billowing cloud-like ceiling of Jørn Utzon's otherwise Islamic-inspired Bagsvaerd Church in Copenhagen; and the poignantly 'missing' dome of James Stirling's Staatsgalerie in Stuttgart. There are, of course, some exceptions – such as the buildings of Frank Lloyd Wright in his dotage – and there are domes by engineers such as Buckminster Fuller and Pier Luigi Nervi. But for our purposes the most significant exception is Oscar Niemeyer's National Congress Building in Brasilia, another twentieth-century parliament building of international repute.

Peter Buchanan

Here too the public has access to the roof via an external ramp to an elevated plaza from which spring a pair of domes. The larger dome, above the Chamber of Deputies, is inverted (so evoking, according to Niemeyer, the cumulonimbus cloud forms of Brazil's high plateau) and the smaller dome of the Senate chamber is merely a formal counterpart to it. Little wonder that Foster was reluctant to reinstate a dome on the Reichstag. But these are now Pluralist times, and Modernist taboos are giving way to more conventional responses to decorum and context.

Chandigarh and the new Reichstag might be thought of as polar opposites. The Reichstag is as technologically sophisticated as the Chandigarh Assembly is primitive (although, more accurately perhaps, both buildings reflect the level of technology then readily available in their respective countries). And while the Reichstag draws in as much natural light as possible, Chandigarh, like Dacca, shuts out the bright glare and heat to become a cool, shadowy refuge. Yet there are also some curious parallels between the two buildings. Both chambers are circular – or implicitly so – in plan, are naturally toplit, and have an emphatic vertical axis crowned by a lantern that announces the presence of the chamber on the roof line. And just as the Reichstag chamber draws warm air up and out through its lantern, so the Chandigarh chamber was consciously inspired by power station cooling towers, which are profiled to channel warm vapours upwards. Furthermore, many of Le Corbusier's design sketches show a ramp spiralling around the exterior of the lantern (3), rising from a roof terrace to which the public would have had access to enjoy solar and lunar festivities.

One of the last generation of architects to be fully educated in the Western Classical tradition, Le Corbusier still valued the distinction between exoteric symbols, the meaning of which could be readily grasped by all, and the esoteric, to be understood only by deserving initiates. Intentionally hermetic, Le Corbusier's symbolism was conscious and complex (far too much so to be discussed here), and its cosmic connections were carefully calculated; for example, a direct shaft of sunlight focuses on a statue beside the Speaker's chair in the Chandigarh chamber on the exact day and hour of the opening of Parliament each year. Such focused shafts of light are a theme in Hindu temples; and the sculptural element of the chamber's roof, which controls the incoming sun, suggests such historical Indian observatories as the Jantar Mantar. Le Corbusier had visited this site and

408

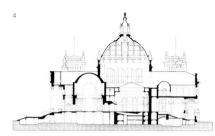

4

5

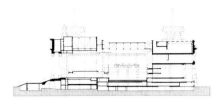

noted in his sketchbook: 'The astronomical instruments of Delhi – point the way: re-link men to the cosmos.' These elements give the assembly building further resonances with local culture and mythology.

Foster's appointment as architect for the Reichstag renovation was not without direct precedent. The Reichstag was originally built as a triumphalist monument to Germany's belated unification and burgeoning imperial power. Yet the country still felt culturally insecure and uncertain of how best to symbolise these twin achievements. Hence, when the Reichstag project was first proposed, the design was put out to an international competition in which the British architect Sir George Gilbert Scott won second prize.

The eventual building (4) was in a bombastic Italianate style, ornamented with German iconography and statues of Teutonic heroes, and capped by a dome (18). Built of steel, clad in copper and glass, and square in plan, this dome was hailed at the time as modern. It rivalled in height and prominence the domes of Berlin's Royal Palace and Cathedral, so announcing the importance of the newly emergent Parliament alongside the established institutions of the Monarchy and the Church.

Following the reunification of Germany in 1990, and the decision to return the seat of government to Berlin and the Bundestag to the Reichstag, Germany again opted for an international competition to select an architect to rebuild the Reichstag. This was to emphasise the country's transcendence of nationalism in favour of international cooperation, as well as its continuing commitment to being enmeshed in Europe. But it probably also revealed again an uncertainty as to how Germany should represent itself and tame or exploit the association-laden hulk of the Reichstag building.

Compounding such conundrums, renovating the Reichstag meant coming to terms with more than one building. Once Norman Foster had won the competition and the design was progressing through numerous revisions and refinements, it must have become increasingly apparent that he was dealing with the memories of, and associations with, four quite different buildings: the original Reichstag; its fire and war ravaged hulk; Paul Baumgarten's 1960s conversion (5); and Günter Behnisch's new Bundestag building in Bonn, completed in 1992.

Of these four, much the least important was the building immediately to hand, Baumgarten's renovation. Ranking equally with both the original and the ravaged

Peter Buchanan

8
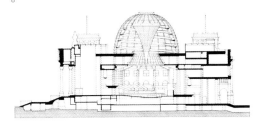

9
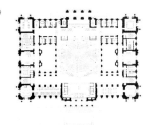

Reichstag was the Bundestag in Bonn, then occupied by the politicians. Contrived as the ultimate expression of democracy, this building forsakes any vertical architectural emphasis in favour of a uniform horizontality and transparency, symbolising openness to scrutiny, accountability and accessibility.

The equation of transparent or glass walls with open political process goes back to Hannes Meyer and Hans Wittwer's entry in the 1927 League of Nations competition (6). This key precedent to the sort of High-Tech architecture of which Foster is the leading exponent, was to have been built of standardised repetitive components that minimised expressions of hierarchy as well as suggesting the factories of the proletariat. Meyer's report stated that: 'If the intentions of the League of Nations are sincere, then it cannot possibly cram such a novel organisation into the straitjacket of traditional architecture – no back corridors for backstairs diplomacy, but open glazed rooms for public negotiation by honest men.'

The transparent enclosure of the Bonn chamber (7) also reveals a bucolic backdrop of landscaped grounds and the Rhine. The ultimate model behind Behnisch's design is, then, not Meyer and Wittwer, but the original seat of democracy, the ancient Athenian Pnyx where political meetings were held in the open air against a panoramic backdrop.

Foster's original design solution at the first stage of the Reichstag competition, drew less on Behnisch's design and more on the temporary arrangement for the 1949 inaugural session of the Bundestag in a converted teachers' college in Bonn. For this occasion bleachers were erected outside the chamber to allow the public to view proceedings inside. Foster's first scheme proposed a podium wrapped around the Reichstag, reaching the top of its original plinth, equivalent to first-floor level. This provided a public esplanade around the building, aligned with the bottom of the huge windows around its *piano nobile*. Rising from the podium were immense columns supporting a canopy that sailed high above the building. Thus was the mighty Reichstag tamed. What appeared to be the lower part of the building was now invitingly open and porous and the historical structure was reduced to the status of a relic on protective display. The building's bombastic rhetoric would lose all its force. Moreover, people promenading on the podium and on the Reichstag's roof would, though outside the building, still come within its embrace, and to a larger degree take command of 'their' parliament.

of course in this
approach
it also easy
to incorporate
lifts w
staircases
from
upper
platform
down
to main
roof level.

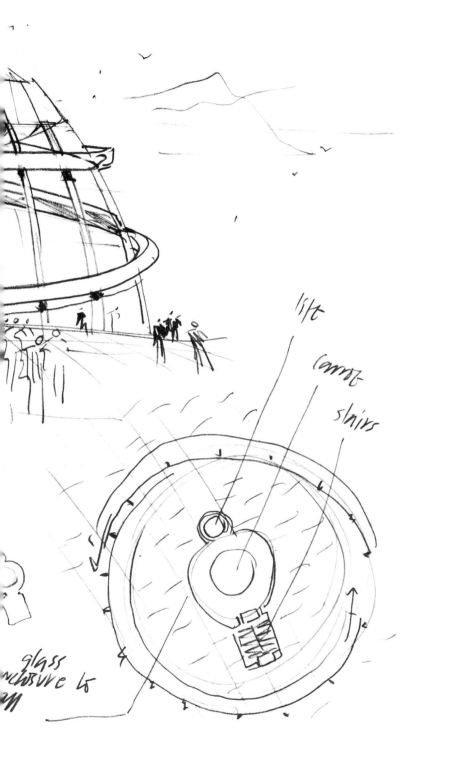

lift

connt

stairs

glass
nclosure to
w

412

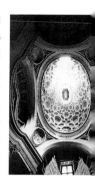

The built solution is very different, not least in being contained within the shell of the old building (8,9). A key design strategy has been to fuse, by bringing into dialogue, contrasting formal themes and their various implicit meanings. The most immediately obvious of these is to be found in the interplay between the thick, heavy and solid enclosure of the existing building and the transparency and lightness of the new insertions. This represents a dialogue of the legacy of the past, couched in Classical rhetoric, with the present's very different aspirations for the future voiced in a more 'space-age' language. The dominant sense is of a forward-looking lightness and buoyant optimism overcoming the heavy and claustrophobic constraints of the past. The renovated building also cleverly combines the vertical emphasis (with its connotations of higher purpose and cosmic connections) found in the chambers of Chandigarh and Dacca with the horizontal emphasis (with its secular and democratic connotations) found in Behnisch's chamber at Bonn. This is clearly apparent in the chamber (13), but it is a theme that recurs in the general organisation of the building and again on the roof.

The result is an aesthetic and technical *tour de force*. Moreover, many aspects of the scheme are symbolically apt and resonant. The light reflector that intrudes into the chamber not only brings energy savings but also makes manifestly clear how it does so (19), thus becoming a potent symbol of very topical concerns. However, many other aspects of the scheme could be construed as being symbolically ambiguous. It is difficult to predict the meanings that might finally be ascribed to these elements, or whether they will remain teasingly uncertain. It is also unclear whether the agreed meanings will be those the public decides ring true, or those it is persuaded to ascribe as intended and therefore correct.

For example, upon entering the Reichstag, members of the public are offered a clear view into, and through, the chamber via the glazed screen that closes the tall lobby, and another at the back of the chamber. This view introduces the theme of transparency and so of the accountability of politicians. Yet this same device could easily be read as a tantalising glimpse that emphasises physical inaccessibility. Such are the quandaries faced both during and after design. The architects did in good faith what was possible, within the constraints set by security demands and the limitations of the existing building, to achieve transparency: perhaps it is now up to critics and the public to interpret the results in similar good faith.

Peter Buchanan

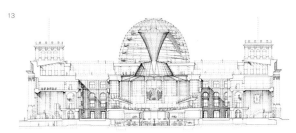

13

For those who can penetrate further on the ground floor, the sense of transparency and openness, and of light and lightness that has been achieved within the massive walls of the old building is amazing. The chamber is flooded with natural light; the space itself seems drawn into the corridors in front of it and behind it and into the courtyards on either side. Here is the horizontal sweep, the views in and out, that in Bonn have been equated with democracy. Yet the space also soars upwards, and the eye is drawn with it, to the lantern and the inverted cone of the reflector that protrudes downwards from it. This, with the light it reflects down and its energy-saving functions, gives an exalted sense of connection to sky and sun, and even to the cosmos. Yet the 'cosmic carrot' of the reflector, with its tapering point stabilised by only the most slender of ties, also lends a sense of the precarious. In this hall, you feel, thought should take wings, and debate be imaginative and responsible, the latter not least because inappropriate comment might be punished by the skewering descent of the rapier-pointed reflector.

Yet, for all the space-age imagery and concern with the environment, both within the chamber and around, the lantern evokes surprising historical associations, with the Baroque no less. The view up through the dome to the people on the ramps is reminiscent of frescoed ceilings, such as those of Veronese, with skies full of leaning and flying people. And the trick of reflecting down so much light (12) would have been the envy of architects such as Neumann and Bernini (11), who might conceivably have added a few *putti* flying around the reflector. Now, perhaps, it is the public – in some celestial realm above the ceiling – who themselves stand in as *putti* constantly circling in a *tableau vivant*.

The compressed circular layout of the seats is not as extreme as the complete circle found in Bonn (and in the self-consciously non-hierarchical chambers of the United Nations Assembly and the European Parliament) which for Behnisch epitomises democracy in both function and symbolism. He imagined politicians forsaking their tradition of speaking from the privileged position of the rostrum and addressing each other from their seats. But when they continued to speak from the rostrum, those behind the speaker had a disadvantaged view. This is why in the Athenian Pnyx, which served also as a theatre, the seating was arranged in a semicircle: in this first democratic forum it was deemed important not just to hear the words of the speaker but to judge the totality of the performance and of the

14>

character who advanced an argument. Now, of course, for such an intimate judge-ment of politicians, most of us rely upon television, that ultimate extension of the horizontal, 'democratic' domain. In the Reichstag, it is through closed-circuit tele-vision that the press, sequestered on the top floor, will follow debates, as will many of the politicians in their committee and faction rooms.

The raised tribunes in the chamber (15), which seat invited members of the public, follow the curved geometry of the seating on the floor below. This was the solution Behnisch had first intended in Bonn, but he discarded it in favour of trib-unes aligned rectilinearly with the walls of the chamber. He reasoned that the pub-lic and press on these galleries are not directly part of the proceedings below, and this divorce should be made symbolically clear. But it could just as convincingly be argued that the invited members of the public are very much part of the proceed-ings: the politicians merely represent their democratic will. Given such a reading, the solution at the Reichstag would seem more truthfully to represent the spirit of democracy than does that in Bonn.

The invited public circulates on bridges that run within the same high-vaulted corridors used by the politicians. The symbolism of this device and the experience it offers – which inevitably informs and adds resonance to any potent symbol – seems again ambiguous: is it a privilege (or a democratic right) to promenade in the same spaces as the politicians, or is the public again simply placed at a tan-talising remove?

Clearly visible from this vantage point are the carefully preserved vestiges of war damage: defaced ornament, the scorch marks of flame-throwers, and Russian soldiers' graffiti. Today, the conservation of all traces of the past has become an almost reflex reaction, although in this context, the decision to preserve the past is probably more easily made by a foreign architect. But again this conservation is a gesture that could be seen as fraught with ambiguities. At one level it can be seen as a mark of maturity, and an unflinching commitment never to forget even the worst of the past. At another level, however, it might be interpreted as verging on collective self-abasement; this applies particularly to the preservation of graffiti, which is the equivalent of tribal or animal territorial markings. To erase the past with a seamless restitution of historical fabric and detail is one thing; not to clean up what are merely territorial markings might be seen as another.

Peter Buchanan

The one part of the building to which the public has free access is the roof, including the interior of the dome (10, 14), the pronounced central axis of which stands against the horizontal sweep of the panoramic view. Traditionally in architecture the roof – as with the original Reichstag – was the realm of gods and heroes, whose images would have adorned the parapets and pinnacles. This was an association that Le Corbusier exploited most explicitly at the Villa Savoye, where the rich disported themselves in Olympian detachment from the world around. On the roof of the Reichstag, against the sky and with Berlin spread out all around, members of the public may feel exalted too as they ascend the ramps within the dome to arrive at a spectacular viewing platform. And yet, again, they may also feel excluded, particularly from the politicians whose activities are visible through the glass ceiling of the chamber below.

The dome fulfils multiple functional purposes. Yet its forms are so striking that they invite speculation as to what they might symbolise, and clear meanings are elusive. Commanding particular attention is the faceted, mirrored reflector. This is reminiscent of that of a lighthouse, although it reflects light down and in rather than out, except when it functions as a beacon after dark, announcing that the Bundestag is in session. Both this – and even more so the computer-controlled mobile sunshade – would have appealed immensely to Le Corbusier, both symbolically and technologically. Not only was he obsessed with cosmic and solar cycles and their symbolic potential, but he was constantly frustrated in his early years because the technology was not yet available to realise many of his pioneering ideas for environmental control systems.

Inside the dome, at the head of the reflector, a wooden bench surrounds the vent through which stale air from the chamber is exhausted. People sitting on this bench look away from each other, making dialogue – the stuff of political process – difficult, while the implied consequence of debate below is that it produces so much hot air, fit only to be whisked into oblivion by upward currents accelerated by the Venturi effect. Such interpretations might be preposterous. But they bring home the impossibility of avoiding the symbolic, particularly with a building like the Reichstag. No matter what functional intention determined its forms, people will inevitably seek and attach meanings to them, and so the architect must anticipate and shape these too.

Yet it is probably the distant view of the new dome atop the Reichstag, an image that will soon symbolise Germany as much as the Capitol dome symbolises the United States or Big Ben symbolises Britain, that will provoke most speculative interpretation. Though it sits comfortably on the old building, it clearly belongs to a very different architectural language and epoch. In contrast to the original dome which, though also glass and steel, seemed to weigh heavily on the Reichstag, the new dome not only looks light but almost seems to be rising as if emerging from the building. Could its egg-like form be seen to symbolise the rebirth of a unified Germany – the eagle has laid?

The dome may also be seen, in a way that reinforces this interpretation, as a belated but apt realisation of the proto-modern vision of a *Glasarchitektur* put forward by the poet Paul Scheerbart and architect Bruno Taut. Scheerbart's utopian novel of that title, published in 1914, claimed that: 'In order to raise our culture to a higher level, we are forced, whether we like it or not, to change our architecture. And this will only be possible if we free the rooms in which we live of their enclosed character. This, however, we can only do by introducing a glass architecture which admits the light of the sun, of the moon and of the stars.' Such a vision was originally hatched in Berlin. But it was realised only in Taut's Glass Pavilion, built for the Deutsche Werkbund Exhibition in Cologne in 1914. This too was crowned by a faceted glass dome around the base of which were emblazoned such aphorisms by Scheerbart as: 'Glass brings us the new era, brick culture only does us harm.'

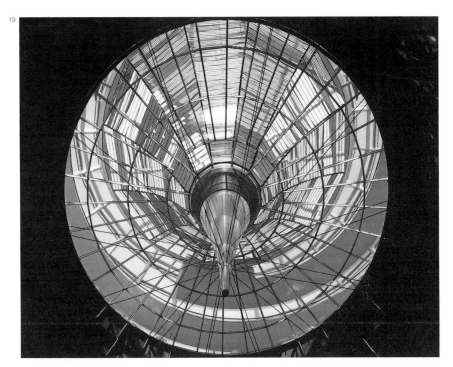

Such associations might suggest that Foster's light and transparent crystal lantern is more essentially German than the heavy Beaux Arts bombast of the original dome, which some parliamentarians argued should be reinstated. This lineage further suggests a reading – even more resonant – of the lantern as a crystalline *Stadtkrone* (17), or city crown, without which, Taut argued, no city could fully achieve its identity. This modern secular and spiritual equivalent of the Gothic cathedral (16) – which Scheerbart and Taut, like Gropius at the time he founded the Bauhaus, saw as symbolising the deepest collective aspirations of the German *Volk* – was dreamt of by its proponents as a new civic and communitarian element that would raise German culture to a new and more emancipatory level.

Even if not consciously intended, are not such resonances with local culture and myth rather similar to those that raise the assembly buildings by Le Corbusier and Kahn into masterworks? And could any symbolic interpretation be a more appropriate encapsulation of the intentions and hopes behind the rebuilt Reichstag?

'The game has changed, and Norman Foster has consistently been able to adapt his architecture to a shifting set of conditions without loss of meaning and humanity.'

Joseph Giovannini

Norman Foster is celebrated for designing buildings detailed with the finesse of a trapeze – daring and even majestic high-wire apparatuses of steel parts tensioned between articulated joints. Whether in projects built for small English towns or for outposts of the global economy, the technological imagery is so consistent that his approach amounts to both an architectural signature and a design paradigm.

Ironically, the poetics of structure in a Foster building – the forces, their convergence, their expression – are based on the prosaics of componentry. From the firm's first years in the late 1960s, Foster Associates produced award-winning buildings put together systematically from off-the-shelf parts: the stock cables, turnbuckles, joists and I-beams were assembled into structures at prices competitive with contractor buildings. The beauty of Foster's structures was cool, and even tough in the way athletes exhibit grace under pressure. The designs are gymnastics frozen in steel – strong, taut, lean.

But people working today in Foster's Commerzbank in Frankfurt appreciate the 53-storey building for other reasons. Finished in 1997, the tallest office tower in Europe may project technological prowess, but occupants know the building better for its neighbourly intimacies. The tower allows daily acts of freedom that are unusual for people confined to the closed environmental canisters that pass today for skyscrapers. Employees can meet for sandwiches and coffee in terraced gardens adjacent to their offices, enhanced by long vistas in nearly all directions. More remarkably, they can simply reach over and open a window to let in fresh air that will cross the floor and rise up through the flue-like atrium, to waft out of windows lining other gardens spiralling up the tower. Natural cross-ventilation may be a commonplace assumption in a house, but in high-rise architecture, where it has invariably been engineered out, the ordinary window is a tender mercy.

Breezes, an espresso and some chatter represent the tip of a different kind of architectural iceberg – gentle, humanistic signs that Foster has predicated the Frankfurt tower on premises belied by the building's urbane technological detachment. Lobby, skin and a logo crown are among the few sections of a high-rise left for the architect to design after the cost engineers and real estate consultants run their figures. As a building type, the office high-rise is the most formulaic of all, a tightly wrapped package with an elevator core centred in a stack of pancake floors, sealed off from the environment by a curtain wall. But at the Commerzbank,

Foster rearranged the usual anatomy of a skyscraper. He moved the elevator core with its bathrooms and stairwells from the centre, leaving it vacant for the 53 storeys, and then triangulated the three sides of the tower around the atrium while carving four-storey gardens out of each side (1).

The terraces, each a small, vertically local park serving its district of offices, fosters a democratic sense of village-like community within the larger geography of the building. By redistributing the central core to the corners of the triangular plan, Foster broke up the normally monolithic mass of the point tower (2) so that each facade varies from the others in both height and volume.

Many successful architects accept the conceptual envelope of a given building type, perhaps pushing it in certain places, but Foster has dared rethink the whole package, including what he calls 'the social dimension'.

The Manchester-born architect first radicalised the morphology of the high-rise with the completion of the Hongkong and Shanghai Banking Corporation building in 1986 (3). At a time when many architects were figuring out how to slip Classicised suits over the steel cage, Foster relegated the usual core of elevators to the corners of a four-poster scheme, liberating the centre for a partial-height atrium. The building became a more porous structure with open plateaux on each floor that allowed easy expansion and contraction within column-free spaces. Foster designed the tower as a stack of bridge trusses supported at the ends by steel masts, and he kept the perimeter walls back from a revealed edge. He lifted the banking hall off the ground with a glass underbelly that sheltered a public plaza whose angled escalators dramatise the entry.

Though simple in its systematicity, the 47-storey cross-section is rich and varied, with double-height storeys regularly interspersed among single-height spaces. By building the structure from an assembly of parts that are not wrapped within a continuous skin, Foster opened what is usually a closed form, creating an armature of change – open, free-span decks filled with light and supplied with conduits for squadrons of mobile computers. He mixed notions of the point tower and office block with principles of the megastructure developed during the 1960s and '70s, in which fixed structure was conceived as a support system for changing configurations. Although the final use of the building remained only offices, Foster originally planned the tower as a small vertical city with restaurants, pool, gym and outdoor

Joseph Giovannini

gardens. As built, an executive restaurant at the top overlooks a helipad, and the glass-roofed plaza has proved popular for demonstrations as well as picnics.

Foster is an architect of flexibility, and his instinct to design for the inevitability of change is rooted both in the unself-conscious factory sheds of England's Industrial Revolution and in the modest steel Case Study Houses of Los Angeles by Pierre Koenig, Raphael Soriano, Craig Ellwood, and Charles and Ray Eames.

While a student at Yale's architecture school in the early 1960s, Foster found the direction he would pursue for most of his career in an industrialised, off-the-peg approach conceived to raise construction standards and minimise costs. In the 1960s such assumptions were common, but instead of following the idealism of Mies van der Rohe's Classicised steel structures, Foster pursued prefabrication. Rather than Mies' godly joints, he preferred California details – that is, more casual connections often determined in the field without any attempt at abstract purity. The Los Angeles houses did not have the closure of Mies' Classical structures but were more open-ended and even *ad hoc*. Mies had cut such a wide swathe that an architect of Foster's generation had more creative room in adjacent territory, and Foster found his path in an architecture built up from parts rather than deduced from any sense of a perfectible whole. Instead of the Miesian temple, Foster adopted the Eamesian Tinker Toy model, which allowed a much looser, more spontaneous approach that also meant plans could be easily changed.

Though Foster would practise the approach with what engineers would call elegance, he did not think of himself as an artist (or even as an engineer). Like the Californians and the anonymous designers of England's industrial sheds, Foster was not shaping one-off forms but inventing and deploying systems. For him, the terrain of creativity was in the selection of the parts and their assembly. Foster's ability to design huge buildings – Chek Lap Kok in Hong Kong (4) is the world's largest airport – rests in part on the infinite extendability of modules. Foster designs fields of integrated parts rather than objects in a field. He does not struggle to stretch figural form beyond the limits of growth. In Robert Venturi's terms, he does not design a duck but creates a shed that he leaves undecorated. The integrity is in the parts and how he balances and sums them.

In architecture as in jurisprudence, precedent tends to become unwritten law, and Foster has often innovated by breaking with precedent. If, by displacing the

424

5

elevator core, he recast the traditional office tower, he also reinvented the traditional airport by reconceiving the usual morphology of its roof. At London's third
airport, Stansted, he removed the air handling equipment and ducts that usually
cram the ceiling, placing them within a service floor, and in so doing, he liberated
the roof of cumbersome weight and volume. Foster devised a four-masted structural pod, with integrated lighting, air ducts and roof struts, which serves as the
basic module for a building conceived as a capacious tent that seems tethered
down rather than supported. Like the architects of the Gothic cathedral, Foster
essentially created a modular bay based on a columnar structure, and repeated
the bay as demanded by the programme. Triangular windows within the delicate
roof structure allow sunlight to spill onto the floor. And Foster uplit the ceiling to
emphasise the floating effect.

Whether in airports, office buildings or museums, Foster often dissociates
the floor-plates from the roof enclosure, creating hangars of open space very
much in the tradition of the industrial shed. At the recently completed Hong Kong
International Airport, spaces are vaulted with a gull-wing ceiling supported on
arched trusses. Without being literal, the lightness of the structure suggests
notions of flight. The graceful roof of the American Air Museum in Duxford is based
on a rotated curve that spans the voluminous space without interior supports.

In section, the roofs often curve into walls, forming light shells covering highly
negotiable interiors. A building like the Daewoo Research and Development
Headquarters in Seoul (5, 6) combines an overarching umbrella shape with Foster's
interest in carving public spaces within the stack of floors. In the serene galleries
of his addition to the Joslyn Art Museum in Omaha, Nebraska, another gull-winged
ceiling springs from a central wall to feather daylight delivered by F-shaped fins
adjacent to linear skylights: the lilting curves add movement to the straightforward
galleries. In many of his open structures, the ceilings reflect and carry the light.

While favouring roofs with a diagrammatic simplicity, Foster is an architect of
complex sections. Just as he does not expose structure for the sake of shape, he
is not a formalist about space: his variations in the section are functional. At the
Commerzbank, the four-storey sky courts break down the social scale of the tall
building as they create micro-environments. The architect reinforces a sense of
community as he advances ecological goals.

An empirical rather than conceptual architect, Foster is uneasy about creating form and formal space without a practical purpose and when the German government required a new dome of symbolic grandeur for the top of the Reichstag, Foster found his design logic in ecological and social pragmatics. He created a mirrored cone within a glass ovoid, to reflect natural light down to the assembly space; the cone also channels air within the chamber's system of natural ventilation. Helical promenades lead the public to a roof terrace, allowing a bird's-eye view into the deliberations below. The criss-crossing paths up the dome are characteristic of the way Foster uses systems of escalators and open stairways inside his buildings to create a democratic sense of community and general liveliness. Stairways are not tightly encapsulated but take part in a process of socialisation already encouraged by sectional designs.

Foster's Carré d'Art in Nîmes (7), a cultural centre next to the ancient Roman temple, the Maison Carrée, perhaps best demonstrates his ability to orchestrate the space, programme and circulation of a building to create a three-dimensional social matrix. On a busy day, the building teems with people wending their way bottom to top between galleries and cafes. The Classical European city is, of course, rich in public spaces, but mostly at street level. Foster draws that civic life into his buildings, vertically creating a social concatenation of libraries, performance spaces and galleries, up to the roof terrace.

At a small scale, the Carré d'Art exemplifies the civic motivations that Foster brought to a series of super-tall structures where he employed the concept of creating an internal urbanism in towers intended for tens of thousands of people. First in 600-metre and 800-metre-tall buildings designed for Tokyo (the larger with an anticipated daytime population of 52,000), then in an even bigger tower in Shanghai, and finally in a more 'modest' 92-storey tower proposed in London (8, 9), Foster developed a series of skyscrapers in which spaces opened sectionally to create interior townscapes.

Buildings at this scale have the critical mass of a city, and just as the city comes to an intense focus at intersections, Foster proposed interior streets and plazas with shops, churches, markets, cafes and theatres at transfer floors, where passengers switch elevators. Nolli, the eighteenth-century Italian cartographer, could well have mapped the sections of these behemoths as he did the piazzas,

courtyards and streets of Rome – open spaces of public activity surrounded by occupied solids. Rather than being exhibitionistic about the technology that makes the super-tall building possible, Foster is searching for ways to humanise the verticality made possible by today's confluences of capital and engineering.

Scale is what distinguishes Foster's current work from that of his California role models, whose work largely remained domestic. From his first projects in the 1960s, Foster had been ramping up in scale, and though he still handles small, prestigious institutional projects, it is the large and very large buildings that distinguish his portfolio. The Hongkong and Shanghai Banking Corporation Headquarters was a signal moment in architectural history because of its originality; within his opus, it marks the start of a globalised practice within an irreversibly globalised economy. (Foster and Partners now operates 24 hours a day, seven days a week, to serve what has become a worldwide clientele.)

His design logic has survived the jump in scale, but quantity has changed his design process. The sheer dimensions and conceptual scope of the Hongkong and Shanghai Bank, for example, meant that it was more expedient, and less expensive, to design the components than to try to find them on a shelf somewhere. In Hong Kong, which is not a manufacturing centre, the constituent 'off-the-rack' parts were shipped to the city, sometimes by air, for assembly, exemplifying the far-flung economy that the Bank itself services.

Still, the technological rhetoric of these very large architectural assemblies is not an end in itself. Foster's contribution is the invention of buildings that are organically whole, buildings rethought from the basic infrastructure down to the bolt. With an appropriate technology and new typologies, Foster integrates not only building systems but also a range of issues that make the buildings complete in many ways – they are green, flexible, socially considerate and buoyant with natural light and fresh air.

What is unique about Foster's practice is the search for the qualities in the astounding quantities that new financial equations have made possible. The game has changed, and Norman Foster has consistently been able to adapt his architecture to a shifting set of conditions without loss of meaning and humanity.

'The public has thus taken full possession of what was once the hidden heart of the building, as if asserting its rights to what now feels like "the people's museum" far more than it ever did before.'

Peter Buchanan

The reclamation of the British Museum's Great Court is far from a self-contained project. Along with its impact on adjacent spaces and those on the floor below, it has resulted in the total transformation of the experience of the Museum. Indeed it has transformed the Museum's essential nature; and it will do much the same for a large area of London around it. These changes correspond aptly with larger moves (produced by new technologies and shifts in social aspirations) sweeping through our culture and affecting every aspect of our lives, institutions and cities.

Built for the edification of all, the British Museum, virtually from the start, harboured at its core a legendary yet secret space accessible only to initiates: the ticketed readers of the British Library. Buried amidst surrounding stack rooms, this space was the famous Round Reading Room. The stack rooms have now been swept away and the domed drum of the Reading Room opened up to public access as the centrepiece of a glass-roofed piazza, the Great Court (1). This court is not only open to all Museum-goers, it is at the heart of a new public route through the building. Moreover, the route and the court, along with its shops, restaurant and the lecture theatre below, are open late, outside Museum hours. So too is the Reading Room, with its public reference library and electronic access to the whole of the Museum's collections. The public has thus taken full possession of what was once the hidden heart of the building, as if asserting its rights to what now feels like 'the people's museum' far more than it ever did before.

Yet both the transformation of the Museum and the feeling (and actuality) of public accessibility go much further. The old British Museum was labyrinthine and disorienting. To reach most destinations it was necessary not only to press through throngs of visitors, but also to thread through strings of galleries, up and down stairs, as one wove a complex route through the building. Furthermore, there was an implied cultural hierarchy: entering and moving through the building in the clockwise direction that feels natural to most of us (hence its replication in supermarket layouts) led visitors through the antecedents to Western civilisation; Oriental and Pre-Columbian cultures were banished to the back of the building, and the ethnographic collection (from pre-civilised cultures) housed elsewhere entirely. Now orientation is crystal clear, as the multi-level Great Court gives direct access to all parts of the Museum; all the collections are immediately to hand and – because accessed as if on spokes radiating from a single hub – each is given equal status.

(If anything, the returned ethnographic collection, in straddling the central axis, is now privileged above others.) Such profound changes bring the Museum closer towards our post-imperial, multicultural age and the anti-elitist spirit of the times.

These changes also reflect recurrent themes in Foster's architecture, which can be detected almost from the beginning of his career. First is an egalitarian drive to dissolve boundaries so that everybody is visually aware of, and shares in, a building's prime facilities. Second is that these facilities often share a single space, or adjacent visually linked spaces, promoting contact between the people using them. In seminal early Foster buildings, such as Team 4's Reliance Controls factory, or Foster Associates' Amenity Centre for Fred Olsen in the London Docks, barriers between white-collar and blue-collar workers, workers and visitors, were eroded. These ideas are explored further in another key early work, the Sainsbury Centre at the University of East Anglia, Foster's first cultural building. Here, the permanent collection, visiting exhibitions, the Art History Department, and a cafeteria all share the same hangar-like space, encouraging interaction between students and teaching staff, visitors from other faculties, and those from outside the University.

With the Great Court, the elaboration of such themes appears to have been latent and inevitable. Using the Great Court as a circulation hub, with public facilities below a glazed roof, might seem an obvious solution. But making the court part of a public route through the Museum, open beyond Museum hours, is somewhat less obvious and must count among Foster's personal initiatives (3). Hence it is instructive that such ideas can already be seen to be shaping Foster's architecture as long ago as 1974, when the Sainsbury Centre – which is also something of a covered piazza or mixed-use urban microcosm – was on the drawing boards.

This leads us to a recurrent theme in Foster's *oeuvre*, which might be dubbed the 'urban room'. Typically this is a large, naturally lit space, which is central to the functioning and experience of a building, and is itself so distinctive in character as to be central to a design's very identity. Most essentially, the urban room is an inward extension of the public realm into a corporate, cultural or institutional building where the public can take possession of that building and/or meet with its more regular users, be they executives, employees or performers. Because the urban room belongs to an institution or corporation, it is not strictly speaking a public space; but crucially it functions and feels like part of the public domain. It

2

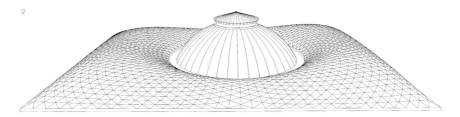

is an architectural type appropriate to today's fragmented cities and society, both compensating for the loss of the conventional public realm and sometimes helping to regenerate this public realm by forging vital new links within it. The Great Court exemplifies most of the characteristics of the urban room, although few members of British Museum staff, such as curators, are likely to be encountered by the public outside the education centre and lecture theatres.

A similarly clear example of an urban room is the foyer of the Gateshead Music Centre. This too serves as a route through the building and includes shops and restaurants while also providing immediate access to all parts of the building. In this case the urban room has been devised to promote interaction between musicians, students from the music school and the public, who have access to the foyer during most of the day. If the Great Court is an intense hub on a new link tying together parts of London, then here the backdrop of the Tyne – conspicuous through the foyer's glass facade – will visually cement a connection between the Music Centre and the city centre on the opposite bank.

In some cases the urban room is made up of contiguous spaces. Although the public might only be admitted to some of them, the crucial sense of taking visual possession remains. For instance, at the Commerzbank in Frankfurt, the public can circulate freely only on the ground floor, through the glass-roofed 'plaza' with its restaurants and cafes, and the lobby of the office tower. But from this lobby the public may look up through the tower's open central shaft and the 'sky gardens' that spiral up around it to create informal meeting places for bank employees. Here the urban room comprises the open shaft and the sky gardens, as well as the lobby and plaza where bank staff might meet employees from the adjacent Commerzbank building as well as those simply passing through.

Another such composite urban room, and an especially significant precedent to the Great Court, is the renovation of Germany's Parliament building, the Reichstag. It too is a huge historical stone building housing a major national institution into which a new glass-roofed, light-filled core has been inserted. However, at the Reichstag it is not artefacts but the politicians who are put on show. Seated in the assembly chamber MPs are visible from the main entrance, which is shared by public and politicians, and from inside the glass dome, where the public circulate above the political representatives who are accountable to them. Here the

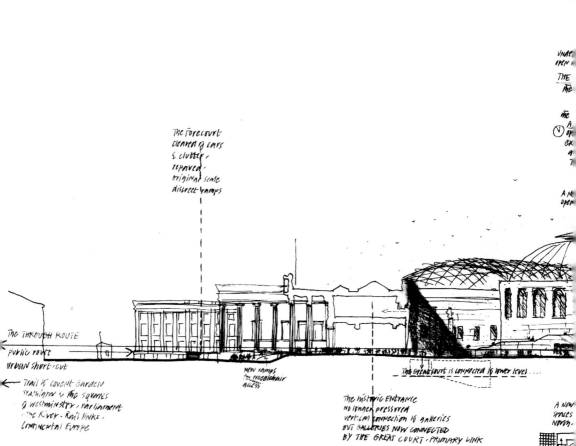

The Forecourt
cleared of cars
& clutter -
repaved -
original scale
discreet ramps

THE THROUGH ROUTE

public route
urban short-cut

← Trail to Covent Garden
Trafalgar & the squares
& Westminster - Parliament
- the River - Rail links -
Continental Europe

New ramps
for wheelchair
access

The historic entrance
no longer preserved
vertical connection to galleries
but galleries now connected
by the Great Court - primary link

The Great Court is connected to lower levels ....

UNDE
OPEN

THE

THE

A
OP
EX
A
T

A NE
open

A NEW
SPACES
NORTH.

THE GRE

CONCEPT · BRITISH MUSEUM · STUDY FOR THREE DIMENSIONAL MODEL

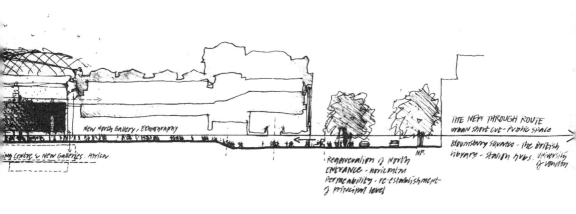

New North Gallery, Ethnography

ng Centre & New Galleries, African

Regeneration of North
ENTRANCE - horizontal
Permeability - re-establishment
of principal level

NF.

THE NEW THROUGH ROUTE
urban short cut - Public space

Bloomsbury savanna - The British
library - Station hubs, University
of London

chamber and dome (extending perhaps to the roof) comprise the urban room. Although public and politicians rarely mix beyond the main entrance, their tantalising proximity emphasises the politicians' public accountability.

The geometry of some prominent new insertions in the Reichstag (in plan, the seating layout in the chamber and the glazed screen that encloses its rear; in elevation, the edges of the dome and light reflector) follows complex dynamic curves very different to anything found in the original building. This is part of an extensive dialectic between old and new. Something similar recurs in the Great Court. Here the ovoid around the original drum and the swinging curves of the chords of the roof structure introduce a dynamic dance of fluid lines in counterpoint to the static rectangles and circles of the old building. The stairs that define part of the ovoid embrace the drum and present it to those arriving from the main entrance, while the welcoming shape invites visitors to climb up to the restaurant terrace. From here one can best appreciate the beautiful whiplash curves of the roof (2), which, together with the aptness of scale of the structural elements and the triangles they define (4), give the roof a gracefulness last seen in Victorian cast-iron structures.

It is significant, however, that this seemingly effortless resolution of geometry was only possible with the help of computer-aided design programs. In fact, it might be argued that the transformation of the Great Court has brought the British Museum into the computer age. This is not simply because the computer was used to resolve structural or environmental issues, or even because it forms the very basis of COMPASS (the Reading Room's electronic version of the collection) and, no doubt soon, other displays. An apt analogue for the old British Museum would have been the book (or the cassette tape); to access something you had to proceed through several chapters or galleries (or wind the whole tape). Now, proceeding from the Great Court, visitors enjoy the same ease in locating any part of the Museum, or any single exhibit, offered to users of the CD-ROM.

The computer, and the electronically globalised world it has brought about, is also profoundly altering the city, certainly the way that it works, if less so the way it looks. A city like London remains a centre of trade, but most manufacturing has moved elsewhere. In its place as key economic sectors (supported by huge and underacknowledged substructures of largely menial labour) are knowledge (information, culture and creativity) and tourism, which in large part comes to partake of that knowledge. Furthermore, now that the computer makes it possible for much work to be done at home, an increasingly important reason to come to work in the city is to meet others. This is the new world for which the Great Court seems so eminently apt as a place of meeting, culture and information exchange, at a prime juncture in intellectual and touristic London.

Amongst the largest covered spaces in Europe, the Great Court has a semi-outdoor feel and a microclimate suited to the generically Mediterranean, informally hedonistic lifestyle sweeping the world, as catered for here most explicitly in the terrace restaurant. Besides being at the heart of the British Museum, these characteristics, together with its bookshop and the events in the lecture theatre, mean that it adds an intense new focus to the knowledge hub of London University and Bloomsbury's learned institutions, bookshops and publishing houses. Inevitably the life in the area, particularly in the evenings, is going to change substantially.

There are bound to be those who will acknowledge all the above and yet feel uneasy about the Great Court, particularly the very immediate access it provides to all parts of the collection and some of the Museum's grandest rooms. For some people such immediacy is trivialising: for them the whole processional route through the fusty, congested galleries was crucial to contextualising and readying themselves to confront the works or culture they wished to study. And the prior progression through smaller rooms lent impact to spaces such as the Egyptian Gallery, or the King's Library, which will be lost when such spaces can be accessed directly from the much larger and brighter Great Court.

It would be wrong to reject such criticism. Although it betrays those who voice it as belonging to the age of the book rather than the CD-ROM, there is probably truth in it and the associated feeling that the cultural realm is being stripped of its depth to assuage charges of elitism. Of course, those who prefer can still circulate through the Museum as they did before. However, vastly increased visitor numbers mean that this option is not open to everybody. The British Museum had to change (the only alternative would have been to introduce charges high enough to discourage visitors from one of the world's great repositories of knowledge and culture). The Museum is to be applauded for having accomplished this change with an architecture that is emphatically and elegantly future-oriented, yet also deeply respectful of the past.

4>

'Foster is as likely to single out a door handle as an example of hi approach to design as he is an airport or office tower.'

Kenneth Powell

For Norman Foster, the twentieth century ended with a flourish. At the millennium, his practice is not only the most prestigious in Britain – it is also one of the largest and most profitable. On the world scene, Foster is critically ranked alongside Renzo Piano and Frank Gehry, Richard Meier and Tadao Ando, Alvaro Siza and Rafael Moneo – as the recent award of the Pritzker Prize confirmed. In terms of the scale and sheer range of their practice, however, none of these figures can quite equal Foster. He is arguably the architect of the millennium, rivalling the late James Stirling, his sometime teacher and mentor, as the most influential British architect of the twentieth century and combining commercial success with critical acclaim to a degree which Lutyens would have thought inconceivable.

The phenomenal success of Foster and Partners is guaranteed to engender envy and sheer malice, particularly in Britain – where quantity and quality are seen as irreconcilable. Hence the gleeful jibes about French stone (at the time of a 'beef war') used at the British Museum, of all places; the media campaign to find fault with the Berlin Reichstag (perhaps the most difficult project Foster has ever tackled); and the prominence given to the Foster projects which allegedly reflect a slipping of standards and are the work of a 'B' team at his office. Such is the potency of the Foster legend, however, that the deficiencies of such schemes are often blamed on an inadequate input from the great man himself. Foster's personal charisma and sheer energy remain central to the office's success, something which even SOM in its greatest years, in the 1950s and '60s, never possessed.

Foster's reputation was first forged back in the 1960s, when he was a partner with Richard Rogers in Team 4. The two men remain good friends, but their partnership was an unlikely one: neither is content to share the starring role. For nearly twenty years, since the time of the Hongkong and Shanghai Bank project in fact, Norman Foster has depended on a small group of fellow directors to make his potentially unwieldy operation work. Most prominent amongst them is Spencer de Grey, whom Foster took back to London as his lieutenant when the other directors were all committed to a long stint in Hong Kong. De Grey, the son of a former President of the Royal Academy, is an adept negotiator, a flawless presenter of projects and a forceful team manager – Foster still depends greatly on his expertise and judgement. Equally vital to the practice, in their different ways, are the other members of the core group – David Nelson, Graham Phillips and Ken

Shuttleworth. 'Key individuals will still play a decisive role in the field of design,' Foster predicted some 30 years ago while extolling the merits of teamwork. De Grey, Nelson, Phillips and Shuttleworth are all 'key individuals', a role which a number of the younger directors of Foster and Partners are also increasingly assuming. The Foster magic is, to no small degree, about good management and a wise use of resources.

It is also, as much as ever, about Norman Foster's personal and passionate sense of conviction, even mission. He could never be a titular president or figure-head. He needs to be involved in the process of design. Given the scale of the practice today, however, his role in a project is often confined to that of initiator of ideas and critical reviewer. He is the individual who sees, on occasions, that a scheme is going wrong, has lost direction, who works late into the night with the team to get it right. Foster is determined still that everything that leaves the office bears a distinctive mark of quality and innovation – he sees open-mindedness and the refusal to produce stock solutions as Foster and Partners' greatest strength. He is genuinely wounded by charges that the office produces 'ordinary' work. Everything it does, he believes, should be extraordinary. In other words, he sets himself a colossal task. Now in his mid-sixties, he shows no signs of retreating from practice: the support he gets from an unusually happy marriage underpins his professional life.

Unlike his old friend (and fellow life peer) Richard Rogers, who has been drawn into New Labour politics and environmental campaigning, Foster has no wish to enter public life beyond the world of architecture and urbanism. His out-look is pragmatic, conservative even. The United States which so impressed him as a young man – a confident, capitalist country, with 'can do' as its prime motto – is still part of his philosophy of life. If Foster keeps his younger colleagues work-ing late into the night developing a project, he can remind them of when he was their age and the legendary Paul Rudolph – still very much a Foster hero – sched-uled design sessions at Yale for 3am!

Born into a poor family in Manchester, Foster is unapologetic about enjoying the material fruits of success, though his executive jet, he insists, is a resource for the office and vital to his personal schedule. Much of Foster's work on projects is done these days at his house in the South of France, with other team members

Kenneth Powell

periodically flown out to work with him. The Reichstag was one project to which Foster's personal input at all levels, from the political and strategic down to detailed design issues, was absolutely critical.

The Reichstag is one of the most striking expressions of Foster's internationalism. Even more than Richard Rogers' earlier success in the Centre Pompidou competition – achieved in partnership with Renzo Piano – Foster's victory in the competition for the Hongkong and Shanghai Bank in 1979 marked a break with the old imperial concerns of British architecture and the advent of a new globalism. Foster Associates (as the practice was then called) was transformed over the next decade from a leading-edge London atelier into a world business.

Even as the Hongkong Bank was rising, Foster Associates was working on competitions in Italy, France, Germany, the USA, Japan and Mexico – where the Televisa Headquarters project was to become an important source for many later projects. Televisa remained unbuilt, but many projects were brought to fruition: the Carré d'Art in Nîmes, 1984-93, for example, an expression of Foster's growing interest in urban design; the Barcelona Telecommunications Tower, 1988-92; the stations for Bilbao Metro, 1988-95 and continuing; a group of buildings in Duisburg, 1988-97; and the Commerzbank in Frankfurt, 1991-97, a job which was significant when it came to the contest for the Reichstag.

The year 1991 was an *annus mirabilis* for Foster. Knighted the previous year, he saw six important projects completed, including the widely applauded terminal at Stansted (begun on site in 1987), the Sackler Galleries at the Royal Academy, and the Crescent Wing at the Sainsbury Centre, Norwich (1, 2). By 1991, however, the British economy was deep in recession and foreign shores beckoned more invitingly than ever. During the following year, Foster secured two commissions which were to dominate the office for some years, the Reichstag and the new Chek Lap Kok Airport in Hong Kong (3).

In theory, the Chek Lap Kok scheme, developed by a consortium of which Foster and Partners was one element, was a design and build scheme, yet it bears the typical Foster imprint of quality and consistency. One of the few man-made structures that can be seen from space, the new airport terminal building (which opened in 1998) occupies a specially constructed island, 6 kilometres long, and is expected to handle up to 90 million passengers annually when the projected second phase is completed. The scheme builds on the lessons of the far smaller Stansted terminal, notably in creating a huge and immediately impressive public space through which all passengers, departing or arriving, must pass.

Modern travel is characterised by routine, the absence of any sense of adventure or drama – indeed, by a sense that the traveller is merely a commodity being processed. Foster has always fought to instil a new drama into travel. The Hong Kong terminal has a powerful sense of direction and movement as passengers are drawn through lofty, barrel-vaulted spaces from the great atrium into the wings of the building. Using a combination of concrete and steel, Foster gives the interiors a dynamic lightness, which is both symbolic and highly practical.

Foster's 'continuing process of discovery, inspiration, invention and innovation', cited by the jury of the 1999 Pritzker Prize, is genuine and is applied to a staggering range of projects, great and small. The Berlin Reichstag, 1992-99, drew on all of Foster's strengths. The choice of the old Reichstag building (badly damaged by the 1933 fire and wartime shelling, and rather perfunctorily rebuilt in the 1960s) as the new home of the German Federal Parliament posed immediate issues of how far such a monument of the 'old' Germany should or could be restored. Santiago Calatrava, among others, came up with the idea of a reinstated dome (though not a copy of the lost dome). The lack of such a feature appeared to be the only deficiency in Foster's competition scheme, which was otherwise the strongest contender.

Foster's incorporation of a dome (6) into the scheme appears, in retrospect, effortless, yet it involved much thought and self-questioning. Determined not to build a meaningless token of homage to the past, Foster developed the dome, in the spirit of his mentor Buckminster Fuller, as a source of natural light and ventilation. It became symbolic not of hierarchy and enclosure (like that of the Kaiserist Reichstag) but of democracy and openness, a tourist attraction, a place where you could go merely to enjoy the view, a people's place. It was a daring move and there were many critics, not only on the Right – the retention of the graffiti (5) left by victorious Russian soldiers in 1945 infuriated some conservatives. It is too early to assess the success of the building in use, yet Foster's dome has become a familiar and popular feature on the Berlin skyline, an important public monument in a city where new office towers dominate.

Kenneth Powell

Back in Britain, Foster spent the second half of the 1990s balancing commercial work against major public commissions including the Millennium Bridge (designed with sculptor Sir Anthony Caro and engineer Chris Wise of Ove Arup), the Greater London Authority building, the British Museum Great Court, and the World Squares initiative. He also turned his attention increasingly to provincial Britain, with projects as far-flung as Scotland, Gateshead and west Wales. Not that international jobs declined. The recent commission from the Museum of Fine Arts in Boston confirms Foster's standing in the field of arts and education, while the practice is a big player in the global commercial field, as its haul of current projects in Korea, China, Australia and in major European cities confirms. Ten years ago, Foster's office had a turnover of £800 million. A decade later, this had quadrupled and in 1998 it had a payroll of 500 – a total which has held steady.

One of Foster's perennial dilemmas is continuing to infuse innovation and experiment into the practice's work. It is Foster, for example, who, inspired by the example of Buckminster Fuller, has personally pushed the 'green' environmental agenda – 'it is not about fashion but about survival', he insists. The low energy Fréjus school, 1991-93, was an important landmark in this aspect of the office's work, with the use of a double-cavity roof to create a solar chimney effect, and generous sunshading used to architectural effect. It was Foster who committed a team to the development of a solar-powered vehicle and who has been an active supporter of the international solar power programme – which reflects his belief in the benign potential of technology, responsibly used. Foster has said of Buckminster Fuller (with whom he worked on various unbuilt projects between 1968 and 1983), that 'he made you believe that anything is possible'. The element of aspiration – a visionary element, even – has never been far removed from Foster's own work.

It is hard to imagine how Fuller would have reacted to a project like the Reichstag. Since Foster completed the Willis Faber & Dumas headquarters in Ipswich a quarter of a century ago – a highly original response to a historical urban quarter – architects have been increasingly drawn into the masterplanning of towns and cities and increasingly obliged to respond positively and sympathetically to history. For Foster, the Carré d'Art was undoubtedly a turning point in terms of working with the past – he was the only one of a group of eminent contenders

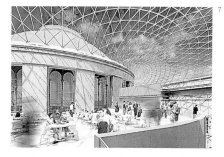

for the commission who really embraced the exquisite Maison Carrée and sought to give it a meaningful new setting. The Royal Academy Sackler Galleries scheme was another landmark, showing how restoration and radical new design could coexist and offering a vignette, in due course, of the potential of the Reichstag. Another massive project which traces its ancestry back to the Sackler Galleries is the British Museum Great Court (7), set to create the largest covered public space in Europe under an ethereal lightweight steel and glass roof (and one of a group of plum Lottery projects won by Foster and Partners). Foster envisages this space as open to all, late into the evening, part of the public domain – like the World Squares project, which he skilfully captured from Richard Rogers (whose campaigning, ironically, had fuelled the idea of taming traffic and creating pedestrian-friendly spaces at the heart of London). Two of Foster's best unbuilt projects, the Hammersmith Transport Interchange, 1977-79, and BBC Radio Centre, 1982-85, can be seen as pioneering attempts, before their time, to extend and civilise the public domain. Foster's many years of work on the site around King's Cross and St Pancras stations in London – where he first tackled major urban planning issues – also ended inconclusively.

Foster is as likely to single out a door handle as an example of his approach to design as he is an airport or office tower. He delights in small projects – domestic interiors, for example, or the installation of an exhibition on 'Modern Britain', at London's Design Museum (4), in which he personally (and unexpectedly) took a leading role. Some would claim that this sort of job is merely an escape from the routine of a large office. Foster and Partners is currently working on at least six sites in the City of London. It is building a tower (8) at London's Canary Wharf to equal the existing tower by Cesar Pelli. It would be unrealistic to claim that all these projects embody the degree of innovation seen, for instance, at Willis Faber. Foster's partner, Spencer de Grey, responds to charges that the office is doing too much and pursuing quantity over quality – 'our defence must be, if we need one, that we can do these jobs better than other architects – we never compromise on quality'.

Few of these schemes, in fact, fit easily into the traditional image of 'High-Tech' design. (The term is one which Foster has always disliked and rejected.) The Hongkong Bank brought Foster close in spirit to the contemporary work of

445

9

10

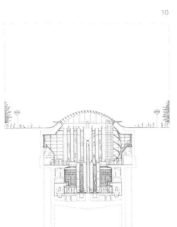

11

Richard Rogers – the project overlapped with Lloyd's of London – but its language of exposed structure and services did not persist in Foster's later work. 'Calm' is a word which Foster tends to use, always positively, of his work. A feeling of calm and order fills the new Jubilee Line Extension station at Canary Wharf (9-11), opened late in 1999, as large as an airport terminal and intended to handle 25,000 passengers per hour. The station has real majesty and its sense of serenity is enhanced by the skilful use of daylight and, after dark, by the quietly dramatic lighting strategy devised by Foster's regular collaborator, Claude Engle.

Not for Foster the more Baroque sense of colour and form seen in Will Alsop's station across the river at North Greenwich. When Foster was pitted against Alsop in the competition for the new home of the Greater London Authority, it was not only the financial equations that impressed. (Foster's building was to form part of a massive office quarter, which he was also masterplanning.) Alsop would have radically adapted an old building. Foster offered London a recognisable symbol of restored local government (12). The scheme went through various permutations, was compared to a glass testicle and a fencing mask, but is likely to become an instant landmark, as much a product of the Blairite era as the Dome.

In Bilbao to inspect his completed metro stations, Foster went to see the new Guggenheim Museum by Frank Gehry. He was immediately impressed and felt that the building was a masterpiece. Back in Britain, he has joined the lobby in favour of Daniel Libeskind's V & A 'Spiral' building. Although stemming from a tradition which is not his, these projects are much to Foster's taste. In his own work, he is striving increasingly for strong and memorable form – witness the Duxford Air Museum, the Daewoo Tower in Seoul and the designs for the Swiss Re tower (15) on the Baltic Exchange site in the City of London. The latter, Foster feels, could be as significant for the 2000s as was Willis Faber for the 1970s, incorporating as it does the low-energy advances of the late twentieth century and a progressive approach to workplace design. The radicalism of the Swiss Re scheme – which looks increasingly likely to be built – compensates for the loss of the earlier Millennium Tower scheme projected for this key site.

Swiss Re could be seen as Norman Foster's attempt to rekindle the excitement of Willis Faber, to capitalise too on a public mood which has been radicalised by Gehry, Libeskind, and the visions of Future Systems. Sixty-five this year, with

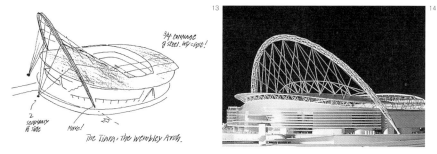

13

14

The Diana, the Wembley Arch.

the Royal Gold Medal (which he won as early as 1983), the AIA Gold Medal and the Order of Merit – an extraordinary honour, granted to few architects – under his belt, Lord Foster is entitled to air his visions. In recent years, he has spoken eloquently of his sources of inspiration: Fuller, of course, Louis Kahn, Paul Rudolph, Serge Chermayeff, Ray and Charles Eames, and Frank Lloyd Wright, whose works he trekked across the United States in all weathers to see more than 30 years ago in company with Richard Rogers. And even before he went to America and found his way of designing, there was the Town Hall in Manchester, superficially an ornate work of the Gothic Revival but also a masterpiece of rational planning and integrated servicing. Foster has no qualms about revisiting his sources and, indeed, his own earlier works, stressing the connections between even the earliest works – the little glazed 'cockpit' at Creek Vean, for example, or the Reliance Controls factory – and those currently at design stage.

Foster is, at heart, a rationalist in the same way that Richard Rogers is a romantic. It was Foster who came to admire the work of Mies van der Rohe. Rogers perceived its formal qualities, but not, in the end, its point. Mies impressed by his consistency. Superficially, at least, Foster has not been overly concerned with consistency. His work has been through a number of transformations and shows no signs of standing still as it responds to the context of place, culture and time. What consistency could there be between – and these are all Foster projects currently under construction – the National Botanic Garden of Wales, a prehistory museum in the Massif Central, a culture complex in Riyadh and a faculty block in Oxford? Foster's rationalism has faced up to the diversity of the world at the millennium. How can the new Wembley Stadium (13, 14) be a purely rational, functional structure? It must express the often irrational excitement of mass spectator sport just as Stansted expresses the excitement of flying. Foster's work is in itself a microcosm of the world of architecture today. At its very core is a belief that the natural world, and the accumulated culture of the ages of which architecture forms a part, demands a great deal of the architecture of the future. Bolstered by the self-confidence that any great architect must have, an optimist through and through but aware of the power of buildings to shape human life for better or worse, Foster is uniquely well equipped to play a central role in defining a continuing role for architects in the twenty-first century.

Kenneth Powell

452   Design for Living
458   Alvar Aalto
462   Social Ends, Technical Means
472   Links: Between Research and Practice
478   James Stirling, Royal Gold Medallist
482   Royal Gold Medal Address
504   Buckminster Fuller
510   Gaudí in Nîmes – the French Connection
516   The Hongkong Bank
524   A Reply to the Prince of Wales
528   Reyner Banham Loves Los Angeles
532   Handrails and Bicycles
538   Flight 347
544   With Wendy
554   F for Frustration
558   The Tate Gallery Lecture
572   The Library: Public Building or Memory Machine?
584   The Microchip and the Zen Garden
588   Building Sights: Boeing 747
592   Otl Aicher
596   Nîmes: Light and Culture
604   Century Tower
610   Architecture and Structure

616   Gordon Cullen
620   Taking Flight
628   Commerzbank: the Social Tower
634   The Human Touch
640   Bilbao Metro
646   Riverside Three
658   Reinventing the Airport
672   The Reichstag Eagle
684   On Flying
694   Lessons From Skiing
700   London: the World City?
706   The Future Office
710   Meeting the Sainsburys
714   The Architecture of the Future
718   In the Thonet Tradition
722   On Tables and Bicycles
728   Pritzker Prize Address
734   Craig Ellwood
738   The Reichstag Energy Story
744   Paul Rudolph
748   Studio Interview
768   Crop Circles
772   Design in a Digital Age

'… the design process
is probably one of our
cheapest commodities.'

Norman Foster

There is a tendency for a certain mystique to develop around such words as 'design', especially 'good design'. This is unfortunate because it tends to cloud the importance that design decisions have in our lives. Virtually everything that is man-made has been subject to a design process involving deliberate choices and decisions. In our Western civilisation that means nearly everything that we see, hear, touch and smell. As in all things this is something that we can do well, badly or indifferently with corresponding end results. To this extent the very quality of our day-to-day living is profoundly influenced by the quality of our design.

Our environment is a compound of many tangible objects and enclosures whose designers may be anonymous, often hidden in bureaucratic and business organisations, or sometimes independent consultants. Their main role, in essence, is problem-solving. It is this fundamental aspect of their work that is so often overlooked.

The 'style' in which the problem is solved is far less important and it is unfortunate that this aspect is often over-emphasised. This dilemma can be seen in two current attitudes. Firstly, there is a public apathy and indifference to the most fundamental aspects of design as they affect our very existence. Secondly, there is a tendency among designers to over-indulge in the more superficial aspects of their trade to the exclusion of key problems. The ensuing dialogue, with its overtones of 'good taste' and mystique, is largely irrelevant to a world going about its business.

As a random example of the above dilemma it is worth considering the 'tower block' of flats in the form that is currently designed and built in Britain. As a design for a family with young children it is chronically unsuitable. Despite all popular conceptions it is not the only way to achieve high densities; students of architecture were drawing up low-rise, high-density schemes six or seven years ago. Nevertheless, it is commonplace for architects and critics endlessly to debate at the level of imagery and detail those 'tower blocks' that are 'good' and those that are 'bad'. Obviously some are better than others at a superficial level; but fundamentally a tower block is a tower block, regardless of whether it is Neo-Georgian, mock-Tudor or plastic-faced.

It is amazing how long outdated design concepts can survive. At least our housing has attempted many new forms and experiments since the Industrial Revolution. By comparison, our design for industry has been virtually at a standstill since the 1800s. We still persist in building management 'boxes' and workers'

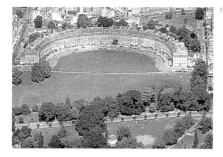 

'sheds' even though this may in fact conflict with the needs of processes, expansion, flexibility and management policies.

Obviously, some types of industries and processes are still rooted in a 'clean and dirty', 'we and they' social structure, but they are a growing exception. The traditional factory building and so-called industrial estate is currently one of our most unpleasant, uncomfortable, inefficient and expensive hangovers from the past.

These examples are only part of a totality. The family living in the tower block may be twenty miles from a major airport but deafened by one of its flight-paths; traffic jams may separate the worker's factory from home; other facilities such as shopping, schools and recreation may be similarly unrelated. It is an indictment of our educational system that we accept such patterns almost without question as the mythical price of progress and frequently continue to regard good design as 'arting up' or cosmetic treatment that can be applied 'after the act'.

At the risk of oversimplification, the designer's task could be summed up as analysing set problems in the widest sense and organising the best available resources to achieve the most high-performance solution in the most economical manner. It follows that the end result will have accommodated and integrated often conflicting and competing requirements. The very core of the problems and the way they are resolved will largely generate the style.

It should not be thought that so fundamental an approach is insensitive to the full range of our spiritual and material needs. Most of the historical places that today delight us were originally a calculated response to well-defined requirements.

For example, Bath was a speculative developers' 'New Town', based on a simple structural system of repetitive cross walls and repeated narrow window openings; an eloquent design totally embracing the social, topographical, technical and financial aspects of its situation (1). It is interesting to compare the scale of our present opportunities and the quality of our own resulting New Towns and speculative developments (2).

In an age of social and technological change the designer's tasks become increasingly complex. The overlaps and interactions between the hardware and software of our time (cars, planes, television, communications, computers) and our building fabric make it increasingly difficult to conceive architecture in terms of the traditional past. However, the age-old definition of architecture as

'Firmnesse, Commodity and Delighte' is still valid even if the 'firmness' is realised by plastic and alloy instead of masonry, and the 'delight' is extended by developments in electronic communications and climatic control.

The scope for new design solutions to meet both established and emerging needs is tremendous. It does not follow that we have to use untried techniques or ideas to innovate. Initiatives taken on a prototype can determine vast potential on the open market. At one end of the scale new planning ideas allied with traditional techniques can often prove as significant as the utilisation of new materials and techniques in isolation. The real scope lies in the fusion of both, whatever the scale of assignment, from product design to city and regional planning, whether one-off projects or vast collective enterprises.

Design innovations, which could change the appearance of buildings and make them more sensitive to our real needs, can spring from a number of sources. These could be broadly classed under new techniques of planning, engineering and management. They can be separated out for examination in more detail, but in reality the design process itself would integrate these and other key factors.

Firstly, new planning techniques. These are needed to satisfy today's rapidly changing social and technological patterns. Our spaces are becoming smaller but very highly mechanised. Like industrial plant it becomes uneconomic not to utilise them to the maximum effect. In planning terms this might mean spaces that have multi-purpose use. We also demand mobility and rapid change. Five-and-a-half million people in the United States are living in trailer homes, and this is increasing at a rate of 300,000 per year.

Obsolescence, whether based on fashion or real change, will have radical implications. Our buildings will have to be planned for flexibility so that they can grow and adapt. As land becomes more precious we must reconcile these needs with buildings that are sensitive to areas of scenic beauty. There is no reason why our present squandering of natural resources, both visual and material wealth, should continue. Intensive coastal development for housing and industry, for example, could be achieved without extending our present 'suburbia-on-sea'.

Similarly, by abandoning out-of-date planning forms, which are currently based on hangovers from the past, we could preserve the genuinely historical parts of our cities and revitalise them with a modern, twentieth-century equivalent.

Secondly, new engineering techniques. Examples of these are new materials, structures, total energy concepts and the feedback of ideas from other sources such as the electronic and aerospace industries. At one extreme we have the large-scale potential – vast areas can be enclosed within lightweight space-frame structures or inflatable plastic membranes (3, 4); full climatic control is feasible; the polar regions could be 'tropicalised' and desert areas cooled.

It is a sad reflection on our society that it takes the stimulus of warfare to promote instant hospitals. A full surgical hospital unit, probably our most complex building type, was dropped by helicopter on barren ground at Tay Ninh (Vietnam) quite recently. Complete with self-contained power-packs, its rubber-coated Dacron walls were inflated and the unit fully operational within a few hours.

Traditional site-based techniques are being replaced by factory-controlled components using new materials to achieve higher standards, speed and value-for-money. Some traditional materials, for example carpets, are being completely reinterpreted by current technology. Mechanical equipment has become a major and fast-increasing proportion of the total building cost. Nevertheless, it is still in a very crude form (it is difficult to imagine anything more crude than our lavatories and waste disposal systems) and we generally insert this equipment into an already obsolete shell, complete with traditional plumbing. At the present time we are still in limbo; half embracing a craft-based past and half aware of the new engineering potential.

Thirdly, new techniques of management. Increasingly complex organisations involved with problem-posing (clients, communities) and problem-solving (designers, contractors, manufacturers) can no longer rely on intuitive judgements. Skilled programming and briefing techniques are becoming increasingly important. Cost and time factors should be welcomed as further performance disciplines. Cost-in-use will become an increasingly critical factor. Our cost planning, often based on first cost in isolation, is quite misleading.

Although the framework for teamwork exists, all too often designers act in isolation, leaving other specialists to 'make it work' in a passive role. The scope for really integrated teams with wide-ranging skills is considerable. Current divisions between design and production will be reduced, involving the designer in new and exciting roles closely allied to industry. Paradoxically, as the organisations involved get larger, the scope for small groups to innovate will increase, either from within or from outside the organisations. Although greater rationalisation will produce sophisticated components and kits-of-parts, there is every reason to suppose that, as in the field of business and politics, key individuals will still play a decisive role in the field of design.

In many ways, the design process is probably one of our cheapest commodities. It allows us the scope to explore many alternatives and possibilities before making any commitment in reality. All too often, however, it is the subject of shortcuts; an unnecessary fringe benefit to which lip service is occasionally paid or a luxury for those prestige occasions. The results we suffer surround us and the loss at all levels is entirely our own.

5

6

'At Aalborg ... on a late autumn afternoon, northern latitude and all, the quality of light was such that only afterwards did I realise that the building was windowless in the traditional sense of the word.'

Norman Foster

At any one point in time a handful of living architects around the world seem to be producing exceptional work. For an architect, it is worth visiting their buildings, not only for the pure delight of the experience but also the certainty of learning something. I never met Aalto but did travel a long way to see his buildings, and were they worth it … and what lessons!

If I visit an exhibition of paintings I always buy a catalogue but somehow never get around to actually using it. I am afraid it's like that with buildings too, so I'll leave it to others to fill in the dates, influences and similar annotations. I'll confine myself to the three-dimensional experience. This starts with Baker House, MIT, some sixteen years ago, and ends with the Aalborg Museum in Jutland, which I saw last year, with several visits to Finland in between.

Thinking back to Baker House, I remember the snake-like geometry splaying views up and down the Charles River, a real back and front with the articulated staircase creeping along the rear wall. It seemed strangely foreign with its small-scale brickwork, but somehow did not impress me in the way that all his other buildings have done since.

Perhaps my first real insight was venturing through the hard streetscape of Helsinki into the Rautatalo (Steel Federation Offices), a tough skin of metal and glass next to the masonry facade of an Eliel Saarinen bank – no token gestures to historicism, just two buildings a generation apart, each uncompromised and an essay in good neighbours. Inside is that well-published toplit urban court with its banks of circular rooflights reminiscent of the Viipuri Library. But the space in reality is somehow quite different from the pictures. There is almost a Mediterranean feeling, with the trickle of water and casual texture of plants over the balconies, a relaxed mix of semi-public and private space. Whether sipping coffee or just wandering through to offices or the adjacent Marimekko shop, the grey, bitterly cold day outside seems very remote.

Moving from there to the Stockmann Bookshop was unintentionally an almost perfect sequence: the same ideas but altogether bigger and bustling with life. Rows of books have a language of their own; but in this setting of layered balconies under those magnificent rooflights I realised, possibly like others, just how much I had really underrated the importance of Aalto. Those rooflights must be the twentieth-century equivalent of chandeliers – sculptural, functional and decorative,

poking upwards into the sky on the outside and hanging down in space inside, a kind of vast glazed container, banks of lights within, but above all a glimpse of sky with the special quality of natural toplighting.

Somehow the writers of the Modern Movement have a particular hobby-horse about the absence of decoration, which always surprises me because it seems that the heroes of the movement indulged in it to their heart's content, and Aalto was certainly no exception. As a key word, decoration is a persistent and humanising thread in all the Aalto buildings that I have seen, whether justified, generated or exploited by the need to acoustically control a space, prevent wear and tear to the base of a column, or eliminate glare and direct light from tungsten bulbs.

Aalto's ability to signal the presence of a building in its setting with simple rugged forms is matched by an ability to break down into detailing with seemingly infinite loving care. So much so that you come away literally recalling the feel of the front-door handle or a leather-covered balustrade railing; not to mention those stools or furniture which still seem as fresh and timeless as ever.

In this respect Säynätsalo comes to mind: a complex of bold shapes rooted in the landscape with the recurring device of grassed terraces and almost Baroque steps (1) which lead to an entrance courtyard and eventually the Council Chamber. Again, no photograph can communicate the feeling of these spaces. The camera actually lies: although physically quite tiny, they have a generosity and presence. One is tempted to say stunning but somehow that does not convey how gentle it all feels. There, there really is a 'there'.

All his buildings have this sense of orientation, possibly because you can always relate back to a key space, which defines the heart of the scheme. At

Aalborg this would surely be the main gallery and its immediately related areas, all beautifully toplit with a rich variety of reflectors, which manipulate and control the light without blanking off the sky or a glimpse of sun (4). On a late autumn afternoon, northern latitude and all, the quality of light was such that only afterwards did I realise that the building was windowless in the traditional sense of the word. By sliding or locking in wall panels, it is possible to tune the gallery areas in a sequence of flowing space or individual compartments.

The use of moveable internal walls occurs in other projects, such as the church at Vuoksenniska. I have not actually seen this building, but it appears to take to dramatic extremes another theme which occurs in Aalto's work: the integration of rectilinear and free-form geometries, not only in plan form, but three-dimensionally. Here the inner skin and outer walls actually separate and pull apart (3).

The Finlandia Hall has all these ingredients, but for me the real importance lies in the masterplan of Helsinki, of which it is but one component. The concept of the green finger, with buildings lining the bank of Töölö Bay penetrating through to and revitalising the centre of the city, shows a vision and breadth far beyond the one-off building.

Aalto would have surfaced as a world leader in his field regardless of circumstance. Nonetheless, his achievements must reflect on a competition system, which clearly works, together with a variety of enlightened clients. In an age more characterised by apologies and mean minds, it is stimulating to view the record of an architect of such strength and integrity.

'The ends are always social
– generated by people rather
than the hardware of buildings.'

Norman Foster

When the Willis Faber & Dumas building was first completed, most magazines began and ended their coverage of the building with pictures of curved glass walls and high technology. Whilst one should not underestimate the importance of such technical means, for me they have never been ends in themselves. The ends are always social – generated by people rather than the hardware of buildings. However, the relationship between ends and means is a vital part of our approach. Together with my known association with Buckminster Fuller, any study of the practice's earlier work, from 1963 onwards (without which it would have been impossible to contemplate this design) should make clear our position on adopting what we believe to be appropriate technologies in achieving social goals.

In a fundamental sense the building is really about people and their place of work. Socially, of course, this is a moving target. Herman Kahn, American futurologist of the Hudson Institute, once made the point that those office buildings that failed to anticipate what he saw as inevitable social changes would simply become obsolete if they did not respond by raising standards and providing a high proportion of amenities. In his view, these were not philanthropic gestures, just the hard cutting edges of changing real estate values. My own experience bears this out.

It is perhaps worth a reminder of the concept – the *parti* – of the Willis Faber building. Essentially, two office floors – for around 1,300 people – are elevated and sandwiched between amenity and support areas above and below them. The ground level comprises a concourse, swimming pool (12), coffee bar, gymnasium, crèche (since changed), mechanical and electrical plant, computer suite and internal truck-loading docks. The roof level comprises a glass restaurant pavilion set in a landscaped garden (8, 11, 13). All the floors are connected and penetrated by a vertical movement space containing banks of escalators (4). This space is filled with palm trees and flooded with daylight from generously glazed rooflights; it forms the centre of gravity of the building and is important functionally, socially and symbolically. Giving it a precise name or label is difficult; the various titles of 'winter garden', 'internal court' or 'atrium' provide clues to its character but do not adequately convey the spirit of the place.

The proportion of amenity area to work area is high, especially if the nearly two acres of roof garden are included. This is due in large part to resource allocation. The emphasis on providing amenities in the workplace and raising standards

represented a virtual about-face from the office buildings of the time, whether prestige one-offs or reach-me-down spec developments. Most office buildings raise standards for the visitor 'front of house' – gobbling up disproportionate slices of funds in the process – and gradually dilute them as you move further 'backstage' towards the users. The reverse is true at Willis Faber. The entrance has exposed concrete structure (enlivened with emulsion paint), studded rubber flooring (the same as the boiler room and lavatories) and demountable metal partitions (like everywhere else). This compares in the two office floors with carpet (the same carpet, incidentally, that was laid in the 1970s) and custom-designed ceilings with glare-free light fittings. This is not a reaction against fine finishes; it is more a question of how you define priorities and reflect them in the allocation of fixed financial resources.

If the workplace is so vital that it determines the priority of finishes, then the spaces themselves are conceived in the same spirit. In a typical office building the working areas are 'out of sight and out of mind'; the only aids to orientation are the floor button you push in the lift, the number on the door. Better-designed versions might have sleeker skins but they are fundamentally the same animal underneath. The reverse is everywhere apparent at Willis Faber. Movement is open, literally in the sun, and social contact is natural and relaxed across the spectrum of the company. Orientation is immediate; you always know where you are. The barriers are few and seldom visual.

A management approach characterised by an open-door policy in Willis Faber's original building is here reflected by a virtual absence of doors. The only planned cellular office – for the Deputy Chairman – was lost *en route* in the design process; and by the same token the 'directors' dining room' became an exercise in furniture design to define a part of the main restaurant. Even that space has now become a 'visitors' dining room'. The kinds of spaces described here are in no manner fixed for the future. Indeed the technology that enables them to work at present also provides the flexibility for them to reflex into quite different patterns.

The plan form and cross-section are a response to balancing and reconciling a range of priorities that are frequently in conflict: namely how to achieve the sympathetic integration of the company and the community. Or, to put it another way, how to incorporate a large new building on the edge of a historical town. The key

factor was to adopt a very low, deep building which enables a commercially viable content to equate with a low profile. There are other significant benefits: for example, fewer, larger floors allow more efficient space utilisation, greater flexibility and far lower energy consumption.

At this point it is worth considering the kinds of outdoor space that typify a town like Ipswich. They must surely be its streets? It seemed to me that so many modern buildings have largely ignored random street patterns by imposing hard rectilinear geometries. That might be appropriate on a greenfield site or in low-density suburbia, but it is alien to dense, complex urban areas (excepting, of course, those cities that come with 90-degree gridiron plans). Apart from destroying the coherence of the street pattern, the leftover spaces produced by such developments tend to be hostile and unuseable. In Ipswich, by pushing the building to the limit of the site boundaries, the original street pattern was reinforced. This is the complete opposite of arbitrary shape making, whether rectilinear or free-form.

The remainder of our townscape proposals are as yet unrealised. Our early drawings show a gravelled urban space with trees, forming a forecourt to the Unitarian Chapel. In the tradition of pedestrian thoroughfares elsewhere in the town it was intended to link this forecourt through the existing passageway to St Nicholas Street to encourage additions to the adjacent shops and restaurants.

The building was the outcome of a team approach in which the key was to shift the traditional roles of those concerned with designing and fabrication. For example, many activities were streamed in parallel in the early stages of the project. This was essential on a crash programme: two years of feverish design and building activity with a minimum run-up period. The client's lawyers described the site as having 'every problem in the book', but we found new ones to swell its pages. During the complexities of demolitions and services diversions, as architects we were more involved in what might be better described as management consultancy than the exercise of any normal design-based skill. In any discussion of 'means' one should not forget the operational and management techniques that we virtually take for granted; management can never be divorced from the design process.

A briefing guide was specifically developed for the project to provide insight into the client's organisation and its working methods. In collaboration with Willis Faber a joint management committee was established to oversee the project; it

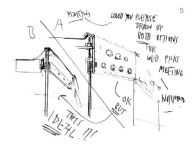

5

was chaired by the Company Secretary and involved the past company Chairman. This working group, with permanent architect representation, was able to co-opt other consultants as necessary. It could monitor progress and review options and had direct communication with the main Board at regular intervals.

This close collaboration began so early in the life of the project that it actually preceded the final definition and purchase of the site itself. We developed many preliminary design strategies in response to varying early site options – some involved closing roads, others spanning over them. It soon became apparent, however, that the real estate process was so volatile that it was impossible to reflex quickly enough with traditional on-off design responses. Allied with a detailed understanding of the brief and its major fixes, careful analysis of ground conditions beneath the building, and an insight into the process of site acquisition, provided the main clues.

We found that an overall column grid of 14 x 14 metres – which kept within an acceptable cost threshold – related well to office planning constraints and allowed us to straddle such fixes as a swimming pool and, if necessary, roads and truck docks. In a building that has no 'back' or 'front', the latter have to be located inside the building, at least if good street manners are to be respected. Furthermore, providing an edge 'necklace' of columns allowed us to tune the perimeter to follow closely the lines of existing street boundaries.

The detailed development of the structure was also influenced by the constraints of mechanical and electrical engineering systems. The consulting structural engineer devised an ingenious modular system based on a specially designed plastic mould. This eliminated downstand beams throughout, which kept the overall height of the building down while providing the maximum flexibility for duct runs and provided a structure that is handsome enough to stand in its own right. This was good for the budget (no need to paste over it) and good for the programme (fewer on-site trades). In its final form the structure was boiled down to remarkably few elements: columns and floor-slabs internally and a necklace of columns with a cantilevered slab at the perimeter.

In designing the structure we also had to anticipate the mechanics of building swiftly and economically on a tight urban site. Ultimately, the structure was the only site-based wet trade. Everything else was shop fabricated to maximise quality

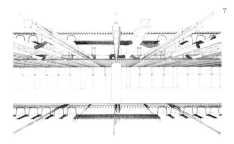

control and speed of erection. These were not the only reasons for using prefabricated elements, although they are fairly persuasive, especially when programme,
cost and attention to detail are considered. A belief and joy in using the materials of
the age, allied with an economy of means, were important additional factors.

This approach also involved a shift in roles because if the product we wanted
was not available 'off-the-peg' (and hardly anything was in the integrated sense of
the word) then we designed a new one and collaborated with the manufacturers to
produce it. This meant secondment to industry where appropriate and the frequent
use of full-scale tests and mock-ups. A brief summary of how some key elements
developed might give an insight into the relationship between design and the management techniques that made our creative goals technically feasible.

The suspended glass wall was a response to the notion that most people are
happier inside a building when they are able to see outside, provided that they do
not suffer some discomfort as a consequence. That concept could no doubt be
phrased in a more scientific manner but it would come down to the same sentiments. Unlike shallow-plan buildings – where a fully glazed perimeter can have a
drastic effect on energy loads – in a deep-plan building such as this the effect is
relatively insignificant. Furthermore, unlike shallow plans where a hole in the wall
will suffice, to ensure that everybody in a deep building (not just those closest to
the perimeter) enjoys visual contact with the outside world, the proportion of glass
has to be generous. This led us to consider several alternative glazing systems
that would combine such qualities of transparency with acoustic and solar control.

An awareness that glass is at its strongest in tension prompted the concept
of a glazed curtain suspended from the top edge of the building. Unfortunately we
were unable to convince anyone outside the office that it was technically feasible.
For this reason all the interior perspectives of that period show a steel mullion system designed for the project and test-bedded in a smaller installation in
Thamesmead. Eventually, however, enough calculations and technical details
emerged to convince specialist suppliers and subcontractors that the idea was
not only viable but also looked very attractive in cost terms (hardly surprising since
it reduced the major elements down to just glass and glue). At this point we found
that industry was so keen to get in on the act that Pilkington (the glazing subcontractor) happily traded design warranties in exchange for rights to our details.

The floor and ceiling systems followed similar development paths; in both cases the design process was driven by a desire to integrate what had hitherto been separate products in single-system solutions. The parabolic light fittings, for example, which are integrated within the ceiling, are designed to accommodate the air distribution and extract grilles for office areas and house sprinkler runs, as well as providing a separate emergency lighting system. Additionally, the power and cable runs on the office floors telegraph through the lighting grid above and below. Compare this with the more usual proliferation (and redundancy) of separate suspended elements, typically brought together on-site in the equivalent of a last-minute shotgun marriage.

Conscious that future flexibility would be thwarted by fixed cable trunking runs (then the norm) and aware that wet screeds take forever to install and cure, we searched for more viable alternatives. The result is a suspended floor system, with continuous lines of easily removable access panels, which was developed by a manufacturer specifically for this project. Our goals were high speed, low cost, optimum appearance and maximum flexibility, although not necessarily in that order (then, as now, it was extremely difficult to consider these factors in a precise hierarchy since they are so closely related).

Similarly, the design development and final definition of facilities and standards was inextricably linked with continuous financial appraisals – quite the opposite of a static brief and cost response. A wide variety of options were examined, always related back to a base yardstick of minimum shell cost. One analogy is the Ford Mustang which, given a basic chassis, could be produced in an infinite variation of models. Alternatives were evaluated with particular sensitivity to cost-in-use. The exterior of the building, for example, is virtually maintenance-free; the glass wall almost wipes its own face and apart from an occasional haircut, the turf roof looks after itself.

Considerable ingenuity was deployed to minimise the on-cost of potential fringe benefits and thereby encourage their introduction. For example, in capital terms a landscaped roof is more expensive than asphalt. However, we beefed it up a little and it provided such a good insulating quilt that we were able to eliminate expansion joints – with their attendant, costly, double rows of columns and piles – across the entire building. Allied to that are considerable long-term energy savings.

For financial justification the building had to be potentially sublettable. Three factors make such an option quite straightforward. Firstly, the internal court with its escalators is capable of functioning as a semi-public space used by all office tenants. Secondly, each floor has four cores enclosing escape stairs and utilities to allow up to four major subdivisions of space from a common access gallery formed by the escalator well. Smaller suites would be possible with shared rather than private toilets. Thirdly, the internal servicing systems allow total subdivision into cellular offices if required.

This design approach is perhaps best characterised as a process of integration, reconciling views and polarities which might otherwise be in conflict. For example: the company versus the community; public versus private; new versus old; time and cost versus quality and innovation; socially acceptable versus commercially viable. Another vital part of the approach is a conscious attempt to pul all those dry objective pieces of the jigsaw (research, statistics, cost plan, site analysis, structural options – the checklist is endless) together with some very subjective joy.

9

10

11

12

'The most relevant technologies now stem from the aerospace industries and it seems no coincidence that events such as the Farnborough Air Show, with its vast array of subcontractors and exhibits, provide more hard-edged clues and inspiration than this year's Sweets Catalogue.'

Norman Foster

Looking back in hindsight, it is clear that the practice's early work developed a consistent range of ideas and themes. However, it is in the nature of the approach that design decisions are almost always rooted in a multiplicity of factors. These could embrace some or all of the following, depending on the project: a positive response to the site context; an interest in the potential benefits of appropriate newer technologies; an awareness of change; a concern for the social implications of architecture; and a belief in movement, natural lighting, transparency and orientation as design ingredients.

In such an approach the building can be seen as an integration of systems rooted in social and technical research. Systems would range from the traditional structural, mechanical and electrical, through to the filigree of interior systems concerned with the flux and change of movement and activities.

The earliest projects were a mixture of traditional materials and industrial components. For example, Skybreak House (2) combines brick cross-walls and flat timber-roof construction with aluminium north-light factory glazing to admit sun into the heart of a flexible deep-plan space. Fine views to the north, and closely adjoining suburban neighbours gave rise to a stepped single-storey section, which was dug into the sloping site. Blinker walls on the boundaries provided privacy from neighbours, and internal cross-walls divided the space into zones offering varying degrees of internal privacy, from enclosed bedrooms to communal areas which could be opened up by means of large sliding panels. The flexibility inherent in the open-ended concept enabled the house to be enlarged later, within the original concept, by growing the bedroom zone independently of the rest.

The Creek Vean waterfront house of the same period exhibits a similar mix of traditional materials with industrial components – in this case blockwork and structural gaskets. The house sits on a south-facing slope, opening up to the sun with fine views out to sea, and closing up more defensively on the public roadside to the north. Entry is via an upper-level bridge, which connects with the toplit gallery/circulation space. The structure is open-ended and expressed both internally and externally. Except for the landscaped roof (shades of a later Willis Faber) such a description would fit exactly the Sainsbury Centre of some ten years later – although the departure points in materials, techniques and flexibility are of an opposite extreme.

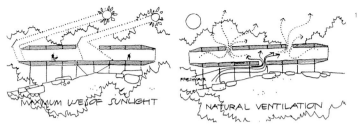

MAXIMUM USE OF SUNLIGHT   NATURAL VENTILATION

These and other one-off houses were seen as prototypes for low-rise, high-density alternatives to more traditional housing models. Although a number of schemes reached the drawing-board stage, this potential was never realised in built form. But while the planning principles held true, there was a growing disenchantment with so-called traditional materials, their anachronisms and the problems of quality control posed by the breakdown of craft traditions. To that extent it is interesting to compare the early schemes with their labour-intensive 'dug-in' sections and dependence on wet trades with later projects for Fred Olsen in Norway.

The Vestby 'offices in a forest' exploited views to the fjord, and pioneered the use of overhead mirrors to catch the low sun (1), just as Creek Vean House responded to the Fal Estuary, and in the same spirit as the factory glazing of Skybreak House. But the similarities end there. The Vestby scheme, rather than being dug-in, sits on raised undercarriages as part of an attempt to conserve the forest and protect it from the ravages of builders' and contractors' plant. Lightweight components, easily transportable through forest trails or moved by helicopter to more remote locations, could be bolted together quickly, with the minimum of fuss, by small teams. This approach embraced the energy concepts to drive the building, and its waste systems were designed to recycle to avoid polluting the fjord.

The turning point in moving from 'traditional' materials to factory-made, lightweight components was the Reliance Controls Factory (3). Whenever possible, elements were designed to do double or even triple duty – for example, the metal roof profile also acted as a lighting reflector for recessed fluorescent tubes as well as performing structurally as a stiff diaphragm. A pavilion form was considered more socially appropriate for a clean and rapid growth electronics industry than the usual workers' shed and management box with its implication of 'us and them', 'posh and scruffy', 'back and front'. Technically such a form also offered a degree of rationalisation, which was more responsive to optimising limited resources of time and money, as well as providing the potential for quick and easy change.

Much of this thinking was taken further in a research project for educational systems, prompted by the 1967 Newport School competition, which expanded a kit-of-parts approach to produce interior layouts that could respond to dynamic change within an infinite variety of plan forms. Essentially these projects were

3

highly integrated and lightweight serviced 'umbrellas' developed with a strong awareness of the SCSD California Schools of that time.

This research was later embodied in a project for IBM, which grouped under one roof a wide variety of functions that would have traditionally sprouted a collection of diverse buildings. Initially it was a head office, with computers, offices, amenities and a communications centre, but it has since been in a constant state of flux. Major internal changes over the years have been helped by the ability to pop in external doors in lieu of the gasketed glazing panels which otherwise complete the external cladding vocabulary.

The programme was so tight on this project (less than a year for design and build) that IBM had assumed that an 'off-the-peg' timber building would be the only answer. The budget had been set accordingly at around half the price of a traditional permanent building. Interestingly, IBM had about half of its total UK accommodation in such temporary structures (similar statistics to the Los Angeles school system), which tells us a great deal about the constant of change. Within such constraints the only solution was an integration of essentially dry systems, which could be likened to a Meccano set. Ironically this produced a permanent building as defined by the owners' and local authority's terms of reference.

The preoccupation with standards in industry and commerce was rooted as much in research into the work process as it was in an interest in social change, and a sensitivity to the proportion of time spent in the workplace. To that extent the

projects for Fred Olsen in Millwall Dock, London, were in our view more interesting socially than technically, notwithstanding their early use of low-brightness lighting systems, heat-and-light-reflective glass and gasketry. Demonstrating a progressive management style more typical of the Scandinavian parent company than the London Docks at the time, the planning cut across existing social divisions and created new working standards with integrated leisure facilities. This democratising process was only realisable by working closely with all the groups involved – unions, middle management in the UK, and senior management in Norway. The proof of the exercise was an ongoing pattern of virtually strike-free activity, in sharp contrast to the industrial strife of the London Docks that surrounded this development.

Probing to determine the users' requirements is an inseparable part of the design process, which helps us to question preconceptions and propose alternatives. For example, a research project for the Spastics Society was concerned with the special problems posed by severely mentally and physically handicapped children. Research into existing buildings highlighted the inadequacy of traditional toilets, given the extreme incontinence common to such children, and the physical and psychological difficulties posed to the staff involved in caring for them. In a prototype school in Hackney (4), pioneered by the Spastics Society with the Inner London Education Authority, the toilets were therefore completely reinterpreted as a glazed central area with low screens for the children's privacy but good views for staff into the adjacent teaching areas and the garden court beyond. By pulling all the ventilating air through this space there were no problems of smells or need for lobbies. (A larger scale version of the same principle of pressurising spaces is used in the Willis Faber building to incorporate the restaurant and pool into a continuous three-storey, two-acre volume.)

At a detailed level the problems of heating and lighting such buildings were quite challenging when it was realised that some children could burn themselves on radiators or suffer eye damage by staring up into bright light sources without being able to raise help. The successful resolution of these and other problems enabled better utilisation of the teachers' time, allowing them to devote their attention to the real priority – the children's therapy.

Perhaps the most minimal exercise in serviced space was the Air-Supported Office for Computer Technology (6). The structure was environmentally engineered

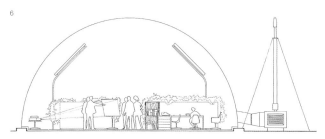

6

to enable 80 people to work for a year in conditions more comfortable than the standard factory shed to which it was attached. This was the first application of an ultra-thin membrane enclosure for sedentary activities. The erection time was under an hour, and the kit-of-parts approach enabled the space to be fitted out in less than a week. The structure was eventually removed to provide a car-park for a new multi-use permanent building which utilised gasketed aluminium and foam sandwich panels derived from the automotive and insulated container industries. This and the later Modern Art Glass project, with its wrap-around cladding, were linked to component developments for the Sainsbury Centre.

The links between research and practice are close and aided by continuous model studies at varying scales, from full-size mock-ups of rooms to testing programmes for prototype components. In 1968 Buckminster Fuller approached us to collaborate on his first UK project, the Samuel Beckett Theatre, which eventually took the form of what could best be described as a submarine under an Oxford quadrangle (5). This collaboration expanded into a wider partnership, which continued to pose radical alternatives to conventional built forms. For example, the Climatroffice was projected at the time of the Willis Faber scheme and demonstrated the potential for grouping a mix of existing buildings and new activities under an all-embracing structural skin to create a total microclimate.

At the time of writing, current work spans a range from large scale urban planning to experimental housing systems. The most relevant technologies now stem from the aerospace industries and it seems no coincidence that events such as the Farnborough Air Show, with its vast array of subcontractors and exhibits, provide more hard-edged clues and inspiration than this year's Sweets Catalogue. Our housing systems project, for instance, is now totally rooted in the alloys, glues and high-strength fixings of the aircraft industry.

'Humanistic considerations must remain the primary logic from which a design evolves.'

Norman Foster quoting James Stirling

President, Ladies and Gentlemen, we're here this evening to celebrate something that really happened a number of years back for many architects and students. Not only in the United Kingdom, but very significantly in Europe, the United States and as far afield as Japan. Namely, the recognition of James Stirling as an architect extraordinary.

By tradition the Royal Gold Medal is awarded well after such reputations have become firmly established, and in comparison with previous years, Jim is a comparatively youthful recipient at 54. The name Stirling has become an architectural byword, but it has also been one of this country's invisible architectural exports in recent years, if that's not too much of a contradiction.

The list of limited competitions won by Jim, from Peru to North America to Germany, is almost endless and in stark contrast with the leaner years here at home; they have produced many influential drawings, in the absence of hard-edged commissions. It is also significant that he is currently working for three American universities and two German institutions.

In recent years the profession in this country has found itself increasingly under attack for its standards, quality and values. It does seem strange that during such a period, an architect of Jim's calibre should be virtually dependent on recognition abroad. Their gain is our loss. On this basis alone, he is now long overdue to receive the kind of formalised recognition that the Royal Gold Medal represents.

Jim really brings together three forces: teacher, draughtsman and designer, all inextricably linked as James Stirling, the architect. Regardless of workload, he has been a visiting professor at Yale for over twenty years now, and it was as a graduate student at Yale that I first came into contact with him. I recall that he was the kind of tutor who refused to say how he would do it, but rather would force you back on your own resources by posing the awkward questions, and quite right too.

Much has been said about Jim's drawings; they seem to exist as abstracts in their own right and yet we know that they are design tools, a means to an end: highly preferable, in my view, to the current unhealthy obsession with architectural drawings as an intellectual substitute for buildings. In the words of Charles Jencks, his drawings show 'the space, the structure, the geometry, function and detail, together without distortion'. Or, as Reyner Banham notes, Stirling made the *all dimensions true* axonometric famous. The drawings are, of course, inseparable

from the buildings, even if they appear as proof that the building has been considered three dimensionally from such diverse viewpoints as a mole with all-seeing
eyes from below, or more likely, from 45 degrees in a helicopter hovering overhead.

It is tempting to try to group the buildings in categories, and even more
tempting to link them by quoting references from the architect or his critics. The
partnership with James Gowan up to 1963 produced distinguished early works.
Everyone has his favourite, and for me the Leicester University Engineering
Building, 1959-63 was a turning point (2, 3), although I enjoyed the earlier projects
with their Corbusian roots, such as the Ham Common flats, the Isle of Wight
house and the Team X Village project, each with overtones of a load-bearing brick
vernacular. But Leicester for me had a tension, an originality and a drama which
was born out of everyday ingredients of materials and function.

The architect sets the nature of circulation and structure to provide insights.
The appropriateness of hard, brittle, reflective surfaces to an outside climate created a new vocabulary for designers worldwide. It was a rediscovered vocabulary
of large-scale industrial glazing, Victorian brickwork and tiles. Likewise one finds
justification for the visible cut and thrust of forces: I remember a column which
seemed to penetrate a lecture hall in a totally arbitrary manner. This was described
by Jim at the time in the following terms:

'The weight of the towers above counterbalances the overhang of the lecture theatre underneath, or to say it another way, the extent of the cantilever of the lecture
theatre is dictated by the amount of weight over. If you removed the top floor, the
building would overturn. No doubt there is a certain architectural quality inherent
in the composition of stable masses; particularly when they're asymmetrical.'

It seems to me that there's a kind of recurring characteristic there – almost
deliberately creating a difficult, if not impossible, design situation, which then has
to be resolved. This results in a kind of studied casualness; and I find this characteristic repeats itself in Jim's work, for example in the apparently random disposition of elements in the Olivetti Training School at Haslemere. And I find this kind
of studied casualness a very English characteristic. It would be an interesting point
to develop by working back in time and citing historical precedents.

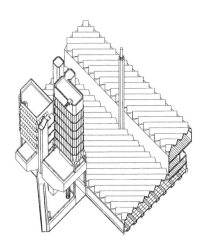

If Leicester belongs to that group of hard, brittle-skinned buildings in the same way as the Cambridge History Faculty and the Florey Building at Oxford, then there are also those projects where structure dominates, such as the unbuilt Dorman Long headquarters (incidentally a personal favourite) through to those more sensuous extruded or moulded buildings, like St Andrew's, the housing at Runcorn or again the Olivetti building. The latter is evocative of the company's own artefacts, and at the same time, quite interestingly, it is pioneering in the application of more advanced materials, such as GRP.

Out of this background of building groups, which evolved in a kind of linear sequence, we come to the current projects, which manifest more urban and historical associations, which I know Jim will be talking about this evening. I particularly like the way that he summed up in a talk in Bologna when he said, and I quote the end of that talk:

'The structural content in architecture is likely to increase as traditional methods of construction decline, and new buildings get larger and more complicated. However, I think it will be ever more necessary for architects not to rely merely on the expression of techniques for the architectural solution. Humanistic considerations must remain the primary logic from which a design evolves.'

If I had to condense that, I would underline the last sentence: '*Humanistic considerations must remain the primary logic from which a design evolves.*' That for me is the key.

It is my honour and delight to support James Stirling for the 1980 Royal Gold Medal for Architecture.

'There are no dogmas for me about whether the structure or services should be expressed or suppressed. I could also add that I do not see a conflict in sharing a passion for the past with a pleasure and anticipation for an architecture of the future.'

Norman Foster

I find the clarity of Sir Henry Wotton's 1624 description of Architecture as 'Firmnesse, Commodity and Delighte' quite refreshing in the light of all the current architectural *isms* – especially in its emphasis on people and their needs for *convenience* and *delight*. Despite the shifts of social and technological change which have been explosive in the last three hundred years, the goals suggested by this description still seem to me to be as valid as ever. I would like to elaborate on this in the context of my own practice.

Before I attempt to do that, it is important that there are no misunderstandings about my own motivations. I practise architecture for the pleasure that I derive from its pursuits – even if, at times, the disciplines and demands seem insuperable. To paraphrase Charles Eames, I like to think that I take my pleasures seriously. In that spirit I should also mention aviation – not for the occasional pleasure that it gives me but because I believe it offers experience and analogies which can inform the world of architecture. As Bucky might say, there is for me a synergetic relationship between the two. I am more at home designing than talking about design, so I shall mostly refer to our own work in order to identify beliefs and attitudes, how they have changed over time and how they are still developing. I shall try to resist the temptation to post-rationalise and make an effort to communicate a reality, which, for me, owes a great deal to pragmatism and intuition.

I have always believed that architecture is about people – at one extreme is the private inner sanctum that it can create, at the other extreme are the outside public spaces, which are in turn created by it. In between such public and private domains the edges can be consciously or unconsciously blurred, to create or modify communities by sustaining, erecting or breaking down social barriers. Such an approach involves value judgements by attempting to ask the right questions; it suggests an interactive process between those who initiate buildings, those who use them, and those who design them – another way of saying teamwork.

It implies challenge. On the one hand, such a process may confirm the status quo, may merely be an audit which rubber stamps an existing model as appropriate for duplication. On the other hand it may lead to building forms that are different, that break with a current tradition, creating fresh possibilities, or hark back to an earlier tradition. It assumes research and an ordering of priorities. In broad-brush terms, such an approach may suggest fragmentation, the creation of several parts

rather than one monolith. Alternatively, the process might lead to integration, the creation of a single entity rather than separate parts. In fundamental terms it might even question the wisdom of constructing a building at all, or suggest thresholds of appropriateness.

It has more to do with optimism than pessimism. It is about joy, and may well be sustained by illusion – the illusion of order in a disordered world, of privacy in the midst of many, of space on a crowded site, of light on a dull day. It is also about quality – quality of space and the light that models it. At some point it involves making a building, and unless we return to the cave it raises the issue of technology, 'the art of making things', to quote Pirsig, the production process as a means to an end. I believe quality – that quality of loving care if you like – has always been a preferred ingredient and is needed more today than ever before.

Architecture exists in a timeframe; it cannot be separated from the past – in tangible terms, the context of site; more intangibly, earlier influences and reference points. But architecture exists quite firmly in the present and assumes an attitude to the future and change. Lastly it cannot be created in a vacuum. The forces that create it are only sustained by resources – time, energy and funds. I should add one further word concerned with the learning curve, those perceived failures, or satisfactions, expected or otherwise – let's call it feedback.

When I wrote this I found myself underlining certain key words and linking them together as threads. The buildings are a complex interweaving of these threads and are attempts to reconcile and integrate issues which are often in conflict: the subjective versus the objective; the humanistic versus the scientific; the qualitative versus the quantitative. I shall try to pick apart some of these threads, firstly to identify influences and then to talk about those social threads and the response of production.

As a schoolboy, my imagination was fired by two architects, Le Corbusier and Frank Lloyd Wright. I was excited by the juxtaposition of past and present in the book *Towards a New Architecture* – the Parthenon and a Caproni Hydroplane on opposite pages for example. Frank Lloyd Wright, through the pages of Henry-Russell Hitchcock's *In the Nature of Materials*, was a more remote fantasy world – science fiction images of shimmering glass in the Johnson Wax building. Over the years my list of architectural influences has grown; Louis Kahn in particular

continues to go up in my esteem (1), Alvar Aalto also. Both of them impress me by the way they handle natural light, particularly from above. It has become fashionable to denigrate the work of such architects – I cannot join in. They were my heroes then and they still are today.

After school I marked time working in the Accountant's Office at Manchester Town Hall, a splendid building by Alfred Waterhouse. I have strong recollections not only of its internal spaces and its presence on Albert Square, but also of its details, the handrails and light fittings, down to the glass-sided water cisterns in the toilets – a building designed through and through. If the Town Hall was a Victorian cave, then I remember being excited by its counterpoint, the tent-like tracery of Barton and Lancaster Arcades (2), the latter sadly demolished in 1980. I can remember citing these buildings in support of our intention with the Willis Faber building over twenty years later.

I passed a further two years doing National Service as an electronics engineer in the Royal Air Force working in a turf-covered hangar, high on camouflage and very low on natural light. There was a certain futility in our struggles. The radar systems that we repaired were designed for propeller-driven bombers; their response was too slow for the new generation of jets. By the time the navigator had established a fix, the aircraft had already travelled a long way to somewhere else. For navigator read architect – there are many obvious analogies about change and the systems that come together to comprise buildings.

Out of the gloom and into the sun. As a late starter I finally sorted myself out and commenced architectural studies at the University of Manchester. The school had a strong emphasis on both history and drawing, traditions that stemmed from Professor Cordingley who continued the revisions of Banister Fletcher. These traditions came together in the formal exercise of measured drawings.

I broke with the mould of measured Classical drawings and discovered a world of vernacular architecture – windmills and barns – and a fascination for the way that things are made and how they work. I was also fascinated by the urban context, which led me to measure, sketch, photograph and make diagrams of a diversity of spaces: piazzas in Tuscan hill towns, quads in Oxford and Cambridge, the Circus in Bath, the Queen's House at Greenwich, Shepherd Market in Mayfair, and many other places.

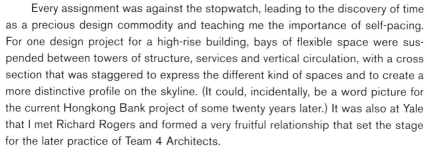

These twin concerns – how things work and the urban context – are interestingly brought together in one of our most challenging projects at the moment, the new headquarters for the BBC. Here the emphasis is on a response that will work for broadcasting as well as the vital urban relationships with Portland Place and All Souls' Church.

After Manchester, a Henry Fellowship allowed me to study at Yale University for a Masters Degree. The influences were diverse: Paul Rudolph, who could only talk about design on the basis of drawings – 'no elevations, nothing to talk about'; Serge Chermayeff, with his pioneering studies published a year later as *Community and Privacy*, philosophical to the point of 'a building – why design a building?'; and Vincent Scully, who introduced me to history as a continuum and opened my eyes to the work of the Chicago School, Frank Lloyd Wright and Louis Kahn.

Every assignment was against the stopwatch, leading to the discovery of time as a precious design commodity and teaching me the importance of self-pacing. For one design project for a high-rise building, bays of flexible space were suspended between towers of structure, services and vertical circulation, with a cross section that was staggered to express the different kind of spaces and to create a more distinctive profile on the skyline. (It could, incidentally, be a word picture for the current Hongkong Bank project of some twenty years later.) It was also at Yale that I met Richard Rogers and formed a very fruitful relationship that set the stage for the later practice of Team 4 Architects.

But America also presented a rich imagery of artefacts, which still continue to fascinate me. The juxtaposition of the Airstream caravan, Ford station wagon and Colorado wilderness alongside the Apollo 17 module, moon buggy and lunar landscape was evocative of autonomy and liberation – a short 30-year hop in time between the earthbound and a 239,000-mile leap into space. Different constraints and different responses – the smooth wrap-around envelope of the Airstream in contrast with the spindly articulated aesthetic of the module (4, 5). (There are some obvious links here to our work with Buckminster Fuller on autonomous dwellings.)

This theme is picked up again in the parallel examples of the Heliostat and the NASA Skylab with their promise of energy harvesting. The latter inspired the concept of scooping sun into the heart of a high, deep building, the banking hall atrium at the base of the Hongkong and Shanghai Bank.

It is not only the hardware of space exploration which stimulates me but also the built spaces that it generates, such as the vertical Assembly Building at Cape Canaveral (6). Alongside this the space shuttle, atop its converted 747 jumbo jet transporter, is a reminder of the extraordinary beauty and performance of new materials that we have discovered through subcontractors to the space programme. I have in mind some of the glass products that we are developing with the Corning Company, as well as the widespread use of aircraft floor construction – equivalent to around a hundred Boeing 747s in the Hong Kong project.

The image of two men carrying a typical floor panel (8) makes points about its inherent lightness and generous dimensions. The expression of the grid that it forms on the floor plane, together with a clearly defined structure both inside and out, suggests how office space might be ordered and broken down to produce a more human scale. There are parallels with traditional Japanese architecture – the manner in which the tatami mat and framed structure articulate interior spaces can be seen quite clearly in the photographs of the Katsura Imperial Villa at Kyoto (9). Having recently been able to study such buildings at first hand, there are many lessons to be learnt about the possibilities of incorporating translucency, achieving a more subtle world in between the extremes of transparency and opacity (back to the exciting possibilities afforded by the new generation of space-age materials and to the tradition of Pierre Chareau's classic Maison de Verre). The layers of screens and changes of level around the edges of these spaces also offer a more interesting sequence of space from outside to inside, and I can sense the potential for such devices in the future.

In spirit I would compare this spatial sequence with the typical Parisian pavement cafe, where the protected edge becomes a transition space – a kind of semi-public/semi-private realm between the interior of a private restaurant and a public thoroughfare; a space with its own special ambience and microclimate.

The image of a bridge, in this case the Golden Gate Bridge at San Francisco (7), has been used as a reference point to make analogies with buildings and to suggest how an expressed structure may work simultaneously at two levels. Functionally the bridge can link one side of the water to the other, while symbolically, it has a presence and exists in its own sculptural right. Its appearance on travel posters and postcards confirms that it can act almost as a signpost, which

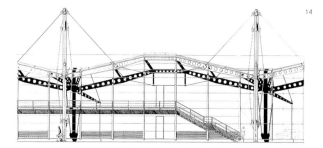

14

to the Piazza della Scala. Images of this space, some of them taken when I was a student, have been used to try to communicate the concept of introducing public spaces and routes into recent projects, thereby blurring the edges between the public and private realms.

It has also been helpful to refer back to historical examples when questioning the nature of vertical movement in modern high-rise buildings; the trip in a typical lift-car is, at best, a third-rate experience. Compare this with the drama of movement through the Eiffel Tower – a dynamic exchange between the space contained by its structure and the vistas beyond (15). Other more modest Victorian examples spring to mind, such as the Bradbury Building in Los Angeles. Here, transparent lifts move through a glass-roofed courtyard to serve the tiers of office floors which ring the site. There are obvious analogies between these examples and the search for more enjoyable movement patterns in the Hongkong Bank project.

This interest in structures extends to include more anonymous tensile ones, such as the agricultural machinery associated with irrigation and grain storage.

Influences of a more indirect kind are evident in the elevation of our recently completed Renault Centre (14). Is its yellow structure sitting in the greenery informed by buttercups (daisies, dandelions, daffodils ...) or the Renault house colour? The truth is that I do not know – the issue is subjective. But a more important question to ask is: is it a friendly and inviting building?

This leads us to the social threads of people and the public and private realms of the sites they occupy, as well as the construction response to those issues, namely the methods of production which have changed over time and in turn influenced the building form. It is interesting to compare two of our first projects – the work of Team 4 which, in 1963, brought together two architect sisters, Wendy Cheesman and Georgie Wolton, with Richard Rogers and myself. The overgrown roofscape of Creek Vean (16), next to the cross-section of a proposed housing development (17), makes a number of points about our earliest work. The individual buildings, although one-offs, were also seen as models for wider application in larger schemes which were sadly unrealised. They attempted an organic response to their sites, closed to the road on the public side and open to views and sun on the private side. They were tight, urban, village-like clusters, anti-sprawl and anti-suburban in spirit. The roof of the house attempts to tie into the landscape, and

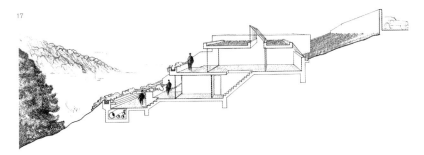

anticipates the public roofscape of Willis Faber, just as the toplighting – a characteristic of those early schemes – also becomes a recurring theme in later work.

The next example, a small electronics factory for Reliance Controls (18), was rooted in the time and cost equations already presented to the client by the building industry in the form of speculative proposals. These proposals all took the traditional form of a management box at the front of the site and a workers' shed at the back. On the grounds of social integration a single building seemed more appropriately democratic and suggested the form of a pavilion, Classical in its simplicity, and more attractive both inside and out than its traditional commercial rivals. At a practical level, the capacity to adjust the mix of production to administration at any time by moving non-structural partitions was certainly closer to the volatile realities of industrial change. In addition the more compact form occupied less of the precious site, and by enclosing more floor area with less wall and roof offered the user better standards within a given fixed cost.

The construction response to these aims was a departure from the traditional wet trades of the earlier work with a new emphasis on so-called component assembly. The drawings suggest a machine aesthetic; the site realities were something else, and closer perhaps to a bent cocoa-tin aesthetic. But more significantly, the technical realisation was in the direction of a greater integration of the systems or parts that comprised the total building. For example, the roof and floor planes were careful attempts to bring together the structure and services, with the profiles of the roof deck acting as a series of reflectors for the runs of light tubes, whilst the floor screed absorbed within its thickness copper heating coils, power trunking and compressed air pipes.

The Reliance Factory was a turning point in our endeavours to integrate social, technical and commercial realities – moves which were taken much further in subsequent work, particularly for IBM.

The next project, for the Fred Olsen Company in the London Docks (19), was a different kind of turning point. Its significance for us lay in our research and questioning of the requirements which might generate a project. In this instance our studies challenged the client's preconceptions and, in effect, said that either they did not need the building that they had commissioned or, alternatively, that it should be a different kind of building somewhere else on the site. This set the

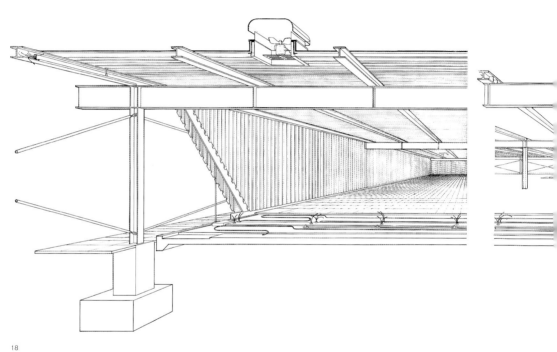

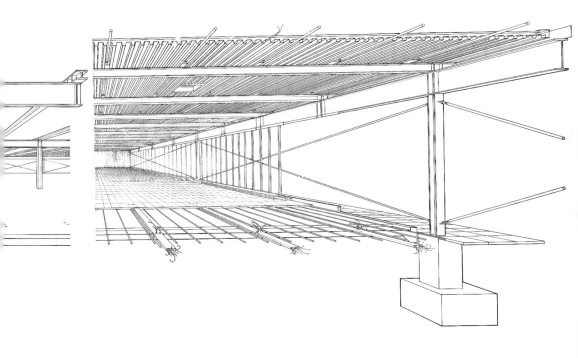

stage for a dialogue with management and the union, and it was out of this that the new project was born.

I have, over time, become increasingly aware of the importance of this early probative phase as a vital and often neglected part of the creative process. Without it, it would certainly not be possible to contemplate projects such as the Sainsbury Centre or the new BBC project where there is no brief as such. For design, in the first instance, is a matter of strategic questioning along with sifting and evaluating development options.

Perhaps one of the most satisfying aspects of the Olsen project was to see the transformation of lifestyle that followed from it. A workforce, supposedly notorious for its vandalism, was apparently transformed to the point of being so possessive about its new building that it would not allow visiting truck drivers to use it because of their 'bad habits'!

I am not suggesting that this apparent miracle in industrial relations, characterised by a virtual absence of unofficial strikes during the working life of the building, was due solely to the architecture; rather it was the result of the integration of a progressive management philosophy and a belief in the value of good communication between people. The building that emerged was a reflection of that philosophy and a shared commitment to it. It also reflected the very personal drive of Fred Olsen and other dedicated individuals behind the venture.

At a personal level the project was significant as the first building that Wendy and I completed as Foster Associates after we disbanded Team 4. It was also influential in the way that Olsen generously opened their doors to such future clients as IBM, Willis Faber and Sir Robert Sainsbury who, in turn, continued that same very helpful tradition.

Technically the Olsen Amenity Centre, with its tighter tolerances and more sophisticated components, gasketry, low brightness lighting and solar glazing, was an advance on Reliance Controls. It also marked a move towards closer links with industry, not only in the development of its glazing system in direct collaboration with American subcontractors but also in its early use of management contracting to achieve projects of increasing complexity on tighter time schedules. This approach has been taken to greater stages of refinement in subsequent projects through to the present time.

The next project, a competition entry for Newport Comprehensive School (20), explored further the possibility of clustering a diversity of activities under one roof to improve social relationships and make better use of the site. The roof was an umbrella, which integrated structure, services and natural light. Its realisation would have involved a range of special product designs, and these formed part of the total competition submission. The project was influenced by the California SCSD school system (21) with its own roots in the Eames House and its stated aim to involve industry through such mediums as performance specifications. We were fascinated by the prospect of higher performance structures which might be realised more swiftly and cheaply. The Air-Supported Office for Computer Technology (22) was a typical built example that followed later.

The Newport school was not built, but it did become a model for a building for IBM – another extraordinarily enlightened client. Their Pilot Head Office in Cosham was realised as a single glass pavilion, compact enough to preserve all the existing trees and create the illusion of a park on the edge of suburbia (23, 24). The mix of activities under this roof has been subject to flux and change ever since its completion over twelve years ago and will probably continue to be so throughout the remainder of its life. Incidentally, although it is a permanent building in the traditional sense of that word, it was rooted in the time and costs associated with temporary off-the-peg structures which, at that time, accounted for half the stock of IBM's real estate, and was constructed at half the cost and in half the time of their so-called permanent buildings.

One of the challenges of the next project, the head office for Willis Faber (25-28) in Ipswich, was to integrate the company into the urban fabric of a market town. The traditional office blocks, high-rise with rectangular geometries that had started to appear on the edges of Ipswich were rejected as hostile and alien to the site context as well as being socially inadequate. There was also a concern to avoid the windswept plazas that seemed to proliferate as wastelands on the left-over site edges of such developments. Instead, a low-rise deep building was proposed, with edges that could meander to follow the curving line of the original medieval streetscape. Such a low-profile, reflective facade could also handle the extremes of scale, from the sweep of a ring road and traffic island through to the calm of a historical Unitarian Meeting House alongside.

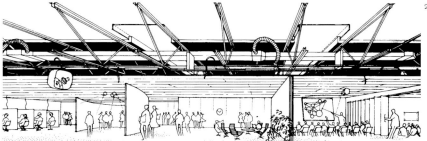

Inside, the building attempted to challenge some of the preconceptions about office buildings, to introduce more joy – sunlight, a swimming pool, roof gardens. The achievement of such luxuries within the realities of a tight commercial budget also presented a special kind of design challenge. The change in level across the site, for example, enabled a pool to be introduced without costly excavation and waterproofing. In similar spirit the roof landscaping was cost-effective in eliminating the need for expensive double structures and expansion joints – not to mention a dramatic reduction in future energy loads.

Movement through the building is by banks of escalators, a kind of magical moving stair, bathed in sunlight and connecting the entrance level with its swimming pool to the roof garden and restaurant pavilion, with the two working floors sandwiched in between. It is significant that, in the client's eyes, this atrium space and the movement to and fro, summed up the spirit of the building. I have often heard Ken Knight – then Company Secretary who, with the close support of his Chairman, headed out the project – explaining to visitors the way in which it effectively knit the company's 1,300 people into a family unit because of the manner in which they would now greet each other in the mornings and evenings compared with life in their past premises with lifts and corridors.

These social endeavours are far more important than the details of a technical realisation which, in my view, have tended to be over-emphasised. However, the building did mark two further stages of construction development. Firstly, the glass wall was a system or product which, following the precedent of the abortive Newport School, was specifically designed for the project and did not emanate from a catalogue. Secondly, the project used extensive prototyping to achieve better on-site quality control both of traditionally based crafts and newer technologies.

This project also raised questions about when it is appropriate to innovate and in what circumstances. Although raised floors were taken for granted in computer rooms, they were unheard of in offices at that time, and to be affordable they required specific product development. They are now, some ten years later, a common feature of many developers' office buildings. More significantly, this feature eventually proved to be a commercial lifeline for Willis Faber by enabling them to cope with growth through the introduction of new office technologies, rather than through building again.

 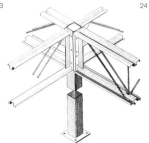

The principles behind Willis Faber can be seen at a larger scale in our project for Hammersmith, which was initiated by the then Chairman of London Transport, Kenneth Robinson, in 1977. The perimeter of the site was to be developed with offices to enclose a vast sunlit public space in the heart of the scheme, surmounted by a translucent membrane roof, recalling our Air-Supported Office for Computer Technology in Hertfordshire completed some eight years earlier. At the corners, entrance gates, reminiscent of the adjoining church tower, incorporated vertical movement and services. More significantly, the existing traffic patterns, which in effect produced a gigantic roundabout, would have been moved over to create instead a new public park.

The scheme hinged on a triangle of forces: firstly, it had to sustain itself financially in the absence of government subsidies; secondly, it had to work operationally as a transportation interchange for buses and tube trains; and thirdly, it had to create something for the community, to work for people. When the individuals and the idealism behind the project changed, and with them the community heart of the project – all to be replaced by a new brief for a typical high street development – we felt it necessary to withdraw. I would call that the threshold of appropriateness, and with the wisdom of hindsight I am now convinced that it really was the right decision for us at that time.

The next project, the Sainsbury Centre for Visual Arts, was concerned with the integration of a private art collection into a new university. At a smaller scale the Sainsbury Centre explored the cross-fertilisation that could be sparked off by bringing together diverse activities under one roof: areas for the display and contemplation of works of art alongside spaces concerned with teaching the history of art, both fused with areas for the public. At a more intangible level there was the desire to create spaces which would at the same time be noble, generous and informally relaxing.

Lighting, both natural and artificial, was a vital ingredient which generated the building's cross-section with its double skins and integrated structure and services. The viability of the project was influenced by maintenance and running costs to the extent of consciously having to 'design out' air conditioning as such. This search for lower energy solutions, coupled with higher performance, led to the transfer of materials and techniques from the aerospace industry to the building

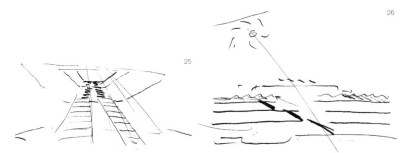

industry. I have used the word 'joy' in connection with spaces but I would also extend it to the tangible qualities of materials; performance is more than just keeping out the rain. Such developments involved the closest cooperation with the University of East Anglia and the personal support of the then Vice Chancellor, Professor Frank Thistlethwaite.

There is a progression from the Sainsbury Centre to the competition that we won for the National Athletics Stadium at Frankfurt. In this case, the roof spanned much further as a very skinny curved membrane which again integrates structure, services and natural and artificial lighting. It is also reminiscent of some of those earlier Team 4 projects in the manner in which it organically digs into the site to create a kind of amphitheatre with landscaping that creeps up the sides to follow the roof line. Both functionally and symbolically, the entrance announces itself more positively as a generous portico and covered outdoor viewing area.

In the competition for the Hongkong and Shanghai Bank headquarters, the local densities and land values made a high-rise building inevitable; indeed Hong Kong is a city of skyscrapers with more of them, I'm told, than anywhere else in the world. It was the very nature of such buildings that we attempted to challenge, their boring inhumanity and anonymity, in which the only apparent difference between the good, bad and indifferent is skin deep and in which every floor is a dreary repetition of the other. Of equal concern was the poverty of public spaces left over at ground level after a further carve-up by road engineers, with the pedestrians very much relegated to third place.

The response to these concerns was to suspend the building in the air. In the process, the ground plane is free to become an expansion of Statue Square, which fronts the site and thereby creates a new public plaza. Widest at the base with its public banking hall, the building narrows down to the summit with its more private areas, the stepped section making an interesting and unique profile against the skyline as well as clearly reflecting the internal organisation and response to light angles. The setbacks are marked by double-height spaces, defined by the deeper structure from which clusters of offices are suspended. These spaces become reception areas, each with their related terraces as 'gardens-in-the-sky'.

Movement is thus through a considered progression of spaces – a sequence from the plaza as a generous outdoor foyer, into a lift, itself translucent within a

28

7

glass tube, to be released in one movement into a main reception space. From there escalators traverse the spaces above and below in a continuous and more gentle manner reminiscent of the Willis Faber building.

There are three main elements: the cage of the building above ground, the cave or vault below ground, and the plaza level, which separates them. The main body of the building above ground is analogous to a vertical cluster of small villages one atop the other, breaking down the scale socially within, and reflecting this clearly on the outside, to achieve a visual breakdown of scale.

Sun is scooped into the heart of the banking hall atrium at the base of the building by a series of reflecting mirrors, to percolate eventually through the translucent glass floor of the plaza to the basement or cave below ground. At night the situation is reversed by light glowing through from below so that the plaza floor itself becomes crystalline and jewel-like.

The first drawing for the scheme was by a geomancer called Koo Pak Ling, whose views about the feng shui of the site were counselled by us on our first visit to Hong Kong. These more subjective influences on the design are powerful and tangible. Suffice to say that the latest model studies of the base of the building clearly echo the spirit of that first sketch in the way in which the building is entered. It has been suggested that the grillages recall a past indigenous architecture; they are also designed to provide typhoon protection as well as being symbolic of the Bank as a secure place.

I am reminded of the checklists which are typical of those used for flying a light twin-engine aircraft. The first list is for when everything is going right, and the second one details the emergency procedures for when things go wrong. There are basically two kinds of pilots: those who take off and are surprised if they have an engine failure, and those who take off and are even more surprised if the engine actually keeps going – they have been conditioned to expect the worst. The aviation fraternity spawns adages such as: 'There are old pilots and bold pilots, but no old bold pilots.' I think it is a bit like that for us architects. We expect the worst, and we try to prepare for it. It is an approach that inspires a healthy respect for testing and prototyping.

This image of a test in progress shows a gentleman on a ladder peering to see if any water is leaking through the joints of the prototype Sainsbury Centre

panel (29). Such test rigs were an important part of the design process and it was essential to confirm that those panels really could perform under extreme conditions before committing to them irrevocably.

The equivalent process in the development of the external wall for the Hongkong Bank project can be seen in photographs of the test programme held at the St Louis-based subcontractors. A tethered Corsair fighter is revved up to blast air and water in simulated typhoon conditions to establish performance limits as well as determining deflections and weather tightness (30).

Another kind of test, using scale models, was undertaken in the wind tunnel of the University of Western Ontario in New London. Such studies provided valuable design criteria for structural loadings as well as informing the nature of the microclimate at the base of the building.

But such tests are not only about things that you can qualify – you are also talking about the qualitative issues. In other words, does the end product look right? Feel good? Give some joy? Does it achieve those architectural aims of breaking down the scale? Providing a filigree of detail? Creating a building which is more human and enjoyable both inside and out? If the answer is no, then those other so-called scientific tests are almost academic.

Another aspect of the process of testing can be seen in the images of large-scale models being studied under an artificial sky in Innsbruck (31). Here, with models and lasers, we were able to explore the possibilities of reflecting sun into the heart of the banking hall space. Would we want a soft diffuse light to wash the edges of the atrium or would we seek the brilliance, hardness and dazzle of a sunbeam? Or a combination of both?

Similar model studies on the glass floor were helpful in indicating qualities of uplighting and translucence, especially when compared with full-size working prototypes which we assembled in our own premises (I now no longer know whether to call it office, studio or workshop – the edges get blurred). We went on to make a film of the test to show those involved in Hong Kong how cleaning and maintenance could be coped with as well as more subjective qualities.

This process of modelling from small scale through to full size continued in the design of the service modules (32), which were originally simulated at a small scale in wood and plastic. This module was subsequently made in those same

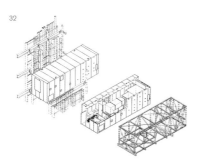

materials as a full-size working mock-up – literally a two-storey-high building in its own right. This was built in Tokyo and formed the basis for the next pre-production prototype, which was assembled in south-west Japan to test out the final steel and aluminium components as well as the engineering systems that it contained. It was not up to performance specification in that first instance and had to be modified, but it was certainly the right place to find out how to make it work rather than on a building site. This partnership with industry made it possible to design down to the detail of ashtrays, ceramic ware, washbasins, door furniture and toilet roll holders.

These modules will eventually be shipped by barge direct from their point of assembly to Kobe and thence by container ship to Hong Kong, to lock into the structural masts which in this photograph can be seen rising some nine storeys into the sky (33). The building is simultaneously being built both upwards and downwards, some three storeys below ground. Although progress photographs give some idea of the ground space which will be liberated at that very busy part of Hong Kong, unfortunately they cannot show how the building will eventually link up with pedestrian pathways and green spaces to the rear as well as with Statue Square to the front.

Our own working spaces are a response to the mixture of traditional activities, such as drafting, as well as to the three-dimensional modelling that I have talked about. This is reflected in high-bay industrial spaces with facilities such as over-head travelling cranes.

The links with production, with actually making things, are really quite important. It would have been impossible for us to produce our own office furniture, itself a model for a later production run, without working on the shop floor with the people who would actually make it. Although they have very much a machine-made aesthetic, the production realities behind these pieces are on the scale of cottage industries.

Two contrasting aspects of the Renault building – its roofscape and the blockwork wall detail – make some points about the range and variety of technol-ogies. For example, the building incorporates materials such as the metallic fabric more normally used to protect the airframe of a Harrier from the heat of its jet engine. To use it on a building to deliver a two-hour fire rating while also respond-ing to movement tolerances, involved special tests to prove the point; the test was, incidentally, stopped after two hours because it could apparently have performed almost *ad infinitum*. But a large part of that building also has a two-hour fire rating provided by the 200mm blockwork wall. I do not see any conflict; it is merely a matter of what is appropriate in the particular circumstances.

I would like to think that the design of the blockwork shows the same concern for quality – the control of quality – regardless of whether the material is traditional or non-traditional. Incidentally, I do not see any conflicts in expressing the structure so manifestly on this building when, at the same time, for equally specific reasons, we are designing the new airport at Stansted with its structure totally enclosed within the external envelope. There are no dogmas for me about whether the structure or services should be expressed or suppressed. I could also add that I do not see a conflict in sharing a passion for the past with a pleasure and anticipation for an architecture of the future.

The final pair of images shows a Caproni high-performance sailplane (34) alongside the solar-powered Gossamer Albatross (35). I have used the analogy of the glider in the past to communicate points about objects which are quite beautiful in themselves; it seems that they can exist abstractly as sculptural objects in their own right. The fact that they can also achieve such high performance with low energy demand is for me expanded by the work of Paul MacCready, who pioneered both man-powered and solar-powered flight. But interestingly, as Buckminster Fuller pointed out when we were together with MacCready some years back at a conference in Aspen, had it not been for a new generation of materials, then such dreams of man-powered flight would still be unrealised.

When challenged about the creative aspects of his work Paul MacCready pointed out that the prime mover was really Henry Kremer, the man who was prepared to set the challenge, establish the rules and put up substantial funds. He felt that such an initiative was truly creative and enabled MacCready and his group to respond to it. MacCready was quick to add that he found himself in the position of a spokesman for the larger team of which he was but a part, and talked of the painstaking struggles that involved so many individuals. I hope that my analogies are clear and that I have left no doubts about our debts and appreciation to those important patrons, without whose initiative we would certainly not be able to exercise our creative skills as architects. Likewise it is especially important that I try to

34

communicate the dedication and enthusiasm that binds us all together, and that the importance of the team – those many diverse individuals – is recognised. That cannot be overstressed.

Finally, two very special people: my wife – a powerful and creative driving force, reticently behind the scenes but undoubtedly my sternest critic – I would like to pay tribute to Wendy; and Bucky … it is difficult to know where to start. It is a privilege to work for and with Bucky, an inspiration for many years and a continuing inspiration. I hope that we will live up to that inspiration and to the standards and traditions of the Royal Gold Medal for Architecture.

35

'Bucky's speech addressed issues of survival – messages that today are even more rel-evant, as his worst predictions are gradually being seen to be accurate. Even now, in the climate of an ecologically more aware culture, his ideas are still far ahead of their time.'

Norman Foster

If I were to write a book about my experience of Bucky I would divide it into chapters, the first telling how we both met and the last telling about our final meeting.

It was James Meller who introduced me to Bucky in 1971. We met at the ICA, which at that time had an elegant wood-panelled dining room overlooking the Mall. In this civilised setting Bucky, James and myself met to talk through a long lunch. Bucky explained that he had been asked to design a theatre under the quadrangle of St Peter's College in Oxford. The prime mover at the college was a professor called Francis Warner and the project was to be backed by such luminaries as the actor Richard Burton. Bucky wanted to find an architect to work with him on the project and James was helping by making some introductions. I had brought examples of our work to show to Bucky and the office was on standby in the hope that he would visit us.

It is only now, many years later, that I realise to what extent Bucky was able to draw me out through that lunchtime conversation without my even knowing it at the time. He got me to reveal attitudes to issues such as design, materials, cost, research and other subjects which ranged far and wide. As it was getting near the time that Bucky had to leave I ventured the thought that he might like to look at the work that I had brought or perhaps to visit our office. Bucky dismissed the idea with a wave of his hand, explaining that he had already decided half-way through lunch that I was the person he wanted to collaborate with and that he did not need to talk to anyone else about the project.

There are many chapters that could be written on the extraordinary insights that Bucky was to offer in the twelve years that elapsed between that first meeting and our last. He was one of those rare individuals who fundamentally influenced the way that you were afterwards to look and to think.

But to move on to the final chapter. Bucky had very kindly agreed to talk on the occasion of my receipt of the Royal Gold Medal for Architecture at the Royal Institute of British Architects in June 1983. I was not to know that it would be the last time that I was to see him alive.

Earlier that day he came into the office, which at that time was a block away from the RIBA in Great Portland Street, having arrived from some far-off corner of the world. His almost perpetual travel schedule was to take him on to the White House in Washington for a major address and then back to his home in Los

Angeles and to the hospital where his wife Anne lay seriously ill. We talked a great deal – jumping from one subject to another and finally focusing on the house project that we were working on together, based on two interconnected geodesic domes, one within the other.

Bucky's speech addressed issues of survival – messages that today are even more relevant, as his worst predictions are gradually being seen to be accurate. Even now, in the climate of an ecologically more aware culture, his ideas are still far ahead of their time.

The following day Bucky came back to the office for a last meeting. James Meller, as almost always, was present, caring, sensitive and attendant to Bucky's needs, worrying about his getting too tired – perhaps he needed a quick catnap or maybe another hot tea? Also on hand was his secretary, Shirley, with whom he had recently started to travel.

Looking back it strikes me for the first time that it was nothing short of a miracle that not so many weeks earlier Bucky had managed to trot around the globe on his own from one destination to another – some of them in the most unlikely and remote corners of the world. I think it had a great deal to do with his presence – everybody would go out of their way to help him and to look after him. In many cases this could be explained as respect by those who knew his eminence. Or perhaps in the hotels that he revisited it might be because he treated the staff so well. (He was very sensitive in the way that he did this – I recall him once handing envelopes to a concierge before his departure, each bearing the name of the individual to whom the enclosed tip and a note of thanks were directed.) But I know that it was nothing to do with his generosity and everything to do with the kind of person that he was. You simply wanted to go out of your way for him because he was so very special – and it was also nothing to do with age.

Our last meeting started with the same dome house project and the assumption that Wendy and I would have one on a country site in Wiltshire and that Bucky and his wife would have another in Los Angeles, both of which would be working prototypes. When Bucky started to talk about his own dwelling Shirley interrupted him, touching his arm gently and delicately suggesting to Bucky that Anne was now so ill that perhaps it might be better to forget the home in Los Angeles. Bucky stopped in his tracks, slightly flustered, and said that of course

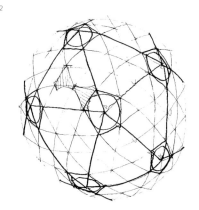

she was right – calling her darling which he often did. It sounds affected when you write it down but when he used it it conveyed a warmth and respect far removed from its intimate use.

We carried on with more talk about the technical aspects of the project. As it drew towards Bucky's departure time we had somehow moved onto a favourite topic – how on earth Bucky at the age of 87 had such energy and drive, running a punishing schedule that would have grounded any one of us not half his age. On this occasion, for the first time, Bucky explained that it was all in the mind and that it was his mental attitude to life that enabled him to set such impossible goals and to realise them. He then added that he could at any time decide to pull the plug and then life would all be over.

Bucky finally departed. As planned he stopped the night in Washington and arrived the following day in Los Angeles to be at his wife's bedside. Bucky died at her side a few days later, on 1 July. Anne followed him within 36 hours. As we said afterwards, he decided to pull the plug. The expression has an unfortunate scientific ring to it – entirely appropriate to the public image of Bucky as a cold technocrat. Nothing could be so far removed from the truth. What was never talked about was his poetic, sentimental and deeply spiritual dimension. That, in the end, was what for me his life, and inevitably his final act, were really about.

4>

'If today, one hundred years later, Gaudí were practising as an architect, then his working methods to determine structural form would still be regarded as revolutionary.'

Norman Foster

In studying Gaudí as a person as well as the architecture that he produced, I became interested in what appeared at first sight to be a pattern of contradictions. On the one hand he was a fervent advocate of the Catalan separatist movement, but on the other he was culturally an internationalist. He defended movements to uphold the rights of workers at the same time as he courted wealthy patrons.

In his approach to structures and materials he would today be regarded as a technocrat, but his architecture was also made possible by recourse to indigenous forms and craftsmanship. The rigour and discipline of his working methods went hand-in-hand with a seeming excess of sculptural expression. In his relationship with the building site he is described as giving orders to the foreman without descending from his open carriage – an imperious attitude quite at odds with his ability to bring together collaborators of diverse skills and even to convert a workforce of artisans into on-site artists.

Although pedantically correct in his early dealings with authority, he later showed scant respect for building ordinances, adding extra storeys and extending beyond site boundaries – challenging the city to demolish or back down. He was the bohemian dandy who died an ascetic recluse, almost begging to sustain the consuming passion of his major project. Ridiculed during his life for buildings that challenged by their very originality, his death was mourned by thousands in a manner befitting a folk hero.

Of course, some of these apparent contradictions can be explained by the evolution of Gaudí as an architect from youth to maturity, but others still persist and I believe that his genius was in part due to an ability to fuse and give architectural meaning to those influences which were seemingly in conflict. In particular, and most relevant to the Nîmes context, is the influence of the French writer and theorist Eugène Viollet-le-Duc. The latter influence – intellectual, rational, Gothic, structured – contrasted with parallel influences from the Mediterranean and North Africa of organic and indigenous forms, romantic allusions and the special qualities of the light in those latitudes. It is through the controlled resolution of those opposing influences – the rational and the romantic – that Gaudí was able to produce an architecture of such poetic force. Perhaps the ultimate contradiction is that although he is now a cult figure, he was, for many years, virtually ignored by otherwise perceptive historians – perhaps because he did not fit comfortably with

the various 'isms' and labels which are invented to package and make meaningful the hindsight of history.

Although Gaudí is frequently grouped with architects of the Art Nouveau movement, he anticipated many of its directions and penetrated beyond its cultural context. The movement was in some respects also anticipated by the moral arguments of Ruskin and the lectures of Viollet-le-Duc at the Ecole des Beaux Arts, in which he offered alternative strategies to the cul-de-sac of nineteenth-century historicism.

As a recently qualified architect, Gaudí wrote that the mission of the architect lay, 'not only in designing grand projects, but also in making them possible ... economically speaking and consequently in being made aware of contemporary production methods and systems ... the most important requirement for an object to be considered beautiful is that it fulfils the purpose for which it is desired.'

This makes an interesting comparison with the following from *Entretiens sur l'Architecture*, published by Viollet-le-Duc in 1863:

'In architecture there are two necessary ways of being true. It must be true according to the programme and true according to the methods of construction. To be true according to the programme is to fulfil exactly and simply the conditions imposed by need; to be true according to the methods of construction is to employ the materials according to their qualities and properties.'

If today, one hundred years later, Gaudí were practising as an architect, then his working methods to determine structural form would still be regarded as revolutionary. His studio constructed many funicular models, which were suspended upside down with strings and weights attached to explore and balance forces within the structure (2). These were later photographed and used as underlays to help produce graphic visualisations of the finished building and its interior spaces.

The early projects, such as the Episcopal Palace in Astorga, were perhaps more obviously derived from the Gothic examples of Viollet-le-Duc, whose restoration work Gaudí had studied first hand at Carcassonne. However, his later and more mature work developed inclined geometries which dramatised side thrusts and in effect eliminated the need for such Gothic devices as flying buttresses. He

3

513

had thus broken free from the restraints of his early inspirations and developed a new and powerful language of space informed by structure.

This approach makes explicable the reported exchange between Gaudí and a visitor to the Sagrada Familia (1, 4) who asked: 'Is this the last of the cathedrals?' To which he replied: 'No, it is the first of a new series.' On the occasion of a major exhibition of Gaudí's work staged at the Société Nationale des Beaux Arts in Paris in 1910, the architect Joan Martorell was given the responsibility of explaining the work and was personally briefed by Gaudí before his departure. Apparently expecting a hostile response from French critics to the parabolic profiles of the four bell towers, the master cautioned that Martorell should on no account argue, but merely confine his response to an explanation that the form 'was a perfection of the Gothic'.

Although Gaudí very rarely travelled outside Spain, one of his most significant journeys was to Andalusia and North Africa in 1887 under the auspices of the Marqués de Comillas, for whom he later designed a Franciscan mission in Tangiers. The organic forms in this project are evocative of the indigenous buildings constructed by Berber tribesmen, which Gaudí must have viewed on his travels. These shapes are a recurring theme in his work, frequently elaborated, twisted and coiled to produce a roof landscape of fantasy images or, as in the Sagrada Familia, a dramatic silhouette of four towers – the very symbol of the city of Barcelona.

It is difficult to imagine Gaudí's architecture outside the Mediterranean region and he expressed the view that the most notable works of art came from the Mediterranean peoples, whom he believed had a more deeply rooted vision of beauty due to their proximity to the sea and the less extreme angle of the sun in those latitudes. Certainly the local quality of light makes meaningful the surface decoration, colour and textures with which Gaudí elaborated his buildings.

This elaboration of detail displays an extraordinary combination of artistic endeavour, technical know-how – particularly in the use of materials – and down-to-earth practicality. For example, the grooves in a carved timber stair were both decorative and anti-slip; the organic patterns of metal bars which form a door would skilfully divide the panes of glass into smaller units at the bottom for greater security and ease of maintenance; the device of doors-within-doors combined the practicality of a small opening with the symbolic formality of the larger unit; ornate grillages were conceived to provide light and views but guarantee privacy from within; the colourfully tiled benches sculpted out of concrete at the Park Güell were a *tour de force*, wonderful to sit on and stunning to behold – the list is end-less to the extent that at least one book and a major exhibition have been produced on the detailed minutiae of his work.

However, these decorative aspects, even at their most expressive, are only part of a much more significant and total concept. His buildings are generated by plans and sections, which spatially are strong diagrams. From these it is possible to anticipate internal spaces and volumes which possess unique and organic qual-ities. To contemplate them in physical reality is a moving experience both intellec-tually and emotionally – a return to that dialogue between the counter-influences of the rational and romantic. In that sense Gaudí's buildings succeed as grand strategies right through, inside and outside, down to the most idiosyncratic detail. Whilst so many architects of the period were applying the trappings of Art Nouveau more like fashionable gift wrapping on otherwise pedestrian buildings, or repeating sterile exercises in academic historical styles, Gaudí was commanding a new and all-embracing vision of space, structure and ornament.

Some years ago, as a visiting examiner at a school of architecture in England, I tried to explain to the students that I did not have any preconceptions about the kind of work that I might commend or criticise. This was an attempt on my part to reassure them that their work would be judged each on its own merits – regard-less, for example, of what materials they had chosen to use. It was a way of say-ing that I would not necessarily find favour with those student projects which might look like the kind of buildings produced by the Foster office, but rather that I would be seeking quality – Was it good of its kind? Did it have integrity? I elabo-rated the point by talking about the buildings of other architects whose work frankly awed me. I gave Gaudí as an example because I had at that time made a recent visit to Barcelona. After my talk it became apparent that the professor in charge of the school was genuinely shocked to find that I could respect and actu-ally learn from an architect whose work was apparently so far removed in every respect from my own. There was obviously a language barrier even though we shared the same mother tongue – he would never really understand what integrity in architecture might mean to me.

4

'Integrity' is defined in my dictionary as 'wholeness, soundness, honesty'. In the world of aviation, which is as about as far removed from Gaudí as is possible to contemplate, I hear pilots differentiating between aircraft and sometimes praising one with the ultimate accolade that 'it is an honest aircraft'. Somehow they never feel it necessary to elaborate or explain what that means. It defies explanation, and yet its meaning is so obvious to them.

The aircraft is a metaphor. The struggle to achieve a building of integrity is not about trying to please the critics or searching for this year's trendy 'ism' or fashionable new overcoats to drape over well-worn models — it is a quest to go deeper, against odds which at times seem overwhelming. In our own humble way that is the link, fragile though it might seem, which makes the pilgrimage to Gaudí meaningful to our work on the competition project in Nîmes.

'I am sceptical of all architecture in which the very nature, the spirit of a building can be tidily isolated from its technology: how can a Gothic cathedral, a Classical temple or a medieval manor house be perceived except by their spaces and the technology that made them possible?'

Norman Foster

I had just boarded a DC-10 at Kai Tak Airport, bound for London, after being interviewed in the departure lounge by a journalist who was writing an article on the new Hongkong and Shanghai Bank building. Because he had requested the meeting at very short notice and time was limited, I asked him what he would most like to talk about. He explained that he had studied architecture in England and had become friends with a number of architects in our office who had worked on the Bank. As a result of these insights he suggested that we could forget about the technology behind the building as he was now thoroughly familiar with it and in any case it had been well documented elsewhere. What he was interested to hear from me was how Chinese mysticism and the philosophies of Buckminster Fuller related to the building.

Important as these and other issues were, I was immediately suspicious of an approach in which the technology of a building could be isolated out from the wider context. I therefore asked him what his views were on the subject and he gave the opinion that the Bank project had stretched the boundaries of technology far beyond that of any other building to date. If, I ventured, that was the case, then why did he think we had chosen to exploit technology to that degree. Quite unintentionally we had reversed roles – I was now interviewing him. But it was the nature of the question that seemed to disturb him more than the reversal of roles. He could not come up with an answer and it occurred to me that he might believe that we had an obsession with technology to the extent that we would indulge in it simply for its own sake. That idea, imagined or real, was so outrageous that I felt compelled to debate it – and so dispel any such notions.

I tried to explain that the building was the outcome both of its context and the technology that made it realisable. The context would embrace all the functional, social and cultural considerations, and the technology would be another way of saying the making of something or the means of production. How then could the very nature of a thing be separated from the way that it had been made – surely each one informed the other? Which comes first, the chicken or the egg?

Was the design concept of the Bank a response to the specific needs of a financial institution moving upwards in the international big league? Or was it a symbol of the colony (1), with its commanding position at the head of Statue Square facing the mainland beyond – a bastion of the established order? Or was it a social

response to the pressures of Hong Kong – the creation of a better workplace and new public plaza? Or was it a regional response steeped in the spirit of the place? Of course it was all of these and many more. At any stage of its evolution it was also quite literally shaped by its buildability – the technology of its production. The appearance of the Bank both inside and out, its internal organisation and the spatial experience that it offered were all defined, ordered and modulated by the structure which supported it and the walls which enclosed it.

The pressures of time also played a part in shaping the building. Given the looming presence of 1997 in a place already noted for its commercial drive and impatience, at least one signal was unambiguously clear: the new building was to be designed and built in the shortest possible time. This pressure had already influenced the choice of materials away from the concrete masts which formed both vertical structure and service cores in the original competition scheme. To reduce time on site these became separate elements of vertical steel structure and independent service cores. The means of production were already an integral part of the set of presentation drawings which were approved by the Board of the Bank in 1981, otherwise it would have been impossible to translate them into more than a million square feet of built space by 1986.

To explain how an undertaking of such magnitude could be achieved within so short a timespan is clearly outside the scope of this article, but four principles can be identified as fundamental to that achievement. Firstly, the site would be more an assembly point than a building site in the traditional sense. Secondly, the building would be conceived and produced as prefabricated elements, manufactured around the world and then shipped or air-freighted to the assembly point. Thirdly, if industries outside the traditional sphere of the construction industry could offer better-performing elements then we would attempt to harness their skills and energies. Fourthly, we would actively collaborate with industry, using mock-ups and testing prototypes to anticipate, as far as possible, the eventual realities on site.

These principles are typical of our approach on other projects; the main difference in this case is a matter of degree. The demanding performance requirements of the Bank, as well as the special circumstances of Hong Kong with its dependence on imports, took these principles to a greater extreme than might have been the case elsewhere – or if more time had been available.

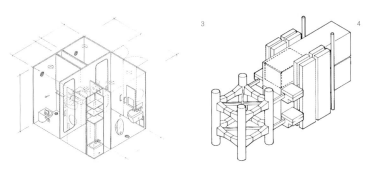

A brief history of the development of one element, the service cores (3, 4), would serve to illustrate the application of this approach. In a traditional building these cores would contain mechanical equipment, toilets, vertical risers and circulation. They would be located in the middle of layered floors with office space on their periphery – all supported by a compression structure. Such cores would be the subject of extensive fitting-out by a vast on-site labour force of construction workers, and this work would occur at the time of maximum congestion towards the end of the building process. Enough time would have to be allowed for each trade to complete its work before the next one could take over. This would be a lengthy process in which quality control would be subject to all the vagaries of site conditions – typhoons included.

By comparison the new Bank building was conceived as clusters of layered space suspended bridge-like from vertical masts with cores on the outboard edges. These cores were built off-site in a factory by a remote labour force who were not normally associated with the construction industry. They were then shipped to the site and clipped onto the building as sealed modules, already fitted out down to the last detail of soap dispensers and taps. Quality was controlled in factory conditions and, by being able to work simultaneously on and off site, the overall timescale for the project was dramatically reduced.

The manufacturers of the service cores were a Japanese consortium of Hitachi, Mitsubishi and Toshiba, names associated with electricity generation, electronics, shipbuilding and engineering rather than construction. Development work proceeded from drawings to large-scale architects' models, full-size timber mock-ups in Tokyo, and eventually to working prototypes in a remote province of Japan. After extensive testing and detail redesign the final versions were agreed; meanwhile in Hong Kong the building structure had barely risen to a height of nine storeys.

A factory production line was set up on a waterfront site in Japan and the completed modules rolled off at a rate of four per week onto barges for shipment to Kobe and onward by container ship to Hong Kong (2). A total of 139 modules were fabricated to contain the air-handling plants and toilets for each floor, as well as 'specials' fitted out to house water storage tanks and gas turbine generators. Each module was constructed as a metal box encased in stainless steel, weighing up to 40 tonnes, and the size of a small two-storey dwelling. In the final stages of

The Prince of Wales is to be congratulated on rallying the nation with his battle cry for the environment and for savaging our appalling legacy of post-war redevelopment. It would be difficult to think of a more powerful weapon for progressive change than the force of an informed public opinion and he is in a unique position to stir people to open their eyes, to question, to look critically and hopefully to seek real quality. The debate is worthy and important and I applaud the headlines. However, the fine print of his message is open to question and as he attempts to move from identifying the symptoms to diagnosing the causes and prescribing the cure, I am fearful of his over-simplistic recipes. They seem to ignore the deeper reality that architecture is but a mirror of social values and technological changes in society at any point in time.

The main targets of his attack are already past history, but it is worth reminding ourselves that there was a strong political will after the Blitz literally to obliterate visions of the past. There is nothing new in that. The Victorians, whom it has now become fashionable to admire, were ruthless proponents of such an approach. In Glasgow they destroyed, virtually without trace, a medieval city on the north bank of the Clyde which Daniel Defoe described as 'the most beautiful little city in Europe'. In its place they erected a heroic vision in which all the major municipal buildings, hospitals and universities were the subject of competitions for architectural quality. The difference between the wave of change then and that after the Second World War was an attitude of mind.

The Victorians had a raw pride, a quest for quality and a confidence to invest in the future, which still shows in those remnants that remain. We should preserve the best of these as part of our heritage, but more importantly we should be asking questions about how it was achieved rather than seeking to copy with mindless pastiche.

The Buddha at the entrance to Frank Lloyd Wright's desert headquarters in Taliesin West has the following inscription: 'Only to a genius or an ignoramus can that which is copied be the equal to that which it copies. Do not copy effects. Seek what the reasons are which give rise to those effects, then you will own your own effects'.

The reasoning in the post-war years was often a search for quantity on a shoe-string as contractors jostled to sell their prefabricated high-rise wares to politicians greedy to score points in the housing numbers game. Architects along with all the other professions were involved as one of the cogs in the system, although they were sometimes conspicuous by their absence – the infamous Ronan Point, for example,

never had one. Developers with their hack architects in tow operated on a hit-and-run basis in a climate of civic indifference and public apathy. If you want proof of this, check the local offices of your Department of the Environment which are most likely housed in some third-rate, speculatively built office block.

The city fathers of the first Industrial Revolution were men of vision, patrons in the real sense of the word, with courage and an optimistic belief in the future. There are never enough such people in any age and as an architect one is painfully aware of the debt owed to those individuals. It needs to be said that architecture can never be achieved by committees, rule books, codes or imposed styles, no matter how well intentioned these are; but can this message ever be repeated too often? There is a vital difference between such heavy bureaucratic impositions and an open democratic forum for exhibitions, public debate and participation in architecture as well as all the other infrastructures of roads and services which combine to make up the totality of our built environment. It is surely only a matter of time before we follow the example of other countries such as France and Germany where culture and the environment have become election issues which politicians ignore at their peril.

As we approach the second millennium and try to gather our national confidence, it is worth noting the quiet but dramatic revolution that is taking place in the process of actually making buildings, because it has far-reaching implications. In the 1960s industrialisation meant standardisation on a vast scale. Production lines had to be justified by huge outputs of identically repetitive items. The monotonous prefabricated buildings across the nation, usually in heavy concrete, are a legacy of that period. But we are now in the process of coming full circle because the new generation of production technology makes it possible to tailor one-off components for a single building. There are no longer any economic benefits in repetitive 'look-alikes'. These components are being manufactured on a global basis and the site becomes the assembly point. Incidentally this has nothing to do with whether a building is faced with stone, metal or glass. Given these emerging realities we, people, are the masters and the machines are the servants. This has the potential for rich creative opportunities as well as more humanistic lifestyles.

There are some ironies here because although our culture is surely about making things, you will be hard-pressed to find anybody in this country to make, for example, a wall to wrap around a city block, whether glass or stone faced. Look at the fine print of any building specification even by those defiantly wanting to buy British. You will find American, Belgian, French, German, Swiss and soon, Japanese suppliers, but not British. However, you will also find a new breed of British developers, far better informed and better travelled than their predecessors, who are responding to the recent shift in consumer demand with a long-overdue desire for higher standards.

On their overseas travels these developers are very likely to bump into British architects who are household names in Europe, Japan, the Far East and the United States but often virtually unknown over here. These architects almost certainly made their mark in those countries because they were either selected for prestigious commissions or invited to limited competitions. Returning to Glasgow, the best modern building and the major tourist attraction in Scotland is the Burrell Collection, which was the subject of an open national competition. It was won by three young architects who have since split, two having emigrated to take up opportunities in Australia and the United States. Do you start to sense a pattern?

Of course the grass can always seem greener on the other side. There are honourable exceptions for every sweeping generalisation. Overseas authorities and clients find much to admire here, and we do have a penchant for self-deprecation. But there are urgent issues, which link our manufacturing decline, the new information industries, leisure, the problems of the inner cities and the architecture that can respond to these crises and opportunities. The Prince of Wales has championed some of these individual causes. He should now be encouraged to immerse himself further in the overlaps between industry, commerce and the arts in some official capacity. Might not the Royal Fine Arts Commission be a good starting point? There was a lunch there last week at which the guest of honour was the Prime Minister, Margaret Thatcher, who is reported as saying:

'Of course, we must preserve, be sensitive to and enhance our architectural heritage – of that there can be no question – but at the same time, and as we are rediscovering our national pride and confidence, we really must try to create new building of equal distinction of our own time and culture. We owe that to posterity.'

'Reyner Banham's background was that of an engineer, and his training in the scholarship of art history at the Courtauld Institute represents two cultures which normally never come together.'

Norman Foster

In 1957 I came across Reyner Banham through a student magazine called *244* which I bought as an undergraduate for the then considerable sum of two shillings. I was in second year and can remember that the history of architecture lectures were a tedious list of dates and events seemingly unrelated to the history of anything except the buildings themselves and totally divorced from the social context which had generated them.

In this magazine Banham had written an article called 'The Lotus and the Gilded Lily' which discussed two cars: the Lotus Mark II designed by Colin Chapman and the Plymouth 1957 saloon by Vergil Exner. Somehow this piece managed to interweave the worlds of Bramante's Tempietto, Sir John Soane's Bank of England, the Coventry Climax, Camembert, Kraft cheese, Peter Pears and Elvis Presley – all into a new vision of the past, the present and the future. That article opened my eyes and my mind at the time and I have never forgotten it.

Reyner Banham's background was that of an engineer, and his training in the scholarship of art history at the Courtauld Institute represents two cultures which normally never come together.

Consider one of his books, *The Personal View of Modern Architecture.* Here, sandwiched between houses by Bruce Goff and Charles Eames and a very obscure town hall in Japan, is the Penguin Pool at the London Zoo by Berthold Lubetkin. He describes this building as an engineer would see it, talking about the skinny concrete ramps being virtually solid steel with a rendering of concrete. He then goes on to describe it in the language of an art historian, with references to the sculptor Naum Gabo and the influence of Constructivism, and other references to the period of its realisation. But there is also another ingredient, which is special to Banham, and that is the entertainment value of his commentary, which always comes with a serious point just below the surface. For example,

'... but chiefly and permanently the Penguin Pool stands up by reason of its entire aptness to its subject matter and purpose. To the best possible advantage it exhibits the pompous, ridiculous behaviour that the penguins unwittingly ape. In honour of their unconscious mockery the penguins were flattered with a rather better building than was available to most English human beings of the period. There must be some moral to this.'

530

Reyner Banham brought together a critical eye with scholarly research and piercing wit. The film of Los Angeles reveals his all-embracing enthusiasm, which still survives today, beyond the context of the early 1970s and before a more cynical age of low-cost mass travel. I could imagine a film that shows the funky side of Los Angeles, or a film about the scale of its urban sprawl, the geography of its freeways and the richness of its diversity. I could see the point of a film about its architecture – indigenous, historical and modern – and about the pioneers who moved there from Europe. But this man brings all these strands together in a single memorable film.

1

'... no detail should be considered too small.'

Designing a handrail might be likened to designing a building. It is important in its own right even though it might be only one of many thousands of components that must come together to complete the whole building, just as the individual building takes its place in the context of the city. Looking back through my own sketchbooks shows how design is a continuous process in which individual elements evolve through constant reworking, even while the building itself is under way. It is an approach that requires concern for the smallest elements; no detail should be considered too small. Also, a handrail, like furniture, is subject to constant physical touch by the users of a building and, as such, it might be seen to demonstrate by its quality – or lack of it – an attitude of mind.

Earlier this year, I was cycling with my eldest son in France and talking to him about this essay. I am fascinated by this man-machine relationship and the racing cycle seemed particularly relevant. Here too is a design that has evolved gradually over time. For example, the junctions between the tubes that make up a frame have been constantly refined and are now very beautifully resolved.

Thinking back to my teenage obsession with racing cycles, the frames have, in relative terms, remained almost static compared to the development of add-on accessories – does this have a familiar echo in terms of buildings? However, new developments with streamlined carbon-fibre and composite frames seem to offer exciting new directions. Consider, for instance, the linkage between the foot and the pedal. Up until quite recently it would be normal to bolt a toe-clip onto the pedal, add a grooved plate to the sole of the cycling shoe, slip one into the other and tighten it all up with a leather strap – a loose and clumsy conversion job on the original concept of a pedal. Compare this to the snap-on device, which is now becoming commonplace (7). By a process of integration, the number of components has been halved, enabling a block on the underside of the shoe to engage onto a minimal clip, which pivots at the end of the traditional crank. This man-machine link is easily made by literally stepping onto the bike. Conversely, by twisting the foot the mechanism is released. It is an immensely satisfying combination, both physically to use and aesthetically to contemplate. I can sense similar satisfaction in the process of architectural design; when, for instance, the old order of separate systems which hold up a building and make it thermally comfortable is superseded by one system of more eloquent simplicity.

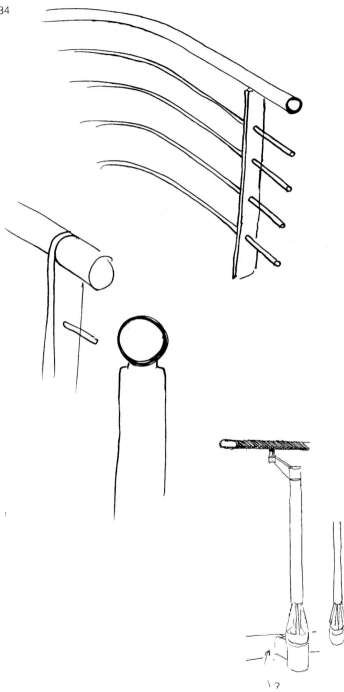

1

2

5

6

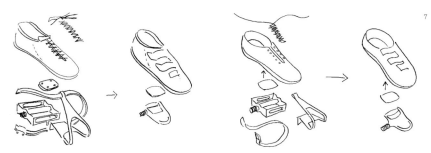

Our conversation continued, branching out in a multitude of directions. One thought linked the evolution of these bindings to competitive cycle racing, rather in the way that motor racing has extended the frontiers of aerodynamics, braking systems, or electronic monitoring of the engine – all of which, in turn, have been fed back into the family car. Another thought concerned the question of technology transfer. Surely the initiative for these bindings had come out of the ski equipment industry? Had this been initiated by sports racing with its links to the commercial competition of the open market? Then there was the game of styling and the dangers of muddling true innovation with pastiche. Wasn't the 'go faster' image of tack-on car spoilers like the worst excesses of so-called architectural 'High-Tech' – both equally gratuitous?

Another thought concerned the funding of research and development programmes, which are commonplace in industry. We already take for granted the many down-to-earth 'spin-offs' from the space race. Unlike the world of industrial production, however, architectural innovation has to be dependent on one individual project, often conceived in competitive circumstances, to generate new ideas. Such special projects become the architectural equivalent of commercial research and development programmes: if they are sometimes individually expensive, surely they should be measured in the context of the wider total market?

Although I referred earlier to the design of handrails being like a building in miniature, the difference of scale can affect the means of realisation. For the larger-scale structure of a building, the architect is largely dependent on the engineer for modelling, calculations and eventual sizing of its members. A handrail, like furniture, can with advantage lend itself to more empirical methods. I recall on the Willis Faber building our vision of the balustrades around the central escalator-well being a minimal vertical cantilever of toughened glass. The concept was proved by suspending, pendulum-like, a bag of sand equivalent to the weight of a large adult alongside a mock-up of the proposed balustrade. This was then swung violently to collide with the glass sheet, which – despite extreme distortion – withstood the most frenzied attacks by the sandbag. It was dramatic proof to the client, building inspector and ourselves that the idea was sound. The final touch was to add a handrail as protection to the exposed glass edge which, if hit by a sharp object, might have fractured. This handrail was designed to relate to that on

9

537

the moving part of the escalator and was slightly soft and generous, encouraging people to lean with their arms on the rail at the edge of the atrium.

I am reminded of Paul MacCready's description of how his man-powered aircraft was designed. Successive versions of this craft were built, each being progressively strengthened where the earlier version had failed under flight testing. Only when a version withstood its required loading was the structure considered correct – any more would have been excessive; anything less, a failure.

The cycle ride meandered in the same way as this conversation until we stopped for a drink in the square of Valbonne. Normally quiet out of the holiday season, the town was alive with the noisy activity of a local cycle race. We had now become spectators, removed from the direct experience of cycling and able to see the harmony between the riders and their machines. This is more than just a physical synergy; there are also visual links between the clothes, equipment and trim. Together, they have the same kind of sparse beauty that I find so moving in the best aircraft.

The start of the race is a flurry of excitement as the competitors commence the first of five circuits, following the motorcycle that will clear the path ahead of them. At the end of the first circuit a clear leader has emerged breaking ahead of the field. As the race progresses his lead increases by seconds, but remarkably he makes it all look so easy; dancing up the hills while the rest seem to strain. It reminds me of those professionals, as diverse as pilots, athletes or even designers, who are so accomplished that they actually make their task look simple – like these new pedal bindings, which look so obvious and direct you wonder why it took so long for them to evolve. But then such simplicity is really quite deceptive.

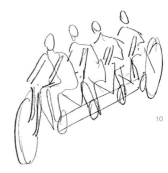

10

Handrails and Bicycles

'Both flight and design involve unseen forces, obey certain rules and for their realisation depend totally on communication.'

Norman Foster

The flight described here brought together three people whose personal inter-action was to help realise the first of a series of monographs on our work. Otl Aicher, in Germany, was the architect of the book and his involvement was an act of friendship. Ian Lambot, from Hong Kong, was the book's publisher and editor; if it were a building project then he would have been both client and contractor.

The flight of a modern aeroplane can be seen as a metaphor for design – the design of a book, of a building or of a piece of furniture. Both flight and design involve unseen forces, obey certain rules, and for their realisation depend totally on communication.

Otl has the concept for a series of documents that will communicate at sev-eral levels; a hierarchy of information in which the reader can scan a visual story or delve deeper through the medium of the written word. Otl is also concerned to reveal the processes behind the work, to show the relationship of drawings, mod-els and prototypes to the final product. He is interested in the comparison between informal sketches, as ideas made visible, and the more formal language of commu-nication that evolves as responsibilities transfer from the private to the public realm.

The book, like the buildings it portrays, is a team effort, initially orchestrated by Otl, then later by Ian in his role as editor. Activities alternate between a studio in Rotis, southern Germany, where Otl lives and works, and a studio in Wiltshire in the West Country of England. Joint working sessions might last a week or just a single intensive day. Spaces are 'wallpapered' with mock-ups of page layouts so the book can be viewed as a continuous sequence or examined a single page at a time. The disciplines that Otl sets as a designer seem initially quite rigid, but as the work proceeds it becomes evident that they provide an overall order within which there is almost infinite scope for choice and variation. Otl's selective eye always seems to be guided by a strong inner philosophy.

The book as a project appears suspended in space and time. At Rotis, Otl, who has a passion for history, provides insights into the past culture of Schwabia and its strong Celtic traditions, which also happen to permeate the West Country of England. The intensity of design activity in Wiltshire is interspersed by long walks to view the prehistoric Ridgeway and Silbury Hill, and the White Horse at Uffington. We speculate that the ancient fortifications of the Ridgeway were part

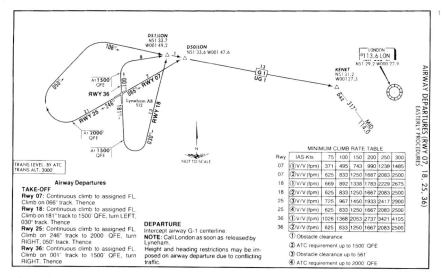

DS1/LON
N51 33.7
W001 49.2

D50/LON
N51 33.6 W001 47.6

106°

LONDON
113.6 LON
N51 29.2 W000 27.9

KENET
N51 31.2
W001 27.3

042° 317°

MID 114.0

B

At 1500'
QFE

RWY 36

050°

246° 181°

RWY 25

066° RWY 07

Lyneham AB
512

RWY 18

030°

At 2000'
QFE

At 1500'
QFE

N
NOT TO SCALE

G 1
UG 1

AIRWAY DEPARTURES (RWY 07, 18, 25, 36)
EASTERLY PROCEDURES

TRANS LEVEL: BY ATC
TRANS ALT: 3000'

Airway Departures

TAKE-OFF
Rwy 07: Continuous climb to assigned FL. Climb on 066° track. Thence
Rwy 18: Continuous climb to assigned FL. Climb on 181° track to 1500' QFE, turn LEFT, 030° track. Thence
Rwy 25: Continuous climb to assigned FL. Climb on 246° track to 2000 QFE, turn RIGHT, 050° track. Thence
Rwy 36: Continuous climb to assigned FL. Climb on 001° track to 1500' QFE, turn RIGHT. Thence

DEPARTURE
Intercept airway G-1 centerline.
NOTE: Call London as soon as released by Lyneham.
Height and heading restrictions may be imposed on airway departure due to conflicting traffic.

MINIMUM CLIMB RATE TABLE

Rwy	IAS-Kts	75	100	150	200	250	300
07	① V/V (fpm)	371	495	743	990	1238	1485
07	② V/V (fpm)	625	833	1250	1667	2083	2500
18	① V/V (fpm)	669	892	1338	1783	2229	2675
18	② V/V (fpm)	625	833	1250	1667	2083	2500
25	③ V/V (fpm)	725	967	1450	1933	2417	2900
25	④ V/V (fpm)	625	833	1250	1667	2083	2500
36	① V/V (fpm)	1026	1368	2053	2737	3421	4105
36	② V/V (fpm)	625	833	1250	1667	2083	2500

① Obstacle clearance
② ATC requirement up to 1500' QFE
③ Obstacle clearance up to 561'
④ ATC requirement up to 2000 QFE

of a defensive system protecting an ancient 'Silicon Valley', for here was the high technology of the day, a source of flint for tools and armaments.

This flight connects these two locations in England and Germany. Ian and I leave Lyneham, a military airbase in Wiltshire, to spend the day with Otl. Although it is a private flight in a small aircraft, it will share the same airspace and operate within the same instrument flight rules as the big jets flying scheduled services. After take-off at dawn, the aircraft, still climbing, passes 7,000 feet to join controlled airspace: a world in which rules, procedures and instrumentation follow internationally agreed standards. The climb to its requested flight level is stepped to fit into the early morning rush-hour traffic, which is now building up around Heathrow and Gatwick.

The aircraft, more than any building so far conceived, is environmentally self-sufficient. At 37,000 feet, with the capacity to climb higher, its occupants shuffle papers and go through the ritual of morning coffee while contemplating the incredible beauty of bright sun and limitless blue sky. This is the poetic and understated component of its performance. The aircraft is now a vessel pressurised to simulate conditions close to those at sea level. With its own sealed air supply, it is comfortably warm despite an outside air temperature more than 60 degrees below freezing.

Safe passage and compatibility with other traffic on this three-dimensional aerial highway, called Upper Green One, is assured by a language of communication which transcends political and cultural barriers. The *en route* charts, with their related arrival and departure procedures, are models of graphic clarity designed for rapid and unambiguous access by the crew and their ground-based counterparts. As the flight proceeds, control is handed over from British to Dutch and, eventually, German centres; the combination of radar, radio and the flight-plan, which was filed some hours earlier, ensures that this event is part of an invisible

2

global network (1, 2). Just over an hour from departure the aircraft descends through cloud, passing 5,000 feet, to leave the relative protection of controlled airspace and, as visual contact is established with the ground, the flight enters the domain of visual flight rules. Here the onus to avoid conflicting traffic passes from the ground controller back to the pilot, on the basis of seeing and being seen. Navigation, which has so far been by electronic aids, is now by eye as ground features are interpreted on a topographical chart showing roads, railways, water and the like to scale – quite different from the graphic abstractions associated with instrument flight rules.

Leutkirch, the destination airfield, comes into view as a single short runway in rolling green countryside: its identity is confirmed from the charts by the relationship of roads and the nearby town. After throttling back and negotiating a visual circuit of the field, the aircraft touches down to complete the flight. Unlike the standard international airport, everything here is simple, direct and friendly – Otl can be seen waiting by his car almost as soon as the aircraft turns off the runway. The arrival formalities are minimal and the group is soon on its way to Rotis.

It is worth comparing the simplicity of the very first airfields with the complexity that we now take for granted in large international airports. Is it merely size that turns airports into those anonymous mazes which are so hostile to users, or can a fresh design strategy recapture the friendly immediacy and orientation of a place like Leutkirch? It seems necessary to keep going back to first principles to question such preconceptions, and historical models are often a valuable inspiration.

However, the lessons from aviation for architecture are not confined to those buildings that host the aircraft and their users: they are operational, concerned with how people work together, as much as technological. An air traffic system has a relatively simple objective: the safe passage of an aircraft from one place to

another. Despite the diversity of professions and interests that are involved – nations, airlines, manufacturers, controllers, pilots, unions and so on – the existence of a shared language of communication with the agreed procedures ensures the achievement of that safe passage.

Similarly, the design process involves many disparate interests and disciplines – clients; architects and surveyors; structural, civil, mechanical and electrical engineers – as well as a host of political and regulatory bodies. Each of these is likely to have its own technical and cultural aspirations and is lacking in any shared language of communication. Even the single line schematics of one of the engineering professions will be incomprehensible to an engineer from a different background. Certainly the education of each skill will have paid scant, if any, respect to the existence of others involved in the total process. Given this state of affairs, one of the earliest tasks on a project is to design operating structures and evolve methods of communication which will unite the separate interests in commonly shared objectives. Only then can the creative process be unleashed.

If all the interests involved are not united in their endeavours then weaknesses become apparent, whether in air traffic networks or the design of buildings. As traffic densities increase, newer technologies emerge to cope with the increased flows, but junctions with earlier systems threaten the total network. Europe, for example, currently has sophisticated computer-managed systems, but each extends only within the limits of its own national boundaries. It is not uncommon for the links between systems to be dependent still on an outdated telephone system. The result is a wasteful and inefficient redundancy of overlapping capabilities

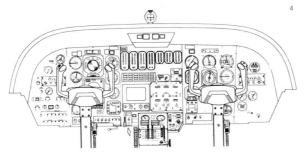

rather than a totally optimised single system. The same dilemmas can appear in the design of a complex building where the weak links are junctions between old and new technologies. These can be the outcome of involving many specialists, each with his or her own area of expertise. In the absence of a shared vision, the result will be a complexity of individual systems each superimposed on the other. The opportunity for a single system of more elegant simplicity will have been lost.

The barriers to a single European traffic network are the politics of national pride. Similarly, the barriers to creating the best design for a building are likely to be the pride of one profession competing for its share of the total, rather than combining its skills in the more worthwhile search for a philosophy of integration. Perhaps this is at the heart of the difference between truly creative teamwork and design by committee.

Both air traffic networks and buildings, like any other human endeavour, have their share of failures; arguably these are inevitable as techniques evolve over time to cope with the stress of seemingly rapid growth and change. It is virtually taken for granted that the way forward to higher levels of safety in air traffic control will eventually be achieved by the reasoned application of new technologies. The same tendencies are apparent in the hardware of flight itself as quieter, more energy-efficient aircraft become available. There is clear potential for the same pattern of progress in architecture, and the world of aviation has much to offer in technology transfer. In these circumstances, there is a certain irony in the proposition that failures in architecture could be redeemed by harking back to a falsely nostalgic vision of the past. That would be akin to suggesting that the difficulties of patrolling the skies by radar should lead back to navigation by road maps. Both propositions are equally absurd.

'It was Wendy who polarised the discussion in her characteristically uncompromising manner: how could you possibly have your heart in a scheme that you knew was not the best one?

Norman Foster

In 1963 I returned to England, after studying and working in the United States, to join Richard Rogers and two architect sisters, Georgie and Wendy Cheesman. We formed a practice based in Wendy's London flat, called Team 4 Architects, which lasted some four years before there was a parting of the ways. Almost from our first meeting Wendy and I had become inseparable, so there was a certain inevitability in our forming a new practice together: after much agonising we chose to call it Foster Associates. The name, with its overtones of a larger plurality, was a gesture of confidence in an uncertain future. Not only were there no associates, there were no commissions to build either.

The first Team 4 projects were mostly for friends and relations. It is only now, looking back, that one can marvel at the courage of those clients, as they subjected themselves to a level of social idealism that was matched only by our lack of real experience. Perhaps the most important asset for a designer, though, is the ability to recognise and accept the limits of personal knowledge, because this leads to the process of posing the right questions to the right people. In those early days this was a relatively slow and linear process, rooted in traditional trades and attitudes. However, the factory for Reliance Controls, which spanned the break up of Team 4 and the formation of Foster Associates, extended this challenge by introducing the commercial reality of time − in addition to financial and engineering constraints − as a fixed and limited resource. It set the stage for a way of working that has since become second nature.

Although all of Team 4's work received wide publicity and even national awards, we were still locked into a vicious circle: without the right kind of work to show, we lacked credibility; but how could we demonstrate credibility without first being given the opportunities? By the middle of 1968, after nearly a year occupied with small-scale conversion work and part-time teaching, Wendy and I − now with two very small sons − were talking about emigrating to a more receptive and open society. In the event, an established contact with the Fred Olsen company in London's Docklands came to the rescue. After long months of 'stop-go' − in competition not against other architects, but with contractors offering a package deal of 'design and build' − Fred Olsen decided to commission us to design his new buildings, a decision which became a major turning-point for us and was pivotal in establishing Foster Associates.

The buildings that arose from this commission were born out of painstaking research into the operational processes of the company and the hardware of its ships, but they were also realised on extremely short timescales. The structures were later to be visited by clients such as Sir Robert and Lady Sainsbury, IBM and Willis Faber & Dumas. These visits were to prove instrumental in securing new opportunities for the future.

When the senior management of Willis Faber came to see the buildings, the outgoing chairman, Johnny Roscoe, was accompanied by Julian Faber, who was soon to take over from him. I introduced them to Mike Thompson, then the dock manager, who was later to become a director of the Olsen company. We sat down in the open office space, contemplating the activities around us, the paintings from Fred Olsen's personal collection that adorned the walls, and the ships beyond.

Johnny Roscoe, an outspoken individual, came quickly to the point: 'Well, is he any good?' he said, pointing at me. Mike Thompson squirmed with embarrassment and I got up to try to leave them to a private conversation. The chairman, persistent and visibly impatient, waved all this aside. Mike Thompson then entered into the spirit of the interrogation and conceded that, perhaps, I rated an 'A minus'. 'That's fine,' was the reply. 'Anything better and I wouldn't have believed it, anything less and it wouldn't be good enough.' Fred Olsen put it a different way – when quizzed about me he said simply: 'He asks the right questions.'

Trying to talk about those early days reminds me that some years ago, Wendy was supposed to have written an equivalent piece. I teased her then about what she might write. 'I'll say that you are a juggler,' she replied. 'You throw the balls higher than anybody else, and you let them fall lower before catching them.' That analogy is appropriate in trying to explain the component of time in the design process, and is perhaps best illustrated by another anecdote. It offers insights into the design process that are as fresh and relevant to us today as they were then.

It was the summer of 1975 and design work was progressing well on the Sainsbury Centre for Visual Arts, planned for the University of East Anglia. We proposed to integrate all the activities – public galleries for the collection donated by Sir Robert and Lady Sainsbury, as well as academic facilities – in one unifying enclosure. This had been greeted initially with some scepticism because it challenged the preconception of a group of separate buildings. However, the principal parties to the venture had been united in this direction and there was a genuine excitement about the richer mix of cultures that would exist under the same roof. After many revisions as the project evolved, the design had finally settled down. The scheme had been approved by the client, the university and the planning authority, and everyone was relatively relaxed.

Behind the scenes, however, we as architects were struggling to resolve the detailed planning. Despite our best endeavours, the clarity of the open galleries was always compromised by the need for solid cores containing boilers, mechanical equipment, toilets and the like. In some ways it was one of the classic challenges in modern architecture: how to handle the relationship between free flexible space and the fixed elements such as toilets, kitchens and mechanical plant. Late in the day, however, we suddenly seized upon a new and exciting solution: by creating a double layer of wall and roof, the space in between could absorb the secondary functions, thereby leaving the primary spaces free and uncluttered. The double wall also had important environmental benefits, shielding the interior from solar gain and reducing the amount of energy required to service the spaces.

In our minds it was as if the original concept had suddenly flowered. It seemed like a new vision. In some ways the scheme responded to many of the directions that had surfaced at the regular design team meetings, but which we had so far failed to express in three dimensions. We rapidly explored the new idea through drawings and study models, which more than confirmed our expectations. To anybody who had felt the pulse of the project it was the culmination of all the work that had gone before.

At the next of our regular design team meetings with all the key individuals involved – architects, engineers and cost consultants – we unveiled the new proposals. As the full implications of the change became apparent, the mood of the meeting became very strained. The shift was so dramatic that it was apparent that it would entail a complete redesign of the structure and cladding. This was a dilemma. Everybody accepted that it was an infinitely better scheme. But dare we put the completion date at risk and threaten the goodwill and confidence of the client by proposing such far-reaching changes at such a late stage? Or should we forge ahead with the existing scheme, knowing that a significantly improved version existed, even if it was only in the mind and on scraps of paper and polystyrene?

To hold to the original date for starting on site would require a supreme effort by everyone. It would require the complete reworking of the many specialist drawings and schedules. Tony Hunt, a good friend and talented engineer whose firm has been responsible for the structures of many of our projects, shared everyone's sentiments. But he suggested that we should maintain our course, save these new directions for some future project, and complete the building to the original design.

It was Wendy who polarised the discussion in her characteristically uncompromising manner: how could you possibly have your heart in a scheme that you knew was not the best one? Furthermore, when it came to the next opportunity, we would all have moved on to newer ideas – each scheme had to be the best thing we could achieve at the time, so 'let's do it now'. By the time the meeting broke up, several hours later, Tony Hunt was already exploring the potential of a new prismatic structure and related panel geometry, which he had begun to sketch out; the services engineers were excited by the prospect of using the space within the structure; and the cost consultants could even see the scope for some savings in the equation.

Within a week of further intensive work, the clients had been persuaded of the new scheme's merits, the university had been consulted and a new application had been submitted for planning permission. All the original tender dates were held and the building works started on site on schedule. Looking back it was obviously the right course of action and no party to the project would ever disagree. In terms of the logistics of striving for the ultimate achievable quality within the fixes of time and cost, it was a supreme juggling act.

I tell the story for several reasons, which would be easy to take for granted, but which may not be so obvious to the reader. Firstly, it illustrates the importance of getting to the core of a situation. Wendy's pithy interventions always brought clarity to our thinking; sometimes only afterwards did this seem obvious and inevitable. But her role in the practice was much wider than her work on the projects. Reticently, behind the scenes, at so many important stages in the evolution of the practice, she was a strong and creative driving force, often sensing the need for change in the spaces we occupied and provoking appropriate actions – but always with kindness and a sense of humour that could verge on the mischievous. All of us took for granted her refusal to compromise on quality in everything the practice did: not just the architecture, but even down to the small things, such as the way a slice of bread might be served. Without Wendy, there would never have been a Foster Associates.

Secondly, the design evolution of our projects is rarely a simple linear route; the process is far more circuitous than might be imagined. Although our tools have become more sophisticated with the introduction of computer modelling, the evolution of a design is still as pragmatic as ever. The computer, like the pencil, is only as good as the person directing it. There is no doubt that the Sainsbury Centre, having undergone that final struggle, emerged as a visually simpler entity. But such simplicity can be deceptive, because the hidden circuitry behind those double walls proved to be far more responsive to the needs of the building and its users than the earlier versions of the design. I still wonder at the contrast between the simplicity of the end product and the complexity of the explorations and debate that led up to it.

The third point to be drawn is that the most important relationship behind any building is that between architect and client. When I went to see Sir Robert and Lady Sainsbury to explain our radical new ideas for the building, like the consultants, their first reaction was one of anxiety: 'Not again!' – how could we propose more changes just as everyone had grown accustomed to the scheme? I urged them to consider the new scheme on its merits; after all, had they too not been responsible for changes during the evolution of the project? Had we not jointly agreed that we would strive to achieve the best possible building within the allotted time and cost? Twenty-four hours later we had a further meeting together and all the implications were set out in painstaking detail. The outcome was an even greater shared sense of purpose and enthusiasm for this new direction.

Over the years Sir Robert and Lady Sainsbury have become valued friends. But throughout our working relationship, their professionalism in the role of client remained undiminished. I can still recall the study tour of galleries in Europe and the United States that Wendy and I made with them at the outset of the project. It was something of a research marathon. Only much later did I discover that each couple had, at the time, confided to their friends that they had difficulty in keeping up the pace set by the others! That tour marked the start of a dialogue based on a common language of standards. No two projects are alike, and the same can be

said for those people who commission them, whether they are individuals, corporate bodies or entrepreneurs. But the most successful projects share to some degree that quality of enlightened concern called patronage – and the Sainsburys were a role model.

Moving forward to the present, the teams now associated with the office, like those of the past, extend from a design-based core to embrace clients, users and a network of consultants and manufacturers. In the larger, more complex projects, which have evolved progressively from the earlier works, it is sometimes necessary to first design operational structures to bring the right people into the process at the right point in time; without a clear definition of needs, there is no basis on which to design. But often an honest 'don't know' is a far more precise acknowledgement of the reality of a situation than some spurious attempt to quantify an unknown future. Unlike the design of artefacts, buildings are conceived in the present for a volatile future but, culturally, they cannot be separated from the context of the past.

Despite the differences between architecture and artefacts it can be helpful to draw comparisons to illustrate a point. Consider the helicopter for example (3, 4). To fly a helicopter you have four controls. In front of the pilot is a stick called the cyclic; you push it forward to go forwards, back to go backwards, to the side to go sideways and so on. Next to the seat is a lever called the collective; you lift it up to ascend and push it down to descend. Depending on the movements of the helicopter it will require continuous adjustments of power, which in the most basic models is achieved by a twist-grip throttle on the end of the collective stick; you wind it up for more power and release it for less. All these control inputs act on the main rotor, which is overhead. Finally, the pilot's feet can move pedals connected to the tail rotor, which enables the helicopter to swivel on its own axis.

The helicopter, unlike a fixed wing aircraft, can describe almost any three-dimensional sequence of movement in space. To do so involves the movement of all the controls simultaneously; the adjustment of one input has consequences for all the others. You can pick apart the theory of this on paper or on a blackboard, but until the physical coordination of all these variables together, at the same time, becomes second nature, you simply cannot fly the machine. The relationship between the four controls is totally interactive.

To return to the design team and the issue of posing the right questions. If the development of a design is seen as a dynamic process in time, then all the variables – for example, massing, materials, inside, outside, structure, heating, lighting, cooling, cost, time – are, like the control inputs to that helicopter, entirely interactive. You cannot change one without affecting some or all of the others. To be able to pose the vital questions and assess the consequences requires a team of specialists who can come together and who are, each in their own way, able to share a vision.

The Sainsbury Centre story tells us something about the nature of communication and the way that individuals interact. It is the camaraderie and chemistry between members of the team that make such heroic efforts possible. I described a situation that was transparent in its openness; if the new idea had not been strong enough, it might well not have survived that cross-examination by the team. But when the idea took root, it was creatively expanded by everyone sparking off each other. The longer the participants are immersed in the design process, the easier it becomes for them to reshape the project at what might seem the eleventh hour. There is nothing capricious in this: it is merely optimising the shared knowledge of the team and using the resource of available time to its best advantage.

There is the potential for misunderstanding in all this. Such an approach is far removed from the grey world of design by committee. Although each individual may become committed to a common point of view, it is the personal chemistry and mutual respect within the team that enables anyone to challenge anything and everything in a forum that is open and volatile, but essentially sympathetic: nothing is too sacred. It is the opposite of much that has been academically taught. Although strong leadership is important, the architect is not handing down from above, passing the parcel to the specialists who wait in line to be told what to do. Each individual has the potential for a creative input. Paradoxically, the architect comes closer to the heart of the project because he is integrated into the 'how and why' of the making of the building. So the process extends out from the architect's studio, to the workplace where real people are making real things. And this must be right, because surely the essence of our culture is the making of things.

I told only part of the aviation story; flying is of course a much more complex interplay of all the senses. Aviation, like architecture, is also subject to legislation and prejudice. The flight can be tracked, via hidden lines of command, by controllers on the ground; they have the legal right of authority, although the ultimate responsibility is still said to rest with the pilot. When disasters occur, whether in airborne or ground-based structures, they provide a field-day for the media. The various parties are individually pilloried with scant regard for the totality of the system that caused the disaster, and of which they form an integral part. A flight, like a building, is only the visible tip of a vast iceberg of infrastructure.

When I fly an aircraft I can, in the same way that I analyse architecture, rationalise the event. Such factors as weight, load capacity, speed, range, fuel consumption and cruising altitude can be quantified into flight times and cost factors. I can even explain an aerobatic flight with blackboard theory. But striving to produce a graceful three-dimensional sequence of manoeuvres in space requires not only a grand decision but also continuous in-flight decisions to refine the performance. The poetic ingredient of flight can lie close to the surface, even if it never emerges in conversation. In the same spirit, every decision in the design of a building is touched not only by reason but also by those intangible and poetic influences. Although unspoken, and often taken for granted, it is this fusion which may explain my own passion for architecture. Like any love affair it is difficult to separate the heart from the mind.

Wendy's response at that design team meeting of 'let's do it now', with the emphasis on the *now*, also explains much about the nature of the practice then and today. I recall my spontaneous dash to the United States when British industry could not produce the goods to maintain the tight time schedule on the Olsen project. It never occurred to me to wait for time-consuming authorisations. Taking the initiative to solve the problem rather than proffering apologies was very much in the spirit of 'doing it now'. That approach possibly explains the cross-section of the present office – with an average age of just 30, and commanding almost as many languages – as well as the early integration of other skills, especially model-making. It is also about the endless quest to improve a working lifestyle.

I am reminded of a group who recently visited our studios, which overlook the Thames. 'Where do you work?' I was asked. I explained that I had the same space as anybody else at one of the long work-benches. 'But why don't you have your own office?' I was asked, almost in disbelief. I tried to explain that it was exactly what I

5

did have, but I shared it with everyone else – I could never have had a space as grand as that just for myself. What I did not say was that the space was symbolic of the team. This has nothing to do with any theoretical attitude: it is simply a good place to be, to work alongside inspirational people. This grand dimension has taken many years to realise but, like all previous spaces that we have occupied, it was envisaged well ahead by Wendy when she identified the present site of Riverside. It is sad that she did not live to see it realised, but I am sure that she approves.

'I have witnessed a culture
of technological success in
the field of space exploration
that is elevated to a level
of spirituality.'

Norman Foster

Why is it impossible to get the toast at the same time as the eggs? And if this is 'mission impossible' for the best restaurants and hotels on the planet, what hope would there ever be of getting hot toast, hot eggs and hot coffee all together at the table at the same time? What is going to make this frustration worse – exploding with impatience? Trying to catch the eye of a waiter who can see everything except the frantic signs that you are making? I can tell you. It's the head waiter – a student of human behaviour who models himself on the worst of his clientele. He not only believes that theirs is the way to behave – it has become a part of him. He is far too grand to actually look at you as he takes an order or listens to your complaint – his eyes are focused on a far more worthy subject somewhere between the opposite wall and the ceiling. His face is frozen – no undignified gestures such as a smile or a hint of welcome or sympathy. Maybe the slightest lift of the chin combined with a raising of the eyebrows.

I could make a long list of such frustrations, but on the sliding scale of this F-word these are short-term affairs. The worst big-league frustrations can last days. Like whodunnits, the main plot has innumerable sub-plots, which themselves would fill a book. There is space here only for a potted version of one such frustration.

This one is set in the Mission Control Centre of Energia, the Soviet agency responsible for space travel, close to Moscow. Together with David Nelson, one of my partners, I have been invited to research a project for them and our visit coincides with the launch of a Japanese cosmonaut to a manned space station. I am well equipped to document our trip with one of those battery-driven, electronically gadgeted cameras – which just happens to choose this trip for its battery to expire.

Remember the good old days of finger driven cameras, wind-up car windows that you could move with a little handle conveniently on the door, and radios with a knob and a dial? Far too simple.

Anyway, 'no problem' say our Russian hosts. A car is summoned and we are off on a hunt-the-battery chase. We go from store to store; we find some boarded up and shuttered after spending hours in traffic to find them. Those that are trading are stocked to overflowing with everything that any consumer paradise could offer – everything, that is, except a battery that will fit this camera.

This is becoming an obsession. We start again the next day fresh for the challenge. Several stores down the list we strike success. The battery is found.

Unfortunately to acquire the battery you have to acquire the camera that goes with it – identical to the one hanging on my shoulder but accessible only to a rouble billionaire (and there are many of them in evidence).

By now I have lost the opportunity to record the extraordinary events that had been taking place between these excursions. I have witnessed a culture of technological success in the field of space exploration that is elevated to a level of spirituality. There is none of the ritual countdowns, the '9 8 7 6 5 4 ...' stuff. Here the understatement belies professionalism of extraordinary proportions. The lift-off is witnessed – the times forecast for the hazardous phase of the mission in hours, minutes and seconds. The audience drifts off to coffee and conversation. There are meetings with ex-cosmonauts turned artists, environmentalists, politicians, saviours of the planet – intelligent and gentle supermen. We go back to witness the critical phase, like people arriving just before the curtain rises, to see a theatre of life and death being played out in outer space. The docking takes place, razor-edged but rendered routine. What could possibly eclipse this experience?

I persuade our hosts that to research our potential project properly we have to see how the cosmonauts train. Rank in this organisation is signified by the number of telephones in an individual's office. We rise up the hierarchy and reach the office of a one-man telephone exchange. We receive clearance to penetrate Space City – an experience that was to render any James Bond film pedestrian by comparison.

We must have a camera that works. There is now a desperate sense of urgency. I give my camera to our Russian hosts – they who alone on this planet have sustained life in outer space year after year aboard the most sophisticated autonomous environments yet devised by man. *Please* make my little camera work!

Well, defeat has to be admitted. Face is lost but I battle on to the end. We summon a car – back to consumer paradise and hard-pressed for time. A small traditional Russian camera is bought at a shocking price that in London would buy the most exotic state-of-the-art trap for any 35mm film. It is boxed down to the detail of a shoulder strap, with no silly nonsense of battery drive – a real camera, which you can advance manually. I leave the shop – back to the hotel – unwrap it – congratulate myself – load it – eyeball the view finder – but wait – there's something not quite right. You guessed it. This camera is coupled to a light meter driven by a battery – and guess what is missing?

2

3

'Investing in infrastructure is rather like designing a building: you cannot do it without a clien organisation to tell you what they need. Similarly, I do not believe you can design transport infrastructure without a political infrastructure to play the same supporting role.'

Norman Foster

I want to talk about my work as an architect and a planner, and the work of the hundred-strong, multi-disciplinary team to which I belong. I shall address the issue of the European Community and the coming of the single European market, but I want to try to do so by way of our own experience, gained through working on projects here and on the Continent.

I would like to begin by describing two projects in Britain. One is the recently completed passenger terminal at Stansted Airport; the other is the ongoing planning project for a new rail transport interchange and redevelopment at King's Cross. In their way, both projects have a European dimension and both were dominated by the same issues: each has a history; each required a return to first principles; and each forms part of a continuing search for more environmentally sensitive ways to build in the future.

To take history first – surprisingly, the design of the new terminal at Stansted was strongly influenced by history, even though the history of air transport is short. Only 50 years ago, for example, Heathrow Airport was nothing more than a military airfield surrounded by open countryside (1). During the next decade it expanded its passenger operations and became London's principal airport, with the more distant Gatwick playing a supporting role. Yet even then, as early as 1953, when a transatlantic flight from Heathrow in a piston-engined Lockheed Constellation (2) was an ordeal that lasted between seventeen and twenty hours, the need for a third London airport had already been identified and Stansted had been proposed as the site for it.

It is here that a European comparison first comes to mind. In France, Charles de Gaulle – the third Paris airport – was not proposed until 1965, more than a decade after Stansted, and yet it began operations in 1974 after a delay of some nine years. Stansted will finally begin operations next month after a delay of nearly 40 years – a delay compounded by three public enquiries, three reports and one false start at another site, Foulness.

The first heavier-than-air flight took place in 1903 and the basic principles of the airport were established soon after. An aerial photograph of Candlas Field, Atlanta, taken in 1925, shows a large area of grass where the aircraft landed and took off; a dirt road used by arriving and departing vehicles; and a shed between the two. There were no 'orientation problems'.

The simplicity of the Atlanta layout makes an interesting comparison with contemporary Heathrow, which looks more like a new town or shopping centre. It is not a place where orientation is obvious. Visitors depend on announcements and graphic sign language to help them move around. You almost need a guide dog.

One of the questions that we asked ourselves at the beginning of the design process was: notwithstanding the complexity of any modern international airport, how far could we get back to the simple logic of the early arrangement? This question informed the shape of our response.

Two images are of interest here. The first shows a photomontage of our proposed terminal at a very early stage to demonstrate its environmental impact (5); the second shows the actual building under construction from the same viewpoint (6). The tree-planting programme at Stansted has been enormous, but the principal means of diminishing the terminal's visual impact was not tree planting but earth movement, a technique which permitted what is actually a two-storey building to appear as a single-storey building from outside.

The model we presented to the board of the British Airports Authority in 1982 and the principle it established held good. You approach the terminal walking towards the aircraft, which you can see, while your baggage is processed through the lower level. One advantage of the simplicity of this arrangement was the way in which direct rail access from Liverpool Street station could be integrated into the building after construction had started, by using the subterranean floor. Over time, as the design progressed, the flat roof started to undulate and it is now supported by a tree-like formation of columns (8), but it is still very close in spirit to the original idea. There is an airfield and a big shed with an access road with car and coach parking in front of it.

The roof at Stansted is unique in its transparency as well as its single level. Its design is dedicated to natural light, with a proportion of the surface glazed to let sunlight in, and 'daylight reflectors' inside that bounce the light back up on to the sculptural shape of the ceiling (7). At night, artificial light achieves the same effect. This arrangement is quite different to more conventional airport terminals of recent years, such as Terminal Four at Heathrow, where the ductwork, suspended ceilings, roof-mounted air-conditioning units and fluorescent lighting involve a lot of structural and servicing redundancy and a great absence of natural light.

All the heavy servicing equipment mounted on the roofs of conventional airport buildings has to be repaired and replaced frequently without the airport itself being closed down. Yet it is actually in the wrong place for easy access. At Stansted we have located all the heavy equipment on the ground where it can be most easily handled. So the unobstructed roof at Stansted is not only about the poetry of natural light, it is also about logistical efficiency.

If Stansted is about space, light and calm in an airport context, I think it achieves these goals in the same way as did the great transport structures of the railway age. The clear spans at Stansted are 36 metres; at Lewis Cubitt's King's Cross station, built in 1852, they were 32 metres. Nineteen years later, William Barlow's great train shed at St Pancras spanned 74 metres, the largest single-span structure in the world at that time.

This comparison brings me to the second major project that I would like to talk about – the proposed redevelopment of King's Cross. The site is a 134-acre stretch of railway land, created by the commercial rivalry between two railway companies in the nineteenth century and running north from their two stations (4). Our planning proposal for the same area has been generated in its turn, if you like, by the railway renaissance that is set to come with the completion of the Channel Tunnel. Our project includes commercial development and a park as the central feature (3), but the driving force is the new international rail terminal itself. An immense task separates these two images. As architects and planners we are only one of a hundred consultancies working on this project, and the programme allows three-and-a-half years of design work before construction even begins.

It is easy to put up a sign saying: 'It could be the only home they ever own'. It is even easier to say: 'Let's build in the Green Belt because it's less difficult there than in the inner city.' But that is not the answer to the problem. There are vast areas of derelict land in inner London, and King's Cross is typical of them in terms of the difficulties it presents. Our masterplan attempts to tackle the issues of inner-city development without taking any of the easy options. It is an immense challenge. How did we approach it?

We began at King's Cross, as we began at Stansted, with a search for the roots of the development. We considered the history of the site, its heritage buildings, the listed gas holders and the intractable canal and railway infrastructure.

Then we considered the urban grain of the surrounding areas. London has its own urban tissue, quite distinct from that of other cities, whether Barcelona, Amsterdam, Washington, Paris or New York. London is permeated with green areas. A ride in a double-decker bus will show you Islington Green, Hampstead Heath, St James's Park, Primrose Hill, Shepherd's Bush – they are all green spaces, large, small, varied, different.

Then if you look at the original King's Cross site, with its canal winding across, and peel away the layers of subsequent railway development, you begin to see how you might bring back some of those freshwater basins in their original form – adapt them for leisure, or use them as a focus for housing. Then the housing could be integrated with offices and slowly a strategy emerges that might knit all these elements together to create a unified community around a 34-acre park, a new addition to London's historical green spaces and probably the first of such a size to be created in over a hundred years.

The focus of the King's Cross development is the rail terminal at its southern tip. In one sense it is the heart of the whole enterprise; in another, it is an entirely separate exercise with a different client – British Rail. The form of the terminal we have proposed was generated by the geometry of the two great nineteenth-century rail termini on the site. It sits between them without touching either – respecting them as historical buildings in their own right. At the same time it opens up new vistas of both these buildings which have, for generations, been blocked by a kind of urban vandalism – typically the temporary structures that still obscure the principal facade of King's Cross.

There is, however, another reason for the transparency of the terminal. It reflects the fact that, like the two great nineteenth-century termini, it too is an iceberg, concealing an even larger complex of infrastructure beneath the ground. What happens beneath King's Cross is a virtual Spaghetti Junction – far more complex, in fact, and without reliable records of any kind. The first underground surveys are actually taking place at this moment.

It is interesting to digress for a moment on the subject of infrastructure. If you compare the percentage of gross domestic product invested in roads and railways in different European countries from 1982 to 1985 you find that Britain trails miserably behind at less than half of one per cent. The average is about three-quarters

of one per cent, and the best performance is West Germany, at over one per cent. A direct comparison between investment in rail infrastructure in Britain and France between 1975 and 1989 tells the same story.

I think it is instructive that, in general, Continental European countries do not look at roads and railways in isolation; they take an overview of all means of transport and think in terms of integrated policies. We, for example, have just over 1,850 miles of motorway and plan a small increase that will take us to just over 2,000 miles by the turn of the century. France already has 2,900 miles of motorway and plans to have 14,000 miles by the year 2,000. People object that such comparisons are unfair because of the difference in population, land area and so on. But even allowing for such factors, there is an enormous disparity.

Investing in infrastructure is rather like designing a building: you cannot do it without a client organisation to tell you what they need. Similarly, I do not believe you can design transport infrastructure without a political infrastructure to play the same supporting role. And this has nothing to do with political leanings Left or Right. If you analyse investment in London's Underground system, for example, it has fluctuated quite independently of the political party in power.

The situation is quite different across the Channel. I will concentrate on France, but I could just as easily compare Britain with Spain, or a Scandinavian country. In France, the political infrastructure, so to speak, starts with the President of the Republic, who involves himself actively with architecture and planning at the level of the *Grands Projets*. Nor is this merely a nominal involvement, as I know from my own experience as a competition assessor. The President awards the commissions for the design of official buildings through a very well-developed competition system dedicated to the achievement of high quality. This pursuit of quality permeates French society. It reaches back through the French system of architectural education so that talented young designers are invited to compete for small-scale projects in local government competitions. In this way young talent is exercised and developed, and it is focused upon architecture centres, such as the Centre Arsenal, one of three such centres in Paris.

There are other architecture centres in France, and throughout Western Europe but Britain thus far has none. The Centre Arsenal was opened in 1988 by the mayor of Paris, Jacques Chirac. Its construction was paid for by commercial developers and the City of Paris, and the city pays the wages of its employees and meets its running costs. In its first year this architecture centre attracted 60,000 visitors to fifteen major exhibitions displaying the work of 570 architects. One of its most popular features is a large model of Paris where any major development project can be displayed and discussed, a process that reflects the intensely democratic nature of the whole process of patronage in France.

My personal insights into architecture in Europe are inevitably confined to those areas where we are currently active. In a number of these places, such as Nîmes and Cannes in France, we are responsible for masterplans as well as buildings, but in all cases the main difference with the way things are done in England is that we are responsible to a single person in authority, frequently the mayor of the municipality. In Continental Europe a mayor is not a figurehead with no real power, as is the case here, but an active politician who can get things done. I would like to give an example of what this means in the case of Barcelona, where we have designed a new telecommunications tower.

Barcelona lies at the foot of a range of mountains, which forms a backdrop to its whole urban development. In order to meet the enormous communications requirements of the 1992 Olympic Games and the expansion of local television and the Spanish telephone service, plans were being made for the erection of something like 30 individual transmission masts on the mountains, with all the problems of electronic shadowing that such aerial 'farms' can create. It was the Mayor of Barcelona who resolved the problem. He said: 'This competitive approach won't work. You must form one company and together we will build one great communications tower. It will also be a public building, open to the citizens of Barcelona. And because this will be such a large project we will throw it open to international competition.'

Now it is impossible to describe the potential for conflict when rival companies are ordered to cooperate in this way. The first thing that happened was that they tried to sabotage the umbrella company by demonstrating that it could not work. There were resignations – I think there were 40 or so changes in the composition of the board in the first year – but the Mayor would not be dissuaded. Somehow, he drove this great project through. It would not have happened without his drive and determination.

The outcome of the Mayor's vision was the competition to design a single tower, which we won (9). We won it with a design that, like our work at Stansted and King's Cross, started with a historical survey. We looked at the evolution of communications structures over time and discovered that they had almost always been modifications or additions to structures built for some other purpose.

Our own approach to the design broke new ground. We proposed a mast that was also a symbol of a new age in that it broke conclusively with the adapted structures of the past. Instead of cantilevering from a base with a diameter of 25 metres, our structure rested upon a central needle measuring 2.4 metres in diameter. The fact that the tower was sited in a national park meant that this tiny footprint was a great advantage. The tensile guys supporting this needle were anchored some distance away and the whole structure was conceptually no more complex than a suspension bridge. Interestingly though, in the Barcelona mast design, the tensile supports began as steel in early proposals but then became Kevlar, a product which is electronically transparent and so does not interfere with signal transmission or reception.

Another unorthodoxy is the way that the various decks for satellite and microwave communications, and the public viewing gallery, are confined to a glass tube in the central section. This gives the Barcelona tower a unique appearance. It is, in effect, a public sculpture as well as a complex piece of technical equipment, but that does not mean that any element of practicality was sacrificed. The British Telecom tower in London took eight years to move from conception to completion. The Eiffel Tower, that miracle of nineteenth-century fast-track construction, was conceived and erected in four years. The Barcelona tower was conceived and authorised in one year, and built in the following two – a performance that I attribute in large measure to the tenacity and forward vision of the Mayor, and to a structural concept which allowed the tower to erect itself, in much the same way that a car aerial does.

Another field we have been involved in recently in Europe concerns urban redevelopment. The city of Duisburg, in Germany, has about 26 per cent unemployment at the moment as a result of the withdrawal of heavy industry from the Ruhr valley. Krupp, Mannesmann and Thyssen have all left, leaving an industrial void and a community in decline. We have been working for a developer and local

10

11

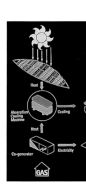

community groups to explore ways to encourage new microelectronic industries to relocate in the area. The site is presently an industrial wasteland, part of which is used as a bus park.

Our proposal in this case hinged on the way in which modern non-polluting electronic industries can be combined with residential development without any harmful effects. Thus we proposed linking an existing park on the site with a business development, housing and a new area of parkland. In this project there is a historical element, as in the other schemes that I have talked about, because we discovered that such mixed-use urban areas were the norm in Germany and elsewhere until the intervention of heavy industry with its concomitant transportation problems, which led to the era of separate zoning. We thought if we could knit together something like the old, pre-industrial zoning relationships, where working and living share the same environment, there would be some exciting possibilities.

Apart from the mixed-use zoning principle, there were three small but important buildings at the heart of our proposal: a Telematic Centre, a Business Promotion Centre (10, 12) and a new Microelectronic Centre (11). The Telematic Centre is the 'brain' of the whole development: it houses all the building management systems, but is also a major public concourse, so it is the focus of interaction between the new industries and the community. The Business Promotion Centre contains exhibition space, a bank on the ground floor, and offices for research institutions and the local authority to use.

Although these buildings could be described as symbols of a new urban fabric, they also reflect a good deal of environmental thinking. The Business Promotion Centre uses a new material with an extremely high U-value patented by the developer, who specialises in low-energy products. Combined with an extensive use of glass and computer-controlled blinds, it gives an excitingly translucent quality to the building but, more than that, because of its excellent insulative properties, it also offers the prospect of a building that can be heated by ambient energy alone.

From northern Germany we move to Nîmes in southern France, where we won an international competition several years ago to design a public arts and media centre, the Carré d'Art, for a site adjacent to the Maison Carrée – one of the best preserved Roman temples (13). Our response was inevitably historical again. We uncovered and studied the ancient Roman planning grid and respected

the surprisingly uniform height and massing of the later buildings that surround the temple. To reassert the original street pattern we designed a very simple rectangular building for the site.

This project has been a long time in gestation, but the time has not been wasted. Since that first project, the city of Nîmes has uncovered a great deal more of its Roman past. In the area surrounding the building, a lot of nineteenth-century additions have been removed to expose Roman paving, and the streets have been pedestrianised. Like the Mayor of Barcelona and many other enterprising mayors across Europe, Mayor Bousquet of Nîmes is a tremendous force for development and investment in the city. When the arts and media centre project finally received government funding, Mayor Bousquet printed hundreds of posters celebrating the courage and determination of the city in pressing for the building (14). It shows, I think, the spirit that animates the city.

Nîmes is also advanced in its understanding of the needs of modern transport planning, and we have been able to help here too. An existing motorway curves around the south of the city but this is due to be replaced by a new motorway following a better route, as well as a new high-speed rail service, the TGV – a reflection perhaps of what I said earlier about French infrastructure investment and its enviable reputation for speed of implementation. Our role in the planning of the new infrastructure at Nîmes has been to study an 8-kilometre stretch of land along the new railway line and explore the possibility of new public parks and lakes and residential areas, as well as a new transport interchange and an enlargement of the airport.

Coincidentally, just as our arts and media centre at Nîmes is now nearing completion, so is our much smaller addition to the Royal Academy here in London. Both these projects began with the challenge posed by an existing historical building, in the case of the Royal Academy, Burlington House itself, together with its nineteenth-century additions. Now an art gallery may not be as complex a building as an airport, but it imposes the same discipline of being required to remain open while building works take place, and thus in some ways it poses similar problems.

Our task was to provide new galleries on the top floor, using the lightwell between the two existing buildings of the Academy both as a means of access and to provide extra accommodation. What was exciting here was the possibility of

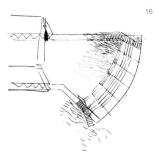

working within this lightwell – a space that would never normally be seen by visitors – and not only using it functionally but, in the process, exposing the garden facade of Burlington House for the first time in more than a century (17).

The original windows of this facade still open onto the lightwell, while the lift and staircase that we have installed permit ease of movement between all levels in a way that does not detract from the function of the grand staircase of the Academy itself. The new Sackler Galleries were designed to provide every advanced-technology climate control and lighting modulation feature, but within the context of a traditional gallery shape appropriate to the age and status of the main Royal Academy building.

Environmental controls are increasingly important in all buildings, not only art galleries. We trace our interest in the subject back to the formation of the practice, and what we call our oldest thatched roof. It is the grassed roof of the Willis Faber & Dumas building in Ipswich, which is 7,000 square metres in area yet acts as a kind of insulation quilt in much the same way as a traditional thatched roof.

This kind of approach can be seen at our new extension to the Sainsbury Centre for Visual Arts at the University of East Anglia. The new Crescent Wing (15, 16) is effectively an underground building, and for this reason it achieves a rate of heat loss only about one-third that of a conventional above-ground structure. By exploiting the slope of the land away from the original building towards the lake, it has been possible to gain an extraordinary lightness inside the building. The crescent of glass provides an uninterrupted view without itself constituting a visual obstruction, rather like the eighteenth-century device of the ha-ha wall.

The internal spaces of this underground building will house an art conservation laboratory, entirely privately financed. Museology and lighting researchers will be able to examine objects under infinitely varied lighting conditions using special installations that do not exist anywhere else in the country. I am sure that nowhere on the Continent would such a project have to be privately funded if there were no equivalent national facility.

Comparison of Continental and British methods and achievements is fascinating and a whole talk could be devoted to this subject alone. There are some interesting comparisons. For example, the National Gallery extension was first projected more than 40 years ago. The British Library, the Mappin & Webb site and

the National Theatre – those too are all 40-to-50-year-old projects. In France they would all have been accomplished in five or six years, and that timespan would have included a competition phase – often an international competition – which we tend to omit over here.

Even if we ignore buildings and concentrate on infrastructure alone, we discover that in Britain the average time needed for the passage of an Act of Parliament to build a railway line or a bridge is five years. Five years from now, in Spain, having won an international competition for a new underground system in Bilbao, we will almost certainly be riding on the trains.

But just as disturbing as these international comparisons, are comparisons over time in our own country. It is instructive to apply the same sort of analysis to nineteenth and twentieth-century projects in Britain. In a most shameful way, the nineteenth century emerges as a far more capable age than our own. For example, our motorway network, which I have already mentioned, was late starting by Continental and United States' standards and only extends to 1,850 miles after more than 30 years of desultory construction. Yet the Victorian railway system covered the 10,700 miles of the present Intercity network only twenty years after the introduction of the first fare-paying passenger train service in 1829. Today, in Europe, they are introducing the TGV network at a similar rate.

The currently much-discussed East London River Crossing, a totally non-contentious scheme, was first projected 45 years ago and still no bridge has been built. Even if the London Crossrail route – which, we are assured, has the highest government priority – proceeds according to plan, it will have taken as long to drive a seven-mile railway tunnel under London as it took the United States to develop an entirely new technology to place men on the moon. And coming back to that five-year lag for an enabling Act of Parliament: it was not always like that in Britain. In 1840, at the height of the Victorian railway boom, Acts of Parliament for the creation of new lines were being passed at the rate of one every 1.2 days. Over the whole of the first twenty years of railway construction in Britain, an Act was passed, on average, every eight days. We, in this country, have a great deal to learn from our own past.

I will finish with an object that has a certain abstract relationship to the theme of my talk this evening: the Vulcan bomber. It is a transitional object – a jet aircraft which marked a quantum leap from the era of its propeller-driven predecessors, but also one that marked a less well-known transition from one system of navigation to another.

Prior to the jet age there was no difference between navigating aircraft or navigating ships, because aircraft were slow enough not to press the navigator to work faster than his methodology allowed. But when the speed of aircraft doubled and trebled, the old navigational system could no longer cope. By the time the navigator had worked out where he was, he was somewhere else. It is a fate that reminds me of today's planning enquiries, legal procedures that go on for so long that those taking part forget what the original issues were because the circumstances have changed and a totally different set of issues has to be addressed. So things move on.

'I grew up in working-class Manchester, an industrial city in the North of England. I remember the local library as a place to escape to ... a quiet haven of peace.'

Norman Foster

As an architect I have been involved in building projects around the world – some very large, some very small indeed. They are quite diverse – art galleries, museums, bank headquarters, offices, an airport, bridges, historical restorations, houses, furniture, even more recently some libraries – in locations as far away as Japan or as close to home as London. So you will see that I do not believe in specialisation.

I have treated this assignment of talking about libraries like any other design project, so my starting point has been to examine their historical roots and to try to identify some possible patterns – past, present and future. As an exploration this led me to suggest the title of – 'The Library: Public Building or Memory Machine?'

The word 'library' originally signified a collection of books arranged for use, and also the building or part of a building where such a collection may be kept. But knowledge is no longer synonymous with books. It could be said that the purpose of a library is to miniaturise knowledge by reducing events and phenomena to accounts of themselves, and to make these accounts instantly accessible.

One suggestion is that the electronic library of tomorrow will be a lights-out, remote-access facility, not a great public building. It is an intellectually appealing proposition. I would like to develop this idea by looking at the historical origins of the library, then to question and finally to demolish the proposition.

The existence of libraries can be traced back to 1600 BC. In ancient times libraries were founded not only for the purposes of study but also for the preservation of single-copy, hand-produced archives against damage or loss by warfare or accident. Thus ancient libraries consisted entirely of original works and were fixed, secure centres of learning to which access was a privilege.

In the ancient world this sort of 'memory' was of enormous importance in keeping track of human events. Records were vast and unwieldy – some painstakingly written or chiselled by hand, and others depicted in mosaic or stained glass. In this wilderness the possession of knowledge of the past was equivalent to power – or knowledge of the future.

The greatest of ancient libraries was the Library of Alexandria, founded by Ptolemy I and built up into a collection of 500,000 papyrus volumes, scrolls and tablets. Ptolemy incorporated some Greek libraries including that of Aristotle, which he purchased. The library survived for 250 years, before it was burned by Julius Caesar. Minor Alexandrian collections survived until the seventh century AD.

From the second century BC numerous libraries were established in Ancient Rome (1) and by the fourth century AD there were 28 Roman public libraries. In Constantinople the Emperor Constantine established a library of 200,000 volumes that also survived until 700 AD. Part of its collection survived for another 700 years.

During the Dark Ages the writings of the ancients survived under Moslem rule in libraries in Constantinople, Alexandria and Baghdad. In one sense the Renaissance was purely the rediscovery of these writings. With the coming of printing, knowledge was more easily miniaturised and replicated. Libraries were thrown open and scholars travelled hundreds of miles to study at them. It took two centuries for the retrieved cosmology of the ancients to be overthrown by the scientific method. Then it was finally established that all wisdom was *not* contained in the past, locked up in dead languages in the ruined buildings, art and writings of the ancient civilisations. Until then the authority of the ancient documents was absolute and the Ptolemaic system held out against the Copernican system. The 'Enlightenment' of the eighteenth century and the coming of the modern world could only occur when observation, hypothesis and experiment overcame the authority of these ancient texts.

With the rise of democracy and the impetus of the Industrial Revolution, libraries became a mass phenomenon. By the end of the nineteenth century there were reckoned to be twelve million books accessible through the public library system in Britain, with 1,250,000 volumes in the British Library alone (4). The Bibliothèque Nationale in Paris (5, 6) boasted 1,500,000 volumes by 1885.

With the arrival of computer access, instant reproduction, electronic communication, microfilming and other techniques, the great public access libraries began to diminish in importance. Instead, a proliferation of private collections and remote access to non-book-based information systems had begun to take place. For example, the new British Library building as completed in 1997 (3) will be only half the size originally planned in 1979.

Declining literacy and an increase in sound and image-based knowledge in the future may mean that libraries will continue to withdraw into their ancient elitist function, accessible only to a few. Some automated, unmanned information systems, which work like libraries, exist already and are maintained by financial markets, television companies, international news organisations and daily newspapers.

The book-based library as we know it was a phase that is already drawing to a close. Information is disassembling into its own sensory components. Just as the library of 1600 BC had no books, the library of 2060 AD may need no books either.

There was a library in the past in China that was supposed to be so valuable that only very few people in the imperial court were even allowed into it. This is a description by Sir John Bowring in his *Travels in China* of 1880: 'I entered the Emperor's library at Ningpo and saw before me hundreds of thousands of volumes, but not a single reader, and it was not in the memory of men that a single book had been allowed to depart from those rooms.' Could this be a description of the inside of the remote access information facility of the future?

According to the Greek historian Siculus, a thirteenth-century BC king of Egypt had a library built in his palace with the inscription above the door 'The Dispensary of the Mind', and sculptures on the walls representing a judge with the image of truth hanging from his neck and many books lying before him. The ruins of this building were rediscovered in the nineteenth century and identified as the Mnemonium or 'house of memory'. In this mnemonic connection, library buildings, indeed all buildings, were as important as their contents. As Frances Yates wrote in *The Art of Memory*:

'There was an art of memory used in antiquity, which consisted of memorising places on real buildings. To these memorised places, images were attached in the imagination, and as the user of the system went, in his imagination, round the building he had memorised, the images which he had placed on the memorised places recalled to him the points that he wished to remember. The ancient orators, including Cicero, used this system for memorising speeches. The fullest description of the use of the system in antiquity is in the anonymous rhetorical textbook, the *ad Herennium*.

'In the Middle Ages the art of memory was moralised; images of virtues and vices, of Heaven and Hell, were impressed on the imagination, on orders of places, as a religious and ethical exercise. In the Renaissance the art of memory had a widespread revival in the form of astrological memory systems, which used the principles of the art, its places and images, in an attempt to organise memory by harnessing it to the occult forces of the cosmos.'

These memory systems, which may go some way to explain the determined presence of ornament on all Classical and Gothic buildings, pre-dated all the modern 'memory systems' of classification, from card indexes to computer files, which are used to access the vast amounts of data in libraries today. The chief difference is that they were 'structural' in the architecture, part of its function and a determinant of its shape and complexity. Modern information systems are completely dissociated from architecture. They are electronic services installed in buildings with no formal demands of their own.

By the end of the eighteenth century, the old architectural art of memory had disappeared so completely that the conscious mnemonic significance of statuary, tracery, stained glass and other decorative architectural features was lost and remains lost to this day. Our non-architectural, electronic, abstract alphanumeric and image systems can be applied to the outside of buildings in the form of advertising hoardings. Perhaps an advertisement on the side of a bus encouraging us to use the Yellow Pages might suggest the correct paradigm for a contemporary memory system, and a computer modem might represent the library ticket of the future?

This Orwellian proposition is intellectually very persuasive, especially at a point in time where the information explosion, which is particularly acute in science and technology, produces an increase in output of 30,000 words per second, doubling the amount of recorded knowledge every seven years. It is a world in which 90 per cent of the scientists that have ever lived are now alive and the growth of literature is directly related to the growth of science.

But there is a paradox. Of the three libraries that we are currently designing in Nîmes (7-9), Cambridge (10, 11), and Cranfield (12-14), the one at Cranfield University is exclusively for scientists. Not surprisingly, of all our clients, they are the closest to the potential that information technology might offer. However, they believe that the traditional form of the library as a building still has an important role to play. I quote a member of the commissioning body:

'The building provides a unique synergy that one cannot really get from interrogating a VDU. It provides what Arthur Koestler described as 'the library angels', i.e. the serendipity that the concentration of materials in one place in an attractive

setting confers on the user. Browsability and helpful librarian intermediaries still have a very important part to play.

'That is why when you first came up to see us I emphasised the vision I had of the library on a winter's evening in which you could see the book, the reader and the VDU all working in harmony. I also saw this very much as what universities are all about, learning from the past and creating new knowledge.'

If I think back to the early days of that project those scientists were very impressed by our scheme for Nîmes, not because of the *médiathèque* part of the project but because of its symbolic presence on a key site in the town. They liked its generous overhanging canopies which marked the prime facade that faces the square and the exquisite Roman temple, the Maison Carrée.

They conceived their library, even within the limits of an Institute of Technology, as part social focus/part gateway. If this can be true of a semi-private institution, then the implications must be far-reaching within the public domain of the town or metropolis. You could advance an argument for such centres of information to be part of the means available to renew and regenerate the outworn areas within our inner cities.

The problem with polarising the library as a memory machine, taking information technology to its ultimate extreme, is that it denies a visual and tactile world where the book is an inspiring object in itself – its smell, its feel, its age, its newness, its own language of typeface and contained images. The 'bookness' of a book has a value of its own – quite beyond the information it contains. Expand the scale and you could reach a point where the concept of the library becomes socially more significant than its contents and the information they contain. I think that this is the point that those scientists intuitively felt about their building when they debated its architectural expression and its location on their campus.

It would be easy to dismiss all this as 'empire building' by politicians and the professions who commission, design, build and finally administer such facilities. But to do so is, in my view, to disregard a very important function of the library. That is its ability to create a good place to be – to attract almost in a religious sense. Maybe the word 'browsability' is at the core of this concept and could best be illustrated with memories of my own childhood.

8

7

I grew up in working-class Manchester, an industrial city in the North of England. I remember the local library as a place to escape to – a quiet haven of peace – a small but quite lofty, toplit building from the nineteenth century. I can recall graduating from the children's section to the areas for grown-ups and dis-covering things by chance – browsing through the world of modern architecture. It was some six or seven years later that I decided to become an architect but I am quite sure that such a decision would have been impossible without that earlier library experience.

So what – technically, architecturally and socially – is my ideal library? It is rooted in a historical past; it attempts to respond to a vision of the present but tries to anticipate an uncertain future. If the only constant is change then such a building must surely have a high degree of flexibility. It should be all things to all people – like the perfect gallery for displaying works of art there will be the right mix of natural and artificial light; maybe like a gallery, that light is tuneable. Quite apart from the humanistic and poetic qualities of natural light there are also the energy implications. We are working on a series of low-energy projects in Germany using new materials that can transmit light but offer extraordinarily high insulation values – the equivalent of a massive masonry wall. You can see through a small part of it but the rest is rather like a traditional Japanese shoji screen in appearance. During the day the inside glows with translucence whilst at night the outside radiates light from within. It really is quite beautiful. I believe it is merely a matter of time before the energy consciousness of buildings becomes a matter of hard legislation – you can already see the signs of this in Germany.

The ideal library, like the most advanced office building, would have clear hori-zontal and vertical zones – freeways in the building – especially below the floor surface where information systems, like the services which drive the building, can weave freely and are accessible for easy change and replacement. We pioneered such thinking in an office building in the early 1970s for Willis Faber & Dumas, cre-ating large open office spaces with the equivalent of a computer floor throughout. In the relatively short period of time since then, these provisions have proved to be commercial lifelines. The building has coped easily with the revolution in office technology – its company profit has multiplied by a factor of nearly sixteen, whilst its competitors have been forced to rebuild or undergo disruptive and expensive

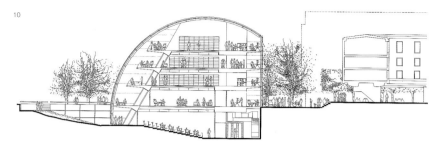

conversion. There is an ironic twist: this year the building was listed with a Grade I preservation order, making it a national monument in the same league as Ely Cathedral. Very flattering, but effectively blocking any more fundamental changes.

At the opening dinner of this conference I sat next to a lady who was involved with a major library project in Barcelona. I asked her about the concept of an ideal library – she suggested the kind of building where you were able to vary the mix between the working areas and the back-up areas. It reminded me of experience with industrial clients who found it very difficult to say in advance how much administrative space relative to production space they might require. This suggested a new kind of building in which the proportion of one to the other could be changed by moving non-structural walls. It is easy to see the same principles being applied to library design.

In a telephone conversation last week with one of the organisers of the conference I tried to find out what the issues might be. Part of the response was: 'What is the ideal shape for a new library?' Regretfully I do not believe that there are any easy answers: put another way I do not believe that there are *any* absolutes. In one urban/political context it may be appropriate to centralise, to make one large building; in another context it may be better to decentralise facilities – to fragment – especially given electronic linkages. In one context it may be appropriate to build high and in another context to build low or deep. Often the value judgements may be subjective – a matter of trade-offs. Why are some warehouses high-rise and others low-rise? They each have their advocates, rationalisations and value judgements.

I talked earlier about our project in Nîmes, which is partly a gallery for contemporary art and partly a library, or to be more precise, a *médiathèque*. In that building the storage area for the most precious contents is below ground level in very deep basements. A few years ago, during the early phase of its construction, there was a terrible storm, which centred over Nîmes for 36 hours. There was flooding on a vast scale – it was a national disaster. Our basement became an instant reservoir, which effectively contained the deluge of water cascading down from the surrounding hills. Without that vast hole the historical Roman temple next to it would have been severely threatened – along with the rest of the central area. It forced everyone to look at the historical records and we identified a pattern of

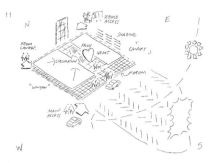

such extreme conditions dating back many hundreds of years. With the client we undertook a total reappraisal of the project.

Our client actually elected to go deeper but also build in more specific forms of flood protection. But you have to remember that given an open site we would probably have never gone down below ground in the first place – we believed and still do believe that it was the only way to knit a large project into the tight urban grain of a historical townscape and not go above the existing skyline. But it also made us look again at that Roman temple, the Maison Carrée. We saw one of the reasons why it might have been elevated one storey above ground, approached by that long flight of steps: maybe that was their way of protecting its sacred contents against the threat of flood. So there really are *no* absolutes.

Perhaps the only absolute is that a library is finally about people and humanistic values. Like the book itself, which transcends its contents, perhaps the concept of the library as a public building, with a diversity of choice for the user (instant information or random browsing), the library as a good place to go (a retreat, an oasis), and as a symbol of the quest for knowledge – perhaps in the end those values are more important than the contents. Maybe that is why we still flock to see that Roman temple two thousand years later, even though it is now only an empty shell.

2

13

14

'If the spaces we create do not move the heart and mind then they are surely only addressing one part of their function.'

Norman Foster

In the past, I have used two images showing an enlarged microchip (1) alongside the Zen gravel garden at the Ryoanji Temple in Kyoto (2), to make points about our work. In Japan more than anywhere else, there is a culture where the old and the new coexist – with integrity and without apology. These two images contrast and complement each other; and they also symbolise a personal attitude to the way in which the new and the old come together.

This attitude permeates our every project, whether it is the conversion of a historical building, the insertion of a new structure into the urban fabric of an ancient town, or a masterplan for growing and regenerating an existing city. In such an approach, every age makes a mark and has its own identity. In one sense there is a break with the past, but that is in itself a powerful and long-standing tradition. Continuity is inherent in the spirit of the new.

These two images also make a point about function. The 'chip' symbolises the flowing of energy within systems. It symbolises a building or a city in microcosm, with systems for the flow of water, waste, air, electricity, information, people, cars, trains or aircraft. But that objective, quantifiable side of the equation is only one part of the function. What about the subjective, the needs of the spirit? Why are the crowds attracted to certain places and spaces? Why do we stand in awe of a rectangle of gravel? Why are we arrested by the sweep of an arch in a cathedral? If the spaces we create do not move the heart and mind then they are surely only addressing one part of their function.

Light is a good example. Any engineer can quantify and produce enough light with which to brighten a passage or by which to read a book. But what about the poetic dimension of natural light – the changing nature of an overcast sky, the discovery of shade, the lightness of a patch of sunlight?

Architecture is a marriage of the functional and the spiritual. These two images bring all these themes together.

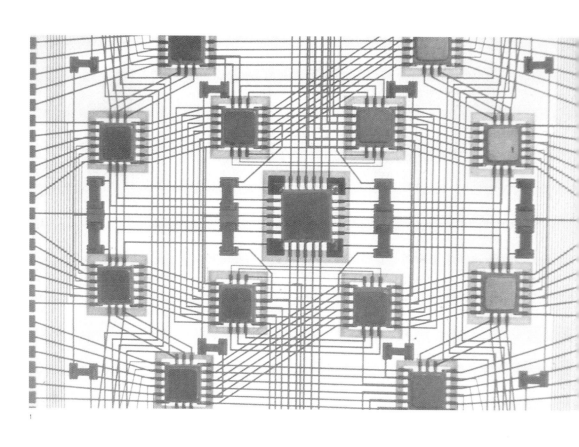

'The fact that we call this an aeroplane rather than a building – or engineering rather than architecture – is really a historical hangover because, for me, much of what we have here is genuinely architectural both in its design and its thinking.'

Norman Foster

What is the essence of a building? Well, it must protect you from the elements – keep you warm when it's cold, cool when it's hot – and it should tell you something about its age, its place in time. This design has a place in time that is without doubt fixed in the second half of the twentieth century. It exudes confidence, style, technology and friendliness in a way that very few others have managed. Most buildings are specialised, but this one is very specialised indeed. It is a jumbo jet.

With about 3,000 square feet of floorspace, fifteen lavatories, three kitchens and a capacity for up to 367 guests, this is surely a true building. But at the same time this machine blurs the distinction between technology and building – and what's more it flies!

It has an extraordinary presence. The tail is higher than a six-storey building. I suppose it's the grandeur, the scale – it's heroic, it's pure sculpture. It does not really need to fly, it could sit on the ground, it could be in a museum. I suspect it is one of those icons of the late twentieth century that future generations will look on in wonder.

The fact that we call this an aeroplane rather than a building – or engineering rather than architecture – is really a historical hangover because, for me, much of what we have here is genuinely architectural both in its design and its thinking.

Once you are inside there are many parallels with modern buildings. Like many offices it is a fixed shell with a moveable interior which is something of an anticlimax. It is really rather bland in many ways. You could say it is in the international hotel style, which I suppose is appropriate – people come and go, it does not have a great deal of character, and it could be almost anywhere.

I am really quite passionate about flying, whether it is in tiny aircraft or giant jumbos like this, which may explain why I protest that most airports are depressingly more and more like shopping centres. You barely see the aircraft and when you do you are inside and the experience of flying is almost anaesthetised with drinks, food and movies. The windows are closed. There is instant music – almost anything to pretend that you are doing something other than flying, which may be what the interior is all about. Somewhere there is a missed opportunity here. The reason is that unlike the exterior, marketing is largely responsible for the interior of this place. However, tucked away from view, there are glimpses of the real thing.

The surprisingly tiny but ruthlessly functional flight deck is a twinkling beauty and the layout is ergonomically efficient. At a more humdrum level, the business-class

toilets are admirably space-efficient and are finely detailed pieces of industrial architecture. Elsewhere there are elegant touches, such as recessed snag-free handles on all the doors. The galleys have a marvellous 'American diner' style – all stainless steel and black plastic – which seems sadly orphaned in a place that usually serves pre-cooked food. Of course safety regulations turn some parts into pure art, and in the end it is this exuberance of technology-as-art that uplifts this assembly of parts.

There is, I believe, a common misconception about architecture and design – the belief that if the forces of nature are allowed to create form then that form will automatically be beautiful (the 'if it looks right it is right' sort of argument). Personally, I think this is nonsense. There is no doubt that an aircraft is an extreme example, but I cannot believe that mere aerodynamics gave this piece of industrial architecture its heroic outer form. This thing was designed. In fact an engineer called Joseph Sutter is credited as the chief designer. It is not decorated; it has style, by which I mean metaphoric elements associated with cultural ideas of speed, efficiency, power, strength, dependability – and yet it is genuinely beautiful. I believe all modern architecture is capable of this intrinsic style and beauty without compromising its function.

These tensions between scale, symbolism and function are purely architectural. Classical and modern buildings often impress by their silhouette alone; when we get closer they lose their impact and when close enough to touch they can be a real disappointment, let down by shoddy workmanship and bad detailing. Only the greatest bear close inspection. On this basis, the Boeing 747 is a monumental achievement. Awe-inspiring in flight, beautiful closer up, and when we reach it, exquisitely detailed.

We don't make buildings on site any more, we make pieces in a factory, bring them to the site and put them together, which is exactly how this aircraft is made – a series of sub-assemblies, little pieces that come together to make the total aircraft.

This is a 1960s aircraft and it first flew in 1969. Its projected life is maybe another 30 years. We think of buildings as enduring. This aircraft is more enduring than a lot of 1960s buildings, many of which are already coming down. Why are they coming down? Because they cannot respond to change. This aircraft's shell is enduring – it responds to change. There is a lot to learn from this building. In one sense you could say it is the ultimate technological building site.

'Otl had a way of working and living in which the creation of a new typeface, the design of a book or a door handle, attitudes to war, politics, writing or communication, how you cut a lawn, were all a related and integral part of a personal philosophy.'

Norman Foster

One day in August I became concerned that I had not seen my friend Otl Aicher since the Christmas holidays. It was three o'clock in the afternoon and I picked up the phone to call him and ask if he was alright. To my surprise, because he travels a lot, he was at home in Rotis, in southern Germany. 'Norman,' he said, 'I've been calling you at Compton Bassett. You never answer and I just wanted to hear your voice.' I explained that I was mostly in London these days and suggested that we meet for dinner – why not straight away, that evening? 'Wonderful,' he said. 'Where are you – in Germany?' I explained that I was in the office in London but could be at Leutkirch (a tiny airstrip close to Rotis) by a quarter past seven his time. I had a long-standing lunch meeting in London the following day, but the time difference would be in my favour so we would be able to have breakfast together, too. It seemed slightly crazy at the time, better perhaps to plan it at leisure in the future. But my diary looked impossible and anyway I had an intuitive sense of urgency.

We had one of those wonderfully spontaneous evenings, shared with his wife Inge and Eberhart, an architect friend who had come from Munich to spend a couple of days cycling with Otl. Early the next morning, the two of us drove to the bakery in the local village to buy bread and pretzels. On the way Otl pulled the car off the road and pointed to a church in the distance. 'That spire, tell me about it,' he said. 'It's leaning,' I replied. 'Exactly, but no one else can see that.' We shared a chemistry, which I still find difficult to comprehend. The time together was all too brief and by mid-morning I was on my way back, after hugging Otl and shaking hands with Eberhart on the apron of the tiny country airstrip.

Within weeks I was back there – dazed, tearful and sad. This time it was the occasion of Otl's funeral. I saw Eberhart after the service, as we stood in line to throw flowers on the coffin. It was surreal, like acting out a part in a silent movie; everyone moving on cue but without being directed; the quiet broken only by the sound of cowbells. Eberhart said that he and Otl had talked long into the night after that dinner about why, out of the blue, I had come so impetuously. 'You must have had a feeling,' he said. Having feelings for such a rare person as a true close friend actually makes it harder to pay adequate tribute. You know almost too much and want to share it all.

Otl Aicher was born in Ulm in 1922. He studied sculpture in Munich and, with Inge Scholl, was instrumental in the founding of the Design College of Ulm, of

which he was later the principal. The story of the school is like a catalogue of the household names of modern product design. In 1952 Otl and Inge married. Knowing them both I find it impossible to talk of one without the other: they seemed intellectually, socially and politically interactive, but they were each strong and individual spirits.

There is relatively little awareness in this country of the resistance movement within Germany during the Second World War, but Inge's brother Hans and sister Sophie were founders of the 'White Rose' resistance movement in Munich and were executed for their beliefs. The family was arrested and the father imprisoned until the end of the war. Inge chronicled the work of the resistance actions by Munich students in her book *Die Weisse Rose*. Published in 1952, this book is still being reprinted.

For the Munich Olympic Games, in 1972, Otl created a new visual language of pictograms, which have since been copied the world over, but never with the same style and directness as the original. His logos, posters, books, exhibitions and graphic communications since then have become cultural milestones; his list of work for companies such as BMW, Braun, Bulthaup, Erco, Lufthansa and Airbus is long and distinguished.

Someone once asked me why I wanted Otl to be the graphic designer for the Hongkong Bank. 'Because he is the best living designer in the world,' I stated. The politics of commissioning did not actually allow us to work together on that particular project, but it did introduce us to one another and was the beginning of a close and inspiring friendship.

In 1972 Otl created a complex of new buildings around an old country farmhouse in Rotis. If he had been an architect, and an individual of less modesty, then this complex of toplit wooden structures would have been well publicised as a classic modern ensemble. It also pioneered ideas about autonomy – by harnessing a turbine to the river and old mill race, the little kingdom of Rotis became energy sufficient and Otl prided himself on being able to manage this community virtually single-handed.

Otl would spend time with us in the West Country and we would likewise escape to Rotis. These were the settings for intensive work sessions, occasionally broken for sightseeing and the paced rituals of food and drink.

Century Tower started in 1986 with a telephone call from a meeting that was taking place in New York. The voice on the other end of the line was a designer from London. Through a network of contacts, I was being invited to Japan by an unnamed person who wished to meet me to discuss a possible project.

My reactions were mixed. I was still suffering the effects of too much long-distance travel during the time that I had been working on the headquarters for the Hongkong Bank, which had recently been completed. Although I enjoyed piloting an aircraft myself, there was little pleasure in boarding a wide-bodied jet every other week. I had therefore promised myself that I would not take on any projects to which I could not fly myself. However, I was touched that somebody would attempt to establish contact with such delicacy; I felt it would be ungracious not to at least make the trip. I vowed to try to keep an open mind.

I was met at Narita Airport by the Japanese intermediary who had been at the New York meeting. We talked on the journey into Tokyo – mostly about my past experiences with Japanese industry on the Bank project, my personal love of traditional Japanese architecture (2, 3) and how much I had enjoyed my limited experience of ryokan or traditional inns. 'Well, the place you are going to stay at now would be too Japanese for me,' explained my companion.

I was soon to see what he meant. The Fukudaya was traditional in the extreme and very exclusive – discreet from the outside to the extent of being invisible. It would be difficult to imagine so extreme a contrast to the Western-style New Otani Hotel, which was close by. From my small room with its glimpse of a minuscule garden it was difficult to imagine that you could be in the midst of a city. It felt like another world – distanced from the twentieth century. After bathing Japanese-style, I was ushered into the next room to meet the client, Mr Akao, his brother (with whom he shared the running of the Obunsha Group) and some of their colleagues (1). It was the start of a long traditional dinner – closer in spirit to a banquet. It was also the start of a new chapter in our architecture.

The conversation flowed through that evening and continued the next day, which started with a Western-style breakfast in another hotel. It ranged far and wide, from contemporary hardware to *Blade Runner*, Richard Long, traditional Korean sculpture, Japanese scrolls, tatami mats, food, colour – even Mr Akao's longer-term ambition to build a house for himself. It shifted around just like the physical context,

without barriers, effortlessly, from the past into the future, weaving between the worlds of East and West, the formal and the informal.

At some point, well into the visit, the project that had been the impetus of my journey must have entered our conversations. I cannot remember when it happened but I do recall that there was no impatience on my part to find out; it evolved out of the chemistry of our relationship in a way that was natural and therefore inevitable.

At the time of writing, Century Tower is a finished building; a house for Mr Akao is under construction on an ocean-front site, and a range of other projects are on the drawing board. Our office in Tokyo feels as if it has always been there. Our architecture has a new dimension. For example, there is the concept of 'Millennium Tower' which projects a community of sixty thousand in a vertical Ginza rising over 800 metres into the sky – more than twice the height of the tallest existing building to date. At the other extreme, in a shipyard in Bremen, Germany, is an ocean-going motor yacht for Mr Akao, which stretches our design skills in other directions.

Our Japanese experience is not only about scale or diversity of opportunity. Like any body of work it cannot be separated from the past out of which it has evolved. However, the work has its own identity – its own inherent Japaneseness.

The influence of place is immediately apparent in any consideration of Century Tower – it is as much rooted in the context of Tokyo and its client as, for example, the Hongkong and Shanghai Bank headquarters is rooted in Hong Kong and in the very nature of the Bank, and as our Carré d'Art in Nîmes, France, is rooted in the urban fabric of Nîmes and the personality of its patron, the Mayor.

Like the Hongkong and Shanghai Bank in Hong Kong, Century Tower is a highly visible structure in Tokyo. If the Bank is symbolic of the strength and accessibility of a powerful institution, then Century Tower symbolises a cultural act of faith by its owner/creator. Mr Akao believed that it should be possible to reconcile the commercial realities of speculative offices with a fresh look at the nature of an office building. Therein lay the beginning of his vital creative role in the project.

Century Tower has been described as marking a new generation of 'intelligent' buildings. This is a reference to the physical performance of the office spaces. But what of its more abstract values, its ambience and image, for example? Though less easy to quantify, these values are no less tangible than the physical needs of the occupants. Both are expressions of a building's intelligence.

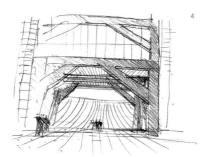

As a building offering space to rent, Century Tower breaks new ground in standards of quality and the technical capability to cope with rapid changes of internal layout. It was ahead of the market place to the extent that it created its own market. The entire building was pre-let ahead of completion – an indication of how its intelligence was perceived in a market that was already saturated with available office space.

But Century Tower is also about a richer mix of activities beyond the usual commercial spaces – for example, the art gallery, pool (5), club, restaurant, tea house and residential areas. These activities generate a richer variety and sequence of spaces. The office tower surrounds a vertical shaft of light and space, which is echoed in the basement. The opposites of light and dark, framed tower and hollowed cavern, are joined together by space and pools of still, reflecting water in the small public places, creating vertical cascades over granite walls (6).

The early sketches of the Hongkong Bank show the original intention, not realised in the final building, to try to tie together the above-ground and below-ground experiences by giving the public plaza a cast-glass floor. Century Tower is the first of our projects to achieve this unity and also explore the medium of water.

Like a temple precinct, the edges of the Century Tower site form a walled enclosure, which conceals the drama of a glass-tented space over the pool and club. It is interesting that so many writers and observers, both Japanese and European, have commented on the Japaneseness of this building. Does the graphic outline of the structure, informed by the spaces within and by the loadings for typhoons and earthquakes evoke historical images? Or is it the more intrinsic quality of serenity that so many have noted? Perhaps it is simply that an appreciation of indigenous architecture finally takes on and infuses the spirit of the new building.

I believe that there is a strong connection between architectural quality and the chemistry of the human relationships that create it. The links between client, architect and builder have, over time, become more complex as consultants and specialist subcontractors have proliferated – a tendency that reflects the increasing complexity of buildings. As more people are involved in the process of designing, the lines of communication have grown, often to be filled by a bureaucracy of committees and procedures. It is hardly surprising that the end product, the architecture, is so frequently compromised and lacking in humanity. There is no substitute

for the inspiration of leadership and trust, starting with an enlightened client or patron and embracing both architects and builders.

For me that trust was immediate at the first meeting with Mr Akao, and it is worth reflecting back on the various ways in which leadership and trust have informed this project at every stage. I can still recall the meeting in a New York hotel in which a single, small, typewritten sheet of paper set out our agreement and was signed by the two of us. There were no teams of legal experts, expensive lawyers and scrutineers, no protracted meetings or mountains of documents – none of the costly and time-consuming procedures which have become normal for projects often far smaller than this. Nothing demonstrated Mr Akao's quality of spirit better than the way in which our relationship began.

The same attitudes, which were also coupled with an absolute rigour, informed the contract between the client and his builder, the Obayashi Corporation. One-third of the cost of the building was paid before work began, one-third when the building was topped-out and the final third on handover. A year after completion all the independent assessments show that the building was exceptional value for money. I can still remember at the time of its construction a building site pristine in its sense of order and craftsmanship, in sharp contrast to my experiences else-where. The question of completing on time and on cost was never in doubt.

The Obayashi organisation is many thousand strong but still masterminded by the man who founded it, with his son following in his footsteps. In a modest way the lines of our own communication and those of the key consultants were equally direct. As a gesture of our confidence, my close colleague and fellow director Chris Seddon moved house and family to Tokyo almost before lines were drawn on paper. My partner David Nelson commuted to Tokyo from London as freely as some peo-ple travel from London to Manchester. He still travels to Japan as if it were next door!

For me the decision to work with Mr Akao was, and still is, an intensely per-sonal commitment. It has, with his blessing, opened doors to a wider involvement in Japan and to many diverse opportunities. Our original motivations were very sim-ple: to try to do our best for somebody who had trusted us, in the hope that we might also learn something along the way. My limited invocations here can only hint at the extent to which our Japanese experience has become ingrained in us – and the sense of joy this extraordinary experience continues to bring us.

'I see no conflict in embracing tradition and new technologies because for me they are both part of a single tradition. The most enduring structures, from any point in time, have always pushed the technology of the day to the limits.'

Norman Foster

I am often asked my views about the relationship between structure and architecture. Is that because the structure in our work assumes an unusual importance? Is our approach different from that of other architects, now or in the past? Does it have something to do with the nature of our work and the relationship that we create between the structure and the spaces which determine the appearance of the buildings, both inside and out?

It is difficult for me to pick apart a process of designing that seems so obvious that I take it for granted. But maybe it is important to state the obvious – to say that structure is influenced by the geography, even the climate of a place, as well as by the needs of the people who generate a building in the first place. How else could you explain the concurrence of the big-span structural steel 'trees' of London's third airport at Stansted and the concrete vaults of the Lycée Albert Camus at Fréjus, in the South of France (1).

At Stansted the base or 'trunk' of the trees is literally rooted in the distribution of air and artificial lighting from the undercroft below (3). The 'branches' spread out to support the most elegantly minimal roof, which serves simply to provide shelter from the elements and to let in light from the sky above (4, 5). Compare this with the massive roof and supporting structure for a traditional airport, with its need to carry the weight of the mechanical equipment above the roof and below it all the usual ductwork, fluorescent lighting, cables and suspended ceilings. By comparison our concept for Stansted is radical, even if it does mark a return to an earlier tradition of less mechanistic structures – suggesting a newer generation of buildings which are elegantly comfortable but also energy conscious.

It is important to note that the motivations here are not just for something that will work better and perform more economically, but also for something that will feel better for those who use the building. The visual dimension of a structure is also its spiritual dimension: how it will look and how it will work become conceptually inseparable throughout the process of design.

Another way of looking at the structure in our building is that it is one of several tightly integrated systems. For example, in the Lycée at Frejus the thermal mass of the heavy concrete vaults is as much a part of the ecology of the building as it is the essence of the structure. Even the roof is a separate element, which hovers above the vaults to protect them from the sun and to encourage the movement of air as

part of the solar stack effect within the building (2). This use of a double roof, thermal mass and natural ventilation by cooling breezes has its roots in the traditional architecture of Islam.

In both of the examples that I have chosen the structure uses commercially available local materials in the most economic manner. There is a tradition of steel structures in Britain but not in the South of France, where the use of concrete is much more sensible. In each case the structure is locked into the environmental concept for the building which, in turn, cannot be separated from the climate of its place. The response to a Northern latitude should be different from that in the Mediterranean region. So in objective terms the structure in almost all of our projects is doing much more than just holding up the building.

The integration of the structure is central to what we strive to achieve as architects, and this is only possible by accepting the engineer as a creative force in the design process. Ideally the engineer will share from the outset the values and aspirations of the rest of the team. Given strong design leadership, there is no conflict in this approach. The idea of a strong united team should never be confused with the impossibility of trying to design by committee. Individuals and teams can share a common passion – committees by their nature are denied such a creative pulse.

But there is also another dimension to structure, and that is the way that it relates to the architecture of the spaces. It does not matter whether a building is about clear open space or whether the space is divided up and cellular by nature, the structure will impart its own order – it will literally structure the space to make it more legible and human in its scale. Perhaps the structure might read through on the exterior to impart an urban scale – to profile the building on the skyline of the city. The most obvious example of this from our past projects would be the Hongkong and Shanghai Bank's headquarters in Hong Kong, and the Century Tower in Tokyo. In both cases the structure allows the shape of the plan to change at different levels up the height of the building. This articulation creates a hierarchy of order and also resolves the issue of light angle restrictions on nearby streets as effortlessly as it copes with typhoon and seismic forces. Thus constraints are turned into opportunities to sculpt the form of the building and in some cases to create the symbol for the place. It is significant that the banknotes in Hong Kong are decorated with images of the Hongkong Bank.

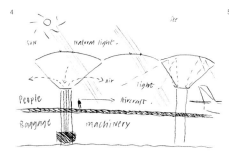

The symbolic value of a structure is nowhere more apparent than in the telecommunications tower that we designed in Barcelona. This project arose out of the political initiative of the Mayor, Pasqual Maragall, who was concerned about the proliferation of towers on the skyline of the mountains of Tibidabo, which dominate the city and major views out from it. You could see what would happen if market forces were given free reign: the giants of regional TV, national TV and Telefonica would each have had their own massive towers, not to mention 30 or more other sizeable masts amidst a forest of microwave dishes. The Mayor demanded one single tower and the abolition of all existing unsightly structures. He proposed that the rival companies should band together to create an organisation that would build, operate and lease space. They would also provide public viewing platforms so that the citizens of Barcelona and visitors could view the city from a new perspective. The site was also ecologically sensitive, encompassing a protected area of forest and a nature reserve.

Our research established what a conventional concrete structure would have looked like – a tapering slip-form concrete tower, massively solid at the base. The effect on the site and skyline would have been brutal (9).

We started from the first principle of communication engineering – to achieve the maximum possible freedom with 'plates suspended in the sky'. We proposed an elegant and slender needle, hollow to carry all the heavy cables and fibre optics, but also supporting platforms aloft, the whole assembly made stable by tensile guy lines raking off to be anchored discreetly in the landscape (8). Integrating consideration for aerodynamic wind forces and structural stiffness transformed the platform shape from a circle to a triangle with curved sides. The form is a revolutionary response to its site and function – but more importantly it has become an established and popular symbol unique to the city of Barcelona.

Like any structure it can also be described in prosaic terms: a slim, hollow concrete shaft with steel platforms made stable by three pairs of steel cables and stiffened by upper cables made of Kevlar, which is an electronically transparent material. All this is prefabricated for fast and clean assembly. The thirteen platforms – equivalent to a domestic block 25 storeys high, weighing 3,500 tons and providing 60,000 square feet of useable space – were assembled on the ground and hoisted up the shaft.

The important thing about the structure was that it grew from two streams of consciousness at the same time. One was the social need, the other was the technological need. Put another way it had to work well and look good – both from close up and from afar. I suppose that is why I can never answer questions such as: 'What is more important, the function or the aesthetics?' For me they are inseparable, the one grows out of the other. This involves manipulation, massaging and finally integration, but never the imposition of one to the detriment of the other.

I would like to continue this theme of the communication tower. More recently we were asked by the Mayor of Santiago de Compostela to design a similar kind of project for a mountain facing his city. Coincidentally the new structure would replace existing facilities, which were unsightly and had defaced the landscape for many years. The relationship between the mountain site and the city is physically close and religiously sacred – Santiago is one of the most important pilgrimage destinations in the Christian world.

It was the symbolic importance of the site that led us to question whether there was a better alternative to a tower on the skyline. By posing such a radical question we were able to demonstrate that a horizontal platform hovering over the mountain forest would not only be more discreet and economical but would do the job even better (7). The dialogue that created this new direction evolved out of the latest advances in the development of communications technology.

I see no conflict in embracing tradition and new technologies because for me they are both part of a single tradition. The most enduring structures, from any point in time, have always pushed the technology of the day to the limits whether they are man-made hills from prehistory, the Gothic stone cathedrals of Europe (6), the magnificent timber temples of Japan, the mosques of Islam, humble barns, or structures from ancient Rome. The list of my personal favourites would be a very long one but in every case the structure is synonymous with the appearance, both inside and out, as well as with the feel, the spirit and the emotional poetry of the buildings. It is also significant that in each of these examples one can rationally analyse the structure with intellectual rigour. That is real integration of architecture and structure – truly the art of necessity.

THE 90's – Another conversion job ?!

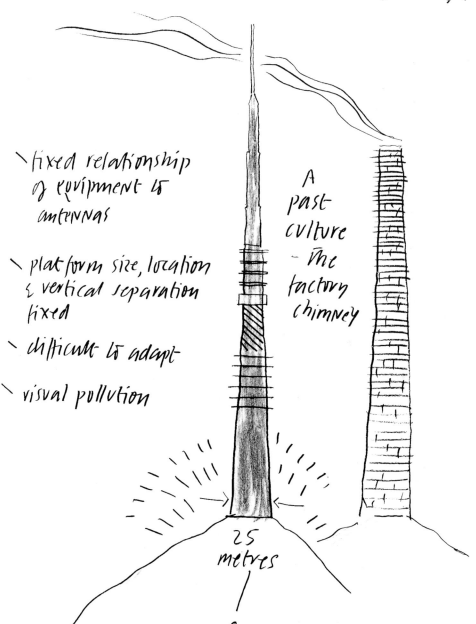

- fixed relationship of equipment to antennas

- platform size, location & vertical separation fixed

- difficult to adapt

- visual pollution

A past culture – the factory chimney

25 metres

'Gordon Cullen was a particular discovery; nearly forty years later I am still entranced by the magic of those sketches.'

Norman Foster

As a youth I had longed to work in some field of design and had for years been interested in architecture. But it seemed an unattainable goal. It was an architect called John Beardshaw in Manchester who opened the door. It was really more a foot in the door, because I was taken on as an assistant to the contracts manager. In the course of my duties I met one of the clients, a building manager for a local textile company. He was cleaning out his office and offered me his collection of old *Architectural Review* magazines.

For me it was as if I had been given a gold mine. I was utterly absorbed and could hardly tear myself away from the images and writings – not only the heroes that I had discovered in my local library such as Le Corbusier and Wright but also new names such as the Smithsons, the Eames, Ralph Erskine and Gordon Cullen.

Gordon Cullen was a particular discovery; nearly forty years later I am still entranced by the magic of those sketches. They influenced not only the way that generations of architects expressed themselves but also the way that they thought – their sense of social values. The messages Gordon Cullen promoted in these early works about the importance of the urban landscape are perhaps more critical to our understanding now than ever before. One also marvelled at Cullen's ability to communicate more with less through his own very personal graphic skills. Many copied his technique, but there was only one Gordon Cullen.

All this led me to approach him many years later after we won the competition for the BBC Radio Centre on the Langham Place site. The combination of historical context with new building and the resulting urban issues seemed an obvious basis for a creative conversation. Through that exchange I met the person behind the Cullen images: he was as enigmatic and elusive as the drawings themselves, and wonderfully inventive.

I was enormously flattered when he later asked me to say some words to formally open an exhibition of his work at the Building Centre in 1985. I cannot remember exactly what I said but I know that it must have been a eulogy about his work and its influence as well as an acknowledgement of the personal debt that I, and so many others, owed him – even down to the way that we pushed our pencils, and so much more that lay behind the lines.

Last month I went to his memorial service at St Joseph's in Ealing to join in silent tribute to a memory that will live on.

I started this piece by mentioning my first boss, the architect John Beardshaw. Without him I would never have discovered Gordon Cullen and may never have had the privilege to become an architect. It is difficult to think of two people who could in every conceivable way be so different from each other. Their paths had never crossed but if they had I think they would have shared a similar brand of impish humour.

Last week I had a sudden impulse to tell John Beardshaw just how grateful I was for the way that he had changed my life when I was twenty by opening that door. Through phone calls to an old friend in Manchester I finally had a number in Peterborough to call. It was his wife who answered the telephone but I was only to discover that he, too, tragically had died earlier this year.

'… how could such a vast shell of concrete, with all its suspended loads of aircraft, sit so delicately, so daringly, upon a sliver of glass?'

Norman Foster

In the lush green countryside near Cambridge in England there is an airfield called Duxford. It is steeped in the history of aviation and its buildings tell the story of two world wars. The traces of this story start in 1917 with elegant timber hangars. Inside there are trusses like a basket-weave of white painted timber as tightly strung as the early biplanes for which they were built.

As the RAF became more established and institutionalised, the buildings grew like a small campus to reflect the ranks and hierarchies of military life. Given the brutal realities of a war machine, the architecture of this battle station is surprisingly understated and deceptively gentle, characteristics which some might say are very British, especially when you realise the connections with the Battle of Britain and heroes such as Douglas Bader, whose 242 Squadron Hurricanes were based there.

But as the war progressed thjs British culture was soon to be overlaid by that of the New World when the first USAAF unit arrived there in 1942. From then until the end of the war, Duxford was home to the 78th Fighter Group, flying over 450 missions in P47s and P51s.

As time overtakes such establishments they generally take on an empty melancholy – a kind of perpetual autumn which is sadly nostalgic. The trim lawns become overgrown, the brickwork crumbles and the paint peels in a suspended state of neglect. Duxford is a thankful exception to such trends because it has been rescued by the Imperial War Museum and will be reborn as a living museum. Not only does it house an exceptional collection of aircraft – from early flying machines through to Concorde – but it is also home to a keen band of enthusiasts who restore and fly historical aircraft and 'warbirds'. Duxford also hosts a spectacular series of air shows throughout the year.

The centrepiece of the collection is a group of American trainers, fighters and bombers – without doubt the best collection of its kind outside the United States. The names themselves chart the history of aviation and war: the Spad, the Fortress, the Superfortress, the Mustang, the awesome B-52 and the U-2 and F-One-Eleven – a reminder of the more recent Gulf War. All together there are 28 examples from the Second World War and ten from later conflicts. Nineteen of these aircraft are still in flying condition.

Given the historical significance of Duxford and its unique collection, it is particularly appropriate that this site should be chosen for a new American air museum.

It will commemorate the vital role of the United States forces alongside the Royal Air Force in achieving victory in the Second World War and will highlight the importance of the Atlantic Alliance and American air power in the post-war world.

Several years ago I was asked by Ted Inman, the Director of Duxford, if our practice could help in the venture, which at that time was only an idea. For reasons that I shall discuss later we felt an immediate sympathy, and this led to our being architects for the project even though there was little in the way of funds to realise it.

One evening in November 1994 I was invited to the Cabinet War Rooms in Whitehall to help promote the fundraising to a group of congressmen from America. My taxi dropped me off in the dark on the edge of St James's Park and I walked to the only patch of light, which was an open doorway on the corner of Downing Street. I had never been there before so I was unprepared for the shock of this underground bunker, which had been the emergency headquarters for Winston Churchill, his War Cabinet and the chiefs of staff of Britain's armed forces during the Second World War.

I found myself at the end of a serpentine line of people, which was flowing down stairways and along a labyrinth of corridors. The spaces were noisy with the buzz of early evening pleasantries as friends were recognised and experiences exchanged. I ran the gauntlet of waiters with trays of champagne and canapes until the line finally ended in a small room filled to almost bursting point. In the centre of the room I recognised Lord Bramall, the Chairman of the Imperial War Museum, and Alan Borg, the Director.

We shook hands and, as Lord Bramall thanked me for turning up, he suggested that I should follow him and speak for five to ten minutes. I was utterly unprepared but stood in rapt admiration as the Field Marshal commanded the room to silence and, with a force given only to the military, directed his speech beyond the confines of the room and out to the lines beyond. My mind raced around, thinking what to say and I scribbled, crossed out and scribbled again on the back of the invitation card. Somehow I managed to write down five or six key words to elaborate as thoughts just seconds before Lord Bramall handed over to me.

Facing the audience I started by saying that this Anglo-American project at Duxford, which involved me as an architect, also touched me in other ways. For example, I had grown up as a child during the Second World War and the memories of that time were still vivid.

In my mind's eye I can still remember holding my mother's hand and peering through the iron railings of a small park where I grew up in the industrial suburbs of Manchester. Standing upright with its nose buried in the ground was the unmistakable shape of a fighter with its RAF roundels painted on the fuselage. I still cannot decide if this was a dream that cannot be forgotten, or whether I imagined a painting by Paul Nash, which had come alive.

I can also remember the sirens that warned of bombing attacks, the barrage balloons in the parks, waking up in the middle of the night in air raid shelters and looking for pieces of shrapnel during the day – totally unaware that not long ago they were lethal fragments of bombs or shells designed to kill or maim.

As I talked through the headlines on the scrap of paper in front of me, my mind silently traced these memories and I moved on to talk about my personal links with America. I explained how I had only just returned from the opening of the first building that we had designed in the United States – the new wing for the Joslyn Art Museum in Omaha, Nebraska. I also thought about how I had felt as a student in the United States over thirty years ago – my debt for the liberation of that experience as well as my gratitude to Yale University and to the many American architects who had influenced me.

Twenty years ago I learned to fly and I have been fascinated ever since by flight. Like many schoolboys before me, I was obsessed by the world of model aircraft and it can be no accident that the machines which give me the most pleasure to fly are themselves like overgrown models. One of the most memorable flights was in a Spitfire out of Duxford – probably the closest that I am likely to come to piloting the classic warbirds which are a vital part of the American Museum collection.

Putting all these strands together, but without narrating the detail, I told the audience that my bonds to this project were therefore much closer than the normal ties between an architect and the building that he designs.

In the few minutes that I had so far been talking I realised that I had scanned back 55 years to the time when the War Rooms had just been completed. This was the week before war with Germany was declared, in September 1939. One of the most important spaces, just around the corner from where we were all standing, was the transatlantic telephone room. It was here that Churchill could speak directly to President Roosevelt in the White House. Using radio telephony, devices known as

3

scramblers turned these conversations into meaningless noise until they were unscrambled at the other end. However, the link was not totally secure until 1943, when a more advanced device developed by Bell in the States was shipped to Britain. Codenamed 'Sigsaly' it was too big to fit in the subterranean spaces of Whitehall and was finally installed in the basement of Selfridges department store in Oxford Street, with an underground cable to make the connection.

I ventured a thought to the audience. Given that all this was relatively recent history, how would the people working in those spaces have reacted, with the Blitz exploding above them, if it had been suggested that in less than 50 years' time a Briton would be selected to design the new German Parliament? If nothing else it was a timely reminder of how rapid the pace of change had become and how easy it is for us to forget, and by forgetting to lose the lessons that history might teach us: too easy for the British to forget that half a million US airmen were based in the United Kingdom during the Second World War; too easy for both countries to forget that 50,000 US airmen gave their lives; too easy to be lulled into a false sense of security in a world which is arguably more unstable today than it has been for longer than a newer generation can remember.

What are the lessons, aside from a renewed sense of urgency to realise this museum? What, in the same spirit, are the lessons for the Reichstag?

I explained how these attitudes had informed the design for the new German Parliament – how by peeling away the layers of history from the old Reichstag we would reveal and preserve the past. How much more compelling and beyond dispute to see a fabric of stone imprinted with the graffiti of a Russian invasion or scarred from its burning by the Nazis. The house of Parliament becomes the house of history, for present and future generations.

It would have been tempting to go off on a tangent, to reflect on a society in Germany so open and progressive that it could look beyond its national boundaries for the design of some of its most significant monuments. There are few political bodies in the world that could accept the symbolism behind our concept – for example a public viewing platform, which looks out over the city and is perched above the main chamber of government. Members of the public are placed physically above the politicians to whom they are answerable, and public and politicians alike can enter the building together through the main western entrance.

It is the same design philosophy that reveals the democratic process of government on the one hand and the artefacts of flight on the other, even if the physical differences are extreme. The new German Parliament is inevitably constrained and limited by the physical jacket of the old Reichstag. By comparison Duxford offers the ultimate greenfield site.

The largest exhibit, the B-52, is the length of two tennis courts and the height of a four-storey building. In our proposed response the new museum describes graceful curves in two directions to span clear over this giant, forming a three-dimensional arch which at its maximum is 90 metres across and 18.5 metres high. This shell, which is made of concrete, will grow out of the landscape on the road side and soar to open out in the direction of the runway, with long views through a vast glass wall to the countryside beyond.

The entrance will plunge through the landscaped base at the lowest end of the structure to propel the visitor into a vast column-free hall. On the edge of this space, a sloping ramp will provide dramatic views of the aircraft, both suspended from the roof and sitting on the gallery floor.

The concept of the roof is derived from the stretched skin structure commonly employed in the construction of the aircraft themselves. The junction between the roof and the foundation will be marked by a continuous strip of glazing to provide natural light as well as adding a dramatic note – how could such a vast shell of concrete, with all its suspended loads of aircraft, sit so delicately, so daringly, upon a sliver of glass? Despite the structural ties binding together shell and foundation, they will appear from the outside to defy reality. But another part of this reality is that this is also one of the most economical ways to house the collection.

As I came to the end of my speech I summarised my main messages. The only important words had to be that it is a desperately worthy cause – that society cannot be allowed to forget the past. But the byline was also about the aviation heritage: if society cannot care enough about the moral argument then please just rescue these aircraft from the accelerating decay that they now suffer from sitting outside in the rain. Rescue them for posterity, not only for their place in history, but because they are simply beautiful objects.

5>

'We not only expect higher standards of comfort and amenity
when we go to work, but we
also expect them to be created
in a socially responsible manner
mindful of the consequences
for future generations.'

Norman Foster

Many of us spend more time at our place of work than we do at home, so the nature of the workplace directly affects the quality of our lives – and indirectly that of our families. Some years ago many people were predicting the paperless office. That has proved to be a myth, despite the widespread use of computers and word processors. Today there is a similar myth, which suggests that we can all work at home and thereby eliminate the need for offices and corporate headquarters. Whilst the technology may exist to create such possibilities, the social need for people to come together is very deeply rooted, notwithstanding teleconferencing, virtual reality and expanded horizons of private time for leisure.

What is changing, however, is the level of our expectations. This is reflected in the so-called 'green revolution'. We not only expect higher standards of comfort and amenity when we go to work, but we also expect them to be created in a socially responsible manner, mindful of the long-term consequences for future generations.

Legislation and attitudes to such issues are more progressive in Germany than in most other countries. The climate of opinion in the city of Frankfurt in particular encourages the pursuit of higher design standards in buildings for both the public and private domain.

To be socially responsible any building should work both from the outside, in the civic context of its site, and from the inside, by responding to the special functions which generate the need for the building. It should also be remembered that function – whether in the public or private realm – also has a subjective and spiritual dimension. How, for example, do you measure the magic of natural light – a shaft of sunlight – or the calming effect of a view of a garden, or the sculptural qualities of a silhouette on the skyline?

The tower for Commerzbank is a response to these and other related concerns. It is a reminder that architecture is about people – their needs and their aspirations. In a time of social and technological change the traditional patterns of how we work, live, play and communicate are called into question. To respond constructively to the challenge of change it is necessary to question the nature of our buildings and how they relate to the traditional structure of our cities.

The new tower starts by challenging the kind of high-rise structure that can be seen in almost any city. Traditionally this has a solid central core of lifts and stairs with a band of office space around the edge. In most buildings like this,

every floor is identical and the city is presented with repetitive facades: there is no life or variety for the office workers inside or for the public spectators outside.

The Commerzbank is a radical reappraisal of the very nature of an office building. Instead of a solid core, the heart of the building is a vertical shaft of open space (5) which expands at intervals up the height of the building into nine large indoor gardens (1). Each of these green spaces is four storeys high; they spiral around the edge of the building to become a dramatic feature, visible from the outside as well as inside.

There are three different kinds of garden – Mediterranean, North American and Asian. Each has its own distinctive character, with planting and large trees as diverse as maples, olives and bamboo. From inside the building these 'gardens in the sky' frame unexpected views of the city beyond (3). The tower's special bridge-like structure allows the gardens to form intervals in each of its sides, uninterrupted by columns, even though they fill an entire facade of the triangular building. As well as helping to create a more human and intimate place to work, the gardens are meeting points and offer the opportunity for a relaxing snack or social gathering. From the outside they break down the scale of the building and offer views, which penetrate from one side to the other across the full width of the building.

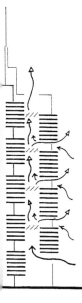

The vertical atrium space and gardens are also part of a unique system of natural ventilation, which, for most of the year, allows the building's users to open windows in the outside wall for fresh air (2). This is one of the energy-saving concepts of the design. There will, of course, be times when the outside temperature is too cold or the winds are too strong. On those occasions the automated building management system will take over and ensure that the internal climate is comfortable and controlled. The lifts which occupy the centre of a traditional tower are moved to the outside corners, where they offer dramatic views of the city and their movement animates the outside of the building.

Many historical cities offer interesting public routes and spaces, which cut through entire urban blocks. In London, for example, there are nineteenth-century spaces such as Burlington Arcade; in Brussels the Galeries St Hubert; and in Milan the Galleria Vittorio Emanuele II, which connects the Cathedral Square with La Scala. Every age in the past offered their equivalent, from the alleys of the Middle Ages to the piazzas of the Renaissance and the kasbahs of the Middle East.

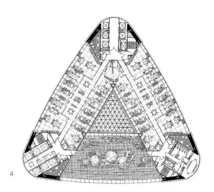

4

In the twentieth century this urban tradition has been sadly neglected. In Frankfurt, however, by working closely with the planners, it has been possible to continue this historical tradition of creating open spaces by making a glazed arcade to link the pedestrian area of Kaiserplatz with Grosse Gallusstrasse. This space offers the citizens of Frankfurt and the employees of the Commerzbank a unique opportunity to stroll, eat and participate in cultural events in a grand space protected from the elements.

The triangular tower (4) is thus knitted into the lower urban blocks and streets at its base whilst from a distance it presents a unique silhouette on the skyline without the need for logos or identifying signs. Although it is special to Commerzbank, and unlike any other tower in the world, the project has evolved from pioneering work on earlier buildings such as the Hongkong and Shanghai Bank headquarters in Hong Kong, Century Tower in Tokyo, and the Willis Faber & Dumas building in Ipswich.

It is difficult to separate the prosperity of Frankfurt from its commercial success in the specialised world of banking. The Commerzbank tower, with its sophisticated systems, is a long-term investment in that tradition.

5

'It seems to me that the best architects of any period not only had an encompassing vision but their passion also permeated the fabric of their creations down to the smallest detail.'

Norman Foster

In 1993 I went to Magdeburg, in what was once East Germany, to give a lecture. Although the Cathedral in the city had been closed to the public under the Communist regime, it had miraculously survived as one of the most outstanding medieval buildings in Germany.

The interior is a magnificent space, which at the time of my visit was entered through a door on one of the long sides of the building. I was intrigued by the handle to this door, which was cast in metal in the form of a stylised bird (2). It was not only good to look at; in its own way it was also eye-catching. But more important and equally memorable was the way in which it sat in the hand – so comfortable and generous.

I remember thinking at the time what a good experience it was just turning the handle and opening that door. It made such a deep impression on me that I arranged for someone to photograph it and to send the images back to the office.

When we accepted the challenge to design a range of door handles for Fusital I was reminded of my experience in Magdeburg and indirectly that was one of a number of influences on the project.

A door handle can be likened to architecture in miniature – it has to work well for those who use it but it must also look good. In another sense it is an important part of the furniture in a building – literally one of the few points of physical contact. In the tactile sense the handle has to feel good. But then it is easy to forget that architecture is about all the senses.

In most of the buildings that we design, including those for our own use, we have consistently specified the classic D-handle with a semi-matt finish in aluminium or stainless steel. The design is intellectually satisfying, sparse and abstract, even though it is acceptably comfortable to use. In that sense it is an excellent compromise with an agreeable economy of production – it is, after all, a simple bent bar.

The appearance of the D-handle conjures up the spirit of an earlier age of functionalism, with strong overtones of the 1930s. It does not, however, offer anything like the satisfaction that most earlier, traditional door handles could offer. If the D-handle is in the tradition of Bauhaus abstraction then those earlier examples are in a tradition of anonymous design that was functional in the ergonomic sense of the word. To put it another way, they fitted well into the palm of the hand.

The sculptural forms that resulted from such considerations assumed a visually satisfying dimension that is far removed from the minimal qualities of the D-handle. Some of the best examples have the sensual qualities that I associate with, say, the flowing sculpture of Brancusi. With a few exceptions they all stem from an age before the period of so-called 'Modern' architecture. Our design exploration for Fusital was, in part, a quest to rediscover this lost tradition.

I am fascinated by buildings from all ages of history and gain pleasure from playing the visiting tourist. It seems to me that the best architects of any period not only had an encompassing vision but that their passion also permeated the fabric of their creations down to the smallest detail. That integrity of concept was true both before and after Mies van der Rohe, but he certainly made the point with the well-quoted remark that 'God is in the details'. I remember, for example, being impressed in Finland by the personal stamp that Alvar Aalto would imprint on the doors of his buildings, through handles that would be customised for each project.

More recently I had the opportunity to study the production of luxury cars. Within the standard design of, say, a Porsche or a Rolls Royce there is an extraordinary latitude to customise the car to one's choice – to such an extent that it ends up being unlike anybody else's car. On the automobile production line it is fascinating to see how the appearance of an interior can be transformed, depending on the final choice of materials – each with their own distinctive colours and textures – even though the forms of the individual fittings are identical.

This experience raises an interesting question about the fittings which come together to create the interiors of buildings. Why is it not possible to have the economic benefits of mass production and still be able to customise fittings such as door handles so that they can be more individually tailored for a project? What other artefacts, besides cars, could we learn from as designers?

One more source of inspiration was the world of penknives. I am compulsively drawn to any shop window that is filled with these objects. In Valencia recently I gazed spellbound at shelves packed with penknives of every shape and size, with handles in a variety of materials that ranged from wood to pearl, plastic and metal, with colours from every hue of the rainbow. The interesting thing about a penknife is that the blades with their mechanism are really the middle of a sandwich, which can be packaged between moulded grips in a variety of materials.

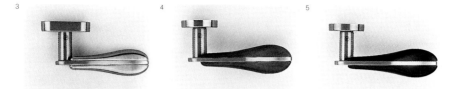

These can be soft, hard, matt or shiny, precious or basic – the choice is extensive and determines the appearance and quality of the end product. Significantly the packaging is not merely cosmetic – the best penknives are a joy to handle, to hold and to contemplate.

Our project for Fusital uses the same principle. The spine of the handle is a flat metal plate attached to a well-engineered locking mechanism. The plate is then sandwiched between mouldings that can be produced in a variety of materials such as metal, plastic in red or white, timber, black rubber or even with a leather covering. The choice of metal for the spine and its finish, together with the nature of the mouldings, determine the final appearance of the handle. Its feel is the outcome of the shape of the mouldings, which are contoured to the hand, and the material from which they are made. The range of options that the end users can choose from is therefore extremely wide. This opens up a new range of creative opportunities for designers.

The concept of this handle is one of separate laminations or layers. In the world of aviation there is a wing section known as a laminar-flow aerofoil, which was developed for high-speed flight. Its qualities of flowing shape and layers have suggested the name of 'Lamina' for this new generation of door furniture.

To write down these influences on the design of the Fusital door handle is to make the process sound like a step-by-step progression. How simple life in a design studio would be if it were that easy. The reality is closer to a game of snakes and ladders. At one point it seemed that the answer might be a single moulded form: this version of the handle was superbly comfortable to use and very beautiful – it looked as if it was derived from the propeller of a vintage ship or aircraft. Some of us fell in love with this design but the production costs would have made it unaffordable.

At the same time we were struggling with the original idea of a spine plate to which additional layers could be added to make up the handle. Intellectually the idea was convincing but the early explorations were unsatisfactory – they either looked or felt wrong. Some had a curiously dated appearance – like throwbacks to the 1950s. There was a profusion of sketches, which gave way to ply and foam full-size models, interspersed with factory-made prototypes. These were fixed to doors in the office to see how they felt. 'Seeing how they felt' is an interesting and

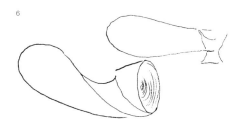

6

relevant play on words. Samples were from time to time passed around the office for comment – generated by innocent questions such as 'Would you specify this handle instead of the usual D-handle?' In its way this proved to be a valuable form of market research.

Our time on this project was determined by an approaching trade fair and the patience of Fusital, which in a good-natured way had been well stretched. At almost the last minute everything snapped into place when one day the pieces of a final prototype arrived in the office from the factory in Italy. It was close to a victory celebration. We were like children playing with our new toys. The mood was infectious and anyone passing by that part of the office was drawn into the game and shared the joy. Since then the concept of 'Lamina' has grown, and sketchbooks bulge to show how further pieces for doors and windows are evolving to extend the product line.

7

Foster On

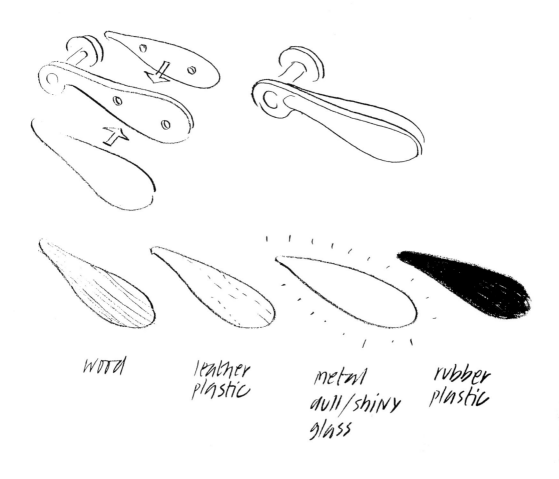

wood

leather
plastic

metal
dull/shiny
glass

rubber
plastic

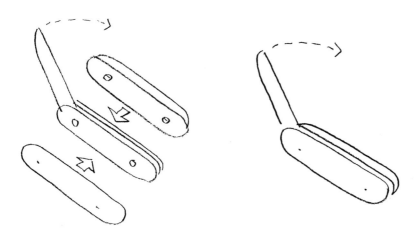

'Quality is an attitude of mind.'

The quality of our architecture influences the quality of our lives – particularly in the places where we live and where we work. But there is also the world in between these places: roads, bridges, filling stations, advertising kiosks, signs, lamp posts, railings and benches – taken together or individually they can scream at us or calm us. We tend to take this public world for granted, as if there can be no control over it, as if it somehow happened by accident. However, like buildings, this 'in between' world is also the outcome of many conscious acts of design. If these have been well thought through and properly coordinated then the effect can be harmonious. But if, as so often happens, all the many different elements are fragmented and there is no overall vision or coordination, then the end result can be chaos.

A metro system is an excellent demonstration of this reality. Normally the engineering of tunnels for trains is seen in isolation from spaces for people – even though the experience for the traveller is a single journey, which starts and ends at street level. The structures above the ground that announce the start and end of the trip are also part of the same event, although they are rarely part of an over-all vision. Metro systems take longer to realise than buildings and are much more dependent on specialised engineering skills. Unfortunately the role of architects in such projects is often cosmetic and limited to fitting-out the spaces with walls and ceilings, just like a conventional building.

The Bilbao Metro is unusual because from the beginning it was conceived as one totality. This was only possible because the Basque government took the unusual step of promoting an international competition. This signalled that there was a strong sense of civic pride in the project, a desire to do it well. For an architect the most critical factor in any project is the aspiration of the client – not the site, the budget, or the size or scale of the project. All of these are nothing if the client does not really care. The political initiative of the competition created the opportunity to combine architectural engineering and construction skills from the outset – to integrate the different disciplines with a shared vision.

In early 1988 we were one of a group of eight competitors, and at that time the project was still only a dream. With my colleagues I had been working franti-cally on our submission which was mostly fine line drawings and models. I had flown to the home and studio of Otl Aicher in southern Germany and persuaded

him to become a member of the team, along with the American lighting consultant Claude Engle. Just before the deadline to submit the proposals I prepared a sheet of small sketches and handwritten notes to summarise our design and the philosophy that lay behind it.

I had forgotten this summary, but looking back now at the report that I wrote in Wiltshire at the time it is even more valid today than it was then. I have selected the following extracts:

A tunnel carved by man through the earth and rock is a very special kind of place. Its shape is a response to the forces of nature and the texture of its construction bears the imprint of man. As found these qualities of shape and texture have a drama – they should be respected, *not* covered up to pretend that it is just another building. You should feel that you are below ground and it should be a special kind of experience.

Part of this philosophy is about the spirit, the poetry and excitement of travel. But it is also a philosophy of reason – practical as well as aesthetic.

Resources such as time and money are precious commodities, which should be used wisely. It is better to do fewer things well. Quality is an attitude of mind. Natural materials such as stainless steel, polished metal and high-grade concrete can wear well physically over time. They are also timeless.

Colour – painted metal or illuminated signs – used sparingly will have the maximum impact. Red commands attention! Red is also rich in local associations.

But the systems below ground are only part of the total metro. On the surface the metro must announce and communicate a presence within the urban fabric of Bilbao. We have searched for a single architectural language, one that will respond with variations to all the different situations.

Glass, beautifully detailed with minimal metal supports, can form building 'crystals' or create gentle infill within existing structures. Glass is a material of our age and our studio has pioneered its applications over many years. The concept is a glass crystal or glass tent over the link to the tunnel. At night it can alter with light from within – a lantern. During the day it is semi-transparent – a minimum intervention. It can modify the climate, keep off rain, be treated to deflect sun (or add grillages), has minimum maintenance, can enclose signs. It becomes an

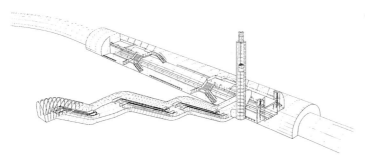

instantly recognisable symbol of the metro from near or mid-distance. But what about from far away and very close up? How can we still recognise the metro? What is its symbol?

Otl Aicher, an important member of our team and an eminent leader in the field of visual communication, has created a symbol for the new metro system based on circles – red circles. This symbol can be used two-dimensionally, to be viewed close up – from the smallest piece of paper, envelope, timetable, poster, throughout all spaces, onto the trains themselves – or three-dimensionally, as sculpture, in the urban landscape for those long-distance views.

These are the ingredients – the tunnel, the glass crystal, the symbol. The ingredients can also be read as symbols of our primeval roots – the cave, the tent and the wheel.

We try to achieve simplicity – a struggle – much more difficult than accepting complexity, but far more poetic and worthwhile.

The most significant change from the competition-winning entry to the finished project was the evolution of the glass crystals which announce the metro in the streetscape. I recall looking again at the Cubist-like pavilions and deciding instead to develop a shape that was evocative of inclined movement from below – a shape that would flow like the subterranean tunnels themselves (4).

These curved glassy structures (5, 6) were to become outward symbols of the hidden network that is buried into the earth. They are emblematic and as unique to Bilbao as are Hector Guimard's Art Nouveau metro entrances of the 1900s to Paris. I could never have imagined at the time I was sketching them that they would eventually be referred to fondly as 'Fosteritos'!

So many subway systems are difficult to negotiate and need a multitude of signs to help you find your way. In Bilbao we tried to make the journey as easy as possible by making the architecture of the spaces legible. The routes 'flow' – like walking through a sculpture of caves that guide you to the caverns of the stations themselves. The decision to make these stations large enough to accommodate mezzanines and staircases above the trains was important (3, 7). Not only is it more dramatic to move in space around a single grand volume in this way, but the concept also offers the flexibility to make changes in the future.

I was privileged to see the project grow from the drawing board through all of the construction phases. There are some experiences in life which are truly unforgettable and mine now include the many underground visits during the tunnelling (1, 2), which was a moving and awe-inspiring spectacle.

When I lecture on this project I show the space shuttle at Cape Canaveral to explain how the Spanish engineers pioneered mobile gantries for the aerospace industries and were able to use the same technology to place the prefabricated concrete panels that formed the tunnels. I also talk about the vast amount of research undertaken to develop protective coatings that would render the concrete vandal-proof against graffiti. For me, the raw power of these concrete-lined spaces has an emotional and spiritual dimension. I would like to think that this has something to do with the way in which the forms are expressive of the enormous forces of nature. Perhaps it is also linked to the primeval echoes that I mentioned in my first concept report.

Since men and women emerged from the cave, the culture of our planet has been about making things. In that sense technology, which could be described as 'the art of making', is a long-standing tradition and as old as our species. However, there will always be some places in the world where this tradition is stronger, and Bilbao, with its Basque heritage, is one such place. Here the industries of engineering, manufacturing, shipbuilding and mining were at the cutting edge of the Industrial Revolution. For the construction of the metro, therefore, most of the elements could be made locally, unlike so many projects, which require skills and materials to be imported from afar.

The future of our cities is linked to our ability to handle physical communication – the ease with which people can move freely and in a civilised manner. The architecture of this kind of infrastructure is critical to urban development. The subway link between the city, the coastal strip and the suburban hinterland is not only significant for Bilbao and the region but it is also a model for the rest of the world.

The 1996 Venice Biennale was called 'Sensing the Future: the Architect as Seismograph'. In the words of the director, Hans Hollein, it was a collection of 'new ideas, trends and visions of the future'. To find this project in the heart of the central pavilion of the Biennale was indeed to 'sense the future'.

5

6

7

'For me, Riverside is a rare combination of a wonderful team and a great place to work.'

Norman Foster

Riverside is a pioneering example of a modern British building, which reintroduces the idea of mixed-use development. By helping to create a new network of pedestrian routes, the project has also played a major role in regenerating the local neighbourhood. Significantly, the building's completion also marked a watershed in the evolution of Foster and Partners, as the practice is now known.

Although it has recently become fashionable to advocate the virtues of mixing uses such as living and working and recreation in one location, there are, at the time of writing, few contemporary examples of these ideas in Britain. It is easy to cite historical examples of such coexistence in the Middle Ages or the Renaissance, even up to the nineteenth century. For example, the tenement buildings of Glasgow combined shops and pubs at ground level, offices immediately above, and then several levels of residential accommodation over that – rising between five and seven storeys in all.

Such compact communities, however, are in direct contrast to most of today's planning guidelines, which specify separate zones for residential, commercial or industrial use, or for leisure and culture. The consequent problems of this approach to urban planning – the social alienation, the need for extensive commuting with all its associated traffic and pollution, and the ecological impact of low-density sprawl – are only now beginning to be fully appreciated.

In the past, it was the blighting nature of heavy industry that was responsible for many of these zoning policies. Today, however, the 'clean' industries – such as microelectronics – and the new service-sector offices and studios are totally compatible with residential areas. In our work in Duisburg, we have demonstrated that the inner city can be revitalised by introducing these newer industries and locating them alongside housing and schools – even creating more green spaces in the process. Furthermore, we have shown that such buildings can be ecologically sensitive and strive towards sustainability.

Riverside was an early example of applying this philosophy to the way that we, as an office, might live and work – a version of trying to practise what we preached. Foster Associates, as it then was, had occupied a variety of office locations in central London. But the word 'office' has always been inappropriate for the way that we design. More than any practice I know, we develop models, full-size mock-ups and prototypes as an integral part of the design process. The modern property market cannot accommodate these realities, with the result that we were forever splitting these activities, one from the other. Even the studio in Great Portland Street, where we were before the move to Riverside, was split, with model-makers on a separate level. Eventually, they overflowed to a warehouse several miles away. It was then that a vision for the future emerged where all of these activities would be integrated, as far as possible, in one space and on one site. Ideally, also, this would be combined with urban living and a riverside perspective.

The search for a suitable location was long drawn out. In the mid-1980s, however, a site was identified on the south side of the River Thames between Albert and Battersea Bridges, opposite Cheyne Walk. In reality, the site was made up of many separate lots, most with decaying industrial structures on them, creating an area of seedy dereliction, which extended up to the edge of the river. On one side was a dock, filled with rotting debris and stagnant water. Working with an enterprising estate agent, a site was finally assembled and then secured with the help of a bank loan.

The next task was to turn the site into a project and, in particular, a home for the practice. So conversations started in earnest with potential developers who might buy the site and create space for the practice to rent. In parallel we were exploring design options.

As architects, with an eye on the potential of the site, it seemed obvious that in a mixed development the flats and offices should share the best views onto the river. It also seemed inevitable that the workplaces would be close to the ground with the living spaces elevated above, where they would enjoy privacy and the best views, as well as command a higher price – which would help the development equation. With the creation of a private courtyard we were able to show that it was possible to provide separate access and security to both those who would work in the building and those who would live there.

However, we were soon to discover an apparently irresolvable conflict. All the financial institutions behind the developers insisted that, for funding purposes, there should be two separate buildings: one for offices, the other for apartments. Worse still, it was argued that the higher-value residential spaces should overlook the Thames and a separate office block should overlook the dock. All our arguments for an integrated mixed-use building were to no avail.

By contrast, the planners and the local authority of Wandsworth were totally supportive. There was a shared enthusiasm to see the dock cleaned up and brought back to life, and European Community funds were pursued for its rehabilitation. In the negotiations that followed, we worked with the borough's Chief Planner to develop a network of pedestrian routes, which would open up the river and the dock to the public with good connections through to the surrounding streets. It was this early planning decision that was to prove so important to the future regeneration of the river and the areas that extended beyond the site.

At this time, quite by chance, I happened to meet David Gabbay, who was one of the developers for the site on the other side of the dock. We agreed to have lunch together. His group was just about to submit a relatively conventional scheme of apartments for planning consent. We got on extremely well together and shared an excellent meal. Over dessert I explained the seemingly impossible dilemma that we faced with our site. To my surprise, he was immediately sympathetic and agreed to help.

David and his then partners eventually became the developer, client and builder of the project. We worked to a very simple formula, which was shaking hands on whatever was agreed. It drove the flocks of lawyers and accountants to despair but it worked.

The apartments were generously planned with virtually no waste circulation or corridors. Sliding windows maximised the view. David's company exercised the right to change details such as the kitchen and bathroom fittings, or the internal finishes, door furniture and staircase detailing. Given that he was taking the financial risk for the apartments – as opposed to the offices, which we would fit out and rent from him – it was difficult to argue the point; and, according to David, most people would do their own fit-out anyway. The fact was that the project was being realised against all the odds and the main priorities were still intact, although the project went through several upheavals – one caused by the collapse of a major subcontractor half-way through the job.

It is easy to look back now, in the light of experience, and demonstrate from conversations with many of the present owners of the apartments that the interiors as originally planned would have commanded a tangible value. But it also has to be conceded that a significant proportion of the flats have been stripped out and

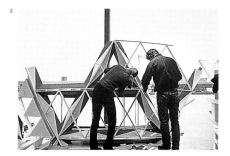

rebuilt – one owner bought three and joined them together to make one huge unit. More recently, another purchased two with the same intention. There was also a delightfully 'extreme' conversion by Claudio Silvestrin – now sadly stripped out – in which he removed just about everything except the supporting columns!

Commercially, the apartments have been extremely successful; not only selling at a period when the market experienced a downturn but also much sought after since and still continuing to change hands at high values. The group of which David Gabbay was a part has since split, but we remain good friends and still enjoy excellent lunches together.

During the early stages of construction, the developer secured an option on a site that backed onto the rear of the project. Plans were hurriedly redrawn and permissions secured to add a two-storey pavilion at the back of the site and build a galleried entrance to the main building, linked to the pavilion by a canopy to create a gateway to the private courtyard.

A grand staircase in the galleried entrance (2) ascends to the main studio space (3) at first-floor level, a two-storey-high volume with good connections to other secondary spaces on a mezzanine level and on the ground floor. The total space offered opportunities for subletting, as well as scope for future expansion, which has since proved to be a lifeline for the practice.

More important than anything else was the opportunity to create a properly integrated studio, which could be tailored to our own special needs. Not surprisingly, it is unlike any other space that I know. Even so, if economic pressures demanded, the main space can be easily converted – by inserting the missing floor – into two storeys of conventional offices, or twelve apartments, or a combination of the two, each served by a separate entrance.

The period leading up to the fitting-out of our new spaces was one of intense debate back in the Great Portland Street office. The design team, headed by Ken Shuttleworth and Howard Gilbey, assumed that everyone would want some degree of privacy in the open space and many versions of carrels were mocked up at full size for comment. The reactions were as positive as they were unexpected – nearly everyone wanted less privacy and more openness. By way of explanation they pointed to the central wall in the existing office, which despite its openings was a substantial division and undermined the concept of optimum communication.

The process of consultation continued and it was from this dialogue that the present rows of big benches were to evolve.

Riverside was realised at a time when the practice faced some of its most difficult challenges. This was in the aftermath of the Hongkong Bank project, which was inaugurated at the beginning of 1986. There was great pressure on the practice to move in its entirety to Hong Kong during this period, especially when the office there was peaking at 120 employees, while the London office had dropped to a mere sixteen. One of my present partners, Spencer de Grey, had made the initial move to Hong Kong to open our start-up office there in 1980. On his return at the end of 1982, virtually all the other key individuals had to leave *en masse* for Hong Kong to follow through the design which had been developed in London. I was torn between commuting to Hong Kong, Japan, America and Europe – all the places where the Bank was being made – and having to start a new practice with Spencer, virtually from scratch.

While the Hongkong Bank was on site – growing simultaneously up into the sky and down into the ground – the London office was completing projects such as the Renault Distribution Centre; winning international competitions such as the Frankfurt Athletics Stadium, the BBC Radio Centre and the Carré d'Art in Nîmes; and competitively securing projects like Stansted Airport and the new headquarters for Televisa in Mexico City. The mental and physical stresses pushed us to the limits. Although we were unaware of it at the time, we were laying the foundations for a better way of working and it is impossible to separate the practice now, in Riverside, from that collective experience which forged very personal bonds.

In 1985 the rest of my present design partners – Graham Phillips, David Nelson and Ken Shuttleworth – returned from Hong Kong, and nearly all the directors in the practice today hail from that critical period in Hong Kong and London.

The regrouping in London could have been an unsettling anticlimax after the triumph of the Bank. Instead, it was the reverse. There was a collective energy and experience eager to tackle new projects and to move forward. It was that same drive which later enabled us to fight off a domestic recession and successfully go out and compete for work internationally.

Begun at the end of 1986, the Riverside project was an opportunity to question everything about the way that we designed, but with a renewed enthusiasm. 5>

Nothing was too important or trivial to merit discussion. Many of the changes that the move achieved were, in retrospect, radical – although we now take them for granted. For example, some of us thought it would be better to have a 'no-smoking' office. The idea was floated, but we never expected it to happen because we assumed one group would feel alienated. To our surprise, however, it was the heaviest smokers, who saw it as an opportunity to help curb their habit, who were the strongest supporters. This hardly seems radical today, but then attitudes have changed since the late 1980s.

Some of the later alterations to the project mentioned earlier, such as the addition of the galleried entrance, were also turned to social advantage. For example, most places of work ensure that the visitor is carefully shielded from the activities within. From the very beginning, our office has been open to scrutiny. Meetings, whether formal or informal, take place in the midst of the creative process itself. The essence of the spaces has always been about lifestyle and communication. In that spirit, the revised entrance dispensed with the traditional waiting area and, instead, the visitor can enjoy the bar, which is the social focus of the office, and drink a coffee, read a newspaper or make a phone call if there is any need to wait.

The double-height glass facade of the main studio space overlooks the river – in terms of shading and solar gain, it was helpful that it was north facing. Along this border, interspersed with whatever models and mock-ups might be under current review (4), are small tables. All day long they are in use, for random meetings or by individuals working quietly on solitary tasks.

On the opposite side of the space is a mezzanine, which contains the three main meeting and presentation spaces, as well as our library – all open and visually connected. Underneath are the model shop and back-up areas – enclosed behind glass where the processes are noisy or there are special requirements, such as dust or fume extraction. Otherwise, almost everyone has a place at a bench – directors, students, partners, model-makers, computer operators, secretaries and architects. The only exceptions are those people working on competition projects, which might require special security, or small overflow groups concerned with accounts and finance.

The materials which enclose this main space are simple: painted concrete, stretched fabric, and carpet tiles for the floor, with its easily removable access panels – essential to cope with frequent changes in layout of computer and communications hardware. It is the calm ambience that surprises most visitors. This is, in part, due to the carefully designed acoustic environment, which can easily cope with up to 250 people, including visitors for meetings, and still ensure privacy.

The tempo of the office changes by the week, the day and the hour. The bar is a lively meeting place from early breakfast time, through lunch to evening drinks. Smaller groups might gather in the early hours, as the office is open twenty-four hours a day, seven days a week. There are no pressures or rewards for working antisocial hours; preferences and attitudes vary between individuals and this is reflected in a degree of choice – the important thing is that people are together when they need to be. Riverside is virtually a self-contained world with its own printing shop and photographic studio.

Although design is centralised in London and management flows out from there, it is impossible to think of the practice in isolation from the network of project offices around the world. The dynamic of Riverside owes much to the interaction and movement between these different places and cultures.

Communication is at the heart of our work as architects. A building must communicate to those who will use it, live in it and look at it. But it must be born out of their needs. There is no substitute for discussion and debate about the issues that will inform the design – this is an essential part of the creative process. Much of that research and exploration has to take place on the home ground of the client and the building users – the two may not necessarily share the same point of view. Often, some of the most important exchanges need neutral space, or the kind of venue where people can interact with models or full-size mock-ups. It would not be unusual, at the start of such a meeting in Riverside, to preview a prototype and suggest changes that the model-makers can implement before the end of the same meeting.

Ultimately, the quality of thinking transcends these practical benefits. The art of architecture can be practised just as successfully out of a bedsit in Hampstead (as my wife Wendy and I did originally) but the shift from that environment to the present one is not only more pleasurable: it has made it possible to contemplate far wider ranges of scale – from large-scale infrastructure projects to individual product design studies for door handles or bath taps. There is also an issue of

principle. It is self-evident that if we suggest that an environment can influence the quality of our lives then we should try to set an example in the environment that we create for ourselves as architects.

If Riverside demonstrates the value of good communication and a sharing of the main space by everyone on an equal basis, this should not be confused with an absence of hierarchy. Every Monday morning at nine o'clock the directors meet at the round table in the far corner of the studio (5). This regular forum reviews every aspect of the practice and makes the critical decisions, such as which projects to accept and which competitions to enter. But there is also an interaction with other meetings that take place and involve a wider body of the practice.

For me, Riverside is a rare combination of a wonderful team and a great place to work. But the ultimate luxury is being able to live and work in the same location. I am not alone in that respect. At different times, for several people in the building, it has been a place to live as well as a place to work. Two individuals that I know of have leased office space in the building and commuted by lift from their apartments above. Others have used the flexibility of their domestic spaces to blur the edges between their private and professional lives.

I have emphasised the importance of communication in the creative process and hinted at the link between creativity and sustained endeavour. The counterpoint to this is the physical communication that Riverside has created locally and how that relates to the wider context of London. For all of us there is contrast and stimulation in being able to move out through the network of pedestrian routes that we have helped to create. Sometimes these generate their own focus of social and commercial activity: for example, at the junction between the local road and the pedestrian path, which leads down from the river, a lively shopping and cafe life has developed which spills out onto terraces overlooking the dock.

There is no road between Riverside and the Thames, unlike the Embankment opposite, which is always busy with traffic. The result for those of us who live in the apartments is the luxury of an unusually calm style of urban living. This is particularly true at weekends when I often equate the experience to that of a rural retreat.

From the apartments, whether they are on the third or eighth storey, you look out across London and not down on it. The skyline is constantly fascinating and punctuated by a surprising amount of greenery. London is essentially a low-rise city and the area of Chelsea and Kensington that the building overlooks is, by European standards, quite dense. But the contact with the sky and the weather is sublime. Another unexpected surprise is the bird-life – for a wide variety of species the Thames seems to be a playspace and aerial highway. Although there is no doubt that one is in the midst of a city, the proximity of Battersea Park and the ease of being able to walk everywhere gives this place a village-like quality.

I find intuitively that the most pleasant routes always take precedence over the others – even though they might be longer. For example, it is a shorter distance to walk to and from the local cinema via Battersea Bridge, but the journey is not as pleasant as using Albert Bridge, and the walk along the edge of the river is much more interesting than by the road which is a part of the other route.

I think most designers would welcome a second chance with any project, whether it is a building or an artefact – I know I would. But, more than any project, I would like other opportunities to explore the integration of spaces for living and working, particularly in an urban environment. Perhaps that is, in part, because I have learned so much from the personal experience of Riverside and because I believe that it offers so many optimistic lessons for the future of cities. But, more than anything, it is because of the sheer pleasure, proximity and privacy that this way of life offers.

7

'... these new terminals are the noble halls of our age, evoking a sense of occasion and bring-ing a new thrill to air travel.'

Norman Foster

Two global urban scenarios are rapidly unfolding. The first of these is the explosive growth of cities: by 2030 more than five billion of the planet's predicted eight billion inhabitants are expected to be living in cities. The second is the shift of growth from the so-called 'developed' to 'developing' countries.

As an example of what this global shift means in comparative terms, in 1939 London was the highest populated city in the world. Ten years later it still shared the big league with cities such as Paris, Milan and Moscow. However, at the turn of the twenty-first century a demographic map of the world reveals that the European cities have receded into a mini-league, while the concentrations of population elsewhere have enlarged and proliferated. This is particularly true on the Asian Pacific Rim.

One of the implications of this shift is migration around the globe on a very large scale. Airbus, for example, anticipates that by 2010 only twenty per cent of air travellers will be business passengers. A key indicator in this respect is the accelerated rate of investment in infrastructure in the Pacific Rim, particularly in airports, which are being built on a hitherto unparalleled scale.

A further shift can be discerned in the nature of such infrastructure projects. The edges between infrastructure and architecture are becoming more blurred. We can see this in structures concerned with information transmission – communication towers and platforms, for example – but we can also see it in structures for physical communication, such as the airport. Is the airport infrastructure or is it architecture? Or is it perhaps inhabited infrastructure? As these edges become less finite, the distinctions between the role of the architect, the engineer, and other professions become similarly blurred. New infrastructure projects are typically becoming more publicly accessible, more multifunctional, less unidirectional. Together these trends have the potential to create a new kind of airport building.

The first generation of airports – such as Hong Kong's Kai Tak, Berlin's Tempelhof, or Le Bourget in Paris – were located close to the city centre. The combination of an earlier age of smaller aircraft and a predominantly low-rise building infrastructure was compatible with an embedded urban airport. However, the pattern with these and similar early developments is that the city, as it expanded, finally engulfed them. Kai Tak probably stretched this model to its logistical and technical limit. The dramatic approach path into the Airport memorably wove in

between the tower blocks that had grown up around it, giving rise to an 'urban myth' about jumbo jets landing with washing hanging from their wings, plucked from the balconies of nearby flats.

In London, the entrepreneurial vision that generated Heathrow's original Terminal One in the mid-1950s and set the pattern for the first generation of large airports around the world, echoed the pioneering spirit of the London Underground in the 1930s. However, that impetus has been lost in the capital, and transportation projects habitually founder in the wake of an overdeveloped and stultifying bureaucracy. Heathrow's planned expansion, in the form of Terminal Five, is mired (perhaps indefinitely) in an official inquiry.

London Heathrow, in terms of international passenger movements, is currently the world's largest airport, with some 40 million visitors per annum. It has evolved over the last 50 years from a military airfield and a cluster of canvas tents nestling amongst market gardens (1), into four major terminals on a site covering 1,100 hectares. In European terms this rate of growth might be considered rapid, but in terms of contemporary Asia it is closer to a snail's pace.

Compare Heathrow with the pattern of Hong Kong's Chek Lap Kok, or Shanghai's Pudong. In one-tenth of the time that it has taken London's airport to grow, Hong Kong has overtaken it by realising even more capacity in a single massive building (3-6). By 2040, Chek Lap Kok's planned passenger capacity, at 87 million passengers and 375,000 aircraft movements per annum, will be the equivalent of Heathrow and New York's JFK Airports combined.

In 1972 the British Airports Authority had the opportunity to anticipate the huge demands that would eventually be placed on Heathrow, and the transport infrastructure that serves it, and to make a bold leap into the future. They almost did it. They identified a site at Foulness, in the Thames Estuary, to the east of London. Foulness, a former army artillery range, offered almost unlimited space – 50 square miles – on which to build a brand new airport, far away from the restrictions of the city.

It was an opportunity to scoop up all of the facilities then existing at Heathrow, together with those that would eventually be provided by the 'second' London airport at Gatwick and what was to become – after 40 years of negotiation and public inquiry – the 'third' London airport at Stansted. Foulness would have been to

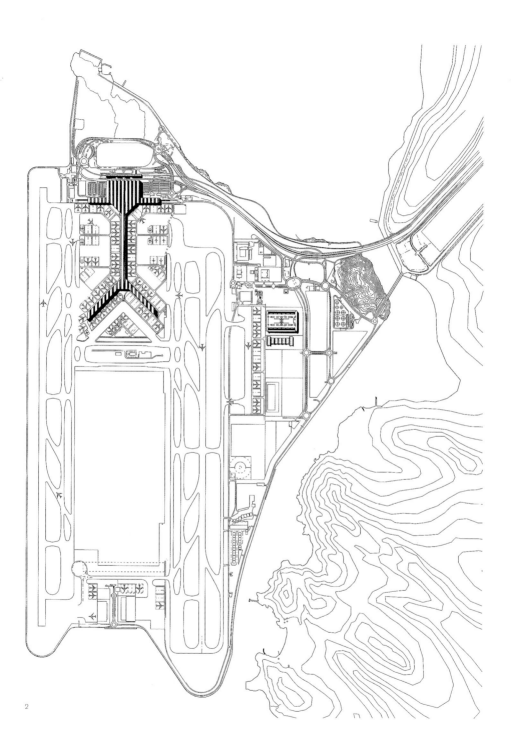

3

4

5

London what Chek Lap Kok is to Hong Kong, and involved similar travel distances. But the opportunity was lost. Construction began in 1973 and was abandoned in the face of entrenched opposition in 1974.

The Asian experience is very different. In Hong Kong, when the time came to select the site for a new airport there was no available land. The site itself had to be created. But far from being an obstacle to development, it became instead the catalyst for the largest construction project of modern times.

In 1992, Chek Lap Kok was a compact mountain island rising out of the sea off the South China coast. In an ambitious reclamation programme that involved moving 200 million cubic metres of rock, mud and sand, the island's 100-metre-high peak was reduced to a flat 7 metres above sea level and expanded to four times its original size. At 6 kilometres long and 3.5 kilometres wide, it is as large as the Kowloon peninsula (2).

From Chek Lap Kok, new road and rail links cross a causeway to Lantau to the south, and continue across two new bridges, including the typhoon-resistant Tsing Ma Bridge – the longest combined road and railway suspension bridge in the world – to reach Hong Kong itself. Thanks to the new railway line, three-lane highway, and Western Tunnel to Hong Kong Island, the entire journey between city and airport can be completed in approximately twenty minutes.

In Hong Kong brand new physical infrastructure is already in place to support the Airport's expansion over the next 50 years. Central London, meanwhile, has only belatedly begun to enjoy dedicated transport links to Heathrow. But even the Heathrow Express has to share ageing intercity and suburban rail tracks.

As London contemplates the nostalgia of its past and trades on a physical infrastructure largely inherited from the age of the horse and cart – long before the onslaught of the car – Hong Kong, which is already less than four hours' flying time from half the world's population, plans strategically for the reality of global expansion and major shifts of population.

In this new world view, airports are the symbolic gateways to a city. In the past these might have been the portals in the castle walls, the harbour quayside or the train terminus. The need to create imposing and symbolically important structures to celebrate these points of arrival and departure would seem to be a constant over time, from antiquity to the present.

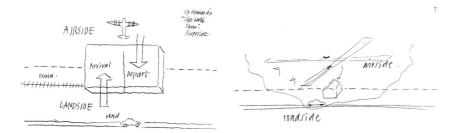

In the newest generation of airports the gateway has to be pushed well beyond the city limits and linked with an umbilical cord of rapid transit. The more remote location not only protects the environment of the core of higher density cities, but creates the opportunity for the airport to expand as a destination in its own right. The rapid transit system can be suppressed below ground and emerge into the heart of a city. Our expansion of Kowloon station to accommodate some 80 million passenger movements a year to and from China has created a fitting gateway to Hong Kong and part of the wider network of ground transportation supporting the Airport.

During this shift from centralisation to decentralisation in airport design we have witnessed a passing phase in which individual airlines have commanded their own customised terminals. But the almost universal model of an airport in the Western world is one of incremental, *ad hoc* growth. Heathrow remains London's principal airport and, although facilities at Gatwick and Stansted are growing, Heathrow is still expected to expand within its original site by adding more and more terminal buildings.

I can recall the previous head of the British Airports Authority, Sir Norman Payne, reflecting on nearly twenty years' experience of London's airports by saying that not once had any of the terminal buildings expanded in the way that their designers had planned. All their predictions had proved to be obsolete, rapidly overtaken by events. At Heathrow the end result is a non-finite architecture of individual structures, each in a state of continuous change and growth, with new ones being squeezed in wherever possible; the only limiting factors in this cycle being land and runway capacity. As a result, Heathrow is closer to the 'concrete jungle' of a 1960s new town than to the planned development of Chek Lap Kok or Osaka's Kansai.

Perhaps the same tendencies will eventually overtake the thrusting Asian economies. Meanwhile the architectural rules are being rewritten by the sheer scale of these single, large-volume buildings, which have evolved from a combination of political will and the appetite to invest in a fresh start. At this size they pose unprecedented challenges and opportunities.

I can trace the lineage of our projects for the airports of Hong Kong, Shanghai and Bangkok back to our design for Stansted Airport (13), which we

began in 1981. Stansted, in turn, can be traced back to the pattern of the earliest airports, such as Atlanta (8), where the progression from landside to airside was a simple walk from your car to your plane, which was always in view (7). But the new airports are not simply bigger versions of this concept: they are transformed by their megascale.

They are also rooted in the thirteen-year collaboration we enjoyed with Buckminster Fuller before his death in 1983 – an alliance which influenced our projects during that time and beyond. This is true not only of those projects that were recognisably geodesic in form, such as the Knoxville Energy Expo and the Climatroffice, but also of the deep-plan office projects, such as the Willis Faber & Dumas headquarters in Ipswich. Aside from an intrinsic concern for the relationship of mass and volume to the building's energy equation, Bucky's influence liberated our attitudes to scale, size and repetition.

The Climatroffice project, dating from 1971, points towards an architecture of 'interiorised' buildings, which live within an envelope so diaphanous that its presence is perceived as being closer to the sky or clouds than to any conventional structure. The form of this minimal envelope is a manipulation of Bucky's optimum sphere, which can envelop the maximum volume within the minimum surface area. It is the sheer scale of the single-volume membrane that reverses the traditional hierarchies. The mechanisms for creating order, orientation and routes through the interior space are independent of the enclosure, which from inside and out is anonymous and without scale, except for that of its surroundings which are reflected on its skin.

The vast new airport terminals have some characteristics in common with these Fuller-influenced visions. The form of an airport terminal is of necessity extruded to provide linear frontage and while the exterior is closer to a traditional building, the interior is increasingly determined by an architecture of individual buildings housed beneath the protective umbrella of a vast lightweight roof. This is an approach that we pioneered with the design of Stansted, which has subsequently become a model for airport terminals worldwide.

When we planned Stansted, we questioned, at the most fundamental level, the nature of a terminal building. Before Stansted, every large terminal essentially followed the same model: the structure would carry huge amounts of ductwork at

9

10

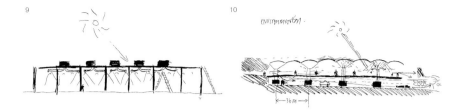

roof and ceiling level to move large volumes of conditioned air (9, 11); and there would be a reliance on artificial lighting, which generated a great deal of heat, and in turn required more cooling, with increasingly large ducts and more and more refrigeration plant. Furthermore, all that equipment had to be supported at roof level, and so the structure had to be enormous. The whole arrangement was incredibly wasteful of energy and other resources.

Stansted represents a departure point, one that was achieved by demonstrating that the old order of the 'serviced shed' could literally be turned on its head. The heavy engineering of mechanical plant rooms, metal ducts and supporting structure that made up the traditional roof are all relocated in an undercroft below the concourse level (10). The undercroft is really the engine room of the building. It contains all the baggage handling and environmental engineering plant and runs beneath the entire floor of the concourse, where it can easily be accessed via a service road. The heating, ventilating, air-conditioning and artificial lighting distribution systems are all contained within the 'trunks' of the building's tree-like structural columns as they rise up from the undercroft, through the floor of the concourse. The result is a lightweight membrane roof, which is freed simply to let in natural light and keep out the weather (12).

Flexibility for change is a vital consideration in such a volatile and expanding industry. This is another reason for the services undercroft. It is analogous to the void beneath a highly serviced office floor, which enables you to reconfigure the cabling to suit different layouts and changing technology. The headquarters building we designed for Willis Faber & Dumas in the early 1970s, was the first in Britain to be equipped with a raised 'aircraft floor' – before Willis Faber it was only computer rooms that had a void below the floor for cabling. Willis Faber is the only British insurance company not to have been forced to move into a new building in the 1980s in order to accommodate new communications technology.

The difference between these two examples is simply one of scale. Instead of cables, in Stansted's services undercroft it is possible to move or replace the hardware of baggage handling systems, electrical generators and heating and ventilation plant. As an example of how far this principle can be stretched, it was possible to insert a mainline railway station in the undercroft for a direct link to the city without disruption, even after the building had started on site.

A terminal building is in some ways also analogous to the aircraft it serves. The investment in a modern aircraft is so great that prolonged downtime for maintenance or upgrading is simply unaffordable. This has design implications. The engines, for example, have a relatively short design life when compared with the airframe, and will be replaced many times in the lifetime of an airliner. So in a modern aircraft, such as a Boeing 747, they are located in separate pods under the wing for ease of access and maintenance. This is in contrast to an earlier generation of aircraft, such as the Comet, where the engines were embedded in the airframe itself, making them very difficult to access.

The modern terminal is locked into a complex international network of flights and connections and is even more sensitive to downtime. It is a 365-day-a-year, 24-hour-a-day operation. The roof of the old-style terminal building, with its short-life elements such as mechanical equipment and light tubes sandwiched between structure and suspended ceiling, was a maintenance nightmare. It was also a serious safety hazard, as the tragic fire at Düsseldorf Airport, in April 1996, demonstrated. In that instance, a fire began in a flower kiosk and spread rapidly through the ceiling void of the arrivals hall, quickly engulfing the terminal. The advent of the undercroft solves all these problems.

There is no doubt that the quality of light and views in a terminal building contributes towards making it more friendly and spiritually uplifting. Added to that, this arrangement also uses much less energy, which is good news both for the environmentalists and the accountants.

At Stansted, natural light floods into the concourse through the glazed perimeter and apertures in the roof vaults. Suspended beneath the vaults are daylight reflectors, which shield the apertures and bounce light upwards onto the ceiling so that it is reflected indirectly at floor level. There is no 'black hole' effect at night. At dusk, as outside lighting levels diminish, artificial lighting hidden at the base of the 'trees' is projected onto the underside of the reflector so that the whole surface glows.

The principles defined at Stansted make a quantum leap in the new generation of airports that we have designed for Hong Kong (14-17), Shanghai and Bangkok. The essence of these large terminals, following the Stansted pattern, is a single roof, flowing freely over a fertile ground plane, on which fully serviced

13

instant buildings can grow within a tempered climate of unbroken space. The possibilities opened up by this evolutionary response to the realities of mass air travel can be grasped as a civic opportunity, or merely exploited for their commercial potential. In the tradition of the great nineteenth-century railway stations, these new terminals are the noble halls of our age, evoking a sense of occasion and bringing a new thrill to air travel.

For many people, however, air travel has become a stressful and confusing experience. In recognition of that fact, these terminal buildings are designed to make the traveller's experience as calm and pleasant as possible. Knowing that one can find one's way contributes greatly to this sense of well-being. The guiding principle was to ensure that the concourse would be a clear logical zone, and that movement through the building, from landside to airside or vice versa, would be as far as possible in a straight line and at a constant level.

At Stansted, for example, you proceed in one fluid movement from the set-down point, through the check-in area, security and immigration controls to the departure lounges, from where you can see the planes standing on the tarmac. From there you are taken via an automatic tracked transit system to the pavilion-like satellite buildings from where you board your aircraft.

In the process you experience two architectural orders. The primary order is the lattice-shelled roof, which is supported on the outstretched branches of the 'trees'. The smaller, secondary, order is the flexible system of free-standing enclosures such as shops, banks and bars which inhabit the space. There are none of the infuriating changes of direction and level that disfigure most major airports.

In Hong Kong, the Airport's natural setting is spectacular. To the south is the backdrop of the Lantau mountains, while to the north, across the water, are the New Territories, also with mountains in the distance. Wherever passengers are within the building, they can enjoy unimpeded views out. The glass sides of the terminal are purposely left clear up to a minimum height of 4 metres, and clutter throughout is eliminated so that sight lines are never blocked.

The design accentuates natural orientation far beyond the Airport itself: you can see the land, the water, and glimpses of the road and rail bridges in the distance, from the terminal; and you can see the aircraft. You know whether your plane is waiting on the 'landside' or the 'waterside' and so you can orient yourself

accordingly. This elemental approach, quite different from the claustrophobic boxes and tunnels that characterise so many airports, brings a sense of pleasure and drama back to the experience of flying.

The lessons of Stansted and Chek Lap Kok are that unimpeded views of the airside and landside, together with the natural order provided by a clear structure, can dramatically reduce the need for complicated signage systems or colour codes. In that sense they are 'analogue' rather than 'digital' buildings, insofar as, like a traditional watchface one can read them instinctively at a glance: there is no awkward conversion process from sign to route. Instead of an apparently life-threatening maze the experience can be friendly, direct and reassuring. Of course, the ultimate clarity of direct movement will always be modified by the inevitable barriers of customs, immigration, security and a degree of retailing. But these buildings are still very much open in spirit.

It is difficult to comprehend the scale of these buildings. Hong Kong's new terminal is so large that – like the Great Wall of China – its distinctive Y-shaped plan form is clearly visible on satellite photographs. At 1.27 kilometres long, and with an area of 516,000 square metres, the terminal building is the largest enclosed public space ever made. Its roof covers 18 hectares – approximately the same area as London's Soho district. Within that, the baggage hall is large enough to contain five Boeing 747s wing tip to wing tip; you could drop the Wembley or Yankee stadiums into it and still have room to spare. And the terminal's plant room alone, at 62,000 square metres, is large enough to contain Stansted's concourse twice over.

But although Chek Lap Kok is an enormous building, in reality it can be thought of as quite compact, because it covers a very small footprint in comparison to the equivalent four terminals at Heathrow Airport, while providing about 48 per cent extra space.

Nonetheless, the logistics behind the management of design and construction at this scale are awesome. To give just a few examples: the detailed design of the superstructure, including the roof, generated a print run of 125,000 drawings – in excess of 100,000 square metres of paper; at the peak of construction, there was a workforce of 21,000 on site; and the sheer size of this temporary community, and its isolation from the mainland, led to the creation of a 'smart card'

15

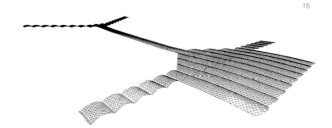

16

cashless society, based in a sizeable settlement of instant short-life hotels, offices and restaurants which sprang up on the island.

It is rare to encompass such extremes of scale and diversity in a single project. Moreover, all this was achieved at a staggering speed. A total design that coordinated all the details of the Airport's functioning, from aircraft parking to air conditioning, from security to shopping, was completed in just 21 months. Then, despite its heroic scale, and the fact that all building supplies had to be ferried to the island by boat, the building's superstructure took only 36 months to complete.

But perhaps the ultimate example of thinking big in Asian terms is the move from the old airport to the new. For a time the authorities ran the two in parallel, while they tested the new airport's technical systems. Once they were satisfied, they changed from one to the other overnight. The whole operation was achieved within six hours. The logistics of that, in terms of moving people and equipment, are truly staggering.

The airport on this new scale assumes many of the properties of an urban settlement, which raises further questions of social responsibilities. Are the prime public spaces the equivalent of a city's main square? Are they to be protected, or squandered like so many places that become saturated with billboards and retailing? Should this inside world be subject to controls and restrictions similar to those that have evolved to cope with urbanisation in the world outside? Or is the terminal to be regarded as a cross between a department store and a theme park? Will the fake, half-timbered 'ye olde pub' that unfortunately graces one London airport ultimately find its equivalent inside an Asian terminal: perhaps a Chinese restaurant in the guise of a plastic junk afloat in space?

Significantly, the British Airports Authority presently makes as much money from retailing as it does from its airport business. Gatwick, for example, attracts half a million visitors a year who are not going to meet somebody, or to say goodbye, but are just going to the airport to shop. Together, the BAA terminals contain more than 60,000 square metres of retail space.

Equally significantly, Chek Lap Kok's shopping centre – which covers an area the size of the original airport at Kai Tak – is the only shopping centre in Hong Kong which has one hundred per cent occupancy. Does the airport terminal in this scenario finally become a market with airline travel as a by-product, a shopping mall which feeds off the captive audiences that follow the new trade routes of industry and leisure?

As cities grow and airports respond to the new centres of population it is worth sounding a cautionary note by recalling how one writer commented on the occasion of the 50th anniversary of London's Heathrow:

'Every human settlement is an organism. But this one, fuelled by the virtually unconstrained power of the market, is a monster out of science fiction, swallowing land and hamlets, continuously recreating itself, permanently ravenous. It can never get enough: enough land, money, noise, dirt, adrenaline, electricity, organisations, car-parks, retail outlets, hotels, people. In this respect it is the image of us, and of our civilisation.'

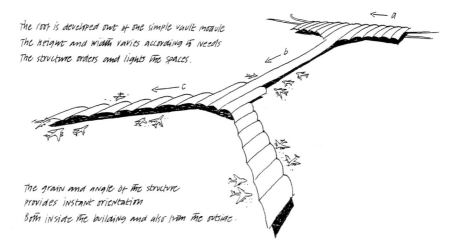

The roof is developed out of one simple vault module
The height and width varies according to needs
The structure orders and lights the spaces.

The grain and angle of the structure
provides instant orientation
both inside the building and also from the outside.

17

'The eagle is such an important feature of the Reichstag chamber that it is impossible to separate the design of one from the other.'

Norman Foster

In April 1996 I was invited to put forward ideas for a new eagle, as part of our project for the transformation of the Reichstag in Berlin. The following month, on 22 May, I presented my first proposals to a meeting of the Building Committee in Bonn.

During the few weeks leading up to the first presentation I had been living in the world of eagles – studying them, reading about them and trying to learn as much about them as possible. I have since spent time observing eagles in their natural habitat.

I could never claim to be an expert but I have studied them in sufficient detail to begin to see the special characteristics that distinguish eagles from other birds of prey. Their profile or silhouette is distinctive whether resting, in flight or diving to attack. These differences can be clearly seen in the photographs and the most telling clues are the spread and geometry of the wings as well as the position of the head. Eagles are so visually appealing and majestic that one starts to understand why they have assumed such emblematic importance in the history of societies around the world.

From my studies of many sources on the subject of heraldry I selected nearly 300 examples of symbolic eagles in order to compare them graphically. The eagle appears as a symbol in the history of Germany as early as 800 AD and it is interesting to trace its many different expressions over time. The more eagles I studied the more I became impressed by the extraordinary variety of mood and character that they projected – equivalent to all the extremes of human nature. The nuance of the way the beak, the eyes or the claws are drawn is particularly significant. Couple the handling of these details with variations in the sweep of the wing or body and the scope for expression is unlimited.

At an early stage in the process I started to list in my sketchbooks the varying attributes and qualities of some of these many eagles from the past. Each one of them projected tangible values, which I assumed mirrored, consciously or not, the ambitions and aspirations of their time. Given these insights what kind of 'new generation eagle' would be appropriate? What values should it project? Going back to my list of attributes I started to underline key words.

First I decided that it should look like an eagle – that it should be *eagle-like*. This might seem obvious but I am surprised how many eagles from earlier periods were more like crows, doves, turkeys or hens. One of the primary roles of the

designer is to transcend the naturalist perspective – to distil the essence of reality through a selective and graphic eye.

The next decision was the state of the eagle – was it to be static and resting, diving to attack its prey or flying? I decided that symbolically it would be better for it to be portrayed in *flight*. This led me later to propose an eagle that was not just flying but was *rising upwards*, like a phoenix reborn and rising from the ashes (1-4).

Then what kind of physical presence should this eagle have – would it be massive and swollen or *lean* and *lithe*? I decided that the latter direction would be more appropriate – but it certainly should not be skinny, rather it should be *strong* and *muscular*.

Finally and most importantly, what qualities should this eagle project – what was its character, its inner self? Well, I suggested that it should not be passive or indifferent – not a bystander or onlooker. On the contrary this new eagle should be *alert, attentive, involved* and *direct*. There are other qualities, which I believed it should embody: *timeless, dignified* and *mature*.

Only by spending much time on observation, contemplation and analysis was it possible to start to paint a word picture of the new eagle. It gave a solid philosophical foundation on which to build an image – to be able to pick up a pencil and start the process of exploration.

In the early stages of sketching I discovered that the essential features were thrown into sharper relief when I filled in the pencil silhouette and made a solid imprint. However, I was not proposing that the final version of the eagle should necessarily be solid black – quite the reverse. But graphically this was a good discipline because it focused attention onto the critical details of beak, eyes, talons and feathers. Even the slant of the neck or bulk of the body is magnified and has a profound effect on the emotional impact of the drawn image. The black on white image has a strong and timeless quality – it seems no accident that as a device it was much favoured in the past.

In the evolution of my design I moved on to explore the idea of perforating the eagle to emphasise the structure of the wings and also to make them visually *lighter* and more *transparent*. Attempts to reverse this visual language lacked the clarity and impact of the traditional heraldic form with its solid silhouette. In the same way attempts to divide the eagle around its centre line were also less convincing.

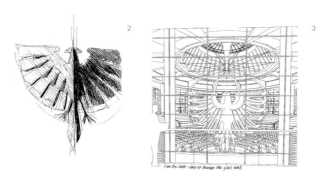

In the background I was aware of the context of the Reichstag chamber. The physical circumstances of the Reichstag are very different from the previous locations for the German Parliament, such as the old Bundestag chamber in Bonn and the new Bonn building by Günter Behnisch. In each of these previous locations the eagle was hung on a wall, always to be viewed from one side only. Accordingly it was a flat and two-dimensional image – even though the surface may have been slightly modulated.

The Reichstag in Berlin could not be more different: because the front and rear walls of the chamber are transparent, with people approaching from both directions – east and west – the new eagle is seen 'in the round'. It therefore needs to be a three-dimensional, sculptural object, free-standing in space.

Although there are exceptions in the past, it is an important tradition for the head of the eagle to look to its right and not to its left. So if you suspend an eagle in space then it will be correct from the front, but from the back it will look as though the head is pointing in the wrong direction. My answer to this dilemma was to place two eagles back-to-back, which was a critical step in the creation of a three-dimensional form.

There was also the challenge of avoiding any suggestion of a double-headed eagle, which has all the wrong historical associations. My first attempts made me aware of this difficulty – but they also suggested new ways forward. An eagle that faces both the West and the East is also symbolic of the act of political reunification. It is difficult to separate the shift of government from Bonn to Berlin from this event. All of our memories are still raw with the recollection of the dividing Wall, which was hard against the east facade of the Reichstag.

Working with computer models of the interior spaces and exterior approaches I explored how large the eagle would need to be when seen from the most important angles. As a sculpture it needs to be large enough to have an appropriate presence but also to have a degree of transparency and lightness – the opposite of a monolithic intervention.

At the end of my presentation in May the response of the committee was encouraging. However, I was reminded about the undesirability of a two-headed eagle. I was also asked about the relationship between the design of the Reichstag chamber and the eagle. I responded with the observation that it was

4>

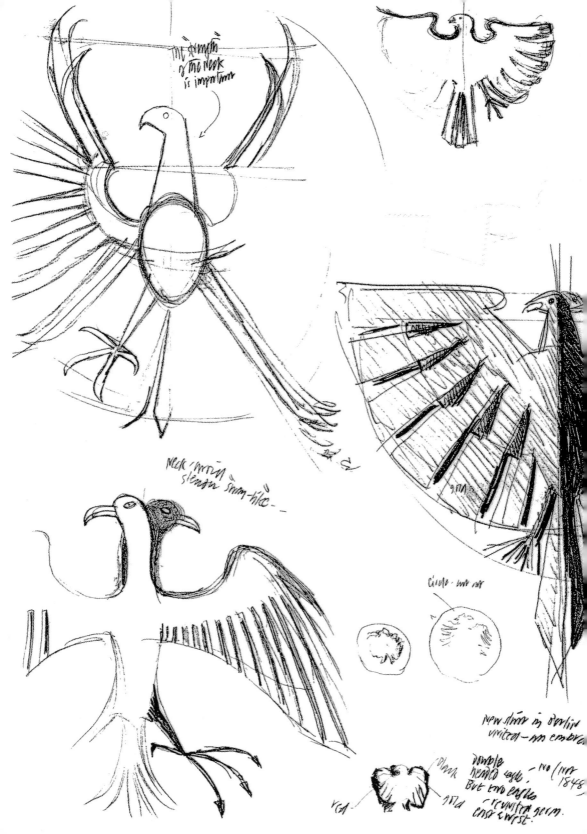

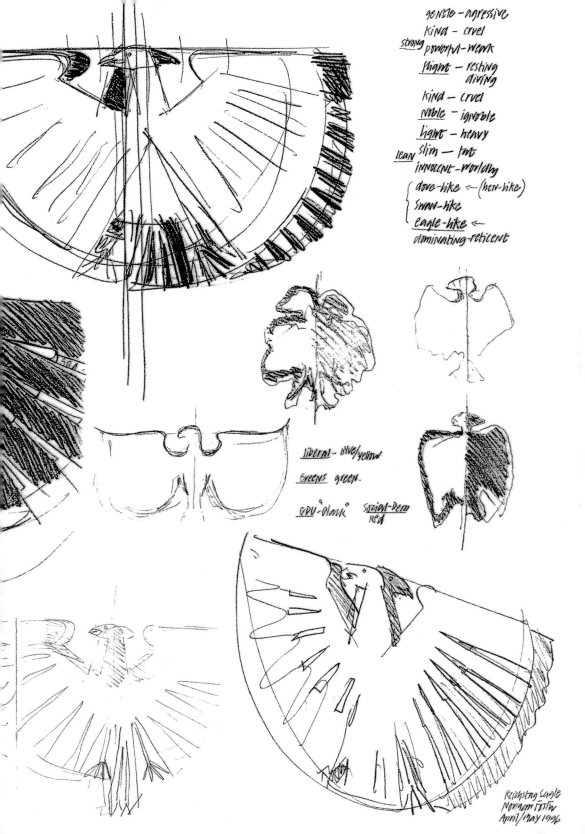

gentle – aggressive
kind – cruel
strong powerful – weak
flight – resting
diving
kind – cruel
noble – ignoble
light – heavy
lean slim – fat
innocent – worldly
dove-like ← (hen-like)
swan-like
eagle-like ←
dominating-reticent

liberal – blue/yellow
Greens green.
CDU "black" Social-Dem red

Reichstag Eagle
Norman Foster
April/May 1996

5 6

wise for the architect of the Bundestag to be given the responsibility for both the symbol of the eagle and the chamber, because in reality they are completely integrated. The eagle is such an important feature of the Reichstag chamber that it is impossible to separate the design of one from the other.

Following that meeting, I continued to refine the outline of the eagle and to explore the potential for colour rather than my earlier concept of grey and silver. In particular I was interested in contrasting the rear surfaces of the eagle in gold or yellow with the front face in black or dark grey. It could then be highlighted with red for the eyes, beak and talons. I felt that this was in a good heraldic tradition and would impart a richness, and a link with tradition in the main chamber.

However, the creation of a new eagle raises such controversy that any step in the design process can be seen by some as contentious. When I discussed the idea of using colour with some of my German colleagues they were concerned that the result might be seen as too nationalistic. However, I was not dissuaded and I pursued the idea in drawings and models. It was a great relief when these same colleagues saw the coloured models and changed their minds.

It was at this point that I was asked to make a second presentation to the President of the Bundestag, Rita Süssmuth, and a smaller group of the Building Committee in Bonn. I made some further revisions to the size of the eagle in relation to the main chamber and redrew this latest version into a selection of three-dimensional computer drawings.

On Thursday 20 June I travelled to Bonn. I showed a summary of the first presentation, then moved on to present a coloured sketch of the eagle and the new three-dimensional model, rendered in black, gold and red. This was accompanied by up-to-date perspectives of the interior spaces with the re-dimensioned eagle.

The response was most encouraging, but I noted two reactions. Firstly, there was a feeling that perhaps the eagle was a trifle too lean and that it could benefit from a little more weight. I agreed with this observation and promised to adjust the profile accordingly. Secondly, from some points of view, the latest eagle could still be interpreted as two-headed, even though it had improved in this respect since the previous stage. I was sensitive to this point and said that I was confident that with further work this issue could be fully resolved. The Committee asked me to develop the eagle further so that it could be presented to a wider audience.

On my return to the office I redrew the outline of the eagle to increase the width of the neck area. This gave it some additional weight and allowed me to superimpose the west-facing eagle over the east-facing one with no hint of double-headedness (5-7). I was sufficiently encouraged by this development to make the transition from freehand drawing to computer trace. A new generation of models was commenced. The first, with the new profiles as plates of foam, explored a light yellow which would be closer to the true gilding that I envisaged for the rear face of the eagle than the dull gold that I had previously shown. The second series used the computer to cut metal profiles. The idea was that the wing feathers could now be slightly curved outwards. This flare would, I hoped, make the eagle more dynamic and sculptural in space.

The eagle I presented to the Building Committee on Wednesday 25 September (8) was a three-dimensional construction, with four layers of metal mesh and stiffening ribs to anticipate the transition to large-scale reality (9-13). The ribs, made of aluminium or steel, provided a supporting structure. They also projected from the surface of the wings, adding more modelling, reflections, sparkle and highlights, as well as casting shadows. Under the effects of differing light conditions they helped to create a further dimension of change during the day, at night and over the seasons. It is important to remember that this sculpture is bathed in light from the mirrors above which deflect light into the main space. The layers of perforated metal allowed a hint of views, giving the eagle an appropriate lightness.

Postscript

Despite the generally supportive stance of the Building Committee, it soon became clear that the eagle was awakening political emotions. These began to affect the design: some were anxious that it should not be perceived as too aggressive; others wanted the talons and beak to be more prominent; others questioned why the existing eagle, designed by Ludwig Gies in 1952, could not simply be retained. There were even those who questioned whether there should be an eagle at all. In an atmosphere of political uncertainty, there was a growing sentiment that Parliament should take something familiar from Bonn to Berlin.

Ultimately the political consensus was for a further redesign, retaining some of the character of the Gies original. We explored variations on the theme of a new,

full-bodied, eagle but that provoked the intervention of the heir to the Gies estate, who would not countenance what he regarded – quite mistakenly – as modifications to the Gies design. Given the opportunity, we could undoubtedly have demonstrated that these objections were groundless, and produced a distinctive new eagle. But with a general election looming on the horizon, MPs were focused on more pressing issues; time for discussion and political energy simply ran out. The decision was made to retain the Gies eagle. It was frustrating, but I could sympathise and in their place would probably have come to the same conclusion.

The eagle that hangs in the chamber today is therefore faithful to Gies' 'fat hen' from the front, but it has been enlarged, made three-dimensional and given a new back view. Naturally, after two-and-a-half years of conceiving and detailing eagles it is disappointing not to have been able to realise a new design. But I remind myself that the 'headline' has always been the Reichstag; the eagle was a fascinating project in itself, but in the context of the whole it was the fine print. However, the translation of the original two-dimensional bird pinned on a wall into a three-dimensional eagle hovering in space is a creative act in itself. I have to say that I am not displeased by the final transformation, although perhaps the London *Times* of 10 February 1999 should be allowed to have the last word. Commenting on the advent of the twin eagles – plump at the front and thin at the back – it said:

'Cynics say [the new eagle] fairly represents the transition from Helmut Kohl, the previous Chancellor, to his successor Gerhard Schröder – a bird that still likes its dinner but is willing to forgo second helpings – a pragmatic weight-watching kind of eagle.'

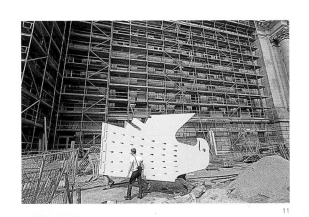

11

12

13

14>

'For the pilot it is difficult to separate the spiritual uplift of the experience of flight from the satisfaction of delicately balancing the physical forces involved in the process.'

Norman Foster

'The aeroplane is the symbol of the new age,' wrote Le Corbusier in 1935 (1). It was during this period that aircraft design was to be revolutionised. Up until then the biplane reigned supreme with its two wings, one above the other, laced together by diagonal struts like trusses inherited from earthbound structures, such as bridges. The fuselage itself followed a similar pattern of triangulated members. In the earliest aircraft this was exposed to the elements but it was eventually covered with canvas like the wings.

Two technological breakthroughs revolutionised the performance and appearance of aircraft. First was the realisation that the outer membrane of cloth could be transformed to become a vital part of the structure. The very earliest examples were sheathed with planks of wood like a boat hull, to be replaced later by skins of metal. The second innovation was to replace the pairs of trussed wings with one single cantilevered wing.

In roughly the same period of time architects and engineers were to transform the appearance of buildings with cantilevered structures which dissolved the boundaries between inside and outside, creating a new concept of space. Frank Lloyd Wright with the thrusting balconies of Fallingwater, built between 1934 and 1937, was to defy gravity at the domestic scale in the same way that skyscrapers, as vertical cantilevers, were charting new territories in the sky.

The 1930s marked a crossover from the time when aircraft structures were inspired by earthly examples to the present time when the roles have been reversed. Today the most advanced engineering of materials and computer simulations is likely to be generated by the aerospace industries. For example, there are new generations of composite and stressed skin structures for bridges and buildings, which could not have happened without feedback from aircraft construction. The computer-aided design systems developed by the aerospace industries to handle three-dimensional complexity have also been absorbed into architectural practice. And it is now commonplace to explore the microclimate around buildings by studying models in wind tunnels using installations and techniques rooted in the world of aerodynamics.

Computational Fluid Dynamics (CFD), the computer simulation of the movement of gases and liquids around and through bodies, was developed by the aerospace, defence and nuclear industries as a 'virtual wind-tunnel'. The technology

enabled these industries to test the aerodynamics of spacecraft or the movement of gases in nuclear cores without incurring the enormous costs or possible hazards of undertaking such tests with real objects.

Because of the complicated mathematical techniques underlying CFD, and the power and cost of the computers needed to drive the software, it remained the preserve of NASA and similar government agencies for two decades. However, within the last ten years the computational power required for CFD has fallen dramatically in price from tens of millions to only a few thousand pounds, making the technology available to industry at large.

The benefit to architecture of CFD is enormous – testing the airflow around and through a building once it has been built is not an option; discovering mistakes during the construction phase is both costly and dangerous. It is now possible, as part of the design process, to conduct virtual tests which can help to optimise a building's reliance on natural ventilation. We were able to exploit this technology in the design of the Commerzbank in Frankfurt, using it to establish the optimum placement, size and angle of the windows and air vents, and the relationship of office floors to the 'sky gardens' that act as the building's lungs. In doing so we were able to prove to our client that the building could be naturally ventilated for a large proportion of the year, thus dramatically reducing its reliance on mechanical ventilation and cooling systems. In practice, we have been able to reduce energy consumption by a third in comparison to conventional office towers.

Just as the history of architecture can be charted by the buildings that move the technology or the thinking forward, it is interesting to trace some of the dramatic changes in the design of aircraft, which have their roots in the work of the pioneering aircraft designers of the mid-1930s. Around this period five British designers were major players on the world stage and they were instrumental in charting the future history of aviation. Ten years later, in 1947, it was possible to glimpse the future and to take stock of the past.

Reginald J Mitchell (1895-1937) was chief designer at Supermarine. He created the legendary Spitfire, famed in the Battle of Britain (2). The Spitfire (of which more than twenty versions were eventually created under the direction of Mitchell's successor at Supermarine, Joseph Smith) was born out of the floatplanes which won three Schneider Trophies and set world speed records.

Following his tragically early death, the obituaries of the time eulogised Mitchell's technical achievements but there were also constant references to the aesthetic delights of his designs – the 'special quality of combining fine lines with great structural strength,' his 'beautiful aircraft' which 'looked a thoroughbred'. The sight and sound of a Spitfire still stirs the heart, and as one of the privileged few who have flown one, I can personally vouch for the fact that the Spitfire is an absolute delight to fly. Remarkably, the RAF continued to fly the final versions of the Spitfire as a front-line service aircraft well into the 1950s – a time when the piston engine had long been superseded by the jet.

Sydney Camm (1893-1966) was a contemporary of Mitchell and created that other classic fighter of the Second World War, the Hawker Hurricane (3). He bridged the transition from the peak of piston engines and propellers to the new era of jet propulsion. In 1953 the first prototype of his Hunter jet fighter, one of the most successful jet fighters ever produced, set a new world record for absolute speed. Camm went on to become the driving force behind the revolutionary Harrier, with its helicopter-like ability for vertical take-off and landing. As I combed the papers of the Royal Aeronautical Society of the 1960s to learn more about him, I was struck by the references to the 'elegant shapes' of his designs, and the comparisons to Sir Christopher Wren and his churches. Charles Richard was quoted as saying: 'In medieval times, all the best designers and engineers were architects. Today many of those who would then have been the best architects are aircraft designers. That is why architecture is not as good as it formerly was.'

George Carter (1889-1969) of the Gloster Aircraft Company worked with Frank Whittle (pioneering designer of the jet engine) to create the Meteor – the world's first operational jet aircraft (6, 8). It made its first test flight in spring 1943 and over the following four years set three new world speed records. Interestingly, Whittle had patented the jet engine as early as 1930, but industry and the Air Ministry proved resistant, refusing to take it up until they were propelled into action by the war effort.

Roy Chadwick (1893-1947) at Avro was responsible for the design of the Lancaster Bomber (4, 5) and its later civil derivative the Tudor – the first civil aeroplane to be pressurised – in which he was to tragically lose his life in a test flight in 1947. The Lanc, as it became known, was the backbone of Bomber Command;

powered by four Rolls Royce Merlin engines, it flew more missions during the Second World War than all the other English heavy bombers combined and, remarkably, continued in service with the RAF until 1956.

Chadwick's sketches pointed the way forward to the delta wing designs of the Vulcan (10) – one of the foundations of the present-day Concorde (9) and the Stealth Bomber (14). Before becoming consumed with the pursuit of aeroplane design, Chadwick was described as 'quite a fair artist and violinist' by a close colleague, who voiced the opinion that his artistic skills were evidenced by his designs. He went on to suggest that although aeroplane design was a science, 'art still contributes and in my opinion and that of others better qualified, an aeroplane that is right looks right and the modern aeroplane is a thing of beauty to appeal to the aesthetic eye'.

Ronald Bishop (1903-89) was head of design for de Havilland and responsible for the all-wooden Mosquito (7). From 1941 until 1944 this was the fastest aircraft in the RAF and, unarmed as it was, it consequently enjoyed the lowest loss rate of any aircraft with Bomber Command. The home-based fighter version defended wartime Britain for three years, downing six hundred enemy raiders and destroying six hundred flying bombs in 60 nights. Bishop was also responsible for the Comet – the world's first jet-propelled airliner (11). This aircraft, more than any other, was to usher in the new era of global communication by big jets.

All of these designers demonstrated great flair during the formative years of aviation, exhibiting what Sir Henry Royce described as 'the ideal temperament for a designer – slow to decide and quick to act,' as well as having 'that infinite capacity of taking pains, which is judged the hallmark of genius'. These were the days when a new aircraft could be flying off the drawing board within a year. The fortunes of companies depended on the quality of their design which in turn rested on the shoulders of their chief designers. No amount of finance or management skills could compensate for inherently poor design. Those lessons are even more valid today when we view the success of companies that lead in design and innovation: it is as true for consumer products as it is for aircraft.

But in the mid-1930s, no matter how brilliant the aircraft designs were, because there was always the uncertainty of demand and the complications of bureaucratic procedures, many of the leading companies were on the verge of

bankruptcy and only survived by diverting their skills into other fields. Westland, for example, was making stainless-steel barrels, and Supermarine used the skilled craftsmen who created boat hulls to make mahogany lavatory seats. This was in the time leading up to the growth of the new war effort.

I grew up during the Second World War and as a child I spent many hours making scale models of the classic fighters and bombers of the period. I am still fascinated by models and looking back, the story of the aero-modelling kits is like history in microcosm. Britain pioneered the concept, but the initiative was seized by others who were better able to exploit the potential of a mass market. For aircraft it was America, for motorcycles and kit models it was Japan and elsewhere in Asia. Kit models today, like the aircraft on which they are based, can be as sophisticated and complex as their forebears were crude and simple.

But aircraft today are infinitely more complex, and design responsibility is spread out through a wide network of subcontractors. These trends were already apparent in the mid-1960s when the changing nature of design was reflected in drawing offices that were already bigger than the full complement of a busy 1925-30 aircraft factory. The same tendencies can be seen today in the design of large and complex buildings such as international airports. The scale of investment limits the number of design offices with the capability to compete on a world scale. Similarly the construction of such structures is spread over hundreds of subcontractors who operate globally; the site is merely an assembly area and the builders rarely build because they have now become construction managers.

Another measure of the increasing sophistication of aircraft design over time is the rise in cost for units of weight. For example in 1925 it was estimated that aircraft cost about £1 for one pound of basic weight. The equivalent for today's airliner, such as the Boeing 747-400, is approximately £160 per pound, while for a modern fighter, such as the Eurofighter Typhoon, the figure is an incredible £2,600 per pound. Even making allowances for inflation, this represents an astonishing increase over 70 years.

Another factor which is common to the worlds of aviation and building is the process of miniaturisation. Relative to its performance the modern aircraft is physically much smaller than its historical counterpart. The same is true of a building type such as the cargo warehouse. The fully automated and very compact HACTL

cargo terminal in the new Hong Kong Airport occupies a footprint of 14.2 acres (5.8 hectares) (12, 13). But if it were spread out as a traditional low-rise shed it would cover one-and-a-half times the footprint of the entire airport terminal.

The American visionary Buckminster Fuller, who designed the geodesic dome, was fascinated by the relationship of ends and means, weight and performance. He drew many comparisons between the advanced technology of flight and the wayward world of buildings. If Mies van der Rohe advanced the spiritual message that 'God is in the details', and 'less is more', then it was Fuller who identified the trend of ever-increasing performance with less and less mass, of 'doing more with less'. His most compelling examples were always drawn from aerospace and communications.

As an architect I can see the same trends. In our design for Stansted Airport we challenged conventional wisdom which up to then had assumed that a terminal roof would be filled with heavy mechanical equipment to light, cool and heat the spaces underneath it. Our innovation was to shrink the mechanical content into a deep void below the floor and to stretch a lightweight metal roof over the entire concourse. It was a classic example of achieving more with less. The problems of uplift from wind were countered by aerodynamic devices at the roof edge – like flaps or airbrakes on an aircraft wing. With an umbrella-like roof whose primary function was to offer protection from the elements, it was then possible to bring sunlight into the heart of the space. The result is far more human and poetic than batteries of fluorescent lights. Furthermore, making free use of daylight has brought significant reductions in energy costs – in architecture I find it difficult to separate the spiritual from the rational.

The same is true of flying. I have flown many hours in high-performance sailplanes which must be the ultimate solar-powered vehicles – capable of using natural up-currents of air to traverse hundreds of kilometres at very high speeds. For the pilot it is difficult to separate the spiritual uplift of the experience of flight from the satisfaction of delicately balancing the physical forces involved in the process. The romance of flight permeates perceptions of aviation – from Malevich, the Futurists and the writings of Antoine de Saint-Exupéry, to the paintings of Robert Delauney and his homage to Blériot, who in turn pronounced: 'The most beautiful dream that has haunted the heart of man since Icarus is today reality.'

If, at their peak, architecture and flight are about the spirit as well as physical practicalities, and the outcome of that fusion is a beautiful object, then there are links between architecture and aviation – even if one form is earthbound and the other traverses the Earth. Aviation started as an offspring of the engineering that makes a work of architecture possible, borrowing freely at the time from the established disciplines. In a remarkably short period it has grown up to be bigger and faster, generating technology and a body of knowledge which are now invaluable to the parent.

Postscript

When I wrote this piece, in 1997, it was a special anniversary year: it was 50 years since the death of Roy Chadwick, since the record-breaking flight of the Gloster Meteor and the end of the production of the Spitfire; and it was the 60th anniversary of the death of Reginald Mitchell. It was also in 1947 that the speed of sound was exceeded for the first time in history.

14

'The true vernacular architecture of its time was often on the cutting edge of available technology, far removed from the romantic associations that might follow in a later age.'

Norman Foster

As an architect I spend my life travelling the world working on projects which, because of their size or complexity, are about pushing the limits. It is perhaps ironic that my private passions – cross-country skiing and the annual Engadin Valley Marathon – are also, in different ways, about pushing the limits.

Downhill skiing is well publicised, and almost everyone knows about the Engadin Valley in Switzerland and its association with the sport. But cross-country skiing, *langlauf,* is probably one of the best-kept secrets in the world – or one of the most misunderstood pleasures, depending on who you talk to. Otherwise it would not be possible for me to assail so many strangers to the sport with my wildly enthusiastic descriptions.

The Engadin Valley has hundreds of kilometres of ski trails, which traverse frozen lakes and climb up and down through forests and across fields. In all kinds of weather throughout the winter months, the valley is alive with two kinds of cross-country skiers – those who glide along grooved tracks 'classic style' and those who ski 'freestyle' on the smoother strip next to the tracks.

I find it impossible to separate aesthetics from any aspect of my life, and *langlauf,* whether classic or skating, can be beautiful to behold – like ballet. But when the theatre for this winter activity is a valley on the heroic and magnificent scale of the Engadin, with its special quality of light – forever changing – then the combination is pure bliss.

Both the Engadin Valley and the sport itself are full of contradictions. It is a paradox that a traditional playground for the rich and famous should also be a setting that has enabled some of the greatest minds to find creative inspiration – Hesse, Mann, Giacometti, Nietzsche and others. What mixture of sport and setting in the world could be at the same time so accessible, so intensely physical and yet so spiritual? It is a unique place that can embrace such polarities.

On most days of the year – whether jogging in a London park, the California desert, the African bush, Hong Kong Mid-Levels or the streets of Sydney and Shanghai – the cross-country Engadin Marathon is in my mind as a point of reference. After long hours in jets with time changes that can turn nights into days, I have to push myself to jog on arrival. I know that it is the only way to ensure that once a year, in the freezing cold of a March Sunday morning in Maloja, I will join up with 12,000 other souls who come together to celebrate their sport.

We start at nine in the morning from the southern end of the valley and travel for 5 kilometres, climbing and descending many metres over the course. The race, like the activity itself, embraces all generations – from Olympic-level athletes at the front to the retired grandparents and less serious addicts who will follow behind.

Consider the range of age and background of the participants and try to imagine their widely differing priorities. The leaders will complete the course in about one hour and twenty minutes, and success or failure will be measured in split seconds. But many, like myself, will be competing for a different kind of pleasure – skiing against their own clocks. For me there is always time to be touched by the humanity of the spectacle: children anxious to pass on refreshment, strangers who cheer from the sidelines. It is difficult to describe the atmosphere – a mixture of celebration, tolerance and vivid colour. Regardless of their finishing times, for the vast majority of participants, the event is a fun-loving celebration.

It is difficult to describe the heightened sense of awareness on a long run. At the last marathon I developed a rhythm on the stretch alongside Samadan Airport – even though I only had one stick at the time – and I remember thinking that it felt close to flying (there are parallels to sailplanes and cross-country soaring). Then there is the way in which the mind can roam freely – from the most profound thoughts to the most prosaic, such as the promise of a beer and sausage at the end; and for those like me who enjoy food and drink, an even greater appetite afterwards!

Then there are other dimensions to the event – the precision of the organisation is awesome. The warm outer clothing that the competitors strip off at the start will be moved to the finish line by trucks, which average about the same speed as the skiers. The flow and separation of vehicles and pedestrians in this operation has many lessons for big cities; and the way in which your clothes always turn up just at the point when you believe they are lost somewhere in the system is uncanny! And how is it that amongst so many thousands of people you always manage to meet friends at the finish?

There is a very satisfying equation between the ends and means of cross-country skiing – you only get out of it what you personally put in, like life itself. Incidentally it still surprises me that just a relatively short time ago I could never have imagined doing what I can now do on skis – a testimony to the patience and

professionalism of my instructors! But there is always a long way to go – like chasing the end of the rainbow.

In the fairly brief history of the race, the speeds have increased dramatically – partly through technique and partly through development of higher-technology equipment (1, 2). I find a tactile and visual delight in this equipment – not only the skis and sticks but also the clothing – the best kind of high technology. The contrast between the dead weight of downhill equipment and the featherweight equivalent of *langlauf* is dramatic. My downhill skis, sticks, and boots, which are agony to walk in, weigh much more than my cross-country gear. Because there is no waiting around in queues or sitting on open chairlifts, the equipment for the cross-country skier is lighter and very much more comfortable. Despite being able to cope with extremes of air and body temperature, perspiration, and great freedom of movement, the clothing is only a fraction of the weight of those bulky parkas and ski suits. Furthermore, when you have to power yourself uphill every gram counts and it shows in the refinement of design. The differences between these two kinds of skiing may be partly philosophical, but there is no escaping the fact that the performance of the independent cross-country skier is directly linked to the advanced technology of the equipment and clothing.

On a typical Engadin winter day, it is interesting to compare the activities of those traversing the cross-country trails at the bottom of the valley and those skiing down the slopes. Aside from the outlay for equipment, the downhill group pays a high price for those facilities that lift them continuously to the top, unlike the cross-country group whose sport costs them virtually nothing. But how do you quantify the poetic difference between queuing for a ski lift and taking a stroll through the woods?

The cross-country skier is liberated from the need for an all-consuming infrastructure. Even the ski trail itself is ephemeral. Almost invisible in winter, by spring it has disappeared into lakes and routes for walkers and mountain bikers.

Although I am privileged to share the pleasures of downhill skiing, I cannot help contemplating, as I ride an elegantly functional chairlift (3), that it consumes a huge amount of energy. For every kilometre that we swish down the slopes with the force of gravity, our quilted bodies, heavy boots, skis, and poles are hauled back up the mountain for a similar distance by a mixture of cable cars, gondolas

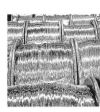

and lifts. It is hardly surprising that those ski passes cost so much money when we consider the outlay and running costs to power systems that for most of the year will lie idle. And although the scale of the mountains in the Engadin dwarfs everything man-made, the urbanisation that relentlessly follows the pursuit of leisure is everywhere apparent and leaves permanent scars on the landscape.

It was Buckminster Fuller who drew attention to the revolution in the world of communication, which has some parallels with my skiing example. He compared the inefficiency of all those tons and tons of copper cable – the infrastructure which not so long ago rested on the sea-bed to connect continents – with the electronic freedom that lightweight satellites and invisible airwaves now offer (4, 5). Fuller never lived to see the tiny mobile telephones that are a logical extension of his many optimistic predictions about society's ability to achieve 'more with less', but in an article written in 1969 Fuller makes the point thus:

'To demonstrate this fantastic improvement in performance, we witness that one communications-relaying satellite of only one-quarter of a ton of material is now outperforming the transoceanic communications capacity and fidelity of 175,000 tons of copper cable. This constitutes a seven-hundred-thousand-fold step-up in communications performance per pound of invested resources.'

In his book *Critical Path*, Fuller wrote about the first flight by a man-powered craft, demonstrating that improved technology would produce more effective results with fewer materials and less energy in quicker times. Some years ago, I met the designer of that aircraft, Paul MacCready, at a conference in Aspen. He talked about how he had achieved the seemingly impossible by going back to the basics of early flying machines and using advanced materials from other technologies. When congratulated, MacCready did not think that he was the most creative force in the equation – he believed that the truly creative act was that of a man called Kremer, who set the challenge and offered a significant prize for the first flight to be powered by human energy. I believe that MacCready's understatement is due partly to modesty, but his point is significant. In any arena, the designer, whether architect or engineer, can only act on the initiatives of those who set the priorities – environmental, political or otherwise.

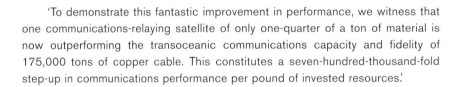

In *Sol Power: the Evolution of Solar Architecture,* Stefan and Sofia Behling similarly emphasise the importance of reference points from the contemporary worlds of communication and recreation. In one chapter they chart indigenous buildings from the past. I am reminded of Bernard Rudofsky's observation in *Architecture without Architects* that 'the philosophy and know-how of the anonymous builder presents the largest untapped source of architectural inspiration for industrial man'.

The true vernacular architecture of its time was often on the cutting edge of available technology, far removed from the romantic associations that might follow in a later age. It is easy to forget, for example, that the concept of an acceptable level of thermal comfort has changed over time. Many instances can be found from the past of solutions that control summer overheating, but there are few that successfully confront the difficulties of heating in winter: the environment for a king in the Middle Ages would be unacceptable to those in many of today's societies who are classed as the poorest. It is surely an irony that the threat of global warming, corrosive pollution, and depleted resources of non-renewable fuels should coincide with a rising demand for thermal comfort.

So what is it that connects the non-building references of our time, such as the cross-country skier, or the mobile telephone, with those indigenous structures of the past? Surely they were all pushing the frontiers of technology by showing ways in which the maximum benefits could be obtained from minimal resources. In the case of those earlier builders, they were, in the best examples, creating synergies between climate, resources and place. They are reminders that current building technology lags behind other sectors and could benefit from greater cross-fertilisation and long-overdue research.

'Londoners cannot negotiate with ease the heart of their city by any mode of transport, and London cannot breathe.'

Norman Foster

It is predicted that within thirty years two-thirds of humanity will be living in cities – a projection which poses entirely new social and technological challenges. Buildings currently consume half the world's energy, with industry and transport accounting for most of the rest. When we consider that just 25 per cent of the world's population presently consumes 75 per cent of the energy, the implications for energy management are obvious.

There is a shift towards super-cities of unprecedented size, especially on the Pacific Rim. It took 130 years for the population of London to grow to eight million people; the population of Mexico City has soared to twenty million in under fifty years. In all their diversity, however, cities around the world have some common problems, and can learn from each other.

London, for example, is a compact and relatively well managed, humanistic city and a potential model for sustainability, particularly because of its high density. There is a close relationship between density and energy consumption and while there are other important factors, such as accessibility and public transportation networks, it is the compact city that offers a lifeline to future sustainability. The key is to focus on what makes a city sustainable.

London is a city that I know well. Over time I have analysed what distinguishes it from other cities around the world, and tried to define what makes it tick. Initially these explorations were *ad hoc*, but recently they have become more systematic. If you look at a map of London (1), it is obvious how graphically different it is from, say, Paris (2) or New York (3). There may be a number of reasons for this, but I find the example of a clock helpful: to me London is an analogue rather than a digital city. On an analogue watch you read the time without reference to numbers. It gives you the time more quickly than its digital equivalent because you skip the conversion process. The position of the hands on the dial is enough.

So, how does this relate to cities? Perhaps it is thus: to get an airport taxi driver to take you to, for example, the Carlyle Hotel in New York City, you must specify its location precisely: Manhattan, at 76th Street and Madison Avenue. Similarly, if I want to be taken to a particular restaurant in Paris the immediate questions are: 'Which arrondissement? What number?'

London is very different. To describe a hotel's location, you might say 'between Berkeley Square and Grosvenor Square', or 'on the edge of Hyde Park,

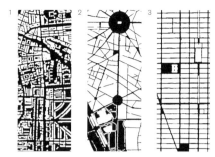

4

near Hyde Park Corner'. The structure of London, with its absence of grids and numerical references, is more organic, having evolved from individual centres that have developed and coalesced over time. Each place has its own green space or, occasionally in the metropolitan centre, its own urban space, such as a square, to define it.

This emphasis on green spaces is reflected in London's extraordinary public transport network. Destinations on the front of buses and the names of many tube stations give clues: Putney Common (4); Parson's Green; Hyde Park Corner; Shepherd's Bush; Hampstead Heath. The intensity of public open space, and the network of links between, is at the heart of the excellent quality of life we can experience in London, notwithstanding the social problems inevitable in any large city.

A walk in Battersea, where I live and work, highlights the density of a London neighbourhood, the open spaces, the rich mix of uses, and the way a river bridge can signal a route and give a visual clue (6, 7). The essence of a city is communication. Individuals come together in close proximity, and their movement to and from those denser areas is dependant on the routes between, say, a square and a park. Wherever we go, we are guided by symbols and signals indicating, for example, metro and railway stations.

Flaws in this system emerge where open spaces are not fully accessible. Sloane Square (5), for example, is an attractive place, but when you are there, navigating a route between passing cars and pushed to its perimeter, you question whether such important spaces should function as traffic roundabouts. Some such spaces have to be partly geared towards traffic, but one cannot help remembering Leicester Square before it was pedestrianised – you could fight the traffic to cross it from one side to the other, but it did not take you anywhere. Now, everyone takes Leicester Square's present form for granted.

Statistically, the results of the changes to Leicester Square have been striking: there is less crime; fewer accidents, and there has been a positive social effect – it has become very civilised. Leicester Square is now the heart of a thriving entertainment district. The diagonal routes across it are important, and the extent of its pedestrianisation means that the entire space is used. It is a complete success story. It is worth noting, however, that the evolution of Leicester Square took nearly twenty years to unfold from the first idea to its eventual realisation.

Today our 'World Squares for All' masterplan for the part pedestrianisation of Trafalgar Square (8, 9), Parliament Square (10, 11), and the surrounding Westminster area in Central London, is being progressed alongside plans for other parts of the city including Regent Street, Soho, Waterloo Plaza, the South Bank and beyond. One of the tools we utilised in developing the World Squares masterplan was the mathematical model and plan of the city developed by Space Syntax at University College, London. This model can demonstrate with clarity the potential for connectivity and easy pedestrian access at street level. It reveals a network of routes ranging from major arteries with the greatest potential for flow and accessibility, down to those that are almost cul-de-sac-like in their dysfunctional relationship with the areas around them.

The variety of our research techniques reflected the many facets of the modern city. The consultant group included traffic engineers and urban designers as well as academics, and it was the wide range of perspectives offered by these different disciplines that allowed us to explore the discrepancy between the picture postcard image of London, and the reality experienced at ground level.

Initial research produced a variety of responses, but above all we learned that any change would involve a balancing act. Improving access had to be balanced with maintaining security; private cars with public transport; the needs of the tourist with those of the Londoner; ceremonial function with the everyday; culture with government business. Additionally, people standing still or sitting down have different needs from people who are moving; local needs may or may not be in conflict with the needs of London as a whole; visual clutter and spontaneity have to be set against legibility and order; design must be balanced with management; and the old with the new.

With all these interests to account for, we had to be analytical, examining traffic flows and accident reports as well as how exactly pedestrians move, or try to move, around the area. The results of this process of study and consultation confirmed the need to reduce the conflict between people and cars. We discovered that few Londoners use the centre of Trafalgar Square, and few people walk the entire ceremonial route down Whitehall, from Trafalgar Square to Parliament Square. Visitors cannot stand back in safety and admire Big Ben, Westminster Abbey and the National Gallery from the most desirable viewpoints. Londoners

8

9

cannot negotiate with ease the heart of their city by any mode of transport, and London cannot breathe.

This central London area has all the potential to be an appropriate urban setting for the civic heart of the nation. Yet today it fails on almost every count. Despite the grandeur of its buildings and the significance of its heritage, it is a dirty and unfriendly environment, dominated by asphalt and the car. It provides no facilities for the millions of tourists who visit it each year and even fewer amenities for Londoners themselves. It is, moreover, incoherently presented: it is hard to find your way around. It contains the vocabulary of city spaces, but lacks the grammar to make sense of those spaces and facilitate communication.

In an area of London that has both variety and great opportunities for grace and cohesion, a further challenge exists: to strengthen connections, both between its different parts and with the rest of the city. This means making its public spaces understandable to pedestrians, including first-time visitors; making accessible the best vantage points for its spectacular views; presenting its buildings and monuments in the most flattering way; and drawing attention both to its centre and to its boundaries along the banks of the Thames and the royal parks.

The heart of London should not simply be an impressive part of our heritage, but also a delightful and comfortable place to inhabit. It is meant to be – as the title of the 'World Squares for All' project so clearly indicates – for everyone. In the words of the Deputy Prime Minister, John Prescott, 'we must reclaim our city centres for people'.

The need to revitalise our cities by improving the urban fabric and achieving a better balance between people and traffic is one of the keys to the future. In the last decade alone, the cities of Barcelona, Berlin, Paris and Amsterdam have shown how the containment of traffic can lead to a better quality of urban life. Even the security-motivated 'Ring of Steel' in the City of London has brought significant benefits to those who work in the financial heart of the capital. As with all such bold initiatives, they have met with some initial resistance, but it is now widely agreed that these schemes have contributed to the economic and cultural vitality of each of those city centres.

Central London requires a similarly bold vision – one that gives priority to people yet recognises the need for movement and access. It is a vision of a higher order of civic environment where Londoners can enjoy their monuments and open spaces together with visitors from across the nation and abroad. A century ago, the Victorians transformed a city of slums, pollution and congestion into a model of civilised urban life. London became the paradigm for cities around the world. Today, 'World Squares for All' and many other urban initiatives offer London a similar opportunity to set an international standard for city living once more. We should be ready to take up that challenge.

10

11

'... we can see a quest for higher environmental standards, for improved levels of amenity and communication in the workplace, and a growing sensitivity to the ecological issues of pollution and energy conservation.'

Norman Foster

Where is the office building going? What in the past have been the driving forces behind architectural change? Is it possible to discern long-term trends, as opposed to the merely transitory and fashionable? Is architectural change progressive – have buildings got better, and if so, why? These questions offer an opportunity to indulge in a degree of retrospection together with some crystal ball gazing.

More than thirty years ago I started design work on my first office project, an operations centre for a Norwegian client, Fred Olsen, in the London Docks. Since then our practice has grown to an international scale and with my colleagues I have been responsible for more than sixty office projects around the world, with workspaces totalling almost 4 million square metres. Of these, 30 are either built or under construction and together they will house around 50,000 people.

Given the diversity of this work, what patterns can be identified? If I had to summarise I would say that the forces of social and technological change continue to drive design. Over time we can see a quest for higher environmental standards, for improved levels of amenity and communication in the workplace, and a growing sensitivity to the ecological issues of pollution and energy conservation.

My experience is that genuine innovation in the field of office design is pioneered by owner occupiers. Fundamental changes, which are seen to stand the test of time, then filter down to be adopted by the market place, and are recreated by those who develop speculatively. For example, in the 1970s our headquarters project for Willis Faber & Dumas, in Ipswich, was considered radical. Flexibility for future change was high on our agenda and was manifested in the provision of access floors and a wide-span structure. Early in its working life the building was easily able to accommodate new information technology which was unheard of at the time of its conception. The necessary cabling was simply fed through the access floors, and teams were able to regroup easily. Many of Willis Faber's competitors were not able to respond so swiftly to change. That project also pioneered the use of low-rise, deep-plan office floors, and improved circulation, using escalators instead of lifts. These features, together with restaurants, a roof garden, and sports facilities, created a new spirit of communication, closer to the atmosphere of a family firm than that of a large head office.

Now, nearly twenty-five years after the completion of that building, we are busy replacing obsolete office towers built in the 1960s with lower-rise structures

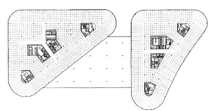 

for progressive developers, such as our building at Tower Place in the City of London (1, 2). Although each is special to its site, the design specifications are remarkably similar to those of Willis Faber – what was once avant-garde has become mainstream.

Willis Faber also pioneered low-energy concepts at a time when 'green architecture' was almost unheard of. Today, a combination of public opinion and political attitude favours ecologically responsive design. Our tower for Commerzbank in Frankfurt was able to optimise the use of its precious city-centre site by addressing social and energy issues, providing an abundance of interior gardens and controlled natural ventilation. In the future, pressure to reduce pollution and fossil-fuel consumption will surely lead increasingly to designs that favour alternative or renewable sources of energy.

It is sometimes difficult to separate fashion in office design from the culture of the office workspace, which can vary from one country to another. In our pilot Head Office building for IBM, in the late 1960s, we challenged the prevailing wisdom of housing the main computer in a separate room. By absorbing it within a single flexible structure we were able to anticipate the decentralisation and freedom of computer usage that has come with the spread of information technology.

Projecting these trends forward one can envisage buildings with even greater flexibility, offering a richer mixture of uses under the same roof. The regeneration of cities is linked to this concept of mixed use on a wider scale. In Cologne we have a major development under construction in which the same structure can be fitted out as offices or apartments: the final usage can be decided at any time during construction or in the future life of the building (3, 4). At pavement level the same universal shell accommodates public facilities such as cafes, restaurants and retail spaces.

This degree of flexibility relates specifically to German office culture, with its emphasis on smaller-scale cellular spaces, although arguably the larger floor-plates favoured in America and Asia could also lend themselves to a different kind of residential subdivision. The tendency towards a more democratic space is also inseparable from these solutions. The social hierarchies may still be in place but they are less likely to be manifested in extremes of space standards, even in traditional office environments.

Inevitably the miniaturisation and domestication of information technology raises the notion that the contemporary office building is a dinosaur destined to oblivion in a world in which we work from home. The concept of the office has changed over the years, working practices have transformed its identity, and I would expect to see those trends continue. But even given greater flexibility to increase leisure time and divide working time between home and elsewhere, I am convinced that there is a deep-rooted need for that social 'somewhere else'. It is this extra dimension to the work cycle that I believe will ensure the future of the 'office', even if we call it by another name.

'... a building is only as good as its client and the architecture of the Sainsbury Centre is inseparable from the enlighten-ment and the driving force of the patrons behind it.'

Norman Foster

It was the morning of New Year's Day 1974 and I was standing in front of the door of number 5 Smith Square, for what I was told would be a brief meeting with Sir Robert Sainsbury about a possible museum project.

Before ringing the bell I remember feeling apprehensive, nervous. I was not to know the extent to which that meeting would influence my future as an architect and also my personal life. As it turned out the 'brief meeting' with Sir Robert carried on through lunch, when I met Lady Sainsbury, and continued to the end of the day.

Although it was more than 25 years ago I can remember it as if it were yesterday. I remember leaving with three impressions. Firstly, their home – surprisingly modest, intimate and discreet. Certainly the architecture was not spectacular, but every space was married with extraordinary works of art – paintings and sculptures. It was a combination of exquisite taste and restraint.

The second impression was the contrast between this very elegant couple and the radical nature of their works of art – especially when I heard how they had discovered them. For example there was a portrait of Lady Sainsbury by Francis Bacon hanging over the fireplace, which was very powerful – almost shocking. Bacon, like Henry Moore and Giacometti, were unknown artists at the time the Sainsburys became their patrons.

Then there was Sir Robert's study, beautifully designed by a young Dutch architect called Kho Lang Ie. Here there were works by anonymous artists, tiny Eskimo carvings for example – objects which, at the time of their acquisition, were not even recognised as works of art in the traditional sense. I think Sir Robert playfully referred to them as his 'toys' (1).

The third impression was how those first conversations ranged so far and wide – I was getting early clues about their way of looking at things, and I do not mean visually: it was as radical as those progressive artists they had encouraged. For me it was a mixture of independence, openness and conviction.

I was later to describe them both as the toughest clients that I had worked for – and I hasten to add that as an architect that was the highest compliment I could pay. Nothing came easily because everything was worked at hard. They made extraordinary efforts to research, to challenge and to support.

I say all this because frankly a building is only as good as its client and the architecture of the Sainsbury Centre is inseparable from the enlightenment and

the driving force of the patrons behind it. It is not surprising then that the resulting building would challenge preconceptions about museums.

For example, we selected a location which at that time was almost in the wilderness of the campus – away from the other arts and next to science – to encourage cross-fertilisation. And as a building it put all the varied functions and user groups – galleries and teaching spaces, students, academics and the public – together in a single space, under a single roof. It was a gallery without walls in the conventional sense (2).

It was also an early example of a low-energy, 'green' architecture. These are fashionable buzzwords today, but at the time the concept of sustainable ecological architecture was unheard of outside a fringe of society, which was mostly occupied by hippies.

I was recently in conversation with the critic, Peter Buchanan, who has identified a concept in our work which he refers to as the 'urban room'. He explains this as a space that is egalitarian, accessible not just to the public but also to other specialist groups – 'urban' because it suggests a 'city microcosm' with all the varied patterns of usage that implies. It is also about the relationship with nature – the movement of air, light and carefully considered views.

When Peter Buchanan made this observation I could see clearly that the Sainsbury Centre was not just our first public building but the first of many 'urban rooms' that our studio has since created. But its influence on our work, and indirectly on the work of others, has also been far reaching in different ways.

For example, if you look up from inside the Sainsbury Centre you will see a structure that gently filters natural light. That is because all the pipes, ducts and machinery that normally occupy the roof, have been discreetly located elsewhere, in the walls and below the floor.

This idea was further developed for Stansted Airport, which has since proved to be a model for a new generation of terminals worldwide, including our own new Hong Kong Airport. In that sense, as well as in other ways, the Sainsbury Centre for Visual Arts was a turning point.

Not too long after that first meeting at Smith Square there was an introductory design session with the Sainsburys and Kho Lang Ie. I knew his work and although we were almost contemporaries he was one of my design heroes. I took

him to one side before the meeting and asked him how I should address Sir Robert and Lady Sainsbury. He laughed and said, 'But of course you must call them Bob and Lisa' – which I did there and then.

It was only afterwards that I realised how over-familiar that must have seemed, because Kho Lang Ie had built his relationship with them over many years. But I think they accepted my rashness with grace, because in all the ways that I hope mattered, it must have been obvious to them that I held them in the deepest respect.

That respect has grown over time and they have merged from client to parent figures. And so today, as they are presented with the Freedom of the City of Norwich (5), is a very privileged occasion on which to say 'thank you Bob and Lisa', and congratulations.

'The architecture of the future
could be the architecture
of today.'

Norman Foster

The architecture of the future will, by necessity, be one that addresses the world's increasing ecological crisis. Architecture can contribute to dealing with this crisis to a degree that few other activities can. Buildings use half of the energy consumed in the developed world, yet virtually every building could be designed to run on a fraction of current energy levels.

Why do we rely so heavily upon artificial lighting when we can easily design buildings that are filled with daylight? Why do we continue to rely upon wasteful air-conditioning systems in locations where we could simply open a window? A holistic approach to architecture – one that sees buildings as the sum of all the systems at work within them – is the start of the solution to our problems. Structure, form and materials each have their part to play in this. Natural lighting and ventilation, recycled rainwater, and heat recycled from lights, computers and people, for example, can all contribute to reducing a building's energy demands.

Applying these methods in the Reichstag, in Berlin, we were able to reduce the building's energy requirements to such an extent that it creates more energy than it consumes. Our integrated energy strategy has also allowed us to reduce pollution; the Reichstag burns renewable vegetable oil, rather than dwindling fossil fuels, which has led to a dramatic reduction in the building's carbon dioxide emissions. If a nineteenth-century building can be transformed from an energy guzzler into a building so efficient that it is now a net provider of energy – literally a power station for its neighbourhood – how much easier is it to design new buildings that make responsible use of precious resources?

However, individual buildings cannot be viewed in isolation. They must be seen in the context of our ever-expanding cities and their infrastructures. Unchecked urban sprawl is one of the chief problems facing the world today. One example will serve to illustrate this phenomenon. In the period 1970-1990 the population of greater Chicago increased by a mere 4 per cent, yet its physical area grew by 50 per cent. Moreover, the peripheral growth of cities is rarely accompanied by integrated public transport networks or other services. Instead, people are forced to travel greater distances by car, creating congestion and pollution.

Higher urban densities provide one solution to this problem – it is surprising to discover that the world's two most densely populated areas, Monaco (3) and Macao (2), are at opposite ends of the economic spectrum. High density – or

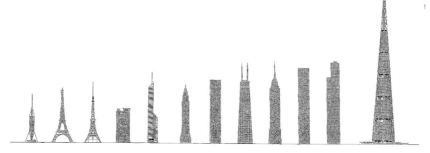

high rise – does not automatically mean overcrowding or economic hardship; it can also lead to an improved quality of life, where housing, work and leisure facilities are all close by.

The Millennium Tower (1, 4) that we have proposed in Tokyo takes a traditional horizontal city quarter – housing, shops, restaurants, cinemas, museums, sporting facilities, green spaces and public transport networks – and turns it on its side to create a super-tall building with a multiplicity of uses. It would be over 800 metres high with 170 storeys – twice the height of anything so far built – and would house a community of up to 60,000 people. This is 20,000 more than the population of Monaco and yet the building would occupy only 0.013 square kilometres of land in comparison to Monaco's 1.95 square kilometres. It would create a virtually self-sufficient, fully self-sustaining community in the sky.

This sounds like future fantasy. But we now have all the means at our disposal to create such buildings. There are no technological barriers to a sustainable architecture, only ones of political will. The architecture of the future could be the architecture of today.

'Furniture is like architecture in microcosm, the big difference being that the time between cause and effect can shrink dramatically – the response time to a decision can be a few weeks or even hours.'

Norman Foster

If I think back to my first days of practice as an architect, my earliest sketches often featured a Thonet bentwood chair. A friend later pointed out that these images always sought to convey a particular lifestyle. The table in the foreground would usually have glasses and a bottle of wine – a suggestion of good taste complemented by the association with classic furniture. Sometimes the chairs would be tubular steel pieces inspired by the early Modernists. I was later to discover that many of this next generation of chairs, bent metal tubes rather than wooden rods, also originated from the factories of Thonet.

At the time I made those early sketches I could never have imagined that nearly 40 years later I would be with the three Thonet brothers in their factory at Frankenberg in Germany, discussing the design of a new generation of furniture for their company. With my colleagues John Small and Mike Holland, I proposed a concept which would combine the advanced production possibilities of today with the Thonet tradition dating back to the nineteenth century. But what exactly was the essence of that heritage?

The answers were to be found in the Thonet Museum, a small building adjacent to the Frankenberg factory. Here it is possible to view those past classics in their extraordinary variety and abundance. How could so many richly sculpted forms be derived from the ostensibly simple idea of bending pieces of wood or metal – and then just screwing them together? This collection is like a treasure trove in a Victorian museum. But all these pieces are simple assemblies from a kit-of-parts.

What we proposed for today's needs is a surprisingly diverse range of individual pieces, chairs and tables, all derived from a limited range of components. Each one is a 'knock-down' assembly of pieces joined together by today's equivalent of the wood screw, but now using a power driven Allen key instead of a screwdriver.

Moving on from steaming lengths of ash into curved forms, or bending steel tubing into Bauhaus-inspired shapes, we have developed a family of aluminium extrusions that can be stretched into curves and joined together with straights. Each one is specifically tailored to its role – a technique that was not available to previous generations of designers.

I am fascinated by the interactive nature of design. If you change one parameter – for example the ergonomic priorities, choice of materials or critical dimensions – then the effect ripples throughout the design to influence all the other criteria.

Furniture is like architecture in microcosm, the big difference being that the time between cause and effect can shrink dramatically – the response time to a decision can be a few weeks or even hours.

For instance, we considered that one version of the chair might feel better with a softer, more tactile point of contact where your hands touch the arms – leather rather than bare metal. But the curved aluminium arm is the very essence of the chair – its identity. How could this be retained and the warmth of a softer, more organic material introduced without compromising the design? I suggested that a strip of leather could be bonded directly onto the metal and to illustrate the point I drew attention to the brown suede belt that I was wearing at the time. This was one of the developments that we reviewed at a follow-up meeting several weeks later. For all of us, clients and designers alike, the outcome was successful and the variation was universally adopted.

However, at that same working session we surveyed the prototype dining table with great anxiety. The structure was very wobbly to put it mildly! There were two tops to consider: one expressed its true thickness, the other had edges that tapered to a finer margin, reminiscent of the cantilevered floor-slabs of our Willis Faber building designed some 25 years ago. The latter looked like a horizontal blade – great! But how to resolve the wobbly structure that was to support it?

By rocking the table to and fro we could identify its points of weakness: the legs and their connection to the horizontal structure. Time was of the essence because we had flown into the local airfield – a very basic landing strip in the middle of hilly country – through a minor snowstorm. Snow ploughs were keeping the runway open and our aircraft was safe in a hangar, but conditions at our destination were more uncertain and the slot time with air traffic control was another fix. A sense of urgency can often be helpful to focus the mind!

I had the idea to double the legs by adding another length of the same extrusion that formed the supports of the chair. We mocked it up with a spacing gap so that you could see that it was a double structure. It may have provided the necessary rigidity but it simply did not look right – so we all rejected it.

Then one of the Thonet brothers suggested trying a different extrusion – only to find disagreement with the others. I was not sure, but I pushed everyone to at least try it. Faces were creased with doubt and somebody started to point at his watch.

I suggested that we went to a DIY store to buy some tools and do it on the spot. The message was received and in minutes two technicians in their overalls arrived from the factory next door and performed the 'transplant'. It looked great but when we pushed it and sat upon it the table was still wobbly – not as much as before but enough to be unmarketable. What next?

First thoughts were to beef it up – add more material, create more fixings. But if you stood back from the table the combination of its slim-edged top and the consistent use of the same family of extrusions was visually convincing – in other words it was looking very good, even if it was a trifle unstable.

The inspiration, at the meeting some weeks earlier which had launched the original concept, was a traditional refectory table. This had led us to a structure framed at the top, with a horizontal crossbar which connected the legs lower down. I suddenly had the idea of cross-bracing the whole structure with a diagonal cable in the plane of the cross bar. First efforts were a crossed diagonal, rather like the structure of the Reliance Controls building dating back almost 35 years.

By this stage we were all on our hands and knees underneath the table, and a simpler version had begun to emerge. The idea was to tension a cable from the top outer edges down to the centre point of the crossbar – an evocative V-shape – that might do the trick. With minutes to go the technicians appeared wielding drills and steel cable. It all happened remarkably quickly; the cable was magically in place and tensioned up. For the first time the table was rock-solid – stronger than we could ever have imagined and looking even lighter and more sparsely structured than before.

The bracing of that table is now as central to its image as it is to the structural stability of the piece. One can draw analogies to earthbound structures and waterborne sailing craft, which have been braced by tension cables in the quest to combine economy and high performance.

I can think of times when an urgent timescale has compromised design but working against the clock has more often than not quickened the creative pulse. That Thonet meeting was a race against two timescales: one, to meet the deadline of a launch at the Cologne Furniture Fair, a mere eight weeks away; the other, to make our snowy departure from Frankenberg.

As a footnote, we managed to fly out on time and launch the product in Cologne.

'Living with the Nomos table
has parallels with owning a
bicycle – you discover the
potential to modify the components. By varying finishes it is
possible to change the appearance, emphasising the frame
or articulating the secondary
structure for example.'

Norman Foster

I live with our Nomos table both at home with my family and in the studio space where I work with my colleagues. In the black-bound sketchbook that I habitually carry around I often doodle variations on the Tecno table – more for pleasure than anything else. So as you can imagine I was overjoyed when Tecno suggested the idea of a new version of the table to mark the millennium. If anything I had too many ideas. But time was a major factor: the millennium was too close to allow for tooling up new components.

With this awareness I went back to the basics of how a table is used. The rectangular and circular-topped versions of the Nomos tables are clearly established favourites – they are already the top-selling line out of all Tecno products. In the quest for another classic shape I worked within the support structure of the existing frame, exploring curved shapes with large sheets of cardboard upon which I drew freehand with a large felt-tip pen. These profiles were later cut out of high-density foam and tested by a group of us sitting around the new 'top'. The resulting smooth curves encouraged better eye-to-eye contact across the table's length, which probably explained why it felt more friendly. It also had no corners – my very mobile daughter of eighteen months has made me quite sensitive to the hazards of sharp edges!

Over a period of weeks, working with colleagues John Small and James Johnson, we finally refined the shape of the top to a point where it was the most promising – both to use and to look at.

Many critics and users have commented on the appearance of the table's frame, suggesting references such as the lunar landing module (1, 4). It is true that a large photograph of this craft adorned the walls of our studio at the time that the table was created, and it still remains a potent symbol. One never knows about subliminal influences but I can recall invoking another image at the time the design was released on the market. This was a grasshopper with its slim body and long gangly legs. I remember buying a Chinese paper version of the insect on a long piece of wire to make an analogy with the world of nature. Perhaps the presence of the table owes much to the dynamic of its splayed feet – an undercarriage that is more evocative of motion than the static columns of a traditional table leg.

The Nomos concept is predated by an earlier foray into furniture design. At a time when our studio was expanding in 1978 we were unable to find any furniture

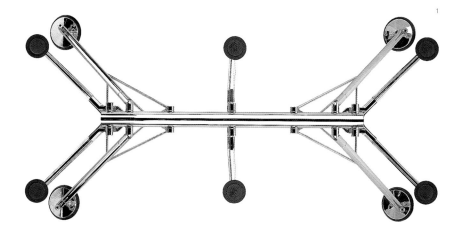

on the market that could respond to our needs – tables that might be adjustable for meetings, drafting or display. We solved the problem by designing our own system. Inevitably, the relatively small production run meant a dependence on hand crafting using a sympathetic workshop – a kind of cottage industry. From these seeds the Nomos system has evolved as a highly automated product, but our experience with the new millennium version is a reminder that the human element is never missing, no matter how sophisticated the process of industrialisation.

Consider the new top for instance. Those freehand curves that I described (2) were mathematically analysed and the corresponding arcs were fed as coordinates into the machine that cuts the glass, using a laser and water jet. Unfortunately the computer seemed unable to make a smooth transfer from one arc to the next – the geometry was momentarily lost. In the end it was faster to use the expedient of hand-guiding the cutting jet over the critical length in question.

It was fascinating to contemplate the significant change of appearance when the familiar support structure of the regular Nomos table was married to its new curvilinear top. This marked a strategic design development, but it was not the only change. The world of two-wheeled machines was another design influence.

Since a teenager I have been keenly interested in bicycles and the detail of their design. My interest was not only tactile and visual – I was, and still am, a keen cyclist. As a youth I would be continually rebuilding my bike – changing a component, adding new tape to the handlebars, substituting different cleats to tidy up the cables and always playing with the colours. This was an organic process, because the machine had not been bought off-the-peg but was, from the start, an assembly of chosen components, which I would tune and upgrade over time.

Living with the Nomos table has parallels with owning a bicycle – you discover the potential to modify the components. By varying finishes it is possible to change the appearance, emphasising the frame or articulating the secondary structure for example.

2

There is a
great New
variation-
easy to
achieve

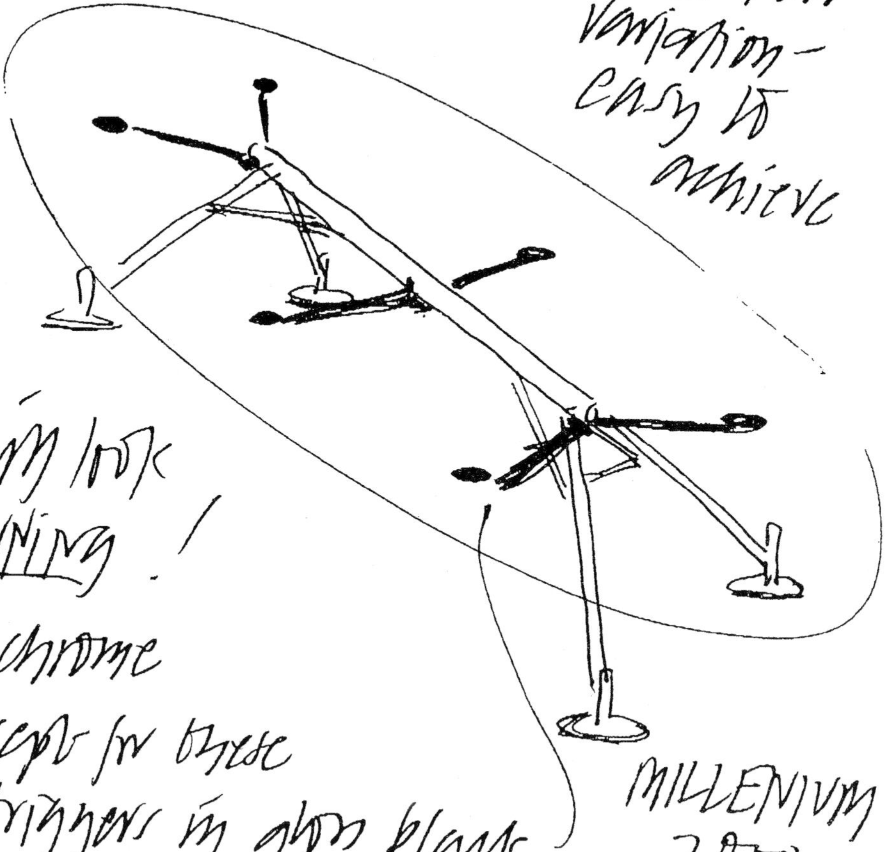

& will look
STUNNING !

All chrome
except for these
outriggers in gloss black

MILLENIUM
2000

red
400

blue 400

yellow
400

white
400

chrome
400

ie each one the
same number.

$40° \times 5 = 2000$

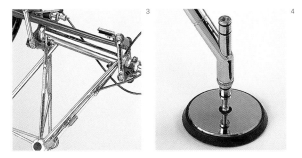

3   4

Coming back to the bicycle, as a youth most of my hard-earned funds would be lavished on this object of desire. I would agonise over the choice of a colour: would the frame be vividly extrovert – a bright red – or a cool white or chrome? Now, many years later, I am fortunate enough to indulge my tastes, both for the visual impact of the bike and for its handling qualities, with the ultimate luxury of being able to exercise a choice for the day: will I take the Ferrari-red road bike with its streamlined composite frame, or the all-black mountain bike, or maybe Alex Moulton's latest creation (3) with its glossy aerospace metal tubes? There is such a luxury of choice – not only in the delight of different riding experiences but also in the aesthetic pleasure of looking at the bicycles lined up in their stands.

Although a static table is in one sense far removed from the dynamic world of the bike there are close parallels with the new Tecno table. Like a bicycle, I have chosen to express the Nomos frame in an extrovert way with a vivid palette of colours – a strong red, a vibrant yellow, a rich blue and a brilliant white. I confined these colours to the spine and legs, which are akin to the primary structure, with all else, such as outriggers and bracing, in bright chrome. Consequently the outward appearance is totally transformed.

But if your choice might tend to the classical, with a preference for the more restrained finishes of the original Nomos table, then there is another version, designed at the last minute, with which to celebrate the millennium. This has a chrome frame with the secondary elements in black – matching the colour of the pads for the glass top and the feet, which cushion the table on the floor. Without doubt this is the coolest!

And again, like the bike, there are the final flourishes that complete the customisation of the table. The handlebars of a bicycle, for example, are bent tubes, and the ends are always plugged with a contrasting element. In a similar way, on the new table I have chosen to cap the ends of the spinal tube with a contrasting plug – unlike the original table with its matching ends, which tended to make the spine look monolithic.

Then there is the question of decals – how far do you go to convey information in the final graphic flourishes? A few months ago I bought a new bike frame, with a beautiful flowing form, which was completely marred by the graphics stridently proclaiming the maker's name. I bought it only on the condition that the

worked with my former Yale classmate, Richard Rogers, under the title 'Team 4'. Richard is still a dear friend and it is wonderful to share so many of the same values more than thirty years later.

Buildings cannot happen without those who commission. Self-evident perhaps, but less evident is the creative contribution of clients. Of course, any architect could name the exceptions, but so often a good client will be a crucial force in shaping a good building. There is certainly a strong relationship between the quality of the architecture and that of the decision-making process that leads up to it. Like any of my architect colleagues I am grateful for those special clients, several of whom are here this evening.

In the best teams the individuals spark off each other. It is the opposite of the architect designing a building and parcelling it out for others to structure and cost. Perhaps this is another example of 'analysis and action' – the exploration of multiple directions in the quest for the optimum solution, or for innovation.

Such an approach is more demanding on all concerned and calls for exceptional consultants, particularly engineers and quantity surveyors. Tonight is a good opportunity to express my appreciation for their highly creative contributions in the past, which I know will also continue into the future.

I am always surprised by how little emphasis schools of architecture, and indeed many architects, place on the process of making buildings. I am deeply suspicious of the class division between those who design and those who construct because in the past they were closely bonded. Surely the means inform the end?

Building sites are hazardous places to work even if they are more and more the point of assembly for prefabricated elements. All the more important, surely, for architects to go to the factories to penetrate the points of production. Not only to learn, and therefore to design on a basis of knowledge, but also to appreciate and pay tribute to those who turn dreams into reality.

Asia has provided us with the opportunity to realise dreams on an epic scale. No land? No problem – make an island. Expand an airport? No – change it to a new one overnight. This scale of thinking is probably the global shift for the future, more out of necessity than choice.

In free thinking we all have our mentors and I was privileged to work with the late Buckminster Fuller – a true master of high technology in the tradition of those nineteenth-century heroes such as Paxton. But Bucky was also the essence of a moral conscience, forever preaching about the fragility of our planet, with a global awareness of ecology which is still ahead of its times. He remains a guiding spirit.

6

So too does the late Otl Aicher from Germany, best known as a graphic designer but in reality a philosopher for whom the correct peeling and slicing of an onion assumed the same significance as designing a building. He was exceedingly good at both activities.

It is interesting how the theme of America with Bucky and Europe with Otl, weaves its way throughout. Even this evening celebrates a prize that originates in America and is being awarded in Berlin, the most European of cities.

A measure of the degree of Germany's 'Europeanness' is the fact that, as architects from the United Kingdom, we could be given the responsibility for the new Parliament here in Berlin. Significantly, it has provided the opportunity to stretch the boundaries on two issues, both particularly important in the future growth of cities: the role of public space and the quest for a more ecologically responsible architecture.

With my colleagues I have been given many creative opportunities in Europe – in Germany, France, Italy and Spain. But my ultimate personal prize was not architectural, although it could not have happened without our Barcelona Communications Tower – it was to win my wife Elena from Spain. I would like to say 'thank you' to Elena: *renaissance* now has a new and profound meaning for me.

Returning to the subject of architectural prizes, I benefited from several foundations, especially the Henry Fellowship, which enabled me to go to Yale University. Inspired by that and similar examples I, with my colleagues, have recently established a foundation to further education and research – and we are grateful for the funds from the Pritzker Prize which will make a substantial contribution to that cause.

It is a great honour to receive the Pritzker Prize, and to share it with so many architect peers whose work I have admired and respected over many years, and I am delighted that several of them are here this evening. In a tradition that dates from the first award in 1979, I would like to join with my predecessors in thanking the members of the jury for their tireless efforts in promoting the ideals behind the prize. Finally I would like to thank the Pritzker family, and especially the late Jay Pritzker, for their enlightened patronage. The award is indeed a celebration of 'architecture in the widest sense'.

7

But as we approach the challenges of the next millennium I cannot help wondering what 'architecture in the widest sense' might mean. Where are the boundaries drawn between those who speak for the design professions, the politicians and industry? Where are the divisions between conscience, provocation and action?

The challenges are awesome. We can already see the growth of a new generation of megacities – urban conurbations of over 25 million people are predicted within the next fifteen years. Not long ago I went to a cultural event in Mexico City and came away with images of a suburb called Chalco (7). It is the size of a European city – with a population of 3.5 million – but there is a significant difference. In Chalco there is no infrastructure – no drainage, no mains water, no sewage system, no gas, no electricity or paved roads. In one sense, however, they are lucky. One hundred million people worldwide have no homes at all. This brings to life the estimate that two billion of the 5.9 billion inhabitants of the planet have no access to energy, except through burning natural materials such as wood or animal waste.

In the industrialised world, half the energy is consumed by buildings; the remainder is divided between transportation and industry, with all the associated problems of pollution. So what happens when the rest of the world catches up – a world that is expected to double in population over the next 50 years?

If those were not challenges enough to the design professions, then surely it is a paradox that we have rapid responses to war, but no such responses to the consequences that follow. Surely the need for instant shelter for the victims of war, oppression or tornadoes should be high on the agenda. However we might divide the responsibilities, we could surely do better than the tented cities which fill the pages of our newspapers (6), let alone the Chalcos of the future.

These, I think, are some of the challenges for 'architecture in the widest sense', in the coming millennium.

'The Eames house, assembled off-the-peg from the Truscon catalogue, still appears radical today, but to Ellwood's eyes, in 1949, it must have seemed exhilaratingly fresh.'

Norman Foster

Craig Ellwood, 1999

I am always wary of naming my heroes, but I can safely say that, were I to draw up such a list, Craig Ellwood would undoubtedly be on it.

Ellwood is an architect with whom I have many sympathies. I first encountered his spare steel structures in the early 1960s when I explored the architecture of Southern California following my year as a postgraduate student at Yale University. I felt an immediate affinity with the work and with the man himself.

Ellwood was something of a maverick. As an architect he was self-taught. As a young man he studied structural engineering at night classes. By day he worked as a cost estimator for a building contractor. The theory he learned in the evening was given practical application on a series of pioneering construction projects, including the Eames and Entenza Case Study houses. It was the Entenza connection that was to give him his first 'big break'.

The Eames house, assembled off-the-peg from the Truscon catalogue, still appears radical today, but to Ellwood's eyes, in 1949, it must have seemed exhilaratingly fresh. But while the Eames' use of structure might be thought of as playful – introducing cross-bracing where none was really required – Ellwood, with his background in engineering, was to develop an architecture that was, by contrast, coolly disciplined.

Ellwood's buildings – not just his houses – have a structural elegance and economy of means that is comparable with those of Mies van der Rohe. But while Mies' structure tends towards the monumental, Ellwood's structure is slender and taut. As Reyner Banham once said: 'You have to wonder how so little steel can support so much roof.'

As with Pierre Koenig and other architects in the Case Study House Program, Ellwood moved on to build industrial and commercial buildings that were as elegant and economical as his houses. His building for Scientific Data Systems is exemplary in this regard. I remember it being published in the February 1967 edition of *Domus* – alongside Team 4's Reliance Controls building – and it having a huge impact on a generation of English architects.

Commissioned by a new technology company in Southern California, Scientific Data Systems was a fast-track building that made brilliant use of prefabricated components. The structure was pushed to the perimeter and the roof trusses punctured the rhythm of its pre-cast concrete panel walls, the resulting slot being glazed to allow glimpses of the outside world. Inside it was a carnival of colours – shocking pinks and lime greens juxtaposed with the primaries, each colour applied to codify a particular element of the building.

Just as architects in the 1920s studying the work of Le Corbusier through the pages of black and white journals were subsequently shocked to learn of its poly-chromy, so too was it a thrill for English practitioners in the 1960s, used to the drab conformity of post-war Modernism, to discover that such an intellectually rewarding architecture could also be so sensuous and joyful. It was a breath of Californian fresh air.

Ellwood had a true artist's sense of colour and scale. And so perhaps we should not have been surprised when in the late 1970s – his work temporarily out of fashion and commissions hard to come by – he abruptly abandoned the strug-gles of practice for the pleasures of painting, leaving California in favour of Tuscany. But art's gain was architecture's loss.

It is ironic that Ellwood is now more highly regarded as an architect than ever before. His exquisite buildings are being appreciated by a new generation of architects. Perhaps they too may come to count him among their heroes.

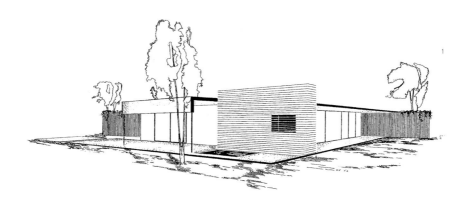

2

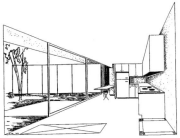

3

4

'In its vision of a public architecture that redresses the ecological balance, providing energy
rather than consuming it, lies one
of the Reichstag's most intrinsic
expressions of optimism.'

Norman Foster

Our work to transform the Reichstag is rooted in four major issues: a belief in the significance of the Bundestag as one of the world's great democratic forums; a determination to make the process of government more accessible; an understanding of history as a force which shapes buildings as well as the life of nations; and a passionate commitment to the low-energy, environment-friendly agenda which is fundamental to the architecture of the future.

Today Germany leads the world in the responsible attitude of its legislation concerning the environment, and the encouragement of renewable energy sources. From the outset our aim was to demonstrate in the Reichstag – a structure that represents the pinnacle of German democratic government – the potential for a wholly sustainable public building, environmentally responsible and virtually pollution free. The design team – Foster and Partners, Kaiser Bautechnik and Kuehn Bauer und Partner, in conjunction with the German Federal Government – developed the brief for an energy-efficient building. The European Commission was extremely supportive and contributed financially towards this challenge to create a model for a more sustainable architecture.

In the reconstruction of the Reichstag, we proposed extensive use of natural light and ventilation, and combined systems of cogeneration and heat recovery. Here minimum energy achieves maximum effect at the lowest cost-in-use. Due to its own modest energy requirements, the new Reichstag is able to perform as a local power station, supplying neighbouring buildings in the new government quarter.

The Reichstag's new cupola or 'lantern', has quickly become a Berlin landmark. Within it, two helical ramps take members of the public to a viewing platform high above the plenary chamber, raising them symbolically above the heads of their political representatives (2). The cupola is both a generative element in the internal workings of the building and a key component in our light and energy-saving strategies, and it also communicates externally the themes of lightness, transparency, permeability and public access that underscore the project.

At the core of the cupola is a 'light sculptor' – a concave, cone-like form which works like a lighthouse in reverse, using angled mirrors to reflect horizon light into the chamber, while a moveable shield tracks the path of the sun to prevent the penetration of solar heat and glare. In winter and at the beginning and end of summer days, when the sun is lower, the shield can be moved aside to allow

softer rays to dapple the chamber floor. At night-time, the process is reversed and artificial light in the chamber is reflected outwards, making the dome glow dramatically so that Berliners will know when the Bundestag is sitting.

The cone also plays an important part in the chamber's natural ventilation system, extracting warm air at high level, while axial fans and heat exchangers recycle energy from the waste air. Fresh air from outside, drawn in above the west portico, is released through the chamber floor as low-velocity ventilation. It spreads out in the room very slowly and gently rises as it heats up. This provides maximum comfort for the occupants and minimises draughts and noise. Power to drive the chamber's exhaust air ventilation system (4) and the shading device in the dome is generated by a hundred solar panel modules with photovoltaic cells (5); these are located on the roof and provide a peak output of approximately 40kW.

Manually and automatically controlled windows, combined with secondary outer glazing, allow natural ventilation to most rooms. These double-layered windows comprise an internal, thermally separated, glazing system and an outer layer which consists of a protective laminated glass pane with ventilation joints. Between these two layers is a void in which a solar shading device is housed. Between half to five times the air volume of a room can be exchanged per hour via this double facade, depending on the weather conditions outside. The double facade also gives a high level of security so that the inner window can remain open whenever required, especially for night-time cooling.

Berlin can be very hot in summer and very cold in winter, and because of its great thermal mass the building responds only slowly to changes in temperature, which is both a problem and an opportunity, allowing passive systems of temperature control to be exploited. Due to the constantly varying number of people using the building, a flexible energy conservation strategy was adopted. The building's inherent thermal mass is used to provide a comfortable base temperature which can be 'topped up' with active heating or cooling using stored energy. This reduces heat load peaks by approximately 30 per cent over conventional methods.

The services installed in the Reichstag in the 1960s, powered by fossil fuel, produced an alarming emission rate of 7,000 tonnes of carbon dioxide annually. Heating the Reichstag today by such means would consume enough energy annually to heat the homes of 5,000 people.

Combined Heat and Power P
Absorption Cooling Plant
Heat Pump
Electrical Power
Heating
Refined Vegetable Oil

We proposed a radical new energy strategy, using vegetable oil, a wholly renewable bio-fuel. Refined vegetable oil – from rape or sunflower seeds – can be considered as a form of solar energy since the sun's energy is stored in the plants (biomass) (1). By using this renewable natural fuel, carbon dioxide emissions are considerably reduced in the long term as the plant absorbs as much carbon dioxide in its lifetime as is released in its combustion. When the oil is burned in a cogenerator to produce electricity it is also remarkably clean and efficient when compared with traditional sources of energy production. In the Reichstag's installation it allows a 94 per cent reduction in the emission of carbon dioxide. Heating and cooling the building will produce, we estimate, a mere 440 tonnes of carbon dioxide per annum.

Surplus heat generated by the Reichstag's power plant is diverted as warm water into a natural aquifer 300 metres below the building, where it can be stored for future use without any impact on the environment at ground level (3). In winter, stored warm water can be pumped up to heat the building; it is also used to drive an absorption cooling plant – rather like a giant refrigerator – which produces chilled water. This, too, is stored below ground and can be pumped back into the building in hot weather to provide cooling via chilled ceilings.

The Reichstag now uses precious natural resources, recycling rather than wasting, to produce a comfortable environment in all seasons. In its vision of a public architecture that redresses the ecological balance, providing energy rather than consuming it, lies one of the Reichstag's most intrinsic expressions of optimism. It is an object lesson in sustainability.

6

Footer On

His enthusiasm, in conjunction with a society that is less hidebound and more receptive to change, produced results that were arguably more extrovertly American than European. It is interesting that Robert Stern, who was both a student and an academic at Yale, might feel that Frank Lloyd Wright was a strong influence on Rudolph's work; and it is difficult to think of a more American architect than Wright. But Rudoph's interest in the relationship between the old and the new and his pronouncements against the insularity of the individual building lost in a sea of cars – his plea for a larger-scale urbanity of public spaces – these were surely European in their inspiration. Perhaps that is why, in his larger urban projects, he always tried to extend the fabric of the building in order to create the 'place' or 'plaza'.

There is also a monumentality about many of his projects – for example, the Art and Architecture Building at Yale (3) – which, combined with the use of sculpted concrete, could be seen as linking back to the works of Le Corbusier. It is significant that conversations and writings about Rudolph often refer to Wright and Le Corbusier as his architect heroes, with Gropius as the revered educator – again the interplay of New World and Old.

Perhaps the strongest common thread that linked Paul Rudolph the architect and Paul Rudolph the teacher was a sense of absolute commitment, a moral imperative in which no effort was spared, however late in the process, to improve the quality of architecture, whether in his own buildings or, by inspiration, in the work of his students. It is an example that will live on in all of those who shared his influence.

3

In 1998, nearly 40 years after my graduation, I contributed to a seminar in London on the special relationship between America and Britain with Yale as a point of reference. I spoke about my time as a student in New Haven – how I enjoyed living next to the school as a fellow of Jonathan Edwards College, which had a garden courtyard that linked to the Yale Art Gallery. At that time the architecture studios were located on the top floor of this building and I was deeply impressed that they were open day and night – a welcome relief from the European hours and attitudes I had left behind in Manchester. As I described this environment to the audience in the seminar I realised that in so many ways it was a word picture of the way that I lived and worked at Riverside, the site of my present practice on the bank of the Thames in London – the studio there is open 24 hours a day, seven days a week and I live above it with an entrance through the courtyard!

'I think that, irrespective of personal circumstances or environment, if you are passionate about an idea, something can come of it.'

This is an edited transcript of an interview conducted by Yoshio Futagawa in London in 1998 and published in a *Global Architecture Extra* on Norman Foster in April 1999.

Futagawa: Can I ask about your parents. What did they do?
Foster: When I was very young my father was a shop manager in a poor area of Manchester. Later, during the war, he was a security guard. Afterwards he worked in a factory as a manual worker.

Futagawa: What were your interests as you were growing up; did you know that you would become an architect?
Foster: As a child I was always interested in sketching and drawing and making things and, like a lot of people that age, I enjoyed making models. I was fascinated by model aircraft and construction kits which were called 'Trix' or 'Meccano' (3).

Looking back it was quite a lonely childhood. At the beginning of my education my parents sent me to a small private school. At the age of eleven I took the Eleven Plus exam and did quite well. As a result I went to the equivalent of a grammar school, which was quite prestigious in the educational system. Most of the children there came from middle-class backgrounds, so socially I was an outsider because in the neighbourhood where I was brought up everyone was a manual worker.

There was a strong work ethic and consequently pressure to leave school early and be a wage earner. This manifested itself in my taking a job in the City Treasurer's Office in Manchester Town Hall (2). For my parents this represented both security and respectability. I stayed there for two years before I was called up for National Service in the Royal Air Force, which at that time was compulsory. Whilst at the Town Hall I studied commercial law and accountancy in the evenings. I realised that this could never be a long-term interest so I opted for electronic engineering in the military and trained to work on airborne radar systems.

At the same time, however, I was developing a growing interest in architecture. At school I had been good at mathematics and physics. I was also good at art, which was unusual because you were not expected, or encouraged, to cross a number of disciplines. As part of my art studies I took a class on architectural history and discovered modern architecture; gradually I began to read further and explore the

subject for myself. I discovered the work of Le Corbusier and Frank Lloyd Wright. I was fascinated by all aspects of design.

Futagawa: Did your parents encourage you to further your education?

Foster: My parents (1) were fantastic. They were very kind and very loving but they did not really understand why I wanted to give up a safe job, although they were in every other sense very supportive. I had to discover for myself, in my own way, my ambitions and interests. That took quite a long time. It was really National Service that gave me a wider perspective and the maturity to enable me to challenge myself.

When I came out of the Air Force, my job in the Treasurer's Office was still open but I delayed going back. I bought time by doing all kinds of jobs: I worked in a factory and in a bakery; I drove a delivery van; I sold furniture; I did anything to earn money and avoid the Town Hall.

Nevertheless it was an important period for me because I found myself. I put myself through a careers examination to try to establish what options might be open to me. The interviews and tests clarified my interests, which were all creative activities: sketching, drawing, or reading about architecture and design. At that point I decided that I would try to work for an architectural firm, but I knew that the only way I could do that was by using my background from the Town Hall to get an administrative position.

I got a job with a Manchester firm as an assistant to the contracts manager. Slowly I got to know the architects in the practice. At first I was in awe of them. But one day I plucked up the courage to engage one of them in conversation. I picked the youngest person there, a student working part time, and asked him what he thought about architecture. I said, 'I'd love to hear what you think about Frank Lloyd Wright,' and he looked at me and said, 'I don't think I know him, is he a student at the college?'

At that moment I realised that in some ways I knew more about architecture than they did. I was curious and knowledgeable about aspects of architecture of which they were not even aware.

Futagawa: Was that due to the poor standard of architectural education at the time?

Foster: No. The reality was that I was actually very well read but it had never struck

5   6

751

N THE NATURE *
)F MATERIALS

HE BUILDINGS OF
RANK LLOYD WRIGHT · 1887-1941

SY HENRY-RUSSELL HITCHCOCK

4

me as anything special. I assumed that if you were an architect, you would know all that I did and much more besides. However, I had a thirst for the subject that was even greater than that of many practising architects, and certainly much greater than I realised myself.

After that I talked to the people in the drawing office more and more. They were very kind and encouraged me to study. They told me that I would have to go to a school of architecture and show my work. The problem was that I had none; I had never done an architectural drawing. And then I had a bright idea. I began to take drawings from the office at the end of each day and do my own versions of them at home. Each morning I would put the drawings back. I was always the last to leave and the first to arrive in the office, so nobody knew that the drawings had disappeared overnight.

I was actually very naive but I had done enough research to know that if I was to stay in Manchester the University was the best place to study. I had visited the studios and talked to the students – there was no doubt about it. Before I applied, however, I decided that I would have to tell my boss. One day, I knocked on his door and said, 'I just wanted to tell you that I am trying to get into the University.' He said, 'But you have to have work to show.' I told him that it was not a problem, that I had lots of drawings. He asked how that was possible. So I explained, and he was amused, and asked to see what I had done.

When I showed him he said, 'You're a square peg in a round hole. Come with me.' There and then he produced a drawing board, a T-square, a book of standards, and a project. That afternoon I became part of the office. And he then tried very hard to persuade me to stay with him and not to study.

That experience was a boost but there were other obstacles. The first and most significant was that, because I had left school early I lacked the necessary academic qualifications to apply for a place on a university degree course. However, at that time the University had what was called a 'diploma course', the only difference being that you did not have to study a language. My next problem was the Manchester Education Authority. They would give me a grant to study at the College of Art but not at the University. In fact they pressured me to go to the Art College but I was determined to go to the University even though I had no money because I knew that it offered a better education.

Studio Interview

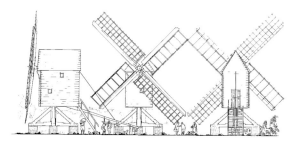

And so I worked my way through university in order to pay the fees. I was a bouncer in a rough cinema; I sold furniture on Saturday afternoons; I did presentation drawings for other architects. During the vacations I worked in a cold store; I drove an ice-cream van; I worked overnight in a bakery. I worked very long hours. It was a very American way of going to school – something unheard of in Europe. And then, through great good fortune, I was lucky enough to win major academic prizes every summer, which were worth quite a lot of money. For example, in my third year I won the RIBA Silver Medal for measured drawings (7, 10), which was worth one hundred pounds. In 1959 that was a lot of money.

I was so highly motivated that when I got into architecture school, nobody was going to stop me. For me, the opportunity to study architecture was the most incredible privilege. I would have paid to do it, which is effectively what I was doing. And so to compete for any prize was quite a challenge.

I used that prize money to fund my travels. I studied Italian Renaissance architecture and visited the Tuscan hill towns as well as exploring work by contemporary Italian architects. I also went to Scandinavia and saw early projects by Jørn Utzon before he did the Sydney Opera House. I saw the work of people who did beautiful pitched roof buildings with slate and brick. I saw all the work of Arne Jacobsen from his earliest buildings to the latest.

Futagawa: Now that you mention some of the architecture you were looking at in your travels, can you tell me if there were any particular styles or trends you were exposed to in school, or were you given a broad range of architectural examples? Earlier you mentioned Le Corbusier and Frank Lloyd Wright; were they the figures you were interested in?

Foster: Manchester University was very traditional. It was nothing like, say, the Architectural Association, or what was then the Regent Street Polytechnic, here in London: I remember visiting the studios there and finding an unbelievably creative environment. Manchester, on the other hand, was very conventional, very disciplined. It was frustrating because you never had the opportunity to debate. You would know what was expected, you would produce the work, it would be assessed, and maybe a week or two weeks later you would get it back with a mark. You would never present your work. There was no dialogue.

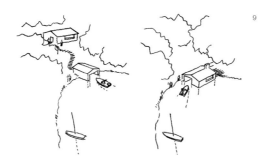

TIHOUSIE – IRETIRIEAT

8

We were still studying the Classical orders and drawing in ink on linen. In the fourth year we had a three-day test and you would be given, for example, an auditorium to design. You had to produce all the drawings, including acoustic diagrams, in just three days. It was very tough in a traditional academic sense, but stylistically it was very limiting.

But it is interesting that even in some of those early student projects I had begun to investigate themes that would become important later on. For example, my very first design project was a boathouse and retreat in the Lake District (8). The expectation was that you would design a shed for the boat and a little cottage alongside to stay in at the weekend. But my design was different. I integrated the boathouse and retreat to form a single building on the waterfront (9). The boat went directly inside the building and the living accommodation was located behind a glass screen facing out onto the river. I was the only student who integrated both the functions in that way.

If you look at the projects in the office today and study their history – whether you take a project such as the IBM Pilot Head Office of 1970-71, or an early one such as the Reliance Controls factory, completed in 1966, or a very recent one, such as Hong Kong International Airport – you will find that they are all about integration.

Reliance Controls (11-13) was a very simple pavilion, but one that allowed the building to grow. It was the opposite of the typical factory of the time, where management and workers were segregated and you could not expand because of this fragmentation. At IBM we challenged the conventional wisdom that the computer should have its own separate 'shrine' and integrated them within the office building. We anticipated the fact that the computer would grow and change, that it was not a sacred object.

The Sainsbury Centre for Visual Arts, a commission we won in 1974, also sought to unify a number of disparate functions – an art gallery, a faculty of art history, a senior common room, a public restaurant – within a single, open, toplit space. Essentially we thought that these buildings would be richer if they were flexible and if the boundaries between functions were broken down.

It has also been suggested that the social dimension in our work comes from my own subconscious, thinking back to the environment in which I grew up, and seeing the possibility of transforming and improving the quality of life for everybody.

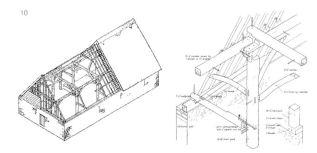

This might be true. At any rate, I think that, irrespective of personal circumstances or environment, if you are passionate about an idea, something can come of it.

At the end of my time at Manchester I applied for a Henry Fellowship, which allows students from America to go to Oxford or Cambridge, and students from British universities to study at Yale or Harvard. I also won a Fulbright scholarship, but the Fulbright would only pay for my travel expenses if I went as a student. The idea back then of being just a student was inconceivable. I had always worked while I studied and I was determined to get a full immigrant visa. That meant I could not accept the Fulbright, so I worked until the last possible moment for that same architectural office in Manchester, and then I flew to the United States on Icelandic Airways, which was the cheapest way to fly.

Futagawa: In some ways it may seem that your time at Yale was the beginning of your career as an architect.

Foster: America was an incredible experience for me in many ways. It was like coming home because instead of being the odd one out, I suddenly fitted in. School was open all hours, from the first day of term to the last, which for me was the greatest luxury. I thought it was fantastic. There were wonderful people at Yale at the time: Paul Rudolph, Serge Chermayeff and Vincent Scully. The grant was very generous, but I was so used to working and studying, and so curious and eager and desperate to see everything, that I worked at a furious pace.

Yale is also where I got to know Richard Rogers, and we became very close friends. Students would work round the clock towards the end of a project, but while everybody else would then collapse and relax, Richard, his wife Su, another friend Carl Abbott, and I would set off in a car and sometimes travel huge distances to visit buildings. And I saw a great deal. I visited other universities, and met Louis Kahn at Philadelphia. I saw all the Frank Lloyd Wright buildings in the Midwest. In fact I travelled so much that I spent money at an alarming rate and had to work even harder to maintain my studies.

Futagawa: Did you and Richard know each other before Yale?

Foster: I first met Richard at a reception for Fulbright scholars before I turned the scholarship down. He had his leg in plaster as a result of a skiing accident. The next

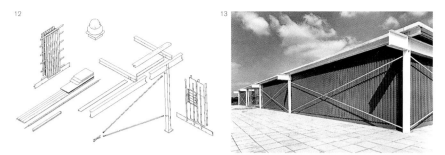

time we met was at Yale. We got along very well. We shared a kind of unspoken language. We even worked on projects together. One was a house for a friend of Richard's, which was very Kahn-like. It was really the beginning of our later collaboration in Team 4, which lasted from 1963 until early 1967.

Futagawa: What kind of work did you do while you were a student?

Foster: I worked on urban renewal schemes for a firm in New Haven. I had studied city planning at Manchester in parallel with architecture and had a planning qualification, so I was able to use those skills on real projects for the first time. Then, in 1961, I got my Masters. I left Yale and set off across the States, as did many of my contemporaries. I ended up in San Francisco where I worked on a large-scale university project for UC Santa Cruz with a group of architects.

I worked for one particular practice but we were in contact with other offices so I was exposed to the work of many people. I got to know the architecture of the whole California school. Occasionally I would travel back to New Haven to advise on some of the renewal projects in the office I had worked with before. Throughout this period, of course, Richard and I kept in touch. We exchanged ideas and talked about working together. Eventually, in 1963, I decided to return to England to make that a reality.

Futagawa: Could you tell me more about what it was like to practise architecture at that time?

Foster: Well, Britain is a very strange place, but I think it has changed a great deal since I started studying and practising. For example, it is a far more open society now than it was then. And although Britain is ambivalent in its attitude towards Europe, there is no doubt that a lot of positive influences and pressures have come from a more confident Europe on the other side of the Channel.

There are always pluses and minuses in being influenced in this way. On the plus side, Britain provides an extraordinary working environment. It is free of the bureaucracy that you find in some European countries, and it is a very balanced society. Therefore, in terms of maintaining an office, it's fantastic. People here have great skills and there is a great spirit. London at the moment is a very lively, interesting place to be.

The architectural profession is now very open in all kinds of ways that it was not when we formed Team 4. At that time, for example, there were those architects who did university work, those who did new town work, those who did commercial work. There were very different kinds of architects who in most cases specialised. Architecture was a closed shop. There was no way of breaking into it.

I remember the early days of the practice. After Team 4 split up, my wife Wendy and I formed Foster Associates. We had so little work that we came very close to leaving Britain. The question was whether or not we would emigrate to North America or Canada. We survived by appealing to a niche in which architects had not traditionally been involved, which was industry.

In order to do that we had to demonstrate that we could offer three things. Firstly, we demonstrated that by playing the open market we could actually build a good building for less than a builder would produce a bad building. We could use our professional skills to research and shop; we could buy a structure here, a cladding there and, since we didn't have a commercial axe to grind, we could justify a fair fee to do it. Secondly, we proved that we could do all of that very quickly. And thirdly, we were able to bring a dimension to the project that a builder never would. We could speak to industrialists in their own language. A client's needs will change, and we were able to use that fact to our advantage by stressing the importance of flexibility. We said: 'You cannot know what you will need tomorrow; the fastest you can build a new factory is a year, and your requirements could be very different in a year from now, or over the life of the building.' Typically we tried to develop a project without permanently locking in how much space was designated for administration, production and so on.

Our work was also socially focused. We explored the idea of a democratic workplace, one that would be rooted in the social realities of the present and the future rather than the past. Of course, as architects, we also wanted to bring these things together in a way that would produce memorable architecture. It is no accident that the Reliance Controls building – which, at 120,000 square feet, was built in nine months, for £5 per square foot – won the first Financial Times Award for Industrial Architecture. It hit every button.

Our work for the Norwegian shipping line Fred Olsen in Millwall Dock was to take these ideas a stage further. We did a number of projects for Olsen and it was

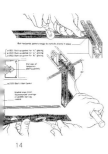

14

a very interesting company. Its main trade was with the Canary Islands. On the out-ward journey from Europe its ships would carry a mixed cargo, and they would return with things like bananas. In order to get the maximum use out of their ships, however, Olsen very cleverly combined this trade with cruises and holidays and inte-grated these two apparently contradictory functions in a complementary way. Interestingly, that was exactly the strategy we advocated for the organisation of their buildings, which is perhaps why they were so receptive to our ideas. The *parti*, of course, goes back to my first-year project for the little boathouse. In our Amenity Building for Olsen we placed the workers and the management together in one building, which was unheard of in the London Docks at that time. We broke all the social barriers.

Our first challenge, however, was to win the client over from the competition, which was not easy. We were not up against other architects, but contractors. The building industry was impenetrable, very different from how it is today.

Typically our competitors would come in and make a presentation and they would talk about how their building would look. Our approach was very different. We would ask questions, listen to what the client wanted and go away. Then we would come back to ask more questions. We made sure we understood the client's objectives in terms of both the functional and social organisation of the company.

The development period for that first Olsen project was incredibly short, and so we had to challenge conventions in other ways too. For example, we could not possibly have designed and prototyped the glazed curtain wall that we wanted in the time available. And so I went on a research trip to the States and brought back a sophisticated system, which used brand new products such as heat-and-light-reflective glass (14, 15).

When they were completed, the Olsen buildings attracted so much attention that we soon found ourselves shortlisted for projects for major companies such as Willis Faber & Dumas and IBM. And when potential clients went to visit our buildings and talked to the managers and workers, they realised how penetrating our under-standing of the needs of those users had been, and the positive effect it had on the design of the building. If you were to ask Fred Olsen what makes us different from other architects, I know he would say that we ask the right questions. I think we have a curiosity, a burning interest in the elements and activities that generate a building.

17

Futagawa: So this kind of questioning and research is a fundamental part of your architectural process?

Foster: Yes. If you jump forward ten years to 1979, when we went out to be interviewed for the Hongkong and Shanghai Bank project, the same sort of thing occurred. After our competitors had left, we stayed on in Hong Kong to discover how banking worked there. We wanted to establish what we could put inside a banking hall. It was only after undertaking that research that we came up with the idea of putting the banking hall up in the air so that you have a glass showcase with a glass underbelly that creates a public space at ground level (16, 17).

That space also created a new social focus in the city. Whenever I go to Hong Kong I take photographs there. At the weekend that public space under the banking hall is the liveliest picnic spot in the city. Significantly, it also allowed the Bank to develop the site at a better than 18:1 plot ratio, which is an extraordinarily efficient use of land. At that time experienced developers in Hong Kong could not achieve better than a 14:1 ratio. We were outsiders but we managed to beat that at our first attempt.

Futagawa: Your early buildings used industrial components partly out of a search for economy. In other words, your research into building technology seemed to be related to a cost-effective way of building. But now it appears that your architectural ideas go far beyond what prefabricated parts can give you. We have talked a little about the Hongkong Bank, which to some degree is a prefabricated building; but it is also one of the most expensive buildings of the century. Has the idea of prefabrication in this case become somewhat ironic, since the use of customised parts tended to make the cost of the building so much higher?

Foster: Your observations are not entirely accurate. The thread that I identified at the beginning runs through the history of the practice and continues today. At Reliance Controls, for example, by using a high degree of prefabrication we were able to raise standards and lower costs. But prefabrication was not – and never has been – a goal in itself. It was simply a means to achieving higher standards for the building and its users in an economical way.

The fact is that all of us spend a very large proportion of our time at work so anything that can help to raise the quality of the workplace is worth investigating. I

might add that we were the first architects to introduce into this country the idea that the workplace could have higher standards, that it could be a pleasant environment, that, for example, you could have views to the outside, or have high-grade amenities. At Olsen we did not just provide the basics, such as showers, but also facilities for table tennis, billiards and television; and we put art on the walls. That might not seem radical now, but in the context of the 1960s these were startling new ideas. In the London Docks at that time, the toilet facilities were disgusting. Workers in industry were treated little better than animals.

In a way, over the years, we have reinvented the workplace, we have reinvented the tall building, and we have reinvented the nature of the airport. If you look at our terminal building at Stansted, you will find that the standard of finishes is astonishingly high compared to the work organised by the British Airports Authority at Heathrow or Gatwick. Yet, remarkably, it cost only 80 per cent of what BAA had been spending per square foot until that time. Stansted was a revolution. It has become the model for airports the world over, including Stuttgart, Hamburg, Kansai and Terminal Five at Heathrow.

Airports after Stansted are very different from those that went before. Hitherto, with very few exceptions, most of them had heavy structures, their roof levels clogged by mechanical equipment (19). They were basically sealed boxes, lit by fluorescent light, with heavy ducts concealed behind suspended ceilings; and they were huge consumers of energy.

Stansted inverted the traditional airport (18). We put the infrastructure on the bottom and not on the top. So, just like a modern office building where you have a raised floor containing all the wiring and so on, at Stansted you have a big flexible void beneath the public concourse. We created a space where you can even accommodate a train station. What happens when you turn the conventional model upside down like that is that you free up the roof. Of course, it keeps off the rain, but it can also let in the sunlight. In the old model you could not do that.

In addition it allows you to make the entire structure much lighter because all the heavy stuff stays on the ground. The roof can therefore be very light. It can be like a tree. Suddenly you can bring daylight in, you can model the form of the roof in relation to the light so that it reflects up or down, and using the airport can be an uplifting experience.

Now the case of the Hongkong Bank was spectacularly different. But again it was revolutionary in terms of a tall building. For the first time you had a skyscraper with no central services and circulation core. As for the economics of the project, you have to understand that the Bank was built during a very sensitive time in Hong Kong's history. It was politically very important for our client that the building should be created without compromise and that it should meet previously unheard-of performance criteria. To this day there is only one building in the world that offers that degree of flexibility and capability as a headquarters tower, and that is the Hongkong and Shanghai Bank.

In short the Bank set performance goals and we had to meet them. Cost did not come after the fact, it was largely determined by the brief. Another major consideration was the fact that Hong Kong produced nothing in the way of building materials. Everything had to be shipped in. Many components were even flown in. And so it was bound to be expensive. Even so, if you take another office building with a very high specification, the new administrative block opposite the Houses of Parliament here in London, you will find that it is costing considerably more per square foot than the Bank. Other buildings, such as Stansted Airport, have used prefabrication to achieve better performance at lower cost, but the circumstances were quite different.

Interestingly, the Bank itself still regards the building as a very good investment. Since we completed it, there have been several changes of senior management, so we now deal with a completely new generation. What is fascinating is that, looking back, they continue to link their consistent financial growth as a bank and their strong world rating directly to the success of the building and the way it has been able to adapt to suit their changing needs.

I should also say something about prefabrication. You might imagine an architect looking for, say, a suspended ceiling system and finding one in a catalogue. You might think that he can just call up and order it off the shelf: wrong. What you do not know is that your ceiling does not yet exist. It is there in the catalogue but if you want to buy it you have to wait while someone manufactures it. The same is true of furniture. If I want an ottoman, a Mies van der Rohe design, I cannot go to Vitra and pick it up with a truck. It exists as a series of drawings and they will make it and deliver it. It is a catalogue item but that does not mean they have it in stock.

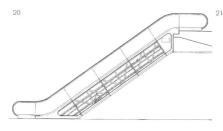

Therefore, if you have enough curiosity and interest in the production process, you very soon discover that you can specify your own ceiling, or your own chair and have it made in the same way. The chances are that you will end up with a better product and the cost will probably not be that different. If you come up with a good design, the likelihood is that your product will appear in someone else's catalogue for another architect to specify in a different context. If you understand that then you start to realise why, if you go to Jim Stirling's Staatsgalerie in Stuttgart, you will find the studded rubber flooring that we developed for Willis Faber. Or go to shopping malls the world over and you will find escalators where you can see the insides moving (20, 21) – they did not exist before we did Willis Faber but now they have become part of a universal building vocabulary.

Futagawa: What about the High-Tech aspect of your work – could you talk more about that?

Foster: We use technology, but not just for its own sake. It is the same with prefabrication. For instance, although you might be able to demonstrate the benefits of prefabricated concrete in the South of France, you cannot build any more economically with it than you can with *in situ* concrete, which is why all our projects in southern France are poured in place. If you go down to Nîmes, to our Carré d'Art, you will find that no concrete beam spans more than six metres. It is very traditional stuff. Local building techniques have determined the outcome of the buildings. The Carré d'Art could not have happened anywhere except Nîmes.

The same is true of other projects. The daylighting concept that forms an essential part of our strategy for the Reichstag was suggested by the uninterrupted skyline of Berlin, where there are few tall buildings on the horizon; the same approach would never work in Frankfurt. The daylighting strategy at Stansted, on the other hand, was a response to a northern climate, and it could never work in Nîmes. Furthermore, the form of the Carré d'Art comes out of the Roman geometry and the cultural roots of Nîmes, in the same way that the shape of Willis Faber, which is amorphous, comes out of the irregular, winding geometry of its medieval market town. They are all very specific to their sites.

That fact is often not appreciated. Instead, people prefer to talk about technology. But if you actually look at it and analyse it, I think you will find that what I am

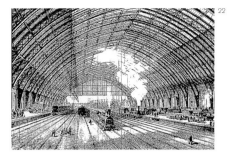

saying is true. In all of these buildings you have a sense of the outside, of the changes in nature and the quality of light – aspects that you cannot quantify. It is very difficult to convey in words the act of design; it involves a lot of value judgements, some of which are practical and some of which are really quite emotional, quite visceral. In truth, a powerful part of ourselves finds its way into design, whether we can articulate it or not. It is not just about technology and efficiency.

For example, at Stansted, if sunlight dapples the floor at a particular time of day, it is because a conscious decision was made that sunlight should be an essential ingredient of the interiors, even if it brings with it some solar gain. It is not accidental. It has all been thoroughly modelled and explored. It comes out of a passion for the quality of that space. Ultimately, even if an airport successfully addresses the mechanics of circulation, of security, of baggage movement, but is a hostile place for the passengers who use it, then it is a failure architecturally. Interestingly, a lot of people say that they use Stansted because they enjoy the experience more than going to other airports.

A policeman once said the nicest thing I have heard about Stansted. He was on security duty when the Queen opened the building. He told me that he had guarded buildings all his life, but Stansted was the first place where he had realised that a building could actually be a beautiful place.

Futagawa: When you were designing Stansted were you thinking about nineteenth-century train stations?
Foster: Of course there is something in that comparison. In the nineteenth century there was a great sense of theatre involved in travel, a sense of occasion (22). It started not when you got on the train but within the station itself. Typically in a modern airport, you are not aware of the aircraft until you finally arrive at the end of a tube somewhere and see your plane standing on the tarmac. At Stansted you can see the aircraft on the airside. On the landside you see the landscaping. This combined transparency is very much about the anticipation and the celebration of travel. It brings some humanity into it.

Futagawa: Stansted is a new type of airport, which reduces the scale of older terminals like those at Heathrow. Perhaps the smaller scale allows your ideas to be expressed more clearly. If you think about Kansai Airport, the scale detracts from what might have been a similar idea. I think the scale really changes the perception of the space inside.

Foster: Stansted follows a masterplan where that front-to-back dimension is part of a building zone. You have the landside with cars and coaches, and you have the airside with terminals. If it grows, it will grow linearly. So you always have a human-scale relationship between the airside and the landside.

I agree that the scale of things really changes the effectiveness of this approach. If the building expands you reach a point where the horizontal dimension is stretched so far that its depth does not allow this kind of visual connection. Our terminal at Hong Kong is much larger than Stansted. The solution there was to elongate the plan, keeping the cross-section relatively shallow. That creates more frontage, which in turn allows continuous views out and helps to lead you in the right direction. You always have this sense of orientation and relationship to the outside. The depth is never too great.

Futagawa: What about the vertical scale?

Foster: There are several factors to be considered: the overall sense of scale, the height of the space, and the ways in which the structure can give it an order and an orientation. Sometimes when we have had the choice of adopting a completely clear span, or having columns going up through the building, we have followed the latter course. The feel of the space is better – more coherent – when you see the columns coming through, although structurally it would have been possible not to use them. They give a sense of order and clarity and drama to the space.

Futagawa: How do you go about determining the size and order of the structure in your buildings?

Foster: Of course today there are all sorts of restrictions that will influence a design. We have to consider structural efficiency, or we might have to allow for a car-park below, which imposes its own discipline. For instance, our studio in London is part of a mixed-use building which contains apartments above, and car-parking below. Somewhere in between the two it had to work as a space for offices – and in the end it has to feel right and you have to feel comfortable with it.

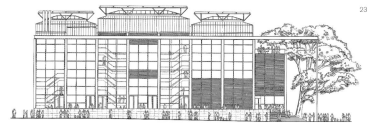

23

Let me give you another example. Recently we won a commission to renew the Free University of Berlin, which was built in the 1960s. The original building is clad in metal panels based on the proportional system of Le Corbusier's Modulor. The only building that Le Corbusier himself did in metal panels that comes to mind is the little Heidi Weber Pavilion in Zurich, which I think is a magical building – the sense of proportion, colour, gridding and modularity is fantastic. The Free University used the same Modulor system, but in comparison, the proportion of the facades and the way in which they come together does not have the same visual elegance.

There is no system that will automatically give you something that looks or feels right. When Le Corbusier used the Modulor it was obviously of great help to him. But I suspect that this was not the case for everything he did. Ronchamp, for example, could not embrace the Modulor. There is not a vertical line or a horizontal plane in it, and yet it has a wonderful quality of space and proportion. And just as some of Le Corbusier's buildings are better than others, any architect will have buildings that are more or less successful. I think it is as much about an intuitive eye as any mathematical formula.

Futagawa: What you say is extremely interesting. When I visited the Carré d'Art (23) for the first time – and maybe my reading is influenced by the little Roman temple opposite, the Maison Carrée – the building seemed to me to be extremely Classical, even though you have used a lot of metal and glass. Your buildings have a highly developed sense of proportion. I sense that you are as much a Classical architect as a High-Tech architect. You use technology as a tool but your designs are not governed by it.

Foster: I am happy to hear you say that. It is an observation that has been made before, and I think that it is quite astute. In fact, after the building was completed, one of the project architects did a drawing to compare its proportions with those of the Maison Carrée (24, 25). It was a playful exercise but it revealed a very close proportional relationship. Later somebody saw those drawings and thought that we had worked out a proportional system based on the Maison Carrée but in fact that was not the case. We designed our building in a way we thought appropriate to its relationship with its context, both in terms of its dialogue with the Maison Carrée and in its own right.

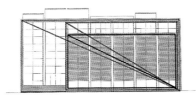 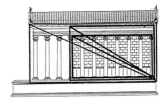

Futagawa: At Nîmes you found yourself in an entirely urban setting. What was your focus there?

Foster: In addition to the Maison Carrée, which is really the historical focus, the social focal points were the Roman arena and the nineteenth-century water gardens. The building, with its entrance on the corner, grew out of an attitude to the urban grain of the Roman origins of the town. That also opened the possibility of walking through the building to a smaller portico at the back where there is a shortcut to the water gardens. The urban grain of the city indicated where the entrance would be. It also helped us in reforming the streets around the building while respecting the specific environment of the Maison Carrée.

In overall terms, we tried to create an urban experience where you would move through almost tunnel-like shaded avenues of trees and explode out into this bright sunlit square. The before and after photographs are very dramatic. Before the Carré d'Art was built this area was very run down. There were no cafes and the Maison Carrée was circled with nineteenth-century iron railings. Our strategy was a deliberate attempt to peel away some of those layers of history in order to reveal others which were more meaningful. We reintroduced Roman paving for example, instead of retaining the nineteenth-century paving. We also took away the parked cars to give the area back to pedestrians.

Futagawa: Your siting and landscape strategy for the Cambridge Law Faculty building seems in tune with certain attitudes at Nîmes and Stansted. Would you agree?

Foster: Yes. In fact, I could talk about Cambridge in the context of Stansted. If you look at the East Anglian countryside where Stansted sits, it is essentially flat and wooded. The airfield slopes down, so one important design consideration was to exploit the slope, especially in terms of access, both for passengers arriving at the concourse level and cargo-handling below, and then access to the aircraft beyond. It is a very rational *parti*, but it also grows out of how you sensitively site a large terminal building in the countryside. In that case, the critical thing was to keep the roof below the tree line.

When we came to the design of the Law Faculty (26, 27) we had to ask ourselves, what is the essence of Cambridge? One of the things that makes it special is its trees and gardens. If you look at a photograph of Cambridge you might get the

occasional spire and various buildings on the skyline, but essentially it is a low, green, garden environment. So our starting point was to preserve the principal trees on the site and the quality of the garden. It is very much about getting a large and complex programme on a site in a very discreet way, which is exactly the challenge we faced in Nîmes.

In Nîmes we placed a large proportion of the building's accommodation under-ground, in order to respect the historical roof line. Similarly in Cambridge, we sought to reduce the visual impact of the building by a combination of methods. Firstly we dug deep into the site, and then we developed an inclined curving glass wall sys-tem that tends to make the facades recede, so that the building appears very much smaller in this context than it actually is. Our approach came directly from a sensi-tivity to the site. I think that a sensitivity to, and understanding of, the culture of a place, or the culture of an organisation – whether you are building a museum, a company headquarters, a governmental institution or a high-rise tower – is a crucial part of the architect's role.

Futagawa: You mentioned high-rise towers. This question of sensitivity to site, and particularly the environment, is highly appropriate in that regard. We have talked about the Hongkong Bank, but you employed a different strategy for the Frankfurt Commerzbank project. Can you talk a little about that?

Foster: The Commerzbank really stems from a desire to reconcile work and nature within the compass of one office building. The design of Willis Faber, with its turfed roof garden, for example, was an early attempt at bringing the 'park' into the office. At the Hongkong Bank we proposed 'gardens in the sky' (28) which unfortunately failed to materialise. The Frankfurt tower was an opportunity to design a building that was symbolically and functionally 'green', and responsive to its city-centre location.

It is the world's first ecological high-rise tower. It is also the tallest tower in Europe at the moment – not that I think that's so significant. What is important is the way in which we developed a strategy that allowed us to place such a tall build-ing in the city and to break down its scale. It rises from the centre of a large tradi-tional city block alongside the existing Commerzbank building. By rebuilding and restoring the perimeter buildings we were able to preserve the scale of the neigh-bourhood at street level.

28

The tower's plan form is triangular, made up from three 'petals' and a central stem. The petals are the office floors. The stem is a central atrium, which provides a ventilation chimney up the building for the inward-looking offices. That led us to a solution where we were able to pull the cores to the corners, which in turn opened up the possibility of breaking the form of the building on the skyline. The interesting thing about the structure is that it allows you to pull out segments and to develop a kind of 'helix' of open gardens rising up the building. Internally it helps to break down the scale of what is in fact a very large institution. It also allows you always to relate to a window and fresh air, and to have a view of a garden wherever you are in the building.

Futagawa: Developing such a project obviously places great demands on your engineers, for example. How does that relationship work?

Foster: Well we don't have engineers in-house; we work with a variety of independent consultants. The same is true across a number of related specialisms. We tend to work very closely with a broad cross-section of talented individuals and we have developed very creative working relationships with them. I like to think that we understand a great deal about many aspects of building, even though we might not practise as structural engineers or in other disciplines.

I believe also that the best architecture comes from a synthesis of all of the elements that comprise a building: the structure that holds it up; the services that allow it to work; the ecology of the building – whether it is naturally ventilated, whether you can open a window, the quality of natural light; the materials used – their mass or their lightness; the character of the spaces; the symbolism of the form; the relationship of the building to the skyline or the streetscape; and the way in which the building signals its presence in the city or the countryside. I think that holds true whether you are creating a landmark or deferring to a historical setting. Successful architecture addresses all these things, and many more.

'... I remember being simply spellbound by the sheer beauty of the complex geometry that had been etched into the smooth table of wheat.'

Norman Foster

My interest in crop circles started around 1981 and was triggered indirectly by our project for the Hongkong and Shanghai Bank. After winning the competition two years earlier, we had established a major presence in Hong Kong and the pace of our activities was building up rapidly. Long-distance flights were already a way of life for me as I commuted between our studios in Hong Kong and London and the main subcontractors in America, Japan and Europe. Heathrow Airport was becoming more like a third home, due to its position between London and our country house in Wiltshire.

My lifestyle changed completely during this period as distance became increasingly dissociated from time. It took almost as long for me to get to the airport through the dense traffic around London as it did to cruise in on the motorway from the West Country.

Consequently, as the pressures of travel increased, I lived more and more in the country where I had also established a small office. Over a period of several years I commuted between London and Wiltshire by helicopter, flying a low-level route which took me over sites marked by the earliest settlements of ancient civilisation – stone circles, ancient burial mounds and the earthworks of Iron Age forts. This heritage has given rise to a variety of cults and theories, with much speculation about invisible lines of energy which have been dubbed 'ley lines'.

At the same time I was discovering a different kind of mysticism in the Asian context of Hong Kong. Here the ancient art of feng shui, with its lines of force and mythology, was a powerful influence on the community – locals and European expats alike. Indeed it had played a role in the design of the Bank – from the earliest days of the design through several stages of construction and fitting-out. The first sketch of the project was made by a geomancer, whose advice I had counselled on my initial visit to the site. Although I am a rationalist to the core I was sensitive to the role of feng shui in the society of Hong Kong. I also had an open mind on the subject.

In between these experiences I was discovering another phenomenon, which seemed to defy rational explanation, and was occurring very close to my home in Wiltshire. This was the sudden appearance of so-called 'crop circles' (5, 6). I can still remember the charge of shock and wonderment when, piloting the helicopter one evening, I came across my first view of a 'formation'. It was in a field close to

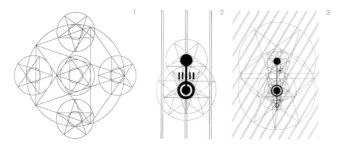

Silbury Hill, the largest man-made earthwork in Europe, the origins and purpose of which are lost in antiquity. The place was called Alton Barnes, a reference point that I used on the final approach of my homeward flight.

I had stayed in London overnight and knew that the field was completely clear the day before. Although there had already been much writing and speculation on the subject of crop circles, I had never seen one; looking back I remember being simply spellbound by the sheer beauty of the complex geometry that had been etched into the smooth table of wheat – dramatically thrown into relief by the low-angle rays of light from a setting sun. It was a stunningly surreal sight.

Over time I saw more crop circles in the same area of my helicopter route – never seeking them out but discovering them by chance. Then, as now, I was not preoccupied by the 'reasons why' – there are as many theories as there are writers on the subject, ranging from the frivolous to the scientific. The debate about whether these formations were the work of practical jokers, aliens, visiting UFOs or acts of God and nature always seemed to pale alongside the sheer poetic beauty of the formations themselves.

It was at this time that I became a close friend of the distinguished German designer, Otl Aicher, whom I had approached to work on the signage for the Hongkong Bank. Otl would stay to work with us in Wiltshire and these would alternate with sessions in his home town of Rotis in Swabia. There were links between both places – Otl was fascinated by Celtic history and he would pore over maps to explain geographic connections. I remember using the helicopter to show him the White Horse at Uffingham – a beautifully abstract creature that had been sculpted in the landscape by scraping away the earth to reveal the white chalk below. Again its origins and purpose were unknown, buried in a long distant past – but graphically it was a haunting image.

I learned much from Otl over the years of our friendship, before his untimely death in 1991. He was a mixture of philosopher, designer and graphic communicator. With his rigorously sparse drawings, mostly in black and white, he was forever demonstrating the power of graphic portrayal over photographic realism.

When I first saw Wolfgang Schindler's collated drawings of crop circles (1-4), the strength of their abstraction reminded me of Otl's work – which is one of the highest compliments that I could pay to anyone.

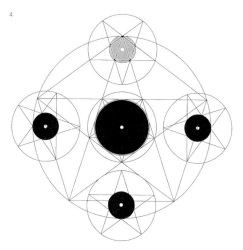

I am intrigued by this urge to translate the perspective of an aerial photograph into a scale drawing. The reverse process is more normal for architects and designers who are continually trying to translate two dimensions into a third – either manually or with the aid of computers. Does the quest for formal plans of these formations aim to fulfil the purpose of geometric analysis or to contemplate their aesthetic subtleties? It does not really matter because the outcome from Wolfgang Schindler is a compelling catalogue of evocative images.

My introduction to the author of this book came through a shared friend, Michael Glickman, who has similarly devoted much time and energy to the same subject. His own line of enquiry has taken him along the same route of planning studies as 'a contemplative exercise, which offers many rewards'. Wolfgang Schindler's work has made these kinds of insight accessible to a wider audience, and with refreshing impartiality.

I could best conclude with a quote from Glickman when he ponders on the aesthetic delights of these formations: 'It is clear to me that an understanding of this most beautiful of phenomena must be based on the response of our eyes and our hearts and not our analytical minds.' I am delighted to share those sentiments.

5

6

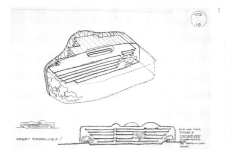

visualisations of yet-to-be-built buildings that are as realistic as photographs. Three-dimensional computer modelling takes this capacity further, enabling us to create virtual reality 'walk-throughs' that take the viewer around and through buildings that do not yet exist. These technologies speed up communications and the design process and enrich the ways in which we can explain the design of a building to a client, consultant or contractor.

Digital technology also aids us in designing buildings with new and unconventional forms that are able to respond to the challenges of building low-energy and sustainable architecture. These new forms, with complex geometries, require building components and construction techniques that have no historical precedent. We therefore need to understand at the earliest stages of design how these new forms can be built. This means that we are talking to the construction industry much earlier than is usual, and drawing upon its expertise to inform the design of the building. There is now a constant flow of information between architect, engineer and building contractor. In this way the design and construction process operates more like a musical jamming session than the 'conductor and orchestra' model of old.

The benefits to architecture of all these developments in terms of efficiency and improved communications are no doubt shared by every branch of industry and the arts. However, uniquely, we now have at our disposal digital design tools that are enabling us to realise buildings which only 30 years ago were beyond our capabilities.

I remember, for example, the initial stages of the design of the Willis Faber & Dumas headquarters in Ipswich, in the early 1970s. One of the principal challenges of that project was to resolve the difficulties of locating a new building on an irregularly shaped urban site; in addition to that was a desire to provide an energy-efficient enclosure.

Our collaborations with Buckminster Fuller – a man who has influenced contemporary thinking about sustainable architecture more than any other – led us to investigate a possible solution in which the site was enclosed within a single, lightweight transparent shell sheltering flexible 'trays' of office floors (1). It was, if you like, a miniature version of Fuller's visionary dome over Manhattan (2), a minimal enclosure capable of creating its own internal microclimate.

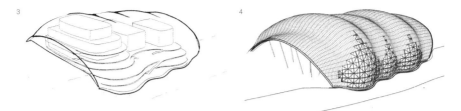

Fuller had already built a number of lightweight spherical structures, most notably for the World Expo in Montreal, and he pursued the model of the sphere because of its geometric efficiency – a sphere has 25 per cent less surface area than a cube of the same volume. But containing the Willis Faber & Dumas site in an optimal way required a fluid, free-form skin, the geometric complexity of which raised technical difficulties which were insurmountable at the time. I recall making a note on one of the sketches: 'Great possibilities! But we lack time and technical expertise.'

Three recent projects serve to highlight how much the world has changed within the last 30 years. Each is far more geometrically and technologically complex than that early proposal for Willis Faber & Dumas, and yet each has been designed in a relatively short period of time, and will soon become a physical reality.

The Music Centre we are currently designing at Gateshead, on Tyneside (5), is a key element in the cultural regeneration of the derelict riverside. It will provide accommodation for the Regional Music School and three auditoria of varying sizes for performances of classical and popular music. Each of the auditoria is conceived as a separate enclosure and they are linked to each other by a concourse, in the form of a covered 'street' on the riverfront.

The budget for the Music Centre is relatively modest, and so it was necessary to design a roof that would shelter the auditoria, the concourse and the music school in the most efficient manner – closely hugging the buildings beneath (3). In 'shrink wrapping' the buildings a free-form shape was generated. However, it was clear that if the roof was to be an economic reality, it would have to conform to geometric rules in order to rationalise the setting out, manufacture and construction of the building components (4).

Previously, if we had presented the cladding contractor with a model of the roof, he may well have thought it unbuildable, or at least extremely costly to build. We made the form correspond to a geometry based on the arcs of nine circles. By altering the radii of the circles we were able to produce a roof form that is economical and that can be more easily understood.

A similar process of geometrical analysis was employed in the design of the new headquarters for the Greater London Authority (GLA), which is being built on the south bank of the Thames adjacent to Tower Bridge. When completed it will

5>

be a model of environmental responsibility; to heat and cool it will consume one-quarter of the energy used by any of the air-conditioned office buildings you can typically find in the City of London.

The unique shape of the GLA building has been generated as a result of rigorous scientific analysis, aiming to reduce solar gain and heat loss via the building's skin, thus reducing the building's energy needs. The building's form is derived from a sphere, but it has undergone a series of geometric modifications (6, 7) so that is now has a shape similar to a rugby ball (8). This achieves optimum energy performance in relation to its site and orientation; in particular minimising the amount of surface area exposed to direct sunlight. The building leans back towards the south, where the floor-plates are stepped inwards from top to bottom, providing natural shading from the most intense direct sunlight.

Analysis of the sunlight hours falling on every part of the building throughout the year has produced a thermal map of its surface that will be expressed in the building's cladding. Where most shading is needed a system of operable louvres will be employed. Less shading is required towards the north-facing facade, where the glazing for the assembly chamber will be clear.

Similar ecological factors have played a decisive role in the equally novel form of the building which we are designing on the site of the Baltic Exchange in the City as the London headquarters for Swiss Re – the world's largest reinsurance company (12). The profile of this tall tower can be likened to a cigar or a bullet – a cylinder which widens as it rises from the ground and then tapers towards its apex. This form responds to the specific demands of the small site: the building appears less bulky than a conventional rectangular block of equivalent floor area; the slimming of the building's profile at its base reduces reflections, improves transparency and increases daylight penetration at ground level; the tapering apex of the tower minimises the extent of reflected sky; and the building's aerodynamic form encourages wind to flow around its facades rather than being deflected to ground level. The relatively small area at ground level also allows the creation of a public piazza with cafes and shops.

'Sky gardens' are central to the building's natural ventilation strategy and build upon the example we pioneered at the Commerzbank Headquarters in Frankfurt. They are created by making six triangular incisions into the edges of the

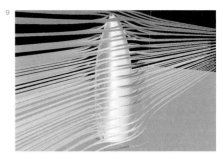

floor-plates so that, in plan, they resemble car wheel-hubs, with six radiating fingers. Each of the 40 stacked floors has been rotated so that the voids spiral around the building's periphery. These will be filled with plants and will help to purify and oxygenate the air in the building.

In each of the projects outlined above, very different functional considerations have produced buildings which all have complex geometries consisting of double curvatures. Without the assistance of new digital technologies, the process of calculating the effects on the buildings' geometries of alterations throughout their design development would have been enormously labour intensive and time consuming.

A relatively new development in computer modelling techniques was employed to assist in the process. Called parametric modelling, it has been developed in the aerospace and automotive industries for designing complex curved forms and is now having a fundamental effect on the design of buildings.

Parametric modelling is an extension of the basic computer-aided design (CAD) package, Bentley Systems' MicroStation TriForma, which is now used throughout the studio. It is a three-dimensional computer modelling process that allows the designer to specify or capture the geometric relationships between design features (10). The parameters that control those relationships can then be modified to generate new versions of the design almost instantaneously.

The process is similar to that of a spreadsheet. By storing the relationships between the various features of the design and treating these relationships like mathematical equations, it allows any element of the model to be changed and automatically regenerates the model in much the same way that a spreadsheet automatically recalculates any numerical changes. As such, it becomes a 'living' model – one that is constantly responsive to change – offering a degree of flexibility never previously available.

During the design of Gateshead, Swiss Re and the GLA building, the parametric model allowed us to alter any aspect of the design and immediately see the result in terms of a modified building form, literally within seconds. In the case of Gateshead, the design team generated more than one hundred alternative roof designs in response to structural, financial and aesthetic issues, sometimes mocking up four or five schemes in a day.

This does not merely herald a quantitative change to the design process in terms of efficiency: it also represents a qualitative change. The rapidity with which alterations can be made to a design generates a greater degree of creative freedom, allowing options to be assessed and taken forward in an organic fashion, providing important lessons along the way. Fully detailed models can be regenerated in a matter of seconds; solid models can be 'sliced' to generate floor-plates. Such models would take hours or even days to create manually.

Our in-house programmers have also extended the capabilities of MicroStation TriForma's software to allow us to rationalise curved surfaces into flat panels. Using this technology, we can generate panelisation studies, which subdivide the curved skin into facets to facilitate the economical production of cladding and glazing elements.

The data produced by the three-dimensional computer model can also be linked directly to numerically controlled model-making tools in order to produce physical models. The compatibility of these technologies avoids any possibility of error in transferring from the computer to the physical model, resulting in models that are extremely accurate.

The conversion of the parametric model into physical models is invaluable in ensuring that errors are discovered early in the design process, when they can be easily rectified, rather than on the building site. For example, during the design of the Swiss Re building we built a large polyboard model of a section of the facade, which is geometrically very complex. In the process we found that two pieces of polyboard would not fit together. But we knew that the dimensions for the parts had come from the computer model and therefore ought to be correct. Going back to the parametric model, we zoomed in very closely and found, indeed, that two lines did not align, alerting us to an anomaly in the geometry.

Importantly, the data from the parametric model can also be exported to structural and environmental consultants for analysis. The findings can then be incorporated into the model to create the next version of the building's design, allowing structural and design decisions to proceed in parallel.

With Swiss Re this enabled us to subject the computer model to 'virtual wind-tunnel' tests to examine airflow around and through the building (9). This was crucial for two reasons: firstly, to assess the impact of wind loads on such a tall

11

structure; and secondly, to test the efficiency of the building's natural ventilation strategy. These studies also showed that the aerodynamic shape of the building will result in improved wind conditions in the locality.

The CAD model works as an electronic drawing board shared by the whole team throughout the design process, but its life extends beyond the design of a building into the construction phase – it is becoming a 'cradle-to-grave' technology. When it comes to building Gateshead, Swiss Re and the GLA building, the computer model, or mathematical formulae derived from it, will serve as the basic tool for the setting out and development of the main building components. The traditional plan, section and elevation drawings can now be extracted from the model, which ensures consistency, but these are no longer adequate to describe the building or to coordinate production and assembly.

We have already used a CAD model in this way during the construction of the Great Glass House for the National Botanic Garden of Wales (11). The building was designed to house more than a thousand species of plants from Mediterranean climates throughout the world. It takes the form of a dome, but because it has an elliptical rather than a circular plan it has a relatively complex geometry, known as a toroid. Its supporting concrete structure is buried underground so that the 'blister' form of the roof seems to grow from the surrounding valley like a glass hillock. The complexity of the geometry meant that conventional architectural drawings could only be effective as an explanatory back up to the three-dimensional computer model.

Some of the most fundamental aspects of our profession are changing as a result of this technology. Our recent experience of the revolution in information technology indicates that the changes will continue to grow in magnitude and speed. A mere twenty years ago, few people could have envisaged that it would be possible to fax a document across the world in a matter of seconds. The growth of e-commerce might well spell the death of the fax machine, just as the fax superseded the telex. Computer screens have already replaced the traditional drawing board – a photograph of our studio, taken shortly after we occupied it in 1990, shows only a handful of computers; today every single workstation has one. We cannot predict how these developments will continue to alter the face of architecture. But we can be sure of one thing: the only constant is change.

12>

Chris Abel
From Hard to Soft Machines
1 Peter Collins, *Changing Ideals in Modern Architecture* (Faber & Faber, London, 1965).
2 Reyner Banham, *Theory and Design in the First Machine Age* (The Architectural Press, London, 1960).
3 Reyner Banham, ibid.
4 Robert Thorne, 'Paxton and Prefabrication', in Derek Walker (ed.), *Great Engineers* (Academy Editions, London; St Martin's Press, New York, 1987).
5 John Heskett, *Industrial Design* (Oxford University Press, New York and Toronto, 1980).
6 Le Corbusier, *Towards a New Architecture*, trans. Frederick Etchells (The Architectural Press, London, 1927).
7 Philippe Boudon, *Lived-in Architecture* (MIT Press, Cambridge, 1972).
8 J F Eden, 'Metrology and the Module', *Architectural Design*, March 1967.
9 John Heskett, op. cit.
10 Gilbert Herbert, *The Dream of the Factory-Made House* (MIT Press, Cambridge, 1984).
11 Chris Abel, 'Ditching the Dinosaur Sanctuary', *Architectural Design*, August 1969; and 'Meaning and Rationality in Design', in G Broadbent, R Bunt, and T Llorens (eds.) *Meaning and Behaviour in the Built Environment* (John Wiley & Sons, Chichester, 1980).
12 Reyner Banham, *Design by Choice* (Academy Editions, London, 1981).
13 David Spaeth, *Mies van der Rohe* (The Architectural Press, London, 1985).
14 John Heskett, op. cit.
15 Ezra Ehrenkrantz, *The Modular Number Pattern* (Alec Tiranti Ltd, London, 1956).
16 G W Cartmell, 'SCSD: Californian Schools Development Project', *RIBA Journal*, August 1965.
17 Chris Abel, 'Modern Architecture in the Second Machine Age: the Work of Norman Foster', *Architecture and Urbanism*, May 1988.
18 Chris Abel, 'Ditching the Dinosaur Sanctuary', op. cit.
19 Arthur Drexler, *Charles Eames* (The Museum of Modern Art, New York, 1973).
20 Chris Abel, 'Modern Architecture in the Second Machine Age: the Work of Norman Foster', op. cit.
21 James Meller (ed.), *The Buckminster Fuller Reader* (Cape, London, 1970).
22 Jean Prouvé, Address delivered at the UIA symposium held in Delft, 6-16 September 1964, in CIB (eds.), *Towards Industrialised Building – Proceedings of the Third CIB Congress, Copenhagen, 1965* (Elsevier, Oxford, 1966).
23 Camillo Sitte, *City Planning According to Artistic Principles*, trans. G R Collins and C C Collins (Random House, New York, 1965).
24 Chris Abel.
25 Quoted in Peter Collins, op. cit.
26 Chris Abel, 'A Building for the Pacific Century', *Architectural Review*, April 1986.
27 Chris Abel, ibid.
28 Chris Abel, ibid.
29 Gordon Vincent and John Peacock, *The Automated Building* (The Architectural Press, London, 1985).
30 Nicholas Negroponte, *Soft Architecture Machines* (MIT Press, Cambridge, 1975).

31 Chris Abel, 'Ditching the Dinosaur
Sanctuary: Seventeen Years On',
in *CAD and Robotics in Architecture
and Construction – Proceedings of an
International Conference, Marseilles,
25-27 June, 1986* (Kogan Page, London,
1986). The same paper is reprinted under
the title, 'Return to Craft Manufacture',
Architects' Journal, supplement on information technology, 20 April 1988.
32 Stafford Beer, 'Toward the Cybernetic
Factory', in H Von Foerster and G W Zopf
(eds.), *Principles of Self-Organisation*
(Pergamon Press, New York, 1962).
33 Chris Abel, 'Ditching the Dinosaur
Sanctuary', op. cit. See also D T N
Williamson, 'New Wave in Manufacturing',
American Machinist, 11 September 1967.
34 Quoted from the *Times Newsletter*,
Council on Tall Buildings and Urban
Habitat, Leigh University, Bethlehem,
December 1983.
35 Chris Abel, 'Ditching the Dinosaur
Sanctuary: Seventeen Years On', op. cit.
36 Werner Blaser, *Furniture as Architecture*
(Waser Verlag, Zurich, 1985).
37 Arthur Drexler, op. cit.
38 Stafford Beer, op. cit.
39 Chris Abel, 'Ditching the Dinosaur
Sanctuary: Seventeen Years On', op cit.
40 William Barrett, *The Illusion of
Technique* (Anchor Press/Doubleday,
New York, 1978).
41 B F Skinner, *Walden Two* (Macmillan,
New York, 1948).
42 Asa Briggs (ed.), *William Morris*
(Penguin Books, Harmondsworth, 1962).
43 David Watkin, *Morality and Architecture*
(Clarendon Press, Oxford, 1977).

44 Colin Murray Turbayne, *The Myth of
Metaphor* (University of South Carolina
Press, Columbia, 1962).
45 Walter Gropius, 'Principles of Bauhaus
Production', in Ulrich Conrads (ed.),
*Programs and Manifestos on Twentieth-
Century Architecture* (MIT Press,
Cambridge, 1964).
46 Chris Abel, 'Ditching the Dinosaur
Sanctuary: Seventeen Years On', op. cit.
47 Norman Foster, 'Hongkong Bank',
Architecture and Urbanism, June 1986.

Francois Chaslin
An Iron Will
1 Le Corbusier, *Towards a New Architecture*, trans. Frederick Etchells (The Architectural Press, London, 1927).
2 Ibid.

Critics' Chorus
Speaking of the Sainsbury Centre
1 Quotes tend to come from the following publications: *Architectural Design*, August 1975; *Architects' Journal*, 5 May 1978; *Architectural Review*, January 1978; *RIBA Journal*, July 1978; *Building*, 7 April 1978; *Glass Age*, May 1978; *Design*, July 1978; *New Society*, 6 July 1978; *Burlington Magazine*, September 1978; *Building Design*, 3 February 1978 and *Building Design*, 8 September 1978.
2 All Foster buildings are one-offs, single buildings, set in disparate environments. If the masterplan for East Anglia University goes the way one must expect, the utter boredom of the single building will become the dangerous boredom of the group.
3 As second best to an adequate architecture.

Kenneth Frampton
On Norman Foster
1 Norman Foster, unpublished text.
2 Reyner Banham, 'Foster Associates', introduction to the catalogue accompanying the Foster Associates exhibition at the RIBA Heinz Gallery, 1979.
3 Norman Foster, 'Social Ends, Technical Means', *Architectural Design* 9-10, 1977.
4 Norman Foster, in Stephan Dobney (ed.) *Selected and Current Works of Foster and Partners* (Images, London 1997).
5 Rudolfo Machado, 'Norman Foster, Urbanist', *Harvard Design Magazine*, Winter/Spring 1999.

Robert Maxwell
The Urban Dimension
1 Denis Donoghue, review of John Updike's *Memoirs*, in *New York Times Book Review*, 5 March 1989.
2 Reyner Banham, 'Foster Associates', introduction to the catalogue accompanying the Foster Associates exhibition at the RIBA Heinz Gallery, 1979.
3 Editorial, *Architectural Review*, September 1975.

Robert A M Stern
The Impact of Yale

1 Norman Foster, quoted in *Advanced
Studies: The Post-Professional Program
at the School of Architecture*, Yale
University, pamphlet (Yale University School
of Architecture, New Haven, 1994).
2 The phrase 'constituent facts' was used
by Sigfried Giedion in his influential book,
Space, Time and Architecture (Harvard
University Press, Cambridge, 1941).
3 Norman Foster, 'Pritzker Prize Address',
7 June 1999, in *The Pritzker Architecture
Prize 1999: Sir Norman Foster* (Jensen
& Walker, Los Angeles, 2000)
4 Paul Rudolph, 'The Architectural
Education in USA', *Zodiac* 8, 1961, quoted
in Stern, 'Yale 1950-1965', *Oppositions*,
October 1974.
5 David McCullough, 'Architectural
Spellbinder', *Architectural Forum*,
September 1959.
6 Norman Foster, 'Pritzker Prize
Address', op. cit.
7 Louis Kahn, 'Remarks', *Perspecta*
9/10, 1965.
8 M J Long, letter to Robert Stern,
11 February 1974, quoted in Stern,
'Yale 1950-1965', op. cit.
9 Stirling's connection with Yale spanned
24 years; he was visiting critic in 1959
and 1961, and from 1966 to 1983 he
was the school's Davenport Professor
for one semester each year.
10 Reyner Banham, 'Morse and Stiles',
New Statesman 13 July 1962, reprinted
in *Architectural Forum*, December 1962.
11 Reyner Banham, 'The History of
the Immediate Future', talk given at the
Architectural Association in London, reprinted
in *RIBA Journal*, May 1961.
12 Banham, 'Morse and Stiles', op. cit.
13 Norman Foster, 'Pritzker Prize
Address', op. cit.
14 Norman Foster, 'Pritzker Prize
Address', op. cit.
15 Richard Rogers, 'Team 4', in Ian
Lambot (ed.) *Norman Foster: Buildings
and Projects*, volume 1 (Watermark,
Surrey, 1991)
16 Paul Rudolph, quoted in Ian Lambot
(ed.), *Norman Foster: Buildings and
Projects*, volume 1 (Watermark, Surrey,
1991) p17.
17 Rogers, 'Team 4', op.cit.
18 Paul Rudolph, quoted in Bryan
Appleyard, *Richard Rogers* (Faber
and Faber, London and Boston, 1986).
19 Rogers, 'Team 4', op. cit.
20 Philip Johnson, quoted in Appleyard,
Richard Rogers, op. cit.
21 Norman Foster, 'Pritzker Prize
Address', op. cit.
22 Rogers, 'Team 4', op. cit.
23 Norman Foster, 'Pritzker Prize
Address', op. cit.
24 Norman Foster, 'Pritzker Prize
Address', op. cit.

Chris Abel is an architectural theorist, critic and educator, based in Malta. He is the author of *Architecture and Identity: Responses to Cultural and Technological Change* and many other publications.
'A Building for the Pacific Century', *Architectural Review*, April 1986
'From Hard to Soft Machines', from Ian Lambot (ed.), *Norman Foster: Buildings and Projects*, volume 3 (Watermark, Surrey, 1989)

Otl Aicher (1922-91) was a graphic designer and co-founder of the Hochschule f,r Gestaltung in Ulm. His work included corporate design for Braun and Lufthansa and he designed the graphics for the Munich Olympics in 1972. His writings on design include *Analogous and Digital* and *The World of Design*.
'A Tree-House', from Ian Lambot (ed.), *Norman Foster: Buildings and Projects*, volume 3 (Watermark, Surrey, 1989)
'Architecture and Epistemology', from Ian Lambot (ed.), *Norman Foster: Buildings and Projects*, volume 2 (Watermark, Surrey, 1989)

Kazuo Akao is Chairman of the Obunsha Publishing Group. In 1986 he commissioned Foster and Partners to build the Century Tower in Tokyo, where the Obunsha Group has been based since the building's completion in 1991.
'A Client's View', from Colin Davies and Ian Lambot (eds.), *Century Tower: Foster Associates Build in Japan*, (Watermark, Surrey, 1992)

Hugh D R Baker is Professor of Chinese at the School of Oriental and African Studies, University of London, where he teaches Mandarin, Cantonese and Chinese Social Institutions. He has carried out anthropological fieldwork in China and Hong Kong. His publications include *A Chinese Lineage Village: Sheung Shui* and *Ancestral Images: a Hong Kong Album*.
'Feng Shui: Applied Technology Chinese Style', from Ian Lambot (ed.), *Norman Foster: Buildings and Projects*, volume 4 (Watermark, Surrey, 1996)

Peter Reyner Banham (1922-88) was Professor of Art History at the University of California, Santa Cruz, and later Sheldon H Solow Professor of the History of Architecture at the Institute of Fine Arts, New York University. His many books include *Theory and Design in the First Machine Age* and *A Concrete Atlantis: US Industrial Building and European Modern Architecture*.
'LL/LF/LE v Foster', *New Society*, 9 November 1972
'Grass Above, Glass Around', *New Society*, 6 October 1977
'Foster Associates', introduction to the catalogue accompanying the Foster Associates exhibition at the RIBA Heinz Gallery, 1979
'The Thing in the Forecourt', *New Society*, 28 July 1983
All texts © Reyner Banham, reproduced by kind permission of Mrs Mary Banham.

Alastair Best is a writer, lecturer and broadcaster. He has edited *Designer* and *Designer's Journal*, written widely on architecture and design for the *Architectural Review*, and wrote the introduction to *Norman Foster: Buildings and Projects*, volume 1.
'The Four Phases of Foster', *Designer*, June 1983
'Foster Development', *Architectural Review*, April 1986

Sebastiano Brandolini graduated from the Architectural Association in London in 1982. He was deputy editor of *Casabella* from 1984 to 1996 and a regular contributor to *Rassegna* and *Domus*. He now runs his own architectural design practice in Milan, and is architectural correspondent of *De La Republica*. He is the co-author of a monograph on Jo Coenen.
'Hong Kong International Airport', *Domus*, October 1998

Peter Buchanan is a writer and critic who trained as an architect. He was deputy editor of the *Architectural Review* from 1983 to 1992 and is the author of *Renzo Piano Building Workshop*, volumes I-IV and *The New Spanish Architecture*.
'Reinventing the Skyscraper', *Architecture and Urbanism*, February 1998
'When Democracy Builds', from Norman Foster, *Rebuilding the Reichstag* (Weidenfeld & Nicolson, London, 2000)
'The Urban Room', expanded version of a text from *The Great Court and the British Museum* (British Museum Press, London, 2000)

Loren Butt is a chartered engineer. From 1968 to 1987 he worked at Foster Associates, of which he became a director. He is now an independent concept designer, specialising in architectural integration of energy design and engineering services for buildings.
'Energy: Issues and Attitudes', from the catalogue accompanying the Foster Associates exhibition at the RIBA Heinz Gallery, 1979

Francois Chaslin is Professor of Architectural Theory at L'Ecole d'Architecture de Lille et des Régions Nord. He is also an architectural critic and former editor of *L'Architecture d'Aujourd'hui*. Currently, he is producing a weekly architectural programme broadcast on the national channel France-Culture.
'An Iron Will', from *Norman Foster* (Electa Moniteur, Milan, 1986)

Doug Clelland is Rouse Professor of Architecture and Urban Design at Liverpool John Moores University and Principal Director of Aire Design.
'Speaking of the Sainsbury Centre', from *AD Profiles* 19, 1978

Theo Crosby (1925-1994) was an architect whose buildings include the reconstructed Globe Theatre on London's South Bank. In 1965 he co-founded the design practice which later became Pentagram. He was technical editor of *Architectural Design* from 1953 to 1962, and from 1990 to 1994 was Professor of Architecture and Interior Design at the Royal College of Art.
'Speaking of the Sainsbury Centre', from *AD Profiles* 19, 1978

Luis Fernandez-Galiano is an architect, writer and educator. He has been Cullinan Professor at Rice University and is now professor at Madrid School of Architecture. He is editor of the journals *Arquitectura Viva* and *AV Monographs* and writes on architecture for the Spanish newspaper *El Paìs*. He is a visiting scholar at the Getty Center of Los Angeles, and a visiting critic at Princeton and Harvard.
'Silence and Memory', unpublished text written in October 1996

Thomas Fisher is Dean of the College of Architecture and Landscape Architecture at the University of Minnesota. He was previously Editorial Director of *Progressive Architecture* and is currently a co-editor of *Architectural Research Quarterly*. His publications include *In the Scheme of Things: Alternative Thinking on the Practice of Architecture*.
'The Industrial Design of Buildings', *Progressive Architecture*, December 1994

Kenneth Frampton
Kenneth Frampton has worked as an architect, architectural historian and critic and is now Ware Professor at the Graduate School of Architecture and Planning at Columbia University, New York. He has written widely on modern and contemporary architecture. His books include *Modern Architecture: A Critical History* (Thames and Hudson, London, 1992)
'On Norman Foster', updated version of an unpublished text written in 1988.

Richard Buckminster Fuller (1895-1983) was an architect, mathematician, engineer and educator. His most famous invention was the geodesic dome – the strongest and most efficient dome ever devised. His many books on architecture and environmental issues include *Nine Chains to the Moon*, *Operating Manual for Spaceship Earth* and *Critical Path*. He received the RIBA Gold Medal in 1968.
'Royal Gold Medal Conclusion', edited transcript of an address given on the occasion of the presentation of the Royal Gold Medal for Architecture to Norman Foster on 21 June 1983, published in *Transactions* 4, RIBA, 1983.

Joseph Giovannini is an architectural designer, critic and writer. He has been a contributor to the *Los Angeles Herald Examiner* and the *New York Times* and to a number of books on contemporary architecture and design, including *Graphic Design in America* and *Los Angeles at 25mph*.
'The Architecture of Norman Foster', from *The Pritzker Architecture Prize 1999: Sir Norman Foster* (Jensen & Walker, Los Angeles, 2000)

Jonathan Glancey is the architectural correspondent for the *Guardian* newspaper, a role he previously held at the *Independent*. He is a contributor to *The World of Interiors*, consultant editor of *World Architecture*, author of *New British Architecture* and *New Moderns*, and regularly appears on television and radio.
'The Eagle has Landed', *Architectural Review*, July 1983
'An Airport Where You Can Actually See the Planes', *Independent*, 13 March 1991
The River God, *Guardian*, 23 August 1999

Ron Herron (1930-94) was an architect and founder member of Archigram in 1960. His most famous works include the Imagination building. He lectured regularly at the Architectural Association in London and was head of the architecture department at East London University.
'Speaking of the Sainsbury Centre', from *AD Profiles* 19, 1978

Robert Hughes is a writer and broadcaster and has been *Time* magazine's art critic since 1970. His books include *The Shock of the New*, *The Fatal Shore*, for which he won the Age Book of the Year Award, and a book of social criticism, *The Culture of Complaint*.
'Lifting the Spirit', *Time*, 19 April 1999
© 1999 Time Inc. reprinted by permission

Charles Jencks is a designer, architectural critic and theorist. He is a visiting professor at the University of California in Los Angeles, teaches part-time at the Architectural Association in London, and lectures widely in the United States, Europe and Japan. His many books include *What is Post-Modernism?*, *Ecstatic Architecture* and *The Architecture of the Jumping Universe*.
'Speaking of the Sainsbury Centre', from *AD Profiles* 19, 1978
'The Reichstag', *World of Interiors*, August 1999

Leon Krier is an architect, planner and architectural critic. He is also an urban development theorist and former adviser to the Prince of Wales. His books include *Architecture − Choice or Fate?*
'Speaking of the Sainsbury Centre', from *AD Profiles* 19, 1978

Vittorio Magnagno Lampugnani is an architect practising in Milan and is Dean of the Faculty of Architecture at the Swiss Federal Institute of Technology in Zurich, where he teaches History of Town Planning. He was editor of *Domus* from 1991-96, and is author of several books, including *Architecture and City Planning in the 20th Century* and *Encyclopaedia of 20th Century Architecture*.
'Hongkong and Shanghai Bank', *Domus*, July-August 1986

Rodolfo Machado is an architect, writer and lecturer. He has held a number of academic positions in the United States, including that of Bishop Professor of Architecture at Yale University and Professor of Architecture and Urban Design at the Harvard University Graduate School of Design. His books include *Monolithic Architecture*.
'Norman Foster, Urbanist', *Harvard Design Magazine*, Winter-Spring 1999

Robert Maxwell is an architect and critic. He is Assistant Professor of Art History at the University of Michigan and was Dean of the School of Architecture at Princeton University. He is a contributor to *Oppositions*, *Casabella* and the *Achitectural Review* and an anthology of his theory and criticism, *Sweet Disorder and the Carefully Careless*, was published in 1993.
'Speaking of the Sainsbury Centre', from *AD Profiles* 19, 1978
'The Urban Dimension', *Casabella*, May 1989

John McKean is Professor of Architecture at the University of Brighton and a contributor to many books and journals on the architecture of Classical Greece, the Renaissance, and the nineteenth and twentieth centuries. He has written books on Walter Segal, Charles Rennie Mackintosh, the Crystal Palace, the Royal Festival Hall, and is currently preparing a volume on Giancarlo De Carlo.
'Speaking of the Sainsbury Centre', from *AD Profiles* 19, 1978
'Gold Standard', *Architectural Journal*, 30 March 1983

Rowan Moore is architecture critic of the *Evening Standard* and former editor of *Blueprint* magazine. He is a qualified architect and has written, broadcast and lectured extensively on architecture. His books include monographs on Nicholas Grimshaw and Norman Foster.
'The Human Figure and the Molecule', *Royal Academy Magazine*, March 1991

Martin Pawley is an architectural writer and critic. He has been editor of the magazine *World Architecture* and contributes regularly to the *Architects' Journal*. He is author of several books including *Terminal Architecture* and *Norman Foster: A Global Architecture*.
'If You Ever Plan to Motor West', *Building Design*, 25 March 1983
'The English School', *Blueprint*, October 1986
'The Years of Innovation', from Ian Lambot (ed.), *Norman Foster: Buildings and Projects*, volume 2 (Watermark, Surrey, 1989)
'Port Side', *Foundation*, Spring 1991
'The Tradition of Big Sheds', *Monografias de Arquitectura y Vivienda*, 1992

Kenneth Powell is a contributor to many architectural journals and was formerly the architectural correspondent for the *Daily Telegraph*. He is consultant director of The Twentieth Century Society. His many books include *Stansted: Norman Foster and the Architecture of Flight*.
'Norman Foster's Triumph', from *New Architecture 4: UK2K, British Architecture into the Millennium* (Andreas Papadakis, London, 2000). Republished here by kind permission of Andreas Papadakis, Publisher.

Malcolm Quantrill is the Distinguished Professor of Architecture at Texas A & M University, Director of the Centre for the Advancement of Studies in Architecture (CASA) and editor of the CASA *Studies in Architecture and Culture*. He has published widely on modern Finnish architecture, and is author of *The Norman Foster Studio*.
'Century Symbol', *Architectural Review*, November 1991

Richard Rogers is an architect and was founder of Team 4 with Norman Foster in 1963. Amongst his most famous buildings are the Centre Pompidou in Paris (with Renzo Piano) and Lloyds of London. He is also a lecturer, author of numerous articles and the book *Cities for a Small Planet*, and chairman of the government's Urban Task Force. He was knighted in 1991 for his contributions to architecture and made a life peer in 1996, taking the title Lord Rogers of Riverside.
'Speaking of the Sainsbury Centre', from *AD Profiles* 19, 1978
'Team 4', from Ian Lambot (ed.), *Norman Foster: Buildings and Projects*, volume 1 (Watermark, Surrey, 1991)

Robert Sainsbury (1906-2000) was a former chairman of Sainsbury's plc and an arts benefactor. He was the founder, with his wife Lisa, of the Sainsbury Centre for Visual Arts at the University of East Anglia. He was knighted in 1967 for services to the arts.
'Royal Gold Medal Introduction', edited transcript of an address given at the presentation of the Royal Gold Medal for Architecture to Norman Foster on 21 June 1983, published in *Transactions* 4, RIBA, 1983.

Deyan Sudjic is the founding editor of *Blueprint* magazine. He is currently editor of *Domus* and architectural correspondent of the *Observer*. He is the former director of Glasgow 1999 and his books include *The Hundred Mile City*.
'Foster Mark Three', from Ian Lambot (ed.), *Norman Foster: Buildings and Projects*, volume 4 (Watermark, Surrey, 1996)

Robert A M Stern is an architect and writer. He is Dean of the Yale School of Architecture. His books include *New York 1900* and *Pride of Place*.
'The Impact of Yale', adapted from a talk at the seminar, 'The Special Relationship: American and British Architecture Since 1945', held at the Paul Mellon Centre for Studies in British Art, London, 29 October 1998

Wilfried Wang has been Director of the Deutsches Architektur-Museum since 1995. He is an architect and is currently Design Critic in Architecture at Harvard University Graduate School of Design. He has written widely on modern European architecture and design, including books on Eileen Gray and Herzog and de Meuron.
'The Constructive Concept', *Building Design*, 25 March 1983

Christopher Woodward is an architect and writer who teaches at The Bartlett Faculty of the Built Environment, University College London. His books include *Computing in Architectural Practice*.
'Willis Faber & Dumas', *Architectural Review*, September 1975 Reproduced by kind permission of Christopher Woodward

Norman Foster was born in Manchester in 1935. After graduating from Manchester University School of Architecture and City Planning in 1961, he won a Fellowship to Yale University where he gained a Masters Degree in Architecture.

Foster Associates was founded in 1967 and is now known as Foster and Partners. Since its inception the practice has received more than190 awards and citations for excellence and has won over 50 national and international competitions.

Major buildings include: Willis Faber & Dumas Head Office, Ipswich, 1975; Sainsbury Centre for Visual Arts, Norwich, 1978; Hongkong and Shanghai Bank, Hong Kong, 1985; Sackler Galleries at the Royal Academy, London, 1991; Stansted, London's Third International Airport, 1991; Century Tower in Tokyo, 1991; Carré d'Art, Nîmes, 1993; Commerzbank Headquarters, Frankfurt, 1997; American Air Museum, Duxford, 1997; and the new Hong Kong International Airport at Chek Lap Kok, 1998.

Recent projects include the German Parliament, Reichstag, Berlin, 1999, the Great Court of the British Museum and the Millennium Bridge, London.

Norman Foster was awarded the RIBA Royal Gold Medal for Architecture in 1983, the Gold Medal of the French Academy of Architecture in 1991 and the AIA Gold Medal in 1994. He was appointed Officer of the Order of the Arts and Letters by the Ministry of Culture in France, also in 1994. In 1990 he was granted a Knighthood in the Queen's Birthday Honours and appointed by the Queen to the Order of Merit in 1997.

In 1999 he became the 21st Pritzker Architecture Prize Laureate and in the same year he was honoured with a Life Peerage in the Queen's Birthday Honours List, taking the title Lord Foster of Thames Bank.

'Design for Living', *BP Shield*, March 1969

'Alvar Aalto', *RIBA Journal*, July 1976

'Social Ends, Technical Means', updated version of an article published in *Architectural Design* 9-10, 1977

'Links: Between Research and Practice', edited version of an essay published in the catalogue accompanying the Foster Associates exhibition at the RIBA Heinz Gallery, 1979

'James Stirling, Royal Gold Medallist', transcript of an address given on the occasion of the presentation of the Royal Gold Medal for Architecture to James Stirling on 24 June 1980, and published in *Architectural Design*, August/September 1980

'Royal Gold Medal Address', transcript of an address given at the presentation of the Royal Gold Medal for Architecture to Norman Foster on 21 June 1983, published in *Transactions* 4, RIBA, 1983

'Richard Buckminster Fuller', text first written in 1983 and published on the centenary of Buckminster Fuller's birth as 'Insights That Last Forever', *Architects' Journal*, 14 December 1995

'Gaudi in Nîmes: the French Connection', unpublished text written in 1985

'Hongkong Bank', *Process Architecture*, 18 March 1986

'A Reply to the Prince of Wales', *Sunday Times*, 6 December 1987

'Reyner Banham Loves Los Angeles', edited transcript of Norman Foster's introduction to the film *Reyner Banham Loves Los Angeles*, broadcast by BBC2 as a memorial to Peter Reyner Banham on 1 May 1988

'Handrails and Bicycles', from Ian Lambot (ed.), *Norman Foster: Buildings and Projects*, volume 3 (Watermark, Surrey, 1989)

'Flight 347', from Ian Lambot (ed.), *Norman Foster: Buildings and Projects*, volume 3 (Watermark, Surrey, 1989)

'With Wendy...', edited version of an essay from Ian Lambot (ed.), *Norman Foster: Buildings and Projects*, volume 2 (Watermark, Surrey, 1989)

'F for Frustration', unpublished text written in October 1990

'The Tate Gallery Lecture', edited transcript of a lecture given at the Tate Gallery on 20 February 1991 and published in Ian Lambot (ed.), *Norman Foster: Buildings and Projects*, volume 4 (Watermark, Surrey, 1996)

'The Library: Public Building or Memory Machine?', transcript of a Bibliothéque keynote address given on 26 June 1991

'The Microchip and The Zen Garden', edited version of a text published in the catalogue of the British Pavilion at the Venice Biennale, September 1991

'Building Sights: Boeing 747', edited transcript of a programme from the BBC series 'Building Sights', published in Ruth Rosenthal and Maggie Toy (eds.) *Building Sights* (Academy Editions, London, 1995)

'Otl Aicher', *Blueprint*, 14 October 1991

'Light and Culture', from Ian Lambot (ed.), *Norman Foster: Buildings and Projects*, volume 4 (Watermark, Surrey, 1996)

'Century Tower', from Colin Davies and Ian Lambot (eds.), *Century Tower: Foster Associates Build in Japan*, (Watermark, Surrey, 1992)

'Architecture and Structure', edited version of an article written for the Architectural Association of Japan, November 1994

'Taking Flight', memoir of a fund-raising speech given in November 1994

'Commerzbank: The Social Tower', unpublished text written in 1995

'The Human Touch', unpublished text
written in 1995

'Bilbao Metro', essay written in October
1996 on the occasion of the VI
International Architecture Exhibition,
'Sensors of the Future: The Architect
as Seismograph in Venice'

'Riverside Three', edited version of an
essay from Ian Lambot (ed.), *Norman
Foster: Buildings and Projects*, volume 4 (Watermark, Surrey, 1996)

'Reinventing the Airport', essay based
on the transcript of a lecture given by
Norman Foster at the UIA in Barcelona
in June 1996

'The Reichstag Eagle', edited version of
a text prepared for a special publication
on the design of the Reichstag Eagle,
presented to Members of the Bundestag
in September 1996

'Gordon Cullen', *Architectural Review*,
December 1994

'On Flying', expanded from an essay written in June 1997 to accompany a first-day
cover of five Royal Mail postage stamps
dedicated to 'Architects of the Air'

'Lessons from Skiing', expanded from
an article written for the Engadin Cross-
Country Ski Marathon Newspaper, 1998

'London: the World City?', *City 20.20*,
February 1999

'The Future Office', transcript of a lecture
given at the MIPIM International Property
Conference, Cannes in February 1999

'Meeting the Sainsburys', transcript of a
speech given on the occasion of the presentation of the Freedom of the City of
Norwich to Sir Robert and Lady Sainsbury,
23 June 1999

'The Architecture of the Future', *Building
Magazine*, 10 December 1999

'In the Thonet Tradition', text written in
December 1999 to celebrate the launch
of a new range of furniture for Thonet at
the Cologne Furniture Fair in January 2000

'On Tables and Bicycles', text written in
December 1999 to celebrate the launch
of a Millennium edition of the Nomos table

'Pritzer Prize Address', edited transcript
of a speech given on the occasion of
the presentation of the Pritzker Prize for
Architecture to Norman Foster on 7 June
1999 at the Altes Museum in Berlin, published in *The Pritzker Architecture Prize
1999: Sir Norman Foster* (Jensen &
Walker, Los Angeles, 2000)

'Craig Ellwood', introduction to a mono-
graphic issue of the international magazine
2G, 1999

'The Reichstag Energy Story', *Spektrum der Wissenschaft*, February 1999

'Paul Rudolph', foreword to Tony Monk *The Art and Architecture of Paul Rudolph* (Wiley-Academy, Chichester, 1999)

'Studio Interview', *Global Architecture Document Extra* 12, 1999

'Crop Circles', introduction to a book on crop circles by Wolfgang Schindler, 2000

'Design in a Digital Age', unpublished text written in 2000

David Jenkins is an architect, editor and writer, now based in the Foster studio. He is a former buildings editor on the *Architects' Journal*, and was editorial director at Phaidon Press, responsible for architecture and design. His books include *Pierre Koenig*, co-written with James Steele.

Mirko Kritzarovic: 720(1,2), 721(4)
Ian Lambot: 136(4), 141(7), 144(10,11),
147(13), 162(1), 175(9), 237(16),
238(17), 280(2), 238(5), 287(3,4),
327(10), 335(2-4), 367(5), 388(7),
395(18,19), 396(20), 422(3), 520(5),
534(3), 535(4), 609(7), 633(5), 758(16)
John Edward Linden: 564(9)
Donald Luckenbill: 746(1,2)
Ken Lui: 608(6)
Meccano Toys Ltd: 750(3)
Magnum/Dennis Stock: 306-7(8),
523(7), 657(7), 662(3-5), 670(16)
Satoru Mishima: 608(5)
MIT Press: 361(13)
James H Morris: 364(1), 583(13,14),
599(2), 602(4), 648(1)
Tom Miller: 303(6), 703(7)
Christan Norberg-Schulz, *Baroque
Architecture*, Faber and Faber, London
1986: 412(11)
John Nye: 135(3), 156(1), 157(2,3),
302(4), 500(30), 501(33), 519(2)
Martin Pawley: 290(1)
Quadrant Picture Library: 117(3-5),
201(11), 590(1)
Paul Raftery: 612(1)
Simo Rista: 460(1)
Richard Rogers: 355(6)
Su Rogers: 316(1)
The Royal Air Force Museum, Hendon:
687(2), 690(6), 691(10,11)
Trustees of the Paul Rudolf Estate: 747(3)
Wolfgang Schindler: 770(1-3), 771(4)
Sealand Aerial Photograhy: 64(1),
151(3), 296(7)
Julius Shulman: 228(5)
Tim Soar: 393(15), 601(3), 602(5)
James Stirling Foundation: 351(4),
480(1), 481(2)

Tim Street Porter: 29(1), 45(1), 86(14),
109(2,4), 173(8), 192(6), 268(2), 269(3),
290(2), 465(4), 468(8), 470(10), 471(13),
476(4), 497(22), 507(3), 508-9(4),
548(1), 757(15), 761(21)
Peter Strobel: 637(3-5), 638(7),
724(1), 726(3,4)
Taylor Woodrow: 766(26)
Tecno: 242(20), 727(5)
Telegraph Picture Library/Mike
Dobel: 238(19)
Jocelyne van den Bossche: 392(13),
470(12)
The Victoria and Albert Museum, London:
222(1), 398(22)
E Viollet-le-Duc, *Lectures on Architecture*,
1881: 170(6)
Vision/Axel Kull: 730(1)
Visum/Rudi Meisel: 413(12), 414-15(14),
426(7), 553(5), 577(6), 578(7), 579(8),
594(2,3), 595(4), 649(2), 652-3(5),
656(6), 674(1), 679(7,8), 680(9,10),
681(11,12), 730 (2), 731(3-5)
Nigel Young: 22-3(2), 47(3), 229(7),
258-9(4), 367(1), 377(3), 394(16),
400(24), 403(26), 416(15), 419(19),
422(1), 427(9), 436-7(4), 441(4),
443(5,6) 445(9), 448(14), 470(11),
568(15), 614(7), 622(1), 625(4),
626-7(5), 630(1), 645(5,6), 650(4),
705(10,11), 709(4), 742(4,5), 743(6),
767(28), 771(5,6), 783(11)

Every effort has been made to contact
copyright holders and the publishers apologise for any omissions, which they will be
pleased to rectify at the earliest opportunity.

Government House, Hong
    Kong 157-8
Gowan, James 351, 480
Grassi, Giorgio 248
Grayburn, Vandaleur 134
Greater London Authority
    headquarters (GLA)
    11, *376*, 377, *446*, 447,
    667, 778
Greenhough, Horatio 221
Greenwich transport inter-
    change, London 377
Grenoble exhibition centre
    94-5, 116
Grimshaw, Nicholas 166
Griswold, Whitney 354
Gropius, Walter 177, 223,
    346, 347, 360, 419, 730,
    745, 747
Guaranty Building,
    Buffalo 399
Guggenheim Museum,
    Bilbao 447
Guimard, Hector 365, 643
Guitart, Josep Maria
    Gil 300
Gunma Museum of Modern
    Art, Takasaki City 57
Gwathmey, Charles 346

H

Ham Common flats 351,
    351, 480
Hammersmith Centre
    19-20, 77, *78-9*, 102,
    120, 187, 444, 497
Hamnett, Katharine 328
handrails 533, *534-5*, 536-7
Happold, Ted 401
Harvard 346
Hawker Hurricane 688, *688*

Hawksmoor, Nicholas 116
Heathrow Airport 559, *560*,
    560, 660, *660*, 663, 664
Hegel, Georg Wilhelm
    Friedrich 216, 217
Heidi Weber Pavilion,
    Zurich 764
Hertzberger, Herman 393
Herzog & de Meuron 376
Hitachi 519
Hitchcock, Henry-Russell
    484
Holden, Charles 121
Holford, Lord 177
Holland, Mike 719
Hollein, Hans 644
Hong Kong 133, 488, *488*
Hong Kong Airport *see*
    Chek Lap Kok and Kai
    Tak Airport
Hongkong and Shanghai
    Bank, Hong Kong 16, 91,
    103, 108, 111-12, 120,
    133-46, *135, 138-9,*
    140, 141, 142, 144, 146,
    147, 149, 155, 158-9,
    161, 161-3, *162,* 166,
    168, 169, 170, 174, *175,*
    178, *179,* 185-6, 187,
    189, *189,* 198-9, 209,
    234-6, *236, 238,* 239,
    246, 277, 285, 299,
    302-3, *302,* 318, 357,
    363, 388, *388,* 395-7,
    395, 396, 422-3, *422,*
    427, 498-500, 516-22,
    519, 520, 521, 523, 651,
    758, *758,* 760
    competition stage 196
    former building 134, *134*
    rejected designs 158, *159*

Hongkong and Shanghai
    Bank, London 328, 377,
    444, *444*
Hopkins, Michael 166,
    171, 731
Horden, Richard 193
Housman, A E 149
Howard, Lord 488
Howe, George 346, 347
Humana Corporation 234
Hunt, Tony 56, 548
Huxtable, Ada Louise 124

I

IBM 75, 491
    Cosham 26-32, *30, 31,*
    33, 74, 82, 90, 150, 166,
    185, 187, 191-2, 198,
    225, 228, *228,* 389, 475,
    708, 753
    Greenford 166, 225
Imperial War Museum 621
Inman, Ted 622
Institut Francais
    d'Architecture 93
Isle of Wight 480
Isozaki, Arata 57
ITN Headquarters, London
    402, *403*

J

Jacobsen, Arne 752
Jacoby, Helmut 316
Jaffé house, Radlett 273
Jantar Mantar 407-8
Japanese architecture *136,*
    137, 186, 234, 284, 605,
    605, 606-7
Jencks, Charles 479
Jewett Arts Center,
    Massachusetts 347

Johnson, Ben 196
Johnson, James 723
Johnson, Philip 75, 177,
    271, 346, 357, 359, 363
Joslyn Art Museum, Omaha
    309, 310, *311, 312, 313,*
    425, 623
Judd, Donald 82
jumbo jet 588-90,
    590, 591

K
Kahn, Herman 393,
    395, 463
Kahn, Lloyd 102
Kahn, Louis 140, 236,
    244, 246, 250, 271,
    272, 346, 348, 349,
    357, 387, 405, 419,
    448, 484-5, 486, 754
Kai Tak Airport, Hong Kong
    659-60, 670
Kansai Airport, Osaka
    664, 763
kasbah, Marrakesh
    488, *488*
Katsura Imperial Villa,
    Kyoto 487, *487*
Kho Lang Ie 711, 712-13
Kikutake, Kiyonori 234
King's College Chapel,
    Cambridge 54
King's Cross masterplan
    187, 196, *196,* 444,
    559, 561-2, *561*
Kline Science Center,
    Yale 357
Knight, Ken 496
Knoxville International
    Energy Expo 233, 665
Koenig, Pierre 360, 423, 735

Koestler, Arthur 576
Koo Pak Ling 499
Kremer, Henry 502, 698
Kurokawa, Kisho 69, 167

L
Lambot, Ian 539
Lancaster Arcade,
    Manchester 485, *485*
Lancaster Bomber
    688-90, *689*
Langham Hotel, London
    99, 120
Larkin Building, Buffalo,
    New York 393
Larsen, Henning 346
Lasdun, Sir Denis 52, 80,
    84, 117, 324
Lavalou, Annelle 94
League of Nations
    408, 409
Le Bourget Airport,
    Paris 659
Le Corbusier 27, 54, 45,
    82, 83, 116, 177, 209,
    222, 244,246, 326,
    345, 403, 417, 685,
    729, 736, 747
    buildings 84, 198, 201,
    222-3, 231, 405, 407-8,
    417, 419, 764
    Vers une Architecture
    169, 400, 484
Leicester Square,
    London 702
Leicester University
    Engineering Building
    480, 481, *481,*
Lewis, Wyndham 53
Libera, Adalberto 250
Libeskind, Daniel 447

Lloyds Building, London
    166, 171, 177, 388, 447
Lock, Max 177
Lockheed Constellation
    559, *560*
Lods, Marcel-Gabriel 93
Loewy, Raymond 223-4
London 375-7, 700-5, *702,*
    703, 704, 705
London Docklands
    Development Corporation
    (LDDC) 18, 187
Long, M J 346, 350
Long, Richard 277
Loos, Adolf 93, 402
Louchheim, Aline B 354
Louvre pyramid, Paris 167
Lubetkin, Berthold 94, 529
lunar module 486, *486*
Lutyens, Sir Edwin 177,
    319, 439
Lycée Albert Camus, Fréjus
    443, 611-12, *612*
Lyons, William 115, 116

M
Macao 13, 715, *716*
MacCready, Paul 130, 502,
    537, 698
McCullough, David 348
Macdonald, Ramsay 178
Machine Age 220-43
Magdeburg 635
Maison Carrée, Nîmes
    250, 330, 364, 393,
    444, 566, *567,* 582,
    597, *602,* 764-5
Maison de Verre, Paris 487
Maison du Peuple, Clichy
    93, *94*
Maki, Fumihiko 403

Malthus, Thomas 130
Manchester 13
Manchester Town Hall
    116, 150, 448, 485,
    749, *750*
Manchester University 117,
    365, 485, 751-3
Mappin & Webb site,
    London 569-70
Maragall, Pasqual 613
Mardall, Cyril 74
Marlborough High Street,
    Wiltshire 488
Martorell, Joan 513
May, Ernst 198
Meier, Richard 326, 439
Meller, James 505, 506
Menil Collection,
    Houston 167
Meteor jet 688, *690*, 693
Mexico City 701
Meyer, Hannes 253, 409
Michaeler House, Vienna
    93, *94*
Middleton Gardens,
    London 488
Mies van der Rohe, Ludwig
    35, 75, 77, 163, 177,
    198, 201, 223, 230,
    263-4, 274, 277, 326,
    357, 391-2, 401, 423,
    448, 636, 692, 735
Millennium Bridge, London
    376, *377, 378-9*, 443
Millennium Tower, London
    426, *427*
Millennium Tower, Tokyo
    13, 716, *716*, 717
Mitchell, Reginald J 115,
    116, 686-8, 693
Mitsubishi 519

Modern Art Glass,
    Greenford 75, *76*, 82,
    166, 225, 250, 291, 477
Molins Machine Company
    238
Monaco 13, 715, 716, *716*
Monadnock Building,
    Chicago 163
Moneo, Rafael 439
Montreal Expo 386,
    386, 775
Montrouge 166
Moore, Henry 711
Morley, David 89
Morris, William 241, 242
Mosquito 690, *690*
Mott Consortium 339, 340
Myer, Val 120

N
Nagakin Tower 167
Nairn, Ian 117
Nash, John 120
Nash, Paul 623
National Botanic Garden
    of Wales 402, 448,
    783, *783*
National Congress Building,
    Brasilia, 406-7
National Gallery extension,
    London 289, 569
National Theatre,
    London 570
Negroponte, Nicholas 236
Nelson, David 301, 302-3,
    304, 439-40, 555, 608,
    651, 730
Nervi, Pier Luigi 406
Neumann, Johann
    Balthasar 413
Neutra, Richard 274, 360

New Statesman 354
New Towns 454, *454*
New York 701 *701*
Newport Comprehensive
    School competition *70*,
    74, 186, 225, 475-6,
    495, 496, *496*
Newton, Isaac 241
Nicholson, Kit 86
Niemeyer, Oscar 94,
    177, 406-7
Nikkei News 285
Nîmes 370-2, *371, 371,*
    567 *see also* Carré d'Art,
    Nîmes and Maison
    Carrée, Nîmes
Nissen huts 51
Nolli 426-7
Nomos furniture 240-1,
    722-7, *724-5, 726, 727*

O
Obayashi Corporation
    13, 608
Obunsha Group 277, 607
Olivetti Training School,
    Haslemere 57, 480, 481
Olsen, Fred 107, 266-8,
    494, 545, 546
Olsen Shipping Line 18,
    186, 474, 545, 756-7
Olsen Amenity Centre,
    Millwall Docks 18-19,
    100, 102, 173, *173,*
    186-7, *187*, 225, 228,
    267-8, *268, 269*, 387,
    387, 388, 430, 476, 491,
    494, *495*, 545-6, 707,
    756, 757, 759
Olsen Country Offices,
    Vestby 152, 237, 474, *474*

Olsen Passenger Terminal,
  Millwall Docks 170, 268,
  268, 389
Otto, Frei 167, 346

P
Pacific Palisades 228, *228*,
  360, *360*
Palais des Machines, Paris
  390, *390*
Palazzo dei Congressi 250
Paley Park, New York
  488, *488*
Palladio, Andrea 116
Palmer and Turner 134
Palmerston Special School,
  Liverpool 82, *83*
Palumbo, Peter 178
Paoletti, Roland 377
parametric modelling
  779-84, *780-1*
Paris 701
Paris Métro 365, *365*, 643
Park Güell, Barcelona 514
Parker, Peter 274
parliament buildings
  404-19
Parliament House,
  Canberra 406
Parliament Square,
  London 703, *705*
Paternoster Square,
  London 252-3, *253*, 324
Pawley, Martin 302
Paxton, Sir Joseph 179,
  222, 238, 390, 398
Payne, Sir Norman 664
Peacock, Frank 273
Pearl River, China 11
Pei, I M 146, 730
Pelli, Cesar 58, 444

Penguin Pool, London
  Zoo, 529
Perspecta 349, 351
Pessac 223
Pevsner, Nikolaus 121
Phillips, Graham 439-40,
  651, 730, *731*
Piano, Renzo 93, 95, 161,
  166, 171, 274, 333, 363,
  388, 401, 439, 441
Pick, Frank 121
Pierson Sage Science
  Laboratories, Yale
  357-9, *358*
Pilkington Glass 467
Pirsig, Robert 101, 484
Plato 203, 204-6, 207, 215,
  216, 217
Porsche, Ferdinand
  189, 200
PPC Company 228
Prado, Madrid 309,
  312, *313*
Prescott, John 704
Price, Cedric 51, 290, 388
Price, Sir Uvedale 167
Princeton 166
Private Eye 111, 113
Process Architecture
  155, 159
Prouvé, Jean 93-5, 101,
  115, 116, 121, 166,
  167-8, 169, 229, 327, 398
Pruitt Igoe 197
Pudong Airport, Shanghai
  660, 664, 667

R
Rautatalo, Helsinki 459
Regent Street Polytechnic,
  London 752

Reichstag, Berlin 9-10,
  305, *305*, *306-7*, 330,
  331, *366*, 366, 381-2,
  382, *383*, 405, 406, 407,
  408-19, *409*, *410-11*,
  413, *414-15*, *416*, *417*,
  419, 426, 431, 434, 439,
  441, 442, *443*, 624-5,
  715, *740*, *743*, 761
  Eagle 672-80, *674*, *675*,
    676-7, *678*, *679*, *680-1*
  energy efficiency 738-42,
    740, *741*, *742*
  old building 408, *408*,
    418, 442
Reliance Controls, Swindon
  74, 107, 152, 186, 187,
  267, 274, 291, 387, 388,
  388, 430, 448, 474, *475*,
  491, *492-3*, 545, 753,
  756, 758, *755*
Renault Centre, Swindon
  89-91, *90*, *91*, 95, *95*,
  96-7, 103, 117, *121*, 170,
  187, 188, 193, 198, 209,
  233-4, *234*, 240, 296,
  397-9, *397*, 490, *490*,
  501-2, 651
Repton, Humphry 84
Retreat, Creek Vean,
  Cornwall 71, 72-3, 74
  see also Creek
  Vean House, Cornwall
Reynolds, Sir Joshua 113
RIBA Journal 27, 29
Rice, Peter 167, 401
Richard, Charles 688
Richardson, Sir Albert 177
Richardson, Henry
  Hobson 349
Ritchie, Ian 167

Riverside, Battersea 317,
376, *376*, 552-3, 646-57,
*648, 649, 650, 652-3,
656, 657*, 747
Robertson, H H 302
Robertson, Sir Howard 177
Robinson, Kenneth 497
Roebling, John
Augustus 129
Rogers, Richard 113, 149-
50, 177-9, *316*, 319, 327,
361, 363, 375, 401, 440,
444, 448
at Yale 152, 271, 315,
346, 356, 357-9,
754-5
buildings 69, 93, 95,
161, 166, 171, 274,
388, 441
collaboration with Norman
Foster 107, 186, 267,
271, 272-3, 274, 291,
315, 356, 357, 439,
486, 490, 731, 755
Rogers, Ruth 274
Rogers, Su 4, 271, 272-3,
274, 355, 356, 754
Roman libraries 574, *574*
Ronan Point 525-6
Rookery, Los Angeles 37
Root, John Wellborn 163
Roper, Lanning 84
Roscoe, Johnny 546
Rosenberg, Eugene 74
Royal Academy of Arts,
London, Foster exhibition
111-13, *112, 113,
320-1*, 322-3
Royal Air Force 485, 749
Royal Institute of British
Architects 27-32

Royal Thames Yacht Club,
London 252
Royce, Sir Henry 690
Rudofsky, Bernard 699
Rudolph, Paul 152, 177,
271, 272, 346-8, *346*,
349, 350, 354, 356-9,
360, 440, 448, 486, 729,
730, 744-7, 754
Ruskin, John 512
Russell, Bertrand 203
Ryoanji Temple, Kyoto,
Zen garden 585, *587*

S
Saarinen, Eero 75, 76, 177,
354, 388
Sackler Galleries, Royal
Academy of Arts, London
177, *178*, 252, *252*, 309,
310, *311*, 329-30, *329*,
403, 441, 444, 567-9,
569, *570*
Sadao, Shoji 386
Sagrada Familia, Barcelona
512, 513-14, *515*
sailplanes 86, *86*, 87,
101, 502, *503*, 692
Sainsbury, Lady 546, 549,
550, 711-13, *713*
Sainsbury, Sir Robert 49,
122-6, 494, 546,
711-13, *713*
Sainsbury Centre for Visual
Arts, Norwich 44, 49-60,
*51, 52, 53, 55, 56, 57,
58, 59*, 65, *66, 67*, 70,
75, 77, 80-1, 84-6, *84,
85*, 102, 116, 117, 122-6,
124, 127, 149, 152, 153,
161, 165, 170, 171,

171, 187, 188, 192-3,
193, 194-5, 198, 199,
209, 231-3, *232, 233*,
237, 250, 291, 323-4,
385, 387, 388, 390-1,
390, 392, 430, 497-8,
546-9, 551, 600, 711-
12, *712*, 753
Crescent Wing *440*, 441,
568, 569
St Andrews 481
St Louis Climatron 385
St Pancras Station, London
390, 444, 561
St Paul's Cathedral, London
252-3, 261, 262-3, *262*,
264, *264, 265*, 375
St Peter's, Rome 130-1
Samuel Beckett Theatre, St
Peter's College, Oxford
385, *476*, 477, 505
Sant'Elia, Antonio 163, 221
Santiago de Compostela
telecoms tower 614
Sänysätsala Council
Chamber 460, *460*
Scharoun, Hans 381
Scheerbart, Paul 35, 381,
418-19
Schindler, Wolfgang 770-1
Schinkel, K F 405
Schlumberger 166
Scholl, Hans 594
Scholl, Inge 593, 594, 595
Scholl, Sophie 594
School Construction
Systems Development
see SCSD
Schweikher, Paul 346, 357
Scientific Data Systems
735-6

Scott, Sir George Gilbert
408
Scottish Exhibition and
Conference Centre,
Glasgow 402-3, *403*
Scruton, Roger 111
SCSD (School
Construction Systems
Development) programme
74, 152, 224, *224*, 225,
274, 360, 475, 495, *496*
Scully, Vincent 271, 346,
348-9, 356, 486, 729,
754
Seagram Building, New
York 103, 395, 399
Seddon, Chris 608
Segal, Walter 101
Seidler, Harry 730
Seifert, Colonel
Richard 375
Sellars, David 346
Sheffield University 351
Shu, Winston 257
Shuttleworth, Ken 439-40,
650, 651, 730, *731*
Siculus 575
Siedlung-Hälen, Berne 74
Silvestrin, Claudio 650
Sitte, Camillo 230
Siza, Alvaro 439
Skidmore, Owings and
Merrill (SOM) 161, 272,
375, 401, 439
Skinner, B F 241
Skybreak House, Radlett
386-7, 473, 474, *474*
Small, John 719, 723
Smirke, Sir Robert 312,
364
Smith, Joseph 686

Smithson, Alison 94,
351, 354
Smithson, Peter 94,
351, 354
Soane, Sir John 179
Socrates 206
SOM *see* Skidmore,
Owings and Merrill
Soriano, Raphael 274,
360, 423
space programmes
221, 486-7
Special Care Unit, Hackney
245, 476
Speer, Albert 217, 381
Spence, Basil 177
Spitfire 115, 686-8,
687, 693
Staatsgalerie, Stuttgart
179, 406, 761
Stansted Airport 153, 187,
233, 255-7, *256, 257,
258-9,* 261-4, *263, 264,
265,* 288-9, *292-3,* 294-7,
294, 295, 299, *300,*
303, 324, 365-6, 399,
399, 425, 441, 442,
502, 559, 560-1, *563,*
611, *613,* 664-8, *666,
667, 668,* 692, 712, 759,
759, 761, 762-3, 765
Stealth Bomber 690, *693*
Stern, Robert A M
9, 363, 747
Stirling, James 57, 69, 94,
177-9, 271, 274, 315,
319, 346, 350-1, 363,
406, 439, *480*
Stockholm Library 406
Stockmann Bookshop,
Helsinki 459-60

Sullivan, Louis 349, 399
Sunday Times building 327
'sunscoops' 143, *144*, 152,
237, *237*, 499
Süssmuth, Rita 678
Swiss Reinsurance
Company, London 11,
377, 447, *449*, 778,
782-3, *785*

T
Tao Hok 522
Taut, Bruno 221, 418, 419
Teague, Walter Dorwin
223-4
Team 4 Architects 9, 74-5,
107, *108*, 161, 186,
272-4, 315, 361, 386-7,
430, 439, 486,
490, 494, 545, 731, 756
Team X Village project 480
Tecno furniture 240-1, *242*,
303, 330-1, 723, 726
Televisa headquarters,
Mexico City 230, 324,
324, 441, 651
Tempelhof Airport,
Berlin 659
Terry, Quinlan 289
Thames Barrier,
London 235
Thames, River,
London 376-7
Thamesmead 392
Thatcher, Margaret 527
Thistlethwaite, Professor
Frank 498
Thompson, Mike 546
Thonet furniture 718-21
Thorton, John 401
Times, London 680

Toshiba 519
Tower Place, London
708, *708*
Townscape 44, 46, 120,
247-53, 465-6
Trafalgar Square, London
19, 703, *704*
244 (magazine) 529

U
UNESCO office, Paris 94
Utzon, Jørn 402, 406, 752

V
van Eyck, Aldo 101
Vanity Fair 319
Venturi, Robert 423
Victoria & Albert Museum,
London 447
Viipuri Library 459
Villa Savoye, Poissy 84,
201, 417
Villette Museum of Science
and Industry, Paris 167
Viollet-le-Duc,
Eugène-Emmanuel 171,
231, 511, 512
Virilio, Paul 94
Vulcan Bomber 690, *691*
Vuoksenniska Church
461, *461*
VW-Audi headquarters,
Milton Keynes 225,
291, *291*

W
Wachsmann, Konrad
51, 223
Wales, Prince of 524-7
Wan Wai Lun 366
Warnecke, John Carl 361

Warner, Francis 505
Waterhouse, Alfred 116,
150, 485
Wates Housing, Coulsdon,
Surrey 273, 386, *387*
Watkin, David 241
Weber, Max 174
Wembley Stadium, London
448, *448*
'White Rose' resistance
movement 594
Whitehead, Alfred
North 203
Whitney Museum project
234, *234*
Whittle, Frank 688
William of Ockham 204
Willis Faber & Dumas,
Ipswich 35-40, *36, 37,
38, 41,* 43-6, *45, 46, 47,*
56, 63-5, *64, 65,* 76-7,
77, 83-4, 102, 104, 108,
117, 135, 137, 149,
150, *151,* 153, 171,
172, 187, 188, 192,
192, 198-9, 200,
229-30, *229,* 247-8,
318, *318,* 324, 390-1,
392-3, *392,* 463-9, *465,
468, 470-1,* 495-7, *498,
499,* 569, 580-1, 666,
707, 774-5, *774*
Wills Tobacco 74
Wilson, Colin St John
346, 351
Wilson, G L 'Tug' 134
Winchester 166
Wise, Chris 334, 376,
401, 443
Wittgenstein, Ludwig 203,
218-19

Wittwer, Hans 409
Wolton, Georgie
(née Cheesman) 107,
272, 361, 386, 490
Woods, Shadrach 346
World Squares for All
masterplan, London
703-5, *704, 705*
Wotton, Sir Henry 483
Wren, Christopher 82, 261,
262, 263, 375, 688
Wright, Frank Lloyd 13,
116, 137, 177, 201, 271,
274, 283, 345, 348, 349,
393, 406, 448, 484,
486, 525, 685, 729,
747, 754

X
XDS plant, El Segundo 74

Y
Yale 271, 315, 344-61,
486, 623, 729-30, 744-7,
754-5
Yates, Frances 575
Yorke, F R S 74
Young, John 273

Z
Zen Garden 585, *587*

Editing: David Jenkins, Philippa Baker,
Christine Davis, Julia Dawson, Gerard Forde

Picture Research: Kate Stirling,
Sophie Hartley, Katy Harris

Design: Thomas Manss & Company with Per Arnoldi
Thomas Manss, Ian Pierce, Ian Davies

Research: Matthew Foreman

Book Production: Turner Libros, Madrid